SONG IN AN AGE OF DISCORD

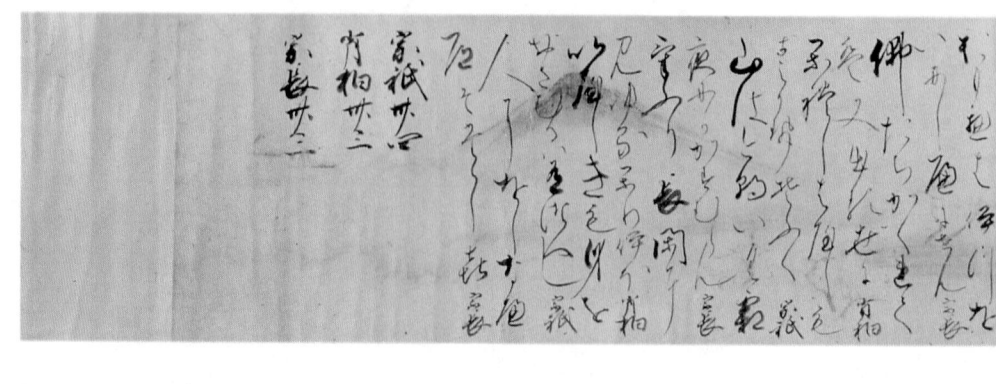

Minase sangin (Three Poets at Minase), scroll, last six verses.

H. MACK
HORTON

Song in an Age of Discord

'The Journal of Sōchō' and Poetic Life in Late Medieval Japan

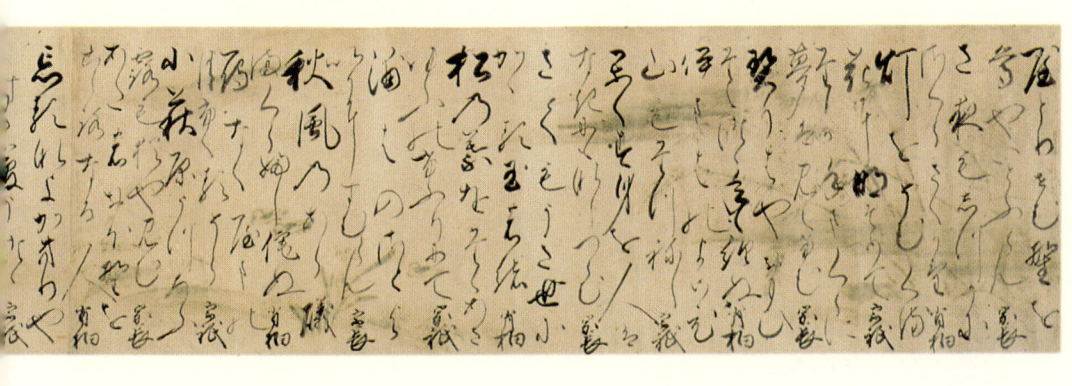

Stanford
University
Press,
Stanford,
California

Stanford University Press, Stanford, California
© 2002 by the Board of Trustees of the
Leland Stanford Junior University

Song in an Age of Discord was published with the assistance of the
Center for Japanese Studies, University of California, Berkeley

Printed in the United States of America
on acid-free, archival-quality paper

Library of Congress Cataloging-in-Publication Data
Horton, H. Mack
   Song in an age of discord : The journal of Sōchō and
poetic life in late medieval Japan / H. Mack Horton
     p. cm.
   Includes bibliographical references and index.
   ISBN 0-8047-3284-1 (cloth : alk. paper)
   1. Sōchō, 1448–1532. Sōchō shuki. I. Sōchō, 1448–1532.
Sōchō shuki. English. Selections. II. Title.
PL792.S58 Z47834 2000
895.6′124—dc21
[B]   99-086682

Designed by Eleanor Mennick
Typeset by Tseng Information Systems, Inc. in 11/14 Bembo

Original Printing 2002
Last figure below indicates year of this printing:
11 10 09 08 07 06 05 04 03 02

To my parents

Harry M. Horton
and
Ann D. Horton

Contents

Preface		ix
Translation of Title-Page Illustration		xiii
List of Abbreviations		xvii
	Introduction	5
Chapter One	"These useless products of my brush": Sōchō and His Journal	11
Chapter Two	"What is to become of me as I travel on my way?": 'The Journal of Sōchō' as Travel Literature	107
Chapter Three	"How I do love a garden": 'The Journal of Sōchō' and the Literature of Eremitism	147
Chapter Four	"A diary of things both serious and frivolous": Poetry in 'The Journal of Sōchō'	195
	Epilogue	293
Appendixes	A. The Imagawa House Lineage	300
	B. Two Early Biographies of Sōchō	301
	C. Major Works by Sōchō	303
	Glossary of Common Nouns	309
	Glossary of Proper Nouns	313
	Notes	319
	Bibliography	369
	Index	403

Illustrations follow p. 150

Preface

Song in an Age of Discord is a companion volume to *The Journal of Sōchō*, a translation of *Sōchō shuki*, the diary of the medieval Japanese linked-verse (*renga*) poet Saiokuken Sōchō (1448–1532). It was conceived as a guide to accompany modern readers setting out with Sōchō on his journeys to castles and temples in the practice of his art. But the diarist was writing at the end of a long and illustrious career, which he pursued largely among political and literary elites during particularly eventful times, and his record of his poetic life expanded to embrace an unprecedented range of subjects, genres, and tonalities. He assumed considerable historical and cultural awareness on the part of his readers, and some of his topical material and elliptical phraseology remains obscure. A modern contextualization of his sprawling, multifarious record necessarily expands commensurately in scope, and while not intended as a free-standing biography of Sōchō or as a synthetic treatment of his entire oeuvre, it assumes something of the character of both. The study is meant to be used in tandem with the translation, and notes on diary passages quoted in the study have generally been relegated to the translation volume.

The book begins with an extended first chapter that situates the journal in terms of its author's life and milieu. Its discussion of the relationships between politics, patronage, and the creative process inherently opposes any notion of *The Journal of Sōchō* as a self-contained cultural artifact and emphasizes instead what Lewis Montrose in "New Historicisms" (1992: 392) calls "the dialectic between the text and the world." The chapter then goes on to introduce the journal in overview, focusing on questions of autobiography and the relationship between the historical author and his literary construct. Like a *ji* or "ground" verse in a renga sequence, Chapter One provides the foundation for the three main chapters, the *mon* or "pattern" verses, that follow.

Each of those subsequent chapters attempts a reading of Sōchō's journal in terms of prevailing norms of genre that Sōchō variously appropriated and reinterpreted while fashioning his own literary portrait. The theory behind the operation applied here is succinctly summarized by Philippe Lejeune (1989: 141): "Literary genres . . . constitute, in each era, a sort of implicit code through which, and thanks to which, works of the past and recent works can be received and classified by readers. It is in relation to the models, to the 'horizons of expectation,' to an entire variable geography, that literary texts are *produced* and then *received*, that they satisfy this expectation or that they transgress it and force it to renew itself."

The norms of travel literature, presented in Chapter Two, were conveniently exemplified in the travel work of Sōchō's teacher, the linked-verse poet Sōgi. Those of eremitic literature, examined in Chapter Three, were employed by two other main figures of the late-medieval linked-verse world, Shinkei and Shōhaku. Sōgi also supplied the template for Sōchō's orthodox poetry, introduced in Chapter Four, as well as for some of his unorthodox or *haikai* oeuvre, as did Sōchō's contemporary, the haikai artist Yamazaki Sōkan. The work of Sōgi in particular forms a *basso ostinato* throughout the study, upon which Sōchō composed his harmonies and his dissonances.

The perspective that underlies this type of inquiry is one of dialogue. Just as the linked-verse art may be conceived in terms of a poetic conversation between the participating poets, future generations, and the poetic past, so does Sōchō's journal initiate a dialogue with his literary predecessors and with his modern readers. These chapters do not posit a teleological argument wherein the works of Sōgi and other earlier artists are construed as inferior models that Sōchō later reinterpreted and improved; Sōchō's attitude toward self-referential writing was in some respects different from theirs, and he chose a different style to express it. The book tries instead to delineate the standards Sōchō received and the dialogue he pursued with them. It is concerned, in short, with establishing the horizons of expectation with which to carry on the dialogue, while at the same time acknowledging the inevitable historicity of Sōchō's position and of our own contemporary site of analysis.

The concern with dialogue has also led to an experiment in applying the thought of Mikhail Bakhtin, whose inquiries into the dialogic concept shape much of his work. Bakhtin's identification in particular of what he calls the "epical" and the "novelistic" modes of discourse provides a useful shorthand with which to compare and contrast Sōchō with his predecessors and contemporaries. The application of modern Western literary theory to a premodern Japanese text

Preface

is always challenging; it was undertaken here in the dialogic spirit, to further expand our appreciation of Sōchō's far-reaching and multivalent discourse. A different project from the one undertaken here might extend the dialogue even further to explore potential ways that these Japanese literary works in turn enrich or alter prevailing interpretations of Bakhtinian theory.

Like ourselves, Sōchō lived in an era in which established values, hierarchies, and interests were being tested, and his journal reflects that excitement and disquiet in its own testing of traditional literary boundaries. The result of that experimentation is a polyphonic and individual record of a time and a personality.

Song in an Age of Discord and the translation of *The Journal of Sōchō* were likewise the result of dialogue with many teachers and colleagues from 1985 to 1997, when the manuscripts went to press. Though it was impossible in either to cite or respond to the many studies on medieval history and culture that have subsequently appeared, I am pleased to acknowledge the individuals who helped bring both volumes to fruition. At the University of California at Berkeley, Helen Craig McCullough and William H. McCullough gave me the initial tools for the project and contributed inspirational models of rigorous theoretical analysis, historical accuracy, and stylistic rigor. In Japan, I was guided by Kaneko Kinjirō, whose devotion to scholarship and dedication to his students is impossible to exaggerate. All three professors have since passed away, and the translation of *The Journal of Sōchō* is dedicated to them, in gratitude and affectionate memory.

My introduction to the work of Sōchō came from Donald Keene, whose seminal studies of the poet's life and art sparked my interest and guided my subsequent inquiry. My colleague Mary Elizabeth Berry was likewise involved in this project from its inception; her knowledge of the Muromachi period and her advice in matters of structure and style were of continual value. I also benefited from the comments and criticism of Steven D. Carter, Lewis Cook, and Esperanza Ramirez-Christensen, who set out before me on the Way of Tsukuba and who share a deep knowledge of Muromachi literature. Christopher Drake, Edward Fowler, and Susan Matisoff read and improved early versions of the text, and Edward Kamens provided valuable perspective. I am also grateful to Haruo Shirane, Karen Brazell, and Thomas R. H. Havens for their remarks on structure, to Irina Paperno for comments on my reading of Bakhtin, and to Kumakura Chiyuki for his innovative spirit of inquiry. In Japan, I was the beneficiary of the prolific historical research of Tsurusaki Hiroo and the poetic scholarship of Okuda Isao. I must also thank (in alphabetical order) Arimitsu Yūgaku, Kidō Saizō, Terry F. Kleeman, Kumakura Isao, Ono Mitsuyasu, Ono Shun, Shimazu Tadao, and Yayoshi Kan'ichi for their advice on specific queries, and Ii Haruki, Nakamoto Tamaki, Tanabe Sōichi, and Tanaka Takahiro for help in acquiring illustrations.

The introductory passage on the history of Sōchō's era was begun at the suggestion of Marian Ury, who also volunteered stylistic advice and continual encouragement. And Terashima Shōichi shared creative insights about the mechanics of poetic analysis and served as a constant resource. They too have since passed away and are greatly missed by their many colleagues and students.

I am also happy to thank Winifred Olsen for painstaking and insightful stylistic recommendations, John Ziemer, Helen Tartar, Pamela Holway, and Sarah Herbold for wise editorial counsel, Eleanor Mennick for her sensitive book design, and graduate student researchers (in alphabetical order) David Averbach, Marilyn Bolles, Gretchen Jones, Christine Shippey, Anne Sokolsky, Joseph Sorensen, and Miki Wheeler. For logistical support in Japan, I am grateful for the generosity of Kanie Hideaki and Kaji Mitsuo, both of Tōkai University, as well as of the library staff of that institution. And for rigorous and artistic translation critique, as well as great personal support, I am indebted to Lisa Sapinkopf.

At its dissertation stage, the project was funded by grants from the Fulbright Foundation, the Japan Foundation, and the Matsumae International Foundation. Later assistance came from the National Endowment for the Humanities and from the Center for Japanese Studies, University of California, Berkeley. This book, and the translation it accompanies, could not have been completed without that support.

Translation of Title-Page Illustration

The title page of this volume reproduces the front and back of the last page of verses (*nagori no ori*) of *Minase sangin* (Three Poets at Minase, subtitled *nanibito* [what kind of person]), a hundred-verse sequence composed by Sōchō, Sōgi, and Shōhaku in 1488. It was a votive sequence dedicated to a shrine at Minase and composed on the 250th anniversary of the death of Emperor Gotoba, a waka and renga devotee who owned a detached palace there. The scroll ends with the *kuage*, the total number of poems by each poet in the sequence. Copy in the hand of Sōchō, on paper decorated with flora and Mount Fuji. Courtesy of Ōsaka Aoyama Junior College.

yadori sen no o uguisu ya itouran	I would find shelter in this field; does the warbler take offense? Sōchō
sayo mo shizuka ni sakura saku kage	In the gentle night, beneath the cherries that bloom in the stillness. Shōhaku
toboshibi o somukuru hana ni akesomete	Upon the blossoms from which I turned away the lamp, the first faint light of dawn. Sōgi
ta ga tamakura ni yume wa mieken	Who was it, arm for a pillow, who had that dream? Sōchō
chigiri haya omoitaetsutsu toshi mo henu	I gave up hope that the vow would be kept years ago. Shōhaku

Translation of Title-Page Illustration

ima wa no yowai yama mo tazuneji	Near my time to die, yet no departure for the hilltop hermitage. Sōgi

kakusu mi o
hito wa naki ni mo
nashitsuran
	In my seclusion,
	others likely think that I
	    am not among the living.
	    Sōchō

sate mo ukiyo ni kakaru tama no o	Even so, it clings to the melancholy world, this cord of life. Shōhaku

matsu no ha o
tada asayū no
keburi ni te
	From nothing but pine needles
	morning and evening,
	    smoke rises.
	    Sōgi

uraba no sato yo ika ni sumuran	In the village by the bay, what can life be like? Sōchō

akikaze no
araisomakura
fushiwabinu
	In the rugged autumn wind
	on the rocky shore
	    I lie awake.
	    Shōhaku

kari naku yama no tsuki fukuru sora	Geese call above the mountains in a moonlit late-night sky. Sōgi

kohagihara
utsurou tsuyu mo
asu ya min
	Dew fading away
	on the field of bush clover—
	    I will see it in the morning!
	    Sōchō

ada no ōno o kokoro naru hito	One with a heart like Fickle Field. Shōhaku

wasuru na yo
kagiri ya kawaru
yume utsutsu
	Do not forget!
	Was it not unto death, our love,
	    be it reality or dream?
	    Sōgi

Translation of Title-Page Illustration

omoeba itsu o inishie ni sen	I find I cannot tell when it all began. Sōchō

hotoketachi
kakurete wa mata
   izuru yo ni
	No Buddha passes away
	but another comes
	   into the world.
	    Shōhaku

kareshi hayashi mo harukaze zo fuku	In withered woods as well the spring wind blows. Sōgi

yama wa kesa
iku shimoyo ni ka
   kasumuran
	Mountains at morning—
	how many frosty nights
	   before this haze appeared?
	    Sōchō

keburi nodoka ni miyuru kariio	Smoke seems to rise serenely from a makeshift hut. Shōhaku

iyashiki mo
mi o osamuru wa
   aritsubeshi
	Even some of humble birth
	surely strive
	   to cultivate themselves.
	    Sōgi

hito ni oshinabe michi zo tadashiki	Righteous is the way that is the same for all. Sōchō

Sōgi   34
Shōhaku   33
Sōchō   33

Abbreviations

The following abbreviations have been used in the text and notes. Full publication information is given in the bibliography, under author or editor where indicated.

GSRJ	*Gunsho ruijū*
JS	*The Journal of Sōchō* (English translation)
KB	*Koten bunko*
KNS	*Katsuranomiyabon sōsho*
KSSMR	*Kokusho sōmokuroku*
KT	*Kokka taikan*
MA	*Muanki* (under Shōhaku)
NKBT	*Nihon koten bungaku taikei*
NKBZ	*Nihon koten bungaku zenshū*
NKT	*Nihon kagaku taikei*
NKZ	*Nihon koten zensho*
OK	*Oi no kurigoto* (under Shinkei)
RJGPS	*Renju gappekishū* (under Ichijō Kaneyoshi)
RSR	*Rengashi ronkō* (under Kidō Saizō)
SA	*San'aiki* (under Shōhaku)
SI	*Suruga no Imagawashi*
SK	*Shirakawa kikō* (under Sōgi)
SKGSRJ	*Shinkō Gunsho ruijū*
SN	*Sōchō nikki* (under Sōchō)
SNKBT	*Shin Nihon koten bungaku taikei*
SNKS	*Shinchō Nihon koten shūsei*

Abbreviations

ST	*Shikashū taisei*
TMK	*Tsukushi michi no ki* (under Sōgi)
UYK	*Utsunoyama no ki* (under Sōchō)
YH	*Yamaga hyakuin* (under Sōchō)
ZGSRJ	*Zoku gunsho ruijū*
ZZGSRJ	*Zoku zoku gunsho ruijū*

SONG IN AN AGE OF DISCORD

Song in an age of concord is peaceful and happy; then government is harmonious. Song in an age of discord is bitter and angry; then government is contentious.

The "Greater Preface" to *The Book of Songs*

Introduction

In the summer of 1522, the linked-verse master Saiokuken Sōchō (1448–1532), then seventy-four, set out on a journey from his residence in Suruga (Shizuoka Prefecture), domain of the Imagawa daimyo. His immediate purpose was to call on his old acquaintance Asakura Norikage, of the Asakura daimyo house in Echizen (Fukui Prefecture) on the northern coast, and there to obtain a donation to help rebuild Daitokuji temple.[1] Both Sōchō and the Asakura had longstanding ties to that venerable Zen institution in Kyoto. Sōchō also doubtless anticipated linked-verse (*renga*) sessions with Norikage, who, like his Imagawa patrons and many other warriors of his day, cultivated a taste for literature. En route the master planned to pause at the shrine to the Sun Goddess at Ise and compose a votive thousand-link renga *hōraku* sequence with one of his disciples at the behest of the dominant warlord in the capital, Hosokawa Takakuni. The entire journey to Echizen was planned mostly as a series of sojourns with poetically inclined warriors, at whose castles Sōchō would trade his cultural expertise for hospitality and protection en route. Such warrior poetasters were eager to be instructed in the way of linked verse by the premier practitioner of the time.

Sōchō had begun his career as a renga master (*rengashi*) just when the country was beginning its descent into the anarchy of the Age of the Country at War (Sengoku jidai) that followed the collapse of the central government, and he had spent the subsequent half-century pursuing his art under the ever-present threat of violence and warfare.[2] Long experience had taught him to expect the unexpected as he traveled between the domains of warriors who might be allies one day and enemies the next. And on this trip his fears were realized. After composing the votive sequence at Ise, Sōchō called on Seki Kajisai, another of his network of friends and patrons among the warrior literati. But when the master bid farewell to his host and attempted to journey further northward, he found that warfare had made the roads impassable. Making a virtue of necessity, Sōchō sent a messenger to the Asakura postponing his visit and remained with Kajisai another ten days, leaving only when that oasis too seemed likely to be engulfed in battle. He retraced his steps to Ise, and thence set out for the capital. It was the beginning of winter when he arrived at a temple in the Daitokuji network south of Kyoto and brought his journey temporarily to a close.

Like centuries of travelers before him, Sōchō recorded his experiences in a travel journal, which a later copyist descriptively if prosaically entitled *Sōchō shuki* (The Journal of Sōchō).[3] But unlike most other literary travelers, Sōchō did not end the document when he arrived at the destination of this particular journey. As a rengashi, Sōchō had spent much of his life on the road, and now in his eighth decade he had perhaps come to the Buddhist realization that distinctions between movement and stasis were in a larger sense illusory. He continued his record for another five years, noting the particulars of his life around the capital, the eventual completion of his visit to Asakura Norikage, and then his return to Suruga in 1524, two years after setting out. But still he continued to write of the cultural events in Sunpu, capital of the Suruga domain, and then of a second trip to Kyoto and back in 1526 to 1527. He finally laid down his brush at the close of that year.

This is a study of that long, desultory, and variegated record. Though Sōchō conceptualized his work to a large extent in terms of earlier literary treatments of travel and reclusion (categories now referred to as *kikō bungaku* "travel literature," and *sōan bungaku* "eremitic literature"), and though he often composed his entries with considerable attention both to fine writing and to a discriminating readership, Sōchō would have seen himself not primarily as a diarist but as a linked-verse poet. And his contemporaries would have concurred. In 1522 linked verse was the most widely practiced form of participatory literature in Japan; it was composed in a variety of styles by court and warrior elites and also by members of the clergy and bourgeoisie. For every one of the hundreds of thousands of verses that survive today, many times that number have vanished. A general knowledge of the complex body of renga rules was a basic element of cultural education, as was the ability to indite an introductory *hokku* verse of seventeen syllables then link alternating fourteen- and seventeen-syllable verses thereafter into sequences of one hundred or even one thousand links. Many who could not even read or write still enjoyed composing renga verses orally. For some, the composition of linked verse became a mania humorously parodied in *kyōgen* plays, and for warriors in particular it became a sign of cultural attainment that helped to legitimize power and status that had been newly won by force of arms.

Little wonder, then, that a poet of Sōchō's stature was universally lionized. A superlative artist, he had also been schooled by some of the finest minds of the entire medieval period. For more than twenty-five years he had been the closest disciple of the great Inō Sōgi, national linked-verse laureate and inheritor of the closely guarded "secret traditions" of the first imperial waka anthology, *Kokinshū*. Sōchō and another famous Sōgi disciple, Botanka Shōhaku, had joined with Sōgi in composing two linked-verse sequences that were soon recognized as classics of the genre, *Minase sangin* (Three Poets at Minase) in 1488 and *Yuyama sangin* (Three Poets at Yuyama) in 1491, and after Shōhaku retired to a hermitage in Sakai, Sōchō became the best known of the post-Sōgi generation of rengashi. Three years before Sōchō set out for Echizen on the first of the journeys he recorded in his journal, the courtier and literatus Nakamikado Nobutane wrote in his own diary that Sōchō was now the linked-verse poet "preeminent in all the realm."[4] Sōchō also enjoyed the patronage of the Imagawa, a particularly venerable and culturally esteemed daimyo house, and he cultivated deep spiritual bonds to the Zen prelate Ikkyū Sōjun, one of the most eccentric personalities yet profound thinkers of his era. Ikkyū was as important to Sōchō's intellectual and spiritual formation as Sōgi, a fact demonstrated by Sōchō's deep ties to Daitokuji, Ikkyū's temple.

But if Sōchō's reputation during his lifetime rested on his abilities as a linked-verse poet, his importance to subsequent literary history derives as much (and some say more) from his journal as from his linked-verse masterpieces. One modern authority on diary literature has judged *The Journal of Sōchō* and *Towazugatari* (The Confessions of Lady Nijō) as the two most notable works of self-representational literature in the medieval era.[5] The work is important for a variety of reasons, not least of which is the portrait it preserves of one of the most gifted minds of the Age of the Country at War.

Equally important is the light the journal sheds on Sōchō's renga practice. For example, though a diary, *The Journal of Sōchō* in places assumes the character of a personal poetry collection (*shū*), a fact recalling the traditionally close relationship between those two genres.⁶ But the journal withal remains quite different from the three separate collections of his own linked verses that the poet also compiled (see Appendix C). The latter were meant as anthologies of what the author took to be his most memorable work; they contain pairs of linked verses and various hokku, with occasional headnotes. The journal, too, includes passages quite similar in nature, but it also preserves extended commentary on certain verses as well as a few verses the poet wished he had revised or had never composed. A much wider vision of the poet's oeuvre develops.

But the diary is less important for what it says about linked verse than for its own character, formed not only of diary passages and lists of personal verses, but also of hundreds of thirty-one syllable *waka* and even a "long poem" (*chōka*), a few linked verses in Japanese and Chinese (*wakan renku*), and snatches of popular song. It contains in addition passages of narrative history, epistolary exchanges, short tales (*setsuwa*), lore about famous poetic places (the standard fare of travel accounts), and even a record of points Sōchō made during a "desultory conversation" (*zōdan*) with one of his warrior patrons. The journal constitutes a compendium in a single volume of nearly all the literary genres in use at the time. The generic breadth of the work is mirrored by its stylistic variety, encompassing passages tossed off in an extemporaneous manner and others written with evident regard for high style. Some sections recall Japanese diaries written in Chinese (*kanbun nikki*); others, the tradition of diary writing in pure Japanese (*wabun nikki*). But most of the account is composed in a terse and elliptical blend of Japanese and Chinese (*wakankonkōbun*) that is at times vigorous and elegant, while at others cursory or obscure. Perhaps most important, *The Journal of Sōchō* includes not only waka and renga in the formal and orthodox style but also a wide variety of the unorthodox or unconventional *haikai* verses that were habitually composed at every level of society but that had been generally excluded until Sōchō's time from works with "literary" pretension.

This breadth of scope and blend of subjects, styles, and registers in a single work was unprecedented in Japanese diary literature. While *The Journal of Sōchō* does not have as much psychological depth as some of the classics of female wabun nikki nor, perhaps mercifully, as much quotidian detail as some of the works of their male counterparts writing in kanbun, it combines elements of each, and with a greater variety of form and content than either. Sōchō, the work shows, was not only a poet but a historian. He was concerned both with creating poetry of lasting value to the linked-verse tradition and also with recording the creative context of those works. He was, in short, interested in linking verse to verse and verse to milieu, in both the elite and the popular cultural spheres.

This is by no means to suggest that *The Journal of Sōchō* represents a triumph of popular culture over the Japanese equivalent of Robert Redfield's "Great Tradition."[7] It was written by a member of the cultural elite, and it deals primarily in terms of elite cultural transactions. And while its pages demonstrate compassion for human suffering at all levels, it is also sympathetic to the interests of the author's patrons. Sōchō's historical accounts in particular are elite, partisan accounts.

The depiction of the artist's inner world is likewise varied, including not only formal and high-minded passages in the neoclassical travel tradition but also personal moments both too light and too dark for the orthodox travel mold. Here too, *The Journal of Sōchō* provides a blend of interiority and exteriority; it reflects in its entirety the unitary and self-oriented quality of waka poetry together with the dialogic, other-oriented nature of linked verse. Of course, the lyricism of the poetry may not have been shared by the man behind it; we explore the written Sōchō through the double prism / prison of the author's informing consciousness and then our own. The literary persona can no more be uncritically conflated with the real man than it can be completely divorced from him.

What follows, then, is a book about a book about a man. In subsequent chapters we will look in more detail at the nature of Sōchō's journal and the various traditions out of which it came, among them the travel diary, the diary of reclusion, and the orthodox and haikai poetic traditions, and suggest how the work mirrors received orthodoxies in terms of genre and how it sets out in new directions. Like a linked-verse sequence, which exists in the interplay between connection to the previous link (*tsukeai*) and development in new directions (*yukiyō*), the journal takes shape through a constant dialectic between attachment to earlier forms of poetic expression and breaking away into new realms of individual creativity, to form in total a unique and multifaceted portrayal of one poet's art world.[8]

CHAPTER ONE

"These useless products of my brush"

Sōchō and His Journal

In its variety of styles and subjects, *The Journal of Sōchō* reflects the confrontational and dialogic character of the era in which it was written. The Age of the Country at War brought far-reaching changes to every level of society; changes occurred in political authority, in agriculture and commerce, in religion, and in learning and the arts. It was an age of constant and often violent clashes between old and new interests, between elites and nonelites, between the center and the periphery. Such clashes often resulted in the displacement of those above and the enfranchisement of those below, a phenomenon often encapsulated in the term *gekokujō* (inferior overcomes superior).[1] Implicit in that overgeneral but pithy formulation is the enormous social fluidity of that century; individuals and ideologies were thrown into greater contact than ever before, resulting at times in conflict and destruction and at others in concord and the creation of new systems and values. For some it was a time of danger; for others, of opportunity; and for all, of crisis.

For Sōchō and other respected practitioners of linked verse, the universal popularity of that art resulted in unprecedented social mobility. He counted among his friends courtiers, warrior aristocrats, and elevated clerics, as well as common samurai and traveling evangelists, both in Kyoto, the imperial capital, and in regions as distant as Kyushu and the far northeast. He was both a witness to and a participant in the social and cultural intercourse that characterized the age.

The Collision of Cultures in the Sixteenth Century

By 1522, when Sōchō began his journal, real governing authority had long since passed from the imperial court to its ostensible military servant, the Ashikaga shogun, and then had largely shifted yet again to warriors like Sōchō's patrons the Imagawa, who were once the subordinates of the Ashikaga government (*bakufu*). The income from public land and private manors that had sustained the court for centuries had by this point been largely usurped by the provincial military, who converted those lands to private fiefs. The imperial house accordingly became progressively impoverished over the four reigns spanned by Sōchō's eighty-four years. Emperor Gokashiwabara, who occupied the throne at the start of Sōchō's journal, was forced to wait twenty-two years for his enthronement ceremony, until the meager imperial coffers could be augmented by donations from military benefactors. After Gokashiwabara's funeral in 1526, which Sōchō reported at second hand in his journal, his son Gonara was forced to institute a national subscription before he could carry out his own succession rites ten years later.[2] The palace had been burned in the catastrophic Ōnin War of 1467–77, as had most of the imperial city itself, and Sōchō wrote in 1526 that much of the site had reverted to summer barley (*JS*: 319).

But the court nevertheless retained a hold on the imagination of warrior elites, who still coveted aristocratic titles (which Sōchō was careful to add after their names when he mentioned them in his diary) and the culture that originally accompanied them. Though Sōchō was of far too humble birth to be able to meet the emperor himself, the imperial court remained for him a very alive and real entity, thanks largely to his close friendship with the doyen of the court literary world of the day, Sanjōnishi Sanetaka. As his aristocratic friend lost his revenue from ancestral estates, Sōchō helped him translate his literary patrimony into a new source of wealth by selling Sanetaka's copies of poems and books to rich provincial magnates like the Imagawa, who considered the words of the courtier to be literally good as gold. As the Sengoku era progressed, more and more courtiers and their families left the capital for the protection of provincial warriors eager to host them, a diaspora that further accelerated the pace of social and cultural collision occurring during that period.[3]

The Ashikaga shoguns, who had come to power by thwarting the last bid for real power by the court in the Kenmu Restoration of 1333–36, had by 1522 lost almost all substantive authority themselves and were manipulated by their own erstwhile subordinates, the daimyo. Sōchō lived during the tenures of five bakufu heads, and only the first, Ashikaga Yoshimasa, died in the capital; the others were all driven out by onetime allies or died in campaigns against them.[4] Like the courtiers they emulated, bakufu officials carried on an active cultural life even as their political power dwindled. Bakufu patronage, in fact, contributed much to the revival of the linked-verse art after it had fallen into temporary decline in the late fourteenth and early fifteenth centuries.

Sōchō is known to have composed verse during at least one shogunal session earlier in his life, but he does not appear to have had personal dealings with Ashikaga Yoshiharu, the incumbent during the years recorded in his journal.[5] It was instead the daimyo, the predominant holders of power, who were the most active of Sōchō's warrior patrons. He received a number of commissions from Hosokawa Takakuni, for example, who held the nominal post of shogunal deputy (*kanrei*) but was the de facto ruler of Kyoto during most of the period covered by Sōchō's journal.

But Sōchō's most important patrons among the military were the Imagawa daimyo and their retainers. Sōchō lived during four generations of Imagawa leaders and actively served three, and much of the time covered by his journal was spent in the Suruga capital. The Imagawa daimyo, their vassals, and their wives profoundly influenced the course of Sōchō's life and his record of it. They will play a major role in subsequent chapters here.

By the time Sōchō began keeping his journal, daimyo like the Imagawa, originally appointed as military constables (*shugo*) to oversee the provinces for the bakufu, had largely broken off from the central government and were consolidating their own local power bases. This involved the large-scale acquisition of proprietary rights into their own hands, rights that had once belonged to temples, other military houses, or courtiers. They then were able to apportion those rights to their own subordinates, whom they vassalized, becoming in the process autonomous and absolute princes in their own domains, *sengoku daimyo*.[6] This was in part a matter of self-defense; in the power vacuum created by the collapse of central authority and the resultant national free-for-all, the provincial barons had no one to rely on but themselves in the face of potential encroachments by their neighbors, who were equally bent on survival through self-aggrandizement. The development of autonomous local domains in turn encouraged the formation of new social relationships, and as the new daimyo divorced themselves from the center and consolidated their own provincial power, they worked to establish new ties with local subordinates.

The most important of these subordinates were *kokujin*, "men of the provinces," who had over centuries set down deep roots in their domains. Many kokujin houses had originally provided estate managers for courtiers or military estate stewards appointed by the bakufu. When the daimyo of their domains began taking power into their own hands, the local kokujin overlords had the choice of either joining in feudal compacts with them or forming leagues of opposition (*ikki*) with their own followers, usually small-scale samurai cultivators (*jizamurai*) and farmers. Since the office of military constable had become heritable by the early fifteenth century, some shugo like the Imagawa developed close ties to their provincial domains, which greatly aided them in strengthening their local support as central bakufu authority declined. But other shugo, particularly those who were in charge of several noncontiguous provinces, were not able to acquire the strong allegiance of local powers, and as the Age of the Country at War progressed, more and more of the old shugo houses fell to their own former servants. Some kokujin families provided the Imagawa with years of staunch support and in the process became important patrons of Sōchō. Others continually opposed Imagawa expansion; Sōchō's patron Imagawa Yoshitada was killed by kokujin in Tōtōmi in 1476. Sōchō was well aware of the dynamics and significance of the kokujin role, and he included the history of one kokujin house, the Asahina, in his journal.

Like the daimyo they either served or opposed, the kokujin too were intent on forging new personal ties with those around them and on building their own power bases, which resulted in new forms of social dialogue. The Imagawa were hard pressed by some of these alliances, and Sōchō's Asahina history concentrates in large part on how the Asahina aided the Imagawa house in overcoming the threat posed by such kokujin to its suzerainty.

As violence increasingly supplanted order and traditional hierarchies, cultivators too began to strengthen their bonds with each other, and they gradually won a measure of self-determination that took the form of *sōmura*, self-governing villages. This was true for craftsmen and artisans as well, who formed guilds (*za*) to manage competition, and also for merchants, particularly those in the port of Sakai, which became a free and self-governing city. Like the rising kokujin, the merchants in Sakai, Kyoto, and other urban centers became a new market for learning and the arts, and both renga and the tea ceremony flourished in those new milieux.

Sōchō's age was one of great energy, derived from both fission and fusion—from destruction and decentralization as well as from agricultural and commercial growth and the formation of new social linkages. The pages of *The Journal of Sōchō* bear witness not only to the devastation and political turmoil of the age but also to the new economic, religious, and artistic encounters then taking place. Despite the periodic famines that brought suffering to thousands, agricultural productivity had gradually increased throughout the Muromachi period (1392–1573), thanks to new strains of rice, cultivation of new lands, and more sophisticated land use. The resulting surplus led to a higher standard of living among many cultivators. Sōchō saw this happening, and he remarked in his journal that the villagers in Ōmi profited by cleverly calculating the best time to send their rice to urban storehouses (*JS*: 122). Surplus also contributed to commerce and urbanization; well before Sōchō's day most cultivators could already make the round trip to a town and back in a day.[7] Markets proliferated and were held more frequently, and even before Sōchō was born, coins had supplanted barter as the preferred medium of exchange nationwide, which further stimulated the variety and amount of goods available. And as commerce increased, so did moneylending, particularly by pawnbrokers (*dosō*) and sake brewers (*sakaya*), two institutions that were protected by the bakufu as a source of taxation but which often became the target of uprisings by those in their debt. Wealth—its acquisition and its preservation—became more and more a focal point of existence, because some segments of the population were being deprived of their traditional means of support while others were recognizing that the collapse of earlier social institutions opened the way to new forms of private enterprise.[8]

Though an artist and a Buddhist priest, Sōchō was not so idealistic as to ignore financial matters, and *The Journal of Sōchō* makes occasional references to money and commerce. He sometimes noted gifts he received from his patrons, and he also made several references over the years to shortages or to theft. And at the end of 1525 he spent an evening chatting with a friend and patron, the warrior Asahina Tokishige, about "frustrations at year's end, the repayment of loans, the allotment of rice stipends, and the lack of enough of anything" (*JS*: 84).

The conversation with Tokishige centers on money and making a living precisely because life at the time was so precarious. While the chance to get on in the world was greater than ever before, so were the risks, and there was little help for the unfortunate or dispossessed. Sōchō took their suffering personally, and his journal presents a vivid picture of contemporary human misery: of friends killed in battle, of dying infants, of lepers, of starving samurai driven to selling their children or even to suicide.

The social mobility of the period, whether up or down, and the concomitant interaction of populations is symbolized by the images of the road (*michi*) and the assembly (*yoriai*). One of the major concerns of all sengoku daimyo was the maintainance of provincial roads, for they were the mechanisms that melded the disparate areas of their holdings into a more defensible and productive unit.[9] The roads carried armies, and the roads carried trade, which could be taxed: during Sōchō's life, toll barriers proliferated to the point where their imposts became prohibitive to commerce, particularly around the capital. Sōchō was no stranger to them himself; after a trip through Minakuchi in Ōmi Province (Shiga Prefecture), he complained: "There are many toll gates in these parts, and as we went along people would should 'Stop! Toll!' at every one . . ." (*JS*: 143).

Traffic on the highways also brought out highwaymen, and merchants learned to band together for safety. Sōchō too occasionally joined a larger group for protection in numbers. Earlier on the same journey he wrote in his journal, "I was warned of bandits in the area around Wakamatsu Pond and Shirutani, and so I traveled in a large company" (*JS*: 120).

It was thus an age not only of tearing apart but of banding together, of communal action, and of strength in numbers. The bakufu polity itself was organized as a confederation with the Ashikaga shogun as primus inter pares, advised by an assembly of elders, the *shugo yoriai*. This was repeated down the social scale, through the ruling council of the Imagawa house to the village assemblies and the guilds. Even the pawnbrokers of Kyoto had their own ruling assembly, the *dosō yoriaishū*. Kokujin joined together into leagues (*kokujin ikki*) to oppose rule foisted on them from above, and villagers formed leagues as well (*tsuchi ikki* or *doikki*), sometimes with samurai as their leaders, to force the reduction of taxes or the cancellation of debts.[10] Eventually great segments of the populace learned in the absence of strong central authority to join together to achieve their demands, resulting in risings by entire provinces (*kuni ikki*). Although such uprisings were occurring less frequently during the years covered by *The Journal of Sōchō*, in part because of the growing control of sengoku daimyo over their domains, they remained a major form both of social contention and of cooperation during most of Sōchō's life. They gave to the age something of a democratic flavor, and they lent a spirit of collectivity or solidarity (*ichimi dōshin*) to participants from diverse backgrounds. And they gave new weight to the popular voice.

As with politics and commerce, the Age of the Country at War also brought confrontation and change to religious life. Sōchō himself was deeply involved in religious affairs because of his own thorough education as a priest, his wide-ranging travels to temples, and his friendships with clerics. Religion and literature were the twin supports of his intellectual and emotional existence, and they were never entirely separate, much less mutually exclusive. His dealings with the religious community reached from the elevated to the common, and his record of that interaction adds another dimension to the dialogic quality of his diary literature. Though trained initially in the Shingon sect of Esoteric Buddhism, he was influenced the most deeply by Ikkyū's brand of individualistic Zen. Zen monks, particularly those of the Gozan (Five Mountains) establishment patronized by the bakufu, were among the religious and intellectual elite and the foremost conduits of Chinese literature, art, and philosophy.[11] At the other end of the religious spectrum were the mendicant monks of the Ji (Time) sect, a brand of popular Pure Land belief, who ministered to the humblest strata of Japanese society and also contributed greatly to the vigorous religious and cultural mix of the period. Sōchō respected the simplicity and the dedication of the Ji sect monks of his acquaintance, to the point where he himself on occasion referred to himself by the Ji sect name Chōa. He also frequented Shinto shrines and was a major influence on the poetic community centered around Ise Shrine, a group whose most famous member was Sōchō's friend Arakida Moritake, who would later become famous for his seminal contribution to the development of haikai linked verse.

The syncretism that marked Sōchō's religious life was characteristic of the age, both in the sense of blending between various forms of Shinto and Buddhism, and also of interaction between the sacred and the secular communities. Zen monks in particular were often versed not only in the sutras and commentaries but also in land management, international trade, and diplomacy. Ikkyū had railed against the growing worldliness and gregariousness of the Zen establishment, and Sōchō shared the fiery prelate's opinion. He took his year-end discussion with Asahina Tokishige as an opportunity to denounce monks who instead of dedicating themselves to achieving enlightenment preferred to pursue self-aggrandizement in the secular world.

But Zen monks were not the only ones who became involved in mundane affairs. Tendai monks of Mount Hiei, for example, had for years maintained not

CHAPTER ONE

only large estate holdings and an army of warrior monks (*sōhei*) but also extensive pawnbroking and moneylending organizations.¹² Religion tinged every aspect of life in the late Middle Ages, but so did a drive for wealth and "blessings in this life" (*genze riyaku*). Ways were found to rationalize the two: the seven gods of good fortune (*shichifukujin*), for example, became "national gods" at this time, beloved by a cross-section of all social classes.¹³ A haikai renga couplet in *Shinsen inu tsukubashū* (Newly Selected Mongrel *Tsukubashū*, no. 368) dramatizes the blend:

fuku o mochi	One should be wealthy
renga o mo mata	and also compose
subeki nari	linked verse!
inore ya inore	Pray, O pray
benzai tenjin	to Benzaiten and Tenjin!¹⁴

Again, the road and the assembly were central agents of that blend. As commerce increased, so did the numbers of priests taking their message further and further into the countryside. These were not only mendicant priests of the Ji sect, who were often the first to reach battlefields and carry out last rites for the slain, but Zen monks, particularly of the Sōtō sect, who popularized Zen teachings in the provinces by providing social services, overseeing funerals, and appropriating elements from Esoteric Buddhism and folk beliefs.¹⁵ While the Gozan Zen temples began to lose vitality as their bakufu patron languished, provincial Sōtō temples prospered, as did those of the Daitokuji network, since instead of shogunal patronage the latter enjoyed the support of provincial daimyo, local samurai, and merchants, all of whom grew in power as time progressed. The older Tendai sect responded to the competition for adherents among the rising popular strata through its own reform movement, which now held out the promise of salvation not only to elites but to commoners as well.¹⁶ Down the road too went evangelists (*shōdōshi*), priests (*etoki hōshi*) who lectured using illustrated tales, nuns from Kumano (Kumano bikuni), and manifold other religious proselytizers, who tailored their religious messages for the common population through the use of entertaining pictures and stories.¹⁷

The road was still a route away from society for some devotees who abandoned their homes and even religious communities for the sanctity of a solitary life divorced from all attachments. But for many other monks and nuns the road brought them into ever greater contact with the affairs of this world. Traffic went both ways, with missionaries carrying their messages to the hinterland, and provincial believers going on pilgrimages to famous temples in or near urban centers. The number of such pilgrims increased markedly during Sōchō's life, and while he approved of them in principle, he counseled Asahina Tokishige to practice economy in his donations to them (*JS*: 84). Monks and nuns also often took to the road to raise subscriptions for their temples from wealthy provincial residents. Sōchō's trip to Echizen was in part just such an errand.

The leagues through which samurai and cultivators had learned to advance their interests often took on religious overtones as well. The most notable cases in point were Ikkō ikki, leagues affiliated with the Ikkō (Single-Minded) sect, another name for True Pure Land Buddhism (Jōdo Shinshū). Its adherents killed the constable of Kaga Province (Ishikawa Prefecture) in 1488 and controlled that domain themselves for nearly a century thereafter. The Asakura holdings, which Sōchō had set out to visit at the start of his journal, bordered on Kaga, and Sōchō's patron Asakura Norikage was embarked on a campaign against the Ikkō sect when he died of illness in 1555.

The increasingly dynamic interaction in Sengoku society thus occurred both vertically across ranks and horizontally across fields of endeavor: some kokujin overlords and cultivators were progressively rising in status while the court and bakufu declined, and religious sects that had once served select elites now ministered to more diverse groups.[18] And as warriors took control of entire provinces, they necessarily assumed command of not only military affairs but also matters of government and commerce, in the same way that men and women of religion became increasingly involved in secular concerns. This is not to suggest that warriors and monks had never crossed lines of status or occupation before, but rather that social collision and collusion grew enormously in speed and dimension during this century of intense change. And this was nowhere more true than in the cultural life of the period, specifically in learning and the arts.

The Age of the Country at War witnessed the wholesale destruction of the capital and its art treasures but also the development of new art forms that are today considered quintessentially Japanese. This was the era not only of the greatest flowering of linked verse, but also of the painting of both Sesshū and the early Kanō school, as well as of the birth of *wabi*-style tea and of *shoin*-style architecture. Sōchō experienced much of this cultural efflorescence personally and was aware of its historical significance. Aside from his linked-verse activities he was also a skilled *shakuhachi* flute player, the owner of Chinese paintings, an enthusiast of nō (*sarugaku*) theater, and a witness to the development of rustic *wabi*-style tea taste.

CHAPTER ONE

The high arts of the period, such as court poetry, tea, nō drama, and ink landscape painting, are known for such qualities as sophistication, understatement, suggestivity, mystery, or elegant simplicity. Some of these characteristics themselves resulted from judicious blends: of the Japanese and the foreign, of the courtly and the rustic, or of the sacred and the profane. But the art of the age was by no means limited to the aesthetic ideals of *wabi*, *sabi*, and *yūgen*.[19] Sōchō was also a witness to and at times a participant in other arts of the period that were characterized not by an ethereal idealism but by an engagement with the human, the hilarious, and the here and now. Among these were *otogizōshi* "companion stories," *kojōruri* and *kyōgen* plays, *Heike* recitation, *kōwakamai* ballad drama, and *kouta* popular songs. Sōchō's enjoyment of the last in particular was well known; he mentions them several times in his journal, and a famous collection of such songs, *Kanginshū*, was once popularly attributed to him. Demonstrative of an increasing interest on the part of elites in the popular affairs of this world was the appearance of genre paintings depicting various trades and occupations (*shokunin zukushie*) and those portraying festivals and daily life in Kyoto, called "scenes in and around the capital" (*rakuchū rakugaizu*). One early extant example of the latter, the Machida screens, dates from 1525 and gives a sense of the appearance of Kyoto exactly during the years covered by *The Journal of Sōchō*.[20] Barbara Ruch has summarized this "other side" of Muromachi culture:

> "Tea, men, and poetry" has a very different ring than does "wine, women, and song." The first three constitute the main ingredients in the history of Muromachi Japan as commonly depicted today. Yet the history of medieval life and literature, and indeed of Japanese culture as we know it today, is inconceivable without the ceremonials and liberations of saké, the fascinations of female artistry, and the social bonding of song.[21]

Both "sides" have always been part of the Japanese cultural matrix; what distinguishes the Age of the Country at War is a new intensity of conflict, dialogue, and transaction between them, and a new willingness to depict them in literature and the other arts.

The Journal of Sōchō is a corrective to any notion of completely separate and exclusive spheres of elite and nonelite cultural practice during the Sengoku period. As in the areas of politics, economics, and religion, the artistic, educational, and recreational life of the era consisted of a mix of discourses and mutual appropriations between high and popular cultural forms.[22] If we continue to refer here for convenience to such binary equations as elite/nonelite or high/popular, it is with the proviso that the cultures of those spheres were by no means entirely mutually exclusive. Both areas were instead constellations of what Herbert Gans calls "taste cultures" and "taste publics." "Taste cultures" consist of "values, the cultural forms that express these values: music, art, design, literature, drama, comedy, poetry, criticism, news, and the media in which these are expressed"; "taste publics" comprise "users who make similar choices of values and taste culture content."[23]

Cultural borrowing between taste publics was a matter not only of appropriation of artifacts of elite taste cultures by nonelite publics but also of the reverse. The profession of the linked-verse master was in large part concerned with the former, that is, with facilitating the acquisition of the elite form of linked verse and its attendant classical literary episteme by newly enfranchised provincial overlords. This symbiosis between warriors and artists was one major reason for the cultural efflorescence of the sixteenth century. Cultural borrowing by taste publics, of course, was nothing new; *Heike monogatari* (The Tale of the Heike), for example, is much concerned with the cultural dialogue between warriors and the Heian court. But such appropriation grew enormously in the Higashiyama (1443–90) and Sengoku eras. Now not only the military but newly prosperous merchants in Sakai, *machishū* townsmen of the capital, and even rising cultivators were attending gatherings to compose verse or to compare varieties of tea, which were sometimes prepared with elegant utensils. Not only warrior aristocrats, but also merchants could now study renga, and some were even acquiring part of the secret traditions of *Kokinshū*, a phenomenon that would have been unthinkable for earlier guardians of the courtly poetic legacy.

Elite taste publics were also coming into increasing contact with nonelites and sharing in or co-opting more plebeian art forms. This too, of course, had been occurring for centuries, three notable late Heian cases in point being Fujiwara Akihira, who depicted lower-class life and entertainments in *Shinsarugakuki*; Ōe Masafusa, who wrote of prostitutes in *Yūjoki*, puppeteers in *Kairaishiki*, and popular tales in *Gōdanshō*; and Emperor Goshirakawa, who studied popular song and anthologized hundreds of examples in his *Ryōjin hishō*.[24] Some of the major elite forms of art in the Sengoku period had borrowed from popular sources. Such borrowing became marked in the Period of the Northern and Southern Courts (Nanbokuchō), itself an era of prolonged violence. The mature form of the nō drama, for example, resulted in part from the combination at that time of courtly poetic elements with popular dance forms, and one early type of high renga was concurrently molded by the courtier Nijō Yoshimoto and his commoner advisor, the monk Kyūsei, through a blend of courtly and certain popular poetic styles. Members of elite circles by no means only engaged in elite forms of art; Sōgi, Sanetaka, and other notable representatives of the high cultural tradition also enjoyed composing popular forms of noncanonical haikai verse. Sōchō made especially important contributions to this particular discourse.

Taste publics in the Sengoku era were becoming progressively porous; already in the fourteenth century the courtier Yoshimoto had instructed the plebeian *sarugaku* actor Zeami in matters of court literature and had been in turn instructed by him in the nō drama. Some time later the secret traditions of *Kokinshū (Kokin denju)* were for the first time conferred on a warrior, Tō no Tsuneyori. A century later the borrowing went backwards, with Sōgi, of middling samurai origins, conferring the traditions on a courtier, Sanetaka.[25] Herbert Gans has referred to this interpersonal exchange across boundaries as "cultural straddling"; Carlo Ginzburg, echoing Bakhtin, has referred to it as cultural "circularity."[26] The images are apt, though the straddling or circularity was plural and overlapping. In the case of appropriation by cultural elites, it is sometimes hard to know when they were engaging in déclassé co-optation and when they were simply demonstrating their membership in a common culture that knew no social hierarchy.[27] When, for example, the Regent Konoe Hisamichi made a version of the popular otogizōshi story *Shuten dōji* (The Wine-Drinking Demon) and sent it to the daimyo of Sagami, it was less a case of the story being adopted from a popular source than of making use of a shared cultural artifact.[28]

Peter Burke is quite right to point out with reference to such blending in early modern Europe that members of the elite were "bicultural," taking part simultaneously in literate high culture and popular, largely oral, tradition.[29] But David Johnson, in reference to cultural interchange in the same period in China, has added the important caveat that elites inevitably participated in that shared popular tradition in a different manner from the unlettered masses.[30] Konoe Hisamichi's perspective on the story of the Wine-Drinking Demon would have been different from that of an illiterate farmer hearing it told by a traveling priest who pointed out scenes from the story on a picture scroll as he narrated. But it is equally dangerous to generalize about the masses; as our mention of wealthy cultivators has already implied, there were also huge status differences and cultural variations among the members of the lower classes which must be kept in mind, for some of those nonelites too were in the process of becoming bicultural or multicultural from, as it were, the bottom up.

Cultural interaction in Sengoku Japan was as complex a phenomenon as it was widespread. Subsequent chapters here will in part be concerned with the social, political, and aesthetic aspects of the fluid cultural matrix as it is demonstrated in *The Journal of Sōchō*.

It is important to add, however, that although The Age of the Country at War was characterized by unprecedented social mobility and cultural intercourse, the separation between elite and nonelite culture was still very much operative. This is as relevant to a cultural characterization of Sengoku Japan as is the notion of give-and-take between taste publics. The relatively low-born Sōgi, for example, might lecture to courtiers, but a face-to-face meeting with the emperor would have been unthinkable. The very distinction, in fact, between the elite and the nonelite in a way helped to foster artistic exchange, for warriors and merchants would have been considerably less interested in the classical literary tradition had it not carried with it the cachet of the privileged and inherently separate courtly estate. As Pierre Bourdieu has observed, "art and cultural consumption are predisposed, consciously and deliberately or not, to fulfil a social function of legitimating social differences."[31]

Again, the road and the assembly were two prominent images and agents of this Sengoku cultural interaction. It was a society in motion, and along with the armies, freebooter warriors, émigré courtiers, fund-raising monks and nuns, shamans and shamanesses, pilgrims, merchant caravans, peddlers, teamsters, corvée laborers, blind masseurs, prostitutes, thieves, and beggars, the roads carried biwa priests, sarugaku and *dengaku* troupes, itinerant entertainers, and of course linked-verse masters. Sōchō himself not only traveled frequently between Suruga and Kyoto but also to Kyushu, to Kamakura and Edo (then a small castle town), and as far as Shirakawa Gate at the northern frontier. At the same time that Japan was becoming politically atomized, with daimyo reigning supreme over autonomous domains, a consolidated national culture was emerging, shaped by elites and nonelites alike.[32]

If the roads facilitated an unprecedented degree of cultural exhange, it was in assemblies that the exchange actually occurred. Despite the long literary tradition in Japan and the spread of writing that accompanied new wealth and leisure, much of the art, entertainment, and learning practiced during the period was still largely communal and oral in nature. It was in groups that linked verse was composed, tea or incense enjoyed, and lectures held. Many of those salon activities were competitive, involving gambling or prizes for the best waka or renga verses or for guessing the provenance of tea or incense varieties. In Sōchō's day, tea was still often prepared in a separate room and then brought in to the guests, but the practice of drinking tea in the same small chamber in which it was prepared was just then gaining popularity. Also enjoyed in groups were tales about heroism or death in battle, or revenge, or tragic love, or miracles associated with temples and shrines, or ghosts, or striking it rich. Sōchō himself recorded in his journal many anecdotes involving either humor or tragedy, demonstrating that a linked-verse master was not only a poet and a teacher but at times an entertainer. There were lectures, too, by definition communal, both on religious topics and on Chinese or Japanese classics. Such lectures might be written down and circulated. Some of the material presented at communal gatherings was more properly called vocal rather than oral, to use Barbara Ruch's distinction, for it involved narratives memorized from written sources and then recited.[33] Such "vocal literature" included the chanting of episodes from *Heike monogatari* by blind priests to the accompaniment of biwa lute, and the presentation of passages from *Taiheiki*, rhythmically delivered by tale-chanting monks. Vocal literature also shaded into the areas of written literature and drama. Diaries of the period often mention works of written literature being read aloud to others, occasionally with commentary added.[34] Sengoku Japan was still a manuscript culture; copies of the great works of literature were rare and expensive, and they were shared orally as a matter of course. This was nothing new, certainly; the structure of *Genji monogatari* (The Tale of Genji) is in parts reminiscent of oral performance practices, and the work was later customarily read aloud to others, often with comments by the person reading.[35] Many of these communal pastimes—waka, renga, the theater, tea, flower arranging—took place in a building set aside for them called a *kaisho* (meeting place), and the arts and entertainments of the period are in consequence sometimes referred to as "salon culture."[36] More prevalent use of lamp oil beginning in the fourteenth century meant that such meetings could increasingly be held at night.

The culture of the salon also overlapped with that of the temple compound and the marketplace, venues that again recall the interactive nature of the religion, art, and entertainment of the period. Some communal activities were held in *muen* or "unconnected" areas where normal status boundaries were disregarded and broader social transaction was encouraged.[37] Likewise in the practice of tea or linked verse, acknowledged differences in social standing did not preclude mutual engagement by the participants. Sengoku Japan still operated largely on a face-to-face, oral basis; lord-vassal ties were deeply personal, as were master-disciple relationships in both religion and the arts. Sōchō worked hard to maintain his wide circle of acquaintances by writing letters, examples of which are preserved in his journal. But he was still obliged to travel constantly, for in the end his art was predicated on communal performance.

Linked Verse

Indeed, the renga art was undoubtedly the prime artistic correlative of the dialectical and agonistic nature of the age. Renga *was* linking: of verses, of people, and of poetic traditions. Linked verse was also intrinsically a metaphor for contemporary social displacement, for just as inferiors were overcoming their superiors, only to be subsequently overcome themselves, so in renga did each new lower verse in time become an upper verse, only to pass from immediate consideration itself when a third verse was added. The orthodox and codified form of renga was a combination of art, religion, and sport, and it could demand of the participants a blend of many of the personal talents essential to success in the world outside the renga session, among them wit, tact, aggressiveness, education, and culture.[38] The successful renga poet in the high tradition had to know the range and limits of the orthodox poetic lexicon, which had developed over centuries of waka usage, and the conventional applications of each poetic topic (its "basic essence," *hon'i*). A good poet needed in addition hundreds of famous earlier waka poems at his mental fingertips if he was to recognize the classical allusion of a neighbor's verse so that he might himself supply an appropriate link. And he essentially had to memorize the hundreds of rules (*shikimoku*) which fill twelve densely printed pages in one standard early modern edition (see Chapter Four). But once the poet had mastered those mechanics he was required to internalize them and then rise above them and concentrate on poetic effect. At the most elevated and formal sessions there was a scribe (*shuhitsu*) in attendance who recorded each verse as it was orally presented and who checked it for infractions of the rules, in order that the poets might be free to focus on artistic considerations. Ideally a renga master (*sōshō*) like Sōchō also participated to orchestrate the literary quality of the sequence by making suggestions and by composing verses at critical junctures himself. A linked-verse session ideally included seven or eight poets, who would join in composing a hundred-verse sequence (*hyakuin*) over the course of a single day.[39] As the poets linked verse to verse, constructing a neoclassical literary universe while vying with each other to be first with the next link, they recreated their own world in miniature, one blended of ancient courtly ideals and cut-throat Sengoku realities.

Just as the linked-verse sequence was a metaphor for the dialogue that characterized the age, so was the membership of each linked-verse session. If the Muromachi era saw the growth of a national literary consciousness, so did that era see linked verse become a national high literary form, in the sense that its greatest practitioners came from all strata of society, from the courtier Sanjōnishi Sanetaka to Satomura Jōha, the son of a temple servant.[40]

There were, however, differences between formal, courtly, bakufu, and commoner renga styles.[41] And there were limits to the social transaction at the linked-verse session.[42] At most formal renga sessions the seating order was fixed according to social rank, and care had to be taken not only by the participants but by the scribe and even by the renga master to avoid offending elevated personages. One tract on renga etiquette, *Renga kaiseki shiki* (Rules for Renga Sessions) by Sōchō's student, the Kantō warrior literatus Nitta Shōjun, devotes considerable space to matters of deportment under just such circumstances.[43] It advises, for example, that

> if you are at a session with men of rank or with experts, do not attempt fine verses; instead you should do your share in a simple manner. Moreover you should exercise caution when it is the place for the guest of honor to compose. Conflict with the ranking participants will be the worst fault of the day; always try to avoid it.[44]

Nor did the social blend at formal renga sessions in Sōchō's time normally extend to women.[45] The genre had been extremely popular among both sexes in the Heian and Kamakura courts, and Izumi Shikibu, Ben no Naishi, her sister Shōshō no Naishi, and Lady Nijō are all known to have composed renga verses.[46] But by the fourteenth century women apparently had generally ceased to appear at elite renga functions, and there is no mention of feminine participation in any of the renga meetings noted in *The Journal of Sōchō*.[47]

For the renga art as for the age, the road and the assembly—travel and meeting—become dominant metaphors. Renga had long been conceived of as a literary correlative for mutability and the ineluctable passage of time, and its poets, as travelers through successive verse-worlds. As Yoshimoto puts it in *Tsukuba mondō* (Questions and Answers about the Way of Tsukuba, c. 1357–72),

> Renga does not link past and future thoughts. Verses pass through the realms of maturity and decline, pleasure and pain one after the next, just as the affairs of this changing world. The poet thinks of yesterday and already today arrives; he thinks of spring and already it is autumn; he thinks of the blossoms and already

the colored foliage has appeared—is this different from the way the blossoms scatter and leaves fall in life itself?[48]

The renga poet became a figurative traveler through time and space as he composed, and the renga master became a literal one as well, as he journeyed from place to place in the practice of his art. The road was Sōchō's *michi*, his poetic way; it was for him both a religious quest and a livelihood. It was a way across the ages, linking past literary and religious traditions with present-day economic and social realities. For Sōchō the monk, the road represented an escape from mundane attachments, a path of renunciation and asceticism (*shugyō*). For Sōchō the Sengoku poet and teacher, it was a route *to* fellow artists, patrons, students, and admirers. Sōchō was at once an eremitic poet-priest after the manner of Saigyō and a new merchant of culture, making his living from literary commerce. Renga masters were Japan's first truly professional men of letters, since they earned their living directly through their art.[49]

Travel literature was therefore perhaps as natural a by-product of Sōchō's poetic life as was his poetry itself. *The Journal of Sōchō* is both a classical travel diary, in the tradition of those written through the centuries by wandering poet-priests, and a literary merchant's daybook that records the products and contexts of its author's cultural transactions.

And just as the road and the hermitage were for the poet-priest complementary forms of renunciation, so for Sōchō were his stationary moments in Suruga and Kyoto of equal importance to his moments on the road, in terms of both his spiritual life and his poetic calling. For Sōchō, both his periods of movement and his periods of stasis were informed by a blend of the religious, the literary, and the commercial, as well as the social and the private. It was perhaps inevitable therefore that his journal should burst the bonds of a pure travel diary and become instead a record of his entire cultural life.

Saiokuken Sōchō

Sōchō's birth and upbringing were premonitory of the role he would later play in linking disparate cultural discourses. He is thought to have been born in Shimada in Suruga Province. The town was located a little more than halfway down the Tōkaidō road from Kyoto, the ancient center of court culture and current seat of the Ashikaga warrior government, and messengers constantly passed through it on their way to and from Kamakura, the base of Ashikaga power in

CHAPTER ONE

Kantō, the eastland. Provincials though they were, the residents of Shimada were well placed to learn of political events in the two centers of national power.

In social status as in location, Sōchō (as he would later be called) was by birth "middle of the road"; his father is thought to have been Gojō Yoshisuke, swordsmith to Imagawa Yoshitada, the Suruga constable. Yoshisuke is said to have been granted the first character of his name as a mark of his lord's special favor.[50] In that age of warfare, the profession of swordsmith was particularly respected; it was perhaps equal in prestige to that of a lower-level samurai. While not himself of warrior status, Sōchō spent his youth in constant close association with the warrior elite of the domain, and he grew to be completely familiar with their values and way of life.

At the relatively late age of seventeen, however, Sōchō became a monk, taking ordination, preparatory discipline, and baptism in the Shingon sect.[51] The training this involved, combined with his later study of Zen, gave him a far more formal and thorough religious background than that possessed by most renga poets, who often donned religious garb pro forma and called themselves priests (*hōshi*).

But the fact that he shaved his head only after reaching young adulthood meant that he also had considerably more experience in secular, warrior life than had priests who entered the monastery as young boys. And he did not entirely abandon the way of the sword even after taking the tonsure, electing instead to travel with the Imagawa armies, most likely as a monk scribe (*shokisō*). Sōchō himself recognized the varied and even contradictory elements of his upbringing, and in his third diary, *Utsunoyama no ki* (Utsunoyama Chronicle), written in 1518 when he had passed the age of seventy, he related that

> though the child of a humble artisan of little skill, I became a priest at seventeen and received ordination, preparatory discipline, and finally baptism. In my twenties, violence broke out in the province and lasted six or seven years. Fighting also continued for three years in Tōtōmi. I mingled with the worldly dust of encampments, but my diet at least was a meager, priestly one of thistles and such.[52]

Traveling with the army deepened Sōchō's practical understanding of military affairs, which he later put to use in the chronicles he wrote for the Asahina, vassals of the Imagawa, and included in his journal.

This blend of war and religion in Sōchō's life was further complicated by his study of poetry, which he also began as a boy. Though literary pursuits were dismissed by some warriors as effeminate and by some monks as delusory, the way of poetry had for centuries been a venerable part of the education of monks and warriors alike, and Sōchō's early experiences in both walks of life would have given him double exposure to the Japanese and Chinese literary classics. An early biography, *Sōchō Kojiden*, records the quite plausible detail that he participated in his first renga session at the age of twelve.[53] The signal event in his early poetic training occurred six years later, when the linked-verse master Sōgi stopped at Imagawa Yoshitada's residence in 1466 on his way east. It was the eighteen-year-old Sōchō who guided the older poet, then forty-five, to the famous local scenic spot (*meisho*), Kiyomi Strand.[54] It was probably this first meeting, occasioned by Sōchō's Imagawa connections, that later prepared the way for him to call on Sōgi and become his disciple. The encounter obviously made a deep impression on the young poet, and more than a half-century later he wrote of the meeting when he revisited the site in 1524 (*JS*: 56–57, see Chapter Two).

Seven years later, in 1473, Sōchō's Imagawa linkage again afforded him the opportunity to meet a poet of considerable renown, Matsushita Shōkō, who like Sōgi stopped in the Suruga capital on a trip through the eastland.[55] Shōkō was the closest disciple of the great poet Shōtetsu, who had taught a generation of poets in the capital, including Sōgi's teachers Sōzei and Shinkei. Again it was Sōchō who took the celebrated guest to Kiyomi, which suggests that the Imagawa already recognized the young man's poetic precocity and that Sōchō was making every use of his Imagawa ties to expand his poetic connections. Reminiscences about that early but formative visit are likewise preserved in *The Journal of Sōchō* (*JS*: 57–58).

Sōchō and the Imagawa House

Sōchō was fortunate to have been associated with the Imagawa because they were uncommonly devoted to artistic pursuits and boasted a long and illustrious history of both cultural (*bun*) and martial (*bu*) accomplishments.[56] That history informs much of the journal. Sōchō's first patron, Imagawa Yoshitada, counted among his forebears Imagawa Ryōshun and Imagawa Norimasa, both of whom left important literary works.[57] Yoshitada emulated their cultural example, though in a far more limited way. *Imagawake ryakki* (Abbreviated Chronicle of the Imagawa House) relates that "he was a spirited and courageous general, accomplished with both bow and horse. He also appreciated waka and renga."[58] A house genealogy, *Imagawa keizu* (Imagawa Lineage), goes so far as to state that "he enjoyed renga and studied with the priest Sōgi."[59] Though these references to Yoshitada's attention to the bun-bu ethic are perhaps exaggerated, it is true that Sōgi's first collections of personal verses, *Wasuregusa* (Grass of Forgetfulness, completed in or before 1474), includes lines that the poet composed at Yoshitada's manor in 1466. It was at that point that the fledgling poet Sōchō guided the older master to Kiyomi Strand.

Yoshitada also contributed to the incipient cultural efflorescence of the Imagawa capital through his marriage to the niece of Ise Sadachika, advisor to Shogun Yoshimasa. The alliance gave Yoshitada a closer connection to the highest reaches of the warrior aristocracy and, by extension, to members of the court. The Kyoto acquaintances of Lady Kitagawa, as his wife came to be known, were later instrumental in arranging for the marriage of their daughter Kitamuki to the court aristocrat Ōgimachisanjō Sanemochi, who became one of Sōchō's close friends. Lady Kitagawa too became one of Sōchō's devoted patrons. For Yoshitada, the alliance had not only cultural but military advantages, for Lady Kitagawa's elder brother was the warrior later known as Hōjō Sōun, who eventually became master of Izu and Sagami. Yoshitada's marriage thus represented a further step in the appropriation by the Imagawa of Kyoto culture that was to advance so much under subsequent generations.

The marriage is thought to have taken place in 1467, when Yoshitada was in Kyoto to reinforce Hosokawa Katsumoto and the Eastern Army at the start of the Ōnin War.[60] Sōchō may have accompanied him.[61] If Sōchō was indeed in Yoshitada's company, then he first experienced the flowery capital that bulked so large in his poetic training just when it was being destroyed in the battles between the armies of Katsumoto and Yamana Sōzen, who favored rival shogunal successors to Ashikaga Yoshimasa. By the end of 1467, the once-great city lay in ruins, and it was described in *Ōninki* as "the lair of wolves and foxes."[62] In the next decade it was reduced to two small fragments, the Upper and Lower Capitals, connected by a narrow strip along Muromachi Avenue. Though the Ōnin War itself gradually dwindled to a close some years after the deaths of Katsumoto and Sōzen in 1473, the capital was the site of sporadic violence thereafter, and later in his life Sōchō left the city several times because of fire and insurrection.

Yoshitada soon returned to his own domain to counter campaigns in the region by the Shiba house, members of the rival Western Army in the Ōnin conflict. He devoted the rest of his life to strengthening Imagawa influence in Tōtōmi (Shizuoka Prefecture), which had been transferred to the constableship of the Shiba house in the early fifteenth century. It is believed that the Imagawa had been granted Tōtōmi holdings by the bakufu in recompense for their services in its defense. Yoshitada's campaign against the Shiba and their allies in that province was another central topic of Sōchō's chronicle.

Toward the end of his journal, Sōchō also included a lengthy document in which he outlined his lifelong patronage relationship with the Imagawa family. While he devoted most of his remarks therein to his dealings with Yoshitada's son Ujichika and grandson Ujiteru, he wrote with regard to Yoshitada that "though I was in no special service to Lord Yoshitada, I was close to him day and night for years" (*JS*: 162). The wording of the passage has led Ijichi Tetsuo to speculate about a homosexual relationship between the two.[63] Such affairs were common among medieval warriors and monks alike, and a number are recounted in *The Journal of Sōchō*.

But when Sōchō was eighteen, his first Imagawa patron was killed in a skirmish with local warlords loyal to the Shiba house. Yoshitada's death in his prime, in 1476, precipitated a succession dispute (Bunmei no naikō) between forces loyal to his five-year-old son Ryūōmaro (or Tatsuōmaro) and those supporting a more mature candidate, Oga Norimitsu, a cousin of Yoshitada.[64] Lady Kitagawa went into hiding with her son and relied on her brother Sōun to bring about a settlement between the forces of the disputants and their respective allies among two rival branches of the Uesugi family, who were each hoping to profit by the conflict at the expense of the other. Sōun effected an agreement between the two sides in 1478 whereby Norimitsu would serve as interim head of the Imagawa house until Ryūōmaro attained his majority. The crisis averted, Norimitsu installed himself in the Suruga capital, and Lady Kitagawa and her son took up residence in the post town of Mariko. But Ryūōmaro's fifteenth year came and went with no indication that the interim leader would relinquish his position. By 1487 the young heir could wait no longer; with Sōun's help he attacked Norimitsu, killed him, and took over command of the Imagawa domain. He assumed the name Ujichika on the occasion of his belated coming-of-age ceremony, then in the following years worked to realize his father's ambitions in Tōtōmi with the aid of his uncle Sōun, while also supporting Sōun's forays into the Kantō region.[65]

The death of Yoshitada was the first important linkage lost to Sōchō, and it closed the first chapter in his life. When Lady Kitagawa and her son went into hiding, Sōchō lost whatever immediate patronage opportunities remained to him in the Suruga capital, and he decided the time was ripe to travel to Kyoto and pursue his education with the master he had briefly met years earlier, Sōgi.

CHAPTER ONE

In making the decision to travel to Kyoto, Sōchō was going back in time, leaving the provinces for the ancient center of Japan's cultural tradition. For more than half a century thereafter, Sōchō's life would oscillate between the center and the periphery, a dual perspective that would be reflected in his journal.

Sōchō and Sōgi

Sōchō was twenty-eight when he set out from the Imagawa domain. He wrote in *Utsunoyama no ki*, "I conceived the desire to see the shrines of the capital, the seven great temples of Nara, and Mount Kōya, and I set out, heedless of the virtue of my own province" (*UYK*: 404). He was not to resettle permanently in Suruga until nearly three decades had passed.

In Kyoto he became Sōgi's disciple and began his true literary apprenticeship. Sōgi was in his fifties in the late 1470s and had returned from his intermittent eight-year sojourn in the east in 1473, having completed his acquisition of the secret traditions of *Kokinshū* from Tō no Tsuneyori in the previous year.[66] He had met the young Sōchō on his own journey in pursuit of poetic mastery; now Sōchō was traveling to Kyoto to study with the older poet. Sōchō would count Tsuneyori's son Tō no Sojun among his close friends.

Sōchō came under Sōgi's influence just as the older poet was well on the way toward becoming the preeminent composer and teacher of linked verse when that form of poetry was reaching the apex of its popularity.[67] In 1474 Sōgi had finished work on *Wasuregusa*, for which Shogun Ashikaga Yoshimasa contributed the title calligraphy in his own hand. Two years thereafter, he completed his major renga anthology *Chikurinshō* (Bamboo Grove Collection). He had by this time become highly respected by both bakufu and courtly poets and was in frequent contact with the court literati Ichijō Kaneyoshi and Sanjōnishi Sanetaka. Sōchō would become heir not only to Sōgi's teachings about poetry and its underlying classical tradition, but also to his network of friends and patrons.

Though none of his pre-Kyoto verses survives, Sōchō no doubt had already become an accomplished poet in order to be able to call upon the master. It was under Sōgi, however, that his poetic art fully matured through constant practice in skilled company. Soon after taking up with Sōgi, Sōchō (then called Sōkan) accompanied him to the domain of the daimyo Uesugi Fusasada in Echigo Province (Niigata Prefecture) in 1478, and then returned with him to Kyoto via the fortress of Asakura Toshikage in Echizen Province in 1479.[68] It was also in 1478 that Sōgi presented Sōchō with a study entitled *Hyakunin isshushō* (Notes on *One Hundred Poems by One Hundred Poets*), consisting of notes Sōgi had taken on lectures by Tō no Tsuneyori in 1471. Sōchō was already taking his place, therefore, in a recognized line of transmission. While at Fusasada's fortress, Sōgi lectured on *Ise monogatari* (Tales of Ise), and Sōchō's record of the lectures, now known as *Ise monogatari Sōchō kikigaki*, is his earliest surviving work.[69]

The following year, 1480, Sōchō accompanied the master to the residence of Ōuchi Masahiro in Suō Province (Yamaguchi Prefecture). If Sōchō had indeed accompanied his lord Imagawa Yoshitada to Kyoto at the beginning of the Ōnin War, he may have encountered the name of Masahiro as one of the main allies of Yamana Sōzen, enemy of Yoshitada and his Hosokawa allies. But Masahiro treated Sōgi, Sōchō, and the others in their company with consummate generosity. The poets later toured the Ōuchi lands in northwest Kyushu, a journey recorded in Sōgi's *Tsukushi michi no ki* (Account of a Kyushu Journey, 1480; see Chapter Two). Sōchō's first extant linked-verse sequences date from that trip, beginning with Bunmei 12 [1480]:8 *Nanimichi hyakuin* (A Hundred-Verse Sequence Entitled "A Kind of Path"), a dedicatory sequence composed in Suō for the Hachiman Shrine there. He was thirty-two at the time.

During those journeys Sōchō learned firsthand the mechanics of patronage and the nature of a professional poet's life on the road. Though he never again traveled to the Ōuchi domains, he was to make at least one other visit to the Uesugi in 1501. The Asakura became a major part of Sōchō's professional network, and he would stay with them at least four more times on his own. It was to visit them in 1522 that he set out on the trip that begins his journal, and they are mentioned in the work a number of times.

Sōgi's literary influence on Sōchō was immense, and it forms at once the reference point and a counterpoint for Sōchō's own career. Sōchō made frequent mention of his teacher's guidance in his own handbooks, many of which were written years after Sōgi's death. In addition, of the more than fifty renga sessions dating before the eighth month of 1502 in which Sōchō participated and for which records remain, all but four included Sōgi as well. Of his debt to the master, Sōchō later wrote:

> For more than forty years I enjoyed a pleasant relationship with Sōgi, a cultivated gentleman, and learned from him the basics of linked verse. Now passed away, he was renowned in the capital, and he associated with both the court and the shogunate. His life spanned more than eighty years. Because of him even one of

no consequence such as myself was able to appear at elevated renga gatherings. How strong must have been our bond in a previous life! On my last trip to Kyoto [in 1516] I was reminded of him often. (*UYK*: 404)

Sōchō and Ikkyū

During the same years that Sōchō was establishing his relationship with Sōgi, he was also receiving instruction from the great Zen prelate Ikkyū.[70] Ikkyū's influence on Sōchō's spiritual development was to be as deep as that of Sōgi on his literary art.[71]

Ikkyū was in his eighties when Sōchō first came to know him, and he had already achieved fame for his incisive intellect, uncompromising reformist spirit, and personal eccentricity. To his hermitage came some of the finest artistic minds of the Higashiyama period. Murata Jukō, acknowledged as the main early formulator of wabi tea, was a disciple and lived for a time in Ikkyū's posthumous subtemple Shinjuan at Daitokuji. He is said to have been deeply influenced by the relationship between Ikkyū's Zen and tea taste.[72] The nō actor Konparu Zenchiku was another student, and he went on to expound theories of fusion between Zen and the nō drama.[73] In painting, members of the Soga school, most notably Soga Jasoku, created under Ikkyū's influence works now counted among the most original of the period.[74] In renga, Sōi and possibly Chiun, two of the Seven Sages of Linked Verse (Renga Shichiken) anthologized in Sōgi's *Chikurinshō*, studied with him.[75] Another disciple is said to have been Yamazaki Sōkan, who reputably compiled the *Shinsen inu tsukubashū* anthology of haikai (see Chapter Four). The great renga poet Shinkei wrote of the Zen master in his *Hitorigoto* (Talking to Myself, 1468), "It is the priest Ikkyū who is acknowledged to stand apart from the rest in thought and deed in the world today."[76]

Ikkyū himself was a painter and shakuhachi player, and he even dabbled in composition for the nō theater. Under his influence his last hermitage, Shūon'an, in Takigi, south of Kyoto, became not only a spiritual retreat but an artistic salon.[77] The artists mentioned, together with subsequent generations of followers inspired by Ikkyū, were central to the formulation of the Higashiyama aesthetic. But it is likely that his disciples were drawn to him less for specific religious or artistic teachings than for his personal charisma and attitude toward life. His emphasis on spiritual substance over empty display and his self-confidence, individualism, and courage of conviction were surely a major catalyst for the many original minds who came to him for guidance.

The young poet could have known Ikkyū for two or three years at most, but the influence of the great priest seems only to have increased over the course of Sōchō's life. Indeed, it may have been Ikkyū who gave Sōchō his sobriquet Saioku or Saiokuken, and Sōchō is referred to as "Disciple of Ikkyū" in one manuscript of the second imperially recognized renga anthology, *Shinsen tsukubashū* (Newly Selected *Tsukubashū*, 1495).[78]

Later, Sōchō would express on three different occasions his desire to die at Shūon'an in Takigi, where he probably spent most of his time with the master.[79] He visited the hermitage during both stays in the Kansai region depicted in his journal, and his trip to the Asakura in Echizen in 1523, likewise chronicled in the journal, was undertaken to raise money for Daitokuji's rebuilding. Sōchō's journal concentrates on his cultural rather than his religious activities, but the fact that three of the main journeys therein are directly related to Takigi, Daitokuji, and Ikkyū's memory gives those trips something of a pilgrimage quality, though in a very understated way.

As opposed to the underlying spiritual aspect of his trips west, Sōchō's journeys east, to Suruga and the Imagawa, are in a sense a return to stronger secular influences. It would be an exaggeration to cast *The Journal of Sōchō* entirely as a literary metaphor for repeated attempts and failures to renounce the secular world. But the dynamic between the sacred and the secular created by the competing attractions of Takigi and Suruga complicated Sōchō's last years and constitutes an animating factor of the diary in which they are recorded.

Poetic Maturity and the Question of Influence

In 1486, a decade or so after he took up studies with Sōgi, Sōchō finally adopted the name by which he is known today. The change of name is indicative of the poetic maturity he had reached by that time. In 1488, for example, he joined with Sōgi and Shōhaku in the composition of *Minase sangin*, probably the most famous hundred-verse sequence in renga history.[80] It was also in 1488 that he produced a commentary on selected segments from *Genji monogatari* entitled *Shijin zanshō* (Remaining Notes on Purple Dust), his first extant piece of original scholarship (as opposed to his notes from Sōgi's lectures). Two years thereafter he wrote his first guides to aspects of renga composition, *Nagabumi* (Long Letter) and *Sōchō kawa* (Sōchō's Talks on Waka, also known as *Mikawa kudari*, Down to Mikawa). Then in 1491, he again joined with Sōgi and Shōhaku in composing another sequence that was to achieve great fame, entitled *Yuyama sangin*.[81] By this

CHAPTER ONE

period he had acquired the renga skill, the lineage of great teachers, and the beginning of a network of influential or wealthy personal contacts he would need to expand his literary activity thereafter.

The reputation of Sōchō's own teacher, Sōgi, was rising concurrently. In 1488 he had been appointed by the bakufu to the posts of Commissioner of Linked Verse at Kitano Shrine (Kitano Renga Kaisho Bugyō), and Laureate (Sōshō), and then in 1495 his career reached what Sōgi himself surely saw as its zenith with the compilation under his direction of the *Shinsen tsukubashū* linked-verse anthology.[82] As Sōgi's disciple, Sōchō was also heavily involved in the long and taxing project; the relatively large number of his own verses in the work, thirty-eight, demonstrates that he had become recognized as a renga master of the first rank.[83]

But in spite of his success in the literary world of the capital, Sōchō decided in 1496 to return to Suruga. He may at that point have already intended to use his considerable poetic notoriety to cultivate the patronage of Imagawa Ujichika, son of his earlier protector, Yoshitada.[84] He stayed in Suruga until the following year then returned again to the capital, only to find that his own cottage had been burned in his absence in the sporadic violence now endemic to the city. A turning point had been reached; Ikkyū was long dead and Sōgi was already in his late seventies, Sōchō himself was fifty, and Suruga held the promise of relative tranquillity and support. It was probably for those reasons that he decided in 1499 to go back again to the Imagawa capital and further his connections with the Imagawa house.

But he did not abandon his old relationships, and in 1501 he agreed to join Sōgi in the Uesugi domain of Echigo. Just as a journey to Echigo was the first of Sōchō's travels with Sōgi, a visit to that province would be the last, for the old master died in the company of Sōchō and another disciple, Gessonsai Sōseki, en route from Echigo to the Imagawa domain in 1502. Sōchō chronicled the master's last journey, death, and burial in his first piece of diary literature, *Sōgi shūenki* (The Death of Sōgi, 1502).

Sōchō did not return to Kyoto immediately after Sōgi's death, choosing instead to live in the Suruga capital of his youth. He wrote of his decision in *Utsunoyama no ki*:

> After I came down to this province of Suruga violence broke out in Kyoto, and the cottage I had lived in there was burned. I went back to the capital only to return here, where I built a house near Ujichika. I planted spring and autumn

trees and other flora, made a large pond, and brought in abundant fresh water. I was blessed with a plentiful crop of rice to tide me over summer and winter, and the smoke from my cooking fire rose morning and evening. (*UYK*: 396)

This was probably the dwelling Sōchō later referred to in his journal as his "lodging by the river" (*JS*: 62).[85] In about 1504, however, Sōchō decided to build a second, more rustic residence in the post town of Mariko across Abekawa river, about five kilometers southwest of Ujichika's fortress, where Lady Kitagawa and her son had taken refuge decades before.[86] This Brushwood Cottage (Saioku) was located on the fief of an important Imagawa vassal, Saitō Yasumoto. Sōchō wrote in retrospect of the project:

> At the beginning of the Eishō era, I decided I wished to live in this mountain cottage and so spoke to Yasumoto. It was quite easily done. That spring, at the start of the third month, at a linked-verse session of Yasumoto's, I composed this:
>
> | yamazakura | The mountain cherries— |
> | omou iro sou | how my longing for them |
> | kasumi kana | is enhanced by the haze! |
>
> By this I meant that I felt my desire for a mountain cottage would be fulfilled and that the haze on the peak and the mountain scenery were making me anticipate it all the more. In the fourth month we selected a spot and built the cottage in the usual way. (*UYK*: 396)

He also recorded his new commitment to life in the east in more personal ways:

> In this province of Suruga I became acquainted with the woman who did my clothes and had two children by her. One was a boy, whom I put under the care of Yasumoto with the intent of making him a priest. I gave him his youth's name. He is now a novice called Jōha, eleven years old. The girl is thirteen. I had meant her for the religious life as well, but a man took a liking to her, and I am told they were betrothed at the end of this year. I am now free from care and will have no regrets at my end. And yet, somehow I still worry about them:
>
> | kore kare ni | Although I am now |
> | kakehanaruredo | separated from them both, |
> | aware nari | I care about them still. |
> | ko o omou yami wa | It is futile to speak |
> | iu kai mo nashi | of the folly of a parent's love. |
>
> (*UYK*: 404)[87]

Sōchō was in his mid-fifties when he became a father. Though Zen monks were expected in principle to live celibate lives, by the late Muromachi period conjugal relationships appear to have been tacitly accepted. Ikkyū himself had established a precedent for such relationships when he took a mistress named Mori (or Shin) in his late seventies.[88]

Sōchō's decision in 1496 to return to Suruga and Imagawa patronage suggests how different his personality and professional goals were from those of Sōgi. Though Sōchō would to the end of his life honor Sōgi's memory and his linked-verse style, there was evidently too much Ikkyū in him to follow the older poet's path to political preferment in the capital. As later chapters here will elaborate, Sōchō's journal is in a sense a literary reification of both the similarities and the differences between himself and Sōgi.

Particularly demonstrative of Sōchō's divergent perspective is his apparent lack of interest in acquiring two of the most important political emblems of literary authority that Sōgi had obtained, which were the secret traditions of the *Kokinshū* anthology and the bakufu-sponsored posts of Commissioner of Linked Verse at Kitano Shrine and Laureate.[89] Sōchō returned to Kyoto many times, and he occasionally participated in officially sponsored poetic activities, but it was Sōseki who became Sōgi's most important successor in the capital.[90]

Certainly Sōchō's decision to return to Suruga was in part pragmatic—the patronage of the impoverished court could be only spiritual in nature, and the shogun was a puppet in the control of other warriors. Life in the capital, moreover, was uncertain and at times dangerous, and even courtiers were leaving for the security of the provinces. And Sōchō was already fifty years old, a traditional watershed when thoughts turned from public pursuits toward private retirement and renunciation. But it also appears that Sōchō did not share Sōgi's ambitions to lead the Kyoto renga world, advise the emperor, and compile an imperially recognized renga anthology.

Sōchō's disinclination to acquire the full set of secret traditions of *Kokinshū* would likewise seem to stem from the same basic divergence in philosophy. Although acquisition of the traditions was considered essential to attaining poetic primacy, Sōchō's references to his own *Kokinshū* studies are extremely self-effacing:

> The late Sōgi pursued the way of poetry with great application and served as tutor to various aristocratic houses. In particular he is said to have conferred the secret traditions individually on their excellencies the Konoe and on Lord Sane-

taka. I lived with him, but for years showed no perseverance and understood not a single page. Finally I acquired a little familiarity with the *Kokinshū* anthology, but only in the most general way, hearing Sōgi lecture on it in the company of Jibukyō Hōgan Taijin of Shōren'in. (*JS*: 81)

Despite his modest disclaimer, however, Sōchō did indeed receive a part of the secret traditions himself. Sōgi's lectures, to which he so diffidently refers, were in fact a very serious affair, taking place over three months in 1492 and 1493.[91] Sōchō thought enough of his own notes of the lectures to present them much later to Imagawa Ujichika's son and heir on the occasion of the boy's coming-of-age ceremony (*JS*: 81). He obviously considered them a significant addition to a warrior house already famous for its commitment to culture.[92]

Some later scholars have taken Sōchō's modesty at face value and assumed he set little store by *Kokinshū* or, in fact, the whole classical tradition.[93] It is nearer to the mark, however, to say that Sōchō combined an absolute respect for the classics with a growing esteem for literary elements that had not previously been valued in the high classical tradition. He would have been deeply shocked at the notion that he held anything but the highest regard for the poetic orthodoxy; he spent decades mastering it and subsequently taught it with uncompromising conviction and thoroughness. He would never have risen to primacy in the renga world had he not. He possessed a deep knowledge of *Kokinshū* as well as of *Hyakunin isshu*, *Ise monogatari*, *Genji monogatari*, and insofar as it was possible in the medieval period, of *Man'yōshū*. His appreciation of *Genji monogatari* was particularly marked; it was at a discussion of the work at Sanetaka's residence in 1485 that Sōchō's friendship with that courtier began.[94] In addition, he wrote two commentaries on Murasaki Shikibu's work, *Shijin zanshō*, referred to earlier, and *Genjichū* (*Genji* Commentary, 1529).[95]

As subsequent chapters will show, Sōchō valued the secret traditions more for the ways they could improve his own poetry than for the status they might convey. To be sure, Sōgi too esteemed the traditions for their poetic content; he and his own teacher Tsuneyori in fact approached them as an instrument for the vocational training of poets rather than simply as an empty cachet.[96] But Sōgi also used the traditions to position himself, a commoner of obscure samurai origins, within the traditional poetic hierarchy and gain entrée into noble houses. This Sōchō did not do. Hosokawa Yūsai, who later received the traditions himself, perceptively summarized Sōchō's position: "Sōchō received the secret traditions of *Kokinshū* but tended not to emphasize them. He said, 'I am a linked-verse poet. Simply passing on the Way for its own sake is meaningless. If one's linked verse improves, that is enough.' "[97] Nor does Sōchō appear to have transmitted the traditions to his disciples, other than the sheets he presented to his Imagawa patrons. He certainly could have passed on what he had learned of the traditions to select poetic disciples had he been interested in establishing a poetic dynasty. But for Sōchō it was poetic composition that mattered above all else.

Sōchō's combination of dedication to the poetic way and distaste for the official perquisites of professional success is indicative of the dual influences of Sōgi and Ikkyū that would have such a marked effect on his journal literature. Of course influence is as much chosen as received, and Sōchō doubtless combined passive influence with active appropriation. And obviously it would be reductive to focus exclusively on those two figures, no matter how individually dominant. Sōchō's thought and art grew out of the entire classical literary tradition, a wealth of religious ideas, his contemporary social and historical milieu, and his native faculties; they were obviously not circumscribed by Sōgi's poetry and Ikkyū's Zen. But of all the debts that Sōchō himself recognized in his journal and that are reflected in its style and attitudes, those of Sōgi and Ikkyū appear the most clearly.

The influence of Sōgi is the easier of the two to discuss, as Sōchō committed so much of the relationship to writing. Sōchō's memories of the master figure time and again in his journal, written a quarter-century after Sōgi's death. Not only did Sōgi help educate Sōchō and shape his literary style, but he also provided a powerful example in terms of his own career and literary philosophy. Sōgi, like Sōchō, was of provincial birth, and he achieved his preeminence through a combination of poetic genius, dedication, and canny careerism, meeting the right people and appearing at influential poetic gatherings. Like many provincial warlords, both Sōgi and Sōchō rose to prominence in the literary community not through hereditary right but through native talent and personal effort. One courtier noted in grudging admiration in his diary how remarkable it was that a "beggar monk" such as Sōgi had risen to the point where he could donate money to the court itself.[98] But Sōgi's devotion to the literary way was not an empty, self-serving pose; he was absolutely committed to the neoclassical poetic orthodoxy and perceived it as a route to dispel the social discord of his time. For the benefit both of his own career and also of his poetic art, he allied himself to the establishment, in politics by cultivating connections to the imperial house and the shogunate, and in poetry by insisting on poetic orthodoxy and the resolute subordination of unorthodox poetic forms such as *kyōka* and haikai. Sengoku society had lost its moorings, Sōgi felt, and he responded by insisting on an absolute neoclassicism and prescriptivity, which would buttress a return to a conservative political order wherein those above would rule those below with principle (*dōri*) and benevolence. Only the orthodox way (*seidō*) could stave off complete social and literary disintegration. He upheld a poetic view that equated orthodoxy with holiness and heterodoxy with heresy. Poetry, religion, philosophy, and politics were one for the old master; he championed a universal and timeless religio-poetic ideal, and he rigidly subordinated the informal, the quotidian, the commonplace, and the topical.[99]

For Sōchō, Sōgi was the personification of lofty ideals and rigid standards. Through the old master he inherited a sense of the venerability and sanctity of the poetic quest and the conviction that it must be preserved and propagated in its purest form. The orthodox way was a universal way; it could be learned by all, and it could restore spiritual form and unity to a chaotic age.

But in his disinclination to establish a poetic dynasty and become doyen of the renga world of the capital, Sōchō diverged from the example of his master. That difference was suggestive of a deeper and even more basic literary divergence between the two artists. Sōgi's literary world was one of consciously chosen and rigidly exclusive *form*. While Sōchō respected and transmitted this poetic formalism in his orthodox renga practice, his self-fashioning in his journal was more descriptive than prescriptive, more inclusive than exclusive, and more multivalent than Sōgi's diary exercises. Where Sōgi patterned his self-representation after a poetic ideal, Sōchō was more inclined to let his self-portraiture find its own form, blended from formality and informality, elegant *ga* and plebeian *zoku*.[100] Surely the influence of Ikkyū was of major importance in this fundamentally different kind of self-fashioning.

Sōchō's dealings with Ikkyū appear to have been of a spiritual rather than literary nature. They were therefore documented far less frequently, perhaps reflecting the Zen injunction of "nonverbalization" (*furyū monji*), because of the inevitable disjunction between signified and signifier. But evidence from the journal, written more than four decades after Ikkyū's death, shows that the Zen priest exerted a tremendous and life-long influence on Sōchō's spiritual development and, by extension, on his literary creativity. Again, Sōchō traveled not only with Sōgi but also at the behest of Ikkyū's temple, Daitokuji, and he made large monetary contributions to that temple as well. In 1524, he found it impossible to return to Suruga before first traveling out of his way to the Shūon'an hermitage to light incense and announce his departure (*JS*: 45–46). And when he returned to Takigi in 1526, he expressed his enthusiasm in poetry:

375	suruga yori	Up from Suruga,
	isoganu hi naku	tarrying nary a day,
	yamashiro no	to Takigi
	takigi o oi no	in Yamashiro, where the weight
	ni o zo karomuru	of my old age is lifted.

(*JS*: 107)

The Journal of Sōchō gives little direct information on the ways in which its author appropriated the teachings and example of Ikkyū. But the images of the great eccentric and his disciple that remain, though necessarily transmitted and transmogrified by the written medium, indicate that the two men shared basic personality traits and perspectives. Both, for example, rejected affectation and hypocrisy and advocated a direct and unadorned expression of perceived truth. Ikkyū was an adherent of the strict Zen taught by the founder of Daitokuji, the monk Daitō, famous for having spent years as a beggar under Gojō Bridge in Kyoto. Daitō's admonitions for the monks studying at his temple demonstrate his "hard Zen" practice:

> If there is one person who leads an upright life in the open fields, dwelling in a simple thatched hut, eating vegetable roots boiled in a broken-legged pot, and devoting his time to single-minded investigation of himself, then this person will meet me face-to-face each day and requite his spiritual obligations. Is there anyone who can afford to be negligent? Press on, press on![101]

But by Ikkyū's day in the mid-fifteenth century, life in Zen monasteries had become secure and formularized, and while that fact on the one hand contributed to the efflorescence of Zen artistic culture, particularly among those temples in the bakufu-sponsored Gozan structure, it also could mean religious laxity.[102]

Ikkyū believed that Zen had become debased, and he scorned the perquisites of office and public recognition as immaterial. Appointed abbot of the Nyoian subtemple at Daitokuji in 1440, he quit after ten days, disgusted at what he judged to be the empty and vain affectation of the contemporary Zen establishment. In his poetry, he denounced the decadence of his day, lamenting, "Who of Linji's [Rinzai's] descendants passes on his Zen properly?" and "There are no true masters, only false ones."[103] Like his teacher Ken'ō, Ikkyū refused to accept a certificate of enlightenment, usually necessary to achieve preeminence in the

Zen establishment, precisely because it was an artificial and secondary manifestation that he deemed totally superfluous in the presence of enlightenment itself, and he refused to bestow one on any of his own students.

At the same time, Ikkyū demanded Buddhist compassion for all things and was incensed by the selfishness of the rich and their insensitivity to the suffering of the disadvantaged, as he shows in the following preface and verse:

> On the last day of the eighth month of the Kōshin year of Chōraku [1460] there was a typhoon and flood, and the people were in misery. But the very same night I heard guests at a drinking party singing and playing music. I could not stand listening to it:
>
> In heavy winds and surging waters, the people suffer;
> At song and dance, pipes and strings, who is it that plays all night?
> The Buddhist Law rises and falls, the *kalpas* wax and wane,
> So be it, for the bright moon too will sink beneath the western
>   tower.[104]

Ikkyū was famous for forms of behavior that were on one level eccentric but on another were unyielding expressions of the Buddhist principle of nonduality (*funi*), which refuses "to grant more than provisional validity to any phenomenal opposite."[105] Such behavior was meant to make others take notice of the hypocrisy or delusion in their own lives. One illustrative anecdote relates that he once entered the city of Sakai carrying a great sword in a scabbard. When asked why a monk needed such a weapon, he drew the sword from the scabbard, revealing it to be made of wood. He then announced that the sword represented the false wisdom of the day, which might be outwardly impressive but which was actually useless.[106]

Ikkyū referred to this untrammeled aspect of his character as *fūkyō* or *kyōfū* (crazy, wild, free-spirited). His deliberately iconoclastic and "irreligious" activities such as drinking, frequenting brothels, and pursuing a love affair have been interpreted as attempts to criticize through manifest irony the outwardly holy but inwardly corrupt nature of the contemporary Zen establishment.[107] Such acts in addition were demonstrations that all things are part of the One and that distinctions between wealth and poverty, sex and celibacy, sobriety and inebriation, sickness and health, and even birth and death, are on a higher philosophical level illusory. Ikkyū wished to effect a return to the rigorous example of the Tang patriarch Linji, who stressed that the One comprised both the sacred and the secular:

> If you love the sacred and hate the secular
> You'll float and sink in the birth-and-death sea.
> The passions exist dependent on mind:
> Have no-mind, and how can they bind you?
> Without troubling to discriminate or cling to forms
> You'll attain the Way naturally in a moment of time.[108]

Ikkyū maintained that to follow the sacred and disdain the secular was to perpetuate illusory distinctions. So too, then, for distinguishing between form and formlessness, orthodoxy and unorthodoxy, in literature as well as in life. Where Sōgi stood for literary orthodoxy and principle, Ikkyū stood for *kyō*, madness, or what Konishi Jin'ichi calls "a life in violation of earthly morality." But for Ikkyū this also involved subsuming all exclusivist orthodoxies into an inclusive, transcendent One.[109] Where Sōgi championed ga, the formal, the precedented, and the canonical, and subordinated zoku, the informal and unprecedented together with the familiar and the everyday, Ikkyū demanded that distinctions between a sacred ga and a secular zoku be collapsed. Bokusai, Ikkyū's first biographer, observed that Ikkyū applied this principle in his daily affairs: "He made no difference between high and low and happily mixed with artisans, merchants, and small children. He treated unknown monks and old followers alike and without favoritism."[110] Konishi points out that in his Chinese *shi* (*shih*) poetry, "Ikkyū brought all these aspects of secular life into the world of shih, and I view this introduction of zoku in a ga art as one indication that movement toward the Late Middle Ages had already begun by this time."[111] It was a direction that Sōchō would pursue in his journal.

But Ikkyū was important to Sōchō and in fact to all his numerous adherents not only for his religious philosophy but also for his outspoken courage of personal conviction. As James H. Sanford observes, much of Ikkyū's writing and behavior was "concerned with nothing other than illuminating the bodily presence of enlightenment."[112] Ikkyū embodied strength of will, and he seems to have succeeded in bequeathing that courage to those who came to him for direction.

Ikkyū thus passed on to Sōchō the courage to reject outmoded forms and to consider things anew. The impact of Ikkyū's thought and personal example pervades the journal of his disciple. Like Ikkyū, Sōchō detested the empty formalism and ostentation of many of the Zen community, as well as what he perceived as an emphasis on money-raising at the expense of hard spiritual practice. In his year-end discussion with Asahina Tokishige in 1525, he wrote:

> Some call today's Zen practitioners a pack of devils, of the lowest guttersnipe sort. Abbots, monks, and novices these days consort with the high and mighty, curry donations from provincial gentry, pursue their austerities only when it suits them, run hither and yon all day, and dally with other practitioners. But who are the masters they practice with themselves? Some say it is far better to repeat the Holy Name. I am more attracted to those who follow a simple and ignorant practice, as I do. (*JS*: 85–86)

Meditation on the Holy Name is the central practice of Pure Land adherents. Ikkyū too professed at one point to have abandoned Zen for Pure Land beliefs: "In an earlier year I humbly received the portrait of the Zen priest Daitō Kokushi. Now I exchange my robes for those of the Pure Land sect."[113]

This disregard for empty display was doubtless a major factor in Sōchō's attitude toward the secret traditions of *Kokinshū*; they were there to improve poetry, he felt, not to serve as some sort of formalistic cachet for advancement in the poetic profession. And in the same way that Ikkyū accepted no certificate of enlightenment himself nor bestowed any, Sōchō did not pass on the secret traditions *qua* secret traditions, unlike Shōhaku, who bestowed his own *Sakai denju* on select disciples. Ikkyū's rejection of the Nyoian abbacy may also have been a factor in Sōchō's decision not to become poet laureate.

And like Ikkyū, Sōchō was outspoken in both his anger and his compassion. He gave vent to his cynicism at the lies and self-deceptions of others in his journal: "Far too many lies are spread about nowadays. I hear people doing nothing but slandering others and, being in their company, I wonder if I will become like them" (*JS*: 169).

Throughout his journal, he demonstrated Ikkyū's sensitivity to the sufferings of humankind of all social levels, and indeed to all living things:

> Item. Consider the low-ranking samurai, starving and with no land to call his own. There is no help for him. He obviously cannot part from his wife and children. Their food runs out, and the woman must draw water and the man must gather brushwood. Their children are taken away before their eyes to slave for others. Their bowing and scraping is pitiful. Driven to that pass, those with self-respect may even do away with themselves. Someone said that to such unfortunates one should give a little something. That is the essence of charity. Of course one must give as well to those who beg by the roadside and wait by houses and gates . . . To none is fate more cruel. (*JS*: 85)

Sōchō imbued his journal with the perception, which he shared with Ikkyū, that distinctions between the lofty and the commonplace were ultimately deluded and meaningless. Sōchō on one level respected the classical literary orthodoxy, but on another, he reacted against the tyranny of external form, and he at times departed from the canonical literary paradigms.

Sōchō too dared to be different and to manifest eccentricity. Though a monk, he openly rejected celibacy as Ikkyū had, siring two children and never concealing his fondness for young men (*wakashu*). Nakamoto Tamaki has pointed to the connection between Sōchō's "craziness" (*kurui*) and Ikkyū's "madness" (*fūkyō*).[114] Sōchō expressed that persuasion in a poem written in his very last years:

negawaku wa	This is my request—
fūtenkan no	that I who have become
waga mi ni te	a crazy eccentric
shinabaya mono ni	may pass away wild and free,
kurui kurui mo	in all things wild and free![115]

It is a mistake to view Sōchō as simply copying Ikkyū's iconoclastic behavior without the underlying philosophy, for that too would have been affectation, and thus anathema. The principle of nonduality, seeing all things as part of the One, and all as equally illusory, helps explain Sōchō's bipolarities—his conservativism and his eccentricity, his textual formalism and his innovation, his solemnity and his wit, his anger and his compassion.

Ikkyū's importance to Sōchō is made very clear in one incident recorded in the journal. It takes place just after Sōchō arrived at Shōrin'an in Yashima, the temple in the Daitokuji lineage where he wintered in 1526–27:

I acquired a portrait of Ikkyū, one in which he is depicted with a sword:

453 uchiharau   How clear and bright
     yuka no atari ni   the sword in its scabbard that stands
        oku tachi no   on the clean-swept floor—
     sayaka ni izuko   nowhere is it clouded
     kumoru chiri naki   by a single speck of dust.

454 kumori naki   A great sword,
     yaiba suzushiki   its brilliant blade
        tsurugitachi   utterly unclouded—
     togishi kokoro no   the clear mirror
     masukagami kana   of his fine-honed mind!

(*JS*: 126–27)

Sōchō's verses demonstrate the importance of the *chinzō*, the portrait of one's Zen master, which served as a tangible reminder of the master-student relationship in a tradition based on unwritten and even nonverbal transmission of the dharma. The image of the pure and "brilliant blade" in the portrait recalls the famous Sakai anecdote of the wooden sword of false knowledge, made even more incisive a metaphor for Sōchō in view of his own youth as a swordsmith's son.[116] Like Ikkyū, Sōchō was able not only to perceive phenomena inclusively and see value in the zoku as well as in the ga, but also to have the courage, perceived by convention as madness, to put that nondualistic perception into literary practice, not in his orthodox renga, but in his journal writing.

To be sure, some of the above correlations may have been actual influences from Ikkyū and others may simply reflect the correspondence of innate and independent character traits that were strengthened by Ikkyū's example. All were no doubt amplified by various other sources. The principle of nonduality, for example, is central not only to Zen but to all forms of Buddhist thought. But Sōchō's lifelong admiration of Ikkyū and service to his successors suggest that the philosophical parallels between the two men were far-reaching and hardly coincidental.

Sōchō was in any case not simply a myrmidon of his spiritual master. He did not exhibit the same level of volatility or eccentricity. Nor did he teach Zen; rather he *used* Zen while living as a rengashi. Where Ikkyū was a priest first and then a poet, Sōchō was a poet, and then a priest (though such a formulation is itself dualistic). And for all Sōchō's exuberance, he fit well into his cultural milieu.

Moreover, the differences between Ikkyū and Sōgi were by no means polar. Sōgi too had lived as a monk for years in a great Zen monastery, Shōkokuji, and is known to have lectured on the Zen creed more than once to as knowledgeable an audience as Sanetaka and to have inspired his listener's admiration.[117] Moreover, Sōchō himself referred to his linked-verse teacher as "Zen Priest Sōgi" (Sōgi Zenji), as did Shinkei and Tō no Tsuneyori.[118] Most importantly, Sōgi too is believed to have associated with Ikkyū.[119] Conversely, Ikkyū too was a man of many talents, skilled not only in poetry but a number of other artistic disciplines. There were many similarities of character between these two most important of Sōchō's predecessors—both were brilliant proponents of their separate ways and pursued them with complete conviction. They were quintessential idealists who brooked no artistic or spiritual compromise. Moreover, both saw their respective professions and indeed their entire society to be in a state of decline and devoted themselves to effecting a recovery. To do so, both looked backwards, Sōgi to the time of his immediate teachers and predecessors, the Seven Sages, and thence back to the great classical tradition, and Ikkyū to the "hard Zen" of his teacher Kasō and then back to the individualists among the Chan practitioners of the Tang period.

Sōchō was nevertheless to some extent walking an ideological tightrope between his two mentors. Sōgi tried to recover the greatness of past poetry by requiring that a poet attain self-expression by first subordinating himself to ideal preexisting models. Ikkyū placed far more emphasis on breaking out of the existing spiritual norms he perceived as bankrupt and decayed. They were in that sense approaching the same goal from opposite directions, one subordinating his "self" to classical icons and the other embracing individualistic iconoclasm. Their characters reflected that contrast—Sōgi was a man of moderation, self-discipline, and personal privacy. He was careful to let others see only those aspects of himself that were consonant with the poet-ideal. Thus we know little of his early life or much about his haikai poetry. Ikkyū, of course, shared the self-discipline of Sōgi, but expressed it through an overlay of eccentricity and abandon.

Without Sōgi, Sōchō could never have used the influence of Ikkyū as effectively as he did—Sōgi provided the classical tools and philosophical ballast; Ikkyū, the spiritual ether, the courage to break the rules at times and trust to instinct and intuition. Sōgi was the gravity; Ikkyū, the centrifugal force.

The separate attractions of those two basic approaches give rise to a vibrant tension in *The Journal of Sōchō*. The combination allowed Sōchō to base his journal on traditional waka and renga and the classic travel and eremitic literary models, yet to treat those genres with an unprecedented individuality.

New Linkages

Sōgi and Ikkyū were not only crucial to Sōchō's literary, intellectual, and spiritual development, they also greatly expanded the young poet's network of patrons and connections. Through Sōgi, Sōchō achieved entrance into prominent courtly and warrior houses and was introduced to the major linked-verse poets of the period. Through Ikkyū, he established ties to the Daitokuji establishment. Those connections, nourished by his native talent and personality, would serve him for the rest of his life, and they figure prominently in *The Journal* of Sōchō, making that work in part a documentary of one poet's interconnected art world.

Among the courtiers that Sōchō met through his relationship to Sōgi, the one with whom he established the closest ties was Sanjōnishi Sanetaka.[120] Seven years younger than Sōchō, Sanetaka is thought to have become acquainted with the renga poet for the first time in 1485, when the courtier was thirty years old and held the Senior Third Rank. Sanetaka recorded in his diary his first meeting with Sōchō, who was then still using his earlier name Sōkan: "Sōgi called. We read 'The Maiden' chapter of *Genji monogatari*. It was marvellous. He was accompanied by Sōkan, who lives with him."[121] Sanetaka had already been acquainted with Sōgi for at least eight years and had listened to him lecture on the classics.

When Sōchō first met Sanetaka, the courtier was already becoming a main figure in the court linked-verse circle during its efflorescence under Emperor Gotsuchimikado and Crown Prince Katsuhito (later Emperor Gokashiwabara). He eventually came to be considered one of the Seven Gentlemen of Linked Verse (Renga Shichishi), a later complement to Sōgi's Seven Sages, which also included Sōchō, Shōhaku, Kensai, and Sōchō's younger colleagues Sōseki and Sōboku, as well as Sōgi himself.

Though born to vastly different estates, the courtier and the renga master shared a bond that seems to have only deepened as the years progressed. Their literary collaborations were varied. They frequently composed linked verse together, one of the more important sequences being *Iba senku* of 1524, which also involved the younger poet Sōseki and is mentioned in Sōchō's journal (*JS*: 44). Sōchō respected Sanetaka's talent as a linked-verse poet enough to request judgments from him. They also often exchanged waka, many of which are preserved in Sōchō's journal. And both men were devoted diarists.[122]

Sōchō also admired Sanetaka's literary scholarship and would attend his lectures, particularly on *Genji monogatari*, when he was in Kyoto. He also relied on the courtier for copies of the classics, including *Eiga taigai* (Essentials of Composing Waka, after 1223?), part of *Genji monogatari*, and *Kokinshū*, the last of which he later presented to the Imagawa house for the first anniversary of the death of Ujichika (*JS*: 162).

But the relationship between the two men was not restricted to matters of literature. Sōchō traveled frequently and was able, like Sōgi before him, to keep Sanetaka apprised of conditions in his dwindling provincial holdings as well as of events in general outside the capital. Sōchō also occasionally helped the financially straitened aristocrat turn his literary reputation to monetary profit by selling to provincial poetasters samples of his calligraphy or classics he had copied (Sanetaka is believed to have copied *Ise monogatari* a remarkable ten times).[123] Provincial potentates like the Imagawa also occasionally sent the courtier gifts of money, which were often conveyed by the renga master. In a diary entry for 1508, for example, Sanetaka recorded that "Imagawa Ujichika sent two thousand *hiki*. Sōchō brought it, arriving today. Unexpected beneficence! It provides some relief in these times of want."[124] Sōchō occasionally brought Sanetaka gifts on his own behalf as well.

But Sanetaka's enormous labor in copying manuscripts in his elegant hand, writing commentaries, and lecturing on the classics was not undertaken solely to support himself and his family as their lands were wrested from them. Like Sōgi, Sanetaka saw the land's cultural patrimony being lost to fire and warfare, and he was personally committed to perpetuating what he could of his courtly heritage. As a linked-verse master, Sōchō was also devoted to the practice and propagation of the orthodox poetic legacy, and that point of view too would have linked him strongly to his courtier acquaintance.

Both men wrote of their relationship with considerable personal warmth. Sōchō is mentioned in *Sanetakakōki*, the courtier's voluminous kanbun diary, more than thirty times.[125] One entry for 1524 in particular shows both the cultural activity they shared and the relaxed good humor that marked their relationship. After a poetry session involving a poem sequence of thirty waka, music was performed:

> The Middle Counsellor Washio [Takayasu] played the *koto* and Lords [Toyohara] Muneaki and [Imahashi] Hiroaki played the *shō*. After the ceremonial nine cups and dumplings, we poured sake for each other. Sōchō enjoyed himself so thoroughly he got up and danced—it was highly entertaining.[126]

Toyohara Muneaki (or Sumiaki), whom Sanetaka mentioned, was another of Sōchō's closest friends in the courtier community.[127] A court musician, Muneaki was also an accomplished poet with whom Sōchō composed linked verse. Sanetaka, Muneaki, and Sōchō also shared similar tastes in wabi-style architecture (see Chapter Three). When Muneaki died in 1524, Sōchō recorded in the journal ten verses in his memory plus a long preface detailing the courtier's career, Muneaki's last letter to him, and ten memorial poems each by Sanetaka and another courtier, Ōgimachisanjō Sanemochi (who was related by marriage to the Imagawa house). In its entirety it is the longest requiem passage in the entire work, which suggests the depth of Sōchō's sense of loss at Muneaki's death.

During the last four decades of Sōchō's life, it was the Hosokawa who were the shogunal deputies and the real power in Kyoto. Though he did not work to become poet laureate or to establish a close relation with the imperial palace or the shogunate, Sōchō did preserve his connection with that house. It may have been through Sōgi that Sōchō first composed with Hosokawa Masamoto, but the Hosokawa had also maintained long ties with Sōchō's Imagawa patrons, having been their allies during the Ōnin War. Sōchō later benefited from the patronage of Masamoto's adopted son, Takakuni. It was at Takakuni's request, for example, that Sōchō and Sōseki composed *Ise senku* in 1522 (*JS*: 15). Sōchō wrote that he undertook the sequence partly in thanks for Takakuni's patronage of Daitokuji (*JS*: 15). And it was probably Sōchō who kept Takakuni and Imagawa Ujichika in contact.[128]

Sōgi was also the conduit through which Sōchō met the leading members of the poetic community. One of the most important of these was Botanka Shōhaku. A monk of elevated court lineage, Shōhaku was five years older than Sōchō, and by 1491 they shared a position at the top of Sōgi's considerable list of disciples, having composed *Yuyama sangin* in that year and *Minase sangin* three years earlier. The two poets not only made linked verses together but from time to time asked each other for criticism of their respective works. In 1504 or 1505, for example, Shōhaku sent Sōchō a solo hundred-verse sequence for critique, and three years or so later Sōchō returned the compliment, asking Shōhaku, as well as Sanetaka, for judgments on a mock linked-verse contest he made out of one hundred pairs of his own verses, *Sōchō hyakuban rengaawase* (Linked-Verse Contest in One Hundred Rounds, By Sōchō).[129] Shōhaku wrote in a postscript that he made the judgments because he found his feeling on reading the verses "impossible to repress" and added that he and Sōchō had been "friends since their youth."[130]

Between two such gifted poets, however, a degree of rivalry was perhaps inevitable. There is no direct evidence of such competition between Sōchō and Shōhaku, but it is strange that Sōchō never mentions any correspondence with Shōhaku in his journal. The advancing age of both men was likely a contributing factor in this, as was perhaps their difference in social status. But it seems odd that Sōchō refers to Shōhaku only once in the entire document, in the context of a memorial service for Nose Yorinori that had taken place years before, despite the fact that Shōhaku lived until the last year it covers, 1527. Sōchō spent much of that five-year period in the Kansai region, and the Shūon'an hermitage where he occasionally stayed was not far from that of Shōhaku. And while Sōchō does not claim that he had received the secret traditions of *Kokinshū* from Sōgi when he writes about them in his journal (*JS*: 81), neither does he mention Shōhaku's reception of them, though Shōhaku himself went on to transmit them to a number of his own disciples.[131]

Renga was itself born of rivalry, with each poet at a session competing with the others to supply the best link. The art is built on the tension between, on the one hand, the mutual understanding among the participants and the united goal of a successfully modulated sequence and, on the other, the desire of each poet to show off his own verses to best advantage. The issue was particularly serious when the poets involved were professionals whose livelihoods depended on their literary reputations. Reviewing the large number of extant sequences attended by most of the great names in renga during Sōchō's lifetime, one recognizes both how essential competition was to the constant improvement of renga as an art form and how intense were the rivalries hidden behind the reserved and decorous verses on the page. A century before Sōchō's heyday, Imagawa Ryōshun had already recognized the potentially vicious nature of the professional linked-verse world: "After the death of the late regent, rengashi have disparaged their friends and promoted themselves alone."[132]

Sōchō himself could be quite volatile at times, but his withdrawal from the capital removed him to some extent from the competitive arena. And by the last decades of his life, his supremacy was in any case universally recognized. The renga poets of the next generation were his respectful subordinates.

One of the most important of these was Sōseki. The son of a blacksmith, Sōseki is thought to have begun his advanced study of linked verse with Sōchō, then later to have become a disciple of Sōchō's own teacher Sōgi. Sōseki later took up residence in Sōgi's hermitage and accompanied him on his last trip from the capital to the Uesugi domain in Echigo in 1500, where Sōchō later joined them from Suruga. Both disciples were present at the master's death, and Sōseki figures prominently in Sōchō's record of it.

Sōseki went on to take Sōgi's place in the renga world of the capital (insofar as the great master could be replaced), while Sōchō removed to Suruga. But they continued to correspond and to compose linked verse together from time to time until Sōchō's death thirty years later.[133]

It seems to have been nearly impossible for the two poets to keep from composing verses when in each other's company, even during the period of national mourning for the deceased Emperor Gokashiwabara in 1526, as indicated by this passage in Sōchō's journal:

Fifth month, sixth day. For a private linked-verse session at Gessonsai Sōseki's:

370   ama ga shita ya   All under heaven
       harema matsu toki   awaits the sun
         satsuki yami   in the fifth-month darkness.

We wondered whether we needed special dispensation to meet for poetry and how often we might do so, but Lord Sanetaka favored us with the opinion that we might compose as often as we liked. He stated that everyone in the realm, even the poorest dweller in the mountains, was stricken with grief and that we might feel free to compose. We did two sequences in succession. (*JS*: 105–6)

After Sōchō's death in 1532, it was Sōseki who led the renga world. His preeminence was short lived, however, for he died the following year. Into his place stepped a poet who had initially studied with Sōseki but then gone on to become Sōchō's closest disciple, Tani Sōboku. Sōboku is believed to have originally come to Kyoto from the Asakura capital of Ichijōdani, and Sōchō may have first met him either at Sōseki's residence or earlier on one of his journeys to the Asakura domain. He made his first recorded appearance in *Jikka senku* of 1516, which, like *Iba senku*, was held at Sōseki's residence. Sanetaka, Shōhaku, and Sōchō also participated along with many others in that important linked-verse sequence. In the same year he traveled with Sōchō to Ise, where the two composed verse with Moritake and others of the Arakida family.

Sōboku's most important appearance in *The Journal of Sōchō* is in connection with a famous two-poet hundred-verse sequence, *Yashima Shōrin'an naniki hyakuin* (A Hundred-Verse Sequence Entitled 'A Kind of Tree,' Composed at Shōrin'an in Yashima), which he made with Sōchō at the latter's winter lodgings in Yashima by Lake Biwa in 1527. The work became one of the classics of the linked-verse art, and Sōboku later produced a commentary on it for one of his warrior patrons. The commentary is so detailed that we will use it later on to introduce the mechanics of the linked-verse session (see Chapter Four).

Sōboku occupied a preeminent position among Sōchō's disciples for several reasons. Not only was he a fine poet in his own right, but he was also a perceptive commentator on earlier sequences and the author of several important renga studies, most notably *Tōfū renga hiji* (Private Matters Concerning Modern Linked Verse, 1542). Much of his annotation and theoretical work was prepared in part for the benefit of his son, who became the renga poet Sōyō. It is at this point that renga personal linkages began to become hereditary, a trend that would become more marked in the Momoyama (1573–1615) and Edo (1615–1868) periods.

CHAPTER ONE

Sōboku's travel journal, *Tōgoku kikō*, is strikingly similar to *The Journal of Sōchō* in its unaffected contemporaneity. In it, he related his own memories of Sōchō, which mirror Sōchō's recollections of his teacher Sōgi in his own journal.

In sum, it was the personal linkage with Sōgi that allowed Sōchō to polish his own poetic gifts and to exercise them in the company of many of the best poets in the capital. It was also through the old master that Sōchō began to build a circle of patrons outside the Imagawa domain. Sōchō in turn helped provide the same opportunities to those who studied with him.

But it was the Daitokuji temple network that Sōchō depended upon when in the Kansai region for long-term lodging and hospitality, which he could not expect from courtiers, warriors, or other linked-verse poets. When Sōchō first met Ikkyū in about 1476, though, Daitokuji was a charred ruin, a victim of the violence of the Ōnin War. Founded in 1326 by Daitō, the temple became independent of the Gozan system in 1445 during the tenure of abbot Yōsō Sōi. Eight years later it was burned virtually to the ground, and Yōsō spent his last years rebuilding it. He did so in part by soliciting donations from wealthy merchant patrons, a worldly enterprise which seems to have been part of the reason he was so reviled by Ikkyū. It is ironic, then, that Ikkyū should have been raised to the abbacy of Daitokuji in 1474 and become responsible himself for raising money to once again rebuild that venerable institution. He expressed in verse the quandary of a rebel against the establishment who was himself now elevated to a position of authority:

> Daitō's descendants have quenched the flickering flame.
> Only a half-thawed lovesong, cold as night, remains.
> Fifty years a rustic wanderer;
> Now mortified in purple robes.[134]

Because of the damaged state of the main temple, Ikkyū spent most of his old age in residence in his last and favorite hermitage, Shūon'an, in Takigi. He died there in 1481, after much of Daitokuji had been rebuilt.[135] Sōchō would have spent most of his time with the master not at Daitokuji proper but at this southern hermitage.

It was at a time when Ikkyū was devoting himself to the rebuilding effort that Sōchō came to know him. Thus it is not surprising that after Ikkyū's death, Sōchō would feel he could best venerate the memory of his old teacher by carrying on that work. The rebuilding of the Sanmon gate would become Sōchō's particular project, and he expended considerable time and personal funds on the enterprise. He made donations on the thirteenth and thirty-third anniversaries of Ikkyū's death, and he also sold certain of his personal possessions to raise money, most notably his own prized copy of *Genji monogatari*.¹³⁶ He noted the sale in an entry for 1525 in his journal:

> To contribute to the reconstruction of the Sanmon gate of Daitokuji, I sold this and that, though nothing special, and finally decided to part with the copy of *Genji monogatari* I had used over the years:

267   kyō yori wa   What further changes
       nani ni kawaramu   will occur from this day forth?
       asukagawa   White waves of old age
       kono se o hate no   at the end of the shallows
       oi no shiranami   of Tomorrow River.

> To the person to whom I let the book go:

268   miru tabi no   Every time
       tsuyu okisoe yo   you take it up let teardrops fall
       tsurezure no   on its leaf-like words,
       nagusamegusa no   grasses that beguiled me
       koto no ha goto ni   when time hung heavy on my hands.

> (*JS*: 74–75)

In 1526 he recorded in his journal witnessing the building process: "Saw the Sanmon gate of Ryūhōzan Daitokuji at Murasakino, for which the posts were raised on the twenty-sixth of the first month of this year" (*JS*: 105). One can imagine the gratification that lay beneath this laconic notation on seeing his long years of effort come to fruition.

Many of the subtemples subsequently built at Murasakino, the site of the Daitokuji complex, were directly funded by rising sengoku daimyo. The older Gozan temples had been supported by the income from temple manors, and that income steadily decreased in the Sengoku period. Patronage from provincial warriors, combined with that from wealthy Sakai merchants, helped Daitokuji recover from the Ōnin devastation and grow prosperous as the Gozan system deteriorated.¹³⁷ One of those merchants donated money for a subtemple (*tatchū*) to the master's memory.¹³⁸ That complex, Shinjuan, was completed in 1491, and it hosted Sōchō on his subsequent visits to the capital. During his last stay in Kyoto in 1526, he mentioned watching work being done on a small lodging called Plum Cottage off to one side of the main structure, where he is thought to have stayed

(*JS*: 111). Shinjuan still owns a set of Seto Tenmoku tea bowls donated by Sōchō in 1523 (Fujii 1979: 63).

The abbots of Shinjuan also served as abbots of Shūon'an in Takigi, and they divided their time between the two institutions. Sōchō knew the fourth abbot well. Named Soshin Jōetsu, he had been Ikkyū's most active assistant in the rebuilding process, which he later continued as abbot. He was aided in that enterprise by his family connections, for he was the nephew of Asakura Toshikage, daimyo of Echizen and devoted patron of Daitokuji.[139] Sōchō served as one of the intermediaries between the prelate and the daimyo house. The Asakura provided lumber for the rebuilding process, floating it six hundred miles around Honshū then up Yodogawa river, in part to avoid the onerous taxes assessed at the many barriers that obstructed the eighty-mile land route.[140]

The rebuilding of the temple became one of the defining projects of Sōchō's own last years. His dedication to that enterprise was doubtless inspired by his sense of obligation to Ikkyū's memory, but he may incidentally have hoped to accrue religious merit himself as his own death approached. And his service to Daitokuji was to some extent also a kind of social security, for he could count on room and board from any of its affiliated temples whenever he had need of it, and he expected that Takigi would be the site of his own final retirement.

When in Kansai, then, Sōchō divided much of his time between Shinjuan in the capital, Shūon'an in Takigi to the south, and Shōrin'an in Yashima to the east across Lake Biwa. The Daitokuji linkage was absolutely central to Sōchō's last years and to the composition of his journal. The abortive trip to the Asakura domain that begins the work was undertaken in part for fund-raising purposes for Daitokuji, and Sōchō later prefaced his account of his later successful round trip to their domain in 1523 with a short history of his role in the financial negotiations.

Shared Daitokuji linkages also facilitated and perhaps even initiated Sōchō's relationships with certain cultural figures in the Kansai area. These included Murata Sōju, successor to Ikkyū's disciple Murata Jukō, the wabi-style tea master. Sōchō recorded in his journal attending a tea ceremony presided over by Sōju (*JS*: 109). And it may also have been the Ikkyū connection through which Sōchō met the famous early haikai specialist Yamazaki Sōkan. The haikai session in which Sōchō pitted several of his verses against Sōkan's took place at Shūon'an in Takigi.

Sōchō the Master

Sōgi's death in 1502 marked the end of the second phase of Sōchō's life. Just as the poet's youth in Suruga had ended with the death of his daimyo patron Imagawa Yoshitada, now, a quarter-century later, the loss of another central personal linkage brought a definitive end to the Kyoto years and precipitated another major change in Sōchō's career. The poet had mastered the traditional linked-verse orthodoxy after the Sōgi model and attained national preeminence himself. Now, in his fifties, he was in a sense his own man, and he of necessity became the main defining force in his own life. Where the acquisition and application of Sōgi's neoclassical perspective had marked his professional life thus far, he henceforth began to examine himself in the absence of a higher authority, even as he continued to propagate the master's teachings among his own students.

Indicative of this shift of focus from Other to Self was Sōchō's new interest in diary literature. His first experiment in that medium, *Sōgi shūenki*, is symbolic of the transition, for it covers the last journey of the master, his death, and then the funeral observations by Sōchō and other literary descendants as they began to cope spiritually and emotionally with the loss of Sōgi and the order he represented. Over the ensuing three decades Sōchō would write four more diaries, culminating in *The Journal of Sōchō* and its short sequel, *Sōchō nikki* (The Diary of Sōchō), covering the years 1530 and 1531. It was only after Sōgi's death that Sōchō completed his first personal poetry collection, *Kabekusa*. Later, as he developed further skill, experience, and self-confidence, he resorted more and more frequently in his poetry handbooks to the use of his own verses as teaching models. Those later works include *Sōchō renga jichū* (Personal Commentary on Sōchō's Linked Verse, c. 1523–28) and *Renga tsukeyō* (Techniques for Linking Verses, 1528).

And yet, even after the death of his master, Sōchō was never entirely autonomous. Though the student had now become the teacher, Sōchō still took pride in his Sōgi lineage and continued to credit the master's teachings and influence in his own renga treatises. Nor was he entirely his own man professionally, for on his return to the Imagawa domains in anticipation of the master's demise, he resumed a patronage relationship with Yoshitada's son that was closer and more demanding than any relationship Sōgi himself had forged with a warrior house. That new link to the Imagawa would serve as a major support for the aging renga master, but it would also prove at times to be constricting, and it finally became a source of worry in the poet's last years.

CHAPTER ONE

Return to Imagawa Patronage: The Politics of Culture

Though it in one sense liberated Sōchō, the demise of the old master and with it the end of the Kyoto focus he represented also meant that Sōchō lost his center. His resumption of direct, immediate ties with the Imagawa marked a recognition of the new importance of the periphery that characterized the age. The Imagawa house was at the time undergoing a parallel shift, cutting its ties to the old political center represented by the Kyoto bakufu and becoming autonomous in its own expanding sphere of influence.

Imagawa Ujichika, after his violent assumption of power through the assassination of his cousin and de facto regent, devoted the rest of his life to securing the gains made by his father in Tōtōmi and then to extending his authority yet further west into Mikawa (Aichi Prefecture). What he gained by the sword, he worked equally hard to consolidate through administrative measures, including cadastral surveys (*kenchi*), beginning as early as 1518.[141] His activities constituted a reorganization of the previous pattern of land tenure and an assertion of Imagawa hegemony over land proprietorship. Ujichika sought as well to exercise similar control over the local landholders themselves and make them direct Imagawa vassals; in the last year of his life he promulgated *Kana mokuroku* (*Kana* Code) to codify and perpetuate the system for his descendants.[142] Nagahara Keiji has called the code the first mature set of house laws (*kahō*) in the Sengoku period.[143] The cadastral surveys and house laws constitute a renunciation of the subordinate role of bakufu constable. The Imagawa were among the few *shugo* daimyo successfully to accomplish the transition to sengoku daimyo status.

In working to assume broad personal control over an independent domain, Imagawa Ujichika was in effect fashioning a principality of a kind, with himself as an independent sovereign. That enterprise required not only military power and administrative skill but also scholarship and cultural accomplishment. Learning and the arts had been seen in the Japanese and Chinese traditions as a necessary adjunct to political power for two thousand years, back at least to the time of *The Book of Songs* (*Shijing*).[144] Such activities, it was felt, improved character and led to enlightened rule. As Imagawa Ryōshun wrote in *Imagawajō* (Imagawa Epistle, c. 1394), "The Four Books and Five Classics as well as treatises on strategy clearly indicate that it is impossible to govern without scholarship."[145]

Learning and the arts also increased prestige and gave an aura of legitimacy to power acquired only recently and by force. In the words of Joseph Alsop, such activities helped to "mark the leaders from the led."[146] In particular, they identified warriors with the old courtly order they were supplanting. As George Sansom observed, "Most of the leading warriors of [the] day wished to be regarded not as upstarts but as well-bred and cultured gentlemen."[147]

Ujichika was acutely aware of the particularly rich literary traditions of his house, and he worked to distinguish himself as a ruler both martial and cultured. One house history, *Imagawa kafu* (Lineage of the Imagawa House), states that "though the way of poetry had been followed by generations of Imagawa leaders, Ujichika was particularly skilled in such pursuits and was also surpassing in strategy, horsemanship, and swimming."[148] He also fostered the cultural development of his capital, formally named Sunpu in about 1520, after the pattern of Kyoto. In his personal scholarly and cultural pursuits he took as his models his ancestors Ryōshun and Norimasa, compiling a sequel to a poetic anthology attributed to Ryōshun, *Nihachi meidai wakashū* (Selections from the Sixteen Collections), in collaboration with Tō no Sojun. In the preface to his sequel, entitled *Shokugo meidai wakashū* (Selections from the Five Later Collections, 1515), he expressed his recognition of the cultural mission incumbent on him: "The scions of this house from generation to generation have with exceptional devotion set their hearts upon the waves of Waka Bay."[149] And of course he composed linked-verse, occasionally under the direction of Sōchō.

Patronage of the preeminent linked-verse poet in the land was one measure of the cultural commitment of the Imagawa family and, by extension, of their fitness to govern. Their self-ennoblement was also furthered by the growth of their connections to the court aristocracy, again through patronage and also marriage. The marriage of Ujichika's sister, Kitamuki, to Ōgimachisanjō Sanemochi was no doubt instrumental in effecting his own marriage into the venerable Nakamikado family, probably in 1505.[150] His wife, best known by the name Jukei that she adopted on taking holy orders after her husband's death, was the daughter of Nakamikado Nobutane, whose ties to the Imagawa went back to the time of Norimasa.[151]

The courtly in-laws of Ujichika and Kitamuki naturally began to look to Suruga for support at a time when their own lands were being wrested from their control; Ōgimachisanjō Sanemochi, his son Kin'e, and Nakamikado Nobutane's son Nobuhide all stayed in the Imagawa capital during Ujichika's lifetime. They further contributed to the cultural renown of the Imagawa house, and all figure in *The Journal of Sōchō*.

Ujichika's support of proud but increasingly impoverished courtiers was made possible in part by the plentiful gold from the Abeyama mines.[152] That gold also allowed Ujichika to establish and preserve links to courtiers such as Sanjōnishi Sanetaka in the capital and to acquire manuscripts and incunabula.

Ujichika's wife, Jukei, encouraged other courtiers to leave Kyoto for Imagawa protection in Suruga, and at least ten made the trip during her lifetime.[153] She also fostered marriage ties between the Nakamikado house and the Imagawa or their vassals. Her daughter became the wife of her nephew, Nakamikado Nobutsuna (grandson of Nobutane), and her niece married Asahina Yasuyoshi, scion of the Asahina house, vice-constables of Tōtōmi and close Imagawa vassals. Through their mother, Ujichika's sons Ujiteru and Yoshimoto were themselves half-courtier.

The fact that the Imagawa were one of the most culturally inclined of daimyo houses no doubt helped promote Sōchō's early poetic inclinations and later led him to return to their domain. Some later commentators, however, argued that Imagawa emphasis on culture proved counterproductive. Ujichika's fourth son, Ujitoyo, is said to have lost Nagoya Castle to Oda Nobuhide in 1532 after he allowed Nobuhide to enter it under the pretext of a renga session.[154] And the Edo-period bureaucrat and moralist Matsudaira Sadanobu was to blame Imagawa Ujizane and his love of poetry for the fall of the Imagawa house only three decades after Sōchō's death.[155]

The Imagawa Laureate and the Linked-Verse Profession

The Journal of Sōchō is among the best sources of information on the practice of linked verse. More specifically, it documents a variety of services Sōchō provided his patron in his capacity as the de facto poet laureate of the Imagawa house. Perhaps the most important of these was the composition of votive renga, when he was accompanying the daimyo on military campaigns or when he was in the Suruga capital. Sōchō mentions several, including the *Shutsujin senku* sequence composed in thanks for the victory of Ujichika and Sōun in Musashi in 1504 (*JS*: 10) and another composed as a prayer for the successful crossing of Tenryūgawa river in the Hikuma campaign of 1517 (*JS*: 11). A third thousand-verse sequence, *Sengen senku* (A Thousand-Verse Sequence at Sengen Shrine, 1514), was an apotropaic composition to protect Ujichika during a *yakudoshi*, a year thought particularly dangerous for him. It was important to have such verses composed by the finest poet available, for their effect on the deities to whom they were addressed was thought to be related to poetic skill.

But Sōchō's services for Ujichika were by no means limited to renga sessions, either for votive purposes or for simple entertainment. We have already seen that he composed chronicles of the Asahina and Imagawa houses. The large number of humorous stories and comic poems (*kyōka*) in *The Journal of Sōchō* suggest that he could also be counted upon by Ujichika and his immediate retainers for an amusing anecdote, especially when on a military campaign.[156] Sōchō was a jack of all literary trades for Ujichika, especially in the early years of their relationship, and he served the daimyo in much the same way that *dōbōshū* (companions) served the Ashikaga shoguns.[157]

Sōchō also performed a variety of services for Ujichika when traveling. As a famous rengashi, he could pass with relative freedom from domain to domain, and he spent a large part of his last thirty years visiting the holdings of other daimyo or local warlords who were eager for the chance to improve their renga skill under the direction of a first-rate linked-verse master. While on those journeys, Sōchō served as a messenger for Ujichika to courtiers such as Sanjōnishi Sanetaka.[158] He also helped Ujichika in his collecting of literary works, as he indicated in his journal: "Over the years I gave various writings to Ujichika as well, either presenting them personally or sending them by messenger" (*JS*: 162).

In the course of his journeys, he no doubt absorbed valuable information concerning the economic, political, and military conditions of other domains. Though Sōchō understandably did not make direct reference to such activities in his journal, he took an interest in the dwellings and fortifications of his hosts, be they close allies of the Imagawa or far-off provincial lords. Note, for example, what he wrote about the area near one fortress where he stayed:

> They say there was a mountain temple here in the past. Might the site be used in battle? A natural shield of cliffs. Pillars of rock to support a gatehouse. It appears to cover fifty square chō around the valley. Here one could confront tens of thousands of soldiers with impunity. (*JS*: 52)

This sort of information was invaluable to Ujichika, who despite his local power and prestige does not appear to have ever been able to travel to Kyoto himself.

On one noteworthy occasion, Sōchō was called on by Ujichika to negotiate with a rival daimyo, Takeda Nobutora, for the release of an army of one of his generals under siege in Kai Province (Yamanashi Prefecture).[159] The task would be difficult, as Nobutora was described in one chronicle as being "brave without peer, and possessed of superlative cunning, but . . . heedless of censure, contemptuous of others, and unrivalled in volatility."[160] Sōchō was an obvious choice for such an errand, with his knowledge of military affairs, his proven loyalty to his

CHAPTER ONE

Imagawa patrons, and his priestly status and literary preeminence.[161] Their faith in their laureate was not misplaced, and Sōchō wrote with understated pride of his accomplishment soon after the event:

> An army from this province was held within a castle called Katsuyama in Kai Province. The local warlords had had a change of heart and the castle was cut off. On the twenty-second of the first month [of 1517] a local warrior and long-time acquaintance of Ujichika came down and said I must parley with the enemy to bring the matter to a close without incident. Since his order was difficult to refuse, I set out for the provincial capital on the twenty-third . . . For fifty days I exercised my aged mind in any number of ways in the negotiations between friend and foe, mixing truth and lies. On the second of the third month, two thousand and more Imagawa troops withdrew without a single loss. On my way back, I spent a night at a temple of the Lotus sect called Minobu.[162] At their request:
>
> | | |
> |---|---|
> | yuki kōri | The ice and snow |
> | yama ya arasou | vie upon the mountains to swell |
> | haru no mizu | the springtime rivers. |
>
> I meant that with the arrival of spring the ice and snow strive to be the first to melt, and then the mountain streams course down. The underlying meaning refers to the peace talks just concluded. (*UYK*: 400–401)

In the immediate Imagawa family, Sōchō was particularly close to Ujichika's mother, Lady Kitagawa, and to his heir, Ujiteru. Perhaps because of his close friendship with her husband Yoshitada, Sōchō remained one of Lady Kitagawa's inner circle and was apparently privy to sensitive confidences.[163] In his journal, he records a farewell interview he had with her in the second month of 1526, just before setting out again for the Kansai region:

> On the ninth, after nightfall, I had an audience and celebratory wine with Lady Kitagawa. She favored me with relaxed conversation on various subjects. She was concerned about matters at home and tears wet her sleeves, which saddened me greatly. She said, "I have explained the situation and know you understand—by all means come back from Kyoto." I replied I would do so soon and presently took my leave. Her generous gifts left me at a loss for words. (*JS*: 90)[164]

Here, Yoshitada's widow shares with Sōchō her concern for the failing health of her son and, by extension, for the stability of the domain. Later, after Ujichika's death, Sōchō would call on Lady Kitagawa to bear witness to his long service to her husband, and he recorded that moment in his journal as well (*JS*: 162).

The journal also documents Sōchō's increasing responsibilities toward Ujiteru as the Imagawa heir came of age. The renga master composed verses with the young man (*JS*: 61) and on occasion provided proxy verses for him to submit under his own name at formal sessions beyond his yet immature poetic capabilities (*JS*: 82). He later appeared regularly at sessions sponsored by the young heir on obligatory poetic occasions such as the Festival of the Weaver Maid (Tanabata) or on nights of the full moon.

Sōchō was particularly active in the role of tutor. Symbolic of that function was his gift to Ujiteru on the advent of his coming-of-age ceremony (*genpuku*) in 1525 of some of the lecture notes on *Kokinshū* which he himself had received from Sōgi. Sōchō writes of the gift with a mixture of humility vis-à-vis the Imagawa heir and understated pride in his literary contributions to the house:

> I sent Ujiteru five books of lecture notes and eight sheets of esoteric oral teachings on *Kokinshū*. I could not but feel embarrassed by their unreliability, and when Ujiteru has passed his twentieth year and become deeply versed in the way of poetry he may see for himself that my notes have no value and discard them. If that occurs, I think he ought to consign them to the flames.

295
  asakeredo   Though it be but slight,
  kikishi bakari o   what I received I bequeath
   kimi wa kore   to you, my lord,
  waga ie no michi ni   that it may be handed down
  tsutaesoenan   and further enrich your house.

         (*JS*: 81)

Sōchō's services to Ujichika obviously far exceeded simple poetic tutelage, and he was compensated accordingly. *The Journal of Sōchō* gives some idea of the size and nature of the rewards he received from the Imagawa themselves and from their vassals, recording gifts from Lady Kitagawa (quoted above) and son Ujiteru (*JS*: 162), clothing from Asahina Yasumochi and Tokishige, and provisions from Saitō Yasumoto. The postscript of *Imagawa kafu* also relates that Sōchō reworked the account into kana from its original kanbun for compensation in "rice money" (*komedai*).[165] Kidō Saizō suspects Sōchō received a fixed income from the Imagawa, though he does not provide supporting evidence.[166] The assumption is a reasonable one, however, in light of the existence of a residence in Sunpu and the relatively comfortable standard of living depicted in the diaries. Sōchō also had the wherewithal to donate by his own reckoning thirty thousand hiki to Daitokuji over the course of his life. And he owned valuable artwork, such as a Yuan-period painting.¹⁶⁷ In his last years, his financial situation seems to have eroded somewhat, but it is unlikely that he was ever truly in want.

But Sōchō's close Imagawa affiliation also hindered his freedom in some ways. Orders from Ujichika were unconditional. In 1524, for example, Sōchō was obliged to cut short a stay with a local lord in Ise Province (Mie Prefecture) to escort a doctor back to Suruga to treat Ujichika (*JS*: 54). His relationship with the Imagawa also meant obligatory renga sessions on formal occasions. And his well-known ties with them no doubt prevented him from widening his circle of acquaintances to include daimyo and kokujin hostile to their house.

New Provincial Relationships

In addition to the material support he received from the Imagawa—whatever its amount and nature—Sōchō's relationship with them also provided security, so necessary in those violent times. Ujichika's support also led to connections with other members of the immediate Imagawa family, access to the Imagawa vassal network in Suruga and Tōtōmi, and introductions to other literary figures in the Imagawa capital.¹⁶⁸ Members of this extended Imagawa circle went on to become personal friends and active supporters of the poet, and they occupy predominant places in his journal.

They included, most notably, the Asahina family, vice-constables of Tōtōmi, and Saitō Yasumoto. The Asahina family, particularly Yasumochi, Tokishige, and Yasuyoshi, are mentioned in *The Journal of Sōchō* nearly as often as the Imagawa themselves.¹⁶⁹ The Asahina were an old family of provincial gentry (*gōzoku*) in Suruga who entered the service of the first Imagawa constable of that province. Asahina Yasuhiro, elder brother of Yasumochi and Tokishige, built and then expanded Kakegawa Castle during the incursions into Tōtōmi by Yoshitada and then Ujichika. Sōchō stayed at that fortress on each of the four Tōkaidō journeys he recorded in his journal. The Asahina also supported the cause of the young Ujichika in his succession battle, and Yasumochi was a trusted aide throughout his life. According to *The Journal of Sōchō*, Yasumochi and Tokishige were Ujichika's foster brothers (or milk-brothers, *menotogo*), a relationship traditionally considered one of the utmost intimacy (*JS*: 161).

Though Sōchō knew Yasuhiro, his close ties to the family originated with Yasumochi and Tokishige. Yasumochi's battle exploits figure prominently in Sōchō's Asahina war chronicle, a document biased, not surprisingly, in favor of its author's patrons. Moreover, part of the section near the end of *The Journal of Sō-*

chō in which he outlines his contributions to the Imagawa is directly addressed to Yasumochi in the form of a letter, which suggests that he was one of Sōchō's most influential supporters.

Sōchō enjoyed an equally close relationship with Yasumochi's younger brother Tokishige, who is afforded a place of honor in the Asahina chronicle for defending Kakegawa Castle (*JS*: 11). It was also Tokishige to whom Sōchō unburdened himself of his various year-end frustrations in the "desultory conversation" mentioned earlier, which is so revealing of the diarist's attitude toward current events and daily life.

The other main source of Sōchō's support in the Suruga domain was Saitō Yasumoto, lord of Mariko Castle. Yasumoto's proximity to Brushwood Cottage made it particularly easy for him to see Sōchō and profit from his poetic guidance. Sōchō's diary of 1509, *Azumaji no tsuto* (Souvenir of the Eastland, 1509), begins, in fact, with a renga session at Yasumoto's without Ujichika:

> I had been meaning to set out for Shirakawa Gate in the springtime haze, but year after year passed.[170] Finally I decided I must in any event go this autumn, and I fixed the date for the sixteenth of the seventh month, sixth year of Eishō [1509].
> On that day, Saitō Kaganokami Yasumoto, who resides next to my thatched cottage, arranged a session for the composition of a single sheet of linked verse. Unable to refuse, I composed this hokku:
>
> | kaze ni miyo | See them in the wind— |
> | ima kaerikon | kudzu leaves that show I will |
> | kuzuha kana | soon be coming home. |
>
> I was simply recalling here the old poem that goes, ". . . growing by our parting path."[171] At the time I was in the country village of Mariko.[172]

For Yasumoto, proximity fostered particularly close ties to Sōchō, but it also meant a greater burden of responsibility. Sōchō explicitly refers to him in *Utsunoyama no ki* as "the donor of my cottage" and duns him outright in a humorous and familiar way for daily necessities:

> I wrote to the donor of my thatched cottage, Yasumoto, requesting various things for the end of the year, and added:
>
> | sumi futako | Two bags of charcoal. |
> | takigi nijippa | twenty bundles of firewood, |
> | tsuto futatsu | radishes, burdock, |

daikon gobō	two straw-wrapped packets of food—
kaeshi o zo matsu	I am awaiting your reply!

(*UYK*: 402)

Sōchō subsequently sends a poem of thanks, in an equally light vein:

kusa no iori	In my thatched cottage,
kazukazu kimi ga	so much evidence, good sir,
kokorozashi	of your kind regard—
okidokoro naki	I find myself at year end
toshi no kure kana	full of both goods and thanks![173]

(*UYK*: 402)

The two men shared family bonds as well, for Sōchō depended on Yasumoto to be the temporary guardian of his son, Jōha (*UYK*: 404). And one of the most affecting passages in *The Journal of Sōchō* involves the suicide of the impoverished warrior Osada Chikashige, apparently Yasumoto's son-in-law, and the votive verse Sōchō composed for the repose of his spirit (*JS*: 72–74).

Travels to Patrons Outside the Imagawa Purview

Although they had a major impact on Sōchō's life and figure prominently in the poet's diaries, the Imagawa house and its vassals constituted only one segment of the poet's growing network of acquaintances. His return to Suruga of course did not mean that he severed his ties with his friends, students, and patrons in the capital or in other domains. He had instead simply changed the base of his operations, so to speak, from Kyoto to Sunpu, while continuing to travel frequently between those two loci. *The Journal of Sōchō* owes its existence to that dynamic. While maintaining his old connections, however, Sōchō was constantly forging new personal links, to friends of friends, to the descendants of old contacts, and to new acquaintances along his travel routes.

Sōchō's sphere of activity in his later years extended from Suruga and Izu Provinces (Shizuoka Prefecture) in the east down the Tōkaidō road to the capital and Takigi, and then north to Echizen. After returning to Suruga in 1496, he spent more than a third of his last thirty-six years outside Imagawa domains.

In nearly all cases, the primary motivation for his travels was of course the practice of linked verse. He frequently served as guest of honor at the linked-verse sessions of provincial warrior poets in particular, composing the difficult opening hokku and then directing the artistic development of the remainder of the sequence. Sōchō also tutored his warrior patrons and wrote renga instruction books for them, as he had for the Imagawa.

One such individual who figures prominently in *The Journal of Sōchō* is Seki Toshimori, lord of Kameyama Fortress in northern Ise Province, to whom Sōchō refers by his artistic name, Kajisai.[174] Kajisai was very likely related to the Ise house, and Sōchō may have first met him through his associations with Lady Kitagawa and with the Hōjō house.[175]

Sōchō records three visits to Kajisai in his journal—one during his attempted visit to the Asakura in 1522, one on his way back from Kyoto in 1524, and a third on his way to Suruga in 1527. He meant to stay with Kajisai in 1526 as well, but warfare en route forced him to change his plans. The passages devoted to his visits with Kajisai give a vivid sense of one particularly close patronage relationship between a provincial warrior and a renga master. For example:

> Seki, of the Popular Affairs Ministry, came from Kameyama in Ise to my travel lodgings in Yashima on the seventeenth of the twelfth month. He came in the snow, in the rush at year's end, and not simply because he happened to be passing by—I was touched by his sincerity. He had sent a letter by courier at the beginning of the month. I thought it was just a pleasantry, but when he went out of his way in the snow, I was speechless. On sending boxes of food to where he was staying, I wrote:

466
>> suzukayama
>> sazo na furitsumu
>> yuki no uchi
>> ika ni koekeru
>> kokoro naruramu
>
>> Through the driving snow
>> that piled ever deeper on
>> the Suzuka Mountains,
>> what feelings were in your heart
>> as you made your way across?

> Soon came his reply:

467
>> suzukayama
>> furiuzumoruru
>> yuki no uchi
>> mimaku hoshisa no
>> michi motometsutsu
>
>> Through the driving snow
>> that fell and covered
>> the Suzuka Mountains,
>> I came searching out a path
>> in my desire to see you.

> He came to visit after dark. Our words together piled deeper than the snow—we sat side by side at the hearth, eating tofu with miso and taking cup after cup of sake. He then returned to his hostel. Five hundred hiki (the cost of five kegs of sake), six loads of charcoal, two baskets of oranges, and various dried foods. My

lodgings were positively cramped. He stayed five days. During that time various people arrived day and night to help about the house. (*JS*: 130)

Seki Kajisai appears to have been devoted to Sōchō as an individual and to the practice of renga, and by supporting his renga mentor he vicariously assisted in the propagation of the art.[176] Provincial warriors like Kajisai were thus a main source of income for Sōchō and other traveling poets. Sōboku, who studied under Sōgi and Sōchō, bore witness in his own travel diary, *Tōgoku kikō*, to the poverty of the capital and the wealth of the countryside. With reference to the ceremonies marking the seventh anniversary of Sanjōnishi Sanetaka's death, Sōboku wrote, "I had wanted to send a token of my feelings, but my circumstances were too straitened. Recently, though, I received from the east a letter and some money . . . ."[177] Sōboku was then able to make a contribution thanks to the support of a provincial magnate who had been his host.

Indeed, daimyo and kokujin alike made extremely significant contributions to cultural expansion in the Sengoku period. Many of the major thousand-verse sequences in which Sōchō participated were sponsored by warrior literati. A renga gathering attended by a number of prominent renga poets entailed considerable expense, including room and board for the scribe and the poets, the elegant paper and writing materials, banquets for the participants and the large audience, travel arrangements and guides, and most importantly, gifts for the poets. The number of handbooks on linked verse would have been much smaller had it not been for the zeal of the warrior audience. Many of those tracts still survive and contribute significantly to our knowledge of contemporary theories on the practice and the reception of the art. In addition, the compilation of *Shinsen tsukubashū*, in which Sōchō participated, was realized in large part through the backing of Ōuchi Masahiro. To be sure, neither daimyo nor kokujin made great contributions as poets to the development of linked verse as literature. But their enthusiasm for the art and their willingness to study and subsidize it constituted an essential source of support for Sōchō and the other true masters who created its enduring monuments.

Certain Buddhist monks and Shintō priests were another main source of support for Sōchō by making available to him the hospitality of their temples and shrines when he was outside the Imagawa domains. They also provided literary and spiritual stimulation and companionship. In addition to his close ties to the Daitokuji temples affiliated with Ikkyū, he enjoyed long-term connections with monks at the Tendai temple of Miidera overlooking Lake Biwa at the foot of

Mount Hiei, with monks of the Ji sect, and with priests at Ise Shrine. All figure prominently in his journal.[178]

The poetic circle at Ise was particularly important from the point of view of Sōchō's literary activity; he is known to have stopped at Ise at least five times in the course of his life, and he figures prominently in *Nikonshū*, a miscellany of waka and renga lore compiled by Arakida Morihira, a priest at the shrine.[179] Sōchō wrote a number of important works at Ise, most notably the votive senku he composed with Sōseki at the request of Hosokawa Takakuni in 1522 (*JS*: 15), and a number of renga handbooks, including *Sōchō kawa*, the first draft of part of *Sōchō renga jichū*, and possibly *Nagabumi*.[180]

Some patrons directly sent Sōchō invitations or requests to call on them; in other cases Sōchō sent letters ahead on his own initiative: "There was a matter I wished to discuss with Seki Minbunotaifu, now called Kajisai, in Kameyama in the same province. I made the necessary arrangements for the journey . . ." (*JS*: 102). Others did likewise when they wished to visit him, often bringing their own provisions. When Seki Kajisai visited Sōchō at Yashima, for example, he first sent a courier two weeks in advance (*JS*: 130). Sōchō likewise sent ahead letters to others on behalf of guests who had come to stay with him.

The renga master was constantly receiving letters, gifts, and requests for hokku verses from distant locations. Those with the wherewithal, like the Asakura, could send a special messenger: "We were met by a mountain ascetic sent by Asakura Tarōzaemon Norikage. I read the letters he brought, and we then accompanied him to lodgings in Hirao. The next morning I wrote a reply" (*JS*: 19).

Sōchō often sent letters via friends or dependable passersby bound for the vicinity of the addressee, as when he wrote "a message entrusted to the monks from Shūon'an in Takigi, who were returning with others from the capital" (*JS*: 60). A letter could thus go through various hands before arriving at its ultimate destination:

> Hōgaiken Dōken has been in Noto Province for the last two years aiding the constable there. Thinking I was in Suruga, he sent a letter there via a blind attendant. I received it in a packet of letters forwarded to me here at Shōrin'an in Yashima, Ōmi Province . . . I sent a reply to Sōseki in the capital, asking him to forward it if he planned to write. It will be difficult to deliver through the snow at the end of the year. (*JS*: 126)

Sōchō in turn conveyed to his hosts the news he acquired on his travels. War made such information both more vital and more difficult to obtain than in times of peace, and Sōchō, as a nationally known rengashi, enjoyed a relative freedom of passage denied military men often in conflict with their neighbors.

When Sōchō's prospective host received word of his desire to visit, he would send back a messenger who then doubled as a guide and escort. A palanquin or horses or both might be provided as well, as they were from the Asahina in 1519. If the trip involved a water journey, a boat might be sent (*JS*: 48). After his stay with his host, Sōchō was often guided to his next stop by his host's men or called for by escorts from the fortress beyond. If the trip was a long one, several guides might escort him in stages. One example of the system working flawlessly occurred on a trip to Seki Kajisai's residence in 1524:

> On the twenty-second we departed, after having been several times detained. A palanquin to Sakanoshita in the Suzuka mountains. Horses for the rest of the company. Sake and food had been left ahead of time for us along the way at Inohana, Tsuchiyama, Uchi no Shirakawa, and Soto no Shirakawa. Our trip through the mountains was unforgettably pleasant. From place to place people came out to guide us, and at the barriers no one challenged us. We arrived at Sakanoshita, where I received another palanquin from Kameyama and rested my aged self from the rigors of the day. That night, an inn at Sakanoshita. I was reminded of the "reed hut" of the vestal's temporary palace in these mountains on her trip east to Ise. (*JS*: 49)

Travel between provinces was more complicated. Sōchō gives as an example the crossing from Tōtōmi to Mikawa in 1526:

> Saw Makino Denzō, in Imahashi, Mikawa Province. I was acquainted with his father and grandfather. Border crossings are difficult, and so he came out with many well-equipped people to greet us. It was impressive. (*JS*: 98)

Travel between rival domains was fraught with uncertainty. Sōchō's reference to bandits in 1526 (*JS*: 120) was quoted earlier. He includes in his journal a particularly vivid account of the dangerous passage he made from the domain of Miyahara Moritaka to that of Seki Kajisai after composing *Ise senku* with Sōseki in 1522:

> Knowing it was likely to snow before long, I decided to set out for the north on the sixteenth. There has been fighting in this province beyond Kumozugawa river and Anonotsu, making it difficult to get from place to place. Beyond where they are fighting lives Seki Minbunotaifu, who is now retired and goes by the name Kajisai. It was arranged that Miyahara Shichirōbyōenojō Moritaka from

Take would provide us with escorts as far as Yawata in Anonotsu, and he personally accompanied us from Yamada to Hirao, where we spent the night.

We left Hirao when it was still dark. It began to rain in earnest about nine o'clock in the morning. The tide was high at Three Crossings, and with that and the wind Kumozugawa river again overflowed. We were accompanied to the town by many people and palanquins from Moritaka. Anonotsu has been desolate for more than ten years, and nothing but ruins remains of its four or five thousand houses and temples. Stands of reeds and mugwort; no chickens or dogs, rare even to hear the cawing of a crow. The wind and rain at the time were terrifying.

Our escorts all returned home and no others arrived to meet us. We lost our way, and after wandering in the wrong direction we hired a local foot soldier on the advice of an acquaintance. The soldier took us two leagues to a place called Kubota. That night the party sent by Kajisai, equipped with palanquins and such, found us. I am amazed we saw the day through safely. (*JS*: 15–16)

Sōchō's travels were occasionally interrupted by battles. Hostilities forced a change of direction on the trip in 1522 that begins his journal, putting an end to his initial attempt to visit the Asakura. Another battle had kept him from reaching the Shirakawa Gate in 1509, the goal of the journey through the Kantō region recorded in *Azumaji no tsuto*.

An outbreak of war between Sōchō's hosts, between the Matsudaira and Makino houses, for example, was an ever-present possibility. Makino Kohaku Shigetoki, lord of Imahashi Castle in eastern Mikawa, was an old friend, and Sōchō stayed with his grandson Makino Denzō on three occasions recorded in his journal, in 1524, 1526, and 1527 (*JS*: 55, 98, 150). But Sōchō was also an acquaintance of the Matsudaira, lords of western Mikawa and Owari. Among them was Matsudaira Kiyoyasu, with whom Sōchō composed renga a few days before doing so with Denzō in 1527 (*JS*: 150).[181] Two years later Kiyoyasu went to war with Denzō and killed him at his fortress at Imahashi. Sōchō was very probably aware of the deadly rivalry between his respective hosts, and interaction with them no doubt required diplomacy and tact.

The speed of Sōchō's travels fluctuated widely. Returning to Sunpu from Kameyama in 1524, for example, he covered approximately 150 kilometers in eight days, including two days of rest, which averages about twenty-five kilometers per day on the road. The longest single day's travel was about thirty-eight kilometers. That compares with the average speed of thirty-six kilometers per day along the Tōkaidō in the Edo period, when the route was well defined and maintained, hostels were available every few kilometers, and the country was at peace.[182] It should also be noted that Sōchō in 1524 was seventy-six years old.

CHAPTER ONE

The speed of Sōchō's journeys was related not only to violence en route but of course to the local terrain, the condition of the road, and the mode of conveyance. He appears to have favored the palanquin for travel, but he remarks of its discomforts:

169	suzukayama	In the Suzuka Mountains
	furisutenu mi no	what is sad about
	kanashiki wa	*not* casting off the world
	oikagamarer	is having my old, bent back
	koshi o kakarete	carried in a palanquin!

(*JS*: 50)

He also on occasion rode a horse, but apparently with no great skill or enjoyment: "In the beginning of the ninth month [of 1524], I rode about four or five chō from here and on the way home fell from my horse. My upper body aches and my right hand is useless" (*JS*: 59).

And of course he frequently walked, though that became increasingly difficult as he grew older: "In my aged decrepitude I have not been fit for walking and have gone nowhere" (*JS*: 110). Difficult terrain and his own infirmities could make travel exceedingly trying at times:

> We proceeded instead to Eight Peaks Pass. Cups of sake here and there with the monks and lay people seeing us on our way. When our escorts arrived from Umedo, we set out to cross the peaks. I had been told that horses and palanquins had for some reason not been allowed this way in years, but my aged feet could not manage it. Someone tried to carry me on his back, but it hurt my chest, cut off my wind, and put me in fear of plummeting into the valley below. So I hired a body of twenty or thirty palanquin bearers from Umedo to carry this old body of mine. They marched past the huge rocks to the left and right and breasted through the waves that coursed down—from time to time I completely lost my nerve. I felt as though I were being borne right through the air. Finally we stopped for the night at a dwelling on the pass. (*JS*: 102–3)

Passage by boat likewise had its frightening moments, but Sōchō seems to have been exhilarated by the combination of the danger and the festive excursion atmosphere occasioned by that form of transporation. Some of the most lively passages in his journal describe stretches crossed by boat. One involves a trip up Ujigawa river on the way to Shūon'an in Takigi:

> As we went upriver from Fushimi toward Uji Bridge, we could see Mizu no mimaki pasture and Yawata Mountain. Kotsugawa and Ujigawa rivers flow to-

gether there to form an expanse as broad as a lake. The people we invited from Kyoto enjoyed themselves, "beating in time on the boat sides," playing shakuhachi and pipes, and singing popular songs like "Water wheels revolving in the Uji's rapids—are they turning over thoughts of this woeful world?" The deutzia on the banks and the irises at the water's edge looked lovely, blooming together. There were innumerable stretches of rapids, and the boatman sang old songs like "struggling against the current at a tow rope's end." We finally put into shore and all alighted, sorry the trip was over. (JS: 46)

In all cases, Sōchō appears to have traveled with a number of others. The image of a solitary poet journeying solely at the dictates of his heart is not appropriate in his case. Most of his stays with warriors lasted only a day or two, or even just part of a day. His sojourns of four months at Asakura Norikage's residence in 1523 and of fifty days at Seki Kajisai's in 1524 were exceptionally long periods, occasioned by his especially close friendships with his hosts.

But there were limits on Sōchō's freedom, imposed by conditions on the road and the necessity to arrange for guides, palanquin bearers, horses, and so forth. Sōchō must have traveled with considerable baggage, including not only clothing, food, and drink to provide against unforeseen delays en route but also paraphernalia related to his profession, including paper and a quantity of poetic reference books. His first work on *Genji monogatari*, *Shijin zanshō*, is believed to have been made for his own consultation while on the road.[183] He perhaps carried with him his personal poetry collections as well, for he writes in both his second collection, *Nachigomori* (Beneath Nachi Falls, 1517), and his third, *Oi no mimi* (Aged Ears, 1526), that he recorded his verses therein to avoid "accidental repetition."[184] But his portable library was small, and we find him relying frequently on his memory during his travels. At Atsuta Shrine, for example, he wrote, "I seem to recall the line *koko mo atsuta no* from the *Latter Hundred-Waka Sequence at the Palace of the Retired Emperor Horikawa*. Probably a misrecollection in my dotage" (JS: 100).

After reaching his destination, Sōchō was usually offered a bath to wash off the dirt from the road and relax from the rigors of the journey. A bath was a luxury, especially if it included medicinal herbs, and Sōchō appreciated the effort enough to make frequent mention of mulberry, herbal, or salt-water baths in his journal.

Then came the nearly inevitable renga session, usually involving one hundred verses, or perhaps merely a "single page" of twenty-two verses if time or the number of poets was insufficient. When he stopped at several hosts' residences in close succession, Sōchō felt the strain of repeated composition, as indicated by this journal entry for 1527: "Though I was asked to compose verses at various other places, I left on the first of this month. It was unconscionable of me to do so, but at my age I could not endure the repeated linked-verse sessions" (*JS*: 148). After the renga sequence was completed, a banquet would often follow.

Sōchō in Old Age, Suruga in Transition

When Sōchō began writing his journal in 1522, he was seventy-four years old. As the preceding examples from that document have shown, he remained a very active traveler and poet well into his eighth decade. Inevitably, however, deaths of friends and his own advancing age made thoughts of the afterlife intrude into his journal more and more frequently as the years passed, particularly when he neared the age of seventy-nine (by the Japanese count), which a soothsayer had divined would be his last. He resolved to meet his end where his spiritual mentor Ikkyū had, at Shūon'an, and he left the Imagawa domain for what he believed would be the last time in the second month of 1526. Sōchō arrived in the capital three months later, after leisurely stays with various provincial warrior patrons along the eastern seaboard, lodged briefly at Daitokuji, then reached Shūon'an in Takigi toward the end of summer.

It was only a few weeks later that he received news of the death of Imagawa Ujichika, the lord he had known and served for more than half a century. Like the deaths of Yoshitada and Sōgi, the daimyo's passing wrought another major change in Sōchō's life.

The poet did not immediately go home on hearing of Ujichika's death, but decided to stay in Takigi until his prophesied last year had come to an end. He observed the necessary obsequies at Takigi, and he requested that Sanetaka arrange for various nobles to contribute poems on books of the *Lotus Sutra* for Ujichika's repose. Sōchō hoped to present them to the Imagawa in person the following year, should he survive. He remained in Takigi into the winter but was then apparently forced to leave for Shōrin'an across Lake Biwa because the warrior Yanagimoto Kataharu and his allies had taken up arms against the incumbent shogunal deputy Hosokawa Takakuni, making the capital and its immediate environs dangerous. As Shōrin'an was also in the Daitokuji network, Sōchō perhaps felt he might meet his end with equanimity there as well. He survived the year, of course. In the second month, however, Takakuni was driven from the capital together with the shogun he manipulated, Ashikaga Yoshiharu. They made camp near that very temple, which may have convinced Sōchō that it was high time for him to return to Suruga.

But Sōchō encountered hostility from some quarters upon returning to the Imagawa domain, and that prompted him to include in his diary a long and impassioned passage in self-exoneration, explaining his actions since the old daimyo died. Included in it is a copy of a letter he had sent to his old friend Asahina Yasumochi:

> A courier bringing news of the death of Imagawa Ujichika on the twenty-third of the sixth month, sixth year of Daiei, arrived at Shūon'an in Takigi from Rinsen'an on the twenty-ninth of the seventh month. I should have gone to pay my last respects on hearing of Ujichika's death, but I was already in my seventy-ninth year and thought it was to be my last, so I had requested leave to prepare for my end at Daitokuji or Takigi. Having done so, how could I simply rush back again? (*JS*: 161)

This passage gave rise to the notion among early biographers of Sōchō that the hostility he encountered was motivated by his failure to return immediately to pay his last respects to his late lord. But a close reading of the subsequent account, which is written in Sōchō's idiosyncratic and at times ambiguous style, suggests instead that the hostility had been directed primarily at the old Ujichika and, after his death, at his heir, Ujiteru. Sōchō seems to have been implicated by association:

587	sa mo araba	Though I told myself
	are to omoedo	if it must be it must be,
	me ni mimi ni	my eyes and ears
	kikite mo mite mo	are surfeited in sight and sound
	amaru kuchi zo yo	with many too many mouths.

I am saddened by the falsehood I encounter everywhere. I have heard nothing but doubts voiced about judgments and policies made after Ujichika suffered his stroke ten years ago. Ujiteru, they continue, is a boy not yet twenty, unstable and willful with those in his service. When I returned to this domain I heard nothing but slander, groundless rumor, and outrageous insolence, some directed even at me. Were it meant for me alone I would not be bothered. It may seem that I am defending them to all and sundry, but I wanted at the very least to plead their case, and I gave free rein to my brush. But I can do nothing about the ever-present rumors, protest them though I will. Anyone can imagine my vexation. I pressed for an investigation several times but it had no effect. Moreover the slanderers came out in the open. In the end nothing could be done, and so I prepared

> to meet my end at my Brushwood Cottage in Mariko. But Mariko is only just across the river from Tegoshi, and people are always coming and going. What painful matters for these aged ears! (*JS*: 163)

Clearly the derogation was directed at the old regime and its successors, and only secondarily at Sōchō, probably because of his long-standing association with Ujichika and his son. The Imagawa probably did not expect him to return from Takigi immediately, since he had apprised them ahead of time of the prediction about his death; in fact, the messenger announcing Ujichika's death very likely did not even leave Suruga until the funeral was over. Sōchō's account also makes it clear that he notified his Asahina friends that he fully intended to return if he outlived the prophecy, and he went on to do so, laden with offerings that were well received.

The sources of the criticism and its precise reasons may never be known; possibly some came from the disaffected relatives of the rival Ujichika had killed in his own succession battle four decades earlier. But life in Suruga clearly was somewhat less pleasant for the old poet than it had been earlier.

Actual power in the domain was now wielded by Ujichika's widow, the nun Jukei, who served as de facto regent for their son Ujiteru during his first two years as daimyo.[185] Sōchō does not appear to have been particularly close to Jukei, as she is never mentioned in the pages of his journal. That fact is surprising since she was the daughter of his friend Nakamikado Nobutane. Sōchō was, of course, a member of the inner circle of Lady Kitagawa, who was Jukei's mother-in-law, and the relationship between such in-laws is notoriously problematic. It seems likely, however, that Jukei harbored no enmity against Sōchō but simply preferred to associate with others of backgrounds more like her own, such as the émigré courtiers who stayed for extended periods in the Imagawa domain.[186]

Sōchō's relationship with Jukei and her circle was probably cordial but distant, given their different tastes and Sōchō's advancing age. Doubtless this made his position in the domain somewhat less stable, but he continued to serve Ujiteru as before, which he surely could not have done had he experienced a serious falling out, and to compose verses at formal renga sessions at Ujiteru's residence.

Sōchō also still enjoyed the favor of his earlier patrons, especially Asahina Yasumochi, Asahina Tokishige, and Lady Kitagawa, and he continued to write both poetical and historical works for the Imagawa. But there is no disguising the increasing loneliness of his last years as his old friends and supporters died one by one, leaving him more and more isolated in a domain with active detractors. Lady Kitagawa died in 1529, and Ōgimachisanjō Sanemochi and Tō no

Sojun in 1530. With the loss of those old acquaintances there was no doubt a corresponding loss of revenue for Sōchō in the form of gifts.

Sōchō wrote of his loneliness in *Sōchō nikki*:

> My mountain cottage during the long rains was tedious. Here I have none for friends save the snails:

samidare wa	In the summer rains
iwa no shizuku no	the snails that come dancing out
maiizuru	from among the drops
katatsuburi o zo	which spill from off the rocks
tou hito ni suru	are the only ones who call.

(SN: 147)

Nor could he travel as he once had; the old poet's physical condition seems to have deteriorated along with the political climate: "I have recently been suffering cruelly from the flux, and to make matters worse I have been having numbness in the legs. I crawl along like a dog crushed by a cart, completely unfit for travel" (*JS*: 163). His loss of mobility cut him off from the provincial gentry who were his second major source of income. In his last diary, *Sōchō nikki*, there are many more waka than renga verses, which suggests a decline in his professional activities.

But Sōchō does appear to have continued to search out new patrons even in his last years. His relatively short excursions to Atami and Odawara, in the domain of the Hōjō, may indicate a growing closeness with that house. Sōchō had known Sōun, its founder, and he was also a longtime acquaintance of Sōun's son Ujitsuna, who had assumed leadership of the house in 1518. Neither Odawara, the site of Ujitsuna's fortress, nor Atami figure in the journal before the death of Ujichika, but each appears three times in Sōchō's writings thereafter, *Sōchō nikki* ending in Odawara in the autumn of 1531. Long in declining health, Sōchō took the waters of Atami for restorative reasons, but his interest in the Hōjō domain after the death of his old patron may not have been due solely to its hot springs.

Sōcho did, however, return to Suruga, and he died at his Brushwood Cottage in Mariko in the following year, 1532.

The Portrait of the Artist

The man who bore the name Sōchō in life and the man who is called "Sōchō" in the work are of course related, as other historical sources will attest. But

CHAPTER ONE

the figure who is portrayed in the pages of an autobiographical work is not only a discovered but a self-created entity whose relationship to the actual writer is not necessarily completely congruent. Self-portraiture is, of course, a construct. Sōchō's journal shares with all autobiographical literature the conundrum that while the writing subject and the written object are the same, the one can never be the exact mirror of the other. Moreover, the depiction of the object by the subject is inevitably on one level true and on another false. Sōchō's journal, like all autobiographical writing, is as Paul John Eakin reminds us, "a special kind of fiction."[187] But it is never entirely fiction, for even lies, both explicit and implicit, premeditated or accidental, tell their own truths about the author.[188] One constantly "performs" one's life, adds Irving Goffman; the written self is simply another lived role, no more true or false than any other.[189]

Problematic though the relationship of the Sōchō of the journal is to the Sōchō who actually lived, the self that is represented in its pages is, as the foregoing comments have suggested, one of remarkable originality. The journal depicts above all else a man of great cultural attainment. He was a master of orthodox waka and renga, but unlike other contemporary writers in the high tradition, he was also willing to depict himself composing and enjoying popular song and lewd haikai poetry. His love of both was legendary.

Sōchō's attitude toward religion was equally diverse, his portrait revealing a mixture of the this-worldly and the other-worldly. As we have seen, the poet was also a trained cleric who spent long periods in monasteries; an early Edo period biographer wrote that for Sōchō, "there was no Zen without renga, nor renga without Zen."[190] The hundred-verse sequence *Yashima Shōrin'an naniki hyakuin*, which Sōchō composed with Sōboku, required two days to complete because he was called to Zen meditation in the middle of the sequence. Passages in his diary show that he accepted the notions of divination and reincarnation as a matter of course:

> My prophesied life span is seventy-nine years, and now, on the first of the twelfth month, I have only thirty nights remaining:

449   eshinazu wa   If I do not die,
            shō kawareru ka   can the life that I now live
               ware yare ya   change to something new?
            kotoshi o kagiru   This year is the limit
             inochi narikeri   of my allotted span.

                                                     (*JS*: 125–26)

Sōchō believed that the living and the dead could on a shadowy level communicate, and that the spirit world could be influenced by human agency, hence his frequent composition of memorial and votive verse. He also made *musō renga*, based on verses vouchsafed to him in dreams.[191] But he also regretted until he died that he had failed in his own estimation to attain a deeper level of enlightenment with regard to nonattachment and nonduality. And yet his diary style, with its inclusion of diverse ga and zoku elements, itself approaches the very nonduality he sought in his religious practice.

Like many clerics of the period, Sōchō combined religious philosophy with canny this-worldliness. He was, after all, a professional poet, and his livelihood relied on a balance of high artistic idealism and the pragmatics of acquiring and pleasing patrons. As earlier pages here have shown, however, he was valued not only for his poetic expertise but also for his talent as a negotiator and political advisor. Such activities required the quick mind and performative abilities that came naturally to a linked-verse poet, as well as a firm sense of political history, which Sōchō demonstrated in the two historical passages in his diary. And, as we have seen, he knew the value of money.

He was passionate in his pursuit of what he perceived to be the truth, either in poetry or Zen. Deeply sensitive to falsehood, he also knew when the truth had to give way to pragmatism, particularly in the area of diplomacy, as when, "mixing truth and lies," he negotiated with the enemy for the release of besieged Imagawa troops.

Sōchō's worldliness also extended to matters of the flesh. As his journal amply indicates, he was fond of young men (*wakashu*). And of course he himself had two children by the woman who looked after him in Suruga. Sōchō nevertheless remained bothered by the contradiction between his love of his children and the Buddhist injunction of nonattachment. But the mere fact that he wrote down and preserved his ambivalent emotions about such mundane concerns distinguishes his literature from that of most of his clerical contemporaries.

Absolutely devoted both to Zen and to renga, Sōchō was outspoken in his denunciation of those in either community who failed to live up to his high ideals. But while he treated those respective ways and their devotees with deep formality and respect, he also clearly enjoyed a party, with sake and song.

He was modest when comparing himself to those he respected, especially of course when he compared himself to his own teachers, as in the passage in which he disavowed all but "a little familiarity" with *Kokinshū*. But he eschewed false modesty, and his journal contains depictions both of shortcomings and of self-praise. Comparing two of his links to two by Yamazaki Sōkan, already famous for his skill at comic verse, he concluded that his own were superior (*JS*: 38–39). Sōboku also recorded a correction of one of his verses by the master, who was proud of what he had done: "[Sōchō's emendation] was divinely inspired. This is exactly what is meant by the expression 'one word worth a thousand pieces of gold.' Sōchō himself joked that it was quite a correction."[192]

As a poet-priest and admirer of Saigyō, Sōchō was at times attracted to the eremitic ethic of solitude, but by personality he was gregarious. His occupation required association with others, and Sōchō was blessed with a wide circle of acquaintances. Letters and poems in his diary (which sometimes appear in the diaries of their senders as well) show that he inspired affection and respect. Sōchō returned their esteem, which makes the memorials he included in his journal after their deaths particularly affecting. These passages become all the more credible in light of the occasional choleric outbursts that Sōchō also preserved in his journal's pages, as in the case of his denunciation of lax priests and of his detractors in Suruga. He also mentioned occasional altercations:

> I had been at odds with someone, but as time passed we were reconciled. On the tenth of the twelfth month, we took part in a renga session together. My hokku:

296   kaze ya haru   Springtime in the wind—
       furutoshi ni tokuru   ice that melts away
         kōri kana   with the old year.

(*JS*: 81)

Motifs and Motivations: Sōchō's Poetic Life

The welter of subjects in *The Journal of Sōchō* do coalesce over time into a few extremely broad and overlapping areas of apparent authorial concern. To be sure, a discussion of "theme" and "narrative" in the case of a diary may appear inappropriate, for both terms may imply a distancing and an overall perspective that would seem to be lacking in the accretive diary format, constructed, as Robert A. Fothergill tells us, of serial imprints "of that day's being alive." But he continues that over a period of time those imprints can combine into "serial autobiography," with certain themes and perspectives gradually becoming clear to the writer as he or she continues the accretive process.[193] That awareness may then feed back into and shape the recording of subsequent events of the diarist's own life. The reader will likewise gradually form a conception of authorial patterns of attention as he or she proceeds through the text.

One main topic that engaged Sōchō throughout the course of the book was, of course, his life as a poet. The great majority of the journal's pages are devoted to the verses Sōchō composed, comments on their interpretation, and the context in which they were created. That context, which often bears a direct relationship to meaning, involves such matters as where the verses were made and with or for whom. Sōchō's motives were partly historiographic; he was interested in chronicling his professional life and contextualizing his professional production.

As more than six hundred poems are recorded in the journal, and as Japanese poetry is by nature lyrical, the journal in its entirety also takes on a basic affective tone. In addition to recording Sōchō's "life as a poet," the work also tends to concentrate on moments Sōchō found emotionally moving. These aspects of what might be called his lyrical or poetic life overlap with the more historiographic details of his artistic career. The term "poetic life" again recalls the fact that literary self-creation is etymologically "poetic," that is, "made." As Louis Renza points out, "autobiography . . . transforms empirical facts into *artifacts.*"[194]

Sōchō's historiographic record of the people with or for whom he composed, for example, shades into more personal and lyrical recollections of friendship and events. Given the dialogic and gregarious nature of linked verse, it is not surprising that Sōchō devoted considerable space to the topic of friendship. His friendships involved courtiers, men of religion, fellow poets, and most often warriors. The predominance of the last group (and the groups are by no means mutually exclusive), portrayed in both their cultural (bun) and martial (bu) manifestations, makes the relationship between the sword and the writing brush a matter of interest throughout the journal.

Sōchō's own advancing years and the loss of friends to old age or to battle make aging and death another major affective concern of the work. This sense of the passage of time and of evanescence is of course central to Japanese poetry and to diary literature in general, but Sōchō's own old age and the violent time in which he lived give the topic a special poignancy in his writing. Episodes dealing with death appear throughout the journal in the form of poetry, anecdotes, and exchanges of letters. A large portion of the waka that appear in the journal were composed in memory of the dead, and many of the renga sequences were votive occasions on death anniversaries.

But despite the work's richness in terms of topics and genre, there remain large areas of Sōchō's existence that he chose to eliminate from his account. Preexisting strictures of genre and received notions of what was apposite in travel and eremitic accounts, as we shall see in subsequent chapters, were very much a factor in those choices. The most important single determinant was the fact that Sōchō was blending the more factual "recording" and the more imaginative "narrative" diary types, to borrow Earl Miner's categorization of the nikki genre.[195] While Sōchō often made excursions into the stark factuality of kanbun nikki, he was also intent on producing a *literary* diary that portrayed his life in a literary way. What Sōchō construed as "literary" was not identical to the formulations of his diarist predecessors, but he nevertheless chose to focus on his life as a poet, and to treat that life in primarily a poetic fashion. Other areas of his experience appear only in passing or are almost completely absent. Though there are a number of waka on religious themes in the work, for example, the modern reader would like to know more about Sōchō's religious philosophy and how he spent his time at religious institutions when he was not composing linked verse. One wishes too that he had written more about his upbringing in Suruga and about his parents and his children, not to mention their mother. And though Sōchō included considerable historical background in his account and more on the economic realities of the period and of his own profession than other diarists in the wabun tradition, one would still like to know more about his reaction to contemporary political developments, about the local customs of the places through which he traveled, and about the histories and personalities of his associates.

The issues that Sōchō did choose to raise allow speculation on some of the author's motives and purposes in keeping his account, although one must bear in mind the proviso of the intentional fallacy, or at least the notion that the work may reveal motives of which the author himself was unaware. One obvious purpose Sōchō seems to have had for keeping his journal was utilitarian, to have handy an aide-mémoire preserving names and places connected with his poetic life. The work recalls in this wise the *chakaiki* kept by tea connoisseurs as records of where and with whom they participated in tea gatherings and which vessels were exhibited. He also evidently used it to record hokku for future use at renga gatherings.

These utilitarian motives were balanced by the conventional "literary" desire to follow the precedent of his own teacher and countless earlier travelers and leave a poetic record of his journeys. Sōchō mentioned several classic diaries of travel in his journal, and he no doubt closely studied the two travel accounts by his teacher, Sōgi. And since one of the reasons he traveled was to seek out places immortalized in the poems of previous generations, it was likewise natural for him to keep a record of his own poems composed at those locations. Keeping a journal was what a literary traveler *did*.

Sōchō, moreover, kept his diary not only for himself but for others. He frequently added or repeated background information that would have been unnecessary had he been writing for himself alone. What writing "for himself alone" would have meant in the context of sixteenth-century Japan is itself problematic; Sōchō may have had little notion of "privacy" as it is construed today. His public motives were doubtless manifold, and they overlap but are not necessarily identical with uses to which his work was subsequently put.

Another purpose of the work, and indeed very likely one of Sōchō's overt motives, was to demonstrate publicly his construction of himself as a man of literature, one who had learned the lessons of earlier elegant, literary travel diaries and who had himself taken his place in that tradition. But Sōchō was also confident enough, and perhaps (in varying measure) brash, eccentric, and blasé enough, to construct a new type of travel self-portrait even as he took his place within that lineage.

And there appear to have been other, more concrete purposes for the work. Inoue Muneo has suggested, for example, that the journal may have been intended in part as a guide to poetry composition for Sōchō's disciples.[196] There were ample precedents for this use of travel accounts, Shōtetsu's *Nagusamegusa* (Consolations, 1418) being one that Sōchō mentions himself. *Tosa nikki* (A Tosa Journal, 935) and *Izayoi nikki* (Journal of the Sixteenth-Night Moon, 1279–80) are also commonly thought to have served that function, at least in part. Detailed explanations of hokku such as the following, which Sōchō from time to time provides, would seem to support Inoue's contention:

> Stayed [at Utsuyama Castle] one day. A renga session was planned, but I excused myself, pleading old age. I only composed the hokku. There were eight or nine people in the first round.

544
    nami ya kore   These breakers
    kazashioru hana   are its crowning blossoms—
    natsu no umi   the sea in summer.

> This refers to the view from the castle. The foundation poem is "The God of the Sea / did not begrudge giving it / to you, my good lords, / this sea plant that he treasures / as a garland for his hair." The words "its crowning blossoms" are in

praise of the castle, which will crown the surrounding provinces in perpetuity. By "the sea in summer," I was describing the cool waves, which are crowning blossoms now that spring has passed, and there are no flowers of any kind. (*JS:* 151)

But unlike *Nagusamegusa*, *The Journal of Sōchō* does not include general poetic theory in its pages. If Sōchō did write his journal to serve as a guide for composing poetry, he was content to provide only empirical instruction; as in most of his other writings on the art of renga, he tended in his journal to teach by example and practice.

That some parts of *The Journal of Sōchō* are more polished than others suggests yet another likely motive for Sōchō's diary writing, the creation of something of personal meaning and literary value to present piecemeal to certain of his hosts on his travels. There were also precedents for this use of diary literature. One of Sōgi's main reasons for composing *Tsukushi michi no ki*, for example, was to give a copy of the work to his host and potential patron Ōuchi Masahiro. Ijichi Tetsuo has also shown that Sōchō presented copies of his earlier travel diary, *Azumaji no tsuto*, in various stages of completion to certain of his hosts as he progressed on the journey.[197] The very carefully constructed accounts in *The Journal of Sōchō* of the author's visits with the warrior Seki Kajisai, for example, suggest that Sōchō presented those portions to his friend.

The praise that Sōchō accords to the literary efforts of his hosts, predominantly military men for whom literature was an avocation, buttresses the theory that Sōchō wanted these men to read at least sections of the work themselves or hear Sōchō's praise of them from others who had read it. Sōchō may also have meant his work to be read in whole or in part by his Imagawa and Asahina patrons.[198] The journal would indeed have been instructive to the young heads of both houses, for military as well as literary reasons. The two long passages on the history of recent campaigns would certainly have been of use to them, as would the occasional remarks on the fortifications of his various military hosts. And given the contemporary emphasis on literary as well as military education for warrior elite, the passages of poetic exegesis too would have been of value.

In addition to its apparent public uses, *The Journal of Sōchō* also includes an overt statement of purpose that points to other, more personal, motivations:

> For the last year or two I have kept a diary of things both serious and frivolous to console myself each day. I know that the years have slipped away, never to return

no matter how fully I am aware of their passing. So I will cast my brush into the waves of old age and write no more from this day forth.

485	makoto ni ya	I have tossed off these lines
	itsuwaru ni ya to	that may be the truth
	iisuteshi	or may then again be lies—
	tsumi saridokoro	where am I to turn
	izuku tazunemu	for that sin to be forgiven?

486	ori ni fure	These useless products
	nagusamefude no	of my brush, from time to time
	nani naranu	my consolation,
	ne wa musubu yume	are the stuff of dreams,
	yuku mizu no awa	the froth on water that flows away.

(*JS*: 136)

The passage constructs a Sōchō who writes to console himself in his old age. Such consolation is apparently derived in part from a heightened awareness of each day's events, generated through the recording of them. The aged Sōchō literally wrote to save his life by fixing it to the page.

This apparent motivation dovetails with the historiographical impulse outlined earlier. The two historical chronicles in part may have been attempts to draw connections between Sōchō's own experience and its larger historical context in order to understand that experience and give it meaning in the larger stream of time. He was perhaps also anticipating his own position when he too would become part of the past. The entire tradition of travel literature, of course, is a dialogue between the past and the present; the author writes to commune with tradition and to understand and in fact to create the present in traditional terms.

But though Sōchō tried to save each day by recording it, he instead became all the more aware of each day's inexorable passage. His writing simultaneously saved each day, creating a past through memory, and accentuated its loss. Despondent, he decided at this point that the self-representational enterprise was counterproductive, and he resolved (for the moment) to throw away his brush.

Sōchō's short-lived resolve to abandon his project was underscored by an awareness of the religious and philosophical conflict implicit in the very process of defining and saving a literary self. His remark that the lines he writes "may be the truth / or may then again be lies" anticipates one of the modern issues in autobiographical theory mentioned earlier, which holds that, as Barrett J. Mandel puts it, "any human verbalizing is a process that by its very nature fictionalizes experience."[199] Sōchō's observation is again related to the Zen doctrine of nonverbalization, which holds that all words are duplicitous; they create a duality between intent and expression. Sōchō's diary writing is therefore an impediment to truth in the context of an epistemology that teaches nonduality. It was perhaps for that reason that Sōchō picked up his brush only infrequently during his sojourns at religious establishments, in addition to the fact that at such times his professional duties as a poet were less onerous.

But Sōchō's statement that his writing may be the truth or may be lies is itself problematic. On the one hand it seems to suggest that he feels there *is* a truth that may be expressed through writing. The verse that follows, however, insists that his writing is "the stuff of dreams, the froth / on water that flows away," a conventional disclaimer that writing, and in fact all worldly phenomena, have only provisional reality. All the events he records in his journal, and perhaps even the distinction between truth and lies itself, are ultimately meaningless according to a nondualistic philosophy.

That perception, of course, can be turned on itself: if one recognizes, as Sōchō claims, that the difference between truth and lies is only provisional, then keeping a diary is no more inherently deluded than not keeping one. Ikkyū would have appreciated the conundrum. Sōchō can at one point elect to cast his brush "into the waves of old age and write no more" but then a few lines later plead the exigencies of etiquette and friendship as an excuse for picking up his brush again and continuing his diary.

Age, Death, and Memory

The motives and conflicts outlined above indicate that Sōchō's purposes for writing and his attitudes about that process were multiple and inchoate. Like the accretive and atomistic nature of the diary form, Sōchō's thoughts and moods changed from day to day, as did his reasons for keeping a journal and what he felt was worth recording therein. That multivalence is nowhere more obvious than in Sōchō's portrayal of his old age and the incipient end of the life he records. The many passages on that overriding concern reflect a complex, contradictory, and constantly changing state of mind. Another of Sōchō's autobiographical motives seems to have been to unburden himself of his conflicted emotions about the end of his life and in so doing, to understand and come to terms with them.

Sōchō's deep awareness of the passage of his own life is apparent on every page; the first poem quoted in his journal establishes this predominant focus:

1   kono tabi wa   Even though I hope
      mata koyubeshi to   I will pass this way again
        omou to mo   on my journey home,
      oi no saka nari   this is the hill of old age.
      sayo no nakayama   Sayo no nakayama.
                                (JS: 7)

His depiction of his trip to the Kansai region four years later is even more colored by that perpective. Believing that he would die at age seventy-nine, he accordingly embarked on his second Kansai journey with the express purpose of meeting his end at either Daitokuji or Ikkyū's hermitage in Takigi, south of Kyoto. He now viewed people and places long familiar to him with the conviction that he was seeing them for the last time. He writes this, for example, about passing the site of Hamana Bridge:

> I then went on to the site of Hamana Bridge. It was washed away some years ago, and the rough waves make for a fearful crossing. Since this is my last journey, I felt somehow both anxious and sad.

345   tabitabi no   Hamana Bridge,
      Hamana no hashi mo   crossed on many a journey,
        aware nari   now gives rise to sadness
      kyō koso watari   at the thought that today will be
      hate to omoeba   the last time I pass over it.
                              (JS: 97)

Some of Sōchō's references to age are relatively neutral:

193   tsuki wa shiru ya   Is the moon aware
      kono iso narete   I have known this rocky strand
        nanasochi ni   for seventy years
      mitsu yotsu made no   and seven with their salty
      aki no shiokaze   autumn breezes off the sea?
                              (JS: 57)

He is even able to laugh occasionally at growing old:

> I wrote this haikai for my own amusement when I was told we were passing Mirror Mountain:

363   kagamiyama   I do not think I will
      iza tachiyorite   stop by and have a look

> mite yukaji
> toshi henuru mi wa
> oshihakaru nari
>
> at Mirror Mountain.
> I already know full well
> I have become an old man!
>
> (*JS*: 103)

The humor of the verse derives from its reference to *Kokinshū* 17: 899:

> kagamiyama
> iza tachiyorite
>   mi ni yukamu
> toshi henuru mi wa
> oi ya shinuru to
>
> I think I will
> stop by and have a look
>   at Mirror Mountain,
> to see whether after all these years
> I have become an old man!

Other references to the passage of the years appear in numerous poetic exchanges on longevity and mutual wishes for its continuation. One such occasion occurred in Suruga in 1525:

> On the last day of the ninth month this autumn, deploring my longevity, I made a poem on the topic of being seventy-eight at the end of the ninth month:

> 274 kyōgoto no
>   nagatsuki o shi mo
>   sakidatsuru
>   oi ni ika naru
>   shizu no odamaki
>
>   Once again today
>   the ninth month passes
>   while this old one remains—
>   how many more years will roll round,
>   like a spool of flaxen thread?

> Matching that were poems by Ōgimachisanjō Sanemochi, his son Kin'e, Imagawa Ujichika, Sekiguchi Ujikane, Ohara Chikataka, Yui Hōgo, and Shueki. (*JS*: 76)

Even when he himself wanted to forget his old age, he was reminded of it by well-meaning friends. On being mindlessly congratulated on his longevity by a group of young temple novices who had no idea of what it means to grow old, he writes:

> One night the young monks were having a few cups of sake as they composed linked verse in Japanese and Chinese in a small dormitory next to Shinjuan. Feeling old and tired by evening, I was resting in the next building when they came and roused me, so I went out. Someone made what was apparently a comic verse:

> 407 shichijūkyūnen
>   korai mare nari
>
>   Seventy years and nine—
>   a rare age, past and present.

I have forgotten the first part of the poem. The young monks all laughed and agreed with the poet. They pressed me for a quick reply, but I was at a loss for words. It then occurred to me that lines from a field song would do perfectly, and I quoted them:

408
koishi no mukashi ya	How I yearn for bygone days!
tachi mo kaeranu	The waves of old age roll away,
oi no nami	never to return;
itadaku yuki	like snow upon my head
mashiraga no	lies my white hair,
nagaki inochi zo	long as this life that
urami naru	fills me full of woe.

Though my years are fêted and celebrated, there is no joy in old age. I wanted to make that very, very clear. (*JS*: 115–16)

He is happiest when he can forget for a moment the passage of time and his infirmities, but such moments are brief and inevitably bittersweet:

The boats that had taken us thus far and those that were to carry us thereafter merged into a single mass—it took me quite out of myself. The next morning I sent this to Shōgakuin with a reed:

361
tsunadenawa	While being pulled
hikare wasureshi	by the tow rope I forgot
oi no nami	the waves of old age,
kyō wa tamoto ni	but I find they have returned
tachikaeritsutsu	to moisten my sleeve today.

(*JS*: 102)

At another point in 1526 he unburdens himself to a sympathetic ear, that of his friend Lord Sanetaka (who was himself over seventy years of age), sending him ten poems on the infirmities of old age and receiving ten replies in consolation. They speak of his physical infirmities, of anxiety about how much time still remains, and of incredulity that old age, once only an abstraction, has come to him as well. Among them are these:

409
yasugenami	My body complains
tachii ni tsukete	in discomfort whether
nagekaruru	at work or at rest,
waga mi wa oi mo	and I find it true indeed
sazo na kurushiki	that old age is filled with pain.

410	yosekaeru	They keep rolling in,
	izuko mo waga mi	though this body is everywhere
	araiso ni	a ravaged strand—
	nani mutsumashiki	what is friendly about them,
	oi no shiranami	these white waves of old age?

413	hito no ue ni	Although one always
	tsune wa kikedomo	hears of it from others,
	waga shiranu	one can never know
	nikuki mono to wa	just how hateful it is,
	oi no tsurenasa	the cruelty of old age.

(JS: 116–17)

Sanetaka responds to each poem as follows:

419	oi no nami	The waves of old age—
	tachite mi ite mi	whether one watches them
	omou ni mo	at work or at rest,
	kaeranu mono to	the months and years roll away
	sugishi toshitsuki	forever, wish what one will.

420	oshikaeshi	Upon reflection,
	omoeba oi zo	I find the waves of old age
	mutsumashiki	friendly things indeed,
	ukimi o sutezu	to come calling on you
	shitaikinikeru	and not forsake you in your pain.

423	hito no ue ni	I think I know
	nashite wa ika ni	how hateful it is
	nikukaramu	for others,
	ware dani oi wa	as I too have become
	akihatenikeri	deeply weary of old age.

(JS: 118)

The deaths of friends are doubly painful for the old man, for they not only deprive him of another of a dwindling group who share his past experience but remind him that he will eventually follow them. The longest groups of waka exchanges in the journal, in fact, are devoted to votive verses composed by Sōchō on the deaths of two close courtier friends, Toyohara Muneaki and Nakamikado Nobutane. Other exchanges are predicated on the certainty of such a parting in the future:

The monk Fukuda Hachirō sent a request in a poem:

507 hitofude no   Whenever you see
     ato miru tabi ni   this remnant of my brush,
         omoiidete   please remember me
     namu amida butsu no   and do not forget to chant
     tonaewasuru na   "faith in Amida."

My response:

508 nareshi yo o   The bond between us
     wasuregatami ni   will never be forgotten,
         omoide wa   but who will be the first
     izure ka saki no   to remember it and chant
     namu amida butsu   "faith in Amida"?
                              (JS: 140)

Sōchō is left feeling more lonely and even embarrassed by his longevity. Here is his reaction to the news of the death of his patron Imagawa Ujichika:

> I can only wonder with shame why I have lived so long and how I will die. Aside from Ujichika, Lords Bōshū and Zushū have passed away as well—how is it that I too did not awake from this dream in the past year?

548 kazoureba   A count of my years
     ware taga tame mo   shows me to be older
         kono kami no   than the others
     shiniokurekinu   who have gone before me,
     kore ika ni semu   and I can do nothing.
                              (JS: 153)

New Year's, the day when according to the traditional count everyone becomes a year older, is especially poignant:

> New Year's Eve. Tonight the spirits of the dead return. . . . At seventy-nine, I made offerings of tea and hot water and lit incense for the many now departed. On kindling the flame:

482 ware zo kono   Here am I,
     michishirube ni shite   on the evening when I should be
         kubeki yoi   the one leading them back,
     mata takimukau   once again kindling the flame
     tomoshibi no kage   and sitting before its light.
                              (JS: 134)

CHAPTER ONE

The Journal of Sōchō presents a very human ambivalence toward the fact of death. One the one hand, Sōchō depicts himself as being attached to life and wondering how much time remains:

476	kyō yori wa	How much longer
	ikite itsu made	will I go on living from today?
	itsu made no	How much longer?
	isogu kata naki	Nowhere now to hurry to—
	yasotose no haru	spring of my eightieth year.
		(*JS:* 133)

But as one who has taken Buddhist vows and admires Ikkyū's Zen teachings, Sōchō also professes to recognize the ideal of nonattachment and the fact of death as a release from suffering:

483	azusayumi	O catalpa bow,
	yasoyi no haru o	in this, my eightieth spring,
	chikara nite	bend back
	hito no sakai o	and from this world of men
	hikihanachite yo	release me with all your might!
		(*JS:* 135)

He also takes refuge from the fear of death in the religious teaching of non-duality, that distinctions between life and death are ultimately equally illusory, and he records a poem by the priest Tenmyō that recommends philosophical acceptance of the pain of growing older:

477	shinau to mo	Whether you want to die,
	ikite itsu made	or whether you want to go on
	arau to mo	living longer,
	mi ni irowaneba	if you do not dwell upon it,
	wazurai mo nashi	you will avoid suffering.
		(*JS:* 133)

But Sōchō ends his journal as he began it, still struggling with his ambivalence toward old age:

On receiving greetings at year's end from a grandfather, father, and grandchild:

617	ōji chichi	Greetings at year's end
	mumago no toshi no	from grandfather and father

kure ni shite	and also grandchild—
arite nasake wa	I am both glad and ashamed
ureshi hazukashi	to have lingered on so long.

(JS: 170)

The Journal in Overview

The poet's basic topics—his poetic life and its approaching end—are treated in his journal not from a uniform but a variety of perspectives. Unlike Western autobiography or some of the Heian female poetic memoirs, Sōchō's "diary" is an accretive personal record.[200] His portrayal of his life's events does not attempt to limit itself to a single theme or fixed interpretation; it is the very indeterminacy and open-endedness of the continuing life story that concerns the author at each point in its unfolding.

The style and structure of the work contribute to the complexities and contradictions in the author's self-portrayal. Sōchō gives the impression of writing when and how the spirit moved, allowing the nature of each entry to reflect his present mood. This is evident in the variation in frequency and degree of temporal remove with which he records events. On journeys he makes more or less regular entries, but once he arrives at his destination he may let months pass, and even so much as half a year in 1525. Often he writes of an event soon after it occurred, but at other times he lets considerable time pass before picking up his brush. Dating is vague at times or nonexistent, and he occasionally repeats material introduced previously.

The general language of the work too is multifold. Most is a blend of native Japanese words and Chinese compounds (wakankonkōbun), with a high degree of variation in the mix of Japanese and Chinese elements. But in addition, Sōchō often resorts to kanbun locutions, and his prose at times reads like a direct transcription of kanbun (*kanbun chokuyakutai*). But some passages, usually those most lyrical in outlook, preserve something of the flavor of classical wabun. Sōchō also at times uses the epistolary style, *sōrōbun*, even when not reproducing letters written to others. The accretive episodes show a marked imbalance, both in terms of the number of lines in the individual units and of the time span between those units. Some are nearly entirely poetry; others are purely prose. He uses short sentences by and large, but they are often highly condensed and elliptical.

Again, much of the subject matter of the diary is topical in content and requires knowledge of the subject under discussion. Ishida Yoshisada in consequence has called the work "difficult to read," but he adds that "it has a spare (*karekitta*) quality that is quite alluring."[201] Modern interpreters of Sōchō often present conflicting views of the meaning of passages. Nakagawa Yoshio insists that the entire final section of the work has been fundamentally misread for the last fifty years due to its inherent ambiguity.[202]

All writing implies selectivity and a shaping consciousness; this is as true for autobiography as for any other form of literature, based though it is on ostensible fact. "Confession of the past," observes Georges Gusdorf, "realizes itself as a work in the present: it effects a true creation of self by the self."[203] Sōchō's authorial hand is manifest in a number of ways in his journal. Selectivity of topic is one way; we have already seen that Sōchō treated a broader range of subjects than previous diaries in Japanese, but he was no means indiscriminate. The degree of remove at which he wrote also invited selectivity—the longer he waited between entries, the more selective he was in recording his material. The choice of what to record and what to omit itself became a form of interpretation.[204] Sōchō knew he was carrying out this operation, as at the end of 1524 when he wrote, "Various things happened before the end of the year, but I have omitted them" (*JS*: 60).

Writing style is another area that demonstrates a high degree of artistic selectivity and variability. The passages that appear to have been written primarily as memory aides seem stylistically perfunctory and tend to be terse factual recitals. But other passages show obvious attention to fine writing—to word choice, the blend of poetry and prose, and the conventions of genre. This will become clear in comparison to other works of travel and hermitage literature.

The Journal of Sōchō contains cursory entries together with others of considered style, and it records events at times with an apparently cavalier disregard for larger structures but at others with a clear eye to the interrelationships between parts. In that it records personal events in an accretive way it corresponds to what would be labeled a diary in the Western sense. But reflecting the author's old age, the journal often shades into passages that in a Western context would be more the province of autobiography, in which the author exercises greater retrospective selectivity in the interest of developing a more cohesive, if variegated, whole. A diary tends to focus on where the author is going; an autobiography, on where the author has been. Traditionally, of course, the Japanese *nikki* could include both; *Kagerō nikki* (The Gossamer Years, c. 974) is a good example, starting as it does as a very clearly shaped and retrospective memoir of love and ending as a diary of more or less current events.

Dialogue Among Genres: The Poetry Collection, Chronicle, Anecdote, and Conversation

The juxtaposition of genres within the diary format is itself a classical tradition. Most notable, of course, is the mix of poetry and prose, "versiprosa," which is a characteristic of most if not all diaries in the Japanese language since Tsurayuki's *Tosa nikki*. This was not only because of the important role of poetry in diary literature but also because the personal, lyrical stance of the waka corresponded well with the ostensibly autobiographical nature of the diary, and because the brevity of the waka medium often required descriptive headnotes (*kotobagaki*) in prose that detailed the personal events that gave rise to the verses that followed. But the diary also routinely admitted other genres to its pages; Edwin Cranston's study of *Izumi Shikibu nikki* (Izumi Shikibu Diary, early 11th c.), for example, emphasizes the "blurred boundaries" between the personal memoir and the poetry collection, the poem-tale, and even the fictional monogatari narrative that complicate the classification of that work.[205] *Ionushi* (Master of the Cottage, mid 11th c.), the next-oldest travel diary after *Tosa nikki*, is actually half travel account and half poetry collection; *Murasaki Shikibu nikki* (Murasaki Shikibu Diary, 1008–10) includes an epistolary segment along with its diary and poetry passages; *Izayoi nikki* concludes with a chōka, and so forth.[206] In the Japanese context, the blurring of genres is underscored by the plethora of alternate titles for variant manuscripts of a particular work. The title *Ise monogatari*, to cite perhaps the best-known example, foregrounds the poem-tale (*uta-monogatari*) aspect of that classic, while the alternate *Zaigo Chūjō no nikki* (Diary of Middle Captain Ariwara of the Fifth Rank) highlights its reputed quality as poetic memoir.[207]

Such linking of genres would seem to be a universal attribute of self-reflective writing; Fothergill might be describing *The Journal of Sōchō* when he remarks of the Western tradition that diaries overlap with "meditations, letters, anecdote collections, occasional essays, rough-drafts, chronicle histories, [and] commonplace books," for Sōchō's text includes, mutatis mutandis, all those modes.[208] The heterogeneity of Sōchō's journal is reflected in the variety of alternate titles that appear on early manuscripts of the work, including *Sōchōki* (The Chronicle of

Sōchō), *Sōchō nikki* (The Diary of Sōchō), *Sōchō kikō* (Sōchō's Journeys), *Sōchō Suruga nikki* (The Suruga Diary of Sōchō), *Sōchō kukuki* (The Chronicle of Sōchō at Eighty-One), and *Sōchō michi no ki* (The Account of Sōchō's Travels).[209] In Hanawa Hokiichi's great Edo-period compendium of Japanese literature, *Gunsho ruijū*, Sōchō's work is included in the diary section, not in that of travel literature.

Travel and eremitic accounts form the two predominant subgenres of Sōchō's diary literature, and they will occupy subsequent chapters here. But his accounts of life in movement and life in stasis are themselves permeated with examples of other genres: the personal poetry collection, the historical chronicle, the anecdote, and the conversation and its related domain, the epistolary passage. While these genres may not have been conceived in the imagination of the period quite as they are today, there were ready models of each available for Sōchō's emulation and interpretation. Sōchō links these modes into his diary narratives, occasionally presenting the same topic in different genres, a technique that increases the complexity and depth of the whole, forming a dialogic gestalt.

The personal poetry collection (*jisen kashū* for waka; *jisen kushū* for renga) has always been related to the diary in Japanese (as opposed to diaries in kanbun), a reflection of the traditional emphasis on poetry in daily literary life. Verses recorded chronologically, with the time and place of composition indicated, may become in themselves a kind of diary, given the self-referential tenor of the Japanese poetic tradition. Some sections in *The Journal of Sōchō* are, in fact, little more than personal linked-verse collections. The record of his round trip from the capital to Echizen, for example, is primarily a list of hokku with prefaces not a great deal longer than those accompanying the verses from the trip that went into Sōchō's third personal poetry collection, *Oi no mimi*. And passages in the journal where Sōchō appends explanatory notes to verses are similar in terms of genre to other poetic commentaries such as *Sōchō renga jichū* and *Renga tsukeyō* that he wrote at about the same time. Such passages provide insights into contemporary literary reception.

The Journal of Sōchō and *Oi no mimi* share a genetic relationship, in that they were compiled simultaneously and contain verses composed on the same journeys, but they were made for essentially different reasons.[210] Although it shares seventy hokku with *The Journal of Sōchō* and one couplet (one *maeku* and one *tsukeku* link), *Oi no mimi* is a collection of the hokku and tsukeku Sōchō most likely considered his best renga verses composed during those years. It complements the journal in that it provides a much broader sample of tsukeku as well as more than seventy additional hokku. The principles of hokku inclusion are clearly different in the two works; fewer than half of those contained in *Oi no mimi* are found in *The Journal of Sōchō*, and the journal records nearly as many other hokku which are not taken into that collection. In addition, many of the shared verses appear in slightly different forms in the two books, and in different order, suggesting editing and rewriting.

Perhaps the most intriguing difference between the two works is that on occasion Sōchō included verses in his journal that he felt were inferior. For example:

A certain person requested a hokku during a visit:

437	wataru se ya	Where are the shallows
---	izuku yasugawa	of Yasu River safely crossed?
	asagōri	Thin ice at morning.

I must decline such requests from this day forth. (*JS*: 122)

The various divergences between *The Journal of Sōchō* and *Oi no mimi* first suggest that neither work served as a source for the other but that both were composed with the aid of yet other rough notes or copies of renga sequences. The journal is by no means simply a commonplace book from which more polished work was meant to be later culled. While the aesthetic quality of a verse seems to have determined whether it would be included in *Oi no mimi*, it was the relationship between the verse and the circumstances of its composition that determined its inclusion in the journal. As the examples throughout this chapter have indicated, Sōchō clearly valued many of the hokku in his diary for their intrinsic artistry, but as often as not he appears to have been equally interested in context: for whom the verse was composed, where and when the session took place, and how the verse reflected those facts. Some verses and their explanatory material are thus added to fill in the narrative continuum; in a sense they resemble *ji* (background) verses added to a renga sequence to make the *mon* (pattern) verses stand out. In addition, *The Journal of Sōchō* often records the attitudes and emotions that gave rise to the composition. Again, in his diary writing, Sōchō was interested in *linkage*, not only verse to verse, but verse to personal and historical context.

The two war chronicles that Sōchō included near the beginning and the end of his journal expand that historical context, and they also provide a public element that complements the work's overall personal perspective. Where the diary in general focuses on art, these two passages concentrate on war; it was war, of course, and not art, that was the major occupation of Sōchō's patrons, and these passages would have held the attention of his warrior readers as much as the linked-verse segments. Together, they suggest another central dimension of Sōchō's life, but one that could not be included in his renga poetry or in more traditional and orthodox types of diary literature.

It will be recalled that Sōchō served the Imagawa not only as a linked-verse master but also as a historian and diplomatic advisor, and that aside from these two chronicles, he was responsible for revising *Imagawa kafu*, a history of the house, into kana from the original kanbun.[211] He also wrote the postscript to the travel chronicle *Fuji goran nikki* (Diary of Viewing Fuji), which was probably composed by Imagawa Norimasa in about 1432. Sōchō's postscript explains the circumstances behind the journey of Shogun Ashikaga Yoshinori to Suruga in 1432 and describes the practical aspects of the trip and the contributions the Imagawa made to its success. As such, it augments the poetic and artistic focus of the diary.

The two chronicles in *The Journal of Sōchō* are not, therefore, isolated instances of historiography but rather good examples of a separate type of writing the author practiced in conjunction with his diary literature, and one that inevitably influenced his nikki approach.

The first account, the "Asahina Battle Chronicle," describes several campaigns that took place during the years from the Ōnin War (1466–77) up to 1522 when the diary begins. Primary in it are Asahina Yasuhiro and his younger brother, Yasumochi. The latter served for a decade after Yasuhiro's death as regent for Yasuhiro's son and successor, Yasuyoshi. Imagawa Yoshitada and Ujichika figure heavily in the account as well. And with the exception of a few lines on Yoshitada's participation in the Ōnin conflict, all the battles in which those warrior rulers figure are purely local in character. The chronicle is therefore descriptive of the new men of the provinces who were carving out personal domains at that time, independent of old central organs of authority.

A notable passage in the chronicle involves Imagawa Ujichika's campaign in Tōtōmi in 1517:

> Ōkōchi and freebooters in this province of Tōtōmi summoned local warriors from Shinano and requested aid from the Martial Defender. They then began seizing lands here and there on both sides of Tenryūgawa river. . . . The next summer, in the latter part of the fifth month, Ujichika set out for [Hikuma] castle. There was a flood at the time and Tenryūgawa river was like a great sea. Ujichika built a pontoon bridge with three hundred and more boats lashed together

with ten or twenty huge bamboo ropes. It was solid as the ground itself. I made a thousand verses in prayer for a safe crossing. The hokku:

7
    minazuki wa   The Waterless Month—
    kachibito naranu   no victor who does not cross on foot,
      seze mo nashi   as there are no waves.

It now occurs to me I ought to have said, "a crossing made by victors, / all of them on foot."

The enemy came out on the far side of the river, and their arrows fell like rain. Tens of thousands of Imagawa troops crossed easily, and the foe pulled back. Ujichika encircled their castle six or seven fold, covering an area about fifty *chō* around. There, from the sixth through the eighth month, he harassed them. The soldiers inside the stronghold resisted for several days, then capitulated on the nineteenth of the eighth month. Ujichika used men from the Abeyama gold mines to undermine the well in the castle, and there was not a drop of water to be had inside. The Ōkōchi—brothers, fathers, and sons—the Ōmi, the Takahashi, and the others in the castle with them, were either killed, cut down and left for dead, or taken prisoner. The fleeing men and women were a pitiful sight. (*JS*: 11–12)

The account is relatively dry and unembellished in exposition, and it is topical in subject, requiring considerable background knowledge that is not directly presented but which Sōchō's contemporaries would have possessed. Many of Sōchō's immediate readers, in fact, would have remembered some of the campaigns themselves or personally taken part in them. Parts of the passage are formulaic, but it contains a degree of drama and emotion as well.

Although the chronicle centers on the local campaigns of a rising provincial house, it is not literature advocating *gekokujō*; Sōchō instead is supporting what he sees as the established order, in which the Imagawa control their domain by historical precedent and juridical rights countenanced by a venerable central government composed of the court and its ostensible servants, the bakufu. Sōchō describes a revolutionary period, but from a generally conservative point of view.

His position as official historian and Imagawa protégé causes him to consciously downplay Imagawa setbacks. Of the Imagawa campaign in Kai (Yamanashi Prefecture), Sōchō writes only, "Ujichika dispatched troops in support of a campaign launched by Takeda Jirō in Kai" (*JS*: 11), failing to point out how near Ujichika's forces came to annihilation while they were besieged at Katsuyama Fortress.

CHAPTER ONE

The "Asahina Battle Chronicle" is thus official history, written by Sōchō the house laureate. And yet the account complements the diary sections of the journal in a number of ways. Sōchō is composing a house history, to be sure, but he does so as a personal witness. When he writes of Ujichika's pontoon bridge that "it was solid as the ground itself" or of the fall Hikuma Castle, where "the fleeing men and women were a pitiful sight," one is led to believe Sōchō was there himself. Sōchō consciously inscribes himself into the Imagawa victories, composing votive renga in prayer for that very bridge, or earlier in thanks for the victory of Ujichika and Sōun in the Kantō region in 1504 (*JS*: 10). The location of the chronicle at the beginning of the diary balances the letter of self-exoneration at the end, so that the reader, on picking up the work and laying it down, is reminded of its author's loyalty and service.

The second historical chronicle appears five years later in the work, just before Sōchō left Shōrin'an in Yashima for Suruga in 1527 (*JS*: 141–42). The account was motivated by the discord in the capital accompanying the rise of Yanagimoto Kataharu and his defeat of Shogun Ashikaga Yoshiharu and his deputy, Hosokawa Takakuni. A much briefer account than the first, it describes violence in the capital from the Meitoku Discord of 1391 through the Ōnin War and up to the flight of Takakuni. Where Sōchō was writing of rising men and local history in the earlier chronicle, he returns here to the capital, the old center of power, and depicts the challenges to established rule. This account too is heavily biased in favor of Takakuni, Sōchō's bakufu patron. But again, though official history, the passage has personal touches that echo the more lyrical diary sections that surround it. Sōchō probably included his description of the discord and its antecedents not out of purely disinterested historical concern, as it was his patron who was defeated (Sōchō never actually uses that pejorative word, of course) and the movements of that patron were influencing his own. It was Kataharu's entry into Kyoto in 1526 that was likely a main reason Sōchō chose to winter at Shōrin'an, safely located across Lake Biwa from the violence in the capital. Then, when Yoshiharu and Takakuni themselves fled for safety across the lake, Sōchō departed for Sunpu.

These two chronicles contrast markedly with the rhythm of the more lyrical whole and would be unthinkable in more orthodox diary accounts. They present the diarist in an entirely different and official context, and yet in an essentially subjective manner. The histories reveal another aspect of the author's variegated life.

But while Sōchō was experienced in writing public history, he was also moved to record the private moments of suffering or amusement that he so often encountered in that volatile age. Whether tragic or humorous, such anecdotes constitute another genre in Sōchō's literary constellation. Interposed in the narrative and structurally discrete, they create a link between Sōchō's journal and tale literature.

Most of the tragic anecdotes (*aiwa* or *hiwa*) deal with warriors. Some, like the description of the deaths of Wakatsuki Jirō and his father, combine glory and sorrow:

> Recently Takakuni's forces chanced to be defeated in battle in Tanba, and Wakatsuki Jirō won fame for his matchless death on the field. Years ago Jirō's father, Wakasanokami, had likewise won fame for his glorious death when he retired alone into the Kawarabayashi Fortress. I saw much of both father and son. They aspired to the poetic way and were frequent guests of Lord Sanetaka. What sadness and pity his lordship must have felt on hearing the news!

472	toritsutae	Those two who handed down
	wakatsukiyumi no	the way of the Wakatsuki zelkova bow—
	ika nare ya	how did it happen
	shinanu ga uchi no	that when they should have lived,
	aranu shinisuru	both so tragically perished?

> "Handed down the way" refers to the father's glory passing to the son. (*JS*: 131–32)

Here the public heroism of the Asahina chronicle is recast in personal and affecting terms. Other accounts, however, depict the tragedy of war without any of the "nobility of failure" of the Wakatsuki example:

> Yoshikawa Jirōzaemon Yorishige, the son of the deputy constable of Awa, came with me to Suruga to escape the animosity of his stepmother. Neither with master nor without, he went to Kai Province in the company of reinforcements for the Imagawa forces there, where he was cut down. He died seven years ago, on the twenty-third of the eleventh month. I sent these to his son Tōgorō:

600	awajishima	Far, far away
	awa to haruka ni	from the island of Awaji,
	shionoyama	upon Sashiide Strand
	sashiidenoiso o	by Mount Shio
	terasu tsukikage	moonlight shines.

| 601 | nanatose no | How melancholy |
| | fuyu zo kanashiki | is this winter, the seventh |

> usuyuki no
> ha bakari no koto mo
> awade kiekemu
>
> since he passed away
> without receiving a boon
> even light as the snow on a leaf.
>
> How sad that without receiving a stipend light as the dew he was cut down together with those who did. I composed the second verse on recollecting the saying "life is frail as a leaf." (*JS*: 166–67)

This is the other face of battle: inglorious and unappreciated sacrifice. It presents war in microcosm and not only amplifies but also subverts the official Asahina tale of martial glory.

But again, one of the most remarkable aspects of *The Journal of Sōchō* is its inclusion of a range of styles and tonalities. In addition to tragic episodes, Sōchō passed along funny stories or experiences, often concluding them with a humorous verse:

> An old friend of mine named Rikijū lives at Gokokuji temple at Higuchi Aburanokōji. He called on me at my place of retirement, and for more than ten nights we slept side by side. He is an extraordinary lie-abed—a Time sect monk who cannot tell the time!
>
> 53 kazoureba
> nanatsu mo mutsu mo
> itsu to te ka
> toki shiranu jishu
> yama wa fuji no ne
>
> Counting up the hours,
> it is past four, now past six—
> when does he think it is,
> that Time sect monk fast asleep,
> as dead to time as Fuji's peak.
>
> (*JS*: 27-28)

Other passages involve the usual annoyances of day-to-day life:

> The paperer Saburōgorō lives near the intersection of Ayanokōji and Muromachi Streets, on the north side. I sent him inquiries from time to time concerning an order of mine, but he would not return the finished work. When I went back to Suruga, he wrote that he had not contacted me because of my outstanding balance. I sent him the remainder:
>
> 302 atsurae no
> kagiri nobosetsu
> kudasaren
> saburōgorō
> tema no sekimori
>
> Herewith is the rest
> of the money for the work;
> will you send it down?
> Saburōgorō, the keeper
> of payments at Hindrance Gate.
>
> (*JS*: 82)

Such episodes show Sōchō's abiding interest in haikai poetry, and they anticipate Edo-period collections of humorous poetry and prose (*hanashibon*).[212]

Sōchō's evident fondness for anecdotes reflects his interest in conversation, be it in actual face-to-face discussion or in the form of letters. He recorded examples of both in his journal. Most notable of the latter is his conversation, introduced earlier, with his friend and patron Asahina Tokishige in 1525, just before the New Year (*JS*: 84–86).

The miscellaneous quality of the episode places it in the category of the "desultory conversation" (zōdan), a prose form exemplified in Sōchō's time by such works as *Kensai zōdan* (c. 1501–10) on renga and *Zenpō zōdan* (c. 1512–21) on nō drama. But where those two works concentrate primarily on matters related to the arts of the authors, the conversation in Sōchō's journal deals with a variety of topics from contemporary life. Harada Yoshioki has characterized the passage as a *zuihitsu* (random essay), reminiscent of Yoshida Kenkō's *Tsurezuregusa* (Essays in Idleness, c. 1330?).[213] One also finds in it overtones of house rules composed by warriors for the instruction of their subordinates and descendants. It shows Sōchō in his role not as a poet but as an experienced and worldly advisor.

The passage displays a medieval conservativism and fatalism, blended with advice for survival and self-help in changing times. One is bound by one's station in life, Sōchō observes, and while those who ignore the dictates of resourcefulness and dedication in their particular occupations are blameworthy, those who can do nothing about their plight must be pitied and helped. Thus Sōchō affords a degree of grudging admiration to merchants who make profit (though they can be selfish philistines), but he cautions that monks and landowners should avoid the temptation to emulate them, as they are not accustomed to commerce and will fail. Those who study Zen are estimable, but Zen monks who do not pursue the religious way with zeal are despicable. Samurai must live frugally, but those who have lost their source of support are to be pitied, as are lepers and beggars.

This discussion with Tokishige invests *The Journal of Sōchō* with yet another vocality, this one literally dialogic since it derives from conversation. It broadens the reader's picture of the diarist's concerns beyond the purely artistic matters that dominate most contemporary self-referential literature, and it provides an exposition of personal philosophy that puts other parts of the work, such as the tragic anecdotes or other isolated remarks on the pragmatics of the author's own profession, into sharper perspective.

Letters, too, are a kind of conversation. Those that Sōchō quotes in his journal introduce yet another tonality. Again, the author is concerned not only with self-preservation but with self-contextualization in his time and his society. Some of the letters are in kanbun, others are in sōrōbun, and few are quoted in their entirety. In their externality, they provide a touchstone of empirical reality, and they contribute to the establishment of a horizon of expectation through which we "read" the author in his relationships with others. In the realm of poetry, Sōchō exploits this multivocality through the medium of poetic exchanges (zō-tōka) that let the reader experience Sōchō as he relates to others in verse, and as they relate to him in their own words. We are introduced to the court musician and poet Toyohara Muneaki, for example, through a poetic exchange in 1524. He dies soon thereafter, and in 1525 we are presented with Sōchō's poetic memorial for him and then a brief prose biography that is next amplified by poetry in another voice, that of the courtier Ōgimachisanjō Sanemochi. Then Muneaki speaks in person, in a kanbun letter written on his deathbed with the aid of an amanuensis. And finally there are ten memorial poems by Sanjōnishi Sanetaka and his epistolary postscript. Sōchō's view of Muneaki is contextualized for the reader through this interplay of subjectivities. Such epistolary segments make up a relatively small portion of the material in *The Journal of Sōchō*, but they too contribute to the dialogism of the whole.

Emergent Inclusivity

The Journal of Sōchō, thus characterized by the interplay of genres, came at the end of a quarter-century of the author's artistic development. After the death of Sōgi, Sōchō showed an increasing tendency to let various styles, tones, and genres coexist in a single work of art. One cannot but see in that development a link to the Buddhist principle of nonduality and to Ikkyū's self-confident synthesis of diverse and often contradictory principles in his own person. This tendency toward a confluence of styles and genres can be traced with marked clarity through Sōchō's diary literature.

Sōgi shūenki (1502), despite having been written somewhat hastily to apprise Sōgi's friends in the capital of the events surrounding the poet's death, is crafted with stylistic finish as a single statement. That is likewise true for Sōchō's second diary, *Azumaji no tsuto* (1509), which is a description of just one journey, with no period of stasis and no haikai poetry. It does, however, admit a good deal more "non-poetic" vocabulary than did *Sōgi shūenki*. And as mentioned earlier, Sōchō may have released versions in different degrees of completion to various patrons named within. In *Utsunoyama no ki* (1518), Sōchō combines the autobiography and the travel diary, mixing memories of decades past with accounts of various recent trips. He also adds three haikai waka verses, but no haikai renga. *The Journal of Sōchō*, begun five years later, carries this inclusivity even further. And his last diary, *Sōchō nikki*, includes half of a hundred-verse renga sequence, something not found even in *The Journal of Sōchō*.

This evolution is characteristic not only of Sōchō's diary literature but of most of his literary production. It is also seen, for example, in his three poetry collections. Over the course of his life, he compiled three large personal anthologies which are progressively freer in format. The first, *Kabekusa* (first version 1505; last version 1512), is carefully arranged along the general lines of the imperial anthologies, being subdivided by topical category as well as by hokku and tsukeku. The second, *Nachigomori* (1517), is divided only by year (1515, 1516, 1517), with hokku preceding tsukeku in each section. There is evidence that Sōchō began to classify this second collection too by poetic category but then chose simply to list the verses more or less chronologically.[214] The last collection, *Oi no mimi* (1526), includes the work of five years divided into only two books, with a single section of hokku at the beginning. Unlike *Kabekusa*, *Oi no mimi* is arranged predominantly according to chronological rather than topical considerations, underscoring its developmental similarity to the diary genre. Sōchō was nearly eighty when he compiled *Oi no mimi*, and a diminution of energy probably contributed to the increasing tendency to let his material find a natural form.

The same trend is seen in Sōchō's late commentary on his own poetry, *Sōchō renga jichū* (c. 1523–28). The first half is classified by topic and the latter not. And as we will later see, the poet's linked-verse style too acquires increasing freedom and even a touch of eccentricity as he ages. There can be no doubt that Sōchō's late works are a conscious blend of the planned and the spontaneous, a disciplined intuition that gradually developed during the course of his career.

The Journal of Sōchō represents the culmination of that process. In that work are combined the polarities and contradictions of the transitional age in which it was written. The chapters that follow will explore those properties in greater detail, as they apply to the travel and hermitage sections of the work and to its poetry.

CHAPTER TWO

"What is to become of me as I travel on my way?"

'The Journal of Sōchō'
as Travel Literature

When Sōchō left Suruga in 1522, he was embarking not only on a passage through the physical terrain of sixteenth-century Japan but also on a journey through time, recapitulating centuries of earlier travels by poets, priests, nuns, courtiers, and warriors who had passed down the Tōkaidō road before him. Their written records of their journeys directly influenced his own attitude toward travel and his writing about it. *The Journal of Sōchō* is deeply indebted to past models of travel literature, but reflecting the time in which it was written, it initiates a dialogue between the past and the present, and between various aspects of the travel experience.

One earlier work in the corpus of travel literature to which Sōchō's work bears a particularly strong relationship is Sōgi's *Shirakawa kikō* (Account of a Journey to Shirakawa) of 1468, the first full-scale travel account by a linked-verse poet.[1] Sōgi wrote the piece during his first trip to the east, the same journey on which he had made the acquaintance of the eighteen-year-old Sōchō. Sōchō surely read and studied the account. It provides an ideal foundation for a literary contextualization of *The Journal of Sōchō* because of similarities of genre, chronology, and the master-disciple lineage of the two authors. But more important, the earlier work constitutes a concise yet thoroughgoing application of the orthodox poetic travel mythos in a prose diary context.

CHAPTER TWO

'Shirakawa kikō' and the Poetics of Travel

Sōgi left for the Kantō region in 1466, when conditions in Kyoto were moving toward the chaos of the Ōnin War. He was forty-five years old, but still a young man by the standards of the renga profession, junior in both years and reputation to a number of other linked-verse masters in the capital, most notably Senjun and Shinkei, with whom he had studied.[2] It was during his six years in the east that he began to establish himself as a leading linked-verse master and to write his first works of renga instruction for culturally inclined eastern warlords.[3] *Shirakawa kikō* was composed therefore at the end of Sōgi's formative years as a renga poet and was a "masterpiece" in the original sense of the word, its style and concerns demonstrating a mastery of the classical norms of the travel genre.

The destination of the journey, as represented in the written account, was the venerable Shirakawa Gate, entryway to the northern provinces and hallowed by earlier generations of poet-travelers. Sōgi recorded just the last stages of the trip, mentioning his earlier stops at Mount Tsukuba and Nikkō only by way of introduction so as not to compromise the narrative unity of the account. The chronicle is quite short, beginning with his departure with a handful of guides and companions in early winter from Shioya in Shimotsuke Province (Tochigi Prefecture). Kantō at the time was split between rival military camps, and the party proceeded through inhospitable country in melancholy and disquiet, lodging with rustic hosts at night. After three days on the road, they reached their destination, expressed in poetry their spiritual fulfillment, and later composed a hundred-verse sequence which Sōgi appended to his travel record.[4]

Shirakawa kikō

Having fulfilled my desire to see Mount Tsukuba and my vow to view Black-Hair Mountain in the dew beneath the trees, I availed myself of the kindness of a certain person and set out from Shioya.[5] A hard, cold rain was falling, and I hesitated, wondering about the way ahead, but I pressed on, for it was not for a traveler to halt. For guides, I had two young, mounted samurai, and there were others along as well on a pilgrimage. As we forged further and further on our way, the sound of the rivers here and there seemed to vie with the cold rain on our sleeves in moving us deeply.

My two guides then turned back, and with only one other guard left with us, I felt even more insecure. When we reached Nasu Plain, the way ahead was filled with grass so tall we could not even see the tip of the warrior's bow. I was disconsolate, thinking that but for our escort we must surely lose our lives on such a road. Though Musashi Plain is likewise of endless expanse, there one can rely on its "grasses of affinity"; here, I felt bereft of support.[6] But then a withered scene of bamboo leaves bent under thick dew brought to mind lines by the Great Minister of the Right, and I began to be moved.[7] Even so, I continued to be assailed by sad thoughts, whereupon I composed:

nagekaji yo	Cease your sorrowing!
kono yo wa tare mo	Know that for all men
uki tabi to	this life is a sad journey
omoi nasuno no	and embrace your fate,
tsuyu ni makasete	fleeting as the dew of Nasu Plain.

My companions expressed their various emotions in poetry as well. At day's end we reached a place called Ōtawara and took lodging in the house of a humble peasant.[8] We were deeply affected by the novelty of making a fire of brushwood kindling, and we remarked in pity to each other of our host's crude table. We spent the night talking of these and other things, weeping and laughing by turns.

Things did not proceed as we wished, but we were loath to abandon our desire to reach Shirakawa Gate. Our aged host was sympathetic, and he loaned us horses and such. With his support we went on our way greatly cheered. The mountains were covered with autumn leaves, which here and there had fallen to earth to rich effect. The miscanthus and cogon grasses in the fields were as those the day before, and the chirping of the insects seemed about to fade away altogether. An expanse of oaks reminded me of the withered field at Hirano, and though I have no relatives in the capital, my tears fell in the autumn wind.[9] I supposed that I alone felt like this, but I found that all in my party were sunk in deep sadness. Stands of *kashiwa* oak at the foot of the far slopes attracted me with their color, and groves of *kunugi* oak made me feel I was passing beneath the shade of Sao Mountain or by the shore of Ōkawa.[10]

Pressing onward, we came to a great river. On the soaring cliffs, leaves of many colors blended with evergreens into the distance. I recalled Ōigawa river back home, and on asking learned this one was called Nakagawa, which again called to mind the scenery of the capital and afforded me some consolation. We feared for our horses' footing as we crossed through the swift whitecaps, but we urged them forward and spray covered our sleeves, just as in the Muko Crossing poem in *Man'yōshū*.[11]

Thereafter we came to another river, Kurokawa. It was somewhat gentler than Nakagawa, and its confluent valley streams were slowed by fallen crimson leaves. Our path was choked with green moss, and birds unknown to me sang nearby—I was consoled only by the recollection that "dwelling here is better."[12] A tree in the depths of the distant forest was so brilliantly colored I wondered if the Mountain Princess had devoted herself to it alone, and entertained by the notion, I found us before long at Yokooka.[13]

CHAPTER TWO

Here too we found lodging with the headman of the village and arranged for conveyance to the Shiragawa Gate. On the road thither the sound of the valley stream and the wind in the pines of the peaks seemed more affecting than they would have elsewhere.[14] The clusters of branches here and there had lost most of their leaves, revealing the cottages of the mountain folk. In the marsh at the foot of the slope stood bent, frost-withered reeds. No one kept watch over the hillside fields where stags call for their mates, and a clapper-rope left to rot beside a tumbledown hut aroused a lonelier feeling than had the clapper still been sounding. As we rode along in conversation, our guide pointed out a tree of especially deep color in the distance that marked the gate. Bereft of all other thoughts, I urged my pony faster, and when I reached the gate, my emotion left me at a loss for words.

Of the venerable Shrines of the Two Deities, one was very splendid, and both its precinct and sanctuary filled one with awe.[15] The other was old and had moss for its eaves and colored leaves for a holy fence. Vines hung down from spindle trees as holy garlands, with only the chill wind to make an offering. As I gazed upon the scene, I could not restrain my tears. I reflected on how moved Kanemori and Nōin must have been when they visited this spot, and though we hesitated to offer our own poor poetic attempts, our feelings overflowed of their own accord:[16]

miyako ideshi	The haze and wind
kasumi mo kaze mo	one saw on setting forth
kyō mireba	from the capital
ato naki sora no	are today trackless dreams
yume ni shigurete	in a sky of winter rain.[17]

yuku sue no	I desire no fame
na o ba tanomazu	from future generations.
kokoro o ya	But I hope to leave
yoyo ni todomen	my heart for ages hence
shirakawa no seki	at Shirakawa Gate.

Sōgi

Taira Tadamori, a friend from the capital, was perhaps even more deeply moved to have come here with me:[18]

omou to mo	I had always meant to go,
kimi shi koezuba	but if you had not set out,
shirakawa no	I might have
seki fuku kaze ya	heard it only from afar—
yoso ni kikamashi	the wind at Shirakawa Gate.

| tazunekoshi | Now I understand |
| mukashi no hito no | the emotions of those |

kokoro mo	who came here in the past—
ima shirakawa no	at Shirakawa Gate,
seki no akikaze	the wind of autumn.
	Bokuō
kogarashi mo	Did the withering wind
miyako no hito no	leave it as a present for you,
tsuto ni to ya	men of the capital,
momiji o nokosu	this scarlet foliage
shirakawa no seki	at Shirakawa Gate?
	Bokurin

The latter two men were from the Eastland, but they shared an attraction to the way of poetry and had longed to visit here.

And so we returned to our lodgings in Yokooka under a moonlit sky, the evening seeming to have been "made to suit the occasion."[19]

The journey as Sōgi describes it is a literary and spiritual experience; the objective is a particularly famous poetic spot, with a series of natural scenes along the way that evoke affective responses through their rich conventional poetic connotations. The narrative is simply and yet effectively unified. The poet first makes clear the danger and hardships of the project: "A hard, cold rain was falling, and I hesitated, wondering about the way ahead" (*SK*: 9). But he draws strength from the established recognition of travel as perseverance ("it was not for a traveler to halt" [*SK*: 9]), and he and his few companions press on despite their feelings of insecurity and sadness. The trip is arduous and slow, the way ahead "filled with grass so tall we could not even see the tip of the warrior's bow" (*SK*: 9) or "choked with green moss" (*SK*: 14), and the gloom is enhanced by "withered grasses," "frost-withered reeds," "bare branches," "chill wind," and the familiar nexus of water images such as cold rain, dew, and tears. But as the journey progresses, the stark, colorless images evocative of the hardships of the road are increasingly infused with the deep hues of the leaves that finally prove related to the gate itself and by extension to the pleasures and rewards of the way of poetry:

> As we walked along in conversation, our guide pointed out a tree of especially deep color in the distance that marked the gate. Bereft of all other thoughts, I urged my pony faster, and when I reached the gate, my emotion left me at a loss for words. (*SK*: 15)

Sōgi and his companions then express in poetry their emotions on reaching the goal of so many poets before them. Only then does the gloom entirely pass away: "And so we returned to our lodgings in Yokooka under a moonlit sky, the evening seeming to have been 'made to suit the occasion'" (SK: 16).

In the context of Western self-representational writing, James Olney has noted that "there are no rules or formal requirements binding the prospective autobiographer—no restraints, no necessary models, no necessary observances gradually shaped out of a long developing tradition and imposed by that tradition on the individual talent who would translate a life into writing."[20] For Sōgi and other writers of medieval travel chronicles in Japan, by contrast, there was a very clear received tradition that required emulation. That tradition developed directly out of travel waka poetry (*kiryoka*). Sōchō himself summarized the "basic essence" of poetic travel in his poetic treatise *Sōchō kawa*:[21]

> When "pillow of grass" appears in the previous verse, one links such sentiments as going as far as one can, knowing not whither; spending a night in a storm on a peak; waking in the dew of a moor and then departing; heading out to sea, then setting course by a distant mountain and landing on a rocky strand; turning one's robe inside out and wishing for a dream of a loved one during a brief rest beneath the moon; being unable to see even the tops of the mountains of the capital; crossing a peak lost in white clouds; thinking of the people in one's distant village; making one's travel bed night after night in the thick dew; crossing Ōsaka, the Mountain of Meeting, in the haze; or listening to the autumn wind at Shirakawa Gate.[22]

Sōchō then lists waka, all but one from *Shinkokinshū*, to illustrate the travel mythos he has outlined. They portray the journey as uncertain and disquieting:

> akeba mata
> koyubeki yama no
> mine nare ya
> sora yuku tsuki no
> sue no shirakumo
>
> Is that the peak
> of another mountain I must cross
> when morning comes?
> White clouds where the moon
> that courses the sky will set.
>
> (*Shinkokinshū* 10: 939, by Fujiwara Ietaka)

> yūhi sasu
> asaji ga hara no
> tabibito
> aware izuku ni
> yado o karuran
>
> In the field of short reeds
> lit by the evening sun,
> a traveler—
> where will he find someone
> to offer him shelter?
>
> (*Shinkokinshū* 10: 951, by Minamoto Tsunenobu)

> kyō wa mata
> shiranu nohara ni
> yukikurenu
> izure no yama ka
> tsuki wa izuran
>
> Once again today,
> I journeyed over unknown fields
> until night fell.
> From behind which mountain
> will the moon appear?
>
> (*Shinkokinshū* 10: 956, by Minamoto Ienaga)

The traveler is lonely and melancholy:

> makura to te
> izure no kusa ni
> chigiruran
> yuku o kagiri no
> nobe no yūgure
>
> With what grass
> for my pillow
> will I exchange vows?
> Going far as I am able
> over the plain at evening.
>
> (*Shinkokinshū* 10: 964, by Kamo no Chōmei)

> nobe no tsuyu
> urawa no nami o
> kakochite mo
> yukue mo shiranu
> sode no tsukikage
>
> Blame it though I will
> on the dew of the fields
> or the waves of the bay,
> moonlight shines on my sleeves
> since I know not the way ahead.[23]
>
> (*Shinkokinshū* 10: 935, by Fujiwara Ietaka)

And he longs for home, which is often the capital, the standard to which the countryside is compared:

> azumaji no
> yowa no nagame o
> kataranan
> miyako no yama ni
> kakaru tsukikage
>
> Would you could tell them
> how I gaze on you tonight
> on the road eastward,
> O moon shining down
> on the hills of the capital.
>
> (*Shinkokinshū* 10: 942, by Jien)

Pervading all is a sense of strangeness; travel means a complete break with the world the author knows. Thus parting poems (*ribetsu no uta*), composed when the poet is torn from familiar people and places, are important enough to constitute a separate poetic category apart from travel in most imperial anthologies.

This was the poetic travel legacy to which Sōgi and all linked-verse poets were heir, put forth in such travel classics as *Tosa nikki*, the *Azuma kudari* (Down to the Eastland) section of *Ise monogatari*, and later *Izayoi nikki* by the nun Abutsu.[24] Through the identification of the essential nature of travel, the experience was codified and rendered knowable and perhaps bearable.

CHAPTER TWO

Utamakura, places immortalized in the poetry of previous generations, are the focus of the traditional travel model; they function both as the motivation for travel and occasionally as a kind of objective correlative of an intangible affective experience. Poets sought out utamakura to commune with the deities associated with those holy places and to reexperience the emotions those places had elicited for earlier generations of poets. An utamakura was spiritually charged. There one could temporarily benefit from the power of the site's eponymous god or gods and raise oneself and one's writing to a state of higher sensitivity and power. When introduced into a travel account, the utamakura elevated the tone of the work, and marked at least the aspiration to fine writing.

Shirakawa Gate was a particularly venerated utamakura that had been immortalized in the Heian period by Nōin, who was also the author of the first extant utamakura guide.[25] Subsequent poets over the centuries often felt compelled to react in some way to Nōin's earlier evocation:

<table>
<tr><td>miyako o ba
kasumi to tomo ni
tachishikado
akikaze zo fuku
shirakawa no seki</td><td>Though I set out
from the imperial city
in the springtime haze,
the wind of autumn now blows
at Shirakawa Gate.</td></tr>
</table>

(*Goshūishū* 9: 518)[26]

Thus when Saigyō, the greatest of the medieval traveling poet-priests, journeyed to Shirakawa more than a century after Nōin's poem was composed, he wrote:

I stopped at Shirakawa Gate on a pilgrimage to the far northern provinces. Perhaps because of the nature of the place, I found the moon more attractive and moving than usual. I wondered when it was that Nōin had composed "the wind of autumn now blows," and in the fullness of my feelings for the past, I wrote this on a post of the gatehouse:

<table>
<tr><td>shirakawa no
sekiya o tsuki no
moru kage wa
hito no kororo o
tomuru narikeri</td><td>The light of the moon
slips through the gatehouse
at Shirakawa,
and one finds it giving rise
to emotions deep and arresting.[27]</td></tr>
</table>

The role of the past in forming Saigyō's perception and the power of the utamakura to heighten the poet's emotion are immediately apparent.

It was in turn Saigyō who personified for later generations the ideal poet-recluse motivated by an intense awareness of the evanescence of all things to make solitary journeys in renunciation of secular concerns. Through the poetry of Saigyō and other hermit-priests, the essential travel mythos was increasingly enriched with metaphysical significance. Travel away from civilization and into nature, in either aimless wandering or on a pilgrimage to a holy site, became a metaphor for the abandonment of worldly desire and the struggle for enlightenment. The way of the traveling priest was the way toward salvation.[28] Saigyō's corpus of travel verses, itself based on the earlier notions of travel, became a classic expression of the essence of hermit-travel, on which Sōgi, Sōchō, and all medieval rengashi based much of their own philosophy and poetic sentiment. In one of Sōgi's collections of personal linked verse, he tells of obtaining seeds from Miyagino bush clover that Saigyō had sent Jien and planting them in his own garden, literally cultivating the memory of the earlier poets.[29]

The basic essence of travel informs to a greater or lesser extent all medieval travel prose and is given particularly thorough expression in *Shirakawa kikō*. It was certainly natural for linked-verse poets, steeped in the poetic tradition, to conceive and depict their journeys in terms of those poetic conventions. For Sōgi, as for earlier poets, travel is wearisome, dangerous, and melancholy, but the fear of leaving the known for the unknown is partially alleviated if the poet can place terra incognita into the context of earlier poetry and thus give it meaningful structure. At Nasu Plain, for example, Sōgi writes: "Though Musashi Plain is likewise of endless expanse, there one can rely on its 'grasses of affinity'; here, I felt bereft of support" (*SK*: 9). "Grasses of affinity" (*yukari no kusa*) is another name for *murasaki* grass, traditionally associated in poetry with Musashi Plain. Without such poetic connections, Sōgi literally has no "affinity" with his surroundings; without those landmarks of literary time and place, the poet is truly lost.

Travel for Sōgi is thus a break with the normal, an ontological shift that sharpens all the emotions. Affective receptivity is at its height at the utamakura; just as Saigyō in his *Sankashū* found the moon "more attractive and moving than usual" at Shirakawa Gate, so does Sōgi move to a higher emotional plane as he approaches the ancient site: "On the road thither, the sound of the valley stream and the wind in the pines on the peaks seemed more affecting than usual" (*SK*: 15).

Of course for the medieval hermit-poet, the ideal life is one of renunciation and of wandering in search of spiritual perfection. For priests like Jien travel is not abnormal but is in fact life itself, neither having any ultimate reality:

> tabi no yo ni
> mata tabine shite
> kusamakura
> yume no uchi ni zo
> yume o miru kana
>
> Life is a journey,
> and while journeying, to sleep
> on a grass pillow
> is to have a dream
> within a dream.
>
> (*Senzaishū* 8: 533)

Sōkyū, the author of *Miyako no tsuto* (Souvenir for the Capital, c. 1350–52), one of the most influential of medieval travel pieces and one which Sōgi almost certainly acquired, includes in his introduction a similar expression: "Reminding myself that there is nowhere one can live in permanence, I set out from Tsukushi on a forgotten day and wandered here and there."[30] But even for the recluse, complete renunciation of the mundane was usually an unreachable ideal. Saigyō himself makes the unavailing struggle for perfection one of his most moving poetic themes.

Sōgi too conceives of his aesthetic journey to a poetic site in terms of the ascetic pursuit of religious discipline (*shugyō*). He is accompanied by others on a religious pilgrimage, and the word he uses for them, *dōsha* (wayfarers), evokes both the way of the traveler and the way toward spiritual enlightenment. The dual nature of Shirakawa Gate as both a poetic and a religious landmark recalls the power ascribed to poetry in the *Kokinshū* preface to "effortlessly move heaven and earth and to mollify unseen spirits and gods," and it completes the central ascetic/aesthetic theme of the work, the search for poetic fulfillment in terms of a demanding religious quest. Related to this is Sōgi's choice of early winter in which to depart. He is surrounded by dying nature as he proceeds on his way, through "withered grasses" and leaves "fallen to earth." Sōgi's account exploits what is perhaps the dominant metaphor in medieval literature, wherein the death of nature recalls the fundamental Buddhist perception of the evanescence of all things.

And in the tradition of travel writing by priestly poets, Sōgi presents his journey as by and large a lonely one. Those who accompany him intrude only infrequently into what is primarily a record of his private emotions. When they do appear, their feelings mirror Sōgi's own. They travel less in each other's company than in communal solitude.[31]

But while artistic motives and religious motifs are thus blended in *Shirakawa kikō*, both the journey and the account place primary emphasis not on the Way of the Buddha but on the Way of Poetry. When Saigyō visits Shirakawa Gate, he first points out he is engaged in religious practice (*shugyō shite*). Sōgi's journey, by contrast, is primarily motivated by the poetic impulse, has as its goal a poetic spot, and is predominately poetic in tone and attitude. The style of the work reflects that poetic priority. It is a classical tour de force, using in its prose essentially the same ancient wabun vocabulary of the poetry, instead of a more colloquial wakankonkōbun mix of Japanese and Sino-Japanese. The very long sentences likewise hark back to earlier models, and they, together with the frequent use of the standard metric pattern of five and seven syllables, give the whole account much in common with the *michiyuki* poetic travel sequences in *Taiheiki* or the nō drama, themselves intimately related to linked verse. In keeping with the high purpose of the work in recording through established convention a visit to a venerable poetic spot, Sōgi has imbued his prose with the deep "conviction" of orthodox *ushin* (lit., "with heart"). Just as his elevated poetic quest implies renunciation of the phenomenal world, so also does his style rigorously excise mundane vocabulary and topics. There is no unorthodoxy or frivolity on the journey to Shirakawa.

Sōgi's approach to the poetic travel mythos corresponds well to what the Russian theoretician Mikhail Bakhtin meant by the term "epic." While Western theoretical concepts generally cannot be expected to apply hermetically to Japanese works of art, Bakhtin's concepts of "epic" and "novel," which he uses in a very specialized and personal sense, provide further tools to help conceptualize and express similarities and differences in Sōgi's and Sōchō's work. It will become apparent that Sōchō in his journal combines Bakhtinian epical elements with others that correspond to the novelistic, in Bakhtin's use of the term.[32]

For Bakhtin, the epical and the novelistic are paradigms found in various genres and in various times. The style of various genres may become novelistic at certain periods in history. At those times, those genres

> become free and flexible, their language renews itself by incorporating extraliterary heteroglossia and the "novelistic" layers of literary language, they become dialogized, permeated with laughter, irony, humor, elements of self-parody and finally—this is the most important thing—the novel inserts into these other genres an indeterminacy, a certain semantic openendedness, a living contact with unfinished, still-evolving contemporary reality (the openended present). (Bakhtin 7)

The epic is what the novel is not; it is characterized not by a sense of contemporary reality but by the past, a past that is closed off and univocal. *Shirakawa kikō*, according to this definition, is heavily epical in orientation.

Sōgi's narrative is profoundly retrospective.[33] The present world is seen through the filter of the past, and Sōgi reacts to what he sees in terms of emotions expressed by those who beheld such sights before him: "But then a withered scene of bamboo leaves bent under thick dew brought to mind poems by the Great Minister of the Right, and I began to be moved" (SK: 9). And again, "As I gazed upon the scene, I could not restrain my tears. I reflected on how moved Kanemori and Nōin must have been when they visited this spot . . ." (SK: 15). Among the places he passes on his way, special mention is afforded utamakura, those intertextual steppingstones that recall an earlier time. Present value lies in what can be interpreted in terms of past experience, and Sōgi travels through a landscape of brilliant but dying color populated less by the living than by gods and ghosts. Samuel Johnson observed, "The use of traveling is to regulate imagination by reality, and instead of thinking how things may be, to see them as they are."[34] Sōgi uses present reality to see how things were in the past.

Bakhtin might have been referring to Sōgi's narrative in stating that "The formally constitutive feature of the epic as a genre is . . . the transferral of a represented world into the past" (Bakhtin 13), and that "the epic absolute past is the single source and beginning of everything good for all later times as well" (Bakhtin 15). Thus only places hallowed by precedent, utamakura, have value in an epical schema. Nasu Plain is not an utamakura and Musashi Plain is; Sōgi is at the former and consequently feels bereft of the emotional support provided by the past. The nearer he approaches to Shirakawa Gate, the more all about him is infused with the sacred aura of that historic landmark.

Sōgi is writing less of a personal past than of one that is shared and universal (in a Japanese context). In this too he fits into Bakhtin's formulation, in which "national tradition (not personal experience and the free thought that grows out of it) serves as the source for the epic" (Bakhtin 13). Sōgi is not interested in his personal evolution on the road to Shirakawa; he is instead engaged by the manner in which he may tie himself into the epic master narrative. He therefore mentions no dates, for dates particularize and de-universalize. For similar reasons he avoids naming his hosts on the way. Likewise he constructs most of the account in a timeless historical present tense, since the past or perfective markers need appear only at the end of sentences, and sentence endings appear only infrequently.

Not only does the epic take place in the past; that past is closed-ended, complete in itself, and sacrosanct. This is another of Bakhtin's criteria for the epic:

> In general, the world of high literature in the classical era was a world projected into the past, on to the distanced plane of memory, but not into a real, relative past tied to the present by uninterrupted temporal transitions; it was projected rather into a valorized past of beginnings and peak times. This past is distanced, finished, and closed like a circle. (Bakhtin 19)

This is not to say that Sōgi, as a fifteenth-century man, is entirely cut off from the epic past; rather, he gives meaning to his present by joining it to the past. Only the overlap matters. Sōgi makes an epic of his present journey, casting it in classical poetic terms. His journey is closed-ended and his observations are consonant with Bakhtin's requirement that they

> transfer to contemporary events and contemporaries the ready-made epic form, that is, they transfer to these events the time-and-value contour of the past, thus attaching them to the world of fathers, of beginnings and peak times—canonizing these events, as it were, while they are still current. (Bakhtin 15)

Sōgi fits his living self into the scenery of his epic description, but only in terms of that scenery's *universal pastness*. His present is not a present qua present; it is instead present as incipient past. The description of "the venerable Shrines of the Two Deities" near Shirakawa Gate becomes in this context a metaphor for the question of time that Sōgi's narrative introduces. The one shrine is ancient, like Kanemori and Nōin a product of an earlier era. The new shrine, like Sōgi, is of the present, but both new shrine and new poet will soon in their turn belong to the past.

Sōgi journeys to Shirakawa to acquire a "memory" of a past he never personally experienced. What he finally senses is the inevitable past-ness of the present, a sense that not only is the past irrecoverable, but that his own present will be as well. The predominant theme of classical poetry is mutability; any attempt to commune with past poetry is ipso facto to accept the irrecoverability of time. Sōgi can approach Shirakawa Gate, the entryway to the past, but he can by definition not pass through it until he himself has passed away.

The closed-ended quality of epic writing corresponds to the closed-ended narrative form of *Shirakawa kikō*. The work has a clearly crafted introduction, development, climax, and conclusion. Conflict, generated by the dangers of the road and the disquiet of the travelers, is in the end happily resolved. The author writes in retrospect; he knows where he is going and what he wants to find at the end. In terms of Western genres, the work is closer to the autobiography than to the diary, because its structure indicates that the author knew all along the outcome of the narrative.

Sōgi's account, moreover, speaks with a single voice and in a single tone. This "monoglossia" is another main element of Bakhtin's epic scheme. The epic admits no linguistic counterpoint, no countervailing verbal resistances. In Sōgi's narrative, other people, other voices seldom appear, and when they do appear, they speak of the same themes, and with the same tonalities and poetic vocabulary as the principal. There is one source of value in *Shirakawa kikō*, and that is the high poetic tradition.

This epic character, constituted of a monoglossic and closed-ended past, makes Sōgi's account very highly mediated. Bakhtin indicates that "in epic, the narrator and audience are of the same time, but the subject, the characters, are utterly distanced" (Bakhtin 14). The schema is complicated in the case of autobiographical writing, of course, since the subject and object are the same individual. But again, the subject and the object in autobiographical genres are never finally identical. There exists what Louis Renza calls an "ironic discrepancy" between the one who writes and the one written about, for the writing subject writes by definition in retrospect and knows what the written object could not know at the time.[35] The ironic discrepancy in Sōgi's work is very great. The subject Sōgi fits the object Sōgi into a highly prescriptive epic formula and rigorously excises elements of experience that do not apply.

Robert Elbaz has referred to literary genres as "ideological grid[s] forced upon consciousness."[36] In the Japanese context, the poetic travel model had always necessitated selectivity, but in the same way that colloquial speech had moved ever further from the classical language of belles lettres, so had the realities of the Age of the Country at War resulted in a move away from a literary ideal that had been developing over the preceding centuries. In Sōgi's writing, however, the ideological grid forms a nearly hermetic seal; as a result, his diary is at times not only selective, but willfully fictitious.

At the time Sōgi wrote his account, for example, travel no longer connoted withdrawal from courtly civilization to the extent it had in earlier periods. The countryside was growing in wealth, and Sōgi had originally left for the Kantō region to tutor provincial magnates in the poetic arts and, more importantly, to acquire for himself the ultimate poetic cachet, the secret traditions of *Kokinshū*. The capital, by contrast, had for years been the scene of very uncivilized power struggles, and soon after Sōgi departed for Shirakawa much of the city lay in ruins. In effect, Sōgi was forced to *leave* Kyoto to complete his own poetic study. In the provinces, he found an immensely enthusiastic audience—it is not an overstatement to say that in the latter fifteenth century, it was the countryside and not the capital that presented the greatest hope of preserving the poetic tradition.

Nor was travel always melancholy, even if warriors and bandits sometimes rendered it dangerous. Linked-verse masters of high repute were everywhere in demand, and Sōgi was as welcome in one house as he was in that of its adversary.[37] Kaneko Kinjirō points out furthermore that the trip probably took more than the three days described in the written account.[38] The travelers were most likely held over in Yokooka where, Sōgi says, "All did not proceed as we wished" (*SK*: 9). Most crucially, Sōgi's first collection of personal verses, *Wasuregusa*, shows unequivocally that the party proceeded to Shirakawa Fortress, where they probably stayed five or six days enjoying the hospitality of their hosts, members of the Yūki house. But according to *Shirakawa kikō*, the party went directly back to Yokooka after reaching the gate. The quest for the Shirakawa utamakura was indeed one of Sōgi's reasons for the trip, but not the only one.

In its very nature, the life of a professional renga master, even more than that of a waka poet, ran counter in many ways to that portrayed in the travel model. To be sure, the linked-verse poet too derived great solace from nature and artistic stimulus from utamakura. But a linked-verse poet normally required a group for the practice of his art, relieving him of the loneliness of the traveler-recluse. Linked verse itself *is* travel literature—renga poets wander through successive verse-worlds of time and space, guided only by the renga rules, unsure of the way ahead. And as in the proverb "on a journey, a companion" (*tabi wa michizure*), a renga journey was made in the company of others. Given his linked-verse sessions, teaching duties, and conversation with his hosts, companions, and escorts, Sōgi could seldom have actually been alone.

Furthermore, for Sōgi and many other professional rengashi, travel was not a once-in-a-lifetime experience causing a profound ontological disjunction. Sōgi visited the Uesugi in Echigo, for example, at least seven times, and spent much of his adulthood on the road teaching poetry and the classics and leading linked-verse sessions, while also serving as an intermediary between court nobles and great provincial houses. Sōgi was used to travel. And according to Sōchō, who accompanied him on several of his long journeys, he often enjoyed it. Sōchō wrote in his *Sōgi shūenki* that his master "parted from us as he did, like the dew on a pillow of grass, because he had been so fond of travel."[39]

Far from being a rejection of the mundane, then, Sōgi's travels were in large

CHAPTER TWO

part undertaken to deepen his connection to it, both for the teaching and practice of his art and for the income to be derived from it. Nor could Sōgi's life in general and his travel in particular have maintained in actuality the uniform seriousness and elegance of tone with which it is imbued in *Shirakawa kikō*. The reader of that work has no inkling of the haikai departures that Sōgi also occasionally made. In fact, except for the appended hundred-verse sequence, the reader would not know from the text of the account that Sōgi was a linked-verse master at all. At this early point in his career, Sōgi still conceived of the travel diary genre entirely in waka terms. It bears repeating that Sōgi's life was oriented toward raising the artistic level of linked verse and conveying its essence to the court, provincial enthusiasts, and his own professional disciples. The deep conviction and traditionalism with which Sōgi approached the task of writing about his journey to Shirakawa was perfectly in keeping with the seriousness of his public cultural position.

It was precisely his strong sense of neoclassical purpose and commitment to an earlier ideal that both imbued his own verse with such conviction and raised the level of the linked-verse sequences he composed with others. In his first renga handbook, *Chōrokubumi*, he wrote, "If you would practice renga, at all times keep in your thoughts and on your lips the deep spirit and beautiful language of the old waka."[40]

The epic quality of *Shirakawa kikō* then, is not absolute; Sōgi the subject and Sōgi the object do inevitably overlap, which means that the past and the present likewise interpenetrate as well. By casting the present in terms of the past and fashioning himself and his world in terms of a neoclassical ideal, Sōgi appears to have been attempting to bring a sense of order to a chaotic world. In its pristine neoclassicism, his travel account serves as resolutely orthodox a model for travel writing as his renga anthology *Shinsen tsukubashū* would later serve for linked-verse poetry.

'The Journal of Sōchō' and the Poetic Travel Legacy

The poetic travel mythos, as exemplified by *Shirakawa kikō*, establishes one horizon of expectation through which one may approach *The Journal of Sōchō*. Sōchō's account satisfies the expectations so established, but it also transgresses them in important ways.

It was of course the tradition of poetic travel writing that inspired Sōchō to begin his account, and though the journal subsequently went on to include segments informed by numerous other genres, it is the stamp of the travel mythos that marks it most significantly. As mentioned earlier, the work actually includes five major journeys—two round trips between Suruga and Kansai, with long diapauses at each terminus, and a trip to Echizen and back that is treated more or less as a single journey. An indication of the influence of the travel-writing imperative on Sōchō's journalistic conception is that when he again set out from Suruga for Kansai in 1526, he initially recorded the trip as a continuation of the journal he had kept since 1522, but he then broke off the narrative and started Book Two, in which he rewrote the account of his departure for Kansai before going on with new material about the second journey. He made that journey the reason for starting the new account. The author clearly conceived of the two books as separate but integrated chronicles.[41] He also reintroduces in Book Two people from Book One as though the reader has never before encountered them. That so many of the extant manuscripts contain Book One or Book Two alone also demonstrates their independence. Iwashita Noriyuki has shown that Sōchō uses the name "Chōa" more often to refer to himself in Book One and "Sōchō" more often in Book Two, and that that practice, together with other factors, makes the latter book slightly more formal in tone.[42] The fact that Sōchō rewrote the beginning of his second journey west also underscores his attention to the literary quality of his account.

The Journal of Sōchō also contains several short records of outings he made while staying with this or that host, including a tour of Washinosuyama taken in 1524 (*JS*: 52), a visit to Daigoji temple and the Hino area in 1526 (*JS*: 113–14), and assorted other short excursions. All those travel passages bear debts of varying degree to the tradition of travel writing exemplified by *Shirakawa kikō*. The introduction to the first journey establishes this tonality:

> In the fifth month of the second year of Daiei, I set out on a journey to the northland with an acquaintance from Echizen. Though Kaeruyama, the Mountain of Returning, reminded me I could not expect to return home again, I pressed onward past Utsunoyama mountain, and when I reached Sayo no nakayama, I composed this:

1   kono tabi wa   Even though I hope
    mata koyubeshi to   I will pass this way again
      omou to mo   on my journey home,
    oi no saka nari   this is the hill of old age.
    sayo no nakayama   Sayo no nakayama.
                    (*JS*: 7)

CHAPTER TWO

The passage reflects Sōchō's disquiet on setting out and his consciousness of his departure as a break from the normal into a venture fraught with uncertainty. His writing here is also characteristically elevated in tone, and he elegantly avoids, as Sōgi did in *Shirakawa kikō*, mentioning the name of his prospective host. Most importantly, he mentions three utamakura, so essential to travel writing, in the first three lines. All three, furthermore, are mountains, which suggest the rugged hardship of the travel enterprise. In addition, the first poem establishes a relationship with Saigyō, who composed the famous verse on which it is based:

> toshi takete
> mata koyubeshi to
> omoiki ya
> inochi narikeri
> sayo no nakayama

> Did I ever think
> I would pass this way again
> as an aged man?
> Long was my alloted span!
> Sayo no nakayama.

(*Shinkokinshū* 10: 987)

Sōchō builds upon the memory of Saigyō throughout the work, referring to him as "that great priest" (*kano shōnin*). From the beginning of his account, Sōchō selectively fashions his literary persona in terms of the foremost exponent of the travel mythos. And again, the poem also allows Sōchō to introduce the fact of his own advanced age, which makes the travail of the journey all the more hazardous. The verse is an emblem for Sōchō's own aged travel persona, and he refers to it five times in his journal. It is for this reason that Sōchō later dilates on the etymology of that toponym, whether it is more correctly referred to as Sayo no nakayama or as Sayo no nagayama, at the end of Book One and again in Book Two (*JS*: 91–92 and *JS*: 96). And he cites as his authority for his interpretation a now-lost travel record he attributes to Saigyō himself. The work, which Sōchō went out of his way to borrow and read, was apparently called *Azuma michi no ki* (Travels in the Eastland).[43]

Sōchō goes on thereafter to invoke the norms of the poetic travel genre periodically through his account. He too presents himself as afraid of what the future holds on the road:

> 13   omoitatsu
> oi koso urami
>   Suzukayama
> yuku sue ika ni
> naran to suran

> How bitter
> to set out at my age across
>   the Suzuka Mountains—
> what is to become of me
> as I travel on my way?

(*JS*: 16)

Here too, Sōchō is fashioning his own verse on an earlier one by Saigyō:

Composed on a journey to Ise:

suzukayama	In the Suzuka Mountains
ukiyo o yoso ni	I cast aside
furisutete	this world of sorrow—
ika ni nariyuku	what will come to pass
waga mi naruran	in this life of mine henceforth?

(*Shinkokinshū* 17: 1613)

Sōchō refers to this poem a second time in his journal as well, underscoring its importance. The poetic tradition as embodied by the memory of Saigyō is nowhere more apparent than when Sōchō visits Saigyō Valley, site of one of the earlier poet's hermitages:

> We crossed Isuzu Mimosusogawa river downstream and walked along the narrow paths between the rice fields of Yamada, pressing through the bush clover and pampas grass withered under a thin frost.
> When we reached the grounds all was quite desolate. Mountain water brought in by a bamboo pipe, pine posts from the days of old, a fence of woven bamboo, a dozen or so nuns in tumbledown quarters, paper coverlets, stitched hempen garments, the smell of anise incense—I felt the past before my eyes and put into verse what arose in my breast:

23
kikishi yori	More poignant the sight
miru wa aware ni	than anything I had heard—
yo o itou	how moving this dwelling,
mukashi oboyuru	so redolent of the past,
sumai kanashi mo	in which he renounced the world.

> I wrote it on a pine fence post and went back to Kenkokuji. (*JS*: 19–20)

Like Sōgi before him, Sōchō here travels not only through space but also time, emphasizing the connection between himself and his poetic heritage. In keeping with the poetic theme, Sōchō's vocabulary remains here almost entirely within the classic kikō lexicon; he presses "through the bush clover and pampas grass withered under a thin frost" just as Sōgi had crossed Nasu Plain and beheld "a withered scene of bamboo leaves bent under thick dew" (*SK*: 9). As he describes the scenes of the past in the language of the past, Sōchō becomes increasingly moved, and he too finally breaks into poetry, investing in the ancient affective-expressive nexus that is the basis of the Japanese lyric tradition.

CHAPTER TWO

Sōchō, as did Sōgi, often interprets his own present in terms of his perception of his poetic forebears, effecting a literary correlative of psychological transference, a reverse mimesis, in which perceived reality imitates past art. Sōchō constantly travels in the company of earlier precedents and convention, engaging in a dialogue with time.

The ancient travel mythos had by the time of Sōgi and Sōchō also translated itself in more practical terms into an elegant travel etiquette. Sōchō, like all poetic travelers, organizes his itinerary partly on the basis of utamakura. He takes side trips to visit famous poetic places, such as Saigyō Valley, and is careful to mention others that his route takes him past. He is also disappointed when circumstances prevent him from seeing ancient places, as on the occasion when he writes, "Fighting has been breaking out from time to time with no warning in this province, so we could not cross Yahagigawa river and the Eight Bridges" (*JS*: 15), a site that had been immortalized by *Ise monogatari*.[44]

Travel etiquette also called for poetry to be composed with hosts, and for an appropriate parting poem to be composed when taking one's leave. Sōchō lived by that ancient xenial code, figured his travels in its terms, and was discomfited when poetic precedent was not observed:

> As we proceeded through Sayonoyama, we met Sugihara Iganokami on his way to the capital. We parted without exchanging any words worthy of note. I stayed in Kanaya that night and sent this to his lodgings in Kakegawa:

546	yume nare ya	Was it but a dream?
	sayo no nakayama	Rather than being left
	nakanaka ni	as betwixt and between
	aimizu wa to zo	as Sayo the "Between Mountain,"
	tachiwakaretsuru	I wish we had not met at all.

> I sent him a few provisions as a small gift. (*JS*: 152)

Again, his travel journal itself is a testament to the strength of the travel writing tradition. But to a far greater extent than Sōgi did in *Shirakawa kikō*, Sōchō introduces contemporary detail into his account and allows it to blend with elements of the kikō mythos. This depiction of the present-as-present rather than present-as-past corresponds to one of the basic characteristics of Bakhtin's novelistic paradigm, which coexists in Sōchō's writing together with more epic moments.

Sōchō departs from the epic poetic tonality of *Shirakawa kikō* directly after the introductory lines ending with the verse on Sayo no nakayama. Here is Sōchō's account of details of his stay at Kakegawa, site of the castle of the Asahina, important retainers of the Imagawa:

> Kakegawa. Stayed at the residence of Yasuyoshi. A construction project is currently under way. The outer castle is about thirteen or fourteen hundred yards in circumference. Around it they have dug a moat and built earthworks, after the manner of the main compound. The ground here is hard as rock; they might as well have built of iron. There is also a moat between the main and outer compounds. The ramparts are so steep it is frightening to look over.
> I composed this hokku at the castle:

2
samidare wa
kumoi no kishi no
yanagi kana

Summer rain—
on cloud-covered cliffs,
willow trees!

(JS: 7–8)

The passage is a blend of old and new subject matter and style. The hokku, with its elegant tone and compressed diction, provides an orthodox poetic climax to the prose description, as was typical of travel versiprosa from Tsurayuki to Sōgi. But the verse is appended to material alien to the high poetic travel tradition; its subject matter is martial and architectural, and its point of view referential and nonlyrical. The prose style is not the recherché neoclassical wabun of earlier accounts but instead a kind of elliptical and vigorous wakankonkō-bun that at times borders on a sort of *kanbun kundoku* shorthand, with brief and sometimes incomplete sentences which may contain more Chinese characters than Japanese kana. The first page of the journal, then, establishes a thematic and tonal concatenation that will characterize the work in its entirety, inaugurating a dialogue between past and present attitudes toward travel and its literary representation.

The dialogue appears for instance in the author's attitudes toward the relationship between the countryside and the capital, the touchstone of value in *Shirakawa kikō* and the classical tradition. Sōchō, it will be recalled, resided in the capital for about a quarter-century; he knew it well, and his nostalgia for it was probably not just a literary construct. That nostalgia nevertheless relates perfectly to the traditional idealization of the capital and its mores. Having arrived in Kyoto at the end of that first trip in 1522, for example, he writes:

369
oi no koshi
kyō zo nobetsuru
toki wakanu

Today I stretched out
my aged, litter-bent back
and was brushed by breezes

hana no miyako	from the capital that blooms
kaze ni atarite	regardless of the season.

It felt good to hear the word "capital." (*JS*: 105)

Sōchō's personal history, however, was in some respects the opposite of Sōgi's. Whereas his master had grown up in the provinces and then taken up residence in the capital, Sōchō grew up in Suruga and then eventually retired to it after living in the capital for several decades. He shows himself to be at home both in the provinces and in the capital, and while he was at ease in the houses of certain court nobles in the imperial city, he also enjoyed the patronage of a powerful provincial house with its own proud literary tradition. Far from being discomfited by the provinces, as Sōgi represents himself to be in *Shirakawa kikō*, Sōchō is as happy to arrive back in Suruga as he is to reach the capital. His journal blends the centripetal and the centrifugal in equal measure. Here he is in 1527, at the end of his second trip to Suruga:

> We crossed Ōigawa river, passed through Fujieda, and reached my cottage in Mariko by Utsunoyama mountain. I left last year at seventy-nine thinking it was to be the last time, but I have once again come through "the narrow path of ivy," my fears instead disappearing. (*JS*: 152–53)

Sōchō is pointing out that his emotions are the exact opposite of those of travelers in the classical tradition, such as Ariwara Narihira in *Ise monogatari*: "Going on, they came to the province of Suruga. When they reached Utsunoyama, the path they must follow was dark and narrow, and overgrown with ivy and maples, filling them with apprehension."[45]

Of course Sōchō still mentions fear on his travels, due to sporadic fighting en route, such as on the rainy night at Anonotsu quoted in the previous chapter, when his party misses the guide who was to escort them through a battle zone (*JS*: 15–16), and also due to the dangers of the terrain, as when he is carried on the backs of porters over a vertiginous mountain pass (*JS*: 102–3). But Sōchō also describes numerous pleasant days on the road in the company of old friends and enjoyable nights at the residences of warrior hosts.

The increasing economic activity in the provinces and the growing social fluidity of contemporary life is also reflected in the pages of Sōchō's writing, while it is largely absent from the epical world of *Shirakawa kikō*, which prefers to see the provinces and provincials by and large in negative terms. Sōgi mentions taking lodging in the house of a humble peasant and of pitying the man's crude fare, or seeing a clapper-rope left to rot beside a tumbledown hut. Sōchō notices this type of detail, but also the economic prosperity of the countryside: "Villagers here [near Yashima] seem to be piling wealth upon wealth, having waited until just the right moment to load their rice on horses and oxen and ship it to the storehouses" (*JS*: 122).

The sense of contemporaneity that permeates *The Journal of Sōchō* is perhaps most evident in the depiction of the author's own activities. He displays himself at once as a traveling poet-priest after the model of Saigyō and as a peripatetic linked-verse master, making a living in the modern world. The blend is complicated by the fact that the tradition Sōchō teaches is the classical tradition, and he lives by the etiquette of both the past and the present. Like Sōgi, Sōchō at times constructs his work and his travel persona around units of poetry and prose centering on an affective response to an utamakura or historic site. But Sōchō's primary form of self-depiction is in terms of his travels from residence to residence in pursuit of his profession, together with the poetry he composes there. Here is a passage that appears after Sōchō has left Kakegawa:

Hamamatsu

Spent two days with the commissioner of the Hamamatsu Estate, now Iio Zenshirō Noritsura. Then went by boat from Yamazaki in that estate past Inasa Inlet to the manor of Bitchūnokami in Hamana, where we had a day's renga:

8   mizu harete   Clear now over the water—
    sora ya satsuki no   the sky has dressed
        amatsutsumi   for the fifth-month rain.

Kachiyama

We crossed Honsaka and were guided to lodgings with the Saigō, then spent a day at Kachiyama, castle of Kumagai Echigonokami. We composed renga:

9   ōchi saku   Bead trees blossom
    kumoi o chiri no   in the clouds, though dust
        fumoto kana   covers the slope below!

Lodgings with the Makino

Near Yawata, at lodgings at the residence of Makino Shirōzaemonnojō, in a field called Honnogahara, we had a day of renga:

CHAPTER TWO

> 10   yuku sode o
>   kusaba no take no
>   natsuno kana
>
>   Grasses tall enough
>   to touch a traveler's sleeve—
>   the summer field!
>
>   (*JS*: 14)

The unit of host's residence and poem becomes a new kind of utamakura, literally so in the sense of *uta* (poem) plus *makura* (pillow) where Sōchō lodges. The use of the host/hokku unit in the travel record helps establish a literary continuum between poetic tradition and contemporary poetic practice. Sōchō often supplies names and dates. We have here a blend of the romantic, universalized poetic past and a particularized present, which when restated in Bakhtinian terms constitutes a combination of epical and novelistic characteristics.

Consider too this passage recording moments on his return trip to Suruga in 1524:

> I heard that Sōseki and two companions had arrived in Sakamoto the previous day to attend a festival, so I sent a messenger to them before dawn. They paid me a visit later in the morning; it was most enjoyable. After we finished a single sheet of verses, sake was brought out, and Tōenbō, an old monk near to receiving his Eighty-Year Staff, played shakuhachi. At night Hyōbukyō took up his shakuhachi as well and performed a few pieces in the *hyō* mode. It brought to mind Shunzei's poem on the sound of pine crickets in the mugwort that he composed for a hundred-waka sequence well after reaching his eightieth year. Near daybreak I returned to my lodgings in Ōtsu.
>
> Ōmi
>
> On the fifteenth, the master of this house, Sōkei, urged us to hold a linked-verse session. Unable to refuse, I began it with this:
>
> 162   yoru nami ya
>   hana no yamagoe
>   natsu no umi
>
>   Breaking billows!
>   blossoms on a mountain pass—
>   the summer sea.
>
> This simply means that the waves at the foot of the hills looked just like blossoms.
>
> Halfway through the session a boat came for me from the residence of Motosu Yamatonokami in Konohama. In a complete flurry while being rowed out, I recalled the hokku I made this spring in the capital at Shōzōbō's linked-verse session:
>
> 163   itsu idete
>   kasumu yama no ha
>   yūzukuyo
>
>   When did it take leave
>   of the hazy mountain crest,
>   the evening moon?

The following verse was composed at this temple:

164	tsuki o nado	I never understood
	matare nomi su to	why the moon always
	omoiken	kept us waiting.
	ge ni yama no ha wa	Now I find how hard it is
	ideukarikeri	to leave the mountain crest!

Was it from *Senzaishū*? I felt just the same as my boat departed. (*JS*: 48–49)

Sōchō's perception and enjoyment of the shakuhachi music is directly related to an interpretation of Shunzei's poem more than three centuries earlier. Sōchō begins here to erase temporal boundaries, both enriching his interpretation—his fashioning—of current experience through comparison with the past, but also creating a subjective interpretation of Shunzei's past on the basis of his own affective present. The next day he is forced to leave a linked-verse session before it is over, and he is again moved to contextualize his experience in terms of an earlier poem describing the same kind of event, using the past to shape the present, and the present to create a kind of romantic hermeneutic of the past. This is very much the process seen in *Shirakawa kikō*. But it is grounded in a thoroughly contemporary structure, where specifics are presented, individuals are named, and an elevated poetic moment can suddenly be complicated by the very prosaic arrival of a ferry boat. Bakhtin's remarks on the novelistic mode of writing are relevant: "Even where the past or myth serves as the object of representation . . . there is no epic distance, and contemporary reality provides the point of view" (Bakhtin 23). Reflecting the turmoil of the age in which he writes, Sōchō's representation is a blend of established practice and challenges to it, a mix of epic and novelistic approaches to the present.

The model of the past is further complicated in Sōchō's case because his long personal memory is also involved. The past is occasionally doubled in Sōchō's account, with the present Sōchō recalling a Sōchō of years before who was in turn recalling a more distant past of, as it were, a collective poetic unconscious. Memory provides an immediate context for present events, and in recording those events in his diary, he also pursues a self-referential dialogue with his own past in a way that a younger author could not. When he visits the utamakura of Kiyomi Strand in 1524, for example, he is moved to recall a journey which he had made as a novice poet a half-century before in the company of Sōgi, who was then on his way to visit Shirakawa Gate:

On the twenty-ninth, I recalled the journey that the late Sōgi made to this province years ago, and since it was the anniversary of his death, I made a single sheet of verses to forget the years:

190	omoiizuru	My sleeve remembers—
	sode ya sekimoru	like the gate it holds the moon
	tsuki no nami	on waves of teardrops.

The poem is based on a hokku Sōgi composed for a single sheet of verses at the gate when I invited him years ago to this temple, Seikenji:

191	tsuki zo yuku	The moon is departing.
	sode ni sekimore	At least hold it on my sleeve,
	Kiyomigata	Strand of Kiyomi!

Thus my verse, "My sleeve remembers." In *Shinkokinshū* this appears:

192	mishi hito no	Hold the image
	omokage tome yo	of my dear one, Kiyomi Strand,
	kiyomigata	in the channel
	sode ni sekimoru	of the waves of tears that slip past
	nami no kayoiji	the gate and course down my sleeves.

Might that have been the poem on which Sōgi based his? (*JS*: 56–57)

The passage is a short embedded travel account in and of itself, in which Sōchō journeys not only through space but through time. His description of the site of the old gate becomes a multilevel dialogue peopled by himself as an old man and as a youth just setting out on the way of poetry, by Sōgi who was then the old master that Sōchō has now become, and by generations of earlier poets who visited the site and left poetic impressions on which both men draw, fitting themselves into the poetic tradition. And Sōchō is aware that like those who have gone before, he too is soon to become a "man of old" who will blend into the collective poetic landscape in the minds of later visitors to the spot. At various points throughout the journal, Sōchō enriches, complicates, and blends in this way present experience with details not only from a past poetic tradition but from his own memory. Unlike the timeless past/present of the epic account, Sōchō's exhibits a heterochrony, to use Bakhtin's term, that includes both a universal past and a personal past that is remembered in the present.

The Journal of Sōchō, moreover, is not closed-ended and fully formed, unlike Sōgi's epic travel construction. Its open-endedness, its "unfinalizability," is another of the work's novelistic qualities in the Bakhtinian sense.[46] As with the characteristic of contemporaneity, most recording diaries are likely to be more or less novelistic in their resistance to closure; what matters here is that Sōchō actively chose this approach and exploited it, in a conscious departure from his teacher's work. The several journeys, both long and short, that make up the journal are to varying degrees smoothed out through a narrative that naturally develops from a journey with a beginning and an end. But the journeys that make up *The Journal of Sōchō* are finally only part of the larger journey of his own life, which is by definition open-ended.[47] Through the course of the journal, travel comes to be depicted less as an ontological break into an epic past than as simply another facet of the poet's life. While Sōchō depicts his departure for Kansai in 1522 in terms of a travel epic, he begins his description of his last departure for Suruga in 1527 with the simple phrase "On the fourth of the third month I left Yashima" (*JS*: 143). After more than a half-century as a renga poet, Sōchō literally and figuratively takes travel in stride, treating it as a fact of rengashi life.

The written Sōgi in *Shirakawa kikō* knows exactly who he is, what he is looking for, and how he will express it; the written Sōchō is, as we have seen, beset by uncertainty and philosophical contradiction, and his style is commensurately variegated. Even when a journey ends, Sōchō continues to write; his journey of the self through time coexists with the journeys of the poet through past and present poetic space and progresses toward the ultimate utamakura of the next world. In that the Sōgi persona affects to know who he is, what he wants to find on his journeys, and how he wants to figure it, the closed-ended, highly crafted style the author chose was the most suitable. Conversely, because Sōchō appears to be primarily interested in the continuing journey of his artistic self, the accretive, open-ended style was perhaps the only one philosophically viable, for the implicit conclusion in such a program is death. Whereas Sōgi wrote a diary of travel, Sōchō wrote the diary of a traveler.

Together with his blending of past and present, and his use of a basically open-ended framework, Sōchō also admits into his account a rich polyphony of voices. There are passages in his journal that are couched in the high, unitary, epic voice of the travel mythos. But Sōchō weaves those moments into an overall vocal mix, a heteroglossia, which Bakhtin identifies as the third main characteristic of the novelistic. This heteroglossia is manifest throughout the journal, both in terms of the voices of other characters that Sōchō introduces into the account and of the blend of tones, styles, and genres in which he himself speaks. The linking of past and present discourses we have just discussed also contributes to the vocal polyphony, lending a kind of temporal heteroglossia—a heterochrony—to the account.

The number of people and voices Sōchō introduces in his journal is very large. Sōchō is at times the lonely poet-priest of the epic travel mythos, but he is more often a traveling rengashi whose business it is to call on others and teach them. Again, linked verse by its very nature blends monoglossia and dialogism, the voices of various poets speaking in a uniform poetic vocabulary but from disparate perspectives. Sōchō at times resents the pull of others, times when he wishes he could indulge in re-renunciation (*saishukke*), the moment when a priest who is still "in the world" strengthens his vows and cuts his last mundane attachments. But he never finally divests himself of worldly ties, and he instead continues throughout his journal to make friendship and loss one of his main themes.

Sōchō's depiction thrives on alterity, variety, and connection—to people, to his own past, to historical context, and to the poetic tradition. There was indeed dialogue in earlier travel works, but it tended to be an intertextual conversation between the narrator and the poetry of the past. This is indeed a type of heteroglossia itself, and one we have seen Sōchō also exploit. And to be sure there are other contemporary voices in *Shirakawa kikō*; Sōgi does record three poems by his companions. The difference between *Shirakawa kikō* and *The Journal of Sōchō* is one of degree; fully one-quarter of the poems in Sōchō's journal are by others, nearly all of which he answers with one of his own. And again, letters he has received also occasionally appear.

The voices of others come from up and down the social scale, further enriching the polyphony of the whole. In the same way that Sōchō introduces more information about the provinces in his account and does so in a more varied manner, so too does he depict a broader cross section of humanity than one finds in Sōgi's work, or for that matter in earlier travel writing generally. Vignettes fill the pages of Sōchō's journal: the common soldier who guides Sōchō's party through the rain (JS: 16); the young men he meets on a beach (JS: 18); the novice monks he listens to as they enjoy themselves at poetry and wine in the next room (JS: 43); the itinerant entertainer-priest whom Sōchō records by name (JS: 100); the neighbors sweeping soot (JS: 127), or pounding *mochi* rice (JS: 131). They all contribute to a sense of Sōchō communing with a living and multitonal world and fashioning his portrayal in terms of that communion.

Common people do of course appear in earlier travel literature as well, though usually only to emphasize what the traveler *lacks*, that is, the refinement and the familiarity of his home in the capital. The commoners in *Shirakawa kikō* serve primarily to remind Sōgi of his own privation. In Sōchō's journal, by contrast, they are allowed to speak, as it were, on their own behalf. Their voices blend with those of Sōchō's friends among the clergy, court, and warrior aristocracy.

The multivalent quality is further enriched by variations throughout the text in the poet's own moods and writing styles. The traveler in the epic tradition tends to be depicted in terms of one tonality, bittersweet and reflective. Sōchō's self-portrait, by contrast, is one of complexity and contradiction, most notably (as we have already seen) in his attitude toward old age, but also in the variety of his reactions to life in general, including fear, pain, and happiness.

Our stylistic discussion of the first page of Sōchō's journal has also already demonstrated the variety of writing strategies he employs, which include passages quite reminiscent of classical wabun in their restricted poetic vocabulary and extended sentences, as well as moments verging on pure kanbun. He most often tends to write in a wakankonkōbun blend, which is itself highly labile, running from the elegant to the perfunctory and from the potently concise to the frustratingly opaque. This style is established by the first sentence of the work, which though it is cast directly in terms of the traditional travel mythos also informs the reader that what follows will not cleave entirely to the elegant and rhetorically ornate wabun mode. It begins as follows: *Daiei ninen gogatsu, hokuchi no ryokō, Echizen no kuni no shiruhito ni tsukite* . . . ("In the fifth month of the second year of Daiei, [I set out on] a journey to the northland with an acquaintance from Echizen . . .") (*JS:* 7). A more complete sentence would read *Daiei ninen gogatsu* ni *hokuchi no ryokō* o *kokorozashi, Echizen no kuni no shiruhito ni tsukite.*[48]

The best of Sōchō's writing demonstrates an artistic blend of old wabun elegance and kanbun concision:

> Jōsū, a monk and shakuhachi musician, was originally a member of the Higashiyama Ryōzen Ji sect. He spent four or five years at Jōfukuji temple at Gojō Higashinotōin and at Daitokuji's Daisen'in, and until recently he maintained a cottage in Sakai in Izumi Province. He made his living from from shakuhachi students and patrons. I happened to be staying in Yamada when he arrived at Ise Shrine on a pilgrimage; he called on me and stayed more than ten days, until I had to leave for Takigi in Yamashiro. They tell me he was fêted thereafter in Yamada morning and evening. Then came the news he had thrown himself into Futami Bay—what could have happened to make him do such a thing? I composed this on learning of it:

33	mujōshin	That one melody
	okosu ikkyoku	"Perceiving the Law of Change"—
	ika ni shite	how could he play it
	fukishizumiken	yet throw himself into the sea?
	ana umi no yo ya	How awfully sad, this world!

I must have been in the Southern Capital when I received the news. I sent the verse to Yamada.

His sister, a nun of the Ji sect, told them several times she would like to have his shakuhachi flute returned to her so that she might sell it to pay for services in his memory. But they never sent it back. No, they never sent back the shakuhachi to exchange for money, mindful of the changing shallows of Tomorrow River. (*JS*: 22)

The short sentences are often fragments ending with substantives. But Sōchō also pays attention throughout to the function of kindred words, employing in the poem *ikkyoku* (one melody), *fuki* (blow / perform), and *ana* (alas / holes [on a flute]), as well as water imagery, using *shizumu* (to sink) and *umi* (meaning both sea and sad). Water and music imagery tie the prose to the poetry, which ends with an embedded reference to a poem by Lady Ise:

Composed when she sold her house:

	asukagawa	Though not a deep pool
	fuchi ni mo aranu	in Tomorrow River,
	waga yado mo	my home as well,
	se ni kawariyuku	having been exchanged for funds,
	mono ni zo arikeru	has turned into shallows.

(*Kokinshū* 18: 990)

This skillful blend of old wabun elegance and new wakankonkōbun concision, unfortunately lost in translation, is but one of several approaches Sōchō uses toward the matter of form and style. Sōchō's writing at times seems purely functional, and at others it demonstrates a clear concern for interrelationships and connectedness, establishing a link, as it were, between his journal style and renga. This is manifest, for example, in the compression and concision of the short sentences as well as in their ellipses and occasional syntactical inversions. The author is fond of ending phrases with a noun for the sake of brevity and impact, just as he does in renga poetry. He is also partial on occasion to such standard waka and renga devices as sound repetition, pivot words (*kakekotoba*), and lines of five-seven or seven-five syllabic meter. Shimazu Tadao and Harada Yoshioki have both suggested therefore that *The Journal of Sōchō* shows a definite movement toward the haibun prose-poetry amalgam of later haikai poets.[49]

In terms of larger construction, Sōchō is less inclined than Sōgi to smooth the elements of his account into a uniform narrative. Indeed, the events of a person's life are infinitely various and resistant to smooth narrative, leaning instead toward, to use Elizabeth Bruss's phrase, "discontinuous structures."[50] It is less plot than character that lends cohesion to such writing. Georges Gusdorf, in fact, insists that "the original sin of autobiography is first one of logical coherence and rationalization."[51] Sōchō's account often seems particularly discontinuous, for the excellence of a poem composed at a particular time or place, rather than the contribution it makes to the overall narrative, may be the main reason for its inclusion. But Sōchō sometimes appears to link constituent verses or events together on the basis of some lexical or topical similarity. One poem on a theme is frequently followed by another on the same theme, and often a serious verse will be coupled with a humorous restatement. Some of the abrupt changes in subject, moreover, prove on closer examination to share overtones, much as in the concatenation of distant links (*soku*) in renga. And throughout the text, one notices associations that occasionally help link otherwise disparate sections, as in this example:[52]

> This area is far from the mountains, and it is not easy to acquire charcoal or firewood. [Nakae Tosanokami's] response to my letter about this difficulty was very kind. In my answer to him, I included this:

438
    sono sato ni   I even feel as though
    sumu kokochi sae   I were living in that village,
      shigaraki no   as the smoke rises
    maki no sumi yaku   from burning charcoal
    keburi tatetsutsu   made of wood from Shigaraki.

> One night I fell asleep at the *kotatsu* and did not notice when the untended flame set my clothing afire. I woke with a start:

439
    toru tokoro   Morning dawned with
    nakute zo akenu   nothing to show for the fire
      katasuso mo   that coursed through my breast
    mune hashiribi no   and my robe as well—
    urameshi no yo ya   what an awful night!

(*JS*: 123)

Such links occur throughout the work; one would not wish to assert that all were planned, but many were likely the result of associations occurring to a trained linked-verse mind as it selected from events recalled at varying degrees of remove.[53]

In terms of form too, then, *The Journal of Sōchō* blends passages that seem cursorily noted with those that are clearly fashioned and interrelated. It is very likely that much of the form of the work simply reflects the progression of Fothergill's imprints "of that day's being alive," with simple chronology constituting the main organizing principle. But again, especially when writing at a remove of weeks or months, Sōchō inevitably selected what he wrote down from a large pool of experience, a process that was doubtless dictated in part by various of the principles that have been enumerated above.

And even in the matter of nonlinearity and random juxtaposition, Sōchō had native antecedents; in the Japanese context, active disregard for seamless narration and extended cohesion is itself an established literary style. If *The Journal of Sōchō* often takes apparent delight in the juxtaposition of apparently unrelated topics, it has precedents not only in kanbun diaries but in zuihitsu, random essays in which the author "follows the brush" and makes formlessness itself an established form.[54] Sōchō indicates several times in his journal that he has written "giving free rein" to his brush, and he mentions reading *Tsurezuregusa*, also a work that includes a plethora of different genres and shows a disinclination to adhere to a single topic or style. In the context of Buddhist teaching, all phenomena, no matter how apparently disparate, are connected. Sōchō was also steeped in Zen practices designed to thwart consecutive thinking in the interest of apprehending higher religious truths.

But again, much the randomness of Sōchō's account, no matter how it can be explained in retrospect in terms of literary precedent, probably simply reflects the commensurate randomness of his or any human life. Felicity Nussbaum points out that the non-narrativity characteristic of autobiographical writing can in fact be a more convincing representation of the events of daily life, before they are arranged in an artificial narrative.[55]

The most important characteristic of Sōchō's heteroglossia from the viewpoint of the history of Japanese travel writing is his innovative blending of orthodox poetry and haikai, and his incipient valorization of the haikai mode. Sōchō admits onto the page elements of experience not condoned by the traditional poetic orthodoxy. That unorthodox quality is most obvious in various of his haikai verses (both haikai waka [haikaika] and haikai renga), which include noncanonical or comic diction or sentiment. That haikai attitude appears frequently in scenes of humor or good cheer. One particularly marked characteristic of Sōchō's writing is its departures from the genteel melancholy of the travel mode. In terms of lexicon and diction as well, the journal departs widely from the standard of what was acceptable in the traditional travel orthodoxy, its haikai renga and kyōka extending to slang and ribaldry. There is no such tonality in *Shirakawa kikō*.

Orthodox and unorthodox vocabulary and tone are often combined in a single episode. One good example occurs in a description of a sojourn at Atsuta Shrine on Sōchō's return journey to Suruga in 1526. It starts out well within the poetic travel tradition:

> A pilgrimage to Atsuta Shrine. All was still around the precinct and neighboring houses, and the wind in the pines lent a feeling of sacredness and awe, bringing to mind the age of the gods. It was the deity of this shrine, they say, who pacified the Eastern Seaboard. The tide rises up to the fence of the shrine buildings. Through the pines I could see Narumi, Hoshizaki, and out over Ise Bay. The view was indescribable.
>
> A linked-verse session at our travel lodgings at Takinobō. Chikuzennokami participated.

351   hototogisu   A waiting cuckoo
         matsu no hagoshi ka   seen through the pine boughs?
           tōhigata   The tidal pool.

> At the request of a priest, I composed this:

352   usumomiji   Waiting to turn
         matsu ni atsuta no   pale red, young ivy leaves
           wakaba kana   amid pines at Atsuta!

> I seem to recall the line *koko mo atsuta no* from the *Latter Hundred-Waka Sequence at the Palace of the Retired Emperor Horikawa*. Probably a misrecollection in my dotage. (*JS*: 99–100)

The focus on the godliness of the place and its history, its quiet solitude, natural scenery, and utamakura, and then the elegant poetry, in part based on earlier poetic precedents, are just as Sōgi would have represented the scene. But then Sōchō shifts from an epic tonality, what Bakhtin calls the "heaven" of high art, to an earthier one of laughter and parody:[56]

> Young men from the shrine, monks, and others went ahead to a pine grove four or five *chō* from here with various things to eat. From time to time there was singing and dancing to drums and flutes. It was quite merry. An entertainer-priest named Shin'eki was most amusing. All then regretfully parted:

353 okinoite   Sharper than the pain
     mi o yaku yori mo   of flesh seared by fiery coals
        oboyuru wa   is the memory
     kyō no atsuta no   of parting from you today
     miya no wakare zo   at the shrine of Atsuta.

> In jest. (*JS*: 100)

The poem is a parody of *Kokinshū* 20: 1104, by Ono no Komachi:

> On Okinoi Miyakoshima:

   okinoite   Sharper than the pain
   mi o yaku yori mo   of flesh seared by fiery coals
      kanashiki wa   is the grief I feel
   miyakoshimabe no   on your leaving this island
   wakare narikeri   to go to the capital.

In the account as a whole, Sōchō first paints an orthodox and elevated picture, then he provides a haikai sequel, much as haikai poetry often followed a renga session or a kyōgen piece followed a performance of nō. The godliness of the shrine and epic poetry is followed by an entertainer-priest and haikai.

This parody of the orthodox tradition is all the more remarkable in that it is combined with poems of the highest orthodox quality which the author fully expected his own patrons and poetic circle to read. Sōchō, and this is a vital point, is beginning here to ascribe literary value not only to the elite poetry and elegant prose sections of his work, but also to more unorthodox moments of poetry and prose. Of course, he by no means sees haikai as the aesthetic equal of orthodox renga. He is careful to label certain poems explicitly as haikai (he also uses the term *zareuta*) or to append a postcript "in jest" (*isshō*), to distance them from his more serious compositions. It is a mistake to conceive of Sōchō, as some commentators have, as simply an eccentric who either had not fully mastered the epic tradition or subordinated it to parody or comedy, rather like Yamazaki Sōkan, anthologizer of the haikai collection *Shinsen inu tsukubashū*.[57] In his own renga verses and in his handbooks, he is an uncompromising proponent of Sōgi's orthodoxy. But Sōchō's decision to include "things both serious and frivolous" in his journal constitutes a major departure from his teacher's diary approach.

The Atsuta verse is, to be sure, a parody to some extent of the *Kokinshū* foundation poem, but it functions not to undermine or ridicule the original, but rather to provide a light intertextuality that at the same time includes a serious expression of sadness. Haikai here is gradually ceasing to be the devalorized term; a selective deconstruction of the hierarchy between what elites conceived to be orthodox and unorthodox is beginning to take place, though within the general context of a continuing late-medieval classicism.

Sōchō thus consciously blends the high and the low, the ga and the zoku. He is at times deeply serious and traditional, even epic; at others he is humorous, parodic, and even lewd. At other times still, he combines the ga and the zoku into novelistic moments that imbue contemporary themes and common lexicon with elements of the high poetic travel tradition. This blend of epical past and novelistic present is the result of a conscious decision to include both "recording" and "narrative" elements.

The Journal of Sōchō, therefore, incorporates elements of the poetic travel tradition of *Shirakawa kikō*, but it also departs from that model in its more contemporaneous, open-ended, and multivocal qualities. This concatenation, this linking of styles and tonalities, is reflected in the competing and dialogic impulses toward the center and the periphery, and toward tradition and iconoclasm, that characterized the age. It is also reminiscent of the diversity of Sōchō's own background, with its influences from the capital and the provinces and from Sōgi and Ikkyū. The blending of so many genres and voices, of orthodox and unorthodox haikai poetry in *The Journal of Sōchō* is particularly significant from the point of view of literary history. The individuality and multidimensionality of Sōchō's self-portrait develop from precisely this inclusivity.

But it is important to note as well that Sōchō's blending of orthodox and unorthodox elements itself has precedents in the body of travel writing. His contribution is less one of introducing a brand-new quality than of pursuing the blend to a a hitherto unprecedented degree. All prose travel writing since Tsurayuki had to a greater or lesser extent deviated from orthodox travel poetry into unorthodox or haikai areas. *Tosa nikki* itself has even been referred to as a kind of proto-haikai prose (*haibun*).[58] In consequence, the diary genre was not considered the equal of Japanese poetry in the traditional literary hierarchy. The unorthodox or zoku quality of the diary genre became even more pronounced as time passed, with Fujiwara Nagako's *Sanukinosuke nikki* (The Diary of Sanukinosuke, completed c. 1109), for example, making new departures into everyday subject matter.[59] Even Sōgi's *Shirakawa kikō* includes greater contemporaneity and diversity of approach than is seen in strictly orthodox travel poetry.

Nevertheless, *Shirakawa kikō* remains one of the most thoroughgoing attempts to incorporate the norms of poetic travel into a prose diary framework. It is actually more classical than the classics of the genre themselves, a neoclassical throwback that in its effort to demonstrate the norms of poetic travel became more prescriptive than its antecedents. Sōgi, one suspects, set out in *Shirakawa kikō* to actively exclude unorthodox haikai elements from the travel narrative in the same way he excluded haikai from his imperial anthology of linked verse. He wrote the account on a journey undertaken to acquire the secret traditions of *Kokinshū*, and he may have conceived of it as an explicit display of the poetic traditions of travel in a prose context. This has made it a useful touchstone for us to use in reading Sōchō's travel diary.

But twelve years after writing *Shirakawa kikō*, Sōgi composed a second travel account, *Tsukushi michi no ki*, that introduced complications into the poetic travel narrative and anticipated some of the directions *The Journal of Sōchō* would later pursue.[60]

The account depicts a journey from the Ōuchi capital, Yamaguchi in Suō Province, to the ancient Kyushu commandery of Dazaifu and other poetic sites, which Sōgi undertook in 1480. Though he is not mentioned in the travel account, Sōchō was a member of Sōgi's party, and he witnessed firsthand the process through which Sōgi welded his experiences into art.

The excursion starts at Yamaguchi in the ninth month, late autumn. The company stops at various literary and historical landmarks and proceeds across the strait to Chikuzen Province (Fukuoka Prefecture) in Kyushu, where it reaches the shrine to Sugawara Michizane at Dazaifu. Sōgi's three poems at the shrine of the exiled court poet, who was later deified as a god of poetry, mark it as the spiritual climax of his journey. The group then proceeds to Hakata and another Sumiyoshi Shrine, then goes by land and water to Iki no matsubara, Hakozaki, and Kashii Shrine, all of which Sōgi had mentioned in his introduction as places he had hoped to see. The account of the return by a different route through Nagato and Suō is kept quite short, and the travelers reach Yamaguchi on the twelfth of the tenth month.

Tsukushi michi no ki represents for many reasons a major departure from *Shirakawa kikō*. It is of considerably greater length, reflecting the corresponding increase in the distance covered and the thirty-six days Sōgi says the trip required.

'The Journal of Sōchō' as Travel Literature

Far more significant for our purposes, however, are the ways it begins to complicate the poetic travel mythos of *Shirakawa kikō*. Most obvious, perhaps, is the greater contemporaneity of the account. Sōgi identifies his various hosts by name, for example, and all along the way he is careful to give specific credit to those who aided him. The numerous references to local administrators in the service of the Ōuchi has led one scholar to characterize the work as "a perfect document for understanding the nature of Ōuchi power in northern Kyushu in the time of Masahiro."[61] *Shirakawa kikō* is nearly useless in this regard. And unlike the case in *Shirakawa kikō*, where Sōgi fashions himself as a traveler in the old waka tradition, he is willing in this later work to depict himself not only at the composition of waka but also at his work as a renga master.[62]

Added to this increased sense of contemporaneity is a greater variety of voices and tones. Other people figure more strongly in this account, and they represent a slightly more varied cross section of life. He also acknowledges the growing cultural role of provincial warriors and clerics, and he tempers somewhat the idealization of the capital and courtly culture that characterized the traditional poetic account.

The author's own voice is more manifold as well. Sōgi's periodic expressions of gratitude to his hosts contribute optimistic moments to this chronicle, in contrast to the generally unrelieved melancholy and disquiet of the Shirakawa narrative. He even admits at one point to being tipsy, a major departure for the usually straightlaced author.

Stylistically, too, *Tsukushi michi no ki* is also considerably closer to *The Journal of Sōchō*. Its sentences are shorter than those in the wabun-influenced *Shirakawa kikō* and they employ more Sino-Japanese compounds. These are characteristics which reflect more current language usage.

In short, by the time of his trip to Kyushu, Sōgi himself has become willing to amplify and complicate the traditional poetic travel model. Kidō Saizō has for this reason remarked that *Tsukushi michi no ki* is one of the few medieval travel works not aesthetically smothered by the weight of tradition.[63]

But Sōgi's second work is still largely indebted to the poetic travel mythos. He writes, "Though it is a fact of life that travel is always melancholy, one still takes consolation in the ancient poems handed down through the ages" (*TMK*: 91). The quest for utamakura continues to be the main reason for the journey:

> I had long wanted to visit the famous sites in the various provinces and had already seen Mount Tsukuba with "no difficulty as I was bent on reaching it," and

> Shirakawa Gate, so hard to pass.⁶⁴ I was then taken by a desire to see Matsura and Hakozaki. (*TMK*: 29)

Of the sites he sees on his way, only those validated in past poetry have literary importance. The best-known example of that poetic prescriptivity is his response to a scene of natural beauty not mentioned in past poetry: "The pines stretched impressively into the distance—they were quite the equal of those at Hakozaki, but since they are not famous, one gave them scant notice" (*TMK*: 92).

The capital, as a de facto and overriding utamakura itself, is still the center of Sōgi's value structure. Despite the increase in provincial detail, Kyoto and its elite culture continues to be the standard against which those details are judged. As in *Shirakawa kikō*, the great mass of humanity remains anonymous. Commoners' lives of unremitting toil are viewed primarily as novel and even picturesque: "Humble dwellings huddled together, with smoke rising faintly. I was moved as I wondered if these were the houses of the fishergirls known for 'gathering seaplant and dipping up brine for salt'" (*TMK*: 72–73).⁶⁵

And true to the poetic travel model, Sōgi's second journey remains closed-ended and structured around a pre-envisioned narrative. It begins in a fixed place, reaches a climax upon the author's arrival at the shrine to Michizane at Dazaifu, then winds down to a predictable conclusion back at the point of departure.⁶⁶

In keeping with its shaped formal quality, the work also has a single theme, the importance of not only martial but also cultural accomplishments to a ruler and his duty to patronize the poetic art in the interest of his people.⁶⁷ This is symbolized in part by the role of the deities of Sumiyoshi Shrine, one main destination of the trip, as guardians of both warrior arts and literature.⁶⁸

A poetic recrudescence was particularly critical in light of the current violence spreading nationwide in the wake of the Ōnin conflict. This is suggested by Sōgi's remarks about a local temple:

> The two-storied gate was half ruined.... I asked why and was told to my sadness that it was the result of over a decade of war. I prayed before the gods asking only their blessing for the way [of poetry]. (*TMK*: 75)

Tsukushi michi no ki is thus at once a recommendation by Sōgi to his patron Ōuchi Masahiro, the recipient of the completed account, to pursue the way of poetry and also one expression of Sōgi's own "prayer for poetic orthodoxy" (*TMK*: 74):

kamigaki no	I place my faith
matsu ni zo tanomu	in the pines of the shrine precinct—
koto no ha mo	may our leaf-like words
sugu naru michi ni	likewise regain the way
tachi ya naoru to	and stand as straight and true as they.

(TMK: 75)[69]

Tsukushi michi no ki in its entirety thus in a sense becomes a piece of votive (*hōraku*) prose to the gods, and it is accordingly elevated and formal in tone.[70] Sōgi summarizes many of his motives and attitudes in a statement of the nature of his poetry:

> Some of my verses expressed reverence, some my prayers for the way of poetry, some my own feelings, some my emotions on seeing the remains of ancient sites that are no more; some were also composed at various places where I found the scenery unforgettable. (*TMK*: 92)

Whereas two of Sōgi's apparent purposes in writing *Shirakawa kikō* had been to demonstrate personal mastery of the basic essence of traditional poetic travel and to attempt to characterize his travel experience in terms of those of earlier poets at an ancient poetic site, the motives behind *Tsukushi michi no ki* amounted to nothing less than an attempt to restore the entire poetic tradition. No less than Sōchō, Sōgi was a product of his changing times; but while Sōchō embraced that change, Sōgi resisted it. Consequently the overall orientation of his work is, despite its inclusion of greater contemporary detail, deeply neoclassical, and Sōgi remains extremely selective and traditional in his choice of style and topic. His values are still essentially those of orthodox poetry, and mundane reality that does not fit that mold is rigorously excised. In essence, *Tsukushi michi no ki* remains one long poem. Sōgi in his work is not so much traveling through later fifteenth-century Nagato or Chikuzen as traversing a carefully crafted series of scenes reminiscent of the ink monochrome works of the painter Sesshū Tōyō, Sōgi's senior by only a year, who was likewise a Shōkokuji monk and who also spent time in Masahiro's domain.

As in *Shirakawa kikō*, Sōgi has fashioned his self according to a neoclassic poetic persona. In terms of depicted stimuli and the emotional responses to them, the self becomes an amalgam of universal and normative values. *Tsukushi michi no ki* is a lofty and ambitious attempt to use the poetic ideals of the past to redeem a chaotic present. It was available to Sōchō as another model for his own work, and it introduces some of the novelistic elements that characterize Sōchō's journal, while retaining on the whole a more traditionally poetic attitude toward the depiction of the self in terms of the travel experience.

Both *Shirakawa kikō* and *Tsukushi michi no ki* serve as particularly important works for establishing a horizon of expectation for Sōchō's journal because of their similarity in time and provenance. They were not, of course, the only travel works that stood to inform Sōchō's conceptualization of literary travel.[71] The influences of Saigyō and *Ise monogatari*, for example, have been noted. It may also be recalled that Sōchō mentions Shōtetsu's *Nagusamegusa* (referred to in the journal as *Azuma michi no ki* [Travels in the Eastland]), a work which contains both travel passages and poetic theory and is itself a good example of the blending of genres.[72] Shōtetsu's student Shōkō too is represented in *The Journal of Sōchō*, and a short portion of his travel diary, *Shōkō nikki*, relating to his visit to Kiyomigata, is paraphrased therein (*JS*: 57–58). And though it is not mentioned in his journal, Sōchō's postscript to *Fuji goran nikki*, the travel diary probably written by Imagawa Norimasa, will also be recalled in this connection. All these and doubtless numerous other travel works informed Sōchō's representation of his own.

But while retaining elements of the neoclassical poetic travel prescription, Sōchō tolerates complexity and dissonance in his account, giving more space to elements hitherto outside the sphere of poetic representation and beginning selectively to invest them with a measure of serious literary concern. The novelistic quality of Sōchō's travel passages in his journal is further increased in the context of the other genres within the work, most notably the passages of "eremitic literature," to which we will now turn.

CHAPTER THREE

"How I do love a garden"

'The Journal of Sōchō' and the Literature of Eremitism

Sōchō had been a Buddhist monk since his youth, and his life was by definition distanced to some extent from the secular world by virtue of his religious vows. That distance increased in his last decades as he aged, left Kyoto, and built his hermitage in Mariko, outside Suruga, where he could live the life of a poet-priest in provincial retirement. A central setting of his periods of stasis in his journal is therefore the "grass hut" (sōan), the traditional locus of Buddhist retirement. But Sōchō was never a recluse; even in his last years, when physical infirmities and sense of an approaching end drew him closer to a renunciation of the secular world, he was still both in the world and removed from it, exercised both by religious asceticism and by mundane concerns. Like his travel passages, Sōchō's sōan passages resonate with a multitude of voices, tonalities, and most importantly, conflicts.

The extended descriptions of travel and hermitage life in *The Journal of Sōchō* are the longest of any work by a medieval renga master. While the author could draw for his travel passages on a rich tradition of travel poetry in the imperial anthologies and on the diaries of Sōgi and earlier poetic travelers, he had fewer canonical models at his disposal for his hermitage descriptions. There is no sōan category in the imperial poetry anthologies or in the renga rules.[1] Hermitage life was, however, a well-known poetic topos frequently used in poetry collections, notably Fujiwara Kintō's collection of Japanese and Chinese verse, *Wakan rōeishū* (c. 1012). It was subsequently addressed by renga poets both in their linked verse and in other literary genres. Sōchō himself left a linked-verse sequence on eremitic life, *Yamaga hyakuin* (One Hundred Verses on a Mountain Hut, 1511), which demonstrates his understanding of the orthodox renga depiction of the sōan topos. In prose, a short essay survives by Shinkei entitled *Oi no kurigoto* (An Old Man's Prattle, 1471) depicting that poet's journey to the Kantō region and life in a sōan there. And Shōhaku left two very short pieces, *Muanki* (Dream Cottage, 1515) and *San'aiki* (Three Loves, 1516), in which he treated the hermitage theme in prose and verse. Sōchō may never have actually seen Shōhaku's short accounts, nor for that matter Shinkei's, but they are again useful in establishing a contemporary horizon against which to read Sōchō's sōan passages.

In a religious context, travel and hermitage life represent complementary forms of nonattachment. The sōan literature of Sōchō, Shinkei, and Shōhaku is therefore heavily tinged with religious concerns, reminding us of William LaFleur's admonition against constructing a "false wall between ideas and art" in medieval literary exegesis.[2] Their depictions of sōan life share much with categories of verse that *were* canonical, specifically, Buddhist (*shakkyō*) poetry and laments (*jukkai*), both of which are basic topical categories in the linked-verse rules. They possess a characteristic skein of poetic conventions which inform sōan writing.

In the same way that Sōchō's travel passages describe both major journeys and short excursions, so do his sōan passages mix sojourns at the residences of patrons, at temples, and in his own Brushwood Cottage (Saioku) in Mariko. In Sōchō's writing there is often no clear boundary between travel and stasis; both reside on a continuum which itself constitutes a literary metaphor for the Buddhist conviction that all life is transitory.

Travel and Repose in the 'Journal'

In his journal Sōchō is embarked on a journey of self-creation, not only through space but also through time; again, his is a diary not just of travel but of a traveler. All of the five long journeys in the diary (which Sōchō distinguishes by the word *ryokō*) involve stays of varying length at the residences of hosts or at temples. Of course, all travel writing includes moments of stasis, but Sōchō's journal is remarkable for the degree to which it blends the two states. Sōchō's seven-week sojourn at the mansion of Seki Kajisai while on his way to Sunpu in 1524 is a case in point (*JS*: 50–54); it is a long period of rest within the context of travel and is itself punctuated by day-trips and the like. Conversely, while ostensibly in residence at Sunpu, Sōchō frequently makes excursions to Okitsu and other nearby sites.

The terminology the author uses to characterize the places he stays suggests their order of importance. His use of the name of his Brushwood Cottage, Saioku, as his own artistic sobriquet underscores the central character of that residence.[3] He also uses a second term, *kankyo* (retreat), in reference both to that hermitage in Mariko and to his residence at Shūon'an in Takigi. Those places are the twin poles of his existence; the Mariko cottage is the focus of his present life as a poet and teacher to worldly patrons after the fashion of Sōgi, and the Takigi residence is filled with memories of Ikkyū and is the focus of his religious and other-worldly aspirations.

Whenever he is not at either of these retreats, Sōchō appears to conceive of himself as being on a journey, and he refers to other places where he stays as "travel lodgings" (*ryōshuku*), including the lodging by the river (perhaps named Rinsen'an) that he inhabits off and on for years in Sunpu; Myōshōan at Shōrin'an in Yashima, where he spends four and one-half months in the winter of 1526 and the spring of 1527; and his lodgings at Daitokuji and Okitsu, where he stays long enough to carry out repairs on both.

But Sōchō also uses the term *sōan* with regard to both his Mariko Saioku and to his lodgings in Sunpu and Yashima, which suggests that he views as qualitatively related the places where he spends extended periods of stasis at the end of various journeys. Because of his ties to the Imagawa on the one hand and the Daitokuji network on the other, Sōchō is more than a guest at all three places. He is almost completely autonomous at Mariko and Sunpu, and much more than a simple passerby at Yashima, and he entertains guests and visitors at all three *sōan*. There are four extended depictions in his journal of his life at these three places, and they constitute the major loci of Sōchō's hermitage literature.[4]

Though travel, as we have seen, provided the impetus to undertake the journal, nearly twice the number of pages and twice the amount of time covered in the completed account depict stationary periods. These passages contrast with the travel sections in a number of important ways. Where Sōchō the traveler was a guest, he is now either a host to other travelers or alone. Letters and poem exchanges with distant friends, frequently involving gifts, figure far more prominently in these passages than in travel segments.

CHAPTER THREE

Not surprisingly, depictions of periods of rest tend to be organized on temporal rather than spatial principles. Where travel sections read "a day in X . . . , a night in Y . . . ," passages in stasis make more frequent references to specific days and months. While utamakura tend to be the major points of reference in travel passages, here that role is assumed more often by significant annual observances (*nenchū gyōji*) such as the New Year, the Festival of the Weaver Maid, or monthly and yearly death anniversaries. Such dates become, as it were, temporal utamakura.

Perhaps because such predetermined occasions during the year occur less frequently than the daily changes that travel often brings, entries made during periods of extended stasis are more sporadic. Tedium too may have encouraged Sōchō's experimentation with a wider range of topics and poetic styles when he was not on the road. The one chōka (*JS*: 62–64), the philosophical discourse with Tokishige at year's end in 1525 (*JS*: 84–86), and most of the anecdotes about death and suffering were written while Sōchō was in residence in Kantō or Kansai.

There is also a direct relationship between travel and choice of poetic style. Renga verses outnumber waka by nearly three to one in the travel sections, while waka outnumber renga by the same ratio in the stasis sections. The predominance of renga in the travel sections is not surprising, since the teaching and practice of that art was for Sōchō a basic travel motive. In stasis, by contrast, Sōchō is often alone, and he has far fewer opportunities to compose linked verse, aside from solo sequences (*dokugin*). About three-quarters of Sōchō's extant renga compositions made in Suruga, for example, are solo sequences. In the letters he exchanges during his periods of rest, the waka is the customary poetic form; linked-verse was not the normal medium of epistolary poetic exchange. All the extensive exchanges of waka with distant friends occur when Sōchō is not traveling.

The distinction in use between waka and renga has an impact on the tone of the passages in which they are featured. Linked verse, being fundamentally a group enterprise, avoids strong individual sentiment that might disrupt the harmony of the session. That is particularly true for the introductory hokku, which must strike a lofty note for the rest of the piece and refer to the season and location in which it is composed. Nearly all the renga in *The Journal of Sōchō* are hokku. This means that the travel sections include many more verses of a public, formal type that focus on the seasons and natural surroundings. The waka included in the passages in stasis run the gamut from formal pieces on set topics

Illustrations

FIG. I   PORTRAIT SCULPTURE OF SŌCHŌ

Courtesy of Saiokuji temple.

Portrait of Sōgi. Courtesy of Kaneko Kinjirō. Thought to be a close likeness of the poet, the portrait bears the following colophon:

Portrait of the Aged Sōgi

utsushioku	Though it seems
waga kage nagara	to show me,
yo no uki o	I find I envy
shiranu okina zo	the old man in the picture
urayamarenuru	who knows not the world's sadness!
yo ni furu mo	This life goes on,
sara ni shigure no	and now too a cold rain falls
yadori kana	upon my shelter!
toshi no watari wa	No one else to make the crossing
yuku hito mo nashi	from the old year to the new.
oi no nami	The waves of old age—
iku kaeriseba	how often will they return
hatenaramu	before they come no more?

The first verse appears in Sōgi's waka collection *Sōgishū* (*KT* 8: 839) and the second, in *Shinsen tsukubashū* (no. 3799, see pp. 160–61). The last two verses, of which the second is by Sōgi, are found in *Sōgi shūenki* (The Death of Sōgi, in Kaneko 1976: 109), written by Sōchō.

FIG. 2
PORTRAIT
OF SŌGI

Portrait of Ikkyū with a red sword. Courtesy of Shūon'an temple and Nakamoto Tamaki. The portrait bears the following inscription:

> For a hundred years, Zen in the Land of the Eastern Sea:
> Downright madmen, utter monsters.
> In all Japan, Zen is no more—
> With whom can I indulge in Zen conversation?
>
> The Zen priest Sōkan painted this picture of my poor self. He asked for a colophon, and I thereupon wrote this out for him.
>
> The former abbot of Daitokuji, seventh-generation disciple of Xu Tang, Ikkyū Sōjun of the Eastern Sea.

In *The Journal of Sōchō*, Sōchō mentions owning a portrait of Ikkyū with a sword (*JS*: 126–27; see also *Song in an Age of Discord*, p. 47). Ikkyū may also have composed for Sōchō the following poem, entitled "Brushwood Cottage" (Saioku), included in the Shūon'an manuscript of Ikkyū's anthology of Chinese poetry *Kyōunshū* (Ikkyū 1976: 221–22):

> Branches and vines entwine Tathagata meditation;
>   old man Zhaozhou preaches on the True Buddha.
> Amid the toil of planting and harvesting, he surely does not know
>   about garnet towers and jade halls.

Zhaozhou was a Zen master of the Tang; he figures in the first chapter of the famous Zen treatise *Mumonkan* (C: *Wumenguan*, The Gateless Gate, 1228), by Wumen Huikai.

FIG. 3
PORTRAIT
OF IKKYŪ
WITH A
RED SWORD

FIG. 4 SŌCHŌ PLAYING THE BAMBOO FLUTE (*SHAKUHACHI*) IN HIS BRUSHWOOD COTTAGE IN MARIKO

From *Tōkaidō gojūsan tsugi* (the Fifty-Three Stations of the Tōkaidō), an Edo-period picture book with illustrations by Utagawa Sadahide. Courtesy of Tanaka Takahiro. For a translation of the accompanying text, see Appendix B.

(*dai*) to expressions of emotion far more personal than would be allowable in a renga setting.

The sōan, therefore, is the site of the greatest interiority in the journal. It is here that Sōchō writes his most personal waka poetry, and by extension where the conflicts between the this-worldly and the other-worldly, life and death, subject and object, attain their most provocative and multivalent representation.

But these differences, while important, are relative. Again, stasis is not the opposite of travel for Sōchō but its complement, and his main concerns—his art, friendship, old age, and death—remain constant whether he is on the road or at rest. This is so even in the passages of extended stasis, depicting Sōchō's life in one of the three residences he characterizes as sōan.

Sōchō's Figuring of the Poetic Sōan Orthodoxy

Although sōan literature per se never constituted a separate genre in the imperial anthologies, a group of images and attitudes had coalesced around the sōan by the time of Sōgi and Sōchō. Among the most famous contributors to the sōan topos in the Japanese context were Saigyō and Kamo no Chōmei.[5] Etō Yasusada observes that "[Sōgi's] verses on the sōan are heavily overlaid with classical rhetoric. They are nearly all repetitions of topics and conceptions already used in waka poetry and in the linked verse of *Tsukubashū* and *Chikurinshō*," which are based on waka precedents.[6] The same was true for Sōchō's poetic sōan vision. As pointed out earlier, waka and renga expressing sōan themes tend to fall into the categories of Buddhist poetry or laments. As he did with travel poetry, Sōchō succinctly explains the basic essences of sōan themes in *Sōchō kawa*:

> When "tired of living in the world" appears in the previous verse, one links such sentiments as listening to gusts of wind in the pines while alone in a mountain temple or a brushwood hut; cleansing one's heart at the sound of a waterfall or a stream beneath the trees; cutting meager firewood or lighting a fire; cupping water from a valley stream and wishing for the True Law; purifying one's deluded heart; gazing at the dew on the grass or the froth on the water and lamenting life; donning simple garments and dyeing them inky black; letting one's sleeves grow mossy as the cliffs; shunning the fragrance of the spring blossoms lest it permeate one's sleeves; closing one's brushwood door even to the brilliance of the autumn moon and desiring an end even to the path of dreams, climbing yet deeper up the steep paths through the crags of the Yoshino mountains; or fashioning a frail dwelling. Or again, recalling a friend after turning one's back on the world; thinking back on the town in which one used to live; longing for the

capital under spring blossoms or the autumn moon; or knowing that there must be some who have succeeded in cutting their last ties to the world.[7]

He then quotes several waka poems from *Kokinshū* and *Shinkokinshū* that elaborate those attitudes. They take as their basis the recognition of the Four Noble Truths of Buddhism, beginning with the recognition that all life is suffering. For Sōchō, Buddhist poetry and laments are inspired by a sense of being "tired of living in the world." The world is a source of pain, increasingly so as one ages, and pain may be alleviated only by severing one's worldly ties. He provides this verse from *Kokinshū* (18: 951) to express the principle:

yo ni fureba	As one grows older,
usa koso masare	life's misery only increases.
miyoshino no	through the crags of fair Yoshino,
iwa no kakemichi	one step after the next,
fuminarashitemu	I will make my way.

Salvation is to be found in nature, for nature teaches one religious truths. Thus Sōchō adduces images such as "listening to gusts of wind in the pines while alone in a mountain temple or a brushwood hut" or "cleansing one's heart at the sound of a waterfall or a stream beneath the trees" or "gazing at the dew on the grass or the froth on the water," for they are all venerable poetic metaphors for the enlightenment that comes from the recognition of evanescence.

But the vow of renunciation is difficult to fulfill:

yamazato ni	I wonder if the hut
chigirishi io ya	in which I pledged to dwell
arenuran	has gone to ruin.
mataren to dani	I never expected
omowazarishi o	to make it wait so long for me!

[*Shinkokinshū* 18: 1757, by Jien]

And even after one succeeds in cutting worldly ties, one finds the ascetic life estimable in its purity and conviction but also lonely and hard:

yamazato wa	It is very true
mono no wabishiki	that life is poor and dreary
koto koso are	in a mountain hamlet,
yo no uki yori wa	but dwelling here is better
sumiyokarikeri	than in the woeful world.

[*Kokinshū* 18: 944][8]

The Literature of Eremitism

> yama fukaku
> sa koso kokoro wa
> kayou to mo
> sumade aware wa
> shiramu mono ka wa
>
> No matter how
> one longs for a dwelling deep
> within the mountains,
> could one ever know how sad it is
> until one has gone and lived there?
>
> [*Shinkokinshū* 17: 1632, by Saigyō]

According to its poetic formulation, a life of renunciation does not provide immediate release; it affords instead a constant struggle with lingering attachments and human desires.

Two decades after Sōchō summarized those essentials of Buddhist poetry and laments in *Sōchō kawa*, he applied them in *Yamaga hyakuin*, his solo hundred-verse sequence on life in his mountain cottage (*yamaga*), composed in the winter of 1511. The hokku on which he based it reads:

> 1   hitome sae
>   fuyugaretekeru
>   yamaji kana
>
> Even passers-by
> have faded away in winter—
> a mountain path.

Yamaga hyakuin is not a typical renga sequence because it was composed by a single poet and because it centers on a single matrix of topics.[9] But it nevertheless represents the sōan topos as it is constituted in orthodox renga verse.

As with Buddhist poetry, the sequence is predicated on a recognition of the evanescence of all things and the poet's own inevitable death:

> 84   yama mo susono mo
>   matsumushi no koe
>
> In the mountains and the foothill fields,
> the chirping of pine crickets.
>
> 85   aki wa mi no
>   ima wa no sumika
>   shirurame ya
>
> This autumn, can they know
> where the dwelling stands
> in which I will meet my end?[10]

❧

> 93   tōkaranu
>   nishibi o sashite
>   tanomu mi ni
>
> In the western sun,
> not so far in the distance,
> I place all my trust.
>
> 94   kyō ka asu ka o
>   oi no yukusue
>
> Will it come today or tomorrow,
> the end of my aged journey?

CHAPTER THREE

He therefore pursues as a man of religion the hard ideal of renunciation of the things of the world:

67	mizu o dani nururu wa to yo o itouran	Is it only water that wets my robe, now that I have renounced the world?
68	asaku shi mo ya wa sumizome no sode	Have they been dyed but lightly, these ink-black monkish sleeves?[11]

❁

96	mukashi wa sasuga haru zo matareshi	In bygone years, to be sure, I could not wait for springtime.[12]
97	kotogoto ni omoisutetaru yado furite	The cottage in which I have renounced all grows old.
98	shizuka ni sumu ya yama no kai naru	It was good to have come to this valley where I live in peace.

Again the poet retires into nature, his sense of religious purpose strengthened by natural metaphors:

43	akatsuki wa arashi o kikishi mado no mae	Dawn twilight at the window where I listened to the gusts of wind.
44	kokoro sume to ya tsuki wa shizukeki	Make your heart as limpid, the quiet moon seems to say.[13]

His mountain hut is simple and rustic:

58	nokiba o araki sasabuki no ie	A house, its eaves roughly roofed with thin, rock-weighted shingles.
59	ashi no ha o magaki no makuzu aki kurete	Kudzu on a fence thatched with leafy reeds— an evening at autumn's end.

And he will sometimes leave his dwelling, again reflecting the complementary nature of the road and the hermitage for one who has turned his back on the world:

45	aki no yo no tabine o yama no oku ni shite	On an autumn night resting from travel deep in the mountains.
46	suge no ne shinogi tsuyu zo kōruru	The dew that coats the sedge roots begins to freeze.

At other times the roles of host and guest will be reversed, and a traveler will visit him:

7	yuku sode mo takaki kakehashi tare naranu	Those sleeves that pass high up on the cliffside footbridge— whose could they be?[14]
8	mine koeku nari ochi no tabibito	He comes across the mountain peak, a traveler from afar.

But the poet nevertheless deeply feels the constant trials of the eremitic life—its poverty, loneliness, and tedium:

49	kurenureba hotaru no terasu matsu no to ni	By the pinewood door lit by fireflies when it grows dark.
50	tsurezure shiruku sashikomoru hito	One learns the meaning of tedium when one dwells in seclusion.

❀

79	tare o kaku hitotsutokoro ni yobukodori	Who is it you are calling to this spot, cuckoo bird?[15]
80	kaeru hito naki michinobe no kure	A path on which none returns, at evening.
81	sato tōki takigi ni iku ka okururan	Far from a village, how much longer will my firewood last?

And despite his resolutions to the contrary, he continues to be pained by his inability to renounce completely mundane attachments and desires:

CHAPTER THREE

23	minahito no hana no tamoto o urayamite	The blossom-covered sleeves of one and all— how I envy them!
24	kasumi no hoka ni yukikaeru miyu	Beyond the haze I watch them come and go.

❦

33	shikibi taku keburi o fukaku mi ni shimete	The smoke from burning star anise penetrates deep into my body.[16]
34	kono yo no koto wa omowazu mogana	Would that I could stop thinking of the affairs of this world!

❦

51	nageku mi wa sutenu shi mo koso aware nare	That I cannot rid myself of this grief-laden life is itself a cause for sorrow!
52	urami no hate ya tada fukaki tani	An end to my regrets? A deep ravine.[17]
53	ika ni sen ato taenu michi mo koi no yama	What can I do? Traces yet remain of the path on Love Mountain.
54	imose chō kawa no otsuru miyoshino	The River of Man and Wife flowing through fair Yoshino.[18]

Yamaga hyakuin exemplifies the blend of Buddhist poetry and laments presented in theoretical form in *Sōchō kawa*. The lament arises from a dual conflict. The first is the purity, even nobility, of a life of renunciation versus the hardship caused in part by lingering ties to the secular world. As expressed in *Sōchō kawa*, one finds oneself "recalling a friend after turning one's back on the world," or "thinking back on the town in which one lived," or "longing for the capital under spring blossoms or the autumn moon." The second conflict is generated by the first, with nature portrayed both as a means toward Buddhist truth and as a potential attachment and obstruction to salvation. The beauty and the pleasures of nature threaten to overcome their salutary significance, creating new attachments to the very world the aspirant seeks to quit. Thus one must live one's days and nights "shunning the fragrance of the spring blossoms lest it permeate one's sleeves," as *Sōchō kawa* states, and "closing one's brushwood door even to the brilliance of the autumn moon." In the Buddhist context, of course, the blossoms and the moon are the most powerful symbols of evanescence and enlightenment.

Sōchō is participating here in a traditional conflation of religious and aesthetic elements that Chōmei three centuries earlier had termed "taste" (*suki*):

> The person of taste scorns converse with the mundane, accepts poverty with equanimity, is moved by the blossoms that bloom, then fall, meditates on the moon that rises, then sets, and in so doing strives always to keep his spirit pure and unsullied by the world. To him the truth of birth and death will become manifest, and attachment to fame and profit will pass away. It is the first step toward the escape that is enlightenment.[19]

It was the gradual recognition of the beauty that could be gleaned from a life of simplicity, hardship, and seclusion in nature that transformed the negative elements of *wabishisa* (poverty or suffering) and *sabishisa* (loneliness) into the aesthetic virtues of wabi and sabi that gradually took shape in the medieval period.

But Chōmei also recognized the danger inherent in that religio-aesthetic paradigm, wherein one becomes attached to the principle of nonattachment itself. That is, of course, the paradox with which he concludes his *Hōjōki*:

> Now my life draws to its end, like the moon sinking toward the mountain crest. Soon I will face the darkness of the Three Ways. What will I have to answer for? The Buddha teaches us to have no attachments. My love for this thatched hut I now take to be a fault. Attachment to peaceful solitude too is an impediment to enlightenment. How can I waste my time discoursing on idle pleasures?[20]

The problem is particularly acute for the hermit who begins to feel an attachment to the literary life and to devote himself to poetry, for such "aesthete-recluses" are in one sense even further removed from the ideal of total renunciation.[21] Some solved the problem by renouncing art itself. As Ishida Yoshisada points out, "The sōan in its most thoroughly religious form is completely devoted to the Buddhist faith and excludes nearly all aesthetic elements."[22] A central question exercising the medieval literary mind, therefore, was how "wild words and fancy phrases" (*kyōgen kigo*) might contribute not only to aesthetic pleasure but also to religious awareness.[23] It was a question to which Shinkei, Shōhaku, and Sōchō were all compelled to respond in their sōan writing.

CHAPTER THREE

'Oi no kurigoto': Shinkei's Ideal Sōan Vision

Shinkei's *Oi no kurigoto* does for the sōan topos what Sōgi's *Shirakawa kikō* did for that of travel; it presents a conflict and a perfect resolution in a style marked by elegant univocal language and total closure. Shinkei composed the work in 1471 at age sixty-five, after having reached the summit of the linked-verse world in the capital.[24] A cleric of the elevated rank of Provisional Archbishop (Gondaisōzu) and long the abbot of the Tendai temple Jūjūshin'in, situated between Kyoto and Ōtsu, he was forced to spend the last thirteen years of his life moving from place to place after that temple burned in 1463. After the fire, he returned to his home province of Kii (Wakayama Prefecture), where he began work on what is perhaps the most famous treatise in the corpus of renga theory, *Sasamegoto* (1463–c. 1464), then went back to Kyoto, where he is thought to have completed the work. He thereafter traveled east in 1467 to escape the Ōnin War. The introduction to *Oi no kurigoto* describes the trip, which he made at the invitation of a Kantō warrior magnate, Suzuki Nagatoshi. What was meant to be only a short stay at Shinagawa in the province of Musashi (Tokyo Metropolitan Prefecture) eventually lasted five years, during which time he traveled to famous utamakura in the east and composed verses with Sōgi, most notably *Kawagoe senku* in 1469. Sōgi later named Shinkei as one of the Seven Sages of Linked Verse. But violence precipitated yet another removal in 1471, this time to Sagami Province (Kanagawa Prefecture), where he lived at the foot of Mount Ōyama in a hermitage, perhaps like the one described in *Oi no kurigoto*, until his death four years later in 1475.

Written at the request of the abbot of a nearby temple, *Oi no kurigoto* begins with a short travel introduction, and then moves on to an extended description of Shinkei's hermitage. One manuscript of the work bears the title *Jūjūshin'in Shinkei kikō* (The Travel Account of Jūjūshin'in Shinkei), reflecting the combination of travel and stasis in the essay, which again emphasizes the renunciatory aspect of both travel and reclusion. The introductory segment, the part with which we will be concerned here, runs in its entirety as follows:[25]

> *Oi no kurigoto*
>
> Some years ago the winds and clouds throughout the land became tempestuous, and there were those who lamented that the light of the passing sun and moon had been forgotten, hearts had become false, and the myriad ways had grown dim. Then chaos beset the world and all under heaven sank into dark-

ness.²⁶ The sovereign and his consort moved their jewelled daises and the regent, great ministers, grand counselors, nobles, and other courtiers hid themselves away in distant regions.²⁷ Thereupon the people looked to save themselves, their feet hardly touching the ground in their confusion; they were like spring blossoms blown by a gust of wind or autumn leaves meeting a withering blast.

When not one blade of grass remained as a refuge for me, a single drop of dew, an acquaintance in the east pressed me to visit, saying it were far better to visit Mount Fuji and the town of Kamakura than to tarry to no purpose in times such as those.²⁸ Since I had desired at the time to make a pilgrimage to the Grand Shrine, I set aside a modicum of days, secured the services of an Ise fisherman and his small craft, and drifted off uncertain in the endless wind and waves of the blue ocean.²⁹ I choked on the mist and haze of the boundless expanse of sea and sky, pillowed my head on the briny seaweed of unfamiliar beaches, and lay wilted in exhaustion upon a rush mat on unknown islands. After dream upon dream while asleep afloat, I reached amid my tears the harbor of Shinagawa in Musashi.

I saw the famous sites and presently determined to set out for home, but the discord in the world had increased, the tumult reaching now to the ends of Kyushu and the depths of the Eastland. And so, bereft of support, I fashioned a hut of salty seaweed on a precarious, rocky strand and slept side by side with sea folk, so unfamiliar to me.

Drifting thus in dreams of travel sleep, I passed five years, during which time the violence in the Eastland grew only worse.³⁰ The clamor of the bows and quivers on both sides seemed like the mountain of blades and the forest of swords in hell, and I felt ever more deeply the rending melancholy of travel.³¹

So I then set out to find a cleft between rocks or a bed of moss where I might for a while forget my cares and escape tidings of the woeful world. At a place called Ishikura at the foot of Mount Ōyama in the recesses of Sagami Province, I found a mossy hut standing these many years.³² I ventured toward it with high hopes and unexpectedly discovered it to be a place unlike either heaven or earth, defying my powers of description. Indeed it would have appealed to those men of wisdom and benevolence who "love mountains and delight in rivers."³³

To the west solitary peaks stretch into the distance, their stands of thin pines and cedars obscuring the setting sun.³⁴ Ten-thousand-foot cliffs of green reach even to my pillow, forming a natural mossy bed. Immaculate green bamboo grow all around, their leaves veiled in the mist, and bird songs sound faintly in the twilight.³⁵ One might think it the garden of Ziyou or Letian, or the hermitage of Wang Zhi or Fei Zhangfang.³⁶ It assuages the pains of my old age and heals my travel ills. The bells that ornament the altar move me to my depths as they tinkle in the wind that blows down from the peak and through the door. So too does the hilltop bell as it echoes faintly through the blinds. I am forever wiping away the tears with my sleeves.

On the south side of the mountain stands a branch shrine of the three at Kitano. The shade of the *nagi* pines and *nara* and *kashiwa* oaks and the narrow path of moss lend it an air of true divinity. Cedar, cypress, and maple stretch away from both sides of the gate and a far-flowing stream swells with pure water, with smooth stones and spray that bathes the moss. Spanning it is an old, canted bridge, its slats crooked as geese in flight.[37] Tiger Ravine in Cathay must have been just so.[38]

To the east are fields stretching clear into the distance, with blue hills beyond. When the autumn flora are no more, the hue of the morning dew and the rueful cries of the evening insects rend the heart. To the north the great peak pierces the azure empyrean, and the force with which clouds and mist boil to the very tissue of the heavens and rain pours down suggests a coiling dragon's lair.[39]

On the distant slopes there are straw-thatched huts standing in the paddies and a solitary village, the eaves of its crude dwellings rising one by the next. Old men work the fields and children gather nuts; no sound is heard save the rustic song of the woodsman returning behind his ox or the plaintive flute of the grass cutter leading his pony home.[40]

As I linger on the old bridge and gaze at the setting sun, the white waves catch the reflection of the moon and wash away profane dust and dirt. When the evening deepens, I retire to my ivied cavern, where the sound of the mountain wind beating against the pines dispels the dream of the phenomenal world.[41]

This self-referential introductory portion of the work is concerned with the violence of the world and the desire to escape it, resembling in structure Kamo no Chōmei's *Hōjōki*.[42] It is interesting to note that *Oi no kurigoto* and *Shirakawa kikō* were written only three years apart, during the violence of the Ōnin and Bunmei eras (1467–87) when the authors were both in the Kantō region. One recalls in this respect the similar dark tone of two of the poets' most famous hokku, paired in *Shinsen tsukubashū* of 1495:

Composed after going down to the Eastland during the tumult of the Ōnin era:

3798   kumo wa nao   Clouds, then chilling rain:
        sadame aru yo no   still more stable
        shigure kana   than these times!
                                    Provisional Archbishop Shinkei

After going down to Shinano at the same time, he composed this hokku on cold rain:

3799	yo ni furu mo sara ni shigure no yadori kana	This life goes on, and now too a cold rain falls upon my shelter!
		Priest Sōgi [43]

Shinkei then invokes the travel model, writing of drifting in "uncertainty," sleeping "bereft of support" in "unfamiliar" places, and feeling the "rending melancholy" of the journey (OK: 370). But there is no peace even at his destination, and after five years of disquiet, he sets out once more, this time in search of "a cleft between rocks or a bed of moss" where he can for a moment forget his cares and "escape tidings of the woeful affairs of the world" (OK: 370).

The poet discovers such a place at the foot of Mount Ōyama. His subsequent description of the hermitage shares much with the sōan life depicted in *Yamaga hyakuin*. As in that work, the Shinkei of the account is distancing himself from the mundane world, and he looks to nature to lead him to greater spiritual awareness: "When the evening deepens, I retire to my ivied cavern, where the sound of the mountain wind beating against the pines dispels the dream of the phenomenal world" (OK: 371). His sōan too is old and moss-covered, and it is located in the mountains, but it has a forest stream nearby, suggestive of washing away the impurity of the world. The flowing water also recalls the river that Chōmei uses in his account as a metaphor for unchanging change. Likewise the seclusion of Shinkei's dwelling is tempered by proximity to a temple, and the "echoes of a hilltop bell coming through the blinds" recall the vesper bell in Sōchō's renga sequence that announces the end of the day and echoes the impermanence of all things:

9	sokohaka to wakarenu kane no iriai ni	A vesper bell heard only faintly at twilight.

So too does the hermit have a distant view, and he can observe people coming and going, reminding him of his own separation from the world of men. Sōchō refers to much the same scenery in *Yamaga hyakuin*:

39	fune kudaru uji no kawanami hi wa ochite	Into the waves of Uji River where boats make their way downstream, the sun sets.
40	hibiki mo sabishi mizu no yūgure	Its echoes too are lonely— water at evening.

CHAPTER THREE

Pervading the account of the sōan *per se* is a quiet satisfaction; Shinkei is grateful to have found at last so perfect a retreat, where he can turn away from worldly cares. There is spiritual peace at his perfect hermitage, and no *jukkai* conflict.

It should be clear from the description that Shinkei's treatment of the sōan, like Sōgi's portrayal of his journey to Shirakawa, is largely epical in quality. For both poets, satisfaction is derived from a withdrawal from a flawed present into a perfect past ideal, that of classical travel poetry for Sōgi and that of earlier poetic sōan and also the Chinese hermit sages for Shinkei. *Oi no kurigoto* is heavily Sinitic in both style and theme, with no waka or renga poetry at all in the passage in question and numerous references instead to Chinese verse—there are at least ten allusions to *Wakan rōeishū* in the introductory segment.[44] Shinkei, like Sōgi, concentrates on aspects of the present that resemble the past; the pleasure he takes from his hermitage derives in part from his conviction that "it would have appealed to those men of wisdom and benevolence who 'love mountains and delight in rivers'" (*OK*: 370). His natural surroundings remind him of "the garden of Ziyou or Letian, or the hermitage of Wang Zhi or Fei Zhangfang" (*OK*: 370). Sōgi travels in a world of the past and treads in the steps of earlier poets; Shinkei too is invoking the values of an earlier time. His spiritual conception of his hermitage lies nearer to Tiger Valley in ancient China than to Ōyama in contemporary Sagami; it is a fantasy ideal "unlike either heaven or earth" (*OK*: 370).[45] So too is the portrayal literary, timeless, and ideal—precise names and dates are not mentioned and contemporary detail is absent.

Like Sōgi's epical account, Shinkei's is finished and closed-ended. This is in part quite natural, as he is writing an essay here and not, like Sōchō, an open-ended diary. But his closure is thematic as well; Shinkei suffers in the world, then finds an ideal solution. In the beginning "the light of the passing sun and moon had been forgotten" (*OK*: 369), and as the poet travels in uncertainty, he "chokes on the mist and haze" (*OK*: 369). But in the end Shinkei is able to "linger on the old bridge and gaze at the setting sun," where "the white waves catch the reflection of the moon and wash away profane dust and dirt" (*OK*: 371). His conflict is with the external world and not within himself; there is no loneliness, and no lamentation at lingering attachments to things he is trying to renounce. Shinkei's sōan is an ideal and idyllic world and, like Sōgi on the way to Shirakawa, he perceives his eremitic quest as one of trial and then complete success, rather than of ongoing and open-ended inner conflict.

Nor is Shinkei bothered by the potential danger of aesthetic attachments, for he is convinced that poetry and religion are a unified way. In a part of *Oi no kurigoto* not included here, he writes that the lover of verse must blend aspects of taste (*suki*) and religious aspiration (*dōshin*), and that he must live in peaceful seclusion (*OK*: 416). The *sōan* for Shinkei is not an escape from aesthetic pursuits; it is a place to go to actively foster them, for they, like nature itself, contribute to religious awakening. His verses, like Bo Juyi's "wild words and fancy phrases," are ultimately put to religious use.

The voice in which Shinkei expresses this point of view is a single, unified voice. In keeping with its thematic look backward to Chinese precedent, the style of the account is rich in Sino-Japanese compounds rather than in the native *wabun* vocabulary of Sōgi's Shirakawa chronicle. Nor does Shinkei admit at any point a dialogic haikai voice to counterpoint or parody his elevated tone.

Shinkei's essay, like Sōgi's travel account, is unified and closed in past time, structure, and voice. Here, too, the "ironic discrepancy" between the writing subject and the written object is very great. And like *Shirakawa kikō*, the work invokes a neoclassical ideal to bring order to the poet's disordered world.

'Muanki and 'San'aiki': Shōhaku's Elegant Retirement

In Shōhaku's description of his hermitage, *Muanki*, and his account of his hermitage life, *San'aiki*, the lofty and ascetic blend of religion and poetry that characterizes Shinkei's work gives way to a light discourse on the pleasures of elegant retirement. The tone is consonant with the genteel tenor of the life of the author.[46] The son of a high-ranking courtier, Shōhaku spent his first years in a courtly atmosphere, but while still a boy he took holy orders. He had the advantage of impressive teachers, including the Rinzai Zen monk and poet Shōjū Ryūtō, the courtier literatus Ichijō Kaneyoshi, and Sōgi, from whom he acquired a large portion of the secret traditions of *Kokinshū*. Distinguished tutelage and native talent rapidly elevated him to a position of respect in renga circles, including that of the court.[47]

In about 1482, at nearly forty years of age, he moved to Ikeda in Settsu Province (Osaka Prefecture), where he built his Dream Cottage (Muan). For reasons of health he relaxed his priestly regimen and became a lay believer (*koji*) in 1511, at which time he adopted the cognomen Botanka, or "Peony." In his personal poetry collection, *Shunmusō*, he recorded a poem exchange with Sōchō on this personal transition:

I sent a letter to the priest Sōchō telling him that I no longer strictly adhered to the Confucian, Buddhist, or Taoist ways and had ceased to shave my head as a monk:

mieba ya na	How I wish you were
onozukara naru	able to see me now
sugata ni te	in my natural state,
itodo kakurenu	beneath a snow-white profusion
yuki no midare o	that is no longer hidden.

The reply:

shiraji kimi	Though you know it not,
yuki no midare no	your words about your
koto no ha ni	snow-white profusion
onozukara naru	nevertheless reveal
sugata miyu to mo	your natural state.[48]

Four years later, in the summer of 1515, Shōhaku wrote *Muanki*, a very short sōan piece about a gift of a work of calligraphy bearing the two characters for Dream Cottage that Shōhaku had received from someone who had acquired it on a journey to China.[49] Shōhaku includes two waka expressing his emotions on receiving the gift, a description of his hermitage, and a third waka. The work appears in its entirety in *Shunmusō* in the form of prefaces (*kotobagaki*) to the three waka. Where *Yamaga hyakuin* provided a poetic model of sōan writing and *Oi no kurigoto* a Sinitic prose account, Shōhaku's *Muanki* is a blend of poetry and extended prose headnotes, in effect, a very short poetry collection.

San'aiki, written in 1516, is a short essay without poetry, beginning with a few autobiographical lines and then passing to a recital of the author's "three loves."[50]

Muanki

Sōshitsu traveled to China and while there had a friend named Zhonghe write the two characters for Dream Cottage (*Muan*) in his skillful calligraphy to bring back for me.[51] I had expected nothing of the kind and was not a little moved:

kashikoshi na	What a splendid thing,
morokoshi made mo	that in far Cathay itself
fude ni sae	it has become known
kikite somekeru	and inscribed with a brush,
yume no iori	this Dream Cottage!

The Literature of Eremitism

I also showed the Chinese calligraphy to Sōho.[52] I was pleased that Sōshitsu had not forgotten me even in a foreign land:

mizukuki ni	Beyond compare
kakeshi chigiri ya	is the bond with one in Cathay,
tagui naki	where I have never been,
minu morokoshi no	brought about through the writing
yume no iori o	of the name Dream Cottage!

My grass hut is surrounded by tall pines and flowering trees, and there is a great boulder in the front garden like a reclining dragon or a fierce tiger. Stones from the seaside are mixed in as well. A crimson plum stands near the eaves. I had it moved from Ashiya years ago. It spans thirty or forty feet. At the side is a well, the draw rope of which extends several yards. With its cover of pawlonia leaves, the well is a fine place to take refuge from the heat. There are blossoms on the myriad trees in all seasons. The delight I take in them morning and evening dispels thoughts of my old age. For that reason I have named my study Cottage of Floral Delights [Rōkaken]:

yume nagara	Though all is a dream,
kokoro wa tomeshi	I find my heart attracted
oiraku no	now in my old age
natsu sabikinuru	to the mountain rocks and trees
yama no iwaki ni	that mellow in the summer.[53]

San'aiki

Recently I became a lay believer. Not strictly Confucian, Buddhist, or Taoist, I no longer shave my head as a monk.[54] Though I spent years in the Nine-Fold Enclosure, I fashioned not long ago a cottage in Inano in Settsu Province and named it Dream Cottage.[55] Myself I call Peony. Though that may seem out of keeping with my station, the name relates to the religious truth that "the myriad things are a part of the one."[56] I never cease to admire the blossoms, delight in incense, and savor wine. The paragons and sages of both the recent past and long ago did likewise, and who from youth to village elder does not do so as well?

Ever since my childhood, I have begrudged each passing moment of a spring evening beneath the moon over the palace.[57] Now and again I have gone into the Yoshino mountains, following in the footsteps of the great Saigyō, and have also beheld the beauty of famous sites in the nearby provinces. On such occasions I have been moved by even the tiny blossoms that mingle with the grasses by a spring roadside, or taken note as I pressed through the lush summer foliage

CHAPTER THREE

of even the briar rose that twines about the fence of a rude hut, or waved my sleeve in greeting to even a solitary flower left in a frost-withered field. Now and again I have been stirred to my depths in the dawn by leaves crimson as the brocade of Chengdu, and I have reclined in the spring breeze that blows through the peaches and damson plums; I let my life be as the dream of a butterfly, and "thinking of the times, I shed tears."[58]

In incense, I consider aloe wood fundamental and favor Ranjatai, Red Dust, Middle River, and other varieties famous in this land from long ago.[59] Among blends, I delight in Plum Blossom, Lotus Leaf, and First Pillow among others, and carry on the competing secret traditions of the various families, making fine gradations in the mixtures.[60] I enjoy their fragrance while composing poetry in the night rain by my companion's pillow and while harmonizing verses in the day to the sound of the wind in the blinds. In moments stolen from worldly affairs, I do nothing else.

Of wines, I have tasted the flavors of Cathay and the Southern Barbarians and tried the *nerinuki* of Kyushu, the Chrysanthemum of Kaga, the excellent wine of Amano, and even the thin and the cloudy.[61] With one cup I dispel a thousand cares.[62] Sometimes I patch my spring robes and drink to abandon, thus protecting myself from the wind and cold.[63] In so doing I have lived to a rare age.[64] And sometimes I dance and dance, and return in my heart to my youth.[65]

The priest Shōjū of Kenninji was the esteemed elder from whom I received my name.[66] His successor Jōan too is an old friend.[67] I asked him to write on these three virtues, and he composed a piece entitled *Three Loves*. I cannot describe the amazement I felt on seeing how marvelous was the result.[68] A youth here eagerly requested I simplify it for him, and because of his earnest wishes I inked my brush and wrote out a part.

> Composed in the last part of the ninth month, Eishō era, Hinoene [1516], aged seventy-three years.

In these two accounts, Shōhaku consciously employs much of the same vocabulary as *Yamaga hyakuin* and *Oi no kurigoto* in fashioning his eremitic persona. He lives in a hermitage in nature, and he admires the ideal of rustic poverty. For Shōhaku too, travel is the complement of the solitary life in stasis, and he models his forays away from his hermitage on traditional eremitic models: "Now and again I have gone into the Yoshino mountains, following in the footsteps of the great Saigyō" (*SA*: 394).

But the philosophy that informs Shōhaku's hermitage life is quite different from the two earlier rengashi examples whose personae are Buddhist priests who have have renounced the world. Shōhaku, by contrast, has become a "lay believer... no longer strictly Confucian, Buddhist, or Taoist." His attitude toward his hermitage life, therefore, reflects neither the high purpose and lingering regret in *Yamaga hyakuin* nor the perfect escape from worldly chaos in *Oi no kurigoto*; it is instead a gracious way of being both in and apart from the world, of rationalizing elements of the sacred and secular, of faith and fancy.

He may admire, for example, the rude hut he passes on his outings, but he does not live in one himself. He enjoys "a great boulder in the front garden like a reclining dragon or a fierce tiger" (*MA*), an effect reminiscent of the fantastic rocks of Chinese landscape architecture, and he has a plum moved there from miles away. Nature, for Shōhaku, is important as religious metaphor, but also largely for its beauty alone. Shōhaku is not embarrassed by "delighting in" his hermitage and its blossoms, and he goes so far as to name his study Cottage of Floral Delights (Rōkaken).[69]

In keeping with his nondual ontology, Shōhaku indulges his three loves "in moments stolen from worldly affairs" (*SA*: 394). And he supplies us with the names of two of his friends. China for Shōhaku is to some extent therefore a real place; the period was, after all, one of Ming trade, much of it centering on the port of Sakai, where Shōhaku spent his last years. Shōhaku's essay shares some of Sōchō's contemporaneity.

By and large, however, Shōhaku, like Shinkei, presents an epical kind of self-fashioning; he creates himself in terms of past ideals, contructed of elements of the Saigyō model and Buddhist and Taoist traditions. His sōan and his "three loves" are expressed for the most part in antique Sinitic terms. The idea of "three loves" itself is probably borrowed from Bo Juyi's three friends: poetry, wine, and the music of the *qin*.[70] Underneath the unassuming and happy-go-lucky surface, *San'aiki* proves on closer reading to be a tissue of allusions to Chinese poetry, and constructed with careful regard for Sinitic parallelism. Shōhaku's carefree retirement and artistic pursuits remind one of the "Seven Sages of the Bamboo Grove" and Chinese reclusive literature beginning with that of the Six Dynasties, also a period of social unrest when many poets abandoned the world for the rustic serenity of the hermitage and the delights of aesthetics and wine.

Though Shōhaku has a friend who has actually been to China, it remains an "orientalism" for him, an exotic land of the great sages and antique traditions. He still sees the continent as a venerable and envied cultural fountainhead. He shapes his present in terms of an epic formulation of the past, and he excludes all elements that cannot be expressed in terms of past models. He steals time from "worldly affairs" to indulge in his three loves, but he gives no hint of the nature of those affairs, or even that he is a renga master. Likewise he makes oblique mention of his unsettled times, but he does so using lines borrowed from the ancient Chinese poet Du Fu. There is no mention that the author behind the eremitic mask had actually gone south and taken up life in retirement at least in part to escape violence in Kyoto.[71]

This too, then, is a closed-ended portrayal, and one in which all conflict has been resolved. Shōhaku implies the reason for this serenity through the names he chooses for himself and for his hermitage. He writes, "Myself I call 'Peony.' Though that may seem out of keeping with my station, it relates to the religious truth that 'the myriad things are part of the one.'" The word "peony" (*botanka*) has a scriptural history as a symbol for the philosophy of nonduality.[72] Likewise his remark that he is "not strictly Confucian, Buddhist, or Taoist" recalls the parable of the "Three Laughers of Tiger Valley" who recognized the unity of the three creeds. For Shōhaku, being in the world or apart from it, admiring a rude dwelling or living in an elegant one, are all "part of the one." So too does the name "Dream Cottage" suggest that life either in the world or out is equally insubstantial and transient. Shōhaku emphasizes this perspective in the Taoist context by quoting the famous line from *Zhuangzi* in which the narrator finally cannot tell if he is a man who dreamed he was a butterfly or a butterfly dreaming he is a man.[73] Unlike Shinkei, who fled the corrupt world for the sanctity of the hermitage, Shōhaku achieves his release through philosophical rationalization, while being both in the world and apart from it. Neither poet is troubled by ongoing conflicts between eremitic resolve and lingering regrets. Shōhaku's unapologetic rationalization of this-worldly and other-worldly elements recalls the all-encompassing Zen of Ikkyū, for whom the monastery and the brothel were both part of a transcendent One.

Shōhaku's is a "unitary" voice, constructed of elevated ideals expressed in lofty Sino-Japanese language. It is, however, a different sort of unitary voice, much lighter in tone and imagery than that used in Sōchō's poetic sequence, with its cold, lonely, and dark images, or in Shinkei's description of his cottage, where the sun seems only to set, never shine. Shōhaku's hermitage presents no lonely, dreary landscape; rather, "there are blossoms on the myriad trees in all seasons" (*MA*). His elegant retirement presents another sōan prescription, and elements of it too are discernible in the multifaceted sōan portrayals in *The Journal of Sōchō*.

The Sōan in 'The Journal of Sōchō'

The complementarity of life in the hermitage and life on the road forms a kind of leitmotif of *The Journal of Sōchō*. The sōan life as depicted in the journal shares much with that evoked in the poetic verses of *Yamaga hyakuin* and the accounts of Shinkei and Shōhaku. Old age and an ever-deepening sense of personal evanescence continually impress upon the poet the necessity of religious retirement, but in an environment of natural beauty and aesthetic satisfaction. But like his travel accounts, his sōan self-presentation is complex and conflicted, dialogic and novelistic; it introduces a multivocality in which elements of all three earlier sōan approaches are included.

The multivalent nature of Sōchō's sōan depiction begins with the fact that it is not one but several places of retirement that he describes, most notably his Brushwood Cottage in Mariko and his lodgings in Sunpu and Yashima. We will begin with the Mariko cottage. The journal begins, however, in Sunpu, not Mariko; Sōchō departs from Sunpu in 1522 and returns there in 1524, and it is not until early 1526 that he returns to his eponymous Brushwood Cottage. He had meant to continue directly to Takigi in Kansai, but he then changes his mind:

> I have maintained a place of retirement by Utsunoyama mountain for some time, and I decided to take up residence there on the twenty-sixth of the twelfth month, after having been away five or six years in the capital:

311
    toshi no kure no
    takigi korubeki
        kadode nomi
    utsutsu no yama no
    yado motomu nari

    Though I only just left
    for Takigi, where I planned
        to cut firewood at year's end,
    I have taken shelter instead
    by Reality Mountain.

> By "though I only just left," I meant that I had set out for Takigi in Yamashiro only a short time ago.

312
    ima yori wa
    chiyo no takigi mo
        korinubeshi
    utsutsu no yama no
    matsu ni makaseba

    From this day onward
    I must cut my firewood
        for the ages here,
    placing my trust in the pines
    of Reality Mountain.

> I repaired the thatched fence, coarse rush blinds, and bamboo flooring of this mountain dwelling and straightaway took up residence. (*JS*: 86)

CHAPTER THREE

"Cutting firewood" (*takigi o koru* or *takigi o kiru*) is a conventional metaphor from the *Lotus Sutra* for the ascetic pursuit of the Buddhist Law (see also *JS* no. 37). The passage establishes a relationship between a simple and rustic dwelling in a natural environment and the pursuit of religious truth. "Utsutsu no yama" suggests both the site of the Mariko hermitage by Utsunoyama mountain and an awakening to the reality (*utsutsu*) of Buddhist teachings. Takigi also recalls the site of the hermitage of Sōchō's own spiritual master, Ikkyū.

Sōchō then goes on to pursue these sōan themes in a series of ten waka poems on the snow which falls the next next day, his emotions shifting from one perspective to another in a manner recalling the progress of a linked-verse sequence (*JS*: 87–88). He first expresses his enjoyment of the scene around his cottage, which once again suggests the ascetic / aesthetic eremitic nexus:

313 waga io wa   Here at my cottage
    kayaya komogaki   the thatched roof and rice-straw fence
      ashisudare   and blinds made of reeds
    suzuro ni yuki o   all seem somehow to set off
    motehayasu kana   the snow to advantage!

But then he becomes melancholy, recognizing his separation from others and wishing for companions with whom to share the scene:

314 haruka ni te   This morning I have
    tachikaeri sumu   returned from far away
      kesa shi mo are   to take up residence,
    furusatobito wa   but no village folk have come by
    niwa no shirayuki   to see the white snow in my garden.

His spirits then revive, and he again takes pleasure in the change the snow has brought to his garden, constructing his verse on the conventional trope (*mitate*) of the snow and its resemblance to cherry blossoms:

315 tateueshi   It brings blossoms
    niwa no iwaki ni   to the trees and the rocks
      hana sakite   that I put into my garden
    izuko aru to mo   and hides the ruder parts
    mienu yuki kana   from view—the snow!

With the next verse Sōchō effects a philosophical amalgamation of his earlier sentiments, making elements of nature itself the friends with whom he had wished to share his garden's natural beauty:

316	yamazato no	These are my three friends
---	mitsu no tomo to ya	here in this mountain village:
	kesa no yuki	the snow this morning,
	kakine no shitodo	the bunting on the fence,
	mado no kuretake	and the bamboo by my window.

Sōchō's friends, however, are not the elegant artistic pursuits of the Chinese literatus Bo Juyi, but instead simple and rustic things of nature. Sōchō is indicating here that his cottage, like that of Shōhaku, is at once a dwelling for pursuing the Buddhist Law and a place of aesthetic satisfaction.

Sōchō's emotions swing back and forth between enjoyment of the snowy scene and depression at its barren coldness. Villagers apparently pass by, but Sōchō does not see them. The forlorn fence they have unknowingly trampled in the deep snow is all that suggests their presence, and it increases Sōchō's sense of loneliness:

317	yuki fureba	Hidden by snow,
---	kakine mo tawa ni	the fence seems to have been
	fuminarashi	trampled underfoot—
	sokohaka to naku	a mountain village where people
	kayou yamazato	make their way uncertainly.

318	tsuta kaede	This mountain path
---	hi no me mo itsu ka	where the ivy and maples
	miyamaji mo	blocked even the sun
	amari arawa ni	now seems altogether stark
	yuki wa furitsutsu	beneath snow that falls and falls.

Sōchō here relates his environment not to Chinese but to Japanese literary precedents, again recalling the passage quoted earlier from *Ise monogatari* where Ariwara Narihira, in his exile from the capital, walked through the ivy and maples, filled with apprehension.

Thoughts of those ancient travelers and their melancholy are suddenly given immediacy by the echoes of another traveler in immediate distress:

319	yo o fukaku	He seems to have lost
---	michi madourashi	his way in the dead of night.
	furu yuki ni	In the falling snow
	tego no yobisaka	out on Maiden-Calling Slope,
	hito toyomu nari	the shouts of someone echo.

CHAPTER THREE

Night then gives way to the half-dark before dawn. As the old poet-priest watches his surroundings disappear under the falling snow, he is perhaps reminded of his own approaching end and also of the "dawn" of religious enlightenment, *sono akatsuki*:

320	morotomo ni	Together,
	kokorobosoku mo	forlornly,
	kiyuru nari	they disappear—
	kakehi no take no	the snow in the bamboo trough
	yuki no akatsuki	and the dawn light upon it.

But then the poet resolves that he will weather this winter of discontent and look forward to the spring, his mind moving in these last three verses from the past, through the present, to the future, when in a few days spring will arrive with the New Year:

321	kasumi tachi	He has set his mind,
	kiyubeki mine no	this aged one, on waiting
	haru o nomi	for the springtime,
	matsu koto ni suru	when the winter snow on the peak
	oi no shirayuki	will disappear in rising haze.

He is brought up short by the realization that on the first of the New Year he will be yet another year older, and his verse again invokes the close relationship between the reclusive life and the pain of old age, his hair white as the snow that lies on the crown of his cottage:

322	yasoji made	This cottage,
	idein koto o	in which I lament having lived
	ureesumu	nearly eighty years,
	yado mo yuki o zo	must likewise be embarrassed
	hazubekarikeru	by the snow that lies upon it.

Several days later the poet returns to Sunpu to take part in observations for the New Year, and then in the second month he again takes up residence in Mariko. He begins with some spring cleaning:

> On the ninth of the second month of the same year [1526], I left Sunpu for Izumigaya valley by Utsunoyama mountain, site of my Brushwood Cottage. I made some improvements, setting in rocks, rerouting a stream, and planting plum trees. While I was about it, I laid down stones to make a fence through the bamboo

beside the cedars and pines. Then I shaved three feet off the side of a pine and wrote:

339	saioku no	I have made a path
	koke no shitamichi	of moss to my grave
	tsukuru nari	at my Brushwood Cottage.
	kyō o waga yo no	I will consider today
	kichinichi ni shite	a lucky day hereafter!

(*JS*: 95)

These comments by Sōchō appear at the beginning of Book Two, after a line or two of appropriately felicitous poetry made in the Suruga capital. It is thus not only a sōan section but the beginning of Sōchō's second trip to Kansai, a bivalence emphasizing yet again the parity of travel and stasis in the mind of the poet-priest and also the balance of kikō and sōan sections of the journal.

The topographical description of Brushwood Cottage corresponds nearly perfectly with the geographical formula set forth not only in *Yamaga hyakuin* (which was very likely written there years earlier) but also with Shinkei's sōan in *Oi no kurigoto*. It is near a mountain, has a stream outside the gate, and is secluded but close to a temple, Bishamondō (*JS*: 153). Sōchō then sets out for Kansai, not to return for a year and a half. He describes his return in 1527 thus:

> On the ninth of the seventh month of this year I came back here again to take up residence. I removed the encircling fence and the rush blinds, and I also took out more than half the stones in the garden creek and in the short cogon grass to use in the retaining wall for the stream outside the gate. I gave instructions for the rest of the stones, which had been strewn here and there, to be rearranged to allow the creek to flow clear. The garden is a great comfort to me. In the evening cool I composed these:

569	kage mo te mo	Aged and bent
	oikagamarinu	are my hands and my reflection,
	aratamuru	although the water
	asaji no soko no	around the new shoots of short grass
	mizu wa moto mizu	is the same as that of old.

570	sumiutsuru	I am filled with shame
	kage hazukashi no	at the ancient face
	uzumoreshi	so clearly reflected
	yomogi ga moto no	in the water I ladle
	mizu wa kumu made	from the place hidden in the mugwort.

(*JS*: 158)

CHAPTER THREE

The garden is at once a reminder of Sōchō's age, indeed a memento mori, but at the same time a comfort to him, reminding him of the natural cycle of death and rebirth that comes to all things. He subsequently pursues the contrast between cessation and regermination:

> At my Brushwood Cottage by Utsunoyama mountain, I dug up some of the rocks about the pond in the garden and converted more than half of it into dry field. There, I planted seeds for young greens:

> 572   mabikina wa   How hard it is,
>   sazareishi ma no   the ground of this mountain field
>   yamabata no   where I plant young greens
>   katashi ya oi no   between the stones—
>   nochimaki no tane   the late-sown seeds of my old age.

> How I do love a garden! (*JS*: 158–59)

He adds more on the next page:

> In my garden I planted soy and adzuki beans, put up a small hut, rigged a bird-rattle, and spent my mornings and evenings in contentment:

> 576   mamemameshiku mo   An old man plants his garden,
>   nareru oi kana   full of beans!

> On picking greens from my garden to send to someone:

> 577   tsumade koso   You should have seen
>   misubekaritsure   these greens before they were picked!
>   asana asana   Morning after morning
>   waga yamabata no   in my mountain field,
>   aki no tsuyukesa   the autumn dew!

> Rain brought out the singing frogs in the "mountain and river" part of my garden. On hearing their song:

> 578   sekiiruru   Chirping in water
>   niwa no yamamizu   that chortles down its channel
>   korokoro to   into my garden,
>   ishibushi kajika   *ishibushi* singing frogs
>   ame susamu nari   frolic in the rain.

> Gradually the wind has begun to blow cold of nights, and in the wakefulness of old age my mind keeps returning to painful thoughts about my various wants:

The Literature of Eremitism

579	ama ga shita	How I wish that
	ari to aru mono	everything under heaven
	naku mogana	simply did not exist,
	sate ya hoshisa no	for if that were so
	tsukuru to omoeba	then all my wants would disappear!

Though I live in quiet retirement, I do indeed hear of events in both the capital and the provinces from pilgrims and travelers who pass by:

580	tabi goto ni	Every time they come
	sate mo te o nomi	to Reality Mountain,
	utsunoyama	I just clap and say, "Really?"
	utsutsu to mo naki	though there is nothing real
	koto o kiku kana	in anything they tell me!

(*JS*: 159–60)

The individual poems, again linked one to the next through a thematic associative process that would come naturally to a linked-verse poet and student of *Shinkokinshū*, elaborate and complicate Sōchō's *sōan* self-figuring. He begins the passage in contentment, happy to work in his garden, but he then again wishes for someone to share it with him in person, not simply by letter. He then again finds solace in the things of nature, especially the frogs singing in the rain. But night brings the cold, made worse by the wakefulness of old age, his many unfulfilled wants, and his simultaneous recognition that those desires themselves are in a Buddhist sense the root cause of suffering. They are wants that not even human companionship can alleviate, for such visitors as do come prove disappointing companions, whose words as often as not "have nothing real."

These depictions of life in his Brushwood Cottage are the most detailed examples of Sōchō's *sōan* writing. But the passages in which he describes his cottages in Sunpu and in Yashima introduce variations of the same *sōan* themes. Despite the considerable time Sōchō spends at his "lodging by the river" in Sunpu, his description of his life there is devoted primarily to epistolary exchanges and to poetry composed for official occasions. At one point, however, he writes a long account in verse (chōka) of his days residing on the outskirts of the city:

A poem I wrote out in my leisure and sent to an acquaintance in the capital:

215	minazuki no	The rainfall today
	atsusa o arau	that washed away the heat
	kyō no ame	of the Waterless Month
	niwa no ikemizu	filled the pond in my garden,

CHAPTER THREE

hachisuba no	and dew now lies
tsuyu wa shiratama	on the lotus leaves like white jewels—
kazukazu no	all the different kinds
utsushi ueoku	of trees and verdant grasses
ki mo kusa mo	I transplanted here
magaki no take mo	and the bamboo by the fence
wakaetsutsu	begin to revive,
kokoroyoge naru	the gladdening leaves
sueha ni mo	at the tips of their branches
oi o nobaete	easing the burdens of age—
toridori ni	but though my cottage
miru wa kotonaru	offers me so rich a choice
yado nagara	of changing vistas,
omou koto to wa	the thoughts that come to mind the most
meshi oashi	are of food, and funds,
nigori kukon mo	and cloudy cups of sake
maremare ni	I sip so seldom—
sasuga ni hito no	to be sure, I have people
ideiri wa	coming and going
tayuru hi mo naku	day after day without fail
miekuredo	to pay me visits
nani motekoneba	but they bring nothing with them,
motenasazu	naught have I to give,
mune nomi sumite	so sated just in spirit
tsurezure wa	I can only ask
oncha o dani to	"Will you take at least some tea?"
iu bakari	meager as that is—
mukashigatari no	trading tales about the past
oi no tomo	with a friend of years,
kataneburi shite	I feel myself start to nod
hatehate wa	and then in the end
tachisaru o sae	I am not even aware
shirazariki	he has departed—
koko ni shimeoku	the thatched-roof cottage
waga io wa	that I am keeping here
suruga no kō no	stands by the capital
katawara ni	of Suruga Province—
takeami kakuru	outside the window that is
madogoshi no	latticed with bamboo,
fuji no keburi wa	smoke from the smudge fires rises
kayaribi no	with Mount Fuji's
yūgao shiroki	over fences blooming white

kakitsuzuki	with "evening faces"—
koiegachi naru	and throughout the neighborhood
atari ni te	chock-a-block with huts,
ichime akibito	the merchants and market maids
sariaezu	raise their voices:
na sōrō imo sōrō	"Greens and potatoes for sale!
nasubi sōrō	I've eggplants for sale!
shirofuri sōrō to	Melons for sale! White melons!"
koegoe ni	one after the next
kado wa tōredo	passing in front of my gate,
itsu to naku	but since my fortunes
waga kyō asu no	(shifting as the shallows
asukagawa	of Tomorrow River
kawarubeki se mo	that vary from day to day)
taenureba	have forborne to flow,
mimi ni nomi fure	I can but sit and listen
sugosu natsu kana	and let summer pass me by.

(JS: 63–64)

The poem is quoted in its entirety here, as we will have other occasions to refer to it. Once again Sōchō is initially inspired to poetry by the beauty of nature, the trees and grasses and bamboo that ease his burdens of advancing age as they spring forth anew after the drought of the "waterless" sixth month. But soon his contentment turns to dissatisfaction, as he contemplates the lack of "food, and funds, / and cloudy cups of sake." He has visitors, but they cannot alleviate his material insufficiencies, and they are evidently not inspiring company, as he nods off before they leave. His house is on the outskirts of the provincial capital, and he watches life pass by at a distance, separated even though contiguous, wanting to be part of life, yet wanting to renounce it.

Sōchō leaves his Sunpu lodgings in the winter of that year, 1525, as we have already seen, staying at Mariko for a while only to return to Suruga for the festivities of the New Year, then once again stopping at Mariko before going west to Kansai. His Mariko cottage functions, therefore, as a retreat from his more engagé life in Sunpu a short distance away, in the same way that Takigi functions as a retreat from his more public life in Kyoto.

Sōchō expects the second trip to Kansai portrayed in the journal to be his last, and Takigi, where Ikkyū died, is to be his ultimate destination. But on arriving in Kansai he goes first to Daitokuji to see how work has progressed on the rebuilding of the Sanmon gate he had worked so hard to help finance. Thereafter he completes his journey to Takigi, arriving on the sixteenth of the seventh month. A verse he composes at this point demonstrates that he views Shūon'an in Takigi as another hermitage (he never calls it a sōan per se, but he does use the terms *sanka* [mountain house] and *kankyo* [retreat]) that offers aesthetic beauty and religious solace:

> Two or three cups with Tōunken, commissioner for this province. I composed this after telling him that we planned to cross the bridge and go down to Takigi:

374
waga io wa	My rustic hut
miyako no tatsumi	lies southeast of the capital,
shika mo sume	with dragons, snakes, and deer.
yo o uji ni shi mo	So though called gloomy Uji,
nani ka kurushimu	what could cause distress?

(JS: 107)

Sōchō plays on *tatsumi* (southeast / dragons and snakes) and on *shika* (thus / deer). His poem shows him at once subscribing to part of the traditional sōan ethic of rustic contentment, while at the same time reworking it in an even more humorous and lighthearted way.

Sōchō needs the spiritual solace the Daitokuji network provides, and though he is forever visiting friends in Fushimi, Uji, Kyoto, and Ōtsu, he never lets too much time pass between periods at Takigi, Daitokuji, or Yashima. His peregrinations remind one of the admonition to the true recluse to avoid living in one place (*issho fujū*), for that too would constitute attachment. Two months after arriving at Takigi he is back at Daitokuji, staying at Ikkyū's Shinjuan subtemple. There too, he helps improve the surrounding gardens:

> At Shinjuan, where I have recently been staying, they are constructing a handsome building called Plum Cottage. A bamboo veranda, east and south wet verandas, running water in the washroom. They put in four or five boulders, planted camellias, bamboo, and azaleas together with the plum, and spread sand as a ground cover. It has a cooling effect.
> Gokokuji at Higuchi Aburanokōji is famous for its plums, and I asked that they send one to Shinjuan. (JS: 111)

But the outbreak of warfare in Kyoto puts an end to Sōchō's quiet days at Daitokuji, and he, like Shinkei and Shōhaku before him, must leave for a more congenial spot further away. He chooses Shōrin'an in Yashima, and departs from Daitokuji at the end of the tenth month, 1526. He travels in a large company

The Literature of Eremitism

because of the danger of highwaymen, stays with friends along the way (his account becoming another short travel segment), and presently arrives at Yashima, where he takes up residence in a subtemple there called Myōshoan.

As a literatus and connoisseur, Sōchō pays no less attention here at Shōrin'an in Yashima to the aesthetics of his reclusion than at any other of his sōan sites. He writes of what must have been his chagrin at the condition in which he found Myōshōan and what he does to repair it, while philosophically accepting what he cannot improve:

> The cottage in which I am staying is badly run down and not fit to withstand storm or snow. I called in a carpenter and he shored it up, but I was a long way from the mountains and timber was scarce, so I had to order it from Katada and Sakamoto. I fixed new reeds to the frame of the reed fence and enjoyed the carelessness of my preparations for my winter confinement:

> 436   azusayumi   Winter seclusion
>   yashima no sato no   in Yashima, a name that brings to mind
>   fuyugomori   catalpa bows.
>   ima o harube to   I wish the plums would blossom now
>   ume mo sakanamu   and proclaim to us the spring!
>
>   (JS: 122)

Once more, his natural surroundings are not only aesthetically pleasing in themselves, but they lead Sōchō to religious and existential reflection:

> In the cold lingering since dawn the snow was falling on the pines and bamboo of Shōrin'an, bending them down. All morning, the cracking of breaking boughs. I was deeply struck by the matter of dreams and illusions:

> 503   nani ka sore   What is that?
>   maboroshi to towaba   were I to ask an illusion,
>   yume ya kore   "It is a dream!"
>   ware maboroshi no   the illusion might reply,
>   nanorigao semu   to introduce itself.

> 504   wakite tare   Who was it
>   futatsu ni nazuke   who separated them
>   iiokishi   and gave them different names?
>   yume ya maboroshi   A dream is an illusion,
>   maboroshi ya yume   and an illusion, a dream.
>
>   (JS: 139–40)

The verses all suggest an aged recluse trying to come to grips with old age and death through philosophical acceptance of the nonduality of all phenomena and recognition that life and death are part of a larger whole.[74]

Most of the rest of the record of his four-month stay at Yashima over the winter of 1526–27 is taken up with visits from old friends such as Seki Kajisai, on whom Sōchō so often called when passing through Ise, and with numerous epistolary exchanges with more distant friends, such as this one with Sanetaka:

487	nagameyaru	As I gaze out toward
	yuki no fumoto no	the snow-covered mountain slopes,
	shiba no io	I wonder how hard
	ika ni fukuran	the wind from Hira's peaks
	hira no neoroshi	must be blowing on your brushwood hut.

In my gratitude for his remembering me in my brushwood travel lodging, I replied:

488	ima zo omou	Now I feel that here,
	hira no neoroshi	where you gaze upon me
	nagamuramu	on my snowy slopes
	yuki no fumoto wa	blown by the wind from Hira's peaks,
	sumubekarikeri	is indeed the place for me to live!

(JS: 136)

Sanetaka in Kyoto looks east at the slopes of the Hira mountains and thinks of Sōchō to the far side of those peaks in Yashima, where the wind blows from off the peaks. Sōchō answers that he will gladly live in Yashima in the cold mountain wind, if there he can be the object of his friend's distant gaze. Here, Sōchō combines the lonely rusticity of the traditional sōan topos with evident enjoyment of human companionship, if only from afar.

But he is still troubled that he cannot bring himself to effect a more thorough renunciation. He writes that Sanetaka's letter "was impossible to ignore," even though he had said earlier that he would write no more after the New Year (JS: 426; see also Chapter One). At Yashima Sōchō greets his eightieth birthday, a moment, it will be recalled, that an earlier prophecy had held he would never experience. His survival seems to strengthen his conviction that a more complete renunciation of the things of this world is incumbent on him, as he is now living, as it were, on borrowed time. Sōchō knows that poetry can be put to religious use, but he also knows that the lines he writes "may be the truth / or may then again be lies," and as he ages he yearns ever more intensely for the religious purity of a life of stricter asceticism.

But he is nevertheless constantly drawn back to the world of men. In the second month the defeated army of Hosokawa Takakuni and the shogun choose a spot very near Yashima to effect their own retreat. Sōchō at that point leaves for Suruga by way of Takigi, where he one last time burns incense before Ikkyū's image, knowing he very likely will never do so again.

Throughout the sōan passages, Sōchō finds in Saigyō his most enduring model for the life of the poet-recluse, as the great poet was for Lady Nijō, Sōgi, and other medieval poets. Sōchō's day trip from Ise Shrine to the site of Saigyō's hermitage in Saigyō Valley in the autumn of 1522, which we looked at earlier in connection with the travel mythos, is in fact a pilgrimage to the sōan of a revered holy master (*JS*: 19–20, see also Chapter Two). Saigyō is the ideal mentor for Sōchō and also his eremitic conscience; just after Sōchō describes the new work he has done at his Brushwood Cottage, converting half of it to dry field and planting young greens, he writes:

> In the same dry field I put up a small hut, then hung a rain cape and rain hat in the alcove and laid straw mats on the floor:

573   omoiyare   Keep me in your thoughts
      waga yamabata no   here in my brushwood cottage
         shiba no io   in the mountain field
      shika no naku ne o   where I listen to the deer calling
      oi no akatsuki   before dawn in my old age.

> This is a response to Saigyō's verse, "The coming of autumn / to distant fields in mountains / cloaked with clouds—/ simply the thought of it . . ." (*JS*: 159)

Sōchō himself lives in "distant fields," and the autumn of 1527 has arrived; he is like those fields thought of with melancholy centuries ago by Saigyō, and Sōchō draws spiritual sustenance by establishing in his own solitude this connection with the earlier master. Like Sōgi in *Shirakawa kikō*, Sōchō is giving his own life meaning by inscribing himself into an earlier tradition. The small hut he fashions may function as a tangible reminder of the earlier ascetic and as a symbol of the goal of more complete renunciation.

Sōchō finds support in his own moments of privation in the thought that Saigyō likewise suffered but persevered. The ten poems he writes on the snow that falls on his Brushwood Cottage end with the following:

323 yuki no uchi   Now beneath the snow,
   tsumioku to iu mo   I understand his advice
    ima zo shiru   about stacking it up.
   hitotsukane ni mo   I do not have brushwood left
   taraji tsumagi o   to make a single bundle.
            (JS: 88)

Sōchō then explains what he means by this verse:

> I was recalling the satisfaction with which that great priest wrote, "While stacking driftwood / in the yard of my cottage / . . . / how little is this year's end / like others I have seen!" He seems to be saying that people's desires can be satisfied with little. (JS: 88) [75]

It is not only the combination of religio-poetic purpose and conflict that inspires the later poet, but also the fact that Saigyō wrote of the pains of old age. Just as Saigyō's famous Sayo no nakayama verse (see the note to *JS* no. 1) is an emblem of Sōchō's own aged peregrinations, so is Saigyō's equally famous verse (*Sankashū* no. 77) on wishing to die on the same day the Buddha entered nirvana a reflection of Sōchō's own desire to find a release from the pain of old age through a death in the faith. This is Saigyō's verse:

   negawaku wa   This is my request—
   hana no moto ni te   let me die in springtime
    haru shinamu   beneath the blossoms
   sono kisaragi no   when the moon is at its fullest
   mochizuki no koro   in that same second month.

The poem is central to Sōchō's sōan self-figuring; he refers to it on three occasions in his journal, the first time just before the New Year of 1523, a few weeks after he arrives in Takigi:

> I hope to end my days at Shūon'an. Even so, I composed the following in private celebration at the end of another year:

37 negawaku wa   This is my request—
   kotoshi no kure no   that I might vanish before
    takigi kiru   the snow on the peaks
   mine no yuki yori   where they cut firewood
   saki ni kienan   in the last days of the year.
            (JS: 23)

The Literature of Eremitism

Sōchō's poem combines a reference to Saigyō's request, while in addition introducing the double concept of cutting firewood as a metaphor for Buddhist asceticism and of doing so at Takigi, where his master Ikkyū also passed away. The firewood image is even more resonant in the context of a wish for death, since the *Lotus Sutra* expresses entry into nirvana "as, when the kindling wood is exhausted, the fire goes out."[76]

In response to a request for a hokku for a memorial sequence, Sōchō again employs Saigyō's verse as his own foundation poem because of its apposite authorship, season, and theme:

> I received a letter from the chief assistant priest of the Inner Shrine at Ise, regarding the thirteenth anniversary of the death of the previous holder of that office, Moritoki. His friends in Uji and Yamada have planned a memorial linked-verse session for Saigyō Valley on the seventeenth of the second month of next year and urgently requested a hokku, so I took up my brush at once and sent them this:

596   ai ni ainu   A rare chance meeting
      sono kisaragi no   in that same second month
      hana no haru   in spring amid blossoms.
                          (JS: 165)

The poet bases his verse on the notion that the anniversary of Moritoki's death, Saigyō's death, and the entry of the Buddha into nirvana all occur with auspicious simultaneity at the height of the spring blossoms.

Sōchō uses the verse for the third time when he is particularly sensitive to the passage of time, the increasing length of his own old age, and the dilatoriness of the dawn of death, enlightenment, and rebirth:

> First of the twelfth month, before dawn—an auspicious verse on my wish at eighty:

606   negawaku wa   This is my request
      kyō gannichi no   today, the first day
      toshi no kure   of the last month of the year:
      ima komu haru wa   let the coming spring
      koke no shita ni te   find me beneath the moss.
                          (JS: 168)

Sōchō thus figures not only his sōan life but also his wish for an end to that life in terms of the past ideal of Saigyō. The great earlier poet is thus a model for

CHAPTER THREE

Sōchō in both major topics in his journal—his poetic journeys and the incipient end of his journey through life.

The other major figure of the medieval sōan literary tradition, Kamo no Chōmei, was likewise a model for Sōchō. While in Kansai in 1526, Sōchō visited Hino and wrote, "I began to feel the past about me, here near the site of Kamo no Chōmei's hermitage and the spot where Lord Shigehira paused, and my tears overflowed" (*JS*: 113). Chōmei's *Hōjōki* was for Sōchō a poignant expression of the eremitic life and the conflict between asceticism and aesthetic attachment. And like Saigyō, Chōmei was both hermit and traveler; both *Kaidōki* and *Tōkan kikō* were variously attributed to him in the medieval period, and Sōchō quotes one of his poems in his demonstration of the travel ethic in *Sōchō kawa*. Though Saigyō was a far more influential informing force on Sōchō's self-conception both on his journeys and in his hermitages, Kamo no Chōmei also contributed to Sōchō's sōan mythos.

Sōchō's self-fashioning in his sōan sections establishes a dialogue between the earlier sōan accounts of Shinkei and Shōhaku as well as with his own poetic portrayal of the sōan in *Yamaga hyakuin*. Occasionally he finds in his sōan security and comfort, much as Shinkei did, and he is moved to write that he spends his "mornings and evenings in contentment" (*JS*: 159). He is also at times pleased by his self-sufficiency:

On hearing families proudly pounding rice for New Year's rice cakes:

481	ōkata no	In my modest
	tabi no yadori ni mo	travel lodging
	kototarinu	I want for nothing,
	tonari no mochi o	and the sound of neighbors
	mimi ni tsukasete	pounding rice cakes strikes my ear.

(*JS*: 134)

At other times, Sōchō becomes more like Shōhaku, blending faith and fancy in a recognition of his hermitage as a place of aesthetic elegance and enjoyment. Sōchō lives amid nature, but it is a nature of his own devising, in the form of the gardens he so enjoys. The poet celebrates his sōan for not only its spiritual but its aesthetic solace, the "fancy," it provides, though his phrase "how I do love a garden" implies a hint of embarrassment that he should be so caught up in material things.

And again at other times, Sōchō ties into the poetic image of sōan life in

Yamaga hyakuin, where lingering regrets are in continual conflict with the conviction that a solitary life within nature is conducive to spiritual self-improvement and contentment. Unlike that depicted by Shinkei and Shōhaku, the eremitic life in *The Journal of Sōchō* is one in which religious and aesthetic contentment is punctuated by moments of pain and lamentation. Sōchō writes at times of material self-sufficiency, but at other times of his various wants; at times of his contentment, but more often of the pain of loneliness and old age. Over the course of the work he longs increasingly to abandon the world for either a stricter eremitic life or for death itself.

Sōchō's sōan portrayal is finally a novelistic one, expanding and combining elements of all three earlier portrayals in the context of an open-ended and unfinalized present. The sōan visions of Shinkei and Shōhaku, like the poetic vision of *Yamaga hyakuin*, are essentially timeless; the accounts of the two older poets are as evocative of ancient China as of late medieval Japan. Since Sōchō's account is constructed both as a chronological "recording" diary and as a work of art, one is not surprised to find that it combines elements of an atemporal epical sōan construct with contemporary detail.[77] Events in Sōchō's hermitages are dateable, and what is more, they are varied; life in the idealized hermitages of *Oi no kurigoto* and *San'aiki* never changes. His hermitages themselves age with the poet, and he shows us how he repairs them, setting in rocks, rerouting water, rebuilding fences, calling in a carpenter, ordering lumber.

Ultimately the sōan for Sōchō is a place of retirement from worldly concerns but also a locus of worldly transaction, just as travel for him is both a renunciatory act of private religio-poetic austerity and a route to secular contact. The example of Saigyō seems to suggest to Sōchō the bivalence in particularly poignant terms. When crossing the Suzuka Mountains, for example, he remarks with humorous chagrin in a verse (quoted earlier in another context) on his own inability to cut himself off from worldly affairs as completely as he believed Saigyō had:

When that great priest crossed these mountains, he composed this:

168   suzukayama   In the Suzuka Mountains
        ukiyo o yoso ni   I cast aside
           furisutete   this world of sorrow—
        ika ni nariyuku   what will come to pass
        waga mi naruran   in this life of mine henceforth?

Full of envy, I wrote:

CHAPTER THREE

169	suzukayama	In the Suzuka Mountains,
	furisutenu mi no	what is sad about
	kanashiki wa	*not* casting off the world
	oikagamareru	is having my old, bent back
	koshi o kakarete	carried in this palanquin!
		(*JS*: 50)

Saigyō viewed the Suzuka Mountains as separating the secular world of the capital from the sacred precinct of Ise and its shrines. Though the episode does not occur when Sōchō is in a sōan, it reflects an awareness of the desirability of re-renunciation, *saishukke*, so central to the sōan ethos, in which one who has already taken religious vows casts off the final mundane bonds. While staying at Shūon'an in Takigi, Sōchō offers a similarly rueful expression of his continued entanglement in secular affairs in response to one of a group of poems from Sanetaka, which reads:

38	nodoka ni te	Your years will surely
	sara ni yowai mo	continue to increase
	nobinubeshi	as you greet
	chiri no hoka naru	the spring in tranquillity
	haru o mukaete	out beyond the mundane dust.
		(*JS*: 25)

Sōchō responds:

43	onozukara	How my thoughts turn
	omou haru kana	of their own accord to peaceful spring,
	nodoka ni te	though I know naught of
	chiri no hoka to wa	living in tranquillity
	waku mi naranedo	out beyond the mundane dust.
		(*JS*: 26)

He later conveys the same sentiments to another courtier, Nakamikado Nobutane:

From Lord Nakamikado:

142	samukaranu	Come up to the warmth
	miyako no haru ni	of spring in the capital,
	takigi o ba	and leave the Takigi
	hiroisute koyo	firewood that you gathered,
	yamazato no tomo	friend of the mountain village.

... I sent this reply:

143   nodoka naru   For the road leading
      miyako no michi ni   to the balmy capital,
      takigi o ba   he would abandon
      hiroi zo suten   his Takigi firewood,
      haru no yamabito   this springtime mountain dweller.

                (JS: 42)

The courtier Nobutane asks Sōchō to come up to the warm capital, where firewood is not necessary. But the use of the word *takigi* in this context carries with it the suggestion to abandon a life of ascetic seclusion and return to friends and society. Sōchō is sorely tempted by the offer.

In short, Sōchō's journal expresses the theoretical contradiction faced by monkish rengashi, who are required by their profession to be in the world but who admire the ideal of reclusion and nonattachment. Unlike the ideal *inja* recluse, who scorns all contact with the secular world, Sōchō and other professional rengashi use their status as monks as a way both to withdraw spiritually from the world and to acquire wider access to it by transcending the restrictions of secular rank and status. Sōchō's conflict is particularly marked, given the strength of the competing imperatives of Ikkyū's Zen and Imagawa daimyo patronage.

And as in the travel sections, this conflict is open-ended and will ultimately be coterminous with life itself. Whereas the conflict between the sacred and the secular is resolved in the closed-ended accounts of Shinkei and Shōhaku, it persists beyond the boundaries of Sōchō's chronicle, leaving both author and reader in doubt about its ultimate solution. Sōchō's conflict here is one step anterior to that in *Yamaga hyakuin*, in which the conflict is between an eremitism already achieved and lingering attachments to a world left behind. Sōchō in his diary is still trying to achieve that retirement, while always being drawn back to the responsibilities, attractions, and desires of secular life. In part, *The Journal of Sōchō* is a prose *jukkai* lament on Sōchō's old age and his continuing attachment to this-worldly affections, writing, and life itself. In the sōan passages these laments achieve their strongest expression.

Sōchō also introduces a vast number of other voices into his sōan account, distancing the work from the more focused portrayals of seclusion which by definition can have but one voice (or as in *Yamaga hyakuin*, one voice per verse). Like the travel sections of *The Journal of Sōchō*, its sōan moments are punctuated

CHAPTER THREE

by the voices of others, through both their visits and their letters. This multiplicity of voices is amplified by the several conflicted tonalities of the author's voice.

The pull between retirement and the affairs of the world exercises Sōchō increasingly throughout the journal. Book Two is written by a man convinced he is in his final year; it shows a mild darkening of outlook, greater religious concern, and occasional flashes of anger.[78] It was natural for Sōchō to begin his diary afresh with his second trip to Kansai in view of its enormous personal implications.

Sōchō tries to find a peaceful refuge three times, and each time he is frustrated. He leaves Suruga for Takigi in 1526, the westward direction of the trip being fortuitously symbolic of his Zen version of the Western Paradise where he expects to meet his end. But violence in the Kyoto area forces him to leave Takigi later that year. His place of winter seclusion in Yashima then proves only an imperfect retreat, where he still hears "news of the disruption in the capital" (*JS*: 122).

When the troops of the shogun and Takakuni camp nearby, Sōchō must leave and return to Suruga. In Sunpu, he again withdraws to distance himself from the unrest and gossip accompanying the begining of the regime of the new daimyo, Imagawa Ujiteru, but news of political discord nevertheless continues to reach him.

Sōchō's response to the intractable conflict between this-worldly and other-worldly desires is itself variegated. At times he shows us a man who is despondent, upbraiding himself for his own spiritual shortcomings:

On making deluded distinctions between life and death:

505	ika ni shite	As at Nakoso,
	nakoso to towaba	why do I say, "Stay away"?
	kokoro yori	It is, of course,
	hoka ni wa suenu	a barrier I erect
	seki ni zo arikeru	only in my own mind.

506	otowayama	I have heard of it,
	kikite mo ika de	as of Otowa Mountain,
	ōsaka ya	but when will we meet?
	seki no konata ni	On this side of the Gate at the Mountain of Meeting
	yasoji henuramu	I have now passed eighty years.

(*JS*: 140)

188

The Literature of Eremitism

Such emotions sometimes give rise to renewed strength of religious purpose, most notably on the occasion when he resolves to throw away his brush. But on other occasions he evidently subscribes to the notion that the writing he does in his hermitage and elsewhere may itself *lead* to enlightenment. Waka with overtly religious themes, such as those on evanescence or the nature of dreams and illusions quoted above, increase in the last two years covered by the journal. His occupation as renga master, of course, by no means ran entirely counter to religious concerns; one of his main duties was the composition of votive verses for dedication at temples or shrines.

And yet in other instances he adopts the solution of Ikkyū and Shōhaku, that when one truly understands the nature of nonduality, the question of renunciation itself becomes immaterial. He is moved to contemplate this solution while staying in a temporary lodging in Okitsu in Suruga:

> I have decided to go east as soon the new year begins, should I live so long, and have taken up travel lodgings at the "Hall of No Renunciation, [Fushain]," near the Okitsu manor. I thought the temple's name curious and made this poor attempt:

588
    oi no nochi
    sute sutezu to mo
      iigatami
    shibashi na ni nomi
    mezuru yado kana

After one grows old
it is just as difficult
   to renounce as not,
so for the moment I will enjoy
the cottage's name alone!

(*JS*: 163)

This observation then leads into another sōan sequence that reflects Sōchō's ambivalent attitude toward life in a hermitage and introduces a self-referential and heterochronic note, comparing this temporary dwelling with the earlier one in Yashima:

> The Hall of No Renunciation needs to have its roof repaired. One evening, when I was wondering what would happen should it rain or hail, I composed:

589
    kozo kotoshi
    sugi no itaya no
      mabara naru
    tsuki ni shigure o
    kikiakashitsuru

This year and last,
beneath the moon that shines through
   the gaps in the cedar planks
of a cottage, I have listened
until morning to the cold rain.

CHAPTER THREE

> Last year at this time I was staying in travel lodgings at Myōshōan, outside the gate of Shōrin'an in Yashima. I recalled how the wind from the Ibuki and Hira Mountains would blow the snow and hail through the thin cedar-plank door of my timeworn cottage, and engaged by the memory, I wrote the poem above to express my aged emotions. (*JS*: 164)

These ruminations on the trials of living lead to another outburst on the pain of life, especially old age, but then immediately to an attempt to come to terms with those trials by recognizing their ephemerality:

> My eightieth year is drawing to a close. In the last days of the tenth month, in distress as I continue to linger on in this life, I composed this:

590
hakanasa wa	If you would know
tsuyu yume awa no	of something evanescent
maboroshi no	as the illusions
hoka o tazuneba	of dew, of dreams, and of froth,
waga mi narikeri	Here is this life of mine.

(*JS*: 164)

Immediately thereafter he buoys himself up with thoughts of the sympathy shown him by others:

> Lord Nakamikado is now in Suruga. I have been taking the brine baths in Okitsu, and he was kind enough to include this verse in a letter to me here:

591
samuki yo wa	In the chilly night,
mukau uchi ni mo	sitting across from embers
uzumibi no	smoldering in the ashes,
okitsu no koto zo	it is to Okitsu
omoiyararuru	that I find my thoughts are straying.

My humble response:

592
akatsuki wa	Before the break of dawn,
ikeru bakari no	as I sit barely alive
okiitsutsu	like the glowing coals
omou koto to wa	at Okitsu, my thoughts dwell
oi no samukesa	on the coldness of old age.

(*JS*: 164)

Then Sōchō recounts the work he has done to make his existence in his sōan physically tolerable and aesthetically pleasing:

Composed in the darkness before dawn at my travel lodging, the Hall of No Renunciation:

593	yosoge ni mo	Even from afar
	sugi no nokiba no	one saw the rough gaps between
	itama arami	the eaves' cedar shakes,
	moranu shigure ni	so I had the roof repaired
	fukasetarikeri	to keep out the chilling rains.

(*JS*: 165)

In the space of a few lines, Sōchō's mind has wandered from thoughts on nonduality, to physical privation, to old age and philosophical acceptance, to friendship and again the cold of his aged dwelling, and finally to his effort to shore up his lodging, and with it, his spirits. He presents a portrait of a man struggling to reconcile the sōan ideal with a variegated and often conflicted life both in and apart from the world.

Even the trip east to which he referred in the introduction to the segment just quoted is double-edged, playing on the notion of leaving the world while at the same time being inevitably drawn to human contact. He writes this verse a few pages earlier:

556	yasoji zo yo	I am now eighty—
	moshi mo nao moshi	if I chance to live longer,
	nagaraeba	if I have that chance,
	iwaki no oku no	I think I will hide myself
	naka ni kakuremu	deep among the rocks and trees.

(*JS*: 155)

But the poem is only half-serious and in itself indicates the secular-sacred conflict, for Sōchō is also referring in a humorous, punning way to an invitation from Iwaki Minbunotaifu Yoshitaka to visit him in Iwaki Province (Fukushima Prefecture). Iwaki is a homophone for *iwaki*, "rocks and trees."

Sōchō's increasing desire to distance himself more fully from the world is symbolized by the changes he makes to his Brushwood Cottage garden. After returning to Mariko in 1527 he converts more than half the garden to dry field, in which he plants young greens (*JS*: 158). This is not an indication of lack of food, though Sōchō may indeed have made use of the produce from it, but rather a conscious attempt to achieve complete simplicity and naturalness in garden art.[79] Compare the understatement of Sōchō's garden to Shōhaku's, with its "great boulder in the front garden like a reclining dragon or a fierce tiger," his "stones from the seaside," and the "crimson plum" that "spans thirty or forty feet," which he had moved from a distant location.

But the increasing simplicity and rusticity of Brushwood Cottage itself combines ascetic and aesthetic concerns, for it reflects the taste of wabi or sōan tea just then becoming popular in the capital. Sōchō was personally acquainted with Murata Jukō's successor, Sōju, who like his teacher was an early proponent of sōan tea taste.[80] Sōchō wrote this in his diary for 1526:

> The so-called "Lower Capital Tea Coterie" practices a style of tea called *suki*, which they hold in four and one-half or six-mat rooms. At Sōju's, there are great pines and cedars inside the gate. All is clear and fresh within the fence. I noticed five or six fallen ivy leaves of deep color:

383   kesa ya yo no   This morning
       arashi o hirou   I pick up last night's storm—
         hatsumomiji   the first colored leaves.

(*JS*: 109)

It is not surprising that Sōchō should have been attracted to sōan tea, for it had much in common with the Zen teachings of Sōchō's teacher, Ikkyū. Murata Jukō, for example, was profoundly affected by the teachings and example of Ikkyū, with whom he studied. *Zencharoku*, attributed to Sen no Sōtan, the nephew or grandson of Rikyū, goes so far as to state, "The Zen-based tea ceremony began with the Zen priest Ikkyū of Daitokuji, because Jukō, of Shōmyōji Temple in Nara, was Ikkyū's religious disciple."[81] Jukō is believed to have lived for a time in Ikkyū's Shinjuan, and he cherished until his death a scroll he received from Ikkyū bearing the calligraphy of the Song monk Yuanwu Keqin, co-author of the Zen classic *Biyanlu* (The Blue Cliff Record). Jukō in turn willed it to Sōju.[82] The correlation between Sōchō's Zen experience and that of Jukō and his followers no doubt contributed to the approach to sōan taste they shared.

The Sōchō depicted in the journal, therefore, appears to feel an increased attraction as he ages to a simpler and more retired life, but one which responds to aesthetic as well as ascetic impulses, and he is constantly engaged by the problem of distancing himself from mundane concerns while continuing to discharge worldly responsibilities. It was the general practice even among Sōchō's lay contemporaries to take Buddhist vows when they advanced in years in order to prepare for the afterlife. Some achieved a solution by pursuing "urban reclusion" (*shichū no kakure*), building retreats that suggested both religious devotion but also aesthetic refinement.[83] Shōhaku's Dream Cottage is in some respects analogous. Sōchō's two closest friends at court in his last years, Sanjōnishi Sanetaka and the poet and musician Toyohara Muneaki, both built small retreats next to their Kyoto residences so they could enjoy the ascetic benefits of rustic and natural sōan life while remaining "in the world," just as Sōchō did, as he tells us in his chōka.[84] Bringing the sōan into the city or tasting the hermit's life while still taking part in secular affairs could be at once an aesthetic choice as well as one route toward resolution of the conflict between secularity and renunciation.

Sōchō's sōan passages, in sum, share elements of all the other rengashi sōan models introduced here, while constituting *in toto* a hermitage literature of a different sort. Shinkei in *Oi no kurigoto* depicts a successful escape from a gloomy world into an ideal haven, and he leaves no doubt as to which he perceives as better. Shōhaku too presents almost exclusively an ideal refuge. Both have achieved their desires and tell their tales from a timeless, serenely closed, and univocal perspective. Sōchō's account contains elements compatible with those epical approaches, but he blends them with other moments of conflict into an open-ended and dialogic portrait of one who is still in process, still dealing with conflicting desires and the competing attractions of the sacred and the profane. His portrayals of sōan life are a mix of religious ideals, aesthetic pleasure, and existential conflict. Sōchō creates a picture of a specific, ongoing, dialogic life, one that both incorporates and reaches beyond the established boundaries of the sōan genre. As such it becomes a literary correlative of the blend of classicism and iconoclasm, religion and quotidian humanism, that characterized the Sengoku Age.

CHAPTER
FOUR

"A diary of things both serious and frivolous"

Poetry in 'The Journal of Sōchō'

    The essential nature of renga is dialogic, its interest and effect resulting from the linking of individual (but mutually influenced) poetic subjectivities. The history of the genre too is one of ongoing dialogue between diverse poetic traditions: the courtly and the popular, the orthodox and the unorthodox, the sacred and the profane. Interaction between those competing traditions increased in intensity throughout the Age of the Country at War, reflecting the unprecedented social and cultural collision of that era. The vigor of the interplay between diverse poetic styles and attitudes is nowhere better preserved than in Sōchō's journal.

    Like his travel and hermitage writing, Sōchō's waka and renga developed directly out of received orthodoxy, which in the case of poetry stemmed from the imperial poetic anthologies, particularly *Kokinshū* and *Shinkokinshū*, as interpreted through the teaching and practice of his teacher, Sōgi. Sōchō was a lifelong advocate of Sōgi's orthodox poetic approach, employing it in his own waka and renga and teaching it to his students. But Sōchō was also uncommonly attracted to unorthodox haikai poetry, which was just at that time emerging from its subsidiary status and beginning to be considered, even by orthodox practitioners, as an independent art form with its own standards, recapitulating the ontogeny through which high renga had gained its orthodox status nearly two centuries before.

CHAPTER FOUR

The more than six hundred waka, renga, and wakan renku included in the journal, almost three-quarters of which are by Sōchō himself, run the gamut from highly formal occasional pieces and deeply serious memorial verses for the dead to fugitive "throw away" (*iisute*) comic efforts composed at convivial drinking parties.[1] Sōchō was one of the first poets to record in a single document of evident literary intent not only the formal verses but also the more spontaneous efforts that comprised such a large part of the poetic interaction of the time but which are now largely lost. When read together with the prefaces and commentaries that often accompany them, they suggest both the range of Sōchō's own literary activity and the variety of social and cultural functions that poetry served in medieval society.

Linked Verse in the 'Journal'

The interactions in Sōchō's diary between orthodoxy and heterodoxy and between the elite and the popular traditions also animate the history of the linked-verse genre.[2] The birth of the art was traditionally traced in part to the mythic exchange of courting songs recorded in *Kojiki* (712) between the male and female gods Izanagi and Izanami, out of whose union the Japanese islands were said to have been formed. Linked verse was therefore seen as coeval with the land itself; Sōchō himself concludes a short treatise on etiquette for the renga session with the pronouncement that "our land came into being out of this poetic way."[3] This purported divine provenance had its popular correlative in ancient transactional courting verses, often of a challenge and response character, between men and women on days set aside for such rituals.[4] The earliest recorded linked verses per se are by courtiers, who, together with the clerical community, were capable of preserving them not only in oral but in written form. The most famous of these is the exchange of nineteen-syllable *katuata* poems between the divine prince Yamato Takeru no Mikoto and his Keeper of the Fires:

>   niibari   After passing
>   tsukuba o sugite   Niibari and Tsukuba,
>   iku yo ka netsuru   how many nights have I slept?

The Keeper of the Fires replied:

>   kaganabete   Counting them up,
>   yo ni wa kokonoyo   of nights there have been nine,
>   hi ni wa tōka o   and of days there have been ten.[5]

The exchange of verses, which combine into a single *sedōka* poem, gave the name The Way of Tsukuba to the linked-verse art. The earliest extant example of two verses of seventeen and fourteen syllables joining to form an amoebic waka appears in *Man'yōshū* (c. 759).[6] The first reference to an actual linked-verse session appears in *Mitsuneshū*, the personal poetry collection of the *Kokinshū* poet Ōshikōchi Mitsune. The collection includes a group of ten verses linked into five waka poems that were probably composed at a gathering to view the autumn leaves in 918.[7] Thereafter the practice of linking two verses into a single waka, now known as *tanrenga* (short renga), became a common form of court entertainment, and select examples of the art begin appearing in imperial waka anthologies starting with the second such compilation, *Gosenshū* (951). Longer chains of verse appeared in the late Heian period, and the hundred-verse sequence (hyakuin) became the norm at about the time of *Shinkokinshū* in the thirteenth century. Though such amoebic poetry was composed by elites and nonelites alike, the written history of the linked-verse genre has concentrated on that practiced by elites, the custodians of written culture. But the tradition of popular linked verse, largely oral in nature, continued throughout the evolution of the genre.

Heian courtly renga was in general a witty game, indulged in after the more serious work of waka composition was completed. Waka was for the ages; renga was for fun. As waka composition became increasingly serious in the late Heian and early Kamakura periods due to the development of hereditary poetic schools and poetry competitions, some courtly linked verse became imbued with the elegant diction and topics of waka, growing further and further removed from the vigorous transactional repartee that had characterized the earlier examples of the art. Ijichi Tetsuo has therefore asserted that it is the earlier form that constitutes the true linked-verse orthodoxy.[8] Courtiers with reputations for serious poetry to protect concentrated on the *ushin* (lit., possessing heart) variety; others chose to enjoy themselves with the lighter type, known as *mushin* (without heart). The dialogue between the two traditions was institutionalized through linked-verse competitions between ushin and mushin teams at court in the reign of Gotoba, commissioner of *Shinkokinshū*. But the emphasis remained on entertainment, and prizes were awarded to the winners.

Nor were the courtly (*dōjō*) and commoner (*jige*) poetic circles ever entirely separate. Indeed, there was increasing interaction between the two groups over time. As noted in Chapter One, for example, the locus of the renga session was conceived of as a space where poets of varying social degree could interact with relatively few constraints. That had been true since the early Middle

Ages, when people of all classes gathered "beneath the blossoms" (*hananomoto*) and linked verses under the direction of masters of commoner background.[9] The cherry blossoms delimited a sacral and largely non-hierarchical space, since it was there that gods were believed to descend.[10] The tradition of commonality extended as well to "hatted" (*kasagi*) sessions, where without even doffing their hats, passersby might link verses to compositions by seated participants. Though the "beneath the blossoms" tradition died out in the fourteenth century, "hatted" sessions continued long thereafter at Kitano and other shrines.[11] To be sure, the poetic style espoused by courtier linked-verse poets was somewhat different from that favored by commoners (and of course to speak in terms of a unitary style for either group is reductive). The courtier Nijō Yoshimoto and the priestly commoner Kyūsei recognized the respective strengths in both strains, the elegant diction and waka-like sophistication of courtly renga and the vigor and strong individual links of commoner verses, and they fostered that blend in their poetry, their renga treatises such as *Tsukuba mondō*, and the first imperially recognized renga anthology, *Tsukubashū* (1356–57).[12]

But while their work sought to achieve stylistic fusion, it resulted in fission as well. Their anthology was a *Kokinshū* of linked verse; it established an elite standard, a high renga orthodoxy. Implicit in their enterprise was the conviction that linked verse was not simply a game but, like waka, a vehicle for the lyric expression of concerns that were at once deeply personal yet universal. Though their anthology collected verses written over a long time period, it concentrated on the elegant (ga) tradition and tended to exclude the more plebeian (zoku) forms of the renga genre. Like *Kokinshū*, *Tsukubashū* did include one book containing haikai, verses that were judged to fall outside the standard of elegance demonstrated by the anthology as a whole but were near enough to that standard to merit inclusion. The anthology did not excise the entire unorthodox tradition. But its definition of haikai was restrictive, limited to those verses that bent the orthodoxy while remaining within its ambit. Two general traditions were thus developing at the same time, one compatible with the Yoshimoto / Kyūsei orthodoxy and another, more zoku in character, that continued to be practiced on a wide scale by commoner poets and at times by courtiers as well, but of which few examples remain. It is a mistake, however, to conceive of a unilaterally hegemonic courtly ushin tradition in competition with and occasionally subverted by an equally exclusive plebeian tradition of parody and laughter. The two genres and the two social strata constantly interacted. Kubukihara Rei has cogently pointed out that even that most ushin of orthodox poetic monuments, *Shinkokinshū*, displays a balance between the ushin and mushin tonalities, the mushin providing a rough-hewn energy, and the ushin then refining that impulse. It is the interplay between these two tonalities that animates Sōchō's journal.[13]

Sōgi continued these dual tendencies toward blending and excision, both in his anthologies and in his own verse. His ushin renga style is generally seen to have developed in large part through the influence of two of the finest linked-verse masters of the previous generation, Sōzei and Shinkei.[14] They were in turn the two best-represented poets in Sōgi's first anthology of renga, *Chikurinshō*, which was meant to help establish a high canon of ushin renga style.[15] Nearly two decades later, Sōgi undertook the task of compiling a second imperially recognized collection of linked verse, *Shinsen tsukubashū*. In this anthology, Sōgi focused on verse from only the preceding six decades, as he viewed the work of the immediate successors of *Tsukubashū* compilers Yoshimoto and Kyūsei as insufficiently orthodox.[16] The verses constitute what Sōgi considered the finest products of the "renga renaissance" that began in the early fifteenth century, a leap in the literary sophistication of the linked-verse art fostered in part through the waka teachings of Shōtetsu and in part through bakufu patronage.[17] Sōgi's *Shinsen tsukubashū* concentrated entirely on the ushin style of renga and, unlike its imperially recognized predecessor, it excluded all haikai poetry, even that defined in terms of ushin standards. Sōgi was thus pursuing in the arena of renga style a project similar to that which he pursued in travel literature in *Shirakawa kikō*: the determination of an ushin prescription.

Sōgi's conception of ushin poetry was based on earlier waka theoretical formulations.[18] In judgments on waka poetry compositions, the term "ushin" had long been used in reference to those verses which responded most completely to the "basic essence" of the topic on which the verse was to be composed. Ushin poetry, therefore, was that which evoked what centuries of poetic tradition had determined was universal to human experience. The term was used in wide and narrow senses; it could refer to orthodox poetry as a whole, or simply to one particular type of verse, especially that favored by Fujiwara Teika in his last years. For Teika, the ushin quality stemmed not only from the gravity and polish of the verse, but from the "deep feeling" of the poet during the process of composition.[19] This emphasis on the correct mental attitude for composing poetry carries directly through to the advice of Sōgi, Sōchō, and others about how to prepare for and participate in an ushin renga sequence. Ushin poetry was therefore a mind-set as well as a poetic type, and as such it infused all orthodox styles, not simply the one Teika labeled the "style of deep feeling."[20] For Sōgi, ushin poetry in its widest meaning transcended the realm of aesthetics; it was instead a way that combined lyricism, religion, and ethics. Ushin poetry was the apex of the poetic endeavor and the estimable goal of any who would set out on the poetic way. His advice in *Azuma mondō* outlines the character of ushin poetry in its largest sense and also employs the word in its more narrow meaning as one of several orthodox styles:

> *Question*: What is the fundamental configuration [*sugata*] of linked verse?
>
> *Answer*: In waka there are ten fundamental styles and perhaps as many as twenty-eight.[21] According to Sōzei, there are ten as well in linked verse. In my humble opinion it would be difficult to reduce that number. But of those ten, the most important ultimately are those of loftiness [*taketakaku*], ineffable beauty [*yūgen*], and deep feeling [*ushin*]. Though linked verse should not deviate from the elegance [*fuzei*] of waka, few poets understand what that concept means. Some poets descend to coarse words and low conceptions, and one may find that in linking to such verses, one is led down the wrong path, forgetting ineffable beauty in spite of oneself. This is a primary difficulty. It is a mark of true skill if one can overcome such problems when they appear and produce a verse with overtones [*yojō/yosei*]. It is the height of misfortune for people to misunderstand this and think of renga as something vulgar.
>
> In short, if you would attain elegance with loftiness and ineffable beauty, you should always study and reflect upon verses like these by Hitomaro and Akahito:

> saoshika no
> tsumadou yama no
> okabe naru
> wasada wa karaji
> shimo wa oku to mo

> I will not cut
> the early rice in the field
> on the hill
> where the stag calls its mate,
> even if the frost settles there.[22]

> mi ni samuku
> aki no sayokaze
> fuku nabe ni
> furinishi hito no
> yume ni mietsutsu

> When the wind
> in the autumn night
> blows chill,
> the one now gone
> appears to me in dreams.[23]

> akikaze ni
> yama tobikoyuru
> karigane no
> iya tōzakari
> kumogakuretsutsu

> The geese
> that fly over the mountains
> in the autumn wind
> become ever more distant
> and disappear into the clouds.[24]

waka no ura ni	When the tide
shio michikureba	rises in Waka Bay,
kata o nami	the tidal pools are covered
ashibe o sashite	and the cranes call as they fly off
tazu nakiwataru	toward the reeds on the shore.[25]
tago no ura ni	At Tago Cove
uchiidete mireba	I round the bend and gaze:
shirotae no	like white cloth
fuji no takane ni	on Fuji's lofty peak,
yuki wa furitsutsu	the snow is falling.[26]

Also consider the captivating verses of poets such as Narihira, Ise, Komachi, Tsurayuki, Tadamine, Shunzei, Lord Gokyōgoku [Fujiwara Yoshitsune], Jichin, Jakuren, Teika, and Ietaka. If one tries to match one's own linked verse to those, its content [*kokoro*] and configuration [*sugata*] will imperceptibly begin to improve. It is just as in the verse "Frolic in the blossoms and their scent will fill your robes" . . .

In renga, one should take as fundamental the verses of Sōzei, Chikamasa, Shinkei, Senjun, and the like, that have deep feeling [*kokoro mo fukaku*] and beautiful language [*kotoba mo utsukushiku*].[27]

For Sōgi, then, ushin poetry in its widest sense, as Etō describes it, was that "which one pursued as an all-encompassing way (michi), venerating loftiness that transcends reality, searching for beauty and truth, and recognizing the poverty of the evanescent self."[28] Sōgi viewed the pursuit of ushin poetry as a search for universals.[29] The same perspective informed his approach to travel writing in *Shirakawa kikō*. His conception of ushin poetry was so compelling that it fixed renga style in time; the ushin verses of his disciples are distinguished less by new directions than by the skill with which they display the Sōgi ushin orthodoxy. Sōgi is generally credited with effecting through his teachings and personal example the most sensitively integrated renga sequences, in which all poets surrendered a degree of individuality to achieve a harmonious blend of subjectivities through the hundred verses. While each poet at the session spoke in his own voice, contributing to the dialogic quality of the whole, those voices were carefully modulated by clearly defined ushin guidelines for both lexicon and content. Under Sōgi, then, renga achieved something of a balance between the dialogic and transactional origins of the genre and the comparatively unitary voice of ushin waka poetry.

This was the renga orthodoxy to which Sōchō was heir, and it informed his own poetic practice and the guidance he provided to others at renga sessions and in his written instruction. The composition of ushin renga was for Sōchō the most important activity depicted in his journal; renga sessions with military hosts or with other renga masters and hokku composed on request were the background against which other events in his life and other literary genres provided sporadic counterpoint.

It is ironic, therefore, that those renga sessions are generally represented in the journal by the hokku verse alone, and only very occasionally by the second and third verse immediately following. In no case are even the first eight verses, which are recorded on the front of the first sheet of recording paper, provided, not to mention an entire hundred-verse sequence. Sōchō was particularly skilled in the art of linking, the essence of the renga genre, and the advice in his handbooks concentrates not only on the construction of each verse but on a variety of linking techniques.

In renga, every link was born of personal poetic inspiration and of interpretation of the link that preceded it. The renga text was thus a quintessential "writerly" text; the maker of each succeeding link became quite literally a producer of meaning of the previous one.[30] Renga interpretation, in fact, begins with the basic maxim that each verse has three meanings: one as a semantically self-contained verse, one when interpreted together with the maeku, and one when it is itself recast as a maeku by the verse that follows.

At the standard renga session, each poet would vie with the others to be the first to compose a link, which he would at the moment of inspiration convey aloud to the scribe and the renga master. The scribe would repeat the verse aloud, mentally check it for infractions of the renga rules, and then, if the renga master concurred, he would write it down. But even as the earlier poet presented his verse, the other poets were already framing potential rejoinders. In *Renga hikyōshū*, Sōchō or one of his co-authors compares the essential competitive nature of linked verse to another favorite pastime of the period: "Linked verse is no different from sending a number of hawks after a bird; the best one seizes the prey, and the rest return without."[31] But the high renga ideal called for individual competition to be mitigated at all times with group cooperation in the interest of a pleasing totality. The blend was orchestrated by the renga master, who not only worked with the scribe to make sure that each verse followed the hundreds of renga rules, but that it fit aesthetically into its place in the sequence.

The balance of competition and harmony, entertaining play and high aesthetic purpose changed, of course, from session to session. The sessions recorded in Sōchō's journal run the gamut from highly formal votive affairs such as *Ise senku*, composed by Sōchō and Sōseki for dedication at Ise Shrine, to extemporaneous comic verses linked over food and wine, such as the Takigi haikai of 1523.

The only verse in any renga sequence for which those characteristics did not necessarily apply was the first verse, the hokku. While subsequent links were generally composed orally and extemporaneously in the heat of the moment and according to the constraints set by the preceding maeku, the hokku could be prepared in advance in isolation, and it initially stood alone.[32] It also responded to certain special referential circumstances. Whereas the succeeding ninety-nine verses bore no necessary connection to the actual conditions prevailing at the session, the hokku was required to indicate the season and the location in which the session was being held and the degree of formality of the occasion (the three requirements being known in sum as the "season, place, and level," *ji-sho-i*). The season was indicated by a "seasonal word" (*kigo*), and the place was often suggested by reference to a local utamakura or nearby scenery. As his journal entries indicate, Sōchō frequently resorted to utamakura references in hokku that he was asked to compose for particularly important sessions that he was not expected personally to attend. Since he was not always able in such cases to be familiar with the local scenery, he could fulfill the place requirement by mentioning a famous local site. The question of level of formality is related to matters of overall tone; whether, for example, the sequence was meant for presentation to a temple or a shrine, for the consolation of the spirit of someone deceased, or for a less exalted purpose.

By Sōchō's time, hokku were normally also expected to contain a *kireji* or "cutting word," such as *ya* or *kana*, that would contribute to the verse's capacity to stand as an independent poetic statement.[33] But while the hokku had to be able to stand alone, it also had to have "linkability," something to which the second, or *waki*, verse could respond. The hokku and waki were often perceived as a greeting (*aisatsu*) between the guest, who was traditionally afforded the honor of composing the hokku, and the host, who responded with the link. The institution of "guest, first verse; host, second verse" (*kyaku hokku teishu waki*) symbolized the interpersonal and dialogic nature of the enterprise.[34]

The hokku, furthermore, set the tone for the entire sequence and had to be appropriately elevated, though the degree of loftiness varied according to the level (*kurai*) of the sequence as a whole. In his *Nagabumi*, Sōchō writes that "since the hokku begins the composition, it will sound weak if it is composed like a regular verse," and he adds in *Amayo no ki* (Rainy Night Record, 1519) that the hokku, waki, and *daisan* (third) verses (as opposed to the generic *hiraku* verses) "should have loftiness and ineffable beauty."[35] These opinions mirror those of Sōgi. The hokku thus tended to be objective and impersonal even by the quality of non-individuation that governed the sequence as a whole. And yet the best hokku avoided stereotypicity and attempted, within the bounds of orthodoxy, to say something new or to express an old thought in a new way. The hokku, therefore, required a particularly skilled poet; this explains why Sōchō was so frequently asked to provide one.[36]

Though there no doubt were many cases of extemporaneous hokku composition, the hokku was thus the least spontaneous of the verses in a hyakuin. It was also less arbitrary than the other verses of the sequence, in that it had to adhere to the rules of season, place, and level. In his journal, Sōchō provides very specific commentary on these referential relationships:

542   unohana ya   Deutzia blossoms—
       nami moteyueru   a garland of waves encircling
       okitsushima   the ocean island.[37]

> Here, I was likening the castle and its environs to an island and the waves to deutzia blossoms that adorn the island's tresses. I was referring to the poem that goes: "It encircles itself / with a garland of white waves / such as the sea god / uses to decorate his hair— / the island of Awaji." (*JS*: 150)

As in this verse, hokku often have two interpretations, a surface meaning of generalized artistic beauty to which the waki verse is linked and an underlying and more referential meaning which is not apparent from the words themselves but is implied and apparent to those at the session. Explanatory material in the way of prefaces and commentaries is thus particularly important in the case of hokku, and personal linked-verse collections normally include notes on time and place of composition for those verses alone. *The Journal of Sōchō* is especially valuable in this wise because its background information on hokku verses is often far more detailed than that included in the poet's personal linked-verse collections.

To provide a more complete conception of the nature of the activity to which so much of the journal refers, it is worthwhile briefly to consider the first eight verses from a renga sequence in which Sōchō was involved. One example is a two-poet work Sōchō mentions in his journal, *Yashima Shōrin'an naniki hyakuin*, composed with his disciple Sōboku in 1527 while he was wintering at Shōrin'an temple east of Lake Biwa.[38] The *Yashima* sequence is particularly useful to us here because it was composed not by a large group of poets but by two gifted renga masters intent on producing artistry and heuristic value, and because Sōboku later composed a commentary for it in which he recorded observations Sōchō made about the composition as it unfolded, as well as remarks of his own. The commentary concentrates less on stylistics than on the process of composition, recapitulating the interpretive work each poet mentally carried out on the preceding verse, the maeku, before framing a reply. In addition to Sōboku's remarks, there survives in a private collection a second, unpublished commentary on the sequence, the Ōta manuscript, which appears to have been compiled by a spectator at the session.[39] Though Sōchō makes no reference to this, he and Sōboku were evidently composing in front of an audience of other poets and disciples.

The two master poets were therefore engaged not only in the production of a written artifact but in an oral performance. Here too, the art of linked verse is a blended art, involving a "writerly" text to be sure, but one that is initially created orally in a performative environment.[40]

Sōchō describes the occasion in his journal as follows:

> Sōboku requested a hokku from Lord Sanetaka. At my travel lodging we added to it a second and then a third verse. Our determination to complete the sequence was sustained by the deep impression made by the hokku, and we finally reached the hundredth link.

489
>
> ume ga ka o
> kieaenu yuki ya
> niouramu
>
> Is there a scent
> of plum blossoms
> in the lingering snow?

> His conception of detecting the fragrance of plums in the snow when one is "deeply tinged with the desire for them" makes a departure from the foundation poem. (*JS*: 137)

Sōboku's commentary on the *Yashima* sequence provides further information for Sanetaka's hokku:

> The meaning of this hokku is that when the spring becomes redolent of plums, the snow is finally supposed to melt. But it stubbornly remains and becomes imbued with plum fragrance itself, to interesting effect. Having the plums blossom within the lingering snow is most engaging. The hokku masterfully finds a new beauty in both the fragrance of the plum blossoms and the lingering snow. Sōchō said that the first five syllables were used particularly effectively.[41]

kokorozashi	Was it since my heart
fukaku someteshi	was so deeply tinged
orikereba	with the desire for them
kieaenu yuki no	that I mistook the lingering snow
hana to miyuran	for blossoms?[42]

This must be the foundation poem.

    Sōchō also said that ending a hokku with the conjectural suffix *ran* must be done with some care, and examples are consequently rare. Lord Sanetaka had requested that I ask Sōchō about it, as he was attempting it for the first time.[43] Sōchō praised the verse, saying it was in no way inferior even to these:

tsuki hososhi	The moon, a crescent.
katsura ya shigeri	Has its laurel tree burgeoned forth
kakusuran	and hidden the rest?
	Senjun[44]

na zo takaki	The renowned full moon—
tsuki ya katsura o	all its laurel boughs
oritsuran	must have been broken off!
	Sōgi[45]

Sōchō counseled that one should compose in a similar mode when using the *ran* ending. (*Yashima* 201)

    Sōboku's comments begin with an explanation of the relationship between Sanetaka's verse and its waka foundation poem (*honka*). Hokku frequently made reference to such poems, both to expand their own connotative world and also to assume an aura of neoclassical waka elegance. Sōboku then goes on to state that Sōchō paid the verse his highest possible compliment, favorably comparing it to verses of similar construction by two of the greatest poets in the renga tradition, his own teacher Sōgi and a teacher of Sōgi, Senjun, one of the Seven Sages. The commentary thus at once elucidates Sanetaka's verse and praises it in terms of the neoclassic ushin tradition, both through comparison to *Kokinshū* and through famous renga verses of earlier generations.

    Sōchō's own entry in his journal regarding the verse, quoted above, provides similar information. He evidently considers the foundation poem too obvious to repeat in full. Sōchō points out that Sanetaka at once refers to the earlier verse and also reinterprets it by suggesting that as opposed to the imagined blossoms of the foundation poem, the plums at Yashima and the snow both actually exist, the plums infusing the snow itself with their fragrance. Sanetaka was able to combine in his verse venerable words with a new conception, and Sōchō and Sōboku in their respective commentaries acknowledge these ideal qualities for a successful hokku.

Sanetaka's hokku responds to the necessary requirements of season and place by referring to the word *ume* (plum), a seasonal word for spring, the season in which the sequence was composed. The word "ume" also gives the title to the sequence.[46] Renga sequences were conventionally identified by the date of their composition and by formulas known as *fushimono*. The fushimono title of the *Yashima* sequence is *naniki*, "what kind of tree," and the answer supplied by the verse is ume, plum tree. Such fushimono were holdovers from earlier renga games in which poets were required to compose as many verses as possible on the same fushimono subjects.

The task of composing the link to Sanetaka's verse fell to Sōboku:

2   akebono samumi   Since the dawn is cold,
     kiiru uguisu   the warbler comes and alights.

As Sōchō's remarks in his journal indicate, both he and Sōboku felt particularly honored to have a hokku from Lord Sanetaka to begin their sequence, and they were both therefore anxious to provide a suitable waki verse. *Nikonshū*, Arakida Morihira's collection of poetic anecdotes centering around Ise Shrine, relates that "they composed twenty waki for the hokku, and Sōchō said all were poor." Finally Sōboku hit on the warbler verse above, and Sōchō judged it "more or less acceptable."[47] Because Sōchō and Sōboku were composing together as master and disciple, they were able to spend time discussing and rejecting alternative verses before selecting this one. Part of the reason for its success is that it elegantly responds to the hokku while at the same time recasting it; where the relationship with the *Kokinshū* foundation poem gives the initially independent hokku a human subject, the point of view of the verse shifts to that of a warbler when connected to the waki. When juxtaposed, then, the two verses may be interpreted, "Because the dawn is cold, the warbler comes and alights on a branch where it may have caught the scent of plum blossoms in the unmelted snow." Such unexpected changes are the essence of the linked-verse art.

Sōboku then goes on to compare the waki to two famous earlier links between a hokku and a waki verse, one pair by Chiun and Shinkei and another by Sōgi and Sōchō. Again his advice, which we need not linger over here, demonstrates that linking occurs not only between verses but between generations, with the poets of different ages joined in a single orthodoxy. While he comments on matters related to meaning and style, he takes it for granted that the reader will know already how to analyze the hokku and the waki in terms of their "topical" and "lexical" categories and understand how such categories must be related to each other according to the renga rules.[48] It is a commonplace of renga composition that each link (*tsukeai*) in a sequence is related both through the sense of the two verses involved as well as through conventionalized relationships between the topical and lexical categories of the verses. The hokku here, for example, falls into the topical category of Spring, as indicated by the words "plum" and "lingering snow" (*kieaenu yuki*). "Plum" also falls into the lexical category of Plants, and "snow" into that of Falling Things. It was second nature for Sōchō, Sōboku, and the spectators at the session to recognize these structural characteristics of the first verse and then to relate them to the renga rules, which stipulate how often certain images may appear in a sequence (the rules of repetition), how long an image or category may or may not continue successively (the rules of duration or seriation), and how many verses must pass before a particular image or category may reappear once used (the rules of intermission). In the case of the *Yashima* sequence, Sōboku's link was conditioned not only by the meaning of the hokku but by the rule of duration directing that verses in the spring category must continue for at least three verses and for no more than five. Even had Sōboku been inclined to add a link whose imagery assigned it to the topical category of Autumn, for example, such a verse would have been proscribed by the rules. The poets would also have to keep in mind that the word "plum" could appear only five times in a sequence. "Snow" could appear only four times in total, and it had to be separated from other words in the Falling Things category by three verses unless followed immediately by one in the verse that followed. And the word "warbler" itself was too brilliant an image ever to be repeated in the hundred verses.

Every poet at the session was expected to have a thorough knowledge of the rules, which had gradually taken shape over the centuries. In the Kamakura period (1185–1333) numerous different sets of renga rules were privately compiled, a phenomenon which doubtless gave rise to discord at renga sessions.[49] Differences were magnified when poets from diverse areas were drawn to the capital in the Kenmu Restoration after the collapse of the Kamakura bakufu. A broadside at the time lampooned the state of affairs, claiming that renga sessions were in disarray due to the mixing of Kyoto and Kamakura poets and that anyone now felt qualified to be a judge for renga gatherings.[50]

To end this confusion, Yoshimoto and Kyūsei compiled a set of rules meant for uniform adoption called *Ōan shinshiki* (New Rules of the Ōan Era) and revised them in about 1374–75. Those rules were refined by Yoshimoto's grandson Ichijō Kaneyoshi in association with Sōzei in 1452, and additional refinements were added by Shōhaku in 1501. Sōchō and Sōboku were using Shōhaku's rules, entitled *Renga shinshiki tsuika narabi ni shinshiki kon'an tō* (New Rules of Linked Verse with Additions, Plus Current Ideas on the New Rules, Etc.).[51] Standardization of the renga rules contributed to the blending of disparate participants at a session and gave linked-verse a foundation for nationwide application. It meant that Sōchō could be generally sure that wherever he went, his fellow poets and students would be operating with the same basic principles in mind.

The rules were initially developed in part to facilitate renga as a game, but in their final form they were meant to enhance the aesthetic qualities of the sequence, helping to modulate the imagistic patterns in order to encourage constant development (yukiyō) and to avoid repetition (rinne, lit. rebirth). Linked verse thus became an existential metaphor, in which poets journeyed through successive verse worlds, the appearance and disappearance of images reflecting the evanescence of all things.

When contemplating Sanetaka's hokku, Sōboku's imagination was also conditioned by traditional waka conventions. These conventions involved not only the basic essences of love, travel, and so forth, but also associations between images that had developed through their juxtaposition in waka poetry. Such associations (*yoriai*) were another fundamental element of the linking process. Sanetaka's use of the word "plum," for example, would have immediately suggested to Sōboku the word "warbler," for the two images frequently appeared together in waka poetry and their association had subsequently been codified in handbooks that listed hundreds of such connections. The most famous of those handbooks of associations was *Renju gappekishū* (Collection of Linked Pearls and Joined Jewels, 1476), compiled by Ichijō Kaneyoshi.[52] Under the word "plum" it lists the following conventional associations: "snow," "warbler," "someone's waving sleeve," "color and fragrance," "moon," "mountain hamlet," "eaves," "fence," "window," "master," "spring of the past," "soon fall," "southern branches," "willow," "cherry," and "eight-fold."[53] The traditional association between "plum," "warbler," and "snow" had been developed through poems such as *Kokinshū* 1: 5:

> ume ga e ni 　　　　Though a warbler
> kiiru uguisu 　　　　alights on a plum branch

> haru kakete
> nakedomo imada
> yuki wa furitsutsu
>
> then raises its voice in song
> in the long-awaited spring,
> the snow continues to fall.

This poem also serves Sōboku as a foundation honka for his waki verse. Such conventional associations may sound arbitrary and artistically stifling, but they were developed over centuries to suggest universal poetic relationships. To absorb the range of associations listed in a renga handbook for a particular image is to understand its conceptual place in the neoclassical poetic imagination.

Doubtless one of the reasons Sōchō approved of Sōboku's final attempt at a waki verse was both because its honka established a particularly close connection to the spirit of the hokku and because the second verse, like the first, was related to one from *Kokinshū*. The second verse thus responds to the classic elegance of the hokku but at the same time departs from the immediate locale in which the sequence is being composed. The third verse is then required to relate only to the second verse and to cut itself off completely from the first. Failure to do so results in a "clash" (*uchikoshi*), the most elementary and serious of rule infractions because it inhibits the sequence from developing in a new direction.

For the third verse of the *Yashima* sequence, Sōchō composed this:

> 3   kasumi tatsu
>   tani no toyama no
>   haru miete
>
>   In the rising haze
>   of the foothills round the valley
>   spring appears.

Sōchō's response is conditioned by the requirement that the Spring topic continue for at least three verses, and he indicates the season with the words "spring" (*haru*) and "haze" (*kasumi*). Because haze is a Rising Thing, another word from that lexical category will have to either appear immediately hereafter or be separated by at least three verses. The word association he uses involves "warbler" (*uguisu*) and "valley" (*tani*), listed for example in *Renju gappekishū* (no. 87). The third verse of a sequence also normally ends in the continuative particle *te*.[54] When juxtaposed with the previous verse, the connotative world of the third verse is again altered and enlarged: "As the dawn is still cold, the warbler comes and alights in a tree in the foothills round the valley where the haze rises; both the warbler and the haze are signs of spring." A synthetic reading of the first three verses together might encourage one to conflate the images of a warbler on a snow-covered plum branch and the rising haze of the foothills, but such an interpretation would be to introduce an uchikoshi into the sequence. Verse three has already taken leave of the world of the first link; here a warbler alights, but the snow and the plum can by definition no longer figure in the interpretative matrix.

Sōboku is explicit on this matter in his comments on Sōchō's link:

> Sōchō said that there is also an established style for the third verse in a sequence. It must be at once well linked to the waki but no less important; the verse should be as lofty as the hokku. Here, the waki combines with the hokku to create a gorgeous image of a warbler alighting on a snowy branch in the cold dawn, suggesting that it was attracted by the scent of the blossoms in the snow. But because of the word "cold" [*samumi*], the third verse will return to the hokku if the place where the warbler alights is not completely shifted. It was for that reason that Sōchō introduced "foothills round the valley" [*tani no toyama*]. The word "valley" naturally links with "cold," but the place where the warbler alights is in the nearby mountains where spring appears in the haze. That locale is different from the earlier one with snow and plums. The style is also appropriately elevated for a third verse. (*Yashima* 203)

A valley remains cold longer since it lies in the shade of the hills that surround it, and as Sōboku indicates, the words "valley" and "cold" are conventionally associated.[55] The foothills that surround a village are warmer, and haze appears there, heralding spring. In the context of the third verse, the warbler is seen as abandoning a cold valley for the warmer foothills. It was another poetic convention for the warbler to leave a valley when spring arrived; the words "warbler" and "emerge from the valley" (*tani yori izuru*) are associated in *Renju gappekishū* (no. 363), on the basis of such verses as *Kokinshū* 1: 14, by Ōe Chisato:

uguisu no	Were it not for the song
tani yori izuru	of the warbler as it emerges
koe naku wa	from the valley,
haru kuru koto o	who would have an inkling
tare ka shiramashi	that springtime had arrived?

The foothills in the third *Yashima* verse become doubly suggestive of spring, therefore, because they are the locus of both the haze and the warbler, two paramount spring images. The word "cold" thus no longer needs necessarily to relate to snow-covered blossoms, and an uchikoshi is avoided. Sōchō has skillfully resolved the difficulty of the word "snow" in verse two, and in addition he has evoked the lofty tone he deems proper for a third verse.

The first three verses of an orthodox renga sequence, known together as the *mitsumono* (lit., three things), are particularly important in a renga sequence; they are elevated and elegant in tone and considerable time is taken in their composition. Collections exist, in fact, of the first three verses alone of various sequences.[56] The fourth through the ninety-ninth verses (the hiraku verses) are more generic, but they become progressively less conservative as the sequence progresses.

The fourth *Yashima* verse, by Sōchō, reads:

| 4 | tsumagi no michi mo | The trails for gathering wood |
| | ato kasuka nari | have likewise grown faint. |

In a normal renga sequence with seven or eight poets, a verse would not normally be linked to another by the same individual. In the case of a two-poet sequence, however, both poets must occasionally link to their own verses; otherwise one poet would compose nothing but seventeen-syllable verses (*kami no ku* or *chōku*) and the other, nothing but fourteen-syllable ones (*shimo no ku* or *tanku*). In the context of the previous verse, Sōchō's composition reads: "In the foothills round the valley the haze brings signs of spring and also obscures the traces of trails for gathering brushwood."

Now that the requirement of three spring verses has been completed, Sōchō is free to either stay in that season or to depart from it. He chooses to depart, composing a verse that is topically categorized as Miscellaneous because it contains no clear word linking it to a season, love, or other established topical category.[57] Nor does the verse contain any specific lexical associations; it relies instead on linking by meaning alone. The poets will have to keep in mind the rule that the word "path" (*michi*) which appears here must not appear again for five verses. In his commentary, Sōboku enlarges on the rationale behind the link, pointing out that as a single verse, the traces of the trails are faint because of dense foliage, but in the context of the previous verse, they are obscured by the spring haze:

> Here "foothills round the valley" become a place where one gathers brushwood. The phrase "spring appears" [*haru miete*] is important. The paths for gathering brushwood are indistinct; this makes the link mean "it seems to have become spring—the traces of the paths are indistinct." The verse by itself means that there are all sorts of paths for gathering brushwood, but where the forest grows particularly thick the traces of such paths are indistinct. (*Yashima* 203)

Sōboku then relates advice Sōchō gave about the desirable tone of the first verses in a sequence:

> The use of "likewise" [*mo*] makes the verse remarkable on its own, while also linking it effectively to the previous one. As a general rule, he said, some verses are not appropriate for the first round even though they link well with the verse before. They should not involve the ostentatious use of foundation poems or lines from tales. One wants them to be very light and simple, but not *too* plain.[58] (*Yashima* 203)

Sōchō's remarks relate to the development of the sequence as a whole. Much of the advice of his own teacher, Sōgi, had been devoted to techniques for melding an entire sequence into a cohesive entity in which new topical and lexical developments between individual links were balanced with an overall orderly development. Contributing to that balance was the concept of "introduction" (*jo*), "development" (*ha*), and "conclusion" (*kyū*), which renga shares with other Japanese musical and dramatic structures. Definitions of the duration of the three segments changed over time; Sōboku explained them as follows:

> The first round [*ichijun*], second round [*saihen*], and the front of the second sheet are the introduction. The back of the second sheet and the third sheet are the development, and the fourth is the conclusion. In addition, on each fourteen-verse sheet the first five verses constitute an introduction, the second five a development, and the final four a conclusion.[59]

Since the "first round" generally includes one verse each by the seven or eight participants, its definition is problematic when only two poets are involved. Consensus defined it as the first eight and sometimes the first ten verses, and as such it roughly corresponded with the verses on the first side of the first sheet. Nijō Yoshimoto wrote in *Tsukuba mondō* that "the front of the first sheet should have gentle verses with unobtrusive syntax."[60] Such verses are therefore restrained, and they do not contain references to love or lamentation. It would be the role of the renga master at a session with a number of amateur poets to decide whether a proffered verse was in keeping with the elevated and conservative nature of the introduction, or whether it was too ostentatious. The Ōta commentary of the *Yashima* sequence, for example, relates that the fourth verse was initially different and included the phrase "even paths where they cut wood" (*ki koru michi sae*). Sōchō then decided that the imagery was too strong for its introductory place in the sequence and changed it. Later in the sequence, Sōchō asked Sōboku to reconsider his initial composition for the ninth verse for the same reason. Although it was well connected with the previous verse, Sōchō felt that it "was not fitting for the first round" and so Sōboku provided another (*Yashima* 205).

That is not to say that all verses on the front sheet were completely understated. For the fifth link in the sequence, Sōboku introduces a rich variety of images:

5	kage utsuru	Reflecting the light
	tsuki no yūshimo	of the moon, evening frost
	muramura ni	here and there.

The verse makes the first mention of the moon, a particularly striking image that should appear once on seven of the eight sides of recording paper but be separated by at least seven verses. Verses that mention the moon tend to stand out in a sequence, and they must be set off by more understated compositions. Links with especially dominant imagery, such as the moon and cherry blossoms, usually fall under the rubric of *mon* or "pattern" verses, and they alternate at irregular intervals with more restrained *ji* or "background" links. The words "mon" and "ji" relate to the terminology of textile design, and their use suggests another way that the poets "weave" the renga sequence together. The renga master paid close attention to the arrangement of mon and ji verses in the sequence and made sure that the former were plentiful enough to make the sequence interesting yet spaced widely enough to retain their impact.

The moon and the frost images mean that the verse falls into the topical category of Autumn, which, like images in the category of Spring, must continue for at least three and no more than five verses. "Frost" belongs in the lexical category of Falling Things, which means that another word in that category will either have to follow immediately in the next verse or be separated by three verses. As the previous Falling Thing was "snow" in verse one, the lexical category may reoccur here in verse five. The word "moon" comes under the lexical categories of Shining Things (which also must be separated by three verses) and Nocturnal Things.

The verse links to the previous to mean "moonlight is faintly reflected in patches of evening frost on the faint traces of the trail where one gathers wood." Sōboku comments that "patches of frost lie on the woodman's path homeward. 'Faint' [*kasuka*] links to 'moonlight' [*tsuki no kage*]" (*Yashima* 204). That association, however, is conceptual rather than canonical, as it is not listed in such *yoriai* handbooks as *Renju gappekishū* or *Renga tsukeai no koto*. In the context of the new link, the "faint traces" are now also traces of moonlight that are reflected on patches of frost on the trail used by woodcutters.

Sōboku then links verse six to his own previous composition:

| 6 | shigurete kawaku | After cold rain, the garden |
| | niwa no akikaze | dries in the autumn wind. |

The word "autumn" (*aki*) keeps the verse in the Autumn topical category, as required by the rules. "Wind" (*kaze*) will have to be avoided hereafter for five verses, and both "cold rain" (*shigure*) and "garden" (*niwa*) may appear only once more in the entire sequence. Like "frost" in the previous verse, "cold rain" is a Falling Thing, which must be separated by more than three verses or appear contiguously, as it does here. It is already apparent how complex grows the task of keeping the rules in mind as the sequence progresses.

In the context of the maeku, verse six means, "After the cold rain, the garden dries in the autumn wind; in the places where it has dried, the moonlight looks like evening frost, and in the places still wet, the moon is reflected." The link between "moon" and "autumn wind" is listed in *Renju gappekishū* (no. 895). Sōboku then elaborates on the verse and the connection:

> There is nothing special about the verse in itself. It has the moon appearing in a garden after cold rain. In the dried spots moonlight makes it look as though frost has formed; where water remains, the moon is reflected. In this way it links with "here and there" [*muramura ni*]. (*Yashima* 204)

The meaning of verse five thus again changes in the context of verse six; where the moonlight before was reflected in the frost, now it simulates frost and at the same time is reflected in the puddles of water that remain after the cold rain in the garden.

The composition of the seventh verse must fall to Sōchō, since the last two verses were composed by his younger colleague. He is obligated to continue the topical category of Autumn, and he does so through the use of "colored leaves" (*momiji*), a word that may appear up to three times in a hundred-verse sequence, and also through the word "take on color" (*sometsuran*).

7	shitamomiji	Tinted lower leaves—
	itsu katsu chiri mo	When did they begin to fall,
	sometsuran	even as they took on color?

Sōchō's link is based on the literary convention that the cold rains of late autumn make the lower leaves the first to turn color and then fall. In connection with the previous one, this verse means, "After the cold rain, the garden dries in the autumn wind; when did the lower leaves begin to fall, even as they took on color?" Sōboku explains the connection as follows:

> Rain fell on the garden's colored leaves, which then dried in the autumn wind. In the verse here, the poet demonstrates his emotional attachment to the tinted leaves by asking, "When did they begin to fall, even as they took on color?" One ought not dismiss this lightly. (*Yashima* 204)

The content of the link is a simple yet profound observation of seasonal change and evanescence; the leaves were tinted by the cold rain and at the same time began to fall even before the poet was aware of the passage of time. The rhetoric of the verse, by contrast, is complex. There is an association between "lower leaves" and "cold rain" which is listed in *Renju gappekishū* (no. 318). That association appears in *Shinkokinshū* 5: 437, by Fujiwara Ietaka:

shitamomiji	Has it been wet through
katsu chiru yama no	by the cold evening rain
yūshigure	on the mountain where
nurete ya hitori	lower leaves at once color and fall?
shika no nakuran	A lone deer crying out for its mate.

Though the image of the deer makes the *Shinkokinshū* poem too different from Sōchō's to be considered a honka, Ietaka's composition may have prompted Sōchō to link "lower leaves" and "at once falling" to the image of "cold rain" in Sōboku's previous verse. Sōchō also uses the verb *sometsuran* to mean both "begin to" in connection with "fall" and also "take on color." And in addition he introduces a pivot word (kakekotoba) that operates between *itsu ka* ("when") and *katsu chiru* ("at once fall").

Sōchō also provides the next link, the last of the "first eight verses" and the final one that we will consider here:

| 8 | tare o matsu to ka | Whom are they awaiting? |
| | mushi no koegoe | The voices of the crickets. |

In the context of the previous verse, the crickets chirp beneath fallen leaves: "Tinted lower leaves—when did they begin to fall, even as they took on color?

Whom are they awaiting? The voices of the crickets." Again the verse is in the topical category of Autumn, as indicated by the word "insects" (*mushi*). There is a foundation poem for this verse as well, and in that context the insects are identified as "pine crickets" (*matsumushi*). Sōboku identifies the foundation poem, *Kokinshū* 4: 203, in his commentary:

> This verse too is one that would occur to few. People do not normally associate "colored leaves" with "pine crickets" [*matsumushi*] as they do with "bush clover" [*hagi*] or "pampas grass" [*susuki*].[61]

momichiba no	Here at my lodging,
chirite tsumoreru	where the colored leaves fall
waga yado ni	and lie deep on the ground,
tare o matsumushi	whom can the pine crickets
kokora nakuran	be awaiting that they sing so?

> It is a shame that today when phrases such as "whom can the pine crickets be awaiting?" [*tare o matsumushi*] or "pine crickets awaiting someone" [*hito o matsumushi*] are used, they are usually meant in the context of love. This foundation poem, like Sōchō's verse, simply shows deep feeling for the pine crickets beneath the colored foliage. (*Yashima* 204)

Here the *Kokinshū* foundation poem provides the justification for associating "colored leaves" and "falling" in verse seven with "whom can they be awaiting" and "crickets" in verse eight. Sōboku also cites the *Kokinshū* poem as proof that the phrase "whom are they awaiting" need not necessarily imply the topical category of love. This is an important point, because a verse in the love category is not appropriate for the "first round" of a sequence.

And so the first eight verses come to an end. The scribe at this point turns over the recording paper and begins to record the fourteen verses that it will include. Sheets two and three also include fourteen verses on their front and back, and the last sheet is the reverse of the first, ending with eight verses, the last of which is called the *ageku*. As indicated by Sōchō's comment that Sōboku's original ninth verse was not in keeping with the requisite tone of the "first round," the ninth and tenth verses were seen as transitional, since they occur immediately after the page is turned.

A sequence was normally composed between dawn and dusk; the *Yashima* sequence took longer, however, because of the detailed discussions that accompanied the links and also because of a break part way through for Zen meditation at the temple where the sequence was being composed. Again, Sōchō was not only a poet but a priest, and he was as devoted to Zen as he was to poetry. The two disciplines were of course complementary in the medieval period; Zen was perhaps particularly well suited to the philosophy of renga since both actively encourage discontinuous thinking in the pursuit of higher intangible truths.

As indicated earlier, however, the conceptual leaps between contiguous verses in renga and the frequent "recasting" (*torinashi*) of one verse by the next are balanced by a regard for an orderly overall development of the whole sequence. Sōchō's teacher, Sōgi, brought this concern for sequencing to its highest level. That concern increased as he aged, and his late work *Yodo no watari* (Yodo Crossing, 1495) analyzes a complete hundred-verse sequence partly to show the course of development from link to link.[62] He was particularly skilled both at producing provocative verses to lead a sequence in new directions when it was becoming stultified and also at composing self-effacing ground verses that sacrificed individuality in favor of a larger developmental pattern. His focus on the overall sequential development of the hundred verses at once allows internal development but imposes closure on the sequence as a whole. One may see in this a correlative in renga terms of the tendency toward epical closure Sōgi exhibits in his approach to self-representational prose.

The developmental mechanisms at work include the jo-ha-kyū and mon-ji sequencing as well as the pattern created by the relative closeness or distance between links. "Close links" (*shinku*) involve obvious and immediate lexical or semantic ties; "distant links" (*soku*) require more analysis to discover where the connection between the two verses lies.[63] Yet another pattern is established by the related concepts of "linking by words" (*kotobazuke*) and "linking by meaning" (*kokorozuke*). Obviously all verses are linked by meaning as well as by words; the distinction relies on whether the link depends more on lexical and/or paronomastic associations or on the overall meaning of the two verses. Sōchō's attraction particularly to distant linking and linking by meaning is implied in his statement, in *Sōchō renga jichū*, that "the link must be summoned by the maeku; it is desirable that it respond to the maeku like an echo in love with the voice."[64]

The artistic development of a hundred-link sequence in turn sometimes required that the rules be violated in the interest of aesthetics. The renga rules of course facilitated the gaming aspect of the renga enterprise, but for Sōgi, Sōchō, and Sōboku, the rules were also a means toward the creation of art. There is less conflict between regulation and creativity in the renga world than might be imagined, since the rules themselves are based on venerable perceptions of fundamental affinities between facts of life and images in the natural world. Following the rules could of course become automatic and result in artistic sterility; indeed, this was the ultimate fate of ushin linked verse in the seventeenth century. But respect for precedent, demonstrated through an observance of renga rules, the use of foundation poems, and attention to basic essences, could be considered less as a constraint on individual creativity than as a route to the personal realization of eternal poetic truths. Renga was thus both recreation and re-creation. This is what Sōboku is getting at in his comment on verse seven, in which Sōchō "demonstrates his emotional attachment to the tinted leaves by asking 'when did they begin to fall, even as they took on color?' One ought not dismiss this lightly." It is a basic essence of the autumn season that cold rains bring color to the leaves, which thereafter fall, serving year by year as a metaphor for the mutability of all things, including the poet himself. The verse expresses a personal apprehension of universality, and that is precisely why Sōboku finds it impressive.

In his composition of ushin renga, therefore, Sōchō's primary goal was not a completely new and individual approach but the recapitulation in personal terms of the renga orthodoxy, particularly as demonstrated in the work of his teacher, which was itself based on earlier models.[65] Sōchō's advice in his early work on linked-verse poetics, *Nagabumi*, mirrors Sōgi's so closely that the examples he cites are sometimes simply reworkings of those of his teacher, who had himself appropriated them from yet an earlier poet. Sōgi quotes in *Azuma mondō* two hokku by the nun Abutsu that he took to reflect ideal simplicity of conception and attention to the appropriate season:

>   kyō wa haya   Already today
>   aki no kagiri ni   it seems we have arrived
>   narinikeri   at the end of autumn.
>
>   kyō wa mata   Once again today
>   fuyu no hajime ni   it seems we have arrived
>   narinikeri   at the start of winter.[66]

In *Nagabumi* Sōchō encapsulates the same ideal of simplicity with the following two hokku, which he ascribes to "a certain person":

>   kyō wa haya   Already today
>   haru no hajime ni   it seems we have arrived
>   narinikeri   at the start of springtime.

kyō wa mata	Once again today
aki kuru koro ni	it seems we have arrived
narinikeri	at the advent of autumn.⁶⁷

    Far from disguising his debt to Sōgi, Sōchō notes it with pride. He writes in *Nagabumi*, for example, that he based his teachings on a work by Sōgi, and in the postscript to *Amayo no ki* he likewise credits that work to the advice of his teacher:

> I composed this volume on matters about which I asked the venerable Sōgi over the years, writing not during the day when distracted by other concerns and prying eyes, but on rainy nights beneath my lamp. I then showed it to Sōgi, and he reviewed it, adding here and there things I had overlooked. Its approach to the way of renga is that of the venerable master himself.⁶⁸

Amayo no ki is related to an early version of *Renga sakurei*, which was written by 1506 and probably also based on earlier advice from Sōgi. But *Amayo no ki* itself is dated 1519, seventeen years after Sōgi's death.⁶⁹ Sōgi in turn based his own instruction and composition on those of his waka and renga teachers.⁷⁰ A focus on accretion rather than originality was characteristic not only of Sōchō but of the entire medieval period.

    Sōchō also wrote commentaries on Sōgi's second and third personal linked-verse collections.⁷¹ It is not at all surprising, then, that Sōchō's hokku in his journal should bear a close resemblance to those of Sōgi. The following are examples of hokku from *The Journal of Sōchō* and Sōgi's *Wakuraba*:⁷²

The Journal of Sōchō no. 171:

yaso no se no	High, the headwaters
minakami takashi	of the eighty rapids.
aki no koe	The sound of autumn.

(*JS*: 51)

Wakuraba no. 1920:

yamamizu mo	Deep, the evening darkness
yūgure fukashi	of the mountain stream.
aki no koe	The sound of autumn.

The Journal of Sōchō no. 214:

    yūsuzumi
    mi mo hi mo samushi
    kawarakaze

    In the cool of evening
    the water, the day, and I are chilled.
    River wind.

        (JS: 62)

Wakuraba no. 1898:

    fukete minu
    hikari mo suzushi
    yūzukuyo

    Seen in early evening too,
    its light is chill.
    The moon of evening.

❀

The Journal of Sōchō no. 358:

    kuina naku
    ashihara kuraki
    asato kana

    The waterrail calls
    in the dark field of reeds
    outside the door at morning!

        (JS: 101)

Wakuraba no. 1883:

    kuina naku
    tani ni yo fukaki
    asato kana

    The waterrail calls
    in the valley still wrapped in night
    outside the door at morning!

❀

The Journal of Sōchō no. 379:

    kiri no asake
    kawaoto kuraki
    harema kana

    In early morning,
    the sound of the river
    through dark gaps in the mist!

        (JS: 108)

Wakuraba no. 1997:

    yuki harete
    kawaoto samuki
    yamaji kana

    In sunlight after snow,
    the sound of the river is cool
    by the mountain path!

❀

CHAPTER FOUR

The Journal of Sōchō no. 387:

  kari nakite   Geese are calling
samuki sora sumu   in a cold and cloudless sky
  ashita kana   at the break of day!

           (*JS*: 101)

Wakuraba no. 1919:

  kari nakite   Geese are calling
 hisaki irozuku   and the oaks are turning color
  hamabe kana   at the seashore!

❦

The Journal of Sōchō no. 582:

  sora midare   Over a troubled sky,
kumo nowakidatsu   clouds come and go
  yukiki kana   in the gathering storm!

           (*JS*: 160)

Wakuraba no. 1939:

  ame shigure   In the chilling rain,
 kaze nowakidatsu   evening with wind rising
  yūbe kana   in the gathering storm![73]

In these examples there is little to choose from between Sōgi and Sōchō—both present a largely impersonal view of nature, concentrating in general on the evening and morning hours (reminiscent of the "beginnings and endings" that Yoshida Kenkō in *Tsurezuregusa* found to be of greatest interest) and on images of darkness and cold. Both share the loftiness, ineffable beauty, and deep feeling that Sōgi requires in *Azuma mondō*, as well as the taste for lonely, monochromatic landscapes so admired by Shunzei, Saigyō, Teika, and Shinkei.

 Another of Sōchō's verses demonstrates the debt explicitly:

80   ariake ya   The moon before dawn—
 sora ni shimogare no   frost-withered against the sky,
  hanasusuki   ears of pampas grass.[74]

           (*JS*: 33)

Sōchō provided a personal commentary on the verse in work he wrote soon after for a warrior patron:

Withered pampas grass under the crescent moon at dawn. Here one gazes at the moon with the thought that it too seems withered in the sky:

mireba ge ni	Gazing out, I feel
kokoro mo sore ni	my heart growing ever more
nari zo yuku	at one with the scene—
kareno no susuki	pampas grass on the withered moor,
ariake no tsuki	the moon before dawn.75

The foundation poem on which Sōchō bases his own verse is by Saigyō.76 As Sōchō's commentary explains, it is both "the moon before dawn" (*ariake [no tsuki]*) and the "ears of pampas grass" (*hanasusuki*) that are "frost withered against the sky" (*sora ni shimogare*). Sōchō's poem is also reminiscent of a passage in Shinkei's *Sasamegoto* that reads:

> In the past, a certain great poet was asked how to compose waka. He replied, "Pampas grass on the withered moor; the moon at dawn." That means to concentrate on what is not expressed in words and to comprehend the state of chill desolation.77

The passage Shikei quotes in turn appears previously in *Bontōanshu hentōsho*, by the earlier renga poet Bontō, the most important disciple of the great renga codifier Nijō Yoshimoto. Bontō, however, attributes the remark to yet an earlier poetic figure, the courtier Fujiwara Mototoshi, a teacher of Shunzei.78 Sōchō's composition establishes him in a poetic lineage reaching back through Sōgi, Shinkei, and Yoshimoto's disciple to his model, Saigyō, and to the ancestors of the Nijō orthodoxy.

But Sōchō obviously did not limit himself to cold and desolate scenes. He was also capable of brilliant polychrome effects:

28	shimo o aya	A frost of damask,
	kozue o tatamu	with leaves at branch tips woven
	nishiki kana	into rich brocade!
		(*JS*: 21)
329	matsu no ha wa	Pine needles
	hana zo mitsu shio	enhance the blossoms in the rising tide
	yamazakura	of mountain cherries.
		(*JS*: 90)

344   sumire saku
    no wa iku suji no
     haru no mizu

The field where violets bloom
is crisscrossed by how many
   springtime rivulets?
     (*JS*: 97)

535   haru ikue
    iwa kakitsubata
     kishi no fuji

Layers of springtime—
irises on the stone palisade,
   wisteria on the cliffs.
     (*JS*: 148)

586   shimo wa kesa
    harau mo oshi no
     uwage kana

The frost this morning—
a pity mandarin ducks
   brush it off their feathers!
     (*JS*: 161)

Other of Sōchō's hokku emphasize the loftiness and grandeur that Sōgi prized:

381   asatoake
    tanomo irozuku
     chisato kana

Outside the door at morning
the fields take on color—
   for a thousand leagues!
     (*JS*: 109)

386   aki no tsuki
    izuko terasanu
     kuma mo nashi

The autumn moon—
on what does it not shine down?
   Nowhere a shadow.
     (*JS*: 110)

The poet elsewhere pays equal attention to nature in microcosm, trading grandeur for precisely observed detail in a manner reminiscent of the Kyōgoku and Reizei poets:

67   yūdachi ya
    makaseshi mizu no
     iwa kosuge

An evening shower—
rivulets of rain run off
   onto rock-pent sedge.
     (*JS*: 31)

177   samidare ni
    masuge no mizu no
     sueba kana

In the summer rains,
water builds on the outer leaves
   of the sedge grass!
     (*JS*: 52)

The thematic concerns, the kokoro, of Sōchō's poetry are expressed through rhetoric (*kotoba*) of considerable variety and finesse. One rhetorical device he finds particularly effective is contrasting two layers or conditions:

8	mizu harete sora ya satsuki no amatsutsumi	Clear now over the water— the sky above dressed for the fifth-month rain.
		(*JS*: 14)

9	ōchi saku kumoi o chiri no fumoto kana	Bead trees blossom in the clouds, though dust covers the slope below!
		(*JS*: 14)

60	iku iwane otowa no tagitsu haru no mizu	Through the serried cliffs of Otowa Falls sound the surging springtime waters.
		(*JS*: 30)

341	kai ga ne wa yuki ni shigururu yamaji kana	There is snow on the Kai peaks and cold rain on the mountain path!
		(*JS*: 96)

This approach juxtaposes two states in a single verse, which is the essence of the linked-verse art. As seen also in his technique of joining episodes or poem pairs in his journal entries, Sōchō as a renga poet tends to perceive his world in terms of binary similarities and contrasts. In *Amayo no ki*, he explicitly emphasizes the desirability of highlighting those contrasts when linking, and he advises the reader as follows: "When the previous verse deals with a person, recast it in your link in terms of a bird or an animal, a plant or a tree" (103) or "when the previous verse deals with someone else, recast it in your link in terms of yourself" (109) or "link water to mountains or mountains to water" (110). Again, combination and development, blending and change are the essence of the art.

Juxtaposition of two states is also effected in some of his verses by the technique of "reasoning," popular in *Kokinshū* as a legacy of Chinese poetry from the Six Dynasties.[79] In such verses evidence presented to the senses leads to cerebration by the poet. Examples include the following:

CHAPTER FOUR

> 72   yuki okite
>   shirayama no na ya
>   tsuki no aki
>
> Even without snow
>   it is worthy of the name White Mountain,
>   under autumn's moon.
>
>   (*JS*: 32)

The verse was sent to a temple connected with Hakusan ("White Mountain") Shrine at Shirayama mountain, which straddles Ishikawa, Toyama, Fukui, and Gifu Prefectures and is famous as a center of mountain asceticism. The foundation poem is *Kokinshū* 9: 414, by Ōshikōshi Mitsune:

>   kiehatsuru
>   toki shi nakereba
>   koshiji naru
>   shirayama no na wa
>   yuki ni zo arikeru
>
> Since no season
>   sees a thaw,
>   the name White Mountain
>   in the land of Koshi
>   was given by its snow!

Sōchō pursues the "reasoning" approach taken in the *honka*, but he suggests further that the name "White Mountain" is also apposite because of the autumn moonlight.

> 365   kasaneage
>   fuji no ne mo isa
>   hototogisu
>
> Were others piled upon it,
>   this peak would still not match Fuji,
>   but how high the cuckoo's cry!
>
>   (*JS*: 104)

The verse describes a cuckoo on Mount Hiei in terms of *Ise monogatari* (22): "Mount Fuji is like twenty Hiei mountains piled one on top of another." But even so, the cry of the cuckoo on the Kyoto mountain sounds high. There is a pun on *ne* (mountain/cry).

> 175   washi no sumu
>   yama to ya tōki
>   hototogisu
>
> Is it because this is
>   the mountain where eagles dwell
>   that the cuckoo is so distant?
>
>   (*JS*: 52)

The verse is a play on Washinosuyama (Eagle Nest Mountain), where the sequence was being composed, and Ryōjusen (Eagle Peak), where the Buddha preached the *Lotus Sutra* in India. It is possible the verse also implies that the cuckoos keep their distance because of the eagles, though that conception borders on *haikai*.

213	hototogisu makoto o kyō wa hatsune kana	The cuckoo! In truth it is on this day instead that we hear the "first song"!
		(JS: 62)

"First song" (*hatsune*) usually refers to the first song of the bush warbler (*uguisu*) heard in the spring, but Sōchō is so moved by the singing of the cuckoo (*hototogisu*) that he would apply the term to that bird instead. In all four of the above cases, part of the "reasoning" is predicated on an awareness of poetic and religious tradition.

The last two examples also demonstrate that some of Sōchō's verses are rich in aural effects and musicality, a characteristic that nicely reinforces the frequent references in the diary to music, musicians, and especially the shakuhachi flute, which Sōchō particularly loved. *JS* no. 175 derives its aural effect from assonance of "o" and "a" and alliteration; *JS* no. 213, from assonance of *o*. Other particularly musical verses include these:

379	kiri no asake kawaoto kuraki harema kana	In early morning, the sound of the river through dark gaps in the mist!
		(JS: 108)
540	haru wa kurenu hototogisu hata hatsune kana	Springtime has ended. There! The first call of the cuckoo!
		(JS: 149)

Sōchō's rhetorical mastery is best demonstrated by so-called *shūku*, which purposefully display technical virtuosity or paronomasia:

79	shinagadori inano o yuki no ashita kana	Off to Inano, a name recalling grebes side by side, in the morning snow!
		(JS: 33)

The verse includes a *makurakotoba* or fixed epithet (*shinagadori*, "grebes side by side"), an utamakura (Inano), and a kakekotoba pivoting between *yuku* ("to go") and *yuki* ("snow"). It also calls to mind a poem from *Shinkokinshū* (10: 910):

	shinagadori
	inano o yukeba
	arimayama
	yūgiri tachinu
	yado wa nakushite

Off to Inano,
a name recalling grebes side by side,
I find as evening mist
rises round Mount Arima
that I have no place to stay.[80]

Another is the following:

348   nami ya yuku
haru no kazashi no
watatsuumi

The waves go out
with spring—floss garlands
on the great ocean.

(*JS*: 98)

The verse includes two kakekotoba, the first pivoting between *nami ya yuku* (the waves go out) and *yuku haru* (go out with spring), and the second between *kazashi no wata* (floss garlands) and *watatsuumi* (the great ocean). It too bears a relationship with an earlier poem, this one from *Ise monogatari* (83–84):

watatsumi no
kazashi ni sasu to
iwau mo mo
kimi ga tame ni wa
oshimazarikeri

The God of the Sea
did not begrudge giving
you, my good lords,
this sea plant that he treasures
as a garland for his hair.

As the above examples have demonstrated, Sōchō frequently bases his compositions on waka foundation poems (honka). This technique of "allusive variation" (*honkadori*) is the focus of his poetic treatise *Sōchō kawa*, and it is the single most frequently used critical term in *Sōchō renga jichū*.[81] In this characteristic too, Sōchō shares the predominantly neoclassical outlook of Sōgi and indeed of his entire era. Of Sōchō's approximately 170 hokku in his journal, roughly a quarter appear to be built on honka. About one-third of those are based on poems from *Kokinshū* and another fifth on those from *Shinkokinshū*. Those statistics do not mean that Sōchō's style is more like the poetry of *Kokinshū* than that of *Shinkokinshū*, but rather that like the *Shinkokinshū* poets themselves, he felt free to draw on the first imperial anthology while recasting it in a contemporary context. He also borrows from *Man'yōshū* and in isolated cases from most of the other of the first eight imperial anthologies (*hachidaishū*) and the ninth one, *Shinchokusenshū*. There are also several references to poems or prose sections of *Ise monogatari*, *Genji monogatari*, and the *Lotus Sutra*, among other sources. He occasionally identifies his source through partial or complete quotation of the honka in the explanatory notes preceding or following the hokku recorded in his diary, especially where the meaning would be obscure unless the allusion were recognized. A case in point is the following:

200	hayashisomete	Praise the bush clover
	iku soma no hana	growing up like mountain timber,
	hagi no tsuyu	dew on its blossoms.

> This was meant as praise of the [young scribe's] accomplished hand and correct demeanor, using the poem (from *Man'yōshū?*) that goes "made from bush clover / growing straight as timber / and just beginning to flourish." I believe that verse uses *somakata* to mean bush clover growing widely dispersed and therefore straight and tall. (*JS:* 59)

In his renga treatises, Sōchō elaborates on honkadori as a linking device, but in his journal, in the nearly complete absence of tsukeku, his remarks tend more toward simple identification of the honka involved and their relation, if any, to the time and place requirements of the hokku.

Sōchō's hokku in sum demonstrate rhetorical and thematic mastery of the orthodox neoclassical renga style. This is not to say, however, that Sōchō's verses show no trace of personality or stylistic development. Such elements are particularly difficult to isolate in the case of linked verse, though, because it is the very nature of the art to deemphasize individuality in the interest of harmony at the session and cohesiveness throughout the sequence. The high form of the linked-verse art, moreover, is predicated on and shaped by a preestablished and contained waka poetic lexicon, and its aim is the realization of waka-inspired ideals and basic essences of universal experience.[82] Hokku, as we have seen, are the most nonindividualized verses of all, since they are almost entirely seasonal in theme and comparatively restrained in expression. And since they are the least spontaneous verses in the sequence, being normally prepared before the session begins, they seldom show even the understated personal elements that tsukeku sometimes do when composed in the heat of the moment as a session continues.

That being said, critics in Sōchō's own time and in later generations have found in his linked verse both conventionality and certain individual characteristics. With regard to Sōchō's hokku, Kidō Saizō focusses on the former quality, calling the three that appear in *Shinsen tsukubashū* "unremarkable."[83] Kaneko Kinjirō, by contrast, feels that many of Sōchō's verses have a "lucidity" (*heimei*) that "touches one in a natural and straightforward (*sunao*) way."[84] Such lucidity and apparent simplicity may mask the technical effort that Sōchō expended in his hokku composition process. Of the roughly seventy hokku shared by *The Journal of Sōchō* and *Oi no mimi*, a number appear in variant forms, indicating that even after writing down a verse, Sōchō would continue to experiment with syntax and grammatical particles.[85]

His journal too gives evidence of his constant efforts to improve his hokku. When he begins his journal afresh at the beginning of 1526, for example, he also rewrites some of the verses that he had also included at the end of Book One. The following hokku, another example of poetic loftiness, appears at the end of Book One:

> First month, twenty-eighth day—for Lord Ujiteru's linked-verse session:

327   fuji ya kore   Here is Fuji—
      kasumi no yomo no   Mount Sumeru circled
      kuni no haru   by lands in spring haze.

> The verse is also meant to imply Suminoyama. (*JS*: 89)

Suminoyama is Mount Sumeru, center of the Buddhist cosmos. The poet has included it through kakekotoba pivoting between *kasumi* (haze) and *sumi* (Sumeru), then through slant rhyme on *yomo* (in all directions, or circling) and *yama* (mountain). "Circled by lands" (*yomo no kuni*) refers to the four lands said to surround Mount Sumeru. Sōchō thus locates Suruga, the province in which Mt. Fuji is located, at the center of the world. When Sōchō recapitulates the first two months of 1526 in Book Two, he rewrites the verse as follows:

> Sixth year of Daiei, in Suruga, on the twenty-eighth of the first month:

338   ama no hara   The field of heaven
      fuji ya kasumi no   and Fuji—Mount Sumeru
      yomo no haru   circled by spring haze.
                          (*JS*: 95)

It is the latter version that he preserves in *Oi no mimi* (no. 120). As only one of the two verses included in his journal could actually have been presented at the session, it is clear that Sōchō too was capable at times of subordinating actual fact to artistic concerns.

Later he himself remarks with self-deprecatory humor on his efforts to rework a verse he composed to mark Sōgi's death anniversary:

First month, twenty-ninth day: the first observance this year of Sōgi's death. After lighting incense:

501	tachikaeri haru ya fuyugomoru kesa no yuki	Spring goes backwards into winter seclusion— snow this morning.
502	haru ya toki fuyugomorasuru kesa no yuki	Is spring early? It was sent back into winter seclusion by snow this morning.[86]

I can see no difference between the two. His shade is no doubt laughing! (*JS*: 139)

Sōchō's colleagues Sanetaka and Shōhaku provided admiring judgments of his verses in *Sōchō hyakuban rengaawase* in 1508. The work consists of ninety pairs of renga couplets, the tsukeku of which were composed by Sōchō, and ten pairs of renga hokku, which the poet arranged in a mock competition in one hundred rounds after the fashion of waka contests between Left and Right teams.[87] He then sent the manuscript to Sanetaka and Shōhaku for their criticism. In this too, it should be added in passing, he was following ancient precedent, established perhaps most notably by the two waka contests *Mimosusogawa utaawase* and *Miyagawa utaawase*, which Saigyō assembled out of his own verses and sent for criticism to Fujiwara Shunzei and Shunzei's son Teika. The nature of the two judges' praise for Sōchō's mature hokku style is apparent in the following:

Round 91

LEFT

fuji no ne wa
ama no hara naru
kasumi kana

The peak of Fuji
in a heavenly field
of haze![88]

RIGHT

mine no yuki
kesa wa kasumi no
fumoto kana

The snow on the peak
in this morning's haze
now lies on the mountain's foot![89]

Sanetaka gave the round to the verse of the Left, deeming it "not the slightest bit inferior to one by the priest Jichin," which he then quotes:

CHAPTER FOUR

> ama no hara
> fuji no keburi no
> haru no iro no
> kasumi ni nabiku
> akebono no sora

> The smoke of Fuji
> trails high in the field of heaven
> and becomes the color
> of springtime haze—
> the sky at dawn.[90]

Shōhaku concurs, observing that "The verse about the peak of Fuji in the field of heaven is of unparalleled distinction."[91] While both men were old acquaintances of Sōchō and thus doubtless inclined to comment favorably on his work, they were also among the leading poetic minds of the day and not given to idle praise. Indicative of their critical integrity was their willingness to differ occasionally with each other in their judgments. For example:

Round 98

LEFT

> aki ya nao
> itsu to mo wakanu
> matsu no iro

> Autumn—yet
> it does not reflect the season,
> the color of this pine.[92]

RIGHT

> hatsushigure
> somete hosu ma ka
> yamameguri

> First cold rain—
> are you waiting for these leaves to dry,
> that you continue round the mountain?[93]

Sanetaka gives the victory to the Right, commenting that while the verse of the Left is "estimable," that of the Right is "of unparalleled excellence."[94] Shōhaku, however, finds both to possess "depth of diction (*fukaki kotoba*) and feeling (*kokoro aru tei*)" and awards a draw.[95]

Critics have also remarked on the overall simplicity of Sōchō's tsukeku. Kidō Saizō has generalized that Sōchō's linking style is "light" (*assari*) and "artless" (*mugikō*).[96] As we have seen, Sōchō often juxtaposes soku verses quite distant in content, giving rise to a quality that Oda Takuji characterizes as "approaching 'linking by fragrance'" (*nioizuke*), a technique later developed by Bashō.[97] The Sōboku commentary on the *Yashima* sequence, however, shows that such "artlessness" is deceptive in its simplicity and is the result of learned rhetorical consideration.

This depth in simplicity was exactly what Sōchō himself looked for both in his own verse and in that of his students. In his treatise *Nagabumi*, for example, he prizes harmony and constant change, attained through simplicity; ostentatious technique, verses difficult to link, and showy effects were to be eschewed. The desired impression was as if "you are hiding your love for someone."[98] One should refrain from sophistry and the exotic, but at the same time avoid the stereotypical and the ordinary.

Though *Nagabumi* is one of Sōchō's early works, he never strayed from that basic orthodoxy. His own verse does, however, show a degree of stylistic development over time. According to a preliminary diachronic analysis by Oda, it took Sōchō considerable time to reach his artistic maturity. Oda finds that his contributions to *Minase sangin* of 1488 have yet to reach the level of his later work, though as Donald Keene points out, the three poets who composed the work, Sōgi, Shōhaku, and Sōchō, "were nearly equals; otherwise, the sequence would surely not have achieved its reputation."[99] Three years later, when the three poets gathered to compose *Yuyama sangin* in 1491, they were equally matched. By the last decade of the fifteenth century, then, Sōchō had clearly reached his poetic maturity.

But he continued to improve thereafter. Oda cites *Iba senku* as exemplary, with more than a few verses qualifying as his best work ever.[100] Sōchō composed the sequence with Sanetaka and Sōseki in 1524 at age 76, and he refers to it in his journal (*JS*: 44). At the same time, however, Oda detects in some of the verses in that work a touch of the willful or eccentric. While this quality is again more difficult to perceive in hokku than in tsukeku, a few of the hokku in *The Journal of Sōchō* certainly appear to stray from the ideal of rhetorical and conceptual simplicity that Sōchō stressed in *Nagabumi*. The following is a case in point:

> We returned to Sunpu. A linked-verse session for the visitors from the capital:

201	sasowareba	Were it invited,
	miyako no fuji no	Fuji would bring autumn snow
	aki no yuki	to the capital.

> What this means is that if Mount Fuji here could be invited to the capital, there would be snow in the capital in autumn. (*JS*: 59)

Sōchō refers to the fact that the capital's own tall mountain, Hiei, has no snow on it in the autumn, while Sunpu's Fuji already does. Snow on Kyoto's Fuji (Hiei) would be *kisetsu chigai*, "inappropriate to the season," and remarked on; in Suruga, it is normal.

Another of these difficult hokku was composed on his second trip to Kyoto in 1526:

354	saki sakazu ki wa natsu kodachi hana mo nashi	In the summer grove, blooming and nonblooming trees, with none in flower.

(*JS*: 100)

The verse at first glance seems a *nanku*, or puzzle, almost daring the next poet to produce a satisfactory link. It also hardly seems in keeping with the celebratory quality a hokku usually has when composed, as this was, while the poet was at the residence of a host. Sōchō accordingly feels obliged to add an explanation: "That is to say that the green shade was better than blossoms. What I meant by *saki sakazu* is that the green shade was the same whether the tree was a blossoming variety or not" (*JS*: 312). Interpreted in that way, Sōchō's reference in the hokku to the location of the session is indeed a flattering one. One marvels at the perspicacity required of the poet responsible for the waki to link such a difficult verse. Surely Sōchō must have elaborated on the meaning of this hokku before or during the session, since his fellow poets were provincial amateurs.[101]

Sōchō also had a tendency to experiment with word order and grammatical particles, sometimes to unusual or perhaps even eccentric effect. Even in the poems of his early maturity, such as those in *Shutsujin senku* (A Thousand-Verse Sequence for the Campaign, 1504), one encounters verses such as the following:

mushi no ne mo
tokorodokoro no
no wa karete

So too the sound of the crickets—
here and there
the field is withered.

tsuyu no nagori ya
yūbe naruran

Is the dew a remnant
of last evening?[102]

The first is a verse set in late autumn, when the chirping of the crickets has withered away like the grasses. The link continues the autumn topical category through the use of the word "dew" (*tsuyu*) and conflates the poet's tears that fell the evening before at the thought of deepening autumn with the dew remaining in the morning. It is less the image that catches the eye than the inversion of the usual word order (anastrophe).[103]

This combination of considered simplicity plus the occasional touch of willfulness or opacity is also seen occasionally in Sōchō's prose style in his journal.

But as Oda points out, the majority of his Sōchō's later work is very much in the clear and lucid style of his early maturity.

Scholars who pioneered the modern study of linked verse earlier in this century have tended to emphasize Sōchō's orthodoxy. Yamada Yoshio, for example, feels that "Sōchō's renga is conservative (*onken*) with no unconventionality (*kibatsu na ten*). It is not the equal of Sōgi's, but it shows the same skill as Shōhaku's. Even of the hokku that appear in collections, the majority are average. Many of his tsukeku, however, are truly superb."[104] Hisamatsu Sen'ichi, by contrast, sees both Sōchō and Shōhaku as the equal of Sōgi, but he adds that their work shows "no further development worthy of note."[105] Sōchō and Shōhaku would probably not have found these judgments entirely pejorative; orthodox composition as good as that of their teacher Sōgi was to be admired.

Sōchō's student Sōboku, who also studied with Sōseki, felt that Sōchō at times was better than the master himself. In a commentary for *Yuyama sangin*, he writes of one verse by Sōchō that "had a style that not even Sōgi could equal."[106] But the remark also indicates that Sōboku considered Sōgi the ideal against whose verses all others must be judged.

Although Sōchō prided himself on his long apprenticeship with Sōgi and based his style on that of the older master, certain differences in their approach to linked verse are indeed apparent. Kidō, for example, has characterized Sōchō's verse, and in fact the verse of all those of the generation after Sōgi, as possessing greater lightness and optimism.[107] In the previous chapter, we found the same characteristic to be true of the eremitic literature of Sōchō and Shōhaku in comparison to that of the earlier poet Shinkei.

Kaneko and Ijichi also find that Sōchō's verse includes far more references to the daily life of the common people than do those of any previous linked-verse poet. One tsukeku that exhibits that quality is the following:

kosu fukaku	Deep within the blinds
koromo no otonai	garments
kasuka ni te	rustle faintly.
tachinū yoi no	Cutting and stitching
tomoshibi no moto	in the evening by the lamp.[108]

Tanaka Takahiro, furthermore, has indicated that the linked verses of Sōchō's old age, particularly those which he composed at the time he was keeping his journal, are richer in themes that seem to relate to the poet's own condition. Poems on the topic of old age, for example, proliferate in Sōchō's late oeuvre, while there is no corresponding increase in Sōgi's late poetry. Sōchō also became a father late in life, it will be recalled, and verses on children also begin to appear more frequently as he ages. Such verses too are unique to Sōchō.[109]

The affinity for the common, the contemporary, and the personal seen in some of Sōchō's verses corresponds well with what we have found to be true of his journal. Predictably, Sōgi's verse, like his travel writing, shows considerably less of this plebeian concern. Sōgi is more devoted to universal ideals and the creation of abstract, classical beauty. While he too occasionally portrays commoners in his verse, Sōgi's perspective in such cases, suggests Etō, is always that of one standing both outside and above.[110] As in his travel prose, Sōgi treats daily life and common people in the abstract, with little personal involvement. Ijichi notes that Sōchō's verse, by contrast, suggests a deeper personal engagement with common themes, more so, perhaps, than that of any other linked-verse poet to that time.[111] This also ties into his interest in the quotidian qualities of haikai, about which more presently.

In his depiction of everyday life and mundane themes, Sōchō is showing in his verse something of the same tendency to personalize writing that he shows in his journal. Obviously one cannot assume that the verses are purely autobiographical; rather they are a mask the poet wears, but one that appears to correspond quite closely to the poet's own situation in life. Sōchō seems to have taken to heart the injunction in *Kokinshū* that poetry has its seed in the human heart, and in *Utsunoyama no ki* he refers to the Chinese preface to that anthology: "Can someone not advanced in years know the true pathos of things? 'A miserable man composes sad verse'; what is not in the heart cannot come forth in words."[112] Where Sōgi transcends, Sōchō engages. This may be what the compiler of *Nikonshū* was getting at when he characterized Sōchō's style as *nuketōritaru*. Though the term, like any one-word evocation of a style, is ambiguous, Kaneko sees it as meaning straightforward and frank, a quality we have already seen carry over into Sōchō's approach to diary prose.[113]

Nevertheless, Sōchō's individual traits are subsumed beneath the more pervasive conservative orthodoxy of his overall approach. As indicated by our earlier comparison of Sōchō's hokku in his journal to those of Sōgi in *Wakuraba*, Sōchō's verses continue throughout his life to reflect in general outline the conservative and orthodox style of his teacher. His insistence on traditional neoclassical tonalities in his own ushin renga verse and in that of others was unchanging.

His advice in his late treatise on renga composition, *Sōchō renga jichū*, emphasizes this approach:

> Look for the aspect of the previous verse that demonstrates a hint of ineffable beauty, and keep in mind the grace (*uruwashiku*) and overtones (*yojō*) of the total conception. . . . Linking one verse to another in a crude (*futsutsuka*) or vulgar (*iyashikaran*) manner is the mark of a base (*muge naru*) individual. "Overtones" result when elegance (*yū*) and deep feeling (*ushin*) materialize from somewhere beyond the actual diction and content of the verse. Not only when you are participating in a renga session but at any time at work or at rest, or on waking in the night, if you pursue the diction and content of the poets of old, those qualities will appear naturally when you set out to compose a link.[114]

This was not idle lip service; *The Journal of Sōchō* shows that he was always careful in his own ushin verse, no matter how unusual the effect toward which he was working, to avoid exceeding the bounds of orthodoxy and good taste. For example:

532   kesa wa tare   Who is it this morning
      waka no matsubara   at Waka Pine Strand? I cannot tell—
      asagasumi   haze at daybreak.

> The temple is near the pine strand of that name. I was concerned about using "this morning" with "haze at daybreak," but I was reassured by similar usages in such lines as "at daybreak this morning." (*JS*: 147)

Sōchō here is concerned lest the words "this morning" (*kesa*) and "morning haze" (*asagasumi*) sound tautological, but he is reassured because the words appear together in *Man'yōshū* 8: 1513, by Prince Hozumi, an unimpeachable locus classicus:

      kesa no asake   At daybreak this morning
      karigane kikitsu   I heard the calls of the geese.
      kasugayama   On Mount Kasuga
      momichinikerashi   the trees seem to have turned to yellow.
      aga kokoro itashi   My heart is overflowing.

Despite his deep interest in unconventional or comic haikai in both waka and renga, Sōchō was in the realm of ushin linked verse a devoted follower of Sōgi, who was in turn absolutely committed to perceiving renga as an art form of equal gravity and expressiveness as orthodox waka. Although ushin verse itself has relaxed moments that may show something of the lightness of haikai composition (one form of haikai itself being within the orthodox ushin ambit), Sōchō was very careful never to introduce outré haikai themes or diction into his ushin composition.

The poet's interest in contemporary and plebeian themes and his frank and perhaps more immediately personal approach to ushin verse establish points of reference between his orthodox renga style and his diary literature. But because Sōchō was trained according to the orthodox Sōgi model, was personally devoted to the expression of ideal and universal truths through renga, and made his living teaching renga to others, it is that genre that is the least intimate and personal of his literary activities. It was perhaps the very exclusivity of the renga medium that required an outlet in the other "voices" of waka composition and diary literature. Sōchō generally used waka, not renga, when he wished to convey poetic matters of more personal concern. It is to that genre that we will now turn.

Waka in the 'Journal'

Although linked verse reached the height of its literary sophistication during Sōchō's lifetime, waka poetry remained a vital, popular, and respected art form. Proof of its continuing importance is provided by the journal itself, which contains more waka than linked verse. *The Journal of Sōchō* is, in fact, comprehensive testimony to the variety of stylistic forms and social functions that characterized the waka activity of the period.

It is a commonplace in literary history that by the sixteenth century the waka had long ceased to develop in terms of originality.[115] But while it is true that waka poetry had achieved literary maturity centuries before Sōchō was born, it continued to engage the finest poetic minds of his era, particularly among the courtier and warrior aristocracies and, of course, linked-verse poets. Though the last imperial waka anthology, *Shinshokukokinshū*, had appeared in 1439, Sōgi was still attempting to obtain backing for a new waka anthology as late as a half-century thereafter. Utaawase poetry contests flourished, enormous personal verse anthologies were compiled, and private correspondence still involved skill at waka composition. Many of the leaders of the waka world of the early sixteenth century are mentioned in Sōchō's journal. These include in particular the courtiers Sanjōnishi Sanetaka and Toyohara Muneaki, and also Emperor Gokashiwabara, Iwayama Dōken, and Konoe Masaie.[116]

Other contributions to waka teaching and practice were made by linked-verse poets, most notably Shinkei and Sōgi, but also Shōhaku and Sōchō.[117] Their activity underscores the traditionally close relationship between the waka and renga genres. The first major codifiers of high renga, Nijō Yoshimoto and Kyūsei, both studied waka assiduously with courtly masters and took as their main goal the inculcation of the renga medium with waka aesthetic standards. Later, the waka poet Shōtetsu became the mentor of an entire generation of renga poets, including Shinkei and three others of the Seven Sages, and his direction had much to do with the renaissance of renga in the early fifteenth century.[118] Knowledge of waka also constituted proof of poetic legitimacy; Sōgi's acquisition of the secret traditions of *Kokinshū* from Tō no Tsuneyori was the single most important stepping-stone aside from native talent in his quest for renga prominence. The study of the history and techniques of the waka was a vital prerequisite for anyone aspiring to skill in linked verse, and much of the curricula professional renga masters laid out for their disciples and amateur students focused on *Kokinshū* and other basic waka collections. As mentioned in Chapter One, rengashi, along with émigré courtiers, were important conduits through which the art of waka was disseminated to the provinces and the noncourtier classes in the late medieval period.

Sōchō's own poetic education was devoted, as we have seen, in large part to learning the waka tradition, and the foregoing analysis of his renga has indicated how deeply enmeshed it was in orthodox waka concepts. Some of the poetic works he in turn went on to write concentrate on waka knowledge, including *Sōchō kawa*.[119] Aside from the many verses in *The Journal of Sōchō*, numerous other examples of his waka survive, and these are probably only a fraction of the total number he composed during his lifetime.[120]

But *The Journal of Sōchō* indicates that for all the enormous influence of the waka tradition on Sōchō's life and renga practice, the two verse forms occupied overlapping but separate spaces in his mental literary terrain. Unlike courtier poets such as Ichijō Kaneyoshi and Sanjōnishi Sanetaka, who though deeply involved in the renga art always viewed it as subsidiary to the waka form, Sōchō considered himself first and last a specialist in linked verse. Renga was for Sōchō the quintessential poetic art, as suggested by the uncompromising remark in *Renga hikyōshū* that it "developed from waka but has greater depth of feeling."[121] The poet also valued waka for its traditional role in social interaction and for its ability to express concerns too directly personal for orthodox linked verse.

The best cross-section of Sōchō's waka activity is of course provided by his journal. The work includes waka ranging from recondite occasional verses for public poetry gatherings to private verses and haikai.[122] Whereas nearly all the renga hokku in the journal are by Sōchō himself, fully a quarter of the waka are by others, though most of those appear coupled with one by Sōchō in the form of poem exchanges.

The most public and formal poems (*hare no uta*) in the diary are by and large occasional in nature, often composed for annual events in Sunpu such as the Festival of the Weaver Maid (*JS* nos. 563–65), or for moments of special importance such as a celebration of Sōchō's longevity (*JS* nos. 274–81). They were also composed in honor of distinguished visitors to the Imagawa domain (*JS*: 56). The bulk of such poems in Sōchō's journal, however, are votive verses to mourn the deaths of friends or important figures or to mark their death anniversaries (*JS* nos. 221–52, 257–62, 303–8, etc.). Such poetry was meant to console the living and benefit the spirit of the deceased. Orthodox renga also sometimes accompanied the waka composed on those occasions.

Much of this type of poetry was composed on topics (*dai*) that were selected by a person who possessed the requisite poetic skill and elevated reputation. The topics were often distributed beforehand to the poets, who then composed at their leisure in private, or they might be provided for extemporaneous (*tōza*) composition on the spot. The verses were subsequently collected into a waka sequence (*tsugiuta*) and often read publicly. Such waka sequences first became popular in the Kamakura period, and they reflect the social and performative quality of so much of medieval artistic life. One typical waka sequence in *The Journal of Sōchō* was composed to mark the first month after the death of Nakamikado Nobutane in 1525:

> I initiated a one-round waka sequence for the monthly anniversary, each verse to begin with one of the syllables from his death poem. I asked Lord Ōgimachisanjō Sanemochi to select the topics for the thirty-one verses. Two of mine were included, one on "the first dew of autumn" and one on "opening a book and encountering the past":

306	aki no kaze ogi no uwaba mo tabi ni shite sode ni ya tsuyu no naren to suran	Like the upper leaves of the reeds in autumn's wind, will these sleeves of mine become accustomed to the dew as I journey on my way?
307	nochi mo oshi aru ka naki ka no	They will be treasured hereafter as well,

isonokami	these faint traces of the brush
yoyo hete kienu	that will not vanish for ages
fude no omokage	long as Isonokami Shrine's.

(JS: 84)

While some waka series, such as this example, were primarily religious and devotional in character, many others, especially those of the impromptu variety, were literary exercises or entertainments held to test the wits of the poets. Some sessions combined elements of both. In the following example to mark the first anniversary of the death of Imagawa Ujichika, a number of different waka sequences were composed:

Impromptu waka on topics at Ujiteru's residence:

557 MOUNTAIN VIEW

tsuki izuru	They remain till dawn
akatsuki kakete	beneath the rising moon
wakarete wa	then depart
irihi ni kaeru	to return with the setting sun—
mine no yokogumo	the clouds trailing around the peak.

558 LISTENING TO CHIRPING INSECTS

yūkaze ni	In the autumn field
suzu no kikoeshi	one heard the tinkle of little bells
aki no no wa	in the evening wind—
furisutegataki	how hard to turn one's back
mushi no koe kana	on the chirping of the crickets!

At the same gathering for the first anniversary of Ujichika's death, a poem was presented in Chinese by the Abbot of Chōrakuji. I composed a verse to harmonize with it, using the third and fourth lines of his poem as the topic:

559
nao jin'ai o todome	His benevolence and love remain,
ringaku ni amaneshi	everywhere in forest and valley.
hana onozukara kōkō ni shite	The blossoms by themselves turn red;
kusa onozukara aoshi	the grasses by themselves turn green.

560
omokage wa	Their appearance
sanagara akashi	is so like him!
iroka ni te	The hue and fragrance
michi no kusa shigeki	of the flowers by the roadside
hana zo kanashiki	fills me with sadness.

For the same anniversary, Lord Nakamikado sponsored a waka sequence on the *kana* syllabary. For the syllable *ri*, I composed:

561   MOUNTAIN DWELLING

> rin'e seba
> mizu kusa kiyoki
> yama no i no
> akanu kokoro wa
> sa mo araba are

> If he is reborn,
> his heart still thirsting for more
> of the pure water and grass
> at the mountain well,
> it is good that it be so.

562

> ryū no sumu
> minakami tsune ni
> haruru hi mo
> kumo kaze ame no
> taenu yama kana

> The headwaters
> where the dragon dwells
> flow down from a mountain
> where even on clear days below
> there are always clouds, wind, and rain!

(*JS*: 155–56)

Here Chinese poetry has also figured in the series, and Sōchō has used lines from it as topics for his own work. In Sōchō's journal, Chinese verses are the general province of the clerical community, who contribute such verses also for linked-verse sessions in Japanese and Chinese (*wakan renku*).

Stylistically, the poems in the journal composed on assigned topics are the most formal and conservative in terms of diction and conception. In tone, therefore, they complement the hokku in the work. This correspondence was well established in classical poetic theory; in *Azuma mondō*, for example, Sōgi relates the earlier observation by the nun Abutsu that "waka uses the topic (*dai*) as its hokku; renga uses the hokku as its topic."[123] The formal waka must correlate with the basic essence of the topic in the same way that a waki verse in renga must respond to the central thought of the hokku preceding it. Sōchō's public waka demonstrates skill in the manipulation of conventional topics, and it avoids exaggerated personal expression or rhetorical eccentricity in the interest of harmonizing with the other poems at the session. Like hokku verses, these formal poems often focus on seasonal topics and are essentially the waka equivalent of the first eight verses of a highly formal renga sequence.

But while Sōchō was capable of producing competent verse of a formal and conservative character, the vast majority of the verses in his journal are what may be considered private in nature, composed for an intimate audience or on the spur of the moment for his own enjoyment or consolation. These private verses reflect the fact that while renga was an exceptionally popular pursuit for groups and, in the form of solo sequences, for individuals, waka was still the usual medium for the direct communication of one's personal emotions. *The Journal of Sōchō* demonstrates the enormous importance of such private verse in the day-to-day lives of cultured individuals. And since etiquette normally dictated a reply in kind, much of this private work appears in the form of poem exchanges.

Many private poem exchanges involve requests for a visit or thanks for the same, such as the following verse sent from Nakamikado Nobutane in Kyoto to Sōchō, who was then in Kansai:

From Lord Nakamikado:

153	oi no tomo	If you are aware
	matsu zo to shiraba	that your old friend awaits you,
	kaerikoyo	then make your way back,
	tago no uranami	even if Tago's billows
	tachi wa yuku tomo	rise up only to depart.

My reply:

154	kimi ni yori	There is not a day
	tago no urawa ni	when the aged billows
	oi no nami	of the Bay of Tago
	omoi shi tatanu	do not rise up in longing
	hi mo zo nakaran	to go coursing back to you.

(*JS*: 45)

Tago Bay is an utamakura in Suruga, Sōchō's home province, which Nobutane uses as a metaphor for Sōchō himself.[124]

Many other such verses are requests for goods or services or, again, thanks for having received a favor:

Miyaki Nyūdō Shinkan heard I was needing a physic of sorrel root and sent this with it:

478	kimi ga tame	For you, good sir,
	fuyu no no ni idete	I ventured out in winter fields
	shinone horu	to dig sorrel roots,
	waga kamiginu ni	and upon my paper robe
	yuki wa furitsutsu	the snow never ceased to fall.

My reply:

479	waga tame ni	The sorrel roots
	motomuru shinone	that you went out and dug for me
	yuki no uchi no	must have been growing
	takana to koso wa	under a cover of snow
	oi mo idekemu	like the bamboo shoots of old.[125]

(JS: 133)

Other poems are sent while on a journey, very like a picture postcard:

Okitsu Hikokurō sent me this poem he composed while at Kiyomi Gate:

272	kiyomigata	At Kiyomi Strand,
	akemakuhoshiki	where one regrets the end of night,
	nami no ue ni	keep the moon
	tsuki no sekimore	from slipping away over the waves,
	sue no shirakumo	white clouds in the distance!

Though it was no reply, I sent him this:

273	kiyomigata	Your words of hope
	sekimoru tsuki no	that the moon be kept from passing
	koto no ha no	over Kiyomi Strand
	nagame o yosuru	were carried to me here
	ochi no shiranami	on white waves from far away.

(JS: 75–76)

Such exchanges run the gamut from verses whose rhetorical formality equals that of his public and occasional work to ones of considerable freedom of expression. His exchange with Imagawa Ujichika is an example of the former:

Ujichika was good enough to send a sprig of blossoming white gentians, with this poem attached:

284	aru ga naka ni	Unlike all the rest,
	kono hitoeda no	how does it happen that
	ika ni shite	this solitary bough
	yuki matsu hana no	blossoms with flower tinted
	iro ni sakuramu	as if waiting for the snow?

My humble reply:

285	kazukazu ni	How could my eye stray
	me ya wa utsuramu	to any of the others?

aru ga naka ni	Unlike all the rest,
mare naru hana wa	this sprig is seen as seldom
udonge ni shite	as the *udonge* blossom.

(JS: 78)

But other exchanges stretch the bounds of ushin poetry, such as the following, sent by one of Sōchō's acquaintances who missed a more formal waka series held earlier:

> On the twenty-eighth at the seaside we held a one-round waka sequence on thirty topics for the visitors from the capital. We composed on topics set by the Former Palace Minister, Ōgimachisanjō Sanemochi, who currently resides in the province. His poem led the sequence. This was sent from Kiyomi Strand by Ohara Chikataka:

188
matsuran to	Thinking they awaited me,
koma no ashinami	I set out, pony prancing,
yoru idete	to where waves rush in
kiyomigaseki ni	at Kiyomi Gate,
hirune o zo suru	but now I nod here napping!

My reply:

189
chigirishi mo	The aged waves
wasurenikeri na	forgot what they had promised
oi no nami	until the tide
asa mitsu shio no	that rises in the morning ebbed,
hirune suru made	and you took your noontime nap!

(JS: 56)

Chikataka had been waiting at the site of Kiyomi Gate to participate in the waka series. Sōchō apologizes for the misunderstanding about the location of the gathering in his reply. Sōchō's verse is very complicated; he casts himself as the aged billows and asserts that they forgot their promise (with overtones of Sōchō's promise to Chikataka) to rise with the morning tide (i.e., to meet at Kiyomi) until the noon ebb, "noon" (*hiru*) then introducing "nap" (*hirune*).

Sōchō wrote another in an even more jocular vein in response to a gift:

> Gokokuji temple at Higuchi Aburanokōji is famous for its plums, and I asked that they send one to Shinjuan. In their answer, they included a reference to the verse "Though it not suffice / I present this rock instead." I composed this in response:

CHAPTER FOUR

| 389 | akanedomo
iwa ni shi kaeba
onajiku wa
tsutsuji o mo nao
soete tabe kashi | If plum trees in place
of a rock "will not suffice,"
please send along
(if it's all the same to you)
some azaleas as well! |

(*JS*: 111)

The verse, not extant, sent from Gokokuji temple probably recast the *Ise monogatari* foundation poem (74), substituting a plum tree for the rock in the honka:

akanedomo   Though it not suffice,
iwa ni zo kauru   I present this rock instead,
iro mienu   for I have no way
kokoro o misemu   to show you the colors
yoshi no nakereba   that are hidden in my heart.

Sōchō pretends to take literally the phrase "though it not suffice."
And other poems sent to friends are outright haikai:

Nakae Tosanokami called at my travel lodging. He brought rice, firewood, money, and such. Spent two nights chatting beside the hearth. After he left, I sent him this:

| 461 | hatsuboku ni
takigi zōji nado
torigushite
tabine no yoi o
sake no yoiyoi | You came equipped
with rice and also with firewood
and coin of the realm—
we rested on our travels
lit by evening's moonshine! |

(*JS*: 128)

In this humorous verse Sōchō puns on *yoi* (evening / intoxication).
And while the vast majority of such poem exchanges are of a felicitous or good-natured character, waka were also occasionally used by Sōchō to convey disappointment or irritation:

Some visitors said they wanted to see the site of the old Kiyomi Gate, and I gave them a letter of introduction to take with them to Seikenji temple. When they returned, they said nothing about the trip to me, so I appended this poem to an answer to a letter from Okitsu Hikokurō:

| 549 | iza saraba
waga na o kaete | If they would be so,
I will try calling myself |

yobite mimu	something different—
sōchō yue ya	was it the name "Sōchō"
tsurenakaruramu	that made them so unresponsive?

550	miyakobito ni	Know that in place of
	tachikawaritsutsu	the people from the capital,
	kiyomigata	the waves that wash
	iwa shiku nami mo	the rocks at Kiyomigata
	omou to o shire	will convey my feelings.

(*JS*: 153)

Sōchō assumes that his letter of introduction was ineffective, and he directs his pique in the verse toward Seikenji. As explored in Chapter One, the poet also uses waka as a medium for expressing to others such personal emotions as friendship, consolation for misfortunes, and, increasingly as he ages, lamentations on his own condition.

Again, in all poetry, as in all writing, content and form combine to fashion a persona that both reveals and masks the informing intelligence behind. But Sōchō's private waka respond more to the empirical events of his everyday life than do his formal renga, which while also inevitably tied to the subjectivity of the poet tend to be directed more toward the evocation of universals of the human condition, as codified by poetic tradition. The poet's personal perspective is inescapable, of course, and even ushin renga verses may reflect his subjective condition, but never to the degree that private waka in the journal do. Because of such verses, the work as a whole assumes an everyday referentiality that is quite different from the diary literature of, for example, Sōgi, which as we have already seen aims toward the same existential universality of orthodox renga verse.

Private poetry exchanges, however, share with renga a sense of dialogue; they are directed to another, and they call out for a link. They are usually not as completely impromptu and performative as renga links, but the waka response is to some extent predicated on the sense and language of the preceding waka verse. Like the formal waka composed on and shaped by the topics set by someone else, the zōtōka exchanges are conditioned by a relationship between the self and the other. The origins of such exchanges, in fact, are conventionally traced to the same archaic question-and-response courting verses that helped shape the renga genre.

The Journal of Sōchō also includes verses written primarily by Sōchō for his own diversion. To be sure, even such intensely personal verses perhaps at times involve another, be it the poet's own objectified alter ego or a hypothesized reader, but they are written in direct response to personal concerns, emotions, and inspirations rather than to verses or poem topics that originated with someone else. Such verses in the journal, as we have already observed, tend toward lamentation and self-consolation, and they deal primarily with the fact of old age, friends who have died, physical pain and infirmity, and meditations on death and the afterlife. While the bulk of the natural description and seasonal verse in the journal is contributed by hokku and formal waka on set topics, many of the deepest human moments are found in Sōchō's private waka compositions. The journal does contain private nature poetry too, of course, but such verse, far more than the hokku, is directed toward the depiction of nature in relation to the poet's own condition. The following group of verses is a case in point:

In the autumn, on having planted bush clover and reeds beneath the eaves of my travel lodging:

253
    kokoro kara   This is an evening
    kurabe kurushiki   when it is hard to choose
        yūbe kana   in my heart between them!
    hagi ogi uete   Wind and dew in the bush clover
    kaze to tsuyu to ni   and in the reeds I planted.

I broke off a branch of bush clover and sent it to someone with this:

254
    teru tsuki mo   The shining moon wove
    yoru no nishiki no   a long brocade by night
        hagi ga hana   of bush clover blossoms—
    orihae kyō ya   I broke them off and today you too
    tsuyu mo miyuran   may see them cloaked with dew.

On hearing the chirping in the garden of bell crickets, perhaps those I caught and then released here last year:

255
    aware koso   How moving the thought—
    tazune hanachishi   could they be the ones that I caught
        sore ka aranu   and then released?
    susuki ga moto no   In the pampas grass
    suzumushi no koe   the chirping of bell crickets.

They chirped for five or six nights, then disappeared. Thereafter the pine crickets started in:

256	tachikawari	In the other's place
	otoranu mono ya	does it move one any less?
	kore naranu	Once the singing
	suzumushi no ne ni	of the bell crickets; now the chirping
	matsumushi no koe	of the pine crickets instead.

(*JS*: 71–72)

Sōchō's private nature poetry also tends to involve a *sentient* nature, and Sōchō's own feelings toward it. Some verses are concerned with the suffering of animals and the afflictions of all forms of life, a theme on which Ikkyū composed as well.[126] Sōchō's anecdote about birds caught in fowlers' nets is illustrative:

> Near my travel lodgings, on the waters off Shina, Konohama, Yamada, and Yashima, boats without number rest their punting poles before their spread-out fowling nets. Watching the rain capes and hats bobbing up and down on the waves in the icy winds from the Ibuki and Hira Mountains, I cannot imagine the evil of taking life to be any worse than the wretchedness of those who cling to it like this. In the dark before dawn, I hear the beating of the waterbirds' wings and the plaintive calls of geese, thwarted in their attempts to land, and I wonder which of them will be caught. Finally I hear them come to water and then their frantic screams as they are trapped in the waiting nets and killed. It is unbearable. I can only stop my ears, my pillow wet with tears:

462	aware naru	How pathetic,
	kari no koe kana	the crying of the wild geese!
	me mo haru ni	As far as the eye can see,
	ami okiwatasu	waves spread with nets for waterfowl
	nami no akebono	at the break of day.
463	nami no ue	The ducks in the reeds,
	tachii makasuru	which once floated freely
	ashigamo no	upon the waves,
	ami no nawate ni	now lie snared in the meshes
	kakarinuru kana	of the waterfowlers' nets!

(*JS*: 128–29)

The style and technique of Sōchō's waka are likewise enormously varied. His public and occasional work tends to be conservative and straightforward in terms of diction, replicating in waka format the simple "lucidity" of his hokku and prose. Those efforts of Sōchō display straightforward syntax, a balance between content and rhetoric, and few ellipses.

He also pays considerable attention to the technique of allusive variation. About one-fourth of his waka compositions appear to be based on earlier poems, with about a third of those honka taken from *Kokinshū* and a fifth from *Shinkokinshū*. These statistics exactly match those for the allusive variation in his hokku, listed earlier. Nearly all of the first eight imperial anthologies are represented, as well as *Man'yōshū*, *Ise monogatari*, *Genji monogatari*, and various other texts. As with his hokku, the preponderance of *Kokinshū* honka in his waka does not compromise Sōchō's basic *Shinkokinshū* orientation; honka in *Shinkokinshū* itself are primarily taken from the first three anthologies, and Shunzei himself stated that "the basic form (*hontai*) of poems should be searched for in *Kokinshū*."[127]

But while Sōchō was capable of composing poetry in a simple and refined style, it is also true that many of his waka verses seem influenced by renga diction. In this they are characteristic of much of the verse of the period, for while waka had indeed reached a pinnacle of development during the *Shinkokinshū* period and another with the appearance of the *Gyokuyōshū* and *Fūgashū* collections, it did not entirely cease to evolve thereafter.[128] Later stylistic developments were in part inspired by the growing popularity of the renga medium and were manifest in even greater syntactical fragmentation and concision, together with a widening of the poetic lexicon. While courtly purists had long resisted the impact of renga on waka stylistics, by Sōchō's era even the most conservative poets had to varying degrees accepted the new words and new syntactical constructions introduced through renga influence. Some of Sōchō's waka show more compression and ellipsis than is normally found in, for example, *Shinkokinshū* poetry, as well as more fragmentation and nominalization.

Perhaps the most interesting parallel to linked-verse technique is Sōchō's tendency to compose waka in pairs on the same theme.[129] That characteristic was introduced earlier with reference to *The Journal of Sōchō* as travel literature. Many of those pairs are interpersonal poetic exchanges, yoked by circumstance rather than by choice. Even those, however, often have the same quality of greeting seen in the relation between a hokku composed by a guest and a waki by the host. Many other poem pairs consist of two verses by Sōchō, a tendency toward coupling that is thoroughly in keeping with a lifetime of thinking in terms of poetic links.

In addition, some of the private waka in *The Journal of Sōchō* show the same bent toward free and even eccentric expression seen in some of his late renga verses. A few of them exhibit particularly convoluted conceptions or constructions and were apparently composed at least in part as puzzles. One example appears in a poetic exchange with a warrior acquaintance in Suruga:

> Yui Mimasakanokami (whose religious name is Hōgo) sent me a bundle of Fuji silk floss as wadding for a paper robe. I sent this off in thanks:

289   naninani ni   Fuji always wears
      tokaku suruga no   a silken cap in Suruga,
        fuji wata no   where one lacks nothing,
      taenu susono ni   but even so I had no cap myself
      yuki wa furitsutsu   for snow falling on foothill fields.

> Hōgo's reply:

290   yuki wa tada   The silken cap
      kesa furu fuji no   that Fuji wears is only snow
        wataboshi   that fell this morning—
      taenu susono mo   and soon you too will wear one
      shibashi matanan   down in those foothill fields.

                            (JS: 79)

Sōchō means that while Fuji is covered with snow like a silken cap all year long, he himself did not have a cap for the winter snow, despite the fact that in Suruga one should be able to obtain almost anything, particularly in view of the proximity to the place of production of *Fuji [no] wata* or silk floss. Then he received the floss from Yui Hōgo. In his response, Hōgo suggests that since snow has only recently fallen on Mount Fuji, adding to its white cap, the foothills too will wear a cap of snow before long, and Sōchō will now have a cap of silk floss to protect himself as well.

Another example of this free and even slightly eccentric mode is the following poem pair referring to New Year's Eve of 1525 and then New Year's Day of 1526:

> Already New Year's Eve:

324   aken toshi no   The eve of the day
      kyō no koyoi ya   on which the New Year begins—
        aratama no   soon I too will know
      kuru to iu hito no   if the things they say are true
      makoto shirubeki   about spirits coming back.

> ... New Year's morning. First calligraphy:

325	kuru to iu	The night they are said
	koyoi mo akenu	to return has now ended.
	tama no o no	If the cord
	taenaba kesa no	of my life had broken—
	haru no awayuki	light spring snow this morning.

(*JS*: 88–89)

In the first poem of the pair, Sōchō is suggesting that he will soon die and become one of the spirits said to visit on New Year's Eve. The second was composed when Sōchō found himself still alive the following day. It is based on *Shinkokinshū* 11: 1034, by Princess Shokushi:

In a hundred-poem sequence, on "concealing love":

tama no o yo	Jewelled cord of life,
taenaba taene	if you are to break, then break!
nagaraeba	If I live on,
shinoburu koto no	I will weaken from the strain
yowari mo zo suru	of concealing my longing.

Sōchō compares the end of life to the melting of morning's light snow. His diction, however, is disjointed, with the quotation from the poem, *tama no o [no] / taenaba*, being inserted in a grammatically elliptical manner. The sense of the poem too is more implied than stated directly, being based on the conception that had the jewelled cord of his life broken, his spirit too would have joined the others who returned to the world on the eve of the New Year, then left like light snow that melts away to nothing in the morning sun.

Waka like these show an overabundance of spirit (*kokoro*) and an inclination to let the framework (*kotoba*) stand in its spontaneous form. Inoue Muneo attributes that characteristic of Sōchō's verse in the journal to old age.[130] It may also in part be the result of Zen teachings about the intuitive, rather than the studied, approach to truth and the equal validity (and nonvalidity) of all representations of reality. Sōchō appears to have saved his most thorough rhetorical craftsmanship for his professional products, his renga.

But again, this tendency is relative; in his public and occasional poetry, as well as in many of his private compositions, Sōchō is very attentive to sophisticated orthodox expression and technical facility. And despite their selective renga influences, Sōchō's waka show no particularly marked tendency to divide into upper and lower hemistiches of seventeen and fourteen syllables.[131] Some do, of course, but not enough to define a clear-cut partiality to that format. The fact suggests that while Sōchō's waka, along with those of most other waka poets of the late medieval period, were influenced by renga technique, the poet remained conscious that waka and renga were separate genres with different, albeit mutually influential, qualities.

Clearly, Sōchō expended a great deal of energy composing waka, although unlike Sōgi, he never compiled a personal waka anthology (*shikashū*). There is, however, an abridged version of *The Journal of Sōchō* entitled *Sōchō michi no ki* devoted only to the waka in the work together with the prose passages that elaborate them. It includes most of the waka and a number of lines not found in the unabridged versions of the text, as well as a few lines from *Sōchō nikki*.[132] As every important poet was almost required by classical precedent to compile a waka collection as a seal of his mastery of the genre, this may have been meant to serve as Sōchō's. But *Sōchō michi no ki* in no way resembles a formal shikashū; with its long prefaces and passages unrelated to any poetry, it is in form more like an *uta-nikki* or a work of travel literature by a waka poet. If it was meant to serve as a personal waka collection, it is an eccentric and informal one at best.

That being said, it remains clear that for Sōchō as for his contemporaries, waka continued to fulfill crucial social and emotional functions. While Sōchō perceived renga as his central vocation, he was capable of rhetorically accomplished formal waka verses and of a great range of private compositions ranging from deeply serious lamentations to comedic haikai. *The Journal of Sōchō* is a particularly important source of such haikai waka, renga, and chōka verses, some of which are devoted to flippant ribaldry, while others manifest their own brand of ushin conviction.

Haikai in the 'Journal'

Sōchō is remarkable in premodern Japanese literary history for the breadth of the poetic oeuvre he preserved for posterity. Not only was he a collaborator in some of the greatest high renga sequences, but he also recorded an unprecedented range of haikai waka and renga, which incorporate words, subjects, or tonalities that test or exceed the boundaries of high poetic orthodoxy. His journal is testimony to its author's versatility. As many as one-quarter of all the waka recorded in the journal can be classified as haikai to some degree. In addition, Sōchō included fifty-six haikai renga composed with other poets at a gathering in Takigi that are vital to our understanding of the historical development of that genre. While Sōchō never compromised his orthodox standards when working in the high style, he found it possible to use the haikai medium not only for jokes and ribaldry but also occasionally for the expression of serious personal concerns.

The importance of haikai in Sōchō's journal was the result of both the poet's own character and the literary tenor of his era. The late fifteenth and early sixteenth centuries were a watershed period in the history of haikai renga, for it was during that time that some of its practitioners began, selectively and tentatively, to stake out an independent position for that genre, one that challenged the prevailing elite perception of that form of poetry as the nonprivileged element in a high-renga hierarchy. The first known anthology of haikai linked verse, *Chikuba kyōginshū* (Hobbyhorse Collection of Mad Song), appeared in 1499, only four years after Sōgi had excised such poetry from his imperially recognized collection of orthodox renga, *Shinsen tsukubashū*.[133] The appearance of the new haikai anthology and the absence of haikai verses in Sōgi's work both demonstrate that haikai renga was by then beginning to be perceived as a qualitatively different art form.

Sōchō played an important role in that development, both through his own work and through his association with others. Included among the fifty-six Takigi verses in his journal are two by the man nearly universally identified as the compiler of the haikai renga anthology later known as *Shinsen inu tsukubashū*, Yamazaki Sōkan, famed throughout the Edo period as one of the fathers of the modern haikai renga genre.[134] Though Sōkan is believed to have composed many of the verses in his anthology, the two recorded in Sōchō's journal, which he may have composed with Sōchō at Takigi, are the only ones that may be attributed to him with certainty.

Sōchō was also personally acquainted with Arakida Moritake, author of the first extant thousand-verse haikai sequence, known as *Moritake senku* (1536–40), and therefore traditionally venerated as another of the founders of modern haikai poetry.[135] Like Sōkan, Moritake was trained in the composition of high renga; he learned the art in part from Sōchō himself, and Sōkan may have as well.[136] The influence of Sōchō on the two poets, together with Sōchō's own haikai activity, has led Konishi Jin'ichi to state, "I personally feel that the father of haikai renga is neither Yamazaki Sōkan nor Arakida Moritake, but rather Sōchō."[137]

Konishi is quite right to stress Sōchō's importance in the development of haikai literature, but there was, of course, no one agent of its birth as a separate literary form. The entire history of Japanese poetry has been one of collision, confrontation, and cross-fertilization between the courtly and the plebeian, the ushin and the mushin, the orthodox and the heterodox, the canonical and the noncanonical. And haikai, whose roots are as ancient as Japanese poetry itself, has embraced a vast range of styles, from those that fall within the ambit of ga poetry to those of zoku orientation. In the case of waka, examples of haikai within the ga tradition were included even in the first imperial anthology. *Tsukubashū* mirrored this in linked verse, incorporating a book of haikai renga that were within the ga sphere.

But from the point of view of courtly waka and renga, the haikai appellation had always denoted the *un*conventional or the *un*orthodox, being defined by practitioners of high culture in terms of what it was not. It was this radical devaluation of the nonprivileged term that began to break down in Sōchō's lifetime; haikai poetry even of the zoku variety began to be written down, collected, and assessed by both elites and nonelites (albeit to varying degrees) as an independent genre with its own norms. To be sure, this was only a nascent development; the preface of *Chikuba kyōginshū* continues to frame the philosophy of its compiler in terms of the high tradition, and its very title, which may be translated as "Hobbyhorse Collection of Mad Song," was chosen in parodic reflection of its high renga antecedent, *Tsukubashū*. But the author of the preface also indicates that the haikai verses collected therein had their own unique value. The collection, he writes,

> is not meant as a guide for those who would look for pears or pick up chestnuts [i.e., pursue unorthodox linked verse]; it is only meant to engage and console the spirit.[138] And yet I consider it something noble, just as even the bark of a village dog is a means to attain enlightenment or the cry of the stag in Yamada is part of the Truth.[139]

Arakida Moritake too relates in his afterword to *Moritake senku* that he composed his sequence to fulfill a vow to Amaterasu, the goddess he served as a priest at Ise Shrine. He consulted an oracle as to whether he should compose a high renga sequence or one in a haikai vein, and he notes that he prayed that the divination sticks would instruct him to choose the latter. Clearly the priest felt that like orthodox renga, haikai constituted an acceptable offering even to the Sun Goddess herself. He then adds the following: "Should haikai simply be undisciplined and comic? It has been the teaching of men of taste through the ages that haikai should provide both flower and fruit [i.e., words and content], show elegance (*fūryū*), and combine correctness with humor."[140]

This evolution was doubtless related in part to the rising power of commoners, the reason often adduced in literary histories.[141] But as we indicated earlier, the phenomenon was in reality far more complex and founded in the fluidity of the period and a growing cultural circularity embracing elites and nonelites alike. Again, it is a mistake to see haikai activity as exclusively the province of the lower classes and high renga as that of the courtly, military, and clerical aristocracies. Nonelites both rebelled against classical culture and craved it; the continuing popularity and rising sophistication of high renga itself was partly due to its embrace by commoners, a phenomenon facilitated by renga masters who were often of that social stratum themselves. Certain forms of haikai, conversely, enjoyed a long tradition at court. It is far more to the point to see the growth of the haikai medium in this period in part as a broad-based cultural reaction to social, political, and economic changes that embraced all levels of society.

It is probably also true that the increasing complexity and rarefication of high renga required a more relaxing outlet, just as courtly haikai had once provided relaxation after poetry contests in the high style.[142] Moritake wrote that the orthodox renga master Kensai, for example, enjoyed composing haikai verses after long renga sessions.[143] It is highly likely that the many pages of renga rules led some aspiring poets to abandon altogether the attempt to apply them and to take refuge in freer haikai composition. Even the most accomplished composers of high waka and renga enjoyed haikai verse, surely in the same way and for much the same reason that kyōgen was enjoyed between nō performances.

Sōchō made a particularly important contribution to the rising social and literary position of haikai by judging it worthy not only of composition but of preservation. But even his teacher Sōgi left examples of haikai verse. Both poets were products and agents of the social and cultural revolution taking place around them at this time, and the similarities and differences in their literary responses to that shared condition are part of our story here. Sōgi anticipates Sōchō in his composition of a full range of haikai, in both the ga and zoku spheres, much as his *Tsukushi michi no ki* is premonitory of some of the directions Sōchō would pursue in his own travel work. But just as he did in the realm of travel literature, Sōchō demonstrated in his approach to haikai a somewhat different response from that of Sōgi to the collision of cultures that marked the period.

THE HAIKAI POETRY OF SŌGI

Sōgi's reputation today rests almost entirely on his ushin teaching and practice. His exclusion of haikai from *Shinsen tsukubashū* is usually cited as evidence of his disregard for the genre. In the early Edo period, however, Sōgi was remembered by some not only as a great poet in the high style but also as one of the founders of contemporary haikai, along with Moritake and Sōkan.[144]

Sōgi also held a prominent place as a haikai poet in the popular imagination. He and Sōchō figure prominently in the early Edo-period collection of humorous anecdotes entitled *Seisuishō*. One characteristic story reads as follows:

> One evening when Sōgi and his disciple Sōchō were walking beside the bay, they came upon a fisherman hauling in nets that were covered with seaweed [*mo*].
> "What do you call that?" they asked. The fisherman replied, "Some say *me*, some say *mo*."
> "That would make a good renga link," Sōgi remarked, and he composed this:

me to mo iu nari	Some say *me*,
mo to mo iu nari	Some say *mo*.

> He then directed Sōchō to provide a rejoinder. Sōchō composed the following:

hikitsurete	Leading home
nogai no ushi no	oxen that were
kaerusa ni	out to pasture.

> Female oxen make the sound *unme* when they low, and male oxen, *unmo*. Sōgi was impressed. Then Sōchō asked the master for a verse in return. He composed:

yomu iroha	Look beside the finger
oshiyuru yubi no	that points to those syllables
shita o miyo	in the *iroha*.

> *Me* comes after the *yu* of *yubi* [finger] in the *iroha* syllabary, and *mo* comes after the *bi*.[145]

Sōgi is by far the best represented rengashi in that collection, with Sōchō next. Some of those tales were later incorporated into an *ukiyozōshi* collection entitled *Sōgi shokoku monogatari* (Tales of Sōgi's Travels through the Provinces, 1685) devoted to purported examples of his wit while on his various journeys. Such humorous accounts linked him in the popular imagination with Ikkyū, who figured in tales of cleverness and eccentricity that were eventually collected and published in the early Edo period as *Ikkyūbanashi* (Anecdotes about Ikkyū, 1668). In actuality, of course, such stories were in general circulation, and most if not all were probably attributed to Sōgi and Ikkyū after the fact. Sōchō's reputation as a haikai specialist was doubtless strengthened in the Edo period because of his well-known relationship to both men.

Though vastly outnumbered by Sōgi's corpus of ushin verses, various haikai renga survive that can be confidently attributed to him.[146] They run the gamut from poetry within the ushin compass, through more adventurous work, to at least one example in a ribald and zoku vein.

His haikai in the ga manner are well represented by forty-six examples that appear at the end of his first anthology of personal verse, *Wasuregusa*.[147] Some of the tsukeku preserved therein were composed for the same maeku, such as the three below:

	hito no kokoro kawaru yo no naka	People's feelings change in this life.
885	toki suguru mi koso muika no ayamegusa	A woman past her prime: sweetflag a day after the festival.[148]

	hito no kokoro kawaru yo no naka	People's feelings change in this life.
890	ōsaka mo hate wa nakoso no sekiji ni te	Even the Mountain of Meeting leads in the end to Gate Come-No-More.[149]

	hito no kokoro kawaru yo no naka	People's feelings change in this life.
915	ukimi sae ima wa no toki ya oshikaran	Even one who finds the world bleak is loath to leave it in his final moments.[150]

In the first pair of verses, the tsukeku responds to the orthodox maeku with a reference to a vernacular proverb, "a day after the festival," more literally translated as "sweetflag on the sixth." The fifth day of the fifth month is the festival of Tango no sekku, when sweetflag plants were hung from the eaves of houses to ward off ill fortune. Sweetflag plants on the sixth are useless. The image here serves as a metaphor for a woman past her prime, for whom a man feels no attraction. The interest of the verse derives not from outré or ribald vocabulary or subject matter, but rather from the clever application of a vernacular metaphor to a very orthodox maeku in order to suggest an unromantic and even cynical treatment of the love category.

The second pair derives its interest from the use of two utamakura and the imagery of travel again as a cynical metaphor for the hopeful first meeting of lovers to their eventual parting at the end of their relationship. "The Mountain of Meeting," Ōsaka, was one of the main sites of entrance to and egress from the capital, made famous through countless poems. The Nakoso Gate stood at the entrance to the far north, in what is now Fukushima Prefecture. The name is homophonic with the imperative phrase *na ko so*, "come no more," which was often used in love poetry.¹⁵¹ Though the basic essence of love involves a final parting, the imaginative and yet cynical introduction of the travel metaphor gives the verse its haikai cast.

Cynicism is the mark of the third pair of verses as well. It contains overtones of a recluse who professes distaste for the world and shuns it, but who still has lingering attachments to it at the time of death. There is no word play at all in the link; the haikai effect is generated simply through the nonidealized apprehension of the frailty of human nature.

The haikai qualities of the verses stand out more clearly when compared to three ushin tsukeku in the same collection that Sōgi composed on the same first verse:

	hito no kokoro kawaru yo no naka	People's feelings change in this life.
335	itsu mo miru tsuki o koyoi no na ni medete	Taking pleasure in the moon one always sees because of its special fame tonight.¹⁵²

| | hito no kokoro
kawaru yo no naka | People's feelings
change in this life. |

363   aki to ieba
         ika naru toki zo
             yūmagure

What time of day
is it that goes with autumn?
     Evening twilight.[153]

❦

      hito no kokoro
    kawaru yo no naka

People's feelings
change in this life.

599   hakanashi ya
        hane o narabeshi
            toribeyama

How fleeting!
A bird whose wings linked with another's,
     now at Toribeyama.[154]

Two of these orthodox tsukeku verses are in the autumn section, and the last is a love lament. The first refers to the night of the "famous moon" (*meigetsu*) on the fifteenth of the eighth month, when one pays it more attention than on other nights. Verse two is based on the first segment of Sei Shōnagon's *Makura no sōshi* (Pillow Book, c. 995–1000, with later additions), which begins "In spring, it is the time just before dawn." Summer, Sei continues, is best for its nights, autumn for twilight, and winter for sunrise.[155] Thus do people's tastes and feelings change through the course of the year. And verse three speaks of the death of one's lover, the smoke of whose cremation rises at Toribeyama. Though the two were once as close as "two birds with the wings of one," the passage of time mitigates the pain of death.[156] Thus do people's hearts change.

As opposed to these verses, which are in keeping with orthodox waka standards of decorum, elegance, and idealized beauty, the haikai verses focus more on the everyday and even evince cynicism toward romanticized waka taste. They derive their effect from either witty word play or a recasting of an idealized sentiment into a more quotidian vein. These haikai verses never cross the boundary, however, into vulgarity, either of lexicon or content.

Conversely, the first of the ushin verses quoted above does seem to depict a trace of amusement at the way opinion and taste are fashioned by habit or tradition. Just as the haikai in *Wasuregusa* skirt the boundaries of the ushin orthodoxy without trespassing beyond them, so may ushin verses show varying degrees of seriousness or lightness. Even the most orthodox renga sequences demonstrate an alternation of heavy and light verses, the latter of which may encroach into the ga haikai domain. One verse by Sōchō in *Yuyama sangin* is a case in point:

saku hana mo omowazarame ya haru no yume	Can the blossoms too help but give thought to it? The dream of spring.
	Shōhaku
sakura to ieba yamaarashi zo fuku	Cherries—no sooner said then mountain winds blow!
	Sōchō

The overall seriousness and literary orthodoxy of the sequence is unquestionable. But Sōchō's link includes a touch of light, haikai-like humor in the conception of the cherries lamenting the wind that starts to blow the blossoms away at the very mention of their name, reminding them that they are as dream-like and evanescent as the spring. The mix of light and heavy links forms another of the developmental patterns that configure any renga sequence. Sōgi's haikai verses in his *Wasuregusa* collection are not very far from ones that could have been composed during similar light moments at an orthodox renga session.[157]

Sōgi made a more marked departure into the haikai modality with his *Sōgi jōji hyakuin*, a hundred-verse sequence in which each verse contains a Chinese compound (*jōji*), the presence of which is not allowed in orthodox linked verse.[158] The sequence is essentially conceived in ushin terms; it departs from ga renga more in its Chinese lexicon than in its subject matter or tone, which is still on the whole quite orthodox. Although jōji renga had long formed a subgenre in Japanese poetry, Sōgi's composition introduces more elements of the familiar and contemporaneous than do earlier jōji works.[159]

The sequence in general follows the standard renga rules, and its first verses show only a very slight deviation from the elevated and understated quality of an orthodox "first eight verses" (the Chinese compounds are italicized):

1	hana niou ume wa *busō* no kozue kana	Fragrant blossoms of the plum upon peerless branch tips![160]
2	yanagi no *mime* wa ge ni ima no toki	The willows are at their best this very moment![161]
3	haru no yo wa kasumi o tsuki no *kibo* to shite	On spring nights haze is of the essence for the moon.[162]

CHAPTER FOUR

4	yuki no *yozan* o yama ni koso mire	Lingering snow is seen on the mountain.[163]
5	iku tsura mo tada *ippen* ni kaeru kari	Countless lines, but one intent— returning geese.[164]
6	tabi no *sujitsu* no sode zo shiraruru	The length of the journey can be told by his sleeves.[165]
7	kaze machite *tōryū* shitaru minatobune	Waiting for the wind, it must pause awhile— the boat in the harbor.[166]
8	tomaya no *uchū* omoi koso yare	In a thatch hut in the rain, sunk in sad thoughts.[167]

But in the middle of the hundred-verse piece, the "development" (ha) section, where renga conventionally shows the most innovation, some of Sōgi's verses begin to comment on everyday life in a way that ventures further from the ushin mold and establishes closer affinities with zoku haikai composition. The following verses (from the back of the third page of the sequence) show that characteristic the most strongly:

67	tokorogara tsuki mo *tohi* ni ya kawaruran	No matter what the place, capital or countryside, is the moon any different?

The verse in isolation evokes the elegant melancholy of a resident of the capital who is traveling in the hinterlands. Except for the Chinese compound *tohi* (capital and provinces), the verse could easily appear in an ushin sequence.

68	sa mo *nangan* no suma no akikaze	How hard a life, in the autumn wind of Suma.[168]

Now the traveler is explicitly Genji, in exile in Suma. The verse is based on a prose allusion (*honzetsu*) to the line in the "Suma" chapter of *Genji monogatari* that reads, "The autumn wind made Suma all the more melancholy."[169] There is a kakekotoba pivoting between *nangan no su* ("how hard a life") and *suma no akikaze* ("the autumn wind of Suma"). Again, the tone of the verse is completely in the ga renga frame. But that begins to change in the next link:

69	tsuyu hodo mo	Hoping for
	rijun omou ni	earnings even light as dew,
	shio yakite	they boil brine for salt.

The use of the word *tsuyu* (dew) keeps this link in the autumn category. It is a close link lexically, with Suma connected to *shio yakite* ("boiling brine for salt") (*RJGPS* no. 559). The elegant and courtly scene of the previous verse now changes to one evoking the poverty of sea folk who eke out a living by selling salt. The word *rijun* (profit) introduces a mundane element unacceptable in orthodox renga.

70	sukoshi no *eko* mo	Spurred by the thought
	kokoro koso hike	of even a little gain.

With verse no. 70 the sequence leaves Autumn for the Miscellaneous category. *Rijun* in the previous verse calls up *eko* (profit or gain) in the link. In creating his next verse, Sōgi recalls the different but related meaning of *eko*, "nepotism" or "favoritism":

71	hitori sumu	A person living alone
	mi ya *rikan* ni mo	may develop
	narinubeshi	the talent for office.

Even though one may hope for favoritism from relatives to advance one's career, a person who lives on his own and learns self-reliance may prove more likely to succeed. By exploiting the other meaning of the word *eko*, Sōgi avoids a direct reference to the penultimate verse, which would have constituted a "clash" (uchikoshi) proscribed by the renga rules. It was essential in renga practice to master the multiple meanings for single words since that was a basic way to construct *yariku*, verses that helped the sequence develop in new directions. Sōgi was a master of such verses, and he devoted part of his handbook *Bun'yōshū* to such vocabulary.

73	urayamashiki wa	A source of envy:
	yoso no *baibai*	another's sales.

Here too then Sōgi creates a link by focusing on a word in the previous verse. Here *rikan*, "talent for office," suggests the homophone *rikan*, "to calculate profits." This pun then calls up the word *baibai*, "sales." But the use of the word in that sense does unavoidably throw the sequence back to verse no. 71, creating a clash which Sōgi ignores either because of the relaxed nature of the session or the principle that even the renga rules may be selectively transgressed in the interest of developing the sequence as a whole. These last several verses have been linked predominantly through kotobazuke, "linking through words," though content connections of course always figure as well.

74	*eiraku* no	So many strings
---	sashi mo ōki o	of Eiraku coins,
	shoji mo sede	and none for himself.

Sōgi continues the theme of commerce in this next verse. Eiraku coins (*Eirakusen*) were minted by the Ming government in China from 1408 to 1424 and were a primary form of currency in Japan during Sōgi's lifetime. Large numbers of such coins could be strung together. Sōgi uses them in a kakekotoba pivoting between *eiraku no sashi* ("strings of Eiraku coins") and *sashi mo* (so many).

While the sequence, therefore, is basically orthodox in its orientation, verses such as those above introduce contemporary details and a range of emotions that could not be expressed even in the haikai-like verses that appear in a ga renga sequence. In their quotidian detail and occasionally cynical wit, they move somewhat closer to zoku haikai expression.

In fact, Sōgi was at times able to throw off his orthodox orientation and compose zoku haikai purely for fun. Sanetaka recorded one such verse in a diary entry for 1499:

> The priest Sōgi came with food and sake. Gensei and Sōchō brought sake as well. We drank an enormous amount. Lord Toshimichi composed a kyōku hokku, which I have forgotten.

fuji wa sagarite	Wisteria hangs about
yūgure no sora	under an evening sky.
	Sōchō

yōsari wa	When night falls,
tare ni kakarite	to whom will she cling
nagusaman	for comfort?
	Sōgi

Everyone roared with laughter.[170]

Sōchō's maeku is completely orthodox and recalls one Sōgi composed for *Yuyama sangin* in 1491:

66	fuji saku koro no tasogare no sora	When wisteria are in blossom, under the twilight sky.

Beneath the shade of the wisteria, a person is even more conscious of the dusk. *Fuji* (wisteria) and *tasogaredoki* (twilight or gloaming) are kindred words.[171] Wisteria, moreover, are often depicted in orthodox verse as hanging from pine boughs.[172]

Sōgi pursues both the "twilight" and "hanging" images in his link, but he personifies the wisteria, with ribald overtones. The verse is even more risqué when *sagarite* is interpreted as *sakarite*, "be in heat." Hence, "whom will she cling to for solace, in heat when night falls." Since diacritical marks were not conventionally used in recording verses, *sagarite* and *sakarite* are orthographically identical in Sanetaka's record.

This verse by Sōgi unimpeachably shows that he composed and enjoyed zoku haikai, as did courtiers with such impeccable literary credentials as those of Sanetaka. This fact makes more credible the attribution of a fragment of a zoku haikai sequence to Sōgi in Kigin's *Shinzoku inu tsukubashū* anthology. The fragment reads as follows:

dō wa amata no tada no yama nado	On Tada Mountain there are many temples.[173]
manjū o hotoke no mae ni tamukeoku	One leaves an offering of *manjū* before the Buddha.[174]
tare mi zo sukū shakuson ya aru	Is there a Sakyamuni to save me?[175]
ito hosoki te ni akagari ya wataruran	Have those slender hands grown more red and chapped?
hibi ni masarite tabi wa taegata	Day after day, how hard is the journey![176]
sekimori no kokoro wa kibishi zeni wa nashi	The toll-gate guard is hard-hearted, and I have no money.

shinobiji naraba	When on a stealthy journey
ten kurō nare	let the sky be dark![177]
na ya tatan	Will rumors arise?
tsuki no sawari o	The hindering moon
mi ni tsukete	upon one's person.[178]

These verses exceed even the wisteria verse in genre detail and in part in vulgarity; if they were composed by Sōgi they are an isolated exception to his normally more circumspect composition; the exception that proves the ushin rule.

There are also tsukeku attributed to Sōgi in *Shinsen inu tsukubashū*, the eponymous predecessor of Kigin's work. For example:

renga no heta no	A mountain village with
ōki yamazato	so many bad renga poets!
tōsei wa	Judging verses these days
nokiba nokiba no	is as hard as telling
takekurabe	one eave from the next.
	Sōgi[179]

These verses, like those in the *Shinzoku inu tsukubashū* and *Seisuishō* collections, cannot be assigned to Sōgi with any certainty and are presented here simply as an added indication of the zoku verses typical of haikai renga of Sōchō's period.[180] They are perhaps more important as another example of the type of work attributed even to Sōgi by later generations of haikai specialists, perhaps to give added historical authority to their own enterprise.

As we have seen, Sōgi's evident interest in various haikai genres was not unusual even among poets of surpassing talent. The examples of his work included here show that he was able and willing to introduce contemporary and plebeian topics and witty wordplay in his verses. And he undeniably played an important role in enhancing the literary quality of the haikai of his age. Etō has shown, for example, that Arakida Moritake referred not only to *Shinsen inu tsukubashū* as he worked on his ground-breaking senku, but also to *Sōgi jōji hyakuin* and to Sōgi's famous ushin thousand-link sequence, *Mishima senku*.[181] It is noteworthy in this respect that the great Edo haikai poet Bashō later named Sōgi along with Sōkan and Moritake as three important progenitors of the haikai way.[182]

But though Sōgi's intellectual investment in haikai is manifest, that genre clearly remained for him separate from his main poetic activity, ushin renga, and absolutely subsidiary to it. He makes this stance very clear in a passage in

Azuma mondō: "When renga poets speak of haikai they are referring to kyōku. Such verses are marked by amusing wit (*rikō*). (Some are included in *Kokinshū*.) Though this too is one type of renga, it may result in vulgarity."[183]

Haikai had ancient precedents and therefore was acceptable to Sōgi in certain situations, but it had the potential for going wrong, for sinking into the realm of common puns and vulgar content. Sōgi was willing to entertain the haikai impulse, but only within strictly defined limits. The poet, finally, was devoted to univocality and closure in both the ushin and mushin spheres; his approach to haikai was exactly the same as his attitude toward the literature of travel.

Sōgi, in sum, recognized the growing popularity of haikai, composed it himself, and saw its value for expressing truths unreachable through orthodox verse. But he also understood its dangerous potential for subverting that orthodoxy. Faced with the very modern dilemma of a decentered canon in an increasingly pluralist society, he reacted in terms of mass culture critique, stressing the need to separate poetic Right from Wrong and to keep to the single True Way (*seidō*).

SŌCHŌ'S HAIKAI RENGA

Like his teacher, Sōchō composed haikai renga in a range of modes, from ga haikai appropriate to ushin renga sequences to zoku verses of the most ephemeral and ribald kind. Sōchō was sympathetic to his master's attitude toward haikai composition, seeing it as a means of expressing contemporary and everyday truths but also as a form of expression that should not be allowed to interfere with the pure ushin orthodoxy. Just as in his travel literature, though, Sōchō gave a larger voice than his teacher did to the here and now, the plebeian, and the oppositional.

Of his haikai in the ga mode, *The Journal of Sōchō* records only two hokku expressly indicated as such by the author. The first:

> Spent the night at Tsujinobō at Shirakawa. Before dawn I heard the cry of a waterrail:

158
> tani fukami
> kuina no meguru
> toyama kana
>
> So deep the valley,
> the waterrail flies round and round
> in the nearby hills!

> This is a haikai verse. (*JS*: 47)

The phrase *kuina no meguru* (the waterrail flies round and round) is somewhat out of the ordinary, and the mention of *toyama* (nearby hills) is in a sense redundant, as hills are already implied by the word *tani* (valley). But there is little that is overtly comic about the verse unless one imagines the bird constrained to fly in tight circles because of the narrowness of the valley; Sōchō in fact feels obligated to label it haikai to point out its slight departure from strict renga orthodoxy.

The second example is labeled not haikai but *zarete*, "for fun":

> That morning a monk from the temple who guided us to Konohama Crossing requested a hokku. For fun:

364	hototogisu	A cuckoo
	shigeru konohama no	at Konohama Crossing
	watari kana	through flourishing leaves!
	(*JS*: 103)	

Sōchō refers to the verse as *zarete* because of the somewhat exaggerated double pun on the place name *konohama no watari* (Konohama Crossing) and *konoha ma no watari* (crossing through . . . leaves). But again there is nothing remarkably outré about the composition. Both of the verses show only the mildest bending of the orthodox rules of diction or conception. Were they not hokku, they could very nearly fit somewhere in the middle of an ushin sequence, again because even formal, orthodox renga show patterns of tonal tension and relaxation.[184]

The Takigi verses in Sōchō's journal are the polar opposites of such ga haikai composition. They are introduced with this preface: "Saw out the old year in an abandoned dormitory beside Shūon'an in Takigi. Six or seven of us gathered around the hearth, and after tofu with miso we composed a number of haikai" (*JS*: 34).[185] The fifty-six Takigi verses represent both a departure from and at times a contestation of ushin norms. In diction they are free of restraints, and in content they treat contemporary or lewd topics with cynicism, iconoclasm, and above all, comedy.

But one must approach the verses with certain caveats in mind. The most important is that of authorship. Only two of the verses in the series are explicitly claimed by Sōchō, and a third (*JS* no. 125) is attributed to him in a version of *Shinsen inu tsukubashū* not in Sōkan's hand.[186] It is certainly possible, however, that all the tsukeku links were Sōchō's, since he quotes very few renga and haikai verses in his journal other than his own, and when he does, he gives the poet's name. More important, none of the tsukeku appears in other haikai collections attributed to anyone else.

Nor is it clear how the session was conducted. It may have been a single long renga sequence from which Sōchō culled his own verses or those he felt particularly worthy of preservation, or it may have been a *maekuzuke* session, in which the poets vied to link tsukeku to various independent and preexisting maeku with no attempt to fashion a longer composition.[187] Some sections of the Takigi sequence do indeed seem to bear more extended interrelationships. But it may indeed have been that the session involved simple maekuzuke linking, because all but three maeku are of fourteen syllables—one would expect a better balance of long and short maeku had the couplets been selected from a longer sequence. In addition, many of the maeku are *nanku*, puzzles that invite a clever solution. It is difficult to imagine how so many such verses could be incorporated into a longer sequence.[188] Sōchō may later have listed related couplets together out of his characteristic concern for renga-like interrelationships. Or perhaps the session involved both maekuzuke and longer sequences.

But whether Sōchō composed all or only certain of the Takigi verses, and whether they were composed as a long sequence or as isolated couplets, it is clear that despite their completely zoku nature, he felt they were worthy of preservation. In subject matter they are even more diverse than those in Sōgi's *jōji* composition, and they delight in human situations and mundane detail.

Many of the verses deal in one respect or another with religion, an understandable focus given the location of the session and the fact that Sōchō and doubtless many of the others had taken Buddhist orders. As opposed to the concentration on evanescence, aspiration, renunciation, and salvation that characterizes the Buddhist verse in the ushin tradition, these verses depict and sometimes pillory unexalted aspects of daily religious life; the flesh beneath the clerical cloth is decidedly and often humorously weak. The attitude of the poet seems at once cynical and amused:

88	kōya hijiri no yado o kau koe.	The voice of a beggar monk from Kōya craving lodging.
89	natsu no yo no yabure kayadō tachiidete	On a summer night, leaving his thatched hut and its torn mosquito net.

(JS: 34)

Mendicant Kōya monks normally begged for lodging as part of their ascetic discipline, but here the ostensible high purpose of the maeku is subverted by the monk's prosaic hope of finding more comfortable lodging away from torment-

CHAPTER FOUR

ing insects. The tsukeku relies for its effect on a kakekotoba pivoting between *kaya* (mosquito net) and *kayadō* (thatched hut).

The monks of Monjuin in the capital, a place Sōchō had once picnicked (*JS*: 21), show even less piety:

90	hannyajizaka no ōkojikidomo	Brawny beggars around Hannyaji Hill.
91	kokoro mina sechibenbō ya monjuin	Are all the monks at Monjuin temple miserly at heart?
		(*JS*: 34)

The verses are linked by the fact that Monjuin is located on Hannyaji Hill. Instead of lofty self-abnegation and charity for others, the monkish community described in the Takigi sequence is motivated by money, by comfort, and even more often, by carnal desire, usually for young catamites. Takigi verses on the topic range from the elegant to the exceedingly vulgar:

100	koshōdō mina hanami o zo suru	Novices all in a group out enjoying the blossoms.
101	chigo kosode yanagi sakura o kokimazete	The lads' short-sleeved robes— willows and cherry trees blending in profusion.
		(*JS*: 35)

❀

102	nyake no atari wa tada kiku no hana	Nothing but asters where the temple boys are.
103	akikaze no fukiage niou tobosogami	The autumn wind wafts a fragrance from the doorway.
		(*JS*: 35–36)

❀

104	torinukashitaru subariwakazō	The young temple boy with the tight ass passed wind!

270

105	motenashi no hara no oto koso kikoekere	And for an extra treat you could also hear his belly rumble!

(JS: 36)

Not even the deities are exempt from lust, as in this humorously irreverent depiction:

122	ware yori mo seitaka wakashu machiwabite	How he waits and waits for the lad Seitaka, taller than himself.
123	fudō mo koi ni kogarakasu mi ka	Even Fudō burns with unrequited love?

(JS: 37)

The impiety and carnality of these depictions of the religious community extend to love in general; here the ethereal noncorporeality of *ushin* love is traded for physical description of the most explicit kind:

94	chigo ka onna ka nete no akatsuki	Is it a boy or a girl fast asleep before dawn?
95	mae ushiro saguru ni tsuki no ariake ni	Feeling fore and aft there beneath the late-rising moon.

(JS: 35)

Other verses deal with adultery, impotence, and prostitution. Classical romance is also parodied:

92	fuzei mo tsukite hiki ya irenan	Out of elegant topics, are they going to retire?
93	hito ni tsuki omoshirogarare fukinikeri	The moon, for them both the center of attention, has sunk out of sight.

(JS: 35)

The moon has gone down, and with it, the lovers' main topic of romantic conversation. The move from the veranda to the bed chamber can only follow. The elegant *Genji monogatari* mood is further undercut by suspicions of ribald double entendre in *ireru* (retire/insert) and the perennial paronomastic favorite *tsuki* (moon/thrust).

Religious and classical parody sometimes go hand in hand; the one verse from the sequence attributed to Sōchō in *Shinsen inu tsukubashū* is exemplary:

124	kami no yo yori no sugi no zungiri	Cut clean through—a cedar there since the age of the gods.
125	chihayaburu miwayamamoto no chayabōzu	At the foot of Mount Miwa, name of divine might, a tea-selling bonze.

(*JS*: 37)

Here Sōchō (if we are to believe the attribution of this verse to him in *Shinsen inu tsukubashū*) first establishes a lofty and sublime tone in his tsukeku with the ancient makurakotoba *chihayaburu* (of divine might) and the utamakura Mount Miwa. He then punctures the expectations of the audience with the last line, which depicts a very modest cleric indeed, and an odd-looking one as well, his head shaped like a flat-topped *zungiri* tea container made from one of the cedars "cut clearly through" (*zungiri*) in the maeku.

Even great figures of the poetic traditions can sometimes become targets of fun:

130	uma ni noritaru hitomaro o miyo	Look at Hitomaro as he sits astride his horse!
131	shimo ni tatsu chūgen otoko hitori nite	Standing beneath, there is but a single man in his service.

(*JS*: 38)

These verses are evocative of a world turned upside down, of a value structure in which the status quo is held up for ridicule, and where the other-worldly romantic idealism of the high medieval tradition is countered by this-worldly laughter and cynicism. Surely there is something in common here with the carnival described by Bakhtin, where medieval Europeans of all classes found release from formal and official strictures in the earthy and even grotesque world of laughter and parody.[189] Such poetry must have particularly appealed to Sōchō, in view of his attachment to the teachings and perspective of the great eccentric Ikkyū, who was at once a great idealist and a great libertine. As we saw in Chapter One,

Sōchō viewed much of the contemporary religious community with contempt for its lax or hypocritical practices, and these verses doubtless offered catharsis through comedy and criticism.

But at the same time that Sōchō was laughing at others, he was also laughing at himself. After all, in his own journal he depicts himself as one of those very priests who enjoys the company of temple lads and who values material prosperity. In these verses Sōchō acknowledges both sides of his own nature and of the world in which he lives; in a nondualistic way he prefers to document both the high and low traditions, rather than to champion one or the other in the manner of either Sōgi or Sōkan.

Sōchō's unusual attraction to haikai complemented rather than compromised his dedication to the high renga way; in orthodox renga he aspired to universals and basic essences; in haikai he found a means to express other facts of life just as universal but for which there was no room in the classical tradition. Haikai renga are not all "comic" by any means. Some of the haikai verses he preserved combine criticism of contemporary practice with evident sympathy. The poem about the Kōya monk leaving his lodging with its torn mosquito net (*JS* nos. 88–89) is one such verse. Whether or not Sōchō actually composed that poem, he was moved to record it for the gentle and sympathetic laugh it evokes about a very human predicament. The same can be said for this link:

110	gojō atari ni tateru amagoze	In the Fifth Ward stands someone in a nun's habit.
111	taga goke no ukarekimi to wa narinuran	Whose wife did that lady of the night used to be?

(*JS*: 36)

In *Genji monogatari*, the Fifth Ward was the residence of Yūgao, the Lady of the Evening Faces, who lived in reduced circumstances after her affair with Tō no Chūjō. Later, the Fifth Ward became a popular place to hire prostitutes, many of whom dressed as nuns. Much of the effect of the tsukeku lies in the pun on *goke*, meaning both widow and prostitute. When a woman's husband died, she had in many cases no other way to support herself than to enter a temple or take to the streets in religious dress, which many men and women of completely secular status donned to escape prevailing social strictures and to cover a multitude of sins. The couplet therefore combines cynicism about the real motivations that drove many to take the tonsure with sympathy for the woman whose misfortune compelled her to take that step.

Nor are the first two verses in the collection at all jocular in tone; they depict instead a genre scene in which the New Year is greeted not with hopeful optimism but with pathos:

82	asu no shiru tama kagiri naru arame kana	Broth for the morning, with just a glint of *arame* sea plant.
83	kao wa shiwasu no haru no hatsuyome	Her face lined in the twelfth month, the new bride greets the spring.

(*JS*: 34)

The fellow-feeling that informs these verses is also evident in the haikai waka in the journal, to which we will turn presently.

But the desire to ridicule or to pity the contemporary human condition was only partial motivation for preserving these verses in the journal. Doubtless Sōchō saved many of the verses, whether by himself or others, out of enjoyment of their wit and style. The poems rely on a number of different techniques for their humorous effect. As pointed out earlier, many involve a riddle in the maeku that requires ingenuity in the link to explain it:

114	omoshiroge ni mo akikaze zo fuku	The autumn wind blows with it a feeling of excitement.

The difficulty here lies partly in the fact that autumn wind in the orthodox tradition is nearly always melancholy, not "interesting" or "exciting." The tsukeku then gives an amusing explanation:

115	tatenarabe tanabata oreru ashihyōshi	The rhythm of feet weaving on a row of looms at Tanabata.

(*JS*: 37)

The autumn Tanabata festival, when the Weaver Maid and the Herdboy have their one annual tryst, does cause excited anticipation, when elegant garments are woven for the occasion on many looms.

Puns and pivot words are another source of amusement, many of which involve lewd double meanings, as we have seen. Such humor also works in reverse, where in response to a maeku whose ribald meaning is altogether obvious, the tsukeku may frustrate salacious expectations with an innocent rejoinder that recasts the earlier verse:

| 118 | hito no nasake ya
ana ni aruran | All her emotions appear
in the word "respectfully." |

To this is added:

| 119 | onna fumi
kashiko kashiko to
kakisutete | A woman's letter,
signed with a careless flourish,
"Most sincerely yours." |

(*JS*: 37)

Here the humor of the first verse derives from the all-too-apparent lewd alternative based on a pun on *ana* (respectfully/hole). "All of one's emotions are / concentrated on a hole." The ribald double-entendre is increased by a play on *nasake* (emotions) and *nasakedokoro* (place of feelings), argot for the female genitals.[190]

The tsukeku links *ana* with *kashiko*, which together literally mean "with awe and respect," the standard concluding salutation in letters written by women. The cleverness of this tsukeku in particular is that it too has ribald possibilities in that *kashiko kashiko* also means "There! There!" *Kakisute* can mean either "write casually" or "dash off a note" but also "dispense with [shame]." *Honi soit qui mal y pense.* Expectation is also frustrated where there is a surprise switch from the sublime to the ridiculous, or where traditional values and set notions are juxtaposed to earthy, inelegant reality. *JS* nos. 124–25 above ("Cut cleanly through—a cedar") are a case in point.

One of the reasons the Takigi verses are so important to Japanese literary history is that fully one quarter of them appear in various versions of *Shinsen inu tsukubashū*, but in most cases with different tsukeku.[191] It is not known when the first version of the anthology was compiled, but its reputed compiler, Yamazaki Sōkan, was probably already famous as a haikai specialist when the Takigi session took place. He certainly may have composed verses there head to head with Sōchō, but we cannot know for certain. The two tsukeku that Sōchō includes in his collection under Sōkan's name may have been composed then and there at Takigi, or they may have been already famous and quoted by Sōchō only to show by comparison Sōchō's success at "solving" the same two difficult maeku. But Sōkan is indeed believed to have lived near Shūon'an in Takigi, and he was himself a disciple of Ikkyū and had ties to that temple. His presence is also the easiest way to account for the presence in *Shinsen inu tsukubashū* of many of the Takigi verses. Harada Yoshioki, in fact, suggests that not only was Sōkan present at Takigi, but that he may have brought many of the maeku with him, thus explaining why so many appear in both his collection and Sōchō's.[192]

But whether Sōkan was present or not, Sōchō explicitly invites a comparison of his haikai skill to that of Sōkan in the last two sets of verses in the collection. Sōchō records the first of the two sets as follows:

132	oitsukan	"I'll catch up with him,
	oitsukan to ya	I'll catch up"—is that
	hashiruran	what he thinks, running?

| 133 | kōya hijiri no | Behind a Kōya monk, |
| | ato no yarimochi | a lancer.[193] |

Sōkan

[132	oitsukan	"He'll catch up with me,
	oitsukan to ya	he'll catch up"—is that
	hashiruran	what she thinks, running?][194]

| 134 | kōya hijiri no | Ahead of a Kōya monk, |
| | saki no himegoze | a young girl.[195] |

My verse is better linked to the sense of "catch up" (*oitsukan*) (*JS*: 38).

Sōkan's link to the first of the two maeku is based on a pun on *oitsuku*, meaning both "catch up" and "pierce his backpack." Kōya monks, often in reality traveling salesmen who affected clerical dress for ease in passing toll gates, were, like their counterparts in American humor, popularly associated with lechery, as in this ditty from *Tatoezukushi* (148):

kōya hijiri ni	To a monk from Kōya
yado kasu na	don't lend a resting place;
musume torarete	don't let him steal your daughter
haji kaku na	and leave you in disgrace!

Both Sōkan's verse and Sōchō's play with the ribald possibilities of the word *tsuku* (pierce or thrust). The point of view in Sōchō's link is problematic; it may be either the monk's or the girl's. The girl, moreover, may be afraid of being overtaken by the monk, but she could as easily be a traveling prostitute, who will not mind being overtaken. She may in fact be the one doing the chasing.

Sōchō had no doubt about the superiority of his own verse. Modern critical opinion, however, is divided on which of the two poets showed the greater skill. Part of the answer depends on personal taste, of course, and in any case modern assessment of haikai skill is extremely problematic. Ushin renga, like ushin waka, aims at universals of human experience, true for all the ages. That is one of the reasons why changes in ushin topics, treatments, and lexicon were often resisted so strongly. Haikai, by contrast, finds part of its value precisely in contemporary language and topicality, both of which are by definition ephemeral. A verse that struck a resonant chord in 1523 may sound very flat today in the absence of its immediate linguistic and social contexts.

Some scholars feel that Sōkan's verse shows more skill as haikai. Tani Hiroshi, for example, states the Sōkan case as follows:

> Sōkan's verse is symbolic of the times and evocative of real life. The link between the maeku and his tsukeku is so close a hair would not fit between, and it provides a good laugh with its pun on *oitsuku* (catch up) and *oi tsuku* (pierce [*tsuku*] his backpack [*oi*]). Sōkan perfectly responds in his tsukeku to the maeku and in a cheerful way catches the very breath of the period.
>
> Sōchō's depiction of a Kōya monk and a traveling prostitute was also a common scene of the period, but the wit displayed in the contrast of the vulgarity of the merchant and the prostitute with their lofty titles *hijiri* [holy priest] and *goze* [gentlewoman or lady] nowhere approaches Sōkan's inclusive and perceptive depiction of the era.[196]

Harada Yoshioki, by contrast, finds for Sōchō:

> Sōkan makes a facile link founded on the word-based relationship between *tsuku* (pierce) and *yari* (lance), and he appears to imply male homosexuality. . . . The verse relies on the pun on *oitsuku* (catch up/pierce his backpack) for its effect. Sōchō's depiction of one of the foibles of male psychology, with the monk attracted to the figure of the young girl and hurrying to overtake her, shows interest, evocative skill, immediacy, and humor. One agrees with Sōchō's own judgment, "My verse is the better linked."[197]

Kaneko Kinjirō presents yet another perspective:

> Sōkan's lancer verse depicts an observed genre scene; Sōchō's verse, praised by the poet himself, presents a psychological evocation of a woman who hurries ahead, frightened that the Kōya monk with a pack on his back will catch her.[198]

The second set of attributed verses is the following:

CHAPTER FOUR

> 135   goban no ue ni 　　Atop the *go* board
> 　　　haru wa kinikeri 　spring has arrived.
>
> 136   uguisu no 　　　　A centerpiece made
> 　　　sugomori to iu 　to look like "a bush warbler
> 　　　　tsukurimono 　　　sitting on its nest."¹⁹⁹
> 　　　　　　　　　　　　　　　　Sōkan
>
> [135 goban no ue ni 　　Atop the *go* board
> 　　　haru wa kinikeri 　spring has arrived.]
>
> 137   asagasumi 　　　　The morning haze
> 　　　sumizumi made wa has yet to reach
> 　　　　tachiirade 　　　　the corners.
> 　　　　　　　　　　　　　　　　Sōchō
>
> Here too, my verse is the better linked. (*JS*: 38–39)

This second shared maeku is another puzzle. Sōkan's solution is generally interpreted two ways. It may be a description of a centerpiece in a decorative alcove (*tokonoma*) for New Year's, made in the shape of a nesting warbler. Such centerpieces were often displayed atop go boards, and they were sometimes made of food, which was later consumed. *Uguisu no sugomori* (bush warbler sitting on its nest) then relates to the words *tsuru no sugomori* (nesting crane), a move in the game of go.²⁰⁰ Sōkan altered "crane" to "bush warbler" because the latter is a seasonal word for spring, and it therefore ties his verse more closely to the maeku. But the verse instead may depict a go game in progress, with Sōkan conceiving of the go stones as bush warbler eggs and of their layout on the board as a decorative centerpiece.²⁰¹ The word *tsukurimono* may not in fact mean "centerpiece" at all, but may instead be a term in go for a series of moves.²⁰²

Sōchō's tsukeku phonetically relates *kasumi* (haze) to *sumizumi* (corners [of a go board]). One interpretation of the verse holds that Sōchō is simply comparing the arrangement of white and black go stones on the board to a painting in which the white spring haze does not penetrate to the corners.²⁰³ But interpretations and assessments of Sōchō's verse vary considerably. Tani again favors Sōkan's solution over that of Sōchō:

> Sōkan shows a fresh grasp of the emotions inherent in a single, concrete human moment, in which two people during their long struggle to survive enjoy a moment of leisure at a game of go in the Muromachi spring, one using the strategy known as "bush warbler's nest." Sōchō's tsukeku shows skill in its connection be-

tween *kasumi* (haze) and *sumi* (corners [of a go board]), but it does not evoke as concrete an image as Sōkan's, with its two people in a room sitting on either side of a go board.²⁰⁴

Harada Yoshioki again sees as much merit in Sōchō's solution:

> To *haru* (spring), Sōkan links *uguisu* (bush warbler), and then because of *goban no ue* (on the top of the go board) in the maeku he metaphorically compares the go stones to bush warbler eggs and conceives of the layout of the stones on the board as a decorative *suhama* (centerpiece for a formal room). It is a witty, word-based link. Sōchō compares the arrangement of go stones on the board to a painting in which the spring haze does not penetrate to the corners. Instead, only touches of white are brushed on the black. This too is intellectual, but it gives an impression of an early spring scene with haze encroaching only slightly. . . . It is indeed an artistic picture rich in poetic feeling. Haikai may have been only a subsidiary interest for Sōchō, but he clearly had his own convictions about how it ought to be composed.²⁰⁵

It may be, however, that Sōchō's link depends for its effect on some contemporary genre detail obvious at the time but now obscure. Neither commentator, for example, links Sōchō's *asagasumi* (morning haze) with *kasumiwari* (territories), a term denoting the spheres of influence of, for example, rival mountain ascetic sects or blind performers (*kengyō*).²⁰⁶ It is possible that Sōchō's tsukeku solves the nanku with a pun on *asagasumi* and *kasumi*[*wari*] (the other's holdings), in this case the areas of the board still controlled by the opponent's black stones. The player of the white stones, which resemble haze, has made inroads into his opponent's position, but has not yet reached the edges (*sumizumi*), another word associated with both a go board and a territory, and which in addition echoes the sound of *kasumi*. Interpreted in this way, Sōchō's high opinion of the verse becomes more justified.

But regardless of contemporary hermeneutical problems, there was evidently no doubt in Sōchō's mind about whose verses were more skilled, and why. As indicated by his remark, "My verse is better linked to the sense (*kokoro*) of 'catch up' (*oitsukan*)," Sōchō believed that regardless of the word-based associations between verses, the tsukeku had to respond to the fundamental sense of the verse preceding it. In this basic emphasis, his haikai practice was compatible with his ushin renga theory, where he counseled, it will be recalled, that the tsukeku must respond to the maeku "like an echo in love with the voice." Donald Keene suggests that "Sōkan almost always links through some verbal association, no doubt the reason why he was so esteemed by Matsunaga Teitoku and his school,

CHAPTER FOUR

but Sōchō's kokorozuke is more closely related to the Danrin poets."[207] Keene's observation is predicated on the assumption, of course, that the tsukeku in the Takigi collection are by Sōchō and that the *Shinsen inu tsukubashū* alternates are predominantly by Sōkan.

But while many of the Takigi links do show a strong content-based connection, word-based connections likewise figure strongly in the Takigi collection. Iguchi Hisashi, for example, observes:

> The links in *The Journal of Sōchō* are generally effected by means of word-play through word-correspondences [*taiōgo*] or kindred words, and through this, a sense of continuity [*renzokusei*] is realized in the second verse. Sōkan, by contrast, creates conceptual changes through a reinterpretation of the maeku or a shift of metaphor, thereby increasing the witty, haikai nature of the link.[208]

But Iguchi goes on to point out that Sōkan (or whoever was responsible for the alternate tsukeku in *Shinsen inu tsukubashū*) also depends on word relationships in his linking: "By using puns to develop the conception of the maeku in an unexpected direction or by taking realistic description as metaphor, or by introducing a resolute vulgarity, Sōkan casts aside the lyric elements of the maeku in favor of concrete, active content."[209]

Both Keene and Iguchi are suggesting that based on a comparison of the different tsukeku responses to the shared maeku verses in *The Journal of Sōchō* and *Shinsen inu tsukubashū*, the tsukeku in Sōchō's collection often tend to pursue the sense established by the maeku and to strengthen that kokoro connection through lexical relationships. The verses shared with *Shinsen inu tsukubashū*, by contrast, tend to favor wide and surprising changes in conception between the maeku and tsukeku. This judgment would seem to be in keeping with Sōchō's own remark about his verse better reflecting the sense of the previous. Sōchō's taste, in a word, retains more of his ushin renga background than does Sōkan's.

The following comparison supports the generalization that the haikai verses in *The Journal of Sōchō* reflect more of the mind-set of an ushin renga poet. The Takigi verses read as follows:

108	kasumi no koromo suso wa nurekeri	The robe of haze is soaked at the hem.
109	nawashiro o oitaterarete kaeru kari	Shooed away from the seed beds where the young rice grows, geese flying homeward.

Most versions of *Shinsen inu tsukubashū* begin with the same maeku, linked thus:

> kasumi no koromo
> suso wa nurekeri
>
>   saohime no
>   haru tachinagara
>   shito o shite

> The robe of haze
> has grown wet at the hem.
>
>   Spring has come,
>   and the goddess Saohime
>   pisses where she stands.[210]

Shimazu comments as follows:

> Sōchō's tsukeku is indeed a good haikai in the way it derives humor (*okashimi*) and realism from chasing the geese away instead of mourning their homeward flight as in elegant waka. But Sōkan takes a potentially refined scene with a robe of haze wet at the lower edges, introduces the goddess Saohime, then suddenly vulgarizes the image by adding "pisses where she stands." The abrupt change is full of comic (*kokkei*) wit. Sōkan would seem to have purposely placed this verse at the beginning of his anthology to signal a new focus on a vulgar and popular esprit, and a critical reaction against renga and its ever-increasing elegance.[211]

Tani Hiroshi sees Sōkan's verse as the one with the greater realism and cleverness:

> At the height of springtime rice planting, when no one has a moment to spare ... a farm girl works so steadily in the field that she must relieve herself where she stands. Had Sōkan been less well acquainted with such scenes of country life, he could never have produced an impromptu tsukeku that responds so effectively to the maeku. In that sense he makes far better use of the haikai renga medium than Sōchō does.[212]

Again, Harada Yoshioki finds excellence in both verses:

> Sōkan's verse derives humor from its utter lack of restraint. But after the initial shock, no sense of beauty develops. His word-based link (kotobazuke) of *haru tatsu* (spring has come) and *kasumi* (haze) shows a professional's skill, and the humor of the verse no doubt greatly amused the others at the session and provided a welcome emotional release in those troubled times.
>
> Sōchō, by contrast, seems to have worked for a different style of humor. In *oitaterarete kaeru* (shooed away ... [the geese] fly homeward) he evokes the sadness of the traveler who watches as the geese are chased out of the paddy fields, the undersides of their wing tips dripping with paddy water, and, wet and mournful, they fly off to the north through the spring haze.[213]

Despite their differences, all three commentators imply that Sōkan's tsukeku is the more earthy and immediately witty of the two, while Sōchō's is the more elegant and closer to formal renga. The judgment is apt; Sōchō's verse still has much in common with two orthodox verses he made almost exactly three years later for *Yashima Shōrin'an naniki hyakuin* in the company of Sōboku:

11	hakanashi ya	How fleeting it is!
	kite mo tomaranu	Journeying through the skies,
	tabi no sora	they come but cannot stay.
12	kasumi no koromo	Cloaked within a robe of haze,
	kari nakite yuku	the geese call as they fly away.[214]

But again, such generalizations are extremely tentative. Other verses already quoted here indicated that Sōchō was equally capable of the earthiness and pungent ribaldry of Sōkan.[215] And many of the verses in Sōchō's collection also involve word-based effects, just like those in *Shinsen inu tsukubashū*. It is certainly perilous to assume that all the Takigi verses are by Sōchō or that he unquestionably preferred them over the alternate tsukeku in *Shinsen inu tsukubashū*; he may never have known about all of the latter, save the two he explicitly attributes to Sōkan. Again, it does seem *likely* that both men were present and later chose their own verses for their own collections, or at least that their collections reflect their respective haikai tastes, but we cannot be sure.

Ultimately, the Takigi verses are more important for their similarities to those in *Shinsen inu tsukubashū* than for their differences. As the foregoing examples have indicated, both are rich in parody, iconoclasm, uninhibited lexicon, ribaldry, and humor, and some are straightforward and even serious expressions of plebeian everyday life. The two collections testify to the central place that both Sōchō and Sōkan occupied in the development of zoku haikai. Sōchō was one of the first renga masters to evince an active concern for preserving such verses; he was proud of his haikai skill and boasted of it in writing, something Sōgi never did. Sōchō was pleased with his last two verses because he found them superior to those of Sōkan, a haikai specialist. By composing haikai renga and preserving it side by side with his orthodox renga, Sōchō was suggesting that while ushin poetry would always be his most elevated activity, he found both modes to be valuable avenues for the expression of different aspects of experience. His pioneering appreciation of the unique possibilities of the haikai medium is seen even more clearly in the haikai he composed in the waka format.

SŌCHŌ'S HAIKAI WAKA

Despite the importance of the Takigi verses to the history of haikai renga, it is the haikai-style waka (*haikaika* or *haikai uta*) that occupy much more of the author's sustained interest throughout *The Journal of Sōchō*. Like the haikai renga, they cover a wide spectrum, from works on the edge of orthodox ga waka to others that rival the Takigi haikai renga for contemporaneity or earthiness. The actual number of haikai waka in the journal depends on how one defines the ga and zoku parameters, but it can be argued that nearly one-quarter of all Sōchō's waka in the diary are in that mode.[216]

And as was the case with haikai renga, Sōchō's interest in such waka was by no means uncharacteristic of superior waka poets through history. Haikaika in the ga ambit are included, of course, even in the prototype imperial poetry anthology, *Kokinshū*. Verses of a more zoku character have also been attributed to such pillars of waka orthodoxy as Saigyō, Reizei Tamemori, and Nijō Yoshimoto.[217] As with haikai renga, however, interest in composing and preserving such waka grew markedly in Sōchō's lifetime, and increasing numbers were included in contemporary poetry collections and diaries.[218] Sanetaka, for example, preserved about two hundred of his own kyōka and about one hundred others sent to him, including some from Sōchō, among the more than seven thousand verses in his personal poetry collection, *Saishōsō* (1501–36).[219]

Sōchō actually uses the term *haikai* with reference to eleven of the waka in his journal, and he marks others with such comments as "in fun" or "amusing" to mark departures from more orthodox work.[220] He also uses the term *kyōka*. Inoue Muneo has pointed out that in this period the word *haikai* was used in a narrow sense to refer to the ga haikai of imperial anthologies, and in a wider sense more or less interchangeably with *kyōka*, which refers to any unorthodox verse.[221] Whereas Sōchō uses the word *haikai* in its widest meaning to describe the Takigi renga verses, he tends to employ it in its narrow meaning when referring to his waka, reserving it for those compositions that while exceeding the bounds of ga haikai in the imperial anthologies do not stray terribly far from ga haikai parameters.

The haikai waka in this conservative mode employ a slight exaggeration or personalization of orthodox sentiment and/or an understated bending of the orthodox lexicon. The following exemplifies the former type, composed when Sōchō's friend, the old abbot of Shūon'an in Takigi, is about to depart for Shōrin'an in Yashima:

CHAPTER FOUR

We spoke of various things and then said goodbye, promising to meet again soon. Whereupon I composed the following:

430
    oinureba
    asu wa ōmi to
      tanomanu ni
    yo wa fukenedomo
    sode zo shigururu

The old cannot count
on meeting on the morrow
in Ōmi,
and though night has not grown late,
a cold rain moistens my sleeve.

A haikai poem, in jest. (*JS*: 120)

Sōchō's poem is based on *Kokinshū* 8: 369, by Ki no Toshisada:

Composed on the night of a banquet at the residence of Prince Sadatoki, when Fujiwara Kiyō was to take up his duties as Vice-Governor of Ōmi:

    kyō wa wakare
    asu wa ōmi to
      omoedomo
    yo ya fukenuramu
    sode no tsuyukeki

Although I know
we can meet in Ōmi
again tomorrow,
is it because the night is late
that dew lies upon my sleeves?

Sōchō's haikai is very like the original; its vocabulary and its topic are quite close to ga parameters of elegance and propriety. Its haikai quality derives from its application of the basic essence of the original poem to a slightly too personal and topical reference to a contemporary situation.

Other verses in the ga haikai style deviate in only the mildest degree from the orthodox lexicon, which itself varied according to poetic school. A verse Sōchō wrote on his emotions in old age is exemplary:

During the Festival of the Weaver Maid, as I sighed over the length of my old age:

566
    negaikinu
    negau ni taenu
      yasoji nari
    kyō zo waga yo wa
    aihate no hoshi

I have often wished
upon them but now at eighty
wishing does no good.
Today ends the two stars' tryst,
the last one that I will see.

A haikai, in jest. (*JS*: 157)

The only aspects of this verse that mark it as haikai are the word *aihate* (end or death), which is not used in orthodox verse, and possibly the slight incongruity of the poet's envisioning his own end in terms of the annual one-night tryst of the Weaver Maid and Herdboy stars.

Like the poem on the subject of meeting again in Ōmi, many of the ga haikaika are based on orthodox foundation poems. Sōchō provides another good example while staying with Seki Kajisai, the Ise warlord whose several meetings with the renga master are recorded at length several times in the journal:

> Since it was impossible to arrange for palanquins, I considered returning to Yamada, but the rain and wind were incessant, so I stayed near Kajisai's residence:

16
>   azusayumi   Today too spring rain,
>   oshite harusame   recalling catalpa bows
>   kyō mo furu   that one bends to string.
>   asu mo furu to te   No doubt rain tomorrow too—
>   yado ya sadamen   shall I take up lodgings here?

> By this I meant that if it were going to continue raining, I would stay on in luxury. I wrote that poem and others in a haikai vein, littering them about my inkstone. (JS: 17)

The verse is a haikai reworking of *Kokinshū* 1: 20:

>   azusyumi   Today fell spring rain,
>   oshite harusame   mindful of catalpa bows
>   kyō furinu   that one bends to string.
>   asu sae furaba   If it but falls tomorrow,
>   wakana tsumitemu   we will be picking young greens.

In lexicon and rhetoric, Sōchō's verse does not deviate far from orthodox poetry. Its haikai quality derives instead from its approach to the foundation poem. Sōchō's poem does not pursue the earlier poem's universal basic essence; it instead uses the earlier work to frame a personal and topical situation. The humor of the verse derives precisely from the unexpected application of the ga orthodoxy.

The haikaika in the more zoku vein that Sōchō composes resemble the Takigi compositions in their complete disregard for ga restraints on lexicon, topic, or general decorum. The humor of the following lies precisely in that opposition:

> In the beginning of the ninth month, I rode about four or five chō from here and on the way home fell from my horse. My upper body aches and my right hand is useless:

CHAPTER FOUR

> 203   ika ni sen
>   mono kakisusamu
>   te wa okite
>   hashi toru koto to
>   shiri nogō koto
>
> What am I to do
> without the hand I write with
>   to console myself?
> How will I hold my chopsticks and
> how will I wipe my behind?
>
> (*JS*: 60)

Some involve earthy puns:

> Having suffered recently from the flux, I wrote this for amusement:
>
> 292   omowazu mo
>   hitatare o koso
>   kitarikere
>   na o ba Kusoichi
>   komeru to iwanu
>
> Before I knew it,
> I "donned a warrior's robe"
>   and have the runs.
> Would the name "Kusoichi"
> put an end to laying waste?
>
> (*JS*: 80)

Sōchō puns on *hitatare* (warrior's robe) and *hita[sura] tare[ru]* (have diarrhea). Kusoichi resembles a samurai name but literally means "shit once," and *komeru* (contain or subdue) has a martial tone.

As in the Takigi haikai renga, there is occasionally parody in the journal's haikai waka:

> First day of the first month, fourth year of Daiei. At Shūon'an, Takigi. Early in the morning I heard someone outside the gate announce that he had left the world and craved admission:
>
> 138   aratama no
>   hatsumotoi kiri
>   hitotose ni
>   kozo to ya iwan
>   koshami to ya iwan
>
> He has shorn his hair
> that he dressed for the new season—
>   though he is the same,
> should we call him last year's scamp,
> or should we call him this year's novice?
>
> (*JS*: 42)

The work is based on Kokinshū 1: 1, by Ariwara Motokata:

> Composed when spring arrived before the old year was out:
>
>   toshi no uchi ni
>   haru wa kinikeri
>   hitotose o
>
> It seems that spring has come
> before the year has ended.
>   Though one and the same,

| kozo to ya iwamu | should we call it last year, |
| kotoshi to ya iwamu | or should we call it this? |

Sōchō's parody plays on *kozo*, either "last year" or "scamp," and on *koshami*, "novice monk," and *kotoshi*, "this year." It is indicative of Sōchō's interest in unorthodox poetry that he should begin his entries for 1524 with a parody of the orthodox tradition, though it has been pointed out that the *Kokinshū* foundation poem itself has a light, witty tone.[222] Sōchō uses the honkadori device here as a comic response to a personal experience, rather like humorous lyrics sung to the melody of a more famous piece. But occasionally the poet will parody the underlying classical tradition itself, turning basic essences upside-down. In one, Sōchō reverses the classical habit of taking pleasure in the cuckoo's call, as exemplified by *Kin'yōshū* (*Sansōbon*) 2: 116, by Gonsōjō Eien:

kiku tabi ni	Each time I hear you,
mezurashikereba	your singing strikes me afresh,
hototogisu	cuckoo bird,
itsumo hatsune no	so it always seems to me
kokochi koso sure	the first call of the season.

The cuckoo (*hototogisu*) was said to vomit blood when it uttered its mournful cry, likened to "ripping cloth" (*reppaku*); hence Sōchō's parody:

Through the middle of the eighth month, the cuckoo sang both night and day, making my mealtimes unbearable:

202
kiku tabi ni	Each time I hear you
mune warokereba	I feel queasy,
hototogisu	cuckoo bird,
hetotogisu to koso	so one really ought to call you
iu bekarikere	"puke-oo bird" instead.

(*JS: 59*)

The verse also involves a pun, almost as lame as that in the translation, on *hototogisu* and *hedo* ("vomit").

As with his more orthodox waka poems, Sōchō wrote haikaika both for others and for himself. Those meant for others are generally more conservative. But whether close to ga or resolutely zoku, the haikai waka differ from the haikai renga in their personal referentiality. Renga verses, whether ushin or haikai, inevitably express on some level the poet's own subjectivity, but only to a limited degree since they are composed in response to a maeku and often about topics far removed from the immediate situation of the poet. Conversely, of course, even the most personal of the haikaika can only be one persona of the poet. But in that they cast off to varying degrees the thematic confines of orthodox verse, the haikaika contain many of the most personal statements in the journal. Whereas the haikai renga are poetic presentations of impersonal, artificial situations, the haikaika are poetic interpretations of what are presented as actual events.

The haikaika in the journal which Sōchō writes to others are meant for close friends. Like his more orthodox waka exchanges, many of these verses involve requests or thanks for favors, and they often involve parodic play that just as in a linked-verse exchange requires recognition of the foundation poem if the humor is to be understood. Some exchanges involve wordplay of a recondite and donnish sort, as in this exchange with the abbot of Shūon'an:

I sent the abbot a small jug of good sake along with my usual haikai waka:

442
  tamadare no   The jewelled flask's wine
  kogame wa mirume   is plentiful as sea plant;
   sono soko wa   pour what you will,
  utsusu ni tsukinu   still more remains in its depths—
  kō wa henubeshi   your life will last a *kalpa*!

  The abbot replied:

443
  anbai kiezu   Of its everlasting flavor,
   ikkō ryōzetsu nashi   one taste brings no two opinions.

           (*JS*: 349–50)

Sōchō's verse recalls *Kokinshū* 17: 874, by Fujiwara Toshiyuki:

In the Kanpyō era [889–98], a number of the men serving in the palace had a flask of wine sent to the apartments of the empress, asking that whatever remained be returned to them. Laughing, the ladies-in-waiting accepted the flask but sent no reply. When the messenger returned and related what had happened, Toshiyuki sent them this poem:

  tamadare no   Whither that jewelled flask?
  kogame ya izura   Like a turtle it went out
   koyorogi no   into the breakers
  iso no nami wake   off Koyorogi Strand
  oki ni idenikeri   and then far into the depths.

But because the haikai medium imposes the fewest stylistic constraints on the poet, Sōchō also occasionally makes use of it to chide humorously or to express strongly felt resentment. This is not to say that such emotions are impossible to convey in the orthodox tradition (in love poetry or laments, for example); they simply may be more outspoken and topical when composed as haikai. For example:

> The priest Sōseki (Gessonsai) sent me a letter that included a waka. One of its seven-syllable lines was missing two syllables. I sent him this:

301
    miyako ni wa   In the capital
    misomoji amari   it seems that there are poems
       hitomoji no   where the usual
    futamoji taranu   thirty syllables plus one
    uta mo arikeri   are seen as two too many!
                     (*JS*: 82)

It is the haikai that Sōchō writes primarily for his own amusement or consolation that show the widest range of expression. Many were composed in response to everyday events:

> Year's end is commonly called "the season," and in this village too I hear families shouting as they pound glutinous rice in preparation for the festivities:

471
    usu kine no   Here in this village
    oto ni nigiwau   that resounds with the pounding
       kono sato ni   of mortar and mallet,
    ikade tabine o   how is one to have the peace
    sumu kokoro kana   that comes from rested travel?

> . . . Twenty-fifth, the night of *Setsubun*. Hearing them throwing beans:

473
    fuku wa uchi e   This night, when one throws beans
    iru mame no koyoi   and cries, "Good fortune in!"
       motenashi o   do all the demons
    hiroi hiroi ya   rush outside to scrabble up
    oni wa izuramu   the feast they are being served?

In the capital, they have a practice for protecting against evil, in which one counts out his age in coins and tosses them out for beggars to pick up as they go by at night. Recalling that, I composed this:

474　　kazoureba　　　　　　Counting up the years,
　　　ware hachijū no　　　　I find I have eighty—
　　　　　zōjisen　　　　　　　　even to drive out evil,
　　　yaku to te ikaga　　　　how could I possibly
　　　otoshiyarubeki　　　　　throw away that many coins?
　　　　　　　　　　　　　　　　(*JS*: 131–32)

As the last verse indicates, old age is also never far from Sōchō's mind, and he will often use haikai to lift his spirits when depressed by his infirmities:

Before dawn, troubled by a cough:

448　　tare zo kono　　　　Who is he, the one
　　　oi no shiwaza no　　　with an old man's habit
　　　　shiwabuki o　　　　　　of coughing
　　　saki ni tatetsutsu　　noisily each time
　　　tsune ni otosuru　　　before he starts to speak?
　　　　　　　　　　　　　　(*JS*: 125)

As we have often seen him do elsewhere, Sōchō is apparently referring here to a classical passage, one from the "Yomogiu" chapter of *Genji monogatari*: "Koremitsu approached and cleared his throat to announce his presence; after coughing (*mazu shiwabuki o saki ni tatete*), an ancient voice inquired, 'Who is it? Who's there?'"[223]

These verses suggest that Sōchō sometimes has recourse to humor to imply deeper and more serious concerns. But other haikaika in the collection show no trace of humor at all, and fall under the haikai rubric simply because of extra-canonical word choice, while being completely serious in subject. The poem that Sōchō writes in response to the cold and rumor-rife atmosphere he finds in Suruga (*JS* no. 587, quoted in Chapter One in another context) is one such verse. Another appears just after his haikai chōka on his hermitage life (*JS* no. 215, quoted in Chapter Three):

Here in the country this summer, heavy rain has been pouring down from morning till night. I have not been able to poke my head outside, and there has been no way even to reach my neighbors:

216　　izuku mo ka　　　　　Is it so elsewhere?
　　　koshiba sumi tae　　　kindling and charcoal used up,
　　　　cha sake tae　　　　　　tea, sake used up,

| miso shio shiranu | miso and salt sight unseen, |
| ame no tsurezure | time hanging heavy in the rain. |

(JS: 64)

Indeed, the chōka on his hermitage life in Sunpu is one of the best single examples in the journal of verses that combine whimsy with seriousness, the high with the low, and the old with the new. This blend is tellingly emphasized through contrast with an earlier travel journal and literary treatise Sōchō himself mentions, *Nagusamegusa*, by the great poet Shōtetsu. When Shōtetsu arrives at Moruyama, very near where Sōchō was later to winter, he remarks, "There is nothing in Moruyama that touches the heart. It is a village in the forest shade, with only the clamor of market maids and merchants."[224] It is not a line Sōchō would have written. In his chōka, that clamor is part of what he enjoys:

> smoke from the smudge fires rises
> with Mount Fuji's
> over fences blooming white
> with "evening faces"—
> and throughout the neighborhood
> chock-a-block with huts,
> the merchants and market maids
> raise their voices:
> "Greens and potatoes for sale!
> I've eggplants for sale!
> Melons for sale! White melons!"
> one after the next passing in front of my gate.

But this contemporaneous and commonplace detail is blended in the same poem with description phrased in language from the classics. Sōchō's "fences blooming white / with 'evening faces'" and his "neighborhood / chock-a-block with huts" relate to a passage in *Genji monogatari*: "'The white ones blooming over there are called "evening faces,"' he said. 'The name sounds so like a person's, yet here they are blooming on this dilapidated fence.' Indeed it seemed a poor neighborhood, chock-a-block with huts."[225]

The poem evokes the lightness of the haikai medium as well as an underlying bittersweet solemnity that is worthy of any of Sōchō's more orthodox efforts. The work begins to show the same blend of elegance and rusticity seen in wabi tea wares and teahouse architecture. This is not parody of the classics; instead, it is a combination of the courtly and the common, or an expression of common themes in a language imbued with some of the grandeur of the ushin poetic tradition.

It must be reiterated in conclusion, however, that Sōchō was always first and foremost an ushin poet; he still viewed that form of composition as the most sublime, and he insisted on orthodox purity both in his own ushin verses and in those of his students. He made that position very clear in regard to one particularly felicitous verse in his journal:

> Today I took my morning and noon meals at Shōrin'an. First calligraphy in celebration of New Year's:

484
> ugoki naki
> chitose no kage no
> haru ni au
> yo o hito mochii
> kagamiyama kana
>
> Steadfast for a thousand years,
> the protector that all extol
> as they greet the spring
> round the mountain that recalls
> mirror rice cakes!

> This province is at peace. I made this New Year's poem in reference to the great respect accorded in both town and country to the constable, whose will prevails. The word *mochiikagami* appears in the "Hatsune" chapter of *Genji monogatari*, I believe. It is *not* haikai. (*JS*: 135)

And yet it is equally clear that both haikai renga and haikaika account for a considerable amount of Sōchō's interest and creative energy. More than any previous major poet who specialized in the ushin medium, Sōchō was devoted both to the composition and to the preservation of an entire range of haikai poetry, and his inclusion of such poetry along with his ushin efforts in a single volume underscored his commitment to that genre and his contribution to its development.

Epilogue

Five years after the last entry was made in *The Journal of Sōchō*, on the sixth of the third month, 1532, the poet passed away at age eighty-four at his Brushwood Cottage in Mariko. A verse reputed to be his death poem is preserved in the *Nikonshū* miscellany:

negawaku wa	This is my request—
omoyu to tōru	for at least a moment
michi bakari	let the way be opened
shibashi yuruse	for the passage of some rice porridge,
mune no sekimori	gate keeper of my stomach![1]

The kyōka, if indeed by Sōchō, suggests that he maintained a Zen-like sense of wry detachment and proportion even in the face of his impending end. As he had done for so many others, disciples and colleagues such as Sōboku and Arakida Moritake preserved his memory in their diaries and memorial poetic sequences. On hearing of the poet's demise, Sanetaka too confided his emotions in his diary: "The priest Sōchō and I were close friends for many years. He was the one true disciple of Sōgi. How tragic—I can only weep tears of old age."[2]

Brushwood Cottage became a pilgrimage spot for later poets, a new poetic site of sorts. Thirteen years after Sōchō's death, a particularly significant anniversary, his disciple Sōboku revisited the cottage he had seen earlier when he accompanied the master back east during the last journey depicted in Sōchō's

Epilogue

journal. He wrote of time spent with Sōchō's son, now called Suian, in his travel diary, *Tōgoku kikō*:

> I decided to visit the cottage at Mariko and asked Suian if he would like to come with me, as it was a lovely day. He waited for me with horses ready. I also invited others who had connections with Brushwood Cottage, but they could not come due to year-end commitments, so we went by ourselves. But that too was pleasant in its own way. As this year is the thirteenth since Sōchō passed away, I had had a hundred-verse sequence in Japanese and Chinese composed at the Konoe residence, and I placed it before Sōchō's image. Reminiscing about him, I found it hard to restrain my tears of old age. The rocks and the stream were unchanged, and the plums and willows he had planted with his own hands were coming into bud here and there, as though the garden had been waiting to welcome us that day. We made our way through the withered ivy to his grave but could find no trace of the poem he had written on a stupa-shaped marker:

saioku no	I have made a path
koke no shitamichi	of moss to my grave
tsukuru nari	at my Brushwood Cottage.
kyō o waga yo no	I will consider today
kichinichi ni shite	a lucky day hereafter![3]

> He jokingly told me about the poem when we came here years ago. Thereafter he changed the gravesite and composed this:

mata tsukuru	I have remade it,
koke no shitamichi	the mossy path to my grave
saioku ya	at my Brushwood Cottage.
nagara no hashi no	Will it someday be as old
mukashi nariken	as the Bridge of Nagara?

> The marks of that were still faintly visible. Going back over the stone bridge that spans the stream, I made this:

utsunoyama	It still spans the stream
tani yuku mizu ni	that flows through the valley
nokorikeri	of Reality Mountain!
mukashi nagara no	The floating bridge of dreams of Nagara
yume no ukihashi	remains unchanged from the past.[4]

Sōchō became for Sōboku what Sōgi had been for Sōchō, and Sōboku passed on the master's poetic pronouncements to his own students, including his son Sōyō. And as the above example from *Tōgoku kikō* demonstrates, Sōboku's travel writing suggests the same blend of canonical poetic lyricism and quotidian directness seen in Sōchō's work.

Sōchō continued to be revered by succeeding generations, poets who had never met him but who remembered him through his poetry and prose. Satomura Jōha, the last important master of ushin renga, mentioned Sōchō frequently in his travel journal *Jōha Fujimi michi no ki* (Account of Jōha's Journey to Fuji, 1567), the passages about the earlier poet far outnumbering those on the ostensible goal of the journey, Mount Fuji. He makes mention therein of a certain *Sōchō michi no ki*, probably *The Journal of Sōchō*.[5] The style of his diary prose, too, is much like that of Sōchō's. For example, on arriving at Sōchō's Brushwood Cottage, he writes:

> When I looked around the hermitage, I noticed an old plaque inscribed "Saioku" in the hand of the priest Ikkyū. A portrait of Sōchō was also hanging there. He had forbidden anyone to paint his portrait while he was still alive, but he said that if a portrait was made after his death it should show him wearing light-green robes under a black cloak.[6]

As the Edo period progressed and ushin renga gave way to haikai renga as the preferred literary vehicle among the most creative poets, Sōchō came to be remembered as an important literary ancestor of the recent past. The first biography to appear on Sōchō was composed in kanbun in 1668 by the cultural historian Kurokawa Dōyū (d. 1691) and is notable for its insistence on the importance of Ikkyū as well as Sōgi in the poet's career. This was followed by a biographical sketch in Japanese by Bashō's disciple Yamaguchi Sodō (1642–1716), composed when the haikai poet passed through Shimada, the town of Sōchō's birth, in 1701.[7] The accounts of Dōyū and Sodō both remember Sōchō for his contributions to ushin linked-verse poetry. But like Sōgi, Sōchō also achieved a posthumous reputation as an important haikai renga precursor. In the nineteenth-century collection of biographies of haikai poets, *Haika kijindan*, for example, Sōgi is placed at the beginning of the first volume and Sōchō at the beginning of the second.[8]

And like both Ikkyū and Sōgi, Sōchō also came to be mythologized in the popular imagination. As remarked on in Chapter Four, the early collection of humorous anecdotes (*hanashibon*) entitled *Seisuishō* contains numerous stories featuring the poet, often in the company of Sōgi. Sōgi and Sōchō are, in fact, the most famous poetic pair in the work. The historical veracity of these stories is highly problematic, but regardless of their degree of fictionality, they indicate that Sōchō was remembered not only as an ushin renga poet but as a skilled and at times earthy composer of extemporaneous witty verse.

There is no single better demonstration of those two sides of Sōchō's literary oeuvre than *The Journal of Sōchō*. It has been the central argument of this book that Sōchō's journal is at once the product and one of the most evocative literary representations of an age of unprecedented cultural collision, written by one who possessed what Bakhtin calls a "dialogic imagination." It is in such "heteroglot" eras, writes Bakhtin, "when the collision and interaction of languages is especially intense and powerful . . . [that] aspects of heteroglossia are canonized with great ease and rapidly pass from one language system to another: from everyday life into literary language, from literary language into the language of the everyday."[9]

We have seen in the foregoing pages that *The Journal of Sōchō* demonstrates just this interaction between language systems. Much of the work remains profoundly conservative, after the example of Sōgi's poetry and prose. This is most notable in the renga passages, where all the participants strive to speak in one stylistic voice. *The Journal of Sōchō* shows that Sōchō was Sōgi's disciple and proud of it; at least in his ushin practice, he does not appear to have suffered from Harold Bloom's "anxiety of influence."[10] He taught the high canonical poetic tradition to others with an uncompromising fervor worthy of a disciple of Sōgi. And he wrote essentially for an audience both of established and of newly enfranchised elites.

But we have also observed that the journal itself combines these renga moments with an unprecedented number of other genres and registers; it insists at times on the standards of the neoclassical canon and at others it begins to decenter that canon just as the nation itself was being decentered. Where renga is many poets speaking with one stylistic voice, *The Journal of Sōchō* is one man speaking in many voices, mixing the orthodoxy, the *sei*, of Sōgi with the elements of unorthodoxy, the *kyō*, personified in part by Ikkyū. Sōchō joins predominantly elite perspectives with moments of the plebeian and commonplace, and he sometimes invests the latter, in a tentative way, with an importance of their own, as if to give literary expression to the nonduality of his Zen master.

It was perhaps both its classical poetry and also its passages that anticipate Edo haibun that account for the interest shown in the journal by later haikai poets. Sections of the journal do indeed seem premonitory of the haibun blend of everyday topics and charged, poetic language—the "everyday elegance" (*zoku naru en*)—that Bashō prized.[11] Indeed, at times Sōchō too, in an inchoate manner, anticipates the later poet's injunction to "elevate the spirit, then return to the mundane."[12] The journal, despite its considerable size, was frequently copied in the Edo period, and numerous manuscripts survive from the mid-seventeenth century onward. It is quite possible that Bashō himself acquired a copy. Harada Yoshioki explicitly traces the beginnings of what he calls "haikai-style prose" (*haikaitai sanbun*) to Sōchō.[13]

In modern times, some critics have judged the journal in terms of the neo-classical aesthetic standard of Sōgi's *Tsukushi michi no ki* and found it to be a good historical source book but wanting in "literary value."[14] Marxist critics on the other hand have found it altogether too elite, missing its chance, as it were, to be more like the work of Yamazaki Sōkan.[15] The real importance of the work lies precisely in its engagement with both perpectives, resulting in a variegated representation of a man and a time that is remarkable in the literature of the period for its individuality and personal voice.

Appendixes

APPENDIX A

The Imagawa House Lineage

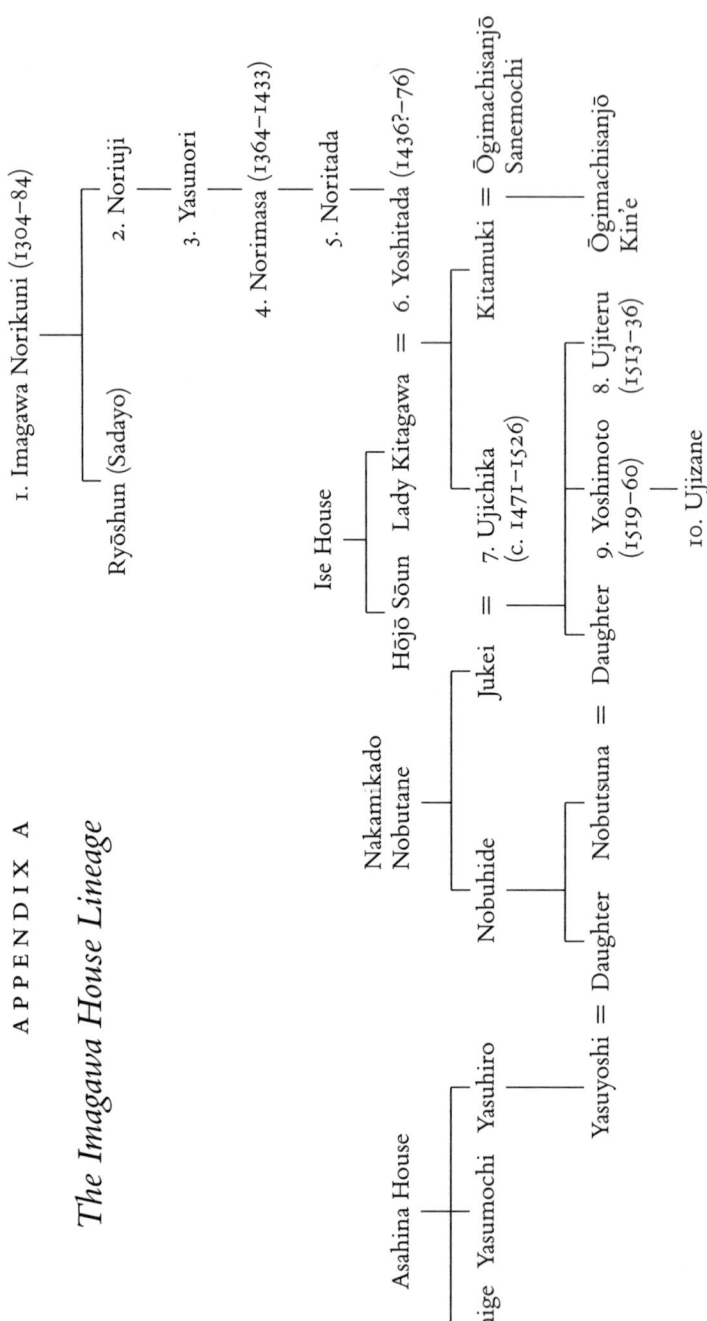

The lineage has been simplified; offspring are listed selectively and not necessarily in order of birth.

APPENDIX B

Two Early Biographies of Sōchō

Biography by Yamaguchi Sodō

This untitled manuscript, dated 1701, is in the collection of Saiokuji temple. There is no printed version available. Yamaguchi Sodō (1642–1716), an early Edo man of letters and haikai poet, was well acquainted with Bashō and members of Bashō's school, as well as with other literati of the period. He was fond of travel and wrote this, the earliest surviving wabun account of Sōchō, while staying in Shimada in Suruga Province.

The lay priest Kyūan Sōchō, master of linked verse, was born in the village of Shimada. His father was Gojō Yoshisuke, and his mother was of Fujiwara lineage. He served Lord Imagawa Yoshimoto in his youth, then for certain reasons took the tonsure and journeyed to the capital, where he studied renga with Shugyokuan Sōgi.[1] When well advanced in his studies, he was granted the *sō* character from Sōgi's name, and he went on to become an authority on the poetic way and ranked with the poetic immortals Hitomaro and Akahito.[2]

He was devoted to travel; he took as his companions the rivers and mountains and found shelter atop cliffs and under trees.[3] His deep love of nature is beyond comment. His blossom-like poetry and prose remain in *Shinsen tsukubashū*, *Hokkoku michi no ki*, and *Utsunoyama no ki*.[4] As with Sōgi and Botanka Shōhaku, many legends about him survive.

At his Brushwood Cottage at the foot of Tenchūzan mountain in the northeastern part of this province stand memorials to the lay priests Sōgi and Sōchō. Someone told me that Sōgi passed away in the Bunki era [1501–4] at Hakone Mountain in Sagami Province and that the date of Sōchō's death is the first year of Kyōroku, third month, sixth day.[5] Very little is known concerning the location of his grave, but the fact of his birth in this village is beyond question. For that reason the residents have long been disposed to provide lodging to travelers of a poetic turn. I too happened to pass by and wrote down what I heard before leaving. Let it be amended at a later date by one of greater knowledge.

> By Buyō Sanjin Sodō,
> Genroku Kanotomi [1701],
> second month, twenty-fifth day.

Biography in 'Tōkaidō gojūsan tsugi'

> This account accompanies the woodblock illustration reproduced in this volume. It appears in a late-Edo picture book depicting the fifty-three stations of the Tōkaidō road, illustrated by Utagawa Sadahide. The manuscript is in the collection of Tanaka Takahiro.

The founder of Saiokuji temple in the town of Izumigawa was the priest Saiokuken Sōchō. He was born in Shimada in [Suruga] Province. He was initially in the service of Imagawa Kazusanosuke Yoshitada. At fifteen he went to the capital, studied with the priest Sōgi, and succeeded him as a famous linked-verse master. At seventeen he took the tonsure, was baptized at Fushain at Daigoji temple, then studied Zen with the prelate Ikkyū of Daitokuji and approached enlightenment.[6] He enjoyed the arts, which he pursued with no thought of profit or self-aggrandizement. In the ninth year of Eishō, he was invited back by Imagawa Ujichika.[7] He built his cottage in this mountain village [of Mariko] and planted bamboo beside the fence:

> iku wakaba   How many, the green buds
> hayashihajime no of bamboo beginning to flourish
> sono no take   in the garden?[8]

A longtime retainer of the Imagawa, [Saitō] Yasumoto, composed the waki verse:

> sumu yado suzushi   The dwelling where he lives is cool.
> matsu no shitamizu Water beneath the pines.

He loved tea and enjoyed the *hitoyogiri* shakuhachi. He died in the fifth year of Kyōroku, on the sixth of the third month, at age 84.

APPENDIX C

Major Works by Sōchō

The following is a list of many of the best-known of Sōchō's works that are available in easily obtainable modern printed transcriptions (unless otherwise indicated), divided by genre and listed chronologically. Printed versions are listed in the bibliography. This is only a fraction of Sōchō's oeuvre; many more examples can be found in printed editions and manuscripts or are known from secondary sources.

Linked-Verse Sequences

1480:8	Bunmei 12 [1480]:8 *nanimichi hyakuin*. With Sōgi and others. Sōchō's earliest extant linked-verse sequence.
1487:10:9–11	*Hamori senku* (also known as *Shugyokuan senku*). With Sōgi, Shōhaku, and others.
1488:1:22	*Minase sangin*. With Sōgi and Shōhaku.
1488:3	*Settsu senku*. With Sōgi, Shōhaku, Hosokawa Masamoto, and others. Sponsored by the warrior Nose Yorinori. No printed edition.
1491:10:12	*Yuyama sangin*. With Sōgi and Shōhaku.
1499:2:25	*Hosokawake senku*. With Ashikaga Yoshitaka, Hosokawa Masamoto, Sōgi, and others. No printed edition.
1504:10:25–27	*Shutsujin senku* (also called *Shin Mishima senku* or *Saiokuken senku*). A solo sequence by Sōchō in gratitude for a successful campaign by Imagawa Ujichika.

APPENDIX C

1516:3:11–13	*Jikka senku*. With Sanetaka, Sōseki, and others.
1518:8:10–12	*Higashiyama senku*. With Shōhaku, Sōseki, and others.
1522:8:4–8	*Ise senku*. With Sōseki. Commissioned by Hosokawa Takakuni and composed at Ise Shrine.
1524:3:17–21	*Iba senku* (also called *Gessonsai senku*). With Sanetaka and Sōseki. Sponsored by Iba (Tanemura) Sadakazu.
1527:1:18	*Yashima Shōrin'an naniki hyakuin*. With Sōboku.

Books on Linked-Verse Composition, Commentaries, Judgments, Etc.

1479	*Ise monogatari Sōchō kikigaki*. Sōchō's notes on lectures by Sōgi.
1488	*Shijin zanshō*. A commentary on *Genji monogatari*. No printed edition.
1490	*Sōchō kawa* (also called *Mikawa kudari*). A book of linked-verse associations.
1490	*Nagabumi* (or *Nagafumi*). An essay on renga composition.
1490	*Shichinin tsukeku hanshi*. Seven poets, including Sōchō, Sōgi, and Shōhaku, providing links to the same difficult maeku, with judgments by Sōgi.
c. 1508	*Renga sakurei*. An essay on renga composition.
1508	*Sōchō hyakuban rengaawase*. One hundred pairs of links by Sōchō, judged by Sanetaka and Shōhaku.
c. 1509	*Renga hikyōshū* (attributed). Renga composition through comparisons.
c. 1514	*Sōchō hikashō* (attributed). Waka commentary.
1515	*Shitakusachū*. A commentary on Sōgi's third personal verse collection.
1519	*Amayo no ki*. An essay on renga composition.
1520	*Guku wakuraba*. A commentary by Sōgi on his second collection of linked verse, with additional commentary by Sōchō.
c. 1522–c. 1528	*Sōchō renga jichū*. Self-commentary on select verses (*Okitsuate* half c. 1522–23; *Mibuate* half, c. 1528 or thereafter).

1528	*Renga tsukeyō*. An essay on linked-verse composition, composed for a member of the Konoe family.
1528	*Genjichū*. A commentary on *Genji monogatari*. No printed edition.
nd	*Kabekusachū*. Commentaries made by disciples, based in part on lectures by Sōchō on his first personal linked-verse collection.

Diaries

1502	*Sōgi shūenki*. A record of the last journey and death of Sōgi.
1509	*Azumaji no tsuto*. A record of Sōchō's journey through the eastland with the intended destination of Shirakawa Gate.
1518	*Utsunoyama no ki* (also called *Oi no higagoto*). A record of various journeys from 1509–17, plus autobiographical passages.
1522–27	*Sōchō shuki* (The Journal of Sōchō). A record of two round trips to Kansai from Suruga, plus shorter journeys and long periods of stasis.
1530–31	*Sōchō nikki*. A record of Sōchō's last years in Suruga, plus short journeys.

Personal Poetry Collections

1505–12	*Kabekusa*.
1517	*Nachigomori*.
1526	*Oi no mimi*.

Miscellaneous

| after 1527 | *Imagawa kafu*. A history of the Imagawa House, rendered into wakankonkōbun by Sōchō. |
| after 1528 | *Fuji goran nikki*. A travel diary, perhaps by Imagawa Norimasa, the postcript of which was later appended by Sōchō for Imagawa Ujiteru. |

Reference Matter

Glossary of Common Nouns

aisatsu 挨拶
aiwa 哀話
azana 字
baibai 売買
bakufu 幕府
biwa 琵琶
bu 武
bun 文
byakudan 白檀
chakaiki 茶会記
chaoyin 朝隠
chinzō 頂相
chō 町
chōka 長歌
chōku 長句
dai 題
daisan 第三
dakurō 濁醪
dengaku 田楽
dō 堂
dō 銅
dōbōshū 同朋衆
doikki 土一揆
dōjō 堂上
dokugin 独吟
dōri 道理
dōsha 道者

dōshin 道心
dōshin 同心
dosō 土倉
dosō yoriaishū 土倉寄合衆
eirakusen 永楽銭
etoki hōshi 絵解法子
fūkyō 風狂
funi 不二
furyū monji 不立文字
fushimono 賦物
fuzei 風情
ga 雅
gachirinkan 月輪観
gekokujō 下剋上
genpuku 元服
genze riyaku 現世利益
gō 号
gōzoku 豪族
haibun 俳文
haikai 俳諧
haikaika 俳諧歌
haikai no uta 俳諧の歌
hananomoto 花の下
hanashibon 噺本
hare no uta 晴の歌
hiki 疋
hiraku 平句

hitoori 一折
hiwa 悲話
hokku 発句
hon'i 本意
hōraku 法楽
hōshi 法師
hotoke 仏
hyakuin 百韻
ichijun 一巡
ichimi dōshin 一味同心
iisute 言捨
ikki 一揆
issho fujū 一所不住
ji 地
jige 地下
jin 沈
jinkō 沈香
jisen kashū 自撰歌集
jisen kushū 自撰句集
ji-sho-i 時所位
jizamurai 地侍
jō 丈
jo-ha-kyū 序破急
jukkai 述懐
kahō 家法
kaisho 会所
kakekotoba 掛詞

Glossary of Common Nouns

kami no ku 上句
kana 仮名
kanbun chokuyakutai 漢文直訳体
kanbun nikki 漢文日記
kankyo 閑居
kanmon 貫文
kanrei 管領
kasagi 笠着
kashindan 家臣団
katauta 片歌
ke no uta 褻の歌
kenchi 検地
kigo 季語
kikō bungaku 紀行文学
kireji 切字
kiryoka 羇旅歌
kōawase 香合
kōdō 香道
koji 居士
kojōruri 古浄瑠璃
koki 古稀
kokkei 滑稽
kokoro 心
kokorozuke 心付
koku 石
kokujin 国人
kokujin ikki 国人一揆
komedai 米代
kotatsu 炬燵
kotobagaki 詞書
kotobazuke 詞付
kouta 小歌
kōwakamai 幸若舞
kuni ikki 国一揆
kurai 位
kyōfū 狂風
kyōgen 狂言
kyōgen kigo 狂言綺語

kyōka 狂歌
machishū 町衆
maeku 前句
maekuzuke 前句付
meigetsu 名月
meikōawase 名香合
meisho 名所
menotogo 乳母子
michi 道
michiyuki 道行
mime 眉目
mitsumono 三物
mochi 餅
mon 文
monzeki 門跡
mushin 無心
musō renga 夢想連歌
nanku 難句
nenchū gyōji 年中行事
neriko 練香
nerinuki ねりぬき
nerizake 練酒
omote hachiku 鼻八句
otogizōshi 御伽草子
rakuchū rakugaizu 洛中洛外図
renga 連歌
rengashi 連歌師
ribetsu no uta 離別歌
rikan 吏幹
rikan 利勘
rinne 輪廻
risei bumin 理世撫民
rosen 路銭
ryokō 旅行
ryoshuku 旅宿
saihen 再篇
saishukke 再出家
sakaya 酒屋

sarugaku 猿楽
sedōka 旋頭歌
seidō 正道
senku 千句
setsuwa 説話
shakkyō 釈教
shi 詩
shichū no kakure 市中の隠
shikashū 私家集
shikimoku 式目
shimo no ku 下句
shinku 親句
shō 升
shōdōshi 唱導師
shokisō 書記僧
shokunin zukushie 職人尽絵
shū 集
shugo 守護
shugo yoriai 守護寄合
shugyō 修行
shuhitsu 執筆
shusse monogatari 出世物語
sōan bungaku 草庵文学
sōhei 僧兵
soku 疎句
sōmura 惣村
sōrōbun 候文
sōshō 宗匠
sugata 姿
suki 好寄
sutemi no gyō 捨身の行
takimonoawase 薫物合
tanku 短句
tanrenga 短連歌
tatchū 塔頭
tawabure uta 戯歌
tohi 都鄙
torinashi 取成
tsuchi ikki 土一揆

Glossary of Common Nouns

tsukeai 付合
tsukeku 付句
uchihirame うちひらめ
uchikoshi 打越
uchū 雨中
udonge 優曇華
ushin 有心
usuzake 薄酒
utamakura 歌枕
utamonogatari 歌物語

wabun nikki 和文日記
waka 和歌
wakankonkōbun 和漢混淆文
wakan renku 和漢聯句
wakashu 若衆
waki 脇
yakudoshi 厄年
yamaga 山家
yojō 余情
yoriai 寄合

yosei 余情
yūgen 幽玄
yukiyō 行様
za 座
zareuta 戯歌
zazen 座禅
zōdan 雑談
zoku 俗
zōtōka 贈答歌
zuihitsu 随筆

Glossary of Proper Nouns

Abutsu 阿仏 (c. 1222–1283)
Amano 天野
Arakida Morihira 荒木田守平
Arakida Moritake 荒木田守武
  (1473–1549)
Asahina Tokishige 朝比奈時茂
Asahina Yasumochi 朝比奈泰以
Asahina Yasuyoshi 朝比奈泰能 (d. 1557)
Asakura Norikage 朝倉教景 (1474–1555)
Asakura Toshikage 朝倉敏景 (Takakage
  孝景) (1428–81)
Ashikaga Yoshiharu 足利義晴 (1511–50)
Ashikaga Yoshihisa 足利義尚 (1465–89)
Ashikaga Yoshimasa 足利義政 (1436–90)
Ashikaga Yoshimitsu 足利義満
  (1358–1408)
Ashikaga Yoshitane 足利義植
  (1466–1523)
Ashikaga Yoshizumi 足利義澄
  (1481–1511)
Asukai Masaari 飛鳥井雅有 (1241–1301)
Asukai Masayasu 飛馬井雅康 (1436–1509)
Asukai Masayo 飛馬井雅世 (1390–1452)
Baika 梅花
"Beichuang sanyou" 北窓三友
Benzaiten 弁才天 or 弁財天
Bo Juyi 白居易 (772–846)

Bokuō 穆翁
Bokurin 牧林
Bokusai 墨斎
Bontō 梵灯 (b. 1349)
Botanka Shōhaku 牡丹花肖柏
  (1443–1527)
Bunmei no naikō 文明の内訌
Caotang ji 草堂記
"Changhenge" 長恨歌
Chiun 智蘊 (d. 1448)
Chōa 長阿
Chōtō 長頭
"Chunwang" 春望
"Chunye" 春夜
Daigoji 醍醐寺
Daiō 大応 (1235–1309)
Daitō 大燈 (1282–1337)
Daitokuji 大徳寺
Dazaifu 大宰府 or 太宰府
Den'a dokugin jōji hyakuin
  伝阿独吟畳字百韻
Dōkō (Dōkyō) 道興 (1430–1501)
Fei Zhangfang 費長方
Fujiwara Akihira 藤原明衡 (989?–1066)
Fujiwara Mototoshi 藤原基俊
  (1060–1142)
Fujiwara Norikane 藤原範兼 (1107–65)

Glossary of Proper Nouns

Fujiwara Shunzei 藤原俊成 (1114-1204)
Fujiwara Tameie 藤原為家 (1198-1275)
Fujiwara Teika 藤原定家 (1162-1241)
Futarasan 二荒山
Geiami 芸阿弥 (1431-83)
Gessonsai Sōseki 月村斎宗碩 (1474-1535)
Gojō Yoshisuke 五条義助
Gokashiwabara 後柏原 (1464-1526)
Gonara 後奈良 (1497-1557)
Goshirakawa 後白河 (1127-92)
Gotoba 後鳥羽 (1180-1239)
Gotsuchimikado 後土御門 (1442-1500)
"Hai manman" 海漫漫
Haikai renga 俳諧連歌
Haikai rengashō 俳諧連歌抄
Hakata 博多
Hirano 平野
Hōjō Sōun 北条早雲 (1432-1519)
Horikoshi Kubō 堀越公方
Hosokawa Masamoto 細川政元 (1466-1507)
Hosokawa Takakuni 細川高国 (1484-1531)
Hosokawa Yūsai 細川幽斎 (1534-1610)
Huxi 虎渓
Iba Sadakazu 伊庭貞和 (Tanemura Nakatsukasanojō 種村中務丞)
Ichijō Kaneyoshi 一条兼良 (1402-81)
Iio Sōgi (see Inō Sōgi)
Ikeda 池田
Ikkō ikki 一向一揆
Ikkyū Sōjun 一休宗純 (1394-1481)
Imagawa Norimasa 今川範政 (1364-1433)
Imagawa Ryōshun 今川了俊 (1326-1420)
Imagawa Ujitoyo 今川氏豊 (c. 1520-36)
Imagawa Ujizane 今川氏真 (1538-1614)
Imagawa Yoshitada 今川義忠 (1436?-76)
Inano 猪名野
Inawashiro Kensai 猪苗代兼載 (1452-1510)

Inō Sōgi 飯尾宗祇 (1421-1502)
Ise haikai kikigakishū 伊勢誹諧聞書集
Ise Sadachika 伊勢貞親 (1417-73)
Ishida 石田
Isuzu Mimosusogawa 五十鈴御裳濯川
Ji 時
Jien 慈円 (1155-1225)
Jijū 侍従
Jōan Ryūsū 常庵竜崇 (d. 1536)
Jōdo shinshū 浄土真宗
Jōgyōji 浄業寺
Jōha 承葩
Jōha (see Satomura Jōha)
Jūjūshin'in Shinkei kikō 十住心院心敬紀行
Jukei 寿桂 (c. 1490-1568)
Jun'a 旬阿
Juntokuin 順徳院 (1197-1242)
Kadoya 角屋
Kakegawa 掛川
Kakinomotoshū 柿の下衆
Kameyama 亀山
Karasumaru Mitsuhiro 烏丸光広 (1579-1638)
Katsuhito 勝仁
Kayō 荷葉
Ken'ō 謙翁 (d. 1414)
Kensai (see Inawashiro Kensai)
Kikka 菊花
Kitagawa 北川 (c. 1442-1529)
Kitamura Kigin 北村季吟 (1624-1705)
Kitano renga kaisho bugyō 北野連歌会所奉行
Koga kubō 古河公方
Kōjin 紅塵
Kokemushiro 苔庭
Kokin denju 古今伝授
Kongōji 金剛寺
Konoe Hisamichi 近衛尚通 (1472-1544)
Konoe Masaie 近衛政家 (1444-1505)
Konparu Zenchiku 金春禅竹 (1405-70?)

Glossary of Proper Nouns

Kōsai 弘済
Kumano bikuni 熊野比丘尼
Kuonji 久遠寺
Kurinomotoshū 栗の下衆
Kurobō 黒方
Kyūan (or Kuan) 久庵 or 久安
Kyūsei 救済 (c. 1281–c. 1375)
Letian 楽天
Linji 臨済 (d. 867)
"Luori" 落日
Lushan 廬山
Makino Kohaku Shigetoki 牧野古白成時
Mansai Jugō 満済准后 (1378–1435)
Mariko 丸子
Matsudaira Kiyoyasu 松平清康
Matsudaira Nobutada 松平信忠
Matsudaira Sadanobu 松平定信 (1758–1829)
Mibuate 壬生宛
Minamoto Sanetomo 源実朝 (1192–1219)
Minamoto Toshiyori 源俊頼 (1055–1129?)
Mitsunaka 満仲
Miyahara Moritaka 宮原盛孝
Mori (or Shin) 森
Murata Jukō 村田珠光 (1422–1502)
Murata Sōju 村田宗珠
Musō Soseki 夢窓疎石 (1275–1351)
Myōshōan 妙勝庵
Myōshōji 妙勝寺
Nagao Magoroku 長尾孫六
Nagao Magoshirō 長尾孫四郎
Nakagawa 中河
Nakamikado Nobuhide 中御門宣秀 (1469–1531)
Nakamikado Nobutane 中御門宣胤 (1442–1525)
Nakamikado Nobutsuna 中御門宣綱 (1511–69)
Nanban 南蛮
Nanquan 南泉

Nasu 那須
Niimakura 新枕
Nijō Yoshimoto 二条良基 (1320–88)
Nikkō 日光
Nisho ga myōjin 二所明神
Nisuiki 二水記
Nitta Shōjun 新田尚純
Nōami 能阿弥 (1397–1471)
Nōin 能因 (b. 988)
Nyoian 如意庵
Oda Nobuhide 織田宣秀 (1508–51)
Ōe Masafusa 大江匡房 (1041–1111)
Oga Norimitsu 小鹿範満
Ōgimachisanjō Kin'e 正親町三条公兄 (1494–1578)
Ōgimachisanjō Sanemochi 正親町三条実望 (1463–1530)
Okitsuate 興津宛
Ōshikōchi Mitsune 凡河内躬恒
Ōtawara (or Ōdarawa) 大俵
Otsuki Masahisa 小槻雅久
Ōuchi Masahiro 大内政弘 (1446–95)
Owa Sōrin 尾和宗臨 (d. 1501)
Ōyama 大山
"Qiwulun" 斉物論
"Qujiang" 曲江
Rakuyō 落葉
Ranjatai 蘭奢待
Reizei Tamekazu 冷泉為和 (1486–1549)
Reizei Tamemori 冷泉為守 (1265–1328)
Renga Shichiken 連歌七賢
Renga Shichishi 連歌七士
Rinsen'an 臨川庵
Rinzai (see Linji)
Rōka Rōjin 弄花老人
Rōkaken 弄花軒
Rokkaku Sadayori 六角定頼 (1495–1552)
Rokushu 六種
Ryōjusen 霊鷲山
Ryūōmaro 竜王丸

Glossary of Proper Nouns

Saigyō 西行 ((1118-1190)
Saioku 柴屋
Saioku Rōjin 柴屋老人
Saiokuken Sōchō 柴屋軒宗長 (1448-1532)
Saitō Yasumoto 斉藤安元
Saka Jūbutsu 坂十仏
Sakai denju 堺伝授
Sakurai Motosuke 桜井基佐
San'ami 三阿弥
Sangyokushū 三玉集
Sanjōnishi Sanetaka 三条西実隆 (1455-1537)
Sanmon 山門
Sanrian 山里庵
Satomura Jōha 里村紹巴 (d. 1602)
Seki Kajisai 関何似斎 (Toshimori 関俊盛)
Sen no Sōtan 千宗旦 (1578-1658)
Senjun 専順 (1411-76)
Sesshū Tōyō 雪舟等楊 (1420-1506)
Shinjuan 真珠庵
Shinkei 心敬 (1406-75)
Shinkyū kyōka haikai kikigaki 新旧狂歌誹諧聞書
Shirakawa 白川
Shōhaku (see Botanka Shōhaku)
Shōjū Ryūtō 正宗竜統 (d. 1498)
Shōkokuji 相国寺
Shokugo meidai wakashū 続五明題和歌集
Shōrin'an 少林庵 or 小林庵
Shōtetsu 正徹 (1381-1459)
Shūa 周阿 (d. 1375?)
Shūon'an 酬恩庵
Sōami 相阿弥 (d. 1525)
Sōboku (see Tani Sōboku)
Sōchō (see Saiokuken Sōchō)
Sōchōji 倉長寺 (originally written 宗長寺)
Sōgi (see Inō Sōgi)

Soga Jasoku 曽我蛇足
Sōho 宗輔 or 宗補
Sōi 宗伊 (1418-86)
Sōkan 宗観 or 宗歓
Sōkyū 宗久
Sōseki (see Gessonsai Sōseki)
Soshin Jōetsu 祖心紹越 (d. 1519)
Sōshitsu 宗叱
Sōshō 宗匠
Sōyō 宗養 (1526-63)
Sōzei 宗砌 (d. 1455)
Sugawara Michizane 菅原道真 (845-903)
Suian 誰庵
Sunpu 駿府
Suruga no saishō 駿河の宰相
Suzuki Nagatoshi 鈴木長敏
Tada 多田
Taijin 泰誰 (d. 1518)
Taira Kanemori 平兼盛 (d. 990)
Taira Tadamori 平尹盛
"Taishang deliangzi" 臺上得涼字
Takeda Nobutora 武田信虎 (1494-1574)
Takigi 薪
Takyōji 建穂寺
Tani Sōboku 谷宗牧 (d. 1545)
Tatsuōmaro 竜王丸
Tenkurō 天九郎
Tenmangū 天満宮
Tō no Sojun 東素純 (d. 1530)
Tō no Tsuneyori 東常縁 (1401-c. 84)
Tobiume senku 飛梅千句
Toyohara Muneaki (or Sumiaki) 豊原統秋 (1450-1524)
Tsukuba no michi 莵玖波の道
Tsukubayama (or Tsukuba no yama, Tsukubasan) 筑波山
Uesugi Fusasada 上杉房定 (d. 1494)
Uesugi Fusayoshi 上杉房能 (d. 1507)
Wang Huizi 王徽子

Glossary of Proper Nouns

Wang Xizhi 王羲之 (321–79)
Wang Zhi 王賈
Washio Takayasu 鷲尾隆康 (1485–1533)
Yamato Takeru no Mikoto 日本武尊 or 倭建命
Yamazaki Sōkan 山崎宗鑑
Yanagimoto Kataharu 柳本賢治 (d. 1530)
Yashima 矢島 or 矢嶋
Yokooka 横岡
"Yongye" 雍也
Yoshino 吉野

Yōsō Sōi 養叟宗頤 (1378–1458)
Yūki Nyūdō Dōchō 結城入道道朝 (Naotomo 直朝)
Yu Jian 玉澗
Yuan Jie 元結 (719–72)
Yuanwu Keqin 圜悟克勤
Zeami 世阿弥 (1363–1443)
Zekkai Chūshin 絶海中津 (1336–1405)
Zen 禅
Zhonghe 仲和
Ziyou 子猷

Notes

Introduction

1. On Sōchō and the Asakura, see Tsurusaki 1969b.
2. Precise dates differ for the Age of the Country at War (also called the Era of Warring States). Those adopted here are 1467–1568, the beginning of the Ōnin War (1467–77) to Oda Nobunaga's entry into Kyoto. Nagahara Keiji prefers to date the period from 1493, when Shogun Ashikaga Yoshitane was expelled from the capital by Hosokawa Masamoto, to 1576, when Nobunaga moved to Azuchi Castle (Nagahara 1983: 18-19). Other definitions end the period in 1573 with the final collapse of the Ashikaga Bakufu, and some go as far as 1615 with Tokugawa Ieyasu's final battle for hegemony at Osaka Castle, or to 1639 with the seclusion laws, and culturally even to the end of the Kan'ei period (1624–44) (Kuwata 1980: i–ii).
3. Donald Keene (1989: 237–41, 1993: 982) has translated the title as *Sōchō's Notebook*.
4. Nakamikado Nobutane, *Nobutanekyōki* 232.
5. Ishida 1965: 21.
6. For a discussion of the relationship between the diary and the poetry collection, see Cranston 1969, Harries 1980, and Konishi 1986, esp. "Kinds of Japanese Prose Compositions," 2: 251–60.
7. Redfield 1956: 41–42.
8. Howard S. Becker (1982: xi) uses the term "art world" to refer to "the network of cooperation" in the context of art as a social phenomenon.

Chapter One

1. The term gekokujō was borrowed from Chinese divination theory (see Yokoi 1979: 33–37).

2. Sōchō's remarks appear in Shimazu 1975: 88–89. All further references to *The Journal of Sōchō* will be cited as *JS*.

3. Christopher Drake (1992) describes this phenomenon in detail in "The Collision of Traditions in Saikaku's Haikai."

4. Ashikaga Yoshihisa died of disease while on a campaign against one of his own constables in Ōmi; Ashikaga Yoshitane was twice driven from Kyoto by his own deputies and died in Awa; and Ashikaga Yoshizumi and Ashikaga Yoshiharu were likewise ousted from the capital by their deputies and died in Ōmi of illness.

5. This was *Hosokawake senku*, 1499:2:25, in which Sōchō particpated along with Ashikaga Yoshizumi (then named Yoshitaka). *RSR* 2: 925.

6. For more on the transition from shugo to sengoku daimyo, see Arnesen 1979, Berry 1982, id. 1994, and Hall 1981.

7. Yamamura 1990a: 379.

8. "Stories of making one's fortune" (*shusse monogatari*), such as *Issun bōshi* and *Monokusa Tarō* became particularly popular in this period. See Yamazaki 1984: 165.

9. Shinjō 1943: 136–37.

10. On ikki, see Davis 1974.

11. See Collcutt 1981.

12. Nagahara 1990: 293.

13. See Okami 1951 and Ruch 1990: 518.

14. Suzuki 1965: 131. Benzaiten is the patron goddess of music and eloquence as well as one of the seven gods of good fortune. Tenjin, the deified Sugawara Michizane, is the god of poetry.

15. Collcutt 1990: 597.

16. On the efforts of the older Esoteric sects to reach out to (and raise subscriptions from) a wider base of parishioners, as well as on the interaction between the older and newer Buddhist sects, see Goodwin 1994.

17. See Ruch 1977.

18. See Weinstein 1973.

19. Barbara Ruch (1990) has made this point in "The Other Side of Culture in Medieval Japan."

20. See Shively in Hall 1991: 733 and Fiévé 1996.

21. Ruch 1990: 531.

22. In fact, such mutual borrowing complicates the very terms "high" and "popular"; Dwight MacDonald (in Gans 1974: 8) entirely rejects the term "popular culture" because works of high culture may themselves be popular.

23. Gans 1974: 10.

24. For partial translations of *Gōdanshō* and *Ryōjin hishō*, see Ury 1993 and Kim 1994, respectively.

25. Kaneko (1995: 46) has suggested that Sōgi's father may have been a member of the Iba house, who served the Rokkaku, daimyō of Ōmi.

26. Gans 1974: 109; Ginzburg 1992: xii. Ginzburg borrows the concept from Bakhtin, whose *Rabelais* is in large part devoted to demonstrating how the interchange of high and popular culture, particularly with regard to the phenomenon of the carnival, informs Rabelais's novels and in fact the entire European sixteenth century.

27. This is what Barbara Ruch (1990: 501) is getting at when she uses the word "popular" not in contrast to "elite" but in reference to "those aspects of a nation's culture valued by most of its citizens, crossing all lines of class, sex, and generation."

28. Hisamichi prepared the work on 1523:9:13 (*Shiryō sōran* 9: 446).

29. Burke 1978: 24ff.

30. Johnson 1985: 39.

31. Bourdieu 1984: 7.

32. The formation of a national culture in the Sengoku age is dicussed in Varley 1990: 458 and Ruch 1990: 501.

33. Ruch 1977: 286.

34. For examples of such diary entries, see Sasaki Kōji 1987.

35. Asukai Masaari, for examples, tells in his *Saga no kayoi* (Saga Visits, 1269) of hearing Fujiwara Tameie's wife, later known as the nun Abutsu, read chapters of *Genji* while providing commentary. See Mizukawa 1985: 61–62. For a translation of the relevant passage from Masaari's diary, see Horton 1993a: 172.

36. Varley 1977. For more on the communal nature of the literature of the period, see Sasaki 1987.

37. See Amino 1977.

38. For a reconstruction of the oral performative nature of the renga session, see Horton 1993b.

39. Though seven or eight participants seems to have been considered ideal, sometimes dozens of poets took part and sometimes only two or three. Solo sequences (*dokugin*) were also frequently composed, but they were a purely literary subset of the essentially oral and performative renga form. There was also considerable variation in speed of composition. Up to four hundred-verse sequences had to be composed in a single day if a thousand-verse sequence (*senku*, actually ten separate hyakuin) was to be finished in the three days ideally allotted. Conversely, when Sōchō was traveling, time and circumstances often allowed only the completion of a single page (*hitoori*, twenty-two verses) or just the first side of the first page (*omote hachiku*, eight verses).

40. For a biography of Jōha, see Keene 1981.

41. Etō 1967: 575.

42. It was, for example, impossible for commoner renga poets, no matter how skilled or respected, to have audiences with the emperor or to compose with him. Sōgi, how-

ever, was occasionally questioned about poetic matters by Emperor Gotsuchimikado via intermediaries, and he was allowed to compose verses with princes and other courtiers. For a discussion of the patronage relationship between Sōgi and Gotsuchimikado, see Kaneko 1993.

43. For a translation of *Renga kaiseki shiki*, see Horton 1993b.

44. Horton 1993b: 510.

45. I use the masculine pronoun throughout with reference to participants at linked-verse sessions. For a review of female participation in linked-verse sessions, see Kaneko 1990: 16–20, and for a chronological listing of known female linked-verse poets and their works, see Okuda 1995.

46. Ben no Naishi and Shōshō no Naishi were remembered for their linked verse by Nijō Yoshimoto in *Tsukuba mondō* 74, 78.

47. In *Tsukuba mondō* (74), Nijō Yoshimoto notes with chagrin, "How sad that these days there are no women composing renga." Isolated records of feminine participation at formal sessions do continue to appear thereafter, but such references are most notable for their rarity. It is likely, though, that women still continued to compose linked-verse informally or in private, in the manner of the husband and wife in the kyōgen play *Mikazuki* (The Winnow Hat). In the Edo period they once again regularly took part in haikai renga sessions.

48. *Tsukuba mondō* 82.

49. Nakamura 1963: 509–10. Courtiers like Shunzei and Teika were certainly seen as specialists in poetry, but they were supported by income from other sources.

50. Saitō Kiyoe (1968: 251) believes that Sōchō was Yoshisuke's third son, as does Ijichi Tetsuo (1936: 15). Takakura Toshiaki (1986: 104), in a more recent and better-documented study, asserts that he was his second son. Sōchō used a number of names during his life. His style (*azana*) was Kyūan (or Kuan), and he first appears in recorded poetry sessions as Sōkan. Although he later adopted the name Sōchō, he also referred to himself as Chōa and Chōtō. His artistic name (*gō*) was Saioku or Saiokuken. Only the former of the two appears in *The Journal of Sōchō*.

51. Sōchō writes in his journal (*JS*: 114) that his religious teacher was the Suruga Counselor (Suruga no Saishō), who received his own religious training at Daigoji in Kyoto. It was long believed that Sōchō too studied at Daigoji (see, for example, the biography in *Tōkaidō gojūsan tsugi* in Appendix B). But Nakagawa Yoshio (1981: 1292) speculates instead that Sōchō was trained at Takyōji, once located in Hattori near Shizuoka City. And Ōtsuka (1987: 176–80) theorizes that Sōchō's name as a young priest may have been Kōsai, the second character relating to that of Mansai Jugō, the abbot of Daigoji, whom the Suruga Counselor may himself have served. See *JS*: 281, n. 150.

52. *Utsunoyama no ki* 404. All further references will be indicated in the text as *UYK*. I have benefited from the translation of a part of this diary in Keene 1977: 261–62.

53. Kurokawa 392. *Sōchō Kojiden* also relates the romantic but unsubstantiated anecdote that Sōgi later saw the two verses Sōchō made at his first renga session at age twelve and prophesied a brilliant career for the boy (Kurokawa 394).

54. Ijichi (1936: 21) and Saitō (1968: 256) both suggest Sōchō also met Shinkei when the latter passed through Suruga to see Mount Fuji on his way east in 1467, but they give no evidence. Saitō (1968: 257) even suggests that Sōchō was present at the composition of *Kawagoe senku*, in which Sōgi and Shinkei participated, but again he provides no proof. Sōchō's early name, Sōkan, does not appear among the poets who composed the thousand verses, but it is indeed possible, though unsubstantiated, that he was a spectator.

55. On Shōkō and his waka activities, see Tsurusaki 1993a.

56. For a brief history of the Imagawa house, see Appendix A of *The Journal of Sōchō*.

57. For a more extended treatment of the cultural achievments of the Imagawa daimyo and their patronage relationships with Sōchō, see Horton 1993c, from which the account here borrows.

58. Quoted in Yonehara 1979: 830.

59. Ibid.

60. Owada 1981c: 987.

61. Ōshima 1962: 39.

62. Quoted in Sansom 1984: 226.

63. Ijichi 1936: 17. An overview of medieval homoeroticism is provided in Childs 1980.

64. The exact date of Ujichika's birth is unsettled, with the dates 1470, 1471, and 1473 advanced. Owada (1983: 142) argues in favor of 1471.

65. On the campaigns of Ujichika and Sōun in Tōtōmi and Kantō, see Akimoto 1984.

66. Sōgi's record of these transmissions is entitled *Kokin wakashū ryōdo kikigaki*.

67. Book-length studies of Sōgi's life include, in chronological order: Araki 1941, Ijichi 1943, Imoto 1974, Konishi 1976, Kaneko 1983, Fujiwara Masayoshi 1984, Morozumi 1985, and Shimazu 1991. The last includes a particularly useful bibliography. For a study of Sōgi's work, see Etō 1967, and for a biography in English, see Carter 1983.

68. On the relationship between Sōgi and Uesugi Fusasada and Fusasada's son Fusayoshi, see Tsurusaki 1988 and a response to that article, Kaneko 1988. Asakura Toshikage is also known as Asakura Takakage.

69. The title *Ise monogatari Sōchō kikigaki* is anachronistic; Sōchō was still known as Sōkan when he wrote it.

70. Two convenient studies of Ikkyū are Nishida 1977 and Ichikawa 1982. In English see Sanford 1981, Arntzen 1986, and Stevens 1993. For a concise introduction, see Keene 1978: 15–25, and for useful background matter, see Covell 1980.

71. On Sōchō's relationship with Ikkyū, see Nakamoto 1967.

72. See Karaki 1982, 16: 415.

73. For more on the relationship between Ikkyū and Zenchiku, see Thornhill 1993: 18–19.

74. See, for example, Arntzen 1986: 29.

75. That is the conjecture of Haga 1948: 36. The relationship between Chiun and Ikkyū is mentioned in the popular legends about Ikkyū known as *Ikkyūbanashi*, but no firm evidence is as yet forthcoming.

76. Shinkei, *Hitorigoto* 473.

77. On Ikkyū's artistic influence, see Nakamoto et al. 1976: 12, 16.

78. The reference appears in the Daiei manuscript (Nakamoto 1967: 266). Sobriquets were often bestowed on artists by eminent monks. Nakamoto interjects a note of caution in the Saioku attribution, however, pointing out that its first use appears more than two decades after Ikkyū's death. But there is also a poem in *Kyōunshū* (Shūon'an ms. in Nakamoto 1976: 221–22) that is titled "Saioku," which tradition holds was composed for Sōchō by Ikkyū. For a translation, see Fig. 3.

79. See *JS*: 32, 178, 466.

80. For *Minase Sangin*, see in particular Kaneko 1985b: 83–187. English translations of the entire sequence are found in Yasuda 1956, Miner 1979: 171–225, and Carter 1991: 303–26, and of the first half of the sequence in Keene 1955, 1: 314–21.

81. For *Yuyama sangin*, see especially Kaneko 1985b: 191–288. For English translations, see Sato and Watson 1981: 254–61 and Carter 1983.

82. Sōgi had been working to realize such a project for two decades. For more on the compilation process of *Shinsen tsukubashū*, see Kaneko 1969: 332–47.

83. That number compares with 123 for Shinkei, 108 for Emperor Gotsuchimikado, 59 for Sōgi, and 31 for Shōhaku.

84. Kidō 1972: 75. There are no records of any return to Suruga before this time, but a passage in *The Journal of Sōchō* suggests that he had remained in periodic contact with the Imagawa house throughout his twenty years in Kyoto: "When Ujichika was a child, I took my leave to spend time at Daitokuji. He showed me great consideration. For twenty years I came and went from the capital and enjoyed his special favor. Everyone must know that. Moreover from time to time I was of service to him" (*JS*: 162). He could not have enjoyed Ujichika's "special favor" had he not been in periodic touch.

85. Nakagawa (1981: 1310–19) believes the "lodging by the river" was Rinsen'an, mentioned later by Sōchō in his journal (*JS*: 161), which later became Sōchōji temple (originally written with the same characters as Sōchō's name).

86. The traditional date given for the construction of Sōchō's cottage in Mariko is 1504, based on the phrase "At the beginning of the Eishō era [1504–21]" (*Eishō hajime no koro*) in *Utsunoyama no ki*. Shigematsu Hiromi (1979: 9–19), however, argues that the date was actually 1506.

87. The foundation poem for Sōchō's verse is *Gosenshū* 15: 1102, by Fujiwara Kanesuke:

> When the Chancellor was General of the Left Bodyguards, he held a banquet after the annual *sumō* contest, which the Middle Captain [Kanesuke] attended. When it was over and people were departing, he invited two or three of high rank to dine with him. After considerable drinking, Kanesuke began to talk of his child, at which time he composed the following:

hito no oya no	Although one's feelings
kokoro wa yami ni	as a parent are not black
aranedomo	as the blackest night,
ko o omou michi ni	still I find that I wander
madoinuru kana	lost in thoughts about my child.

The verse is referred to in the "Kiritsubo" chapter of *Genji monogatari* (1: 34), among others. See also Kaneko 1969. Jōha later took the name Suian and lived in Suruga, where Sōchō's disciple Sōboku visited him in 1544 on the journey recorded in Sōboku's *Tōgoku kikō* (Journey to the Eastern Provinces, 1545) (827). See the Epilogue.

88. Monks of the True Pure Land (Jōdo Shinshū) sect also often married and lived with their wives in religious communities. See Dobbins 1989.

89. Had he stayed in Kyoto, Sōchō would have been the obvious successor to the latter posts after they were vacated in 1501 by Inawashiro Kensai. A legend in *Zoku haika kijindan* of 1832 states that Sōchō had the opportunity to become laureate but declined even an imperial command to take the office. See Takeuchi 1987: 213.

90. Sōseki, who had continued to live in Sōgi's Shugyokuan cottage in the capital after the master's death, succeeded to the positions of Commissioner of Linked Verse at Kitano Shrine and Laureate in 1511, after a ten-year hiatus when no one appears to have filled those positions. See Kaneko 1971: 112–13.

91. Taijin, of the Shōren'in imperial temple (*monzeki*), attended the lectures with Sōchō, and a portion of his notes survives. See Arai 1976: 49.

92. The old version of *Shizuokashi shi* (History of Shizuoka City), though perhaps over-proud of its native son, does indeed give Sōchō a place in the lineage of the secret traditions. See Tsuge 1931, 1: 339.

93. Araki Yoshio (1947: 60), for example, writes, "Sōchō's lack of application to the secret traditions . . . [and his] attitude toward the classics suggests his plebeian character."

94. Kaneko 1976: 117.

95. *Genjichū* is also known as *Genji monogatarishō*.

96. I am indebted to Lewis Cook for this interpretation of *Kokin denju*.

97. Hosokawa Yūsai's remarks were made over five years from 1598 to 1602 to Karasumaru Mitsuhiro, who later transcribed them in *Jiteiki* (or *Niteiki*, Deep in the Ear, 1598–1602) 197.

98. The courtier Otsuki Masahisa made the remark in his diary *Masahisakyōki* (Diary of Lord Masahisa, 1490:11:4), quoted in Konishi 1991: 453, n. 62.

99. On the role of Chinese divination theory in the formulation of Sōgi's amalgamation of politics and poetics, see Konishi 1991: 447–61.

100. Ga refers to what is elegant, sophisticated, and, to use Konishi Jin'ichi's formulation, "precedented," that is to say based on set standards of taste. Zoku, by contrast, refers to the plebeian, the everyday, and the "unprecedented" or without set standards. See in particular Konishi 1984: 14, 58–63, 212–26.

101. Daitō's admonitions, in Kraft 1992: 116–17.

102. The third Ashikaga shogun, Yoshimitsu, was moved to admonish such monks publicly:

> Both elders and ordinary monks must be carefully checked for [attendance at] the three daily services. [If they are absent,] they must be removed from the temple rolls, and elders must not be promoted. In the Zen sect, advancement comes with the practice of Zen discipline (*zazen*), and those who have been repeatedly negligent shall be expelled from the temple. (Grossberg and Kanamoto 1981: 55)

103. Ikkyū 1976: 93, 159. Linji (J: Rinzai) was the founder of Rinzai Zen and a master Ikkyū particularly revered. Note also the colophon Ikkyū composed for the portrait that illustrates this volume.

104. *Kyōunshū* 191, in Ikkyū 1976: 167.

105. Sanford 1981: 41.

106. The anecdote appears in *The Chronicle of Ikkyū*, in Sanford 1981: 91–92.

107. Nishida 1977: 97.

108. Linji, in *Linjilu* (Linji Record). Translated in Sasaki 1975: 23.

109. Konishi 1984: 214.

110. Bokusai, *Tōkai Ikkyū Oshō nenpu*, translated in Sanford 1981: 116.

111. Konishi 1991: 384. Likewise Haga Kōshirō (1948: 30) sees Ikkyū as a harbinger of the end of the Medieval period, and he summarizes his perception of the great monk's importance as follows:

> What Ikkyū hated most was the hypocrisy of splendid appearances and superficial piety. What he respected most was human nature . . . His recovery, or liberation, of human nature, too long alienated by unnatural forms and precepts, meant a revolution in the medieval world view. In that sense Ikkyū was a precursor of Early Modern [Kinsei] naturalism and humanism.

112. Sanford 1981: 43.

113. Ikkyū 1976: 93, 181. Daitō was the founder of Daitokuji.

114. Nakamoto 1967: 270.

115. *Sōchō nikki* 145. All future references will be cited as *SN*.

116. The portrait accompanying this volume depicts Ikkyū with a red sword. For more on these two poems, see *JS*: 126–27.

117. *Sanetakakōki* (Diary of Lord Sanetaka, 1474–1536), 1495:11:16 (3: 132) and 1496: 10:6 (3: 299).

118. See Sōchō's *Kabekusa* (Wall Grass, 1505–12) as well as Fujiwara Masayoshi 1983: 67 and Araki 1947: 227.

119. Nishida 1977: 180.

120. On Sanetaka, see Haga 1960 and Hara 1978. For a summary of entries from his diaries *Sanetakakōki* and *Saishōsō* (Grasses of Recrudescence, 1501–36) that mention Sōchō, see Tsurusaki 1993b.

121. *Sanetakakōki* 1485:7:19 (1b: 608).

122. In addition to his kanbun diary *Sanetakakōki* and his poetry diary *Saishōsō*, both rich sources of information on aristocratic life, Sanetaka left a travel journal, *Kōya sankei nikki* (Diary of a Pilgrimage to Kōya, 1524).

123. For more on this economic symbiosis, see Okuno Takahiro 1952.

124. *Sanetakakōki* 1508:7:6 (5: 68). One *hiki* equalled ten copper cash (*mon*) or .86 *shō* (1.5 liters of rice) in 1522, according to *Dokushi biyō*. 100 *shō* equal one *koku*. The actual value of the hiki, however, differed by region.

125. Yonehara 1979: 857.

126. *Sanetakakōki* 1524:2:20 (6a: 142).

127. For a bibliography of Muneaki's works, see Itō Kei 1969.

128. See Tsurusaki 1978: 2.

129. On the genre of *rengaawase*, see Carter 1984.

130. *Sōchō hyakuban rengaawase* 93.

131. The truncated traditions Shōhaku passed on to select disciples are known as the *Sakai denju*.

132. Imagawa Ryōshun, *Rakusho roken* 409. Sōzei and Shinkei had a particularly rancorous relationship, and Sōgi fell out temporarily with Kensai over the compilation process of *Shinsen tsukubashū*. It may also have been because of personal infighting that Sakurai Motosuke had none of his verses included in that anthology. See Kaneko 1967.

133. Two notable sequences mentioned in *The Journal of Sōchō* were *Ise senku* of 1522 and *Iba senku* of 1524. Sōseki later wrote a travel account of his journey to Ise to participate in the former sequence. Entitled *Sano no watari* (Sano Crossing, 1522), it is written in an ornamented style much like Sōgi's *Shirakawa kikō*. *Iba senku* is also known as *Gessonsai senku* because it was held at Sōseki's residence, Gessonsai.

134. *Kyōunshū* (trans. Sanford 1981: 63, to which this brief summary is indebted).

135. Shūon'an was built on the site of Myōshōji, the first temple of Daiō, founder of Ōtōkan Zen (named after its founders Daiō, Daitō, and Kanzan), the line to which Daitokuji was affiliated, and it was therefore doubtless symbolic in Ikkyū's imagination for a return to an earlier and purer form of Zen practice.

136. Sōchō donated 3 *kanmon* for the thirteenth anniversary of Ikkyū's death in 1493, as compared with 1 kanmon from the tea master Murata Jukō, 500 mon from the haikai poet Yamazaki Sōkan, and 100 mon from the nō playwright Konparu Zenpō. He donated 7 kan 150 mon for the thirty-third death anniversary in 1510, as compared with 1 kanmon for Sōkan. See Haga 1948: 37–38. For photographs of the donation lists, see Yoshikawa Ichirō 1955, front matter. Legend has it that the copy of *Genji monogatari* Sōchō sold was made by the great early medieval literatus Fujiwara Teika, but that is unsubstantiated. See, for example, Takeuchi Gengen'ichi, *Haika kijinden* 214. Takeuchi's work dates from 1816.

137. On the relationship between the Gozan establishment and the Daitokuji lineage, see Collcutt 1990.

138. The merchant in question was Ikkyū's longtime friend and supporter Owa Sōrin.

139. See Yokota 1957.

140. Covell 1980: 249.

141. For more on Ujichika's *kenchi* and other administrative policies, see Owada Tetsuo 1984a.

142. For studies of Imagawa *Kana mokuroku* and its importance, see Ozawa Seiichi 1977 and Matsudaira Norimichi 1982.

143. Nagahara 1975: 52–53.

144. *The Book of Songs* includes this verse, for example: "The cultured (C: *wen*; J: *bun*) and martial (C: *wu*; J: *bu*) Ji Fu—the myriad states make him their model." See "Sixth Month" (Liuyue), in *Shikyō* 2: 83. See also Legge 1871: 283.

145. *Imagawajō*, In Ozawa Tomio 1985: 241.

146. Alsop 1982: 59.

147. Sansom 1984: 158.

148. *Imagawa kafu* 154–55.

149. Imagawa Ujichika and Tō no Sojun, *Shokugo meidai wakashū*. See Yonehara 1979: 840 and Inoue 1987: 220–21. "Waka Bay" (Wakanoura), a famous poetic site in Wakayama Prefecture, was frequently used as a metaphor for the waka art.

150. Owada (1983: 160) suggests the marriage took place in 1505 or 1508; Yonehara (1979: 842) thinks it was the former.

151. For reviews of Jukei's life, see Adachi 1931 and Kurosawa 1975. Imagawa Norimasa had transmitted to Nobutane certain traditions of *Man'yōshū* (Owada, et al. 1981: 1208).

152. Ōgimachisanjō Kin'e's journey to Suruga, for example, required a gift of ten thousand hiki in "travel money" (*rosen*) from the Imagawa leader (Owada, et al. 1981: 1218). The mines also supported Ujichika's military efforts, and Sōchō wrote of them in connection with the Hikuma campaign (*JS*: 12).

153. For a list of those aristocratic guests, see Owada, et al., 1981: 1219–220.

154. For details on Ujitoyo's loss of Nagoya Castle, see *Nagoya kassenki* (Nagoya Battle Chronicle) 104–07.

155. Matsudaira Sadanobu, *Shizuka naru amari* (In an Excess of Quiet) 331.

156. See "Rengashi no hanashi," in Shimazu 1973: 300–14.

157. The most famous *dōbōshū* were the "Three Ami" (San'ami), Nōami, Geiami, and Sōami, who served Yoshinori and Yoshimasa. Ōtsuka Isao (1987: 180–81) suggests that Sōchō's alternate name, Chōa, which shares the *-a[mi]* suffix frequently adopted by *dōbōshū*, reflects his similar role in the Imagawa house.

158. The first reference to such an errand is found in Sanetaka's diary, *Sanetakakōki*, in the entry for 1505:8:11 (4b: 440–41), where Sanetaka judged a collection of Ujichika's poems and then sent them back via Sōchō. Another reference from three years later (1508:6:28 [5a: 62]) shows Sanetaka sending to Ujichika, again through Sōchō's offices, a copy he had made of *Ise monogatari*.

159. For a detailed account of this campaign, see Mizaki 1983.

160. *Kai no kuni rekidaifu* 2: 273.

161. There were ample precedents for employing clerics as negotiators; Musō Soseki served in that fashion during negotiations between the Northern and Southern Courts, and Yoshimitsu used Zekkai Chūshin to treat with the Ōuchi in 1399.

162. Kuonji, in Minobu, Yamanashi Prefecture, is the headquarters of the Nichiren (Lotus) sect.

163. For more on Lady Kitagawa, see Nagakura 1978.

164. Saitō Sakae (1985), in a popularized and at times fictional account, asserts that Sōchō was at one time sexually involved with Imagawa Yoshitada, and for a brief time after his death, with Lady Kitagawa. The claim is perhaps plausible, but unsubstantiated.

165. *Imagawa kafu* 159–60.

166. Kidō 1972: 77.

167. By Yu Jian. See Yamanoue Sōji, *Chaki meibutsushū* 473–74. See also Kuwata 1969: 261 and Tsurusaki 1973b.

168. For lists of Imagawa vassals, see Yamamoto and Owada 1984 and Ōtsuka 1977.

169. See Matsumoto 1980.

170. Sōchō makes reference to *Goshūishū* 9: 518, by Nōin, quoted on p. 114.

171. Sōchō also quotes this hokku in his first collection of verses, *Kabekusa* (1505–12) and, in slightly different form, in *Utsunoyama no ki*. The honka is *Shūishū* 6: 306:

    wasuru na yo   You must not forget
    wakareji ni ouru   that when the autumn wind blows
    kuzu no ha no   through the kudzu leaves
    akikaze fukeba   growing by our parting path
    ima kaerikon   I will soon be coming home.

The autumn wind blowing through the kudzu leaves reveals their white undersides, to elegant effect. Kudzu is thus traditionally associated with the verb *kaeru*, "to turn over," and to its homophone, "to return home."

172. *Azumaji no tsuto* 770.

173. Sōchō puns on *okidokoro naki*, "full of emotion" and "no place to put anything."

174. On Seki Kajisai, see Tsurusaki 1971a and id. 1979.

175. Tsurusaki 1979: 11.

176. Kajisai had dealings with many other men of letters besides Sōchō, notably Asukai Masayasu, son of Asukai Masayo, compiler of the last imperial waka anothology. The relationship between Kajisai and Masayasu is described in Masayasu's own travel journal, *Fuji rekiranki* (Account of Sightseeing at Fuji, 1499).

177. *Tōgoku kikō* 805.

178. On the relation between Ji sect priests and renga, see Nagai 1960, Okami 1940, and Tsurusaki 1987a. The waka commentary *Sōchō hikashō* (Private Notes on Waka, By Sōchō, c. 1514), which Sōchō is believed to have written, is thought to have been meant for Ji sect monks (Kishida 1980b: 61).

179. *Nikonshū* bears a preface dated 1595. On the Ise poetic circle, see *RSR* 2: 664–69, Okuno Jun'ichi 1975, and Tsurusaki 1997.

180. The preface of *Sōchō kawa* (9) says it was written for Ise poets: "During my stay of more than twenty days at Yamada in Ise, some young people came to brighten my hours in my travel lodging. In the course of our talk, they asked about . . . renga in the capital."

181. For more on Sōchō's kokujin acquaintances in Mikawa, see Suzuki Mitsuyasu 1973 and Shingyō 1977. On Matsudaira Kiyoyasu, see Yokoyama 1978. The Matsudaira family member in question is given in Sōchō's journal only as Matsudaira Jirōzaburō, whom the Shōkōkan manuscript of *The Journal of Sōchō* identifies as Nobutada (Shimazu 1975: 125). Suzuki Mitsuyasu (1973) points out, however, that in 1523 Nobutada was forced to retire due to the loss of the support of his housemen (*kashindan*) and to hand over leadership of the family to his son Kiyoyasu. On 1526:4:19 Kiyoyasu moved his headquarters from Anjō in Mikawa to Okazaki Castle, which is where the meeting described in *The Journal of Sōchō* took place. It is thus clear that the Jirōzaburō Sōchō mentions is Kiyoyasu (the grandfather of Tokugawa Ieyasu).

182. Calculations are based on the distances between stations of the Tōkaidō cited in Ōkuma 1979. He gives thirteen to fourteen days as the average time it took to cover the 495 kilometers of the Tōkaidō. Sōchō's route did not exactly match the Edo Tōkaidō, however, and the figures I have used are only approximations.

183. See Ii 1980: 1207–08.

184. *Nachigomori* (Kitano Tenmangū ms.) 352 and *Oi no mimi* 128.

185. On Jukei's regency, see Kubota Masaki 1977 and id. 1978.

186. One such individual was the poet Reizei Tamekazu, with whom Ujiteru studied

poetry for years. For more on the relationship between the Imagawa and the Reizei houses, see Semoto 1983. Tamekazu's years in Suruga do not coincide with those covered in Sōchō's diaries, but Sōchō knew him personally and asked him for a verse in honor of the first anniversary of Ujichika's death in 1527. See Yonehara 1979: 865.

187. Paul John Eakin, in Lejeune 1989: ix. See also Eakin 1985.

188. Cf., for example Jean Starobinski (Olney 1980: 75): "No matter how doubtful the facts related, the text will at least present an 'authentic' image of the man who 'held the pen.'" Note also Powys (in Pascal 1960: 71): "The truth remembered is the only truth that matters."

189. Goffman 1959: 252. He sums up his argument in this sentence: "The general notion that we make a presentation of ourselves to others is hardly novel; what ought to be stressed in conclusion is that the very structure of the self can be seen in terms of how we arrange for such performances."

190. Kurokawa Dōyu, *Sōchō Kojiden* 394.

191. In 1526, for example, Sōchō mentioned receiving one such musō verse from Sōgi, then more than twenty years in the grave (*JS*: 127).

192. Sōchō and Sōboku, *Yashima Shōrin'an naniki hyakuin* 208.

193. Fothergill 1974: 2.

194. Renza 1980: 269.

195. Miner 1969: 10.

196. Inoue 1987: 397.

197. On the extant manuscripts and manner of composition of *Azumaji no tsuto*, see Ijichi 1973.

198. Iwashita Noriyuki (1978: 19–23) has suggested that Book One may have been partly meant for the instruction of the young head of the Asahina house, Yasuyoshi, and Book Two may have been written in part to demonstrate the author's long service to the Imagawa and to exonerate himself for not returning to Sunpu immediately on Imagawa Ujichika's death.

199. Mandel 1980: 53.

200. Roy Pascal (1960: 3) makes the following distinction: "autobiography is a review of a life from a particular moment in time, while the diary, however reflective it may be, moves through a series of moments in time."

201. Ishida 1970: 156.

202. Nakagawa 1981: 1319–41.

203. Gusdorf 1980: 44.

204. Patricia Meyer Spacks (1976: 15–16) gets at the relationship between choice and interpretation when she writes:

> We assume that the happenings of autobiography are more or less given, although the writer obviously selects among his memories and shapes them to his pur-

poses. Events in autobiography, then, do not create character in the same way as events in fiction. Yet one may feel that the central character in autobiography has created a self, then written the book to validate the creation. The writing itself may constitute the creation.

205. Cranston 1969: 125.
206. For *Ionushi*, see Zōki; for *Izayoi nikki*, see Abutsu-ni as well as McCullough 1990: 340–76; and for *Murasaki Shikibu nikki*, see Murasaki and also Bowring 1982.
207. For an English translation of *Ise monogatari*, see McCullough 1968.
208. Fothergill 1974: 3.
209. For information on these and other manuscripts, see Shimazu 1975: 195–97.
210. *Oi no mimi* includes 143 hokku and 1,393 tsukeku composed from the spring of 1522, just before the beginning of *The Journal of Sōchō*, through 1526, the last datable hokku having been made for Sōgi's death anniversary, the twenty-ninth of the seventh month. Shigematsu Hiromi (*Oi no mimi* 5) suggests Sōchō put the collection into its final form while wintering at Shōrin'an temple in 1526–27, a year before the end of the journal. For a study of *Oi no mimi*, see Iwashita 1985.
211. The version of *Imagawa kafu* that remains today, however, was rewritten in 1576 from memory by a descendant of the man who had originally requested the wakankonkōbun version from Sōchō (the original had been lost in 1569 in the destruction accompanying the invasion of Tōtōmi and Suruga by Takeda Shingen and Tokugawa Ieyasu). The extant version is therefore only an approximation of Sōchō's work. Predictably, *Imagawa kafu* is very like the "Asahina Battle Chronicle" in style and narrative structure, and some passages correspond quite closely. *The Journal of Sōchō* may even have been used to recreate *Imagawa kafu* after the original was lost.
212. Shimazu 1973: 295. For translated examples from one such *hanashibon*, Anrakuan Sakuden's *Seisuishō*, see McElrath 1971.
213. Harada 1979: 385–93.
214. On *Nachigomori*, see Iwashita 1976.

Chapter Two

1. There are ten extant travel works by renga masters:

Sōgi	*Shirakawa kikō*, 1468	
"	*Tsukushi michi no ki*, 1480	
Sōchō	*Sōgi shūenki*, 1502	
"	*Azumaji no tsuto*, 1509	
"	*Utsunoyama no ki*, 1518	
Sōseki	*Sano no watari*, 1522	
Sōchō	*Sōchō shuki*, 1527	

Sōboku	*Tōgoku kikō*, 1545
Jōha	*Jōha Fujimi michi no ki*, 1567
"	*Jōha Amanohashidate kikō*, 1569

Some of the above works contain non-travel segments as well. Ishida Yoshisada (1958: 34) believes the list should also include *Ise Daijingū sankei ki* (1342), by Saka Jūbutsu, an early renga poet but not a professional rengashi. For an English translation, see Sadler 1940. There are also short travel sections in *Bontōanshu hentōsho* (1417) by the rengashi Bontō, *Hitorigoto* (1468) by Shinkei, *Oi no kurigoto* (1471), also by Shinkei, and *Sōchō nikki* (1530–31). Ishida views travel works by rengashi as one of four categories of medieval travel literature: works in the poet lineage (*kajinteki keitō no mono*), works in the courtier lineage (*kuge keitō no mono*, i.e., *kanbun* diaries), works by those in intermediate social strata (*chūkanteki kaikyū no mono*), and works in the rengashi lineage (*rengashiteki keitō no mono*). Fukuda Hideichi (1975: 454–76) does so as well. For a short introduction to rengashi and travel, see Okuda 1977.

2. Another of Sōgi's main influences, Sōzei, had died earlier.

3. Those early renga handbooks were *Chōrokubumi*, written at the request of the warrior Nagao Magoroku (for whom it is named) in 1466, and then *Azuma mondō*, written for Nagao Magoshirō in 1467.

4. The translation that follows is based on the manuscript in Kaneko 1976. A hundred-verse sequence is appended to the original work, but it is not translated here. I have also referred to Imoto 1974. For an English version of the entire work, see Carter 1987b. All future references to *Shirakawa kikō* will be cited as *SK*.

5. Mount Tsukuba, in Ibaraki Prefecture, is a famous poetic site and the eponymous mountain of the linked-verse art, the "Way of Tsukuba" (Tsukuba no michi). Black-Hair Mountain (Kurokamiyama), another name for Futarasan Mountain, is near Nikkō Shrine in Tochigi Prefecture. Sōgi refers to his visit there in terms of a love trope taken from *Man'yōshū* 7: 1241:

nubatama no	Crossing at morning
kurokamiyama o	Black-Hair Mountain, name dark
asa koete	as leopard-flower seeds,
yamashitatsuyu ni	I find my clothing moistened
nurenikeru ka mo	by dew beneath mountain trees.

6. *Murasaki* is also known as "grass of affinity" (*yukari no kusa*) through association with *Kokinshū* 17: 867:

murasaki no	Because of one shoot
hitomoto yue ni	of *murasaki* grass,
musashino no	I feel fondness
kusa wa minagara	for all the plants and grasses
aware to zo miru	on the plain of Musashino.

7. Sōgi refers to Minamoto Sanetomo, the Great Minister of the Right, whose personal poetry collection *Kinkaishū* includes the following (nos. 348 and 252):

mononofu no	It glances off
yanami tsukurou	the wrist guard
kote no ue ni	of the warrior
arare tabashiru	as he puts his arrows in order—
nasu no shinohara	hail on the bamboo of Nasu Plain.

asajihara	In the thick dew
tsuyu shigeki niwa no	on the field of cogon grass
kirigirisu	a cricket chirrs
aki fukaki yo no	beneath the moon late at night
tsuki ni nakunari	deep in autumn.

8. Ōtawara (or Ōdarawa) was in Tochigi Prefecture, Nasu District.

9. Hirano field, in Kyoto's Kamigyō Ward, is mentioned in such verses as *Shūishū* 10: 592, by Kiyohara Motosuke:

Composed when Minamoto Tōfuru was blessed with a child:

oishigere	May it flourish,
hirano no hara no	the little cedar growing
ayasugi yo	on the field of Hirano,
koki murasaki ni	until it may become cloaked
tachikasanubeku	in deepest purple.

The little cedar (*ayasugi*) grows dark red in the winter, hence its use here as a metaphor for the child, who, it is hoped, will someday rise to high rank and wear purple. Sōgi may also be using the general word for oaks here, *hahaso*, to recall its partial homophone *haha*, mother, which he then follows by his remark on having no relations in the capital. Socho also used the word *hahaso* in that sense in *JS* no. 56. If Sōgi was indeed using *Shūishū* 10: 592 as a foundation poem, then its mention of *murasaki* further intensifies his sense of connection to the scene by association with the "grasses of affinity" of *Kokinshū* 17: 867 (see note 6 above). *Hahaso* oaks were also associated in poetry with Ishida in Kyoto, which was also called "Eastland" (Azumaji) since it was a point of origination for eastern journeys.

10. *Kashiwa* (Quercus dentata) and *kunugi* (Quercus acutissima) are both species of *hahaso* oaks. Sōgi may be recalling any one of a number of poems that link oaks with Sao Mountain (north of Nara) and Ōkawa river (near Ise Shrine).

11. *Man'yōshū* 7: 1141:

mukogawa no	Was it because
mio o hayami ka	of Muko River's fast current

akakoma no	that I was drenched
agaku tagichi no	with water splashed by
nurenikeru ka mo	my chestnut pony's hooves?

12. *Kokinshū* 18: 944:

yamazato wa	It is very true
mono no wabishiki	that life is poor and dreary
koto koso are	in a mountain hamlet,
yo no uki yori wa	but dwelling here is better
sumiyokarikeri	than in the woeful world.

13. The Mountain Princess (Yamahime) was believed to be responsible for bringing fall foliage to the mountains. Yokooka is in Nasu District, not far from Shirakawa Gate.

14. A connection may be implied here with Isuzu Mimosusogawa river at Ise Shrine and the peak behind, about which Saigyō recorded the following poem in his *Mimosusogawa utaawase* (round 36):

fukaku irite	I made my way
kamiji no oku o	deep into the recesses
tazunureba	of Mount Kamiji,
mata ue mo naki	and on the highest peak of all,
mine no matsukaze	wind in the pines.

15. There were two shrines at the spot, one devoted to the gods of Sumiyoshi in Settsu and one to the god of Tamamatsu in Kii, hence their name Nisho ga Myōjin, "Deities of the Two Sites." They are situated, however, some distance from the location of Shirakawa Gate, which Sōgi may or may not have actually reached.

16. Both Taira Kanemori and Nōin composed famous poems on Shirakawa Gate. Kanemori's appears as *Shūishū* 6: 339:

On passing Shirakawa Gate in the Distant North:

tayori araba	Had I the means,
ikade miyako e	how I would like to send word
tsugeyaramu	to the capital,
kyō shirakawa no	telling that I passed today
seki wa koenu to	Shirakawa Gate!

Nōin's verse appears as *Gosenshū* 9: 518 (quoted in the text on p. 114).

17. The poem is a response to Nōin's earlier sentiments. Nōin's verse is the only one not from *Shinkokinshū* that Sōchō included in his *Sōchō kawa*.

18. Nothing is known about Sōgi's companions Taira Tadamori, Bokuō, and Bokurin.

19. Sōgi ends his account with a phrase redolent of one in the second "Wakana" chapter in *Genji monogatari* (6: 139) spoken by Yūgiri with regard to the setting for autumnal

music: "The sky seems to have been made to suit the occasion." Sōgi hereafter appends a hundred-verse sequence composed by himself, the three men just mentioned, and a certain Jun'a, who was perhaps an escort for the group.

20. Olney 1980: 3.

21. Another good statement of the basic essence of travel may be found in Sōboku's *Shidō kuhon* (Four Ways and Nine Stages) 378.

22. *Sōchō kawa* 20.

23. Ietaka employs the familiar trope of moonlight reflected on sleeves wet with tears.

24. Kaneko (1969: 704–10) has shown that the sense of sadness (*kanashi*) of travel is even stronger among linked-verse poets in *Shinsen tsukubashū* than it was for those in the earlier *Tsukubashū*.

25. I use the term utamakura to mean famous sites hallowed in poetry. Originally the term related not only to sites but to various elements of the general poetic lexicon. It is used in that sense in *Nōin utamakura* (n.d.). Furthermore, not all *meisho* (or *nadokoro*, famous places) qualified as utamakura. But by the time of the *Toshiyori zuinō* of Minamoto Toshiyori and *Godaishū utamakura* of Fujiwara Norikane, the term utamakura had become limited to poetic places. See Katagiri 1983: 5–19.

26. Legend, now largely discounted, holds that Nōin may have only pretended to make the trip to Shirakawa. See, for example, the poetry miscellany *Guhishō* (late Kamakura period) 301. Sōkyū referred to the verse in his *Miyako no tsuto*, as did Sōchō in *Azumaji no tsuto* (see p. 65).

27. *Sankashū* 1126. *Sekiya* (gatehouse), *moru* (slip through), and *tomuru* (stop or arrest) are all kindred words.

28. I do not mean to suggest that this point of view only developed in the medieval period, but rather that it flourished at that time in tandem with the earlier travel constructs. The salubrious effects of unsullied nature in the pursuit of enlightenment were given particularly famous expression a millennium before in the *Lotus Sutra* (*Hokekyō* 1: 198):

> The Tathagata has already left
>   The burning house of the Three Worlds;
> Serenely he lives in quietude,
>   Peacefully he dwells in the forests and fields.

29. *Shitakusa* (Undergrowth, 1493, rev. ed. 1496) 180–81. *Shitakusa* is Sōgi's third personal poetry collection.

30. Sōkyū, *Miyako no tsuto* 348.

31. The presence of others requires an English translation to employ the first person plural, making the experience sound much more communal than in the Japanese, where number distinctions are not mandatory.

32. See "Epic and Novel: Toward a Methodology for the Study of the Novel," in Bakhtin 1981: 3–40. All further references to this work are cited in the text as Bakhtin. Two useful introductions to Bakhtin are Morson and Emerson 1990 and Holquist 1990.

33. For a fine description of Sōgi's neoclassicism, see Carter 1988.

34. Chapman 1952, letter no. 326.

35. Renza 1980: 271.

36. Elbaz 1983: 199.

37. During his stay in the east, Sōgi composed poetry not only with members of the Yūki house, who were allied with the Koga Kubō, the renegade line of shogunal deputies, but also with Uesugi and Nagao supporters of the rival Horikoshi Kubō. It was, in fact, at the invitation of a local warlord, Yūki Nyūdō Dōchō (whose lay name was Naotomo), that Sōgi embarked on his Shirakawa journey, though he does not name him in the text.

38. Kaneko 1983: 125.

39. *Sōgi shūenki* 115, in Kaneko 1976: 115.

40. Sōgi, *Chōrokubumi* 113.

41. The phrase quoted earlier in another context, "For the last year or two I have kept a diary of things both serious and frivolous" (*JS*: 136), was written in 1527, and it thus does not apply to Book One, written in 1522 to 1526.

42. Iwashita 1978: 19. Although the overlapping section in Book Two repeats four of the poems recorded in Book One, each passage contains poems not in the other. One of the shared poems (*JS* no. 325) appears in a significantly reworked form in Book Two (*JS* no. 338), and it is the latter version that Sōchō included in his personal verse collection *Oi no mimi* (120). Sōchō also deleted a personal account of Lady Kitagawa and an equally personal poetic exchange with Asahina Yasumochi but added references to two utamakura not mentioned in the Book One account. Shimazu Tadao (1975: 200) suggests that there may have been another lost journal covering the intervening two years between Book Two and the later *Sōchō nikki*, although no evidence for such a book survives. *Sōchō michi no ki* includes the waka sections of *The Journal of Sōchō* and then a short section of *Sōchō nikki*, but with three intervening original lines found in neither of the others. The fact, however, that no other original passages appear would seem to imply that no diary for the intervening years was ever written.

43. The reading of the characters in the title of Saigyō's purported work is speculative; Sōchō renders the title in two different ways in the text (Shimazu 1975: 77 and 80).

44. The site was so named "because of the eight bridges spanning the river that branches out there like the legs of a spider" (*Ise monogatari* 9).

45. *Ise monogatari* 9.

46. On "unfinalizability," see Morson and Emerson 1990: 36–40.

47. This is perhaps why *Gunsho ruijū* classes Sōchō's journal not as kikō but as nikki.

48. The non-elliptical version appears in Shimazu 1973: 292.

49. Shimazu 1973: 293 and Harada 1979: 405.
50. Bruss 1976: 164.
51. Gusdorf 1980: 41.
52. Kishida Yoriko (1982: 12) has noticed similar linked-verse influences in *Sōchō hikashō*, which Sōchō may have written.
53. The linking of pairs of episodes is not only a linked-verse technique; Kunisaki Fumimaro has discovered a pattern of such thematic links in *Konjaku monogatari*. See Konishi 1991: 134.
54. See Chance 1990.
55. Nussbaum 1989: 16–17.
56. Bakhtin 1984: 21
57. See, for example, Miner 1979: 44–49 and Araki 1947: 60.
58. See, for example, Konishi 1951: 1–7.
59. Konishi 1991: 114. For a translation of *Sanukinosuke nikki*, see Brewster 1977.
60. All future references to *Tsukushi michi no ki* will be cited as *TMK*. The length of the account makes it impossible to present here; for an English translation, see Katō 1979.
61. Kawazoe 1982: 264–65.
62. A pilgrimage to the Tenmangū shrine at Dazaifu had been traditional for rengashi since the time of Kyūsei and Shūa in the fourteenth century. See Kaneko 1983: 206.
63. Kidō 1984: 232.
64. *Shinkokinshū* 11: 1013, by Minamoto Shigeyuki:

tsukubayama	Though gentle hills
hayama shigeyama	and wooded hills abound
shigekeredo	on the way to Tsukuba,
omoiiru ni wa	they pose no obstacle
sawarazarikeri	to one bent on reaching it.

65. *Man'yōshū* 3: 278, by Ishikawa Shōrō:

shika no ama wa	The fishergirls
me kari shio yaki	of Shika are so busy
itoma nami	gathering seaplant
kushige no ogushi	and boiling brine for salt
tori mo minaku ni	that one never sees them comb their hair.

Sōgi writes "dipping up brine for salt" (*shio kumu*) instead of "boiling brine for salt" (*shio yaki*).

66. The form of the whole appears to have been considerably influenced by linked-verse techniques, which deepen the poetic tone of the whole. Most obvious is the inclusion of renga hokku in the body of the text. Sōgi is the first author in the tradition of poetic travel to record hokku in a travel account, and he employs them with sophistica-

tion. At one point he also comments on how a hokku is to be interpreted, reflecting his role as a renga teacher. The increased value Sōgi ascribed to the linked-verse medium is demonstrated by the numerical parity that the two poetic forms are afforded in *Tsukushi michi no ki*, each represented by eighteen examples, the total matching the thirty-six days the trip is said to have taken. Kaneko (1983: 207–10) has also shown how Sōgi very likely patterned his account on the thematic transitions (*yukiyō*) of a renga sequence, from travel through seasonal poetry (restrained of course by the fact that the trip took place in only the ninth and tenth months) to love, an unexpected subject that Kaneko theorizes was an exaggeration of reality to satisfy the structural demands of linked verse.

67. Kaneko (1969: 332, and id. 1983: 211–15) suggests that *Tsukushi michi no ki* was also intended as a veiled expression of Sōgi's hope to secure Masahiro's backing for a new imperial anthology of waka poetry, which in addition might include some of Sōgi's own verses. On his second trip to Yamaguchi in 1489, Sōgi made a direct request of Masahiro to that effect in the wake of the sudden death of the project's previous patron, Shogun Ashikaga Yoshihisa. The project was eventually abandoned, at which point Sōgi acquired Masahiro's cooperation in undertaking a renga anthology instead.

68. Sōgi reminds Ōuchi Masahiro, the recipient of the completed account, of his responsibilities as both a military and civil leader: "I believe that one who would rule the land should show special consideration to the will of these deities" (*TMK*: 44). The pursuit of poetry and the worship of the art's tutelary gods is in fact a prime way for the ruler to "order the world and solace the people" (*risei bumin*). Sōgi advances the same notion in *Chōrokubumi* (112–13):

> In *Shinkokinshū* it says, "[The waka] is the great foundation with which to order the world and solace the people; it is the guide for the appreciation and enjoyment of things . . . ." If one's heart strays even a little from the way, how can one pacify the land and think of the people?

69. Kaneko 1983: 194–99. Again, compare *Chōrokubumi* (113): "As it is the way of poetry that 'stirs heaven and earth and moves unseen spirits and gods,' it can never be realized without honesty."

70. This usage recalls the theory that utamakura themselves may have originally been holy places where travelers were required to perform rituals for the resident gods. Utamakura poems thus originally may have had a votive use. See Okumura 1977: 12–13.

71. Fukuda and Plutschow (1975) identify and describe fifty travel works that date from before or during Sōchō's lifetime.

72. Shōtetsu's work is not to be confused with a lost *Azuma michi no ki* that Sōchō attributes to Saigyō (see n. 337, 43).

Chapter Three

1. It is only recently that hermitage literature has begun to be investigated as a distinct literary genre. For a bibliographical survey of the literature of reclusion, see Horton 1989: 745–49.
2. LaFleur 1983: 18.
3. As remarked upon in Chapter One (n. 50), the name Saiokuken, by which Sōchō is now known, never appears in his own diaries. He refers to his hermitage as Saioku, and Sanetaka calls him Saioku Rōjin. It is unclear from what source the redundant suffix *ken* derives.
4. The four major sōan portrayals occur at Sunpu in 1525 (*JS*: 62–75), at Mariko at the end of that year (*JS*: 86–88, repeated in different form in Book Two [*JS*: 95–96]), during his "winter confinement" in Yashima in 1526–27 (*JS*: 122–41), and on his second return to Mariko in 1527 (*JS*: 152–53). Sōchō also spends periods at Takigi (*JS*: 22–29, 34–43, 107–8), and in Kyoto (*JS*: 111, 115–16).
5. Sōan are also described in *Senjūshō*, *Kankyo no tomo*, and of course *Hōjōki*. For a discussion of the typical sōan formulation in these works, see Ishida 1970: 7–15.
6. Etō 1967: 270.
7. *Sōchō kawa* 22.
8. Sōgi also referred to this poem in *Shirakawa kikō*.
9. Sōchō alludes to the unusual nature of the sequence in his postscript:

> In winter confinement at my mountain dwelling, I was struck by how passersby, like the grasses, had faded away. I made a hokku on that perception, then continued adding verses, each one on my life therein. The many infractions of the rule against repetition made for a most displeasing result.

Sōchō's remark stems from the fact that since the entire sequence focuses on the topic of a mountain dwelling, some of the renga injunctions against topical repetition have been compromised. Renga on single topics, like hundred-waka sequences on single topics, nevertheless were an established subgroup of the art, just as solo sequences were (see Drake 1992: 46).

10. The link is based on *Shinkokinshū* 16: 1560, by Fujiwara Shunzei:

> Composed for a hundred-waka sequence ordered when he was well past eighty:

shimeokite	Mark that plot for me
ima ya to omou	for I feel my end is near—
akiyama no	in the mugwort
yomogi ga moto ni	of the autumn mountains,
matsumushi no naku	pine crickets call.

11. The poet plays on the ambiguity of "water" in the previous verse, where it refers also to tears; now it relates as well to "dyed."

12. The verse is based on *Shinkokinshū* 6: 701, by Fujiwara Sanefusa:

isogarenu	How heavy my heart
toshi no kure koso	now that I am not caught up
aware nare	in New Year's bustle.
mukashi wa yoso ni	In springtimes past would I
kikishi haru ka wa	have simply looked on from afar?

13. This verse refers to the Esoteric Buddhist practice of *gachirinkan*, in which the adept gazes at the moon and attempts to make his own heart similarly pure and still.

14. The verse is based on *Shinkokinshū* 10: 953, by Fujiwara Teika:

tabibito no	In the autumn wind
sode fukikaesu	that blows back the sleeves
akikaze ni	of the traveler,
yūhi sabishiki	how lonely in the evening light
yama no kakehashi	look the cliff-side foot-bridges.

15. The cuckoo was believed to lead spirits to the underworld, and its call instilled in the listener intimations of mortality.

16. The mention of *shikibi* (star anise), which is used at temples, implies that the speaker has taken religious vows.

17. This verse alludes to *sutemi no gyō*, killing oneself in the pursuit of religious enlightenment.

18. Though in seclusion, the poet still suffers the pangs of love. Yoshino was a famous place for both cherry blossoms and for secluding oneself from the world. Compare, for example, *Shinkokinshū* 17: 1619, by Saigyō:

yoshinoyama	For one who knows
yagate ideji to	that he will not soon return
omou mi o	from Mount Yoshino
hana chirinaba to	do they yet wait, thinking
hito ya matsuran	he will come back when blossoms fall?

19. Kamo no Chōmei, *Hosshinshū* 6.9 (p. 278). See also Hare 1989.
20. Kamo no Chōmei, *Hōjōki* 38–39.
21. On the problem of Buddhism and art, see Mezaki 1985.
22. Ishida 1970: 80.
23. Buddhist salvation required the full energy of the aspirant; it was not to be diffused in the pursuit of belles lettres, which could also be construed as fictive, and therefore as lies. The simultaneous pursuit of religious enlightenment and poetic practice was

from a strict Buddhist point of view contradictory. The Tang-Dynasty poet Bo Juyi attempted to solve the problem by donating his poetry to a Buddhist library in the hope that though those verses were from a religious point of view no more than "wild words and fancy phrases," they might also have Buddhist merit. See, for example, LaFleur 1983: 1–25 and Childs 1985.

24. For an overview of Shinkei's life, see Kaneko 1982, and on Shinkei's last years, see Shimazu 1972. In English, see Ramirez-Christensen 1994.

25. The translation is based on the Shoryōbu ms. in Kidō 1972-, 3: 367–85. A second version of the work, based on the Jingū Bunko manuscript, is edited by Shimazu Tadao (see Bibliography). The Shoryōbu manuscript is the more complete. The latter half of the translated portion of the work also appears with a short commentary and an approximate translation into modern Japanese in Tsurusaki 1987b: 144–45. *Oi no kurigoto* is titled *Kokemushiro* (Bed of Moss) in some manuscripts. See also Itō 1972. The translation of this section in Ramirez-Christensen (1983: 153–54, 272–75) is based on the Jingū Bunko manuscript. All future references to *Oi no kurigoto* will be cited as *OK*.

26. This refers to the outbreak of the Ōnin War in 1467.

27. Emperor Gotsuchimikado removed to the Muromachi Palace in the eighth month of 1467.

28. Suzuki Nagatoshi was a retainer of the Ōta who resided in Shinagawa. Five of his verses appear anonymously in *Shinsen tsukubashū*. Shinkei left Kyoto in the fourth month of 1467. He stayed in Ise for some time, then went east to Shinagawa. This section is much like that found in Shinkei's earlier work *Hitorigoto* (1468). The passage resembles one in *Hōjōki* (30): "On reaching the age of sixty years, when one's dew-like life is about to pass away, I again built a shelter frail as a tree's outer leaves." "Dew" and "leaf" are kindred words.

29. "Hai manman" (The Endless Sea), by Bo Juyi, includes these lines (Saku 1978, 1: 245–46):

> Penglai has been but a name since ages past;
> One knows not where to search for it on the distant, hazy ocean.
> The sea is endless, the wind vast . . . .

30. The five years to which Shinkei refers were 1467–71.

31. The passage refers to one of the punishments of hell, in which the damned are made to walk on sword points.

32. Mount Ōyama, in central Kanagawa Prefecture, was for centuries a center of mountain asceticism. Shinkei's hermitage was probably located near the site of Jōgyōji temple. See Tsurusaki 1987b: 145.

33. Shinkei quotes from the "Yongye" chapter of *Lunyu* (the Confucian *Analects* [J: *Rongo* 85]): "The man of wisdom delights in rivers; the man of benevolence delights in mountains."

34. *Wakan rōeishū* no. 501, by Bo Juyi:

>The evening mountains that obscure the setting sun
>>stretch blue into the distance;
>the autumn river that soaks the heavens
>>flows white far away.

35. *Wakan rōeishū* no. 430, by Bo Juyi:

>The hazy leaves are vague, veiled,
>>deepening into shades of night;
>the wind-swept branches are soughing, desolate,
>>resembling the sound of autumn.

Wakan rōeishū no. 431, by Zhang Xiaobiao:

>On the ground where Ruanjie whistled,
>>Someone walks through moonlight
>at the spot that Ziyou beheld,
>>birds dwell in the haze.

36. Ziyou was the style of Wang Huizi, son of the fourth-century poet and calligrapher Wang Xizhi. He so loved gardens that he had bamboo planted even when staying at a temporary residence. Letian was the style of Bo Juyi. Shinkei perhaps refers to the natural scenery around Bo Juyi's cottage on Mount Lu (Lushan). Wang Zhi, who lived during the Jin dynasty (265–419), is said to have become so engrossed in watching a game of chess in the mountains that he did not notice the passage of time until the handle of his axe had rotted away. Fei Zhengfang, who lived during the Latter Han dynasty (25–220), learned the Taoist arts while living deep in the mountains.

37. *Wakan rōeishū* no. 744, by Bo Juyi:

>The Suzhou boat has aged,
>>its dragon prow grown dull;
>The Wangyin Bridge is canted over,
>>its planks crooked as teeth or flying geese.

38. Tiger Ravine (Huxi) is the site of the religious parable of the "Three Laughers," wherein two friends go to visit a third who has vowed never to step beyond the valley confines. But the valley hermit does so inadvertently while conversing with his visitors, and all three break into laughter at the realization that from the point of view of the doctrine of nonduality all such intellectualized distinctions are in a higher sense meaningless. The account also symbolizes the underlying unity of Taoism, Buddhism, and Confucianism. See Rosenfield 1977.

39. *Wakan Rōeishū* no. 412, by To (Miyako Yoshika):

> The clouds vanish from the azure empyrean:
> > the tissue of heaven dissolves;
>
> the wind ripples the clear waves:
> > the water's surface wrinkles.

Wakan rōeishū no. 753, from *Wenxuan* (Selections of Refined Literature, c. 520–26):

> How can one who plays with the pebbles in the shallows
> > and does not peer into the deep pool of jade
> > ever know the place where the black dragon coils?
>
> How can one who dallies in the decrepit village
> > and does not venture into the capital
> > ever know the place where heroes dwell?

The lair of the black dragon was said to contain vast wealth.

40. *Wakan rōeishū* no. 556, by Du Xunhe:

> The fisherman in his boat at evening
> > casts his line by this shore and that;
>
> the herdboy lying on his ox's back
> > blows a flute that echoes in the cold.

Wakan rōeishū no. 559, by Seimei (Ki no Tadana):

> The sun has sunk over the mountain path,
> > and one hears the woodsman's song
> > and the herdboy's flute;
>
> the birds fly home to their nests in the valley
> > and one sees naught but the haze in the bamboo grove
> > and the mist in the pines.

41. *Wakan rōeishū* no. 552, by Kan Sanbon (Sugawara Fumitoki):

> I seek him in a dream late at night
> > in an ivied cavern beneath the moon;
>
> I walk in his footsteps in the spring evening
> > in the dust before a willowed gate.

42. A disquisition on poetry occupies the latter three-quarters of *Oi no kurigoto*. Shinkei's commentary resembles in some respects *Sasamegoto* in concentrated form, dealing with the contemporary state of waka and renga verse, the merits of the poetry of the *Shinkokinshū* period, the work of Shōtetsu (Shinkei's waka teacher) and of Nijō Yoshimoto's renga advisor Kyūsei, and aspects of linked-verse composition.

43. Sōgi's verse is based on *Shinkokinshū* 6: 590, by Nijōnoin Sanuki:

> A winter verse from *Sengohyakuban utaawase*:

>   yo ni furu wa   How painful
>   kurushiki mono o   to grow old in this world!
>   maki no ya ni   Yet the first cold rains
>   yasuku mo suguru   fall then pass by my pinewood cottage
>   hatsushigure kana   without a care.

Both verses play on furu ("to go on living" or "to grow old" / "to fall" [as of rain]). For more on these two verses, see Kaneko 1985a: 38–50.

44. It is also very possible that Shinkei read and appropriated elements of Bo Juyi's record of his hermitage on Mount Lu, entitled *Caotang ji*, not to mention other works of Chinese eremitic literature. For a convenient edition of Bo Juyi's essay, see Yanase 1980, and for English translations, see Strassberg 1994: 34–37 and Watson 1994: 7–17. *Wakan rōeishū* and the reception of Chinese recluse poetry in late Heian Japan are discussed in Smits 1995.

45. Li Chi (1962–63: 241) writes in the context of Chinese eremitism that "fear of the danger and discomfort of living in the wilderness . . . had gradually been replaced during the third and fourth centuries by a love for mountains and secluded valleys as an attraction in themselves. This fresh viewpoint was stimulated by the spread of Buddhism. The Buddhist practice of withdrawal from life appealed to recluses and reinforced the earlier tradition of retiring from world affairs." Alan Berkowitz (1989: 403) calls this Six Dynasties phenomenon "Buddhist-imbued reclusion."

46. On Shōhaku's life, see Hosoi 1959, Kidō 1971, id. 1972, and Tsurusaki 1976a.

47. With Sōgi and Sōchō, it will be recalled, Shōhaku composed two renga sequences which became classics of the genre, *Minase sangin* (1488) and *Yuyama sangin* (1491), and he contributed to the compilation of *Shinsen tsukubashū* (1495). In his *Renga shinshiki tsuika narabi ni shinshiki kon'an tō* (1501) he revised the renga rules of Nijō Yoshimoto and Ichijō Kaneyoshi.

48. *Shunmusō* 937.

49. Kubo 1966.

50. In 1513 Shōhaku had asked Jōan Ryūsū, Shōjū's successor, to write an account in kanbun of Shōhaku's hermitage life and his "three loves"—flowers, incense, and wine. For a printed text of the kanbun version, see Shimazu and Shigematsu 1965. Shōhaku rewrote the account in wakankonkōbun with the title *San'aiki* in 1516, a year after he composed *Muanki*.

The translation of *Muanki* is based on the *GSRJ* text. Another printed version is found in *Fusō shūyōshū* 3: 88–89. The *SKGSRJ* was collated with the latter. *Muanki* also appears in the form of prefaces (kotobagaki) in Shōhaku's personal poetry collection, *Shunmusō* 937. All future references to *Muanki* will be cited as *MA*.

51. Nothing is known of Sōshitsu and Zhonghe. Shōhaku adopted Muan as his own artist's name (gō).

52. The *Fusō shūyōshū* text uses a variant character for the name. Sōho's identity is unknown; all texts refer to him as *dōshin* (colleague), but it is unclear whether he is Sōshitsu's colleague, Shōhaku's, or both.

53. The *SKGSRJ* text gives *tomeji*, which does not seem to make sense. *Tomeshi* is given in the *GSRJ* version.

54. The text literally says "made my appearance natural" (*sono katachi shizen ni shite*), which alludes to Shōhaku's relaxation of his priestly strictures in 1511.

The translation of *San'aiki* is based on the *GSRJ* text. Printed versions also appear in *SKGSRJ* and *Fusō shūyōshū* 3: 89–90. All future references to *San'aiki* will be cited as *SA*.

55. Shōhaku mentions the "Nine-Fold Enclosure," the imperial palace, in reference to his aristocratic birth. Inano was located near Ikeda, close to what is now the border of Osaka and Hyōgo Prefectures. He had begun using the name Dream Cottage in reference to himself by 1484 (*RSR* 2: 525). He later left Ikeda because of warfare, but returned probably in early 1513 (*RSR* 2: 534).

56. Though no longer a monk, Shōhaku was still a lay believer (*koji*), and he quotes the phrase "the myriad things are a part of the one" (*banbutsu ittei*) to demonstrate that his elegant style, "Peony," is not entirely inappropriate to his religious condition. Jōan writes in the Chinese version of *San'aiki* as follows: "He calls himself 'Peony.' He took that from Nanquan, who . . . said 'looking at the blossoms of this [peony] is no different from having a dream'" (Shimazu and Fujita 1963: 41). The passage relates to the Buddhist principle of nonduality. But the name Peony is also based simply on Shōhaku's love of flowers. The Chinese version goes on to state, "He took as his sobriquet (*gō*) 'Peony' since it is the king of the myriad flowers. The virtue of the king encompasses all men. By favoring the peony, therefore, the lay believer [Shōhaku] expressed his love of all flora" (ibid. 45).

57. This is a reference to "Chunye" (Spring Night) by Su Dongpo (Kubo, Shaku, and Iwatare 1978, 6: 591):

> A moment of a spring evening
>   is worth a thousand pieces of gold;
> the blossoms have a pure fragrance,
>   the moon is clouded.

58. "Reclined in the spring breeze that blows through the peaches and damson plums" may be a reference to *Wakan rōeishū* no. 39, by Sugawara Michizane: "On the third day of the last month of springtime; the sky is intoxicated with the blossoms of the peaches and damsons now at their height."

"The dream of a butterfly" refers to the "Qiwulun" chapter of *Zhuangzi*:

> Some time ago Zhuangzhou dreamt he had become a butterfly, a butterfly fluttering free. He felt happy and at ease, but did not know he was Zhuangzhou.

> Suddenly he awoke and found with a start he was Zhuangzhou. Thereupon he could not tell whether he was Zhuangzhou who had dreamt he was a butterfly, or the butterfly dreaming he was Zhuangzhou. Yet there must have been a difference between the two. This is called one thing becoming another.

The parable is said to demonstrate the futility of making dualistic distinctions. See Abe, et al. 1976: 185–86.

"Thinking of the times, I shed tears" refers to "Chunwang" (Spring Vista) by Du Fu (Suzuki Torao 1978, 1: 373–73):

> The country is destroyed,
>   but the mountains and rivers remain;
> in the spring citadel,
>   the grasses and trees grow thick.
> Thinking of the times,
>   I shed tears at the blossoms;
> mourning my separation,
>   I am saddened by bird songs.

59. The two basic types of incense are those made solely from aromatic wood, such as aloes (*jin*) or sandalwood (*byakudan*), and those that are blends of various plant and animal ingredients. The latter, which may include aromatic woods in their composition, are known as *nerikō*. The incense-matching competitions (*takimonoawase*) held in the Heian period involved nerikō. On the role of nerikō in *Genji monogatari*, see Gatten 1977. In the fifteenth century, it became fashionable to match types of incense made from imported aloe wood (*jinkō*) alone. *Ranjatai*, Red Dust (Kōjin), and Middle River (Nakagawa) are all examples of jinkō. Those comparisons of types of incense were known as *meikōawase* or simply *kōawase*. Sanetaka, the founder of the Sanetaka style of incense ceremony, was the judge at a meikōawase in 1501, in which Shōhaku also participated. Sanetaka added a postscript to the written record, part of which reads as follows: "Takimonoawase have a long history in our country, but it was unheard of in earlier ages to take aloe wood alone and discriminate between various samples on the basis of their depth or shallowness" (*Meikōawase* 599). It was Shōhaku who made the fair copy of the record, and overtones of Sanetaka's lines may be sensed in *San'aiki*. For more on the way of incense (*kōdō*), see Hayakawa 1943.

60. Plum Blossom (Baika) and Lotus Leaf (Kayō) are two of the famous "Six Scents" (Rokushu), the others being Chamberlain (Jijū), Chrysanthemum (Kikka), Fallen Leaves (Rakuyō), and Black (Kurobō). First Pillow (Niimakura) is obscure, but it appears in Hayakawa 1943: 87, in a list of traditional scents with particularly elegant names.

61. Shōhaku's reference to wines of China and Southeast Asia (Nanban or "Southern Barbarians"), as well as his emphasis on incense made from imported aloe wood, re-

flects the international trade during that period, much of which was focused on the port city of Sakai. *Nerinuki*, also called *nerizake*, was a generic type of white sake. The *nerinuki* of Hakata in Kyushu was particularly famous. Amano was a superior sake made in Kawachi Province (now part of Osaka Prefecture) at Kongōji on Mount Amano (Kawachi Nagano City, Osaka Prefecture). "The Chrysanthemum of Kaga" is mentioned along with Amano as a "renowned wine" in, for example, Oze Hoan's *Taikōki* ([Chronicles of the Regent, c. 1625] 3: 274). "Chrysanthemum" and "wine" are classed as associated words in Matsue Shigeyori's *Kefukigusa* ([Splitting Hairs, 1645] 147), an early Edo guide to renga and haikai composition. "The thin and the cloudy" refers to *usuzake* and *dakurō* (the latter also called *doburoku*), both cheap, low-grade varieties of sake.

62. A reference to "Luori" (Setting Sun), by Du Fu (Suzuki Torao 1978, 2: 365–66):

> Cloudy wine, who made you?
> One cup dispels a thousand cares.

63. This is a reference to "Qujiang" (Twisting River), by Du Fu:

> Having left the court, day by day I pawn my spring garments;
>   daily by the river I get drunk then go home.
> I have old debts for wine wherever I go;
>   as rare now as long ago is a life of seventy years.

This translation of Du Fu's verse follows the interpretation in Yoshikawa 1977–83, 5: 172–74. Shōhaku seems to imply that he patches his robes in order to pawn them for wine (as does the official who has left court service in Du Fu's poem), relying then on drink rather than robes to stave off the cold.

64. "A rare age" translates *koki*, an elegant expression for the age of seventy. Shōhaku was seventy (by the Japanese count) in 1513, the date of the kanbun version of the *San'aiki*, and seventy-three when he wrote the Japanese version. The phrase here also continues the reference to "Qujiang."

65. There is a lacuna in the *GSRJ* text; I have inserted "dance" (*mai*) on the basis of the *Fusō shūyōshū* text. The line is a reference to "Taishang deliangzi" (On the Estrade, Receiving the Character *Liang*), by Du Fu (Suzuki Torao 1978, 2: 663–64):

> In my old age, one cup suffices;
> who will feel for me as from time to time I dance on and on?

66. Shōjū Ryūtō was the younger brother of Tō no Tsuneyori, who transmitted the secret traditions of *Kokinshū* to Sōgi. He lectured on the Chinese collection *Santishi* (J: *Santaishi*, Poems in Three Styles, 1250) at Sōgi's residence, Shugyokuan, and was also a friend of Sanetaka. It is unclear which name he conferred, but Kidō (*RSR* 2: 542–43) thinks it was "Shōhaku."

67. Jōan Ryūsū was a son of Tō no Tsuneyori and nephew of Shōjū. He not only wrote the kanbun version of the *San'aiki* but also the colophon for an extant portrait of Shōhaku. See Higuchi 1954: 56–58.

68. The *GSRJ* text gives "be confused" (*mayou*); I have substituted the similar character for "describe" (*nobu*) on the basis of the *Fusō shūyōshū* text.

69. The author adopted the name Rōka Rōjin (Old Man Who Delights in Flowers) as one of his artistic sobriquets.

70. Bo Juyi's "Beijuang sanyou" (Three Friends of the Northern Window) begins as follows (Saku 1978, 3: 290–91):

> What am I doing
> today beside my northern window?
> Happily I am with my three friends.
> And who are those three friends?
> When I take leave of my qin, I take up my wine,
> and when I take leave of my wine, I make poems.
> I bring out my three friends, going from one to another
> and back to the first, never stopping.

Like Shinkei, Shōhaku was probably well acquainted with the tradition of Chinese hermitage literature, and he too had very likely read Bo Juyi's record of his cottage on Mount Lu. Shōhaku's essays also bear striking resemblance to some by the Tang poet Yuan Jie, who likewise rhapsodized about constructing or naming pleasant cottages situated amid fantastic rocks and marvelous scenery. See Strassberg 1994: 117–19. Though it is beyond the scope of this study, the impact of Chinese prose styles on both Shinkei and Shōhaku invites further research.

71. *RSR* 2: 523.

72. *RSR* 2: 532.

73. Berkowitz (1989: 404) points out that "it was not requisite that a Daoist priest renounce all worldly functions."

74. See the translation of *The Journal of Sōchō* for notes on the apposite foundation poems that give further depth to these verses by Sōchō.

75. The verse Sōchō quotes is by Saigyō (*Shinkokinshū* 6: 697):

> mukashi omou   While stacking driftwood
> niwa ni ukiki o   in the yard of my cottage
> tsumiokite   I recall the past—
> mishi yo ni mo ninu   how little is this year's end
> toshi no kure kana   like others I have seen!

Though some commentators have understood Saigyō to mean by this poem that he is unfavorably comparing his present privation as a recluse with the plenty he once enjoyed in secular life, Sōchō instead takes Saigyō to mean that less is more and that a life of renunciation is in the end more worthy. Perhaps the poem can be read both ways, thereby emphasizing both the satisfaction and the simultaneous trials of eremitic life. Sōchō's commentary, however, leaves no doubt as to his own positive interpretation of Saigyō's renunciatory statement.

76. Hurvitz 1976: 40.

77. A combination of the epic and the novel, the centripetal and centrifugal, is itself novelistic; Gary Saul Morson and Caryl Emerson (1990: 30) point out that "these categories are themselves subject to the centrifuge."

78. Tsurusaki Hiroo (1978: 18) has contrasted the depiction of Sōchō's brilliant career in Book One and his setbacks in Book Two with the tone of resignation that seems to characterize much of *Sōchō nikki*, written in 1530–31.

79. Tsurusaki 1978: 2.

80. The courtier Washio Takayasu later visited Sōju's cottage in Kyoto in 1532 and wrote in his diary *Nisuiki* (1532: 5), "I was most impressed by the style of his mountain hut. It is indeed a place for reclusion within the city. Sōju is the standard-bearer of today's men of [tea] taste" (quoted in Moriya 1984: 72). While the taste of Sōju and his predecessor Jukō still had much in common with shoin tea, Sōchō's mention of four and one-half mat rooms demonstrates the basic shift in orientation that they and their followers were initiating, as does Takayasu's use of the term "mountain hut."

81. Sen no Sōtan, attrib., *Zencharoku* 243. Ishida Yoshisada (1969: 246) insists that it is the sōan and not Zen that is the fountainhead of wabi taste: "Wabi taste is expressed in the sōan. It was born of eremitic life in the early middle ages and cultivated by that life thereafter; in that period it can have had absolutely no contact with Zen." But while it is certainly true that the sōan aesthetic began its development before it could have been influenced by Zen ideas *per se*, its connection with Buddhism in a larger sense is obvious. Secondly, as indicated by Sen Sōtan, the development of wabi tea no doubt owes much to the influence of Ikkyū's Zen on Murata Jukō.

82. See Kuwata 1969: 265.

83. Urban reclusion may be related to the Chinese eremitic concept of "recluses in society" who, as Li Chi (1962–63: 234) points out, "did not seclude themselves from society; nevertheless they regarded themselves as *yin* [recluses] because their attitude was basically opposed to that of other officials. As might be expected, these 'recluses in society' were Taoists and followed the advice of Lao Tsu and Chuang Tsu to abandon oneself to the tide of the times and avoid revealing one's difference from other men." The concept was also doubtless buttressed by the example of Vimalakirti, which suggests that a Boddhisattva need not renounce the world. See LaFleur (1983: 107–15) and Berkowitz (1989: 278). Berkowitz (1989: 11) writes of this "hiding within the court" (*chaoyin*) that "the cognoscenti of the bon mot grafted Zhuangzi's philosophical Taoist detachment

(and soon also Vimalakirti's worldly Buddhism) onto the Confucian trunk of propagating the Way through service, and thus obfuscated any intellectual distinctions between private life and official employ . . . ." See also Parker 1995 and Smits 1995.

84. Sanetaka wrote in his diary of a six-mat study he acquired in 1502 (*Sanetakakōki* 1502:6:6, 4: 23). He moved it to his mansion, decreased its size to four and one-half mats, and located it in a walled garden in the corner of his property, hence its name Kadoya, "Corner Dwelling." Toyohara Muneaki named his retreat, located in the garden of his Kyoto mansion, "Cottage in a Mountain Village" (Sanrian). He wrote the following verse about it in his personal poetry collection (*Shōkashō* no. 1077):

> yama ni te mo A hidden cottage
> ukaramu toki no for when even mountains bring
> kakureya no respite from gloom—
> miyako no uchi no my hut beneath the pine trees
> matsu no shitaio here within the capital.

Chapter Four

1. For a chronological typology of the poetry in the journal, see Horton 1989: 532–34.
2. For introductions to the history of the linked-verse genre, see Kidō 1958, Kaneko 1987, and Shimazu 1979.
3. See "Ten Vexations of Linked Verse" (*Renga jūmuyaku*) in Horton 1993b: 512.
4. These courting songs, called *utagaki* in the west and *kagai* in the east, occurred on fixed days and often consisted of a challenge by the woman and a response by the suitor; the success of his suit might depend on the skill of his reply. See Kimura and Iguchi 1988 and Drake 1992.
5. *Kojiki* 217.
6. The seventeen-syllable verse, composed by a nun, and the fourteen-syllable reply, composed by Ōtomo Yakamochi, one of the compilers of the anthology, appear together as *Man'yōshū* 8: 1635.
7. For the verses in *Mitsuneshū*, see *KT* 3: 36.
8. Ijichi 1953. See also Drake 1992.
9. Shimazu 1979: 360–62.
10. For more on the sacred quality of the renga space, see Okami 1955.
11. Kaneko 1987: 96. Saka Jūbutsu mentions both *hananomoto* and *kasagi* sessions at Ise in his *Ise Daijingū sankeiki* of 1342, translated in Sadler 1940. Hananomoto is mentioned on pp. 32–33 and kasagi on pp. 73–74.
12. Kyūsei's renga teacher was the hananomoto renga master Zenna (n.d.), but Kyūsei also studied waka with the courtier Reizei Tamesuke. Konishi (1991: 427) points out that "unlike Zenna, [Kyūsei] infused his renga with the ga of waka." Some of Zenna's

verses were even edited by Yoshimoto and Kyūsei to make them more reflective of the high style the two editors were creating.

13. Kubukihara 1985: 73.

14. Ijichi Tetsuo (1955: 285) believes that Sōgi benefited in particular from the technical and rhetorical skill of Sōzei and the harmonious beauty of his links, combined with the deep emotionalism and elegance of Shinkei's approach. Etō (1967: 537) concurs, arguing that Sōgi successfully combined the technical interest (*omoshiroshi*) of Sōzei with the "cold and withered" (*hiesabi*) overtones of much of Shinkei's work.

15. *Chikurinshō* is believed to have been compiled as a preliminary contribution to Ichijō Kaneyoshi's planned successor to the *Tsukubashū* renga anthology. See Kaneko 1993: 74. It also contributed to the primacy of the "Seven Sages of Linked Verse" that it included, and by extension it added to the reputation of their anthologizer and disciple. The manuscript of Kaneyoshi's anthology was lost in the Ōnin War, and Kaneyoshi was never able to reconstruct it. The task of compiling an imperially recognized sequel to *Tsukubashū* eventually fell to Sōgi himself.

16. Fukui 1969: 307.

17. *RSR* 1: 27–28.

18. For a comparison of ushin renga and ushin waka, see Hisamatsu 1948.

19. Brower (1985: 411) comments, "In the narrow sense of one of the ten styles, [ushin] is generally interpreted as a highly subjective style in which the speaker's feelings pervade the imagery and rhetoric of the poem." This subjectivity, however, is expressed in terms of universal basic essences that transcend individual idiosyncracy. The question is not simple subjectivity, but how effectively one can harmonize one's mind with universal basic essences.

20. Teika writes with regard to ushin verse in *Maigetsushō* (129), for example, that "this style of composition applies to the other nine styles as well." For a translation of *Maigetsushō*, see Brower 1985.

21. Teika's *Maigetsushō* sets forth ten waka styles, and *Guhishō* and *Sangoki*, both of which were once attributed to Teika, add eighteen others.

22. *Shinkokinshū* 5: 459, where it is attributed to Hitomaro. It is a variant of *Man'yōshū* 10: 2220.

23. *Yoshitadashū* (also called *Sotanshū*) 243, the personal poetry collection of Sone Yoshitada. The verse was attributed to Hitomaro in other sources, such as *Guhishō* and *Kirihioke*, the latter another text once thought to have been written by Teika.

24. *Shinkokinshū* 5: 498, where it is attributed to Hitomaro. It is a variant of *Man'yōshū* 10: 2136.

25. *Shinkokinshū* 18: 1634, by Akahito (also *Man'yōshū* 6: 919).

26. *Shinkokinshū* 6: 675, by Akahito. It is a variant of *Man'yōshū* 1: 318.

27. *Azuma mondō* 226–27.

28. Etō 1967: 506.

29. This point is made in Kidō 1958: 39–40, for example.

30. On "writerly" texts, see Barthes 1977.

31. Sōchō et al., *Renga hikyōshū* 169. Ijichi (1985: 15–16) writes that this collection is by Sōchō, and Yunoue Sanae agrees, in his commentary to a manuscript facsimile edition (in Kaneko 1978–83, 9: 5). Kaneko has suggested, however, in a personal communication that other Sōgi disciples were probably also involved in the composition of the work, but that it reflects Sōchō's views.

32. There were cases in which the order of composition for the first part of the sequence would be fixed ahead of time to insure that each participant would be represented in the finished sequence, and verses of this "first round" (*ichijun*) were sometimes circulated in advance to give the poets time to compose. But even in such formalized compositions, all the verses after the hokku were composed with reference to the preceding link.

33. Jōha identifies twenty-two kireji in his *Shihōshō* (Ultimate Treasure Notes, 1627). He requires one in the hokku without exception, for a hokku "without kireji sounds like a regular verse (*hiraku*), which will not do" (*Shihōshō* 237).

34. An example of this formulation is found in Jōha's *Renga kyōkun* (c. 1582) 267. See also Yakame 1983.

35. *Nagabumi* 192 and *Amayo no ki* 1236.

36. This fact was recognized as early as *Yakumo mishō* by Juntokuin, which contains an early collection of renga rules: "The hokku for a session must be composed by someone competent. An unskilled poet must not be allowed to compose it" (*Yakumo mishō* 22).

37. Cf. *JS* nos. 357 and 544.

38. All future references will be cited as *Yashima*.

39. The second commentary, considerably shorter than that by Sōboku, is an unpublished manuscript in the collection of Ōta Takeo.

40. For a description of the oral performative aspects of orthodox renga composition, see Horton 1993b.

41. The accusative *o* is positioned so that it allows *kieaenu* (lingering) to apply first to *ume ga ka* (a scent of plum blossoms) to imply "the fragrance does not disappear," then to connect with *yuki* (snow) to suggest "the lingering snow." Here and elsewhere, ume is translated "plum," though "apricot" is more botanically accurate.

42. *Kokinshū* 1: 7.

43. Sōboku brought Sanetaka's hokku to Yashima from Kyoto. Part of the reason for the conjectural *ran* is that Sanetaka did not know for certain what the scene was like at Yashima, but he was nevertheless required to evoke both the season and the location of the session, as well as its level of formality. He therefore inquires whether one smells the scent at Yashima.

44. *Shinsen tsukubashū* 19: 3711. The verse appears in *Chikurinshō* (no. 1679) with the preface "From a solo hundred-verse sequence, on the summer moon." According to Chi-

nese legend, a *katsura* (laurel or Judas tree) five-hundred *jō* (1,500 m) in height grows on the moon. In some examples of Japanese poetry, the hue of the autumn moon is attributed to the yellow laurel leaves, e.g., *Kokinshū* 4: 194, by Mibu no Tadamine:

hisakata no	Is it because
tsuki no katsura mo	the leaves on the laurel tree
aki wa nao	also change color
momiji sureba ya	that the moon in the heavens
terimasaruramu	shines more brightly?

But in the renga verse here, the comparative dimness of the summer moon is attributed to the lush green leaves of the laurel impeding its light.

45. The verse is included in Sōgi's third personal collection of linked verse, *Shitakusa* (732). It appears with another bearing the preface, "On the fifteenth of the eighth month, at a session at the residence of Taira Shinzaemonnojō." See also *Sōgi hokkushū* no. 1081. "The renowned full moon" is the full moon of the eighth month. Here Sōgi suggests its perfect roundness is because it is not hidden by the laurel branches, which have all been broken off. His verse may include a celebratory meaning based on the Chinese expression "to break off a branch of the moon laurel" (in Japanese, *tsuki no katsura o oru*), meaning to succeed in the official examinations.

46. On "titles" of waka and renga, see Miner 1990: 670–72.

47. Arakida, *Nikonshū* 1: 191.

48. "Topical" (also referred to as "thematic") categories include Spring, Summer, Autumn, Winter, Love, Travel, Lamentation, Buddhism, Shintō, and Miscellaneous. "Lexical categories" include Mountains (*sanrui*), Dwellings (*kyosho*), Waters (*suihen*), Falling Things (*furimono*), Rising Things (*sobikimono*), Shining Things (*hikarimono*), Nocturnal Things (*yabun*), Plants (*uemono*), Animals (*ugokimono*), Human Relations (*jinrin*), Famous Places (*nadokoro*), and Clothing (*irui*). For a detailed explanation of the linking process and reading a sequence by the renga rules, see Carter 1987a and also Konishi 1975 and Miner 1979.

49. For a list of different sets of renga rules, see Konishi 1991: 281.

50. *Nijōgawara no rakusho*, in *Kenmu nenkanki*, in *SKGSRJ* 19: 754.

51. A well-organized text of the final Shōhaku revision, with an index, may be found in Yamada and Hoshika 1985: 1–11. For an overview of the rules, see Kaneko 1987: 189–271, and for an English translation, see Carter 1987: 41–72.

52. All future references to *Renju gappekishū* will be cited as *RJGPS*.

53. *RJGPS* no. 300.

54. See, for example, Jōha, *Shihōshō* 240.

55. Another handbook of associations, *Renga tsukeai no koto* (no. 12), explicitly links *tani sato* (valley village) with *nokoru yuki* (remaining snow).

56. For one example, see *Kitanosha ichimanku onhokku waki daisan shidai narabi ni jo*,

which lists the first three verses of one hundred hyakuin composed on the eleventh of the second month of 1433 at Kitano Shrine.

57. Some of the basic words associated with each of the four seasons, love, and other topical categories are listed at the end of the *Renju gappekishū* handbook.

58. On the concept of plain (*uchihirame*) verses, see Shimazu 1973: 257–66 and 1987: 153–54.

59. Sōboku, *Tōfū renga hiji* 164.

60. Nijō Yoshimoto, *Tsukuba mondō* 86.

61. "Colored leaves" and "bush clover" are associated in *RJGPS* no. 233.

62. See also Konishi 1991, 3: 462–66.

63. Konishi further distinguishes between "close-distant" and "distant-close" and also between "somewhat ji" and "somewhat mon" 1991: 463–64. For a discussion of ji and mon, shinku and soku, see Konishi 1975: 51–53 and Carter 1983: 46–53.

64. *Sōchō renga jichū* 95. Sōboku's son Sōyō later stated that "distant linking" was one style Sōchō particularly favored. See *Sōyō yori kikigaki*, in *RSR* 2: 585.

65. Ijichi Tetsuo (1955: 286) judges Sōchō to be "the poet who best carried on Sōgi's renga style."

66. Sōgi, *Azuma mondō* 218.

67. Sōchō, *Nagabumi* 192.

68. Sōchō, *Amayo no ki* 1236.

69. On the relationship of *Amayo no ki* and *Renga sakurei*, see Shigematsu 1981 and *RSR* 2: 591–94.

70. On the accumulative nature of medieval poetic theory, see Kishida 1982.

71. The collections are entitled *Wakuraba* (Blighted Leaves, 1481, rev. 1485) and *Shitakusa*, and the commentaries are *Guku wakuraba* (My Ignorant Blighted Leaves, 1520) and *Shitakusachū* (Undergrowth Commentary, 1515). The collections and their commentaries are extant.

72. *Wakuraba* verse numbers are taken from *Guku wakuraba*, Kaneko 1979.

73. These verses are selected from Uzawa 1956: 9–10.

74. *Oi no mimi* no. 84.

75. This is from the *Okitsuate* (To Okitsu) section of *Sōchō renga jichū* (156–57). Shigematsu (1973: 29) believes that the *Okitsuate* section was probably begun in 1522 while Sōchō was in Ise and completed at about the time he entered the *ariake ya* verse (*JS* no. 80) in his journal, at the end of 1523. The *Mibuate* (To Mibu) section of *Sōchō renga jichū* probably dates to 1528 or thereafter (ibid.).

76. Saigyō, *Saigyō Shōninshū* 555.

77. Shinkei, *Sasamegoto* 175.

78. Bontō, *Bontōanshu hentōsho* 1049.

79. See Konishi 1978.

80. The verse is a variant of *Man'yōshū* 7: 1140.

81. On *Sōchō renga jichū*, see Shigematsu 1973, and for more on Sōchō's use of honka as a linking device, see Uzawa 1961.

82. There were, of course, differences between the two genres; the renga lexicon was somewhat more inclusive than that of waka, and its diction even more compact. And of course waka itself varied according to school. See Shimazu 1955.

83. *RSR* 2: 587.

84. Kaneko 1990: 169. Among the examples he gives are *JS* nos. 344, 387, and 582, quoted above.

85. For example, compare *JS* no. 9, *ōchi saku / kumoi o chiri no / fumoto kana* with *Oi no mimi* no. 23, *kumo kakaru / chiri no fumoto no / ōchi kana*, and *JS* no. 213, *hototogisu / makoto o kyō wa / hatsune kana* with *Oi no mimi* no. 106, *hototogisu / makoto wa kyō o / hatsune kana*, among many other examples.

86. Both verses recall the Naniwazu poem in the *Kokinshū* preface. See *JS*: 287, n. 192.

87. See Carter 1984 for an introduction to linked-verse contests.

88. The verse is a reworking of the topic explored in *JS* nos. 327 and 338, quoted above.

89. *Sōchō hyakuban rengaawase* 86. Sōchō perceives the haze as constituting the ground, out of which the peak of Fuji soars. The snow on the peak therefore now extends to the "ground" constituted by the haze. The verse is based on this by Gokyōgoku Yoshitsune (*Akishino gesseishū* no. 202):

hisakata no	Ikomayama,
kumoi ni mieshi	seen in the clouds
ikomayama	far off—
haru wa kasumi no	in spring the haze
fumoto narikeri	has become the mountain foot!

90. *Sōchō hyakuban rengaawase* 86. Jien's verse is *Shinkokinshū* 1: 33.

91. *Sōchō hyakuban rengaawase* 87.

92. The pine is always green regardless of the season, and now that the other leaves have changed color, the green stands out with even more brilliance.

93. *Sōchō hyakuban rengaawase* 91. The poet inquires of the cold rain if it is because it waits for the leaves it tinted to dry that it goes around the mountain wetting the others.

94. *Sōchō hyakuban rengaawase* 91.

95. Ibid. The translated passages show there is no justification for the following remark in Miner (1979: 46): "The troublesome fact is that Shōhaku and such others as Sanjōnishi Sanetaka (1455–1537) could be so specific in their criticism. They faulted [Sōchō], particularly, for his opening stanzas." The assertion that follows, "Sōchō's technique of joining stanzas was also faulted, and that is a more serious matter," is also incorrect. It is based on one sentence by Sanetaka (*Sōchō hyakuban rengaawase* 26) translated in Miner as:

"It is an attractive thing to add to those white clouds on the hill of Kazuraki some flowers blooming. But to say that Kazuraki is distinct with flowers blooming is extremely odd." The sentence should read: "There is nothing unusual in linking the blossoms of Kazuraki to white clouds about the mountain peak, but to say that Kazuraki stands out with its blossoming cherries is particularly interesting." See also Ramirez-Christensen 1981.

96. *RSR* 2: 587.
97. Oda Takuji 1947: 65.
98. Sōchō, *Nagabumi* 192.
99. Keene 1977: 267.
100. *Iba senku*, also known as *Gessonsai senku*, was a famous thousand-verse sequence in which Sōchō, Sōseki, and Sanetaka participated. Held over the course of five days (1524:3:17–21), it was sponsored by the warrior-literatus Iba Sadakazu, also known as Tanemura Nakatsukasanojō, who was a lieutenant of Rokkaku Sadayori, constable of south Ōmi. Sadakazu contributed a token number of verses to the sequence. The work is extant. See also Tsurusaki 1969a and 1976b. Sōchō included a large number of verses from the sequence in *Oi no mimi* (see Iwashita 1985).
101. Sōboku, in *Tōfū renga hiji* (163), gives evidence that hokku were, in fact, regularly discussed beforehand:

> In Kyoto, from the time of Kensai down through that of Sōchō and Sōseki to the present, the order of the first round has been established after the hokku is composed. Thereafter, verses are sent around to the participants one after another by letter box three to five days in advance. During that time, each person takes his verse to a skilled poet for consultation.

102. *Shutsujin senku* 540. Oda singles out *Shutsujin senku* as typical of Sōchō's mature style. A solo votive sequence that Sōchō composed in thanks for a victory in battle by his patron Imagawa Ujichika, the work includes a large number of verses that Oda considers superb. Sōchō records the circumstances of its composition in his journal (*JS*: 10). For a detailed analysis of the work, see Harada 1979.
103. In more normal word order, the verse would read *tsuyu ya yūbe no / nagori naruran* (see Harada 1979: 329).
104. Yamada 1932: 108.
105. Hisamatsu 1976: 452.
106. *Yuyama sangin*, in Kaneko 1985b: 254.
107. *RSR* 2: 571.
108. The verses are quoted in Ijichi 1955: 290.
109. Tanaka 1993.
110. Etō 1967: 530.
111. Ijichi 1955: 291.
112. *UYK* 404. The quotation from the Chinese Preface (*Manajo*) reads, "a comfort-

able man composes a happy poem; a miserable man a sad one" (trans., McCullough 1985b).

113. Kaneko 1990: 170.

114. *Sōchō renga jichū* 95–96.

115. One modern critical study dismisses the waka of the era with the pronouncement that "the period of the *Fūgashū* [1349] brings the last splendors to the tradition of Court poetry which, from the fifteenth century, sinks steadily into an age of darkness." The unnamed study is quoted in Brower and Miner 1961: 413.

116. Sanetaka's *Setsugyokushū* and Gokashiwabara's *Hakugyokushū* were known together with Reizei Masatame's *Hekigyokushū* as the "Three Jewelled Collections" (*Sangyokushū*), considered the most outstanding of the period. Toyohara Muneaki's *Shōkashō* and Sanetaka's *Saishōsō* were also well known. Shimazu (1953) sees considerable individuality in the three jewelled collections, which were essentially dismissed by earlier modern critics as derivative.

117. For a short introduction to the waka of Shinkei and Sōgi, see Miner 1968: 140–43. Inoue (1969: 52) singles out Sōgi, Shōhaku, and Sōchō as the major contributors among rengashi to the waka tradition of the late fifteenth and early sixteenth centuries.

118. See Brower 1992.

119. *Sōchō hikashō* is devoted entirely to that genre, but its authorship is disputed. See Kishida 1980b and id. 1982. Sōchō is also believed to have composed a commentary entitled *Hyakunin isshuchū*. Shigematsu (1982: 119) mentions the work.

120. The journal mentions one such important lost sequence, which Sōchō asked Sanetaka to critique:

> While I was at my leisure in Suruga, in my Brushwood Cottage in Mariko, Utsunoyama, someone showed me a hundred-waka sequence Lord Sanetaka composed the previous winter on topics chosen by Iwayama Dōken from lines in *Kokinshū*. I modelled a sequence on his and when last in the capital, I took it to him. He was good enough to look it over, and he singled out forty-two for praise. His poem at the end:

429	ika ni shite	How did it happen
	shigure furinishi	that my leaf-like words, rained on
	koto no ha o	by chill showers,
	aranu iro ni mo	came to be so richly dyed
	somekaeshikemu	in these uncommon colors?

> I am undeserving of such praise. (*JS*: 119)

His pride in the critical recognition of them by a respected authority bears witness to the importance Sōchō attached to his waka compositions.

Among Sōchō's surviving waka are part of a hundred-verse sequence sponsored by

Sōgi and dedicated on 1496:3:23 to Sumiyoshi Shrine in Nagato Province (Yamaguchi Prefecture) in celebration of the completion of *Shinsen tsukubashū* (cited in *RSR* 2: 923); *Ei gojisshu waka*, composed for Mishima Shrine in 1525 at the request of the Hōjō; *Chōka* (a collection of 195 waka made in 1530); and an undated collection simply entitled *Wakashū*.

121. *Renga hikyōshū* 162.

122. I use the term "public poetry" to translate *hare no uta*, verse composed with the expectation of a wide audience, and "private poetry" to translate *ke no uta*, verse meant for a select few or the self alone. Public poetry is usually "formal" in that it follows orthodox ushin strictures for diction and content; private poetry may be formal or to varying degrees informal, implying a relaxation of formal standards. See Brower and Miner 1961: 18–19 and McCullough 1985a: 3.

123. Sōgi, *Azuma mondō* 22.

124. The exchange is based on a foundation poem, *Kokinshū* 11: 489. For details, see *The Journal of Sōchō*.

125. Shinken's verse is based on *Kokinshū* 1: 21. Sōchō's response refers to the legend of Mengzong, one of the twenty-four paragons of filial piety. For details, see *The Journal of Sōchō*.

126. Ikkyū's poems on the death of sparrows in Covell 1980: 180–83 are exemplary.

127. Fujiwara Shunzei, *Korai fūteishō* 104.

128. For details on the development of waka during this period, see Inoue 1987 and Carter 1981 and id. 1989.

129. Examples of such pairings quoted here are *JS* nos. 253–54, 255–56, and 462–63.

130. Inoue 1987: 283.

131. This fact is pointed out by Uzawa 1961: 82.

132. Shigematsu Hiromi, the editor of the printed version of *Sōchō michi no ki*, thinks Sōchō probably compiled the work himself because it shows that he had both *The Journal of Sōchō* and its sequel *Sōchō nikki* close at hand and because the additional lines in the work are in Sōchō's style (Shigematsu 1983: 337–38). It is just as possible, though, that it was assembled by a disciple sensitive to the lack of a suitable shikashū among his teacher's credentials.

133. *Chikuba kyōginshū*, compiled anonymously, contains 20 hokku and 217 couplets, about forty percent of which are also found in *Shinsen inu tsukubashū*, though often in different form.

134. *Shinsen inu tsukubashū* (often abbreviated *Inu tsukubashū*) is believed to have first been compiled sometime in the 1530s. Yamazaki Sōkan is almost universally believed to be the compiler because four early versions of the anthology are in his hand, and because extant poem strips bearing the first poem in the anthology are signed by him. See Kimura and Iguchi 1988. Early manuscripts bear such titles as *Haikai rengashō* or *Haikai renga*. The work went through numerous editions and enlargements; the Daiei ms.

(*Haikai rengashō*, in Kimura and Iguchi 1988), for example, contains 94 hokku and 161 couplets, and the Tōkyō Daigaku Toshokan ms. (*Shinsen inu tsukubashū*, in Suzuki Tōzō 1965) has 47 hokku and 335 couplets. The Suzuki edition also contains verses from other manuscripts besides those in his base text. The various versions of *Shinsen inu tsukubashū* include poems attributed to Sōgi, Sōchō, Kensai, Sōseki, Sōzei, Moritake, and other linked-verse masters, as well as to Sōkan himself.

135. *Moritake senku*, also known as *Haikai no renga dokugin senku* or *Tobiume senku*, was composed by Arakida Moritake in 1536 then revised, reaching its final form in 1540. *Arakidashū* is an anthology of verses by members of the family. See Hamachiyo 1961.

136. Yamada 1951: 165. Moritake's personal poetry collection *Gatten no ku* (Jingū Chōkokan), dated Tenbun 9:12:25 (early 1541), contains verses singled out for praise by Sōchō and other rengashi.

137. Konishi 1976: 171.

138. "Those who would look for pears or pick up chestnuts" refers to the Kurinomotoshū (lit., those beneath the chestnut tree), meaning those who pursue mushin linked verse, in contrast to the Kakinomotoshū, those who follow Kakinomoto (lit., those beneath the persimmon tree) Hitomaro, i.e., orthodox ushin poets. The author of the preface uses "look for pears" (*nashi o motome*) as a parallel device because "pears" and "nothingness" are homophonic and because "pears" and "chestnuts" are related poetic words.

139. *Chikuba kyōginshū*, in Kimura and Iguchi 1988: 12.

140. Iida 1977: 234.

141. See Kimura and Iguchi 1988: 286 and Etō 1967: 540.

142. Fukui 1969: 315.

143. *Moritake senku* 234.

144. Kitamura Kigin, for example, in the preface to his haikai anthology *Shinzoku inu tsukubashū* (New Sequel to the Mongrel *Tsukubashū*, 1660), notes with regard to his own haikai antecedents that "in the period that followed [*Tsukubashū*] there appeared the hundred-verse sequence of Sōgi and the thousand-verse sequence of Moritake, but *Inu tsukubashū* by the priest Sōkan of Yamazaki stood out in particular" (quoted in Etō 1967: 553).

145. Sōgi refers to the traditional *iroha* order of syllables ("asaki *yume* miji, (w)e*hi mo sezu*"); in the absence of diacritics, *hi* can also be read *bi*, hence *yubi* (finger). Anrakuan Sakuden, *Seisuishō* 1: 16.

146. The attribution of haikai waka to Sōgi is problematic and will not be dealt with here.

147. For a study of these verses, see Yunoue 1972, to which the following is indebted.

148. *Wasuregusa* 169.

149. *Wasuregusa* 170.

150. *Wasuregusa* 174.

151. Sōchō uses both toponyms in *JS* nos. 505 and 506 (see Chapter Three).

152. *Wasuregusa* 63.

153. *Wasuregusa* 68.

154. *Wasuregusa* 115.

155. Sei Shōnagon, *Makura no sōshi* 63.

156. "A bird whose wings linked with another's" (*hane o narabeshi*) recalls Bo Juyi's "Changhenge" (A Song of Unending Sorrow), which ends with these lines: "We told each other secretly in the quiet midnight world / That we wished to fly in heaven, two birds with the wings of one, / And to grow together on the earth, two branches of one tree" (trans. Witter Bynner, in Birch 1965: 269).

157. On haikai within the renga sequence, see Tanaka 1969 and Saitō Yoshimitsu 1979.

158. The earliest extant examples of *jōji* linked verses appear as tanrenga in *Shūishū*, and there are two extant hundred-verse *jōji* sequences antedating Sōgi's: *Den'a dokugin jōji hyakuin* of 1414 and an earlier but undated text attributed to the codifier of high renga himself, Nijō Yoshimoto. For a history of the subgenre, see Ozaki, Shimazu, and Satake 1985: 16–18, to which the discussion here is indebted.

159. There is also an extant sequence entitled *Wakan kyōku* (Mad Verses in Japanese and Chinese) from 1486 (Etō 1967: 575). It was composed at court, the hokku having been made by Emperor Gotsuchimikado. This is not, however, a *jōji hyakuin*, but rather a sequence of alternating verses in Japanese and Chinese.

160. An early spring verse (*ume*, plum). *Niou* may mean "be fragrant" or "glow"; Shimazu (in Ozaki, Shimazu, and Satake 1985: 23) believes the former sense takes precedence here.

161. A spring verse (*yanagi*, willow). *Mime* 眉目 (looks or features) is not strictly a Chinese compound but rather a *jūbakoyomi*, one character (*mi*) using the Chinese pronunciation (*on yomi*) and the other (*me*) the Japanese (*kun yomi*). Read completely in *on yomi*, the compound is *bimoku*, meaning "eyebrows and eyes," "facial appearance," or a person of beautiful features. Thus when apprehended aurally, the word refers to appearance; when the characters are read visually, a stronger connection between *yanagi* (willow) and its kindred kun yomi word *mayu* (eyebrows) is established (yanagi is associated with both *mayu* [*RJGPS* no. 308] and *me* [*RJGPS* no. 534]). The link is effected through the association between ume and yanagi (*RJGPS* no. 300).

162. A spring verse.

163. A spring verse (*yuki no yozan*, lingering snow). *Yuki* (snow) is associated with *tsuki* (moon) (*RJGPS* no. 12).

164. A late spring verse (*kaeru kari*, returning geese). All the geese have but one intent, that of flying north to their summer home.

165. A miscellaneous verse (no season); travel. Tears of homesickness and travail stain the worn sleeves of one on a long journey.

166. A miscellaneous verse (no season); travel. *Minatobune* (boat in the harbor) is one

of the many words not found in the first eight imperial waka anthologies but nevertheless frequently used in renga. It gradually appears in late waka anthologies as well. *Sode* (sleeves) links with *minato* (harbor) (*RJGPS* no. 660).

167. A miscellaneous verse (no season); travel. *Tomaya* (thatch hut) is linked with *fune* (boat) and *ame* (rain, expressed in the compound *uchū*) (*RJGPS* no. 184). *Ame* comes under the lexical category of Falling Things, occurrences of which must be separated by three verses. As the last Falling Thing in the sequence was *yuki* (snow) in verse four, another such word may appear here. In *Sōgi sodeshita* (Sōgi's Notes Carried in the Sleeve, c. 1480–89, p. 254) he writes that "'thatch hut' and 'reed hut' are not appropriate for the first eight verses." That the term appears here shows the slightly relaxed haikai quality of the sequence.

168. Suma and "capital" (*miyako*, implied in *tohi*) are linked (*RJGPS* no. 162), and Suma and *shio yaki* are linked as well (*RJGPS* no. 559).

169. *Genji monogatari* 4: 48.

170. *Sanetakakōki* 1499:3:15 (3: 628–29).

171. *Fuji no uraba* (wisteria leaves) and *tasogaredoki* (twilight) are linked in *RJGPS* no. 75.

172. One example is *Shinkokinshū* 2: 166, by Ki no Tsurayuki:

Composed on wisteria hanging in pine boughs:

midori naru	Though the wisteria
matsu ni kakareru	hangs down from pines
fuji naredo	that are ever green,
ono ga kokoro to zo	it has now burst into bloom
hana wa sakikeru	and proclaimed the season as its own!

173. The Tada area of Hyōgo Prefecture included a number of shrines and temples (*dō*) related to the Minamoto family, as well as mines that did much to support them. There may be a pun on *dō*, copper.

174. This is a *yotsude* (four-hand) link connecting *dō* with *hotoke* (Buddha) and *tada* with *manjū*, a connection to the ballad-drama (*kōwakamai*) *Mitsunaka* (which may also be read Manchū or Manjū), about Tada no Mitsunaka, a member of the Heike, enemies of the Minamoto.

175. This is another yotsude link, connecting *manjū* with *miso* and *hotoke* with *shakuson*. The verse by itself means "Is there someone like Sakyamuni who will save me?" But the poem can also read *taremiso sukū shaku son ya aru*, which means "Will they cheat when ladling out the *taremiso* sauce?"

176. In the context of the maeku, *hibi ni masarite* also means "the cracks spread day by day."

177. This refers to a nocturnal secret visit to a lover. The link may have been effected in part through a reference to *Ise monogatari* (18):

hito shirenu	How I wish
waga kayoiji no	that each and every night
sekimori wa	when I travel down the road
yoiyoi goto ni	to my lover in secret,
uchi mo nenanan	the gatekeeper would be fast asleep!

178. The next line of the same *Ise monogatari* passage reads: "He was secretly visiting the Nijō Princess, but rumors reached her brothers, who had her guarded, or so it is said." The notion of rumors helps link this verse to the previous. In addition, *ten kurō nare* (let the sky be dark!) leads to *tsuki no sawari* (hindering moon), which also means "menstruation." Ten kurō also leads to tenkurō, a type of lance made in the mid-fourteenth century by Tenkurō in Ōmi. Terashima Shōichi suggests that this pun relates then to *tsuki*, either "moon" or "thrust," bringing in the overtone of sexual intercourse during menstruation (personal communication).

179. *Haikai rengashō* no. 195, in Suzuki Tōzō 1965: 209. The original reads *tōsei wa / nokiba no kishi no / takekurabe*, which is obscure. Suzuki suggests it was a mistake for *nokiba nokiba no*, which is how it is reproduced here. *Takekurabe* (comparing heights) was also a technical term in linked verse for judging tsukeku. But the verses in this mountain village are all uniformly bad; it is no different from trying to tell the eaves of one house from those of the next.

180. Verses attributed to Sōgi in one manuscript may appear as anonymous in another. For example, the first and last of four verses listed with no attribution in the Tōkyō Daigaku Toshokan ms. of *Shinsen inu tsukubashū* (Suzuki Tōzō 1965: 75) appear with Sōgi's name in the Tenri Toshikan ms. of *Shinkyū kyōka haikai kikigaki* (Kimura and Iguchi 1988: 325). And in yet another manuscript (*Ise haikai kikigakishū*, in Suzuki Tōzō 1965: 241–42) one of the above verses given to Sōgi appears with Sōchō's name instead. The confusion in attribution suggests that many verses were most likely in common circulation and were simply attributed to famous literary wits after the fact.

181. Etō 1967: 580–82. Moritake himself mentions his debt to *Mishima senku* in his afterword (*Moritake senku* 234).

182. Bashō's remarks appear in *Sanseizu no san* (Colophon for a Painting of Three Sages, 1692–93).

183. This passage would seem to be based in part on one in *Kirihioke* (289): "The haikai style is one of amusing wit. It makes sport of things, ascribing feelings to things that have none and words to things that cannot speak." "Vulgarity" translates *ashiki* (lit., bad). The line in brackets appears only in certain manuscripts. Kidō and Imoto 1964: 224–25.

184. Sōchō also includes a few ga haikai verses in his late treatise *Sōchō renga jichū*. For comments on them, see Uzawa 1961: 81–83.

185. For more on this sequence, see Araki 1947: 95–99, Harada 1979: 356–70, Inazawa 1973, Keene 1977, Kidō 1984: 340–50, Shimazu 1969: 176–81, and Tani 1952.

186. Kidō Saizō (1984: 343) warns against assuming all the tsukeku are Sōchō's, and

he suggests Sōchō may have written down the verses he felt were the best of those made at the session, regardless of which poet or poets composed them. Shimazu Tadao (1969: 173) suggests that Sōchō was not the author of the very lewd verses in the collection, and Inoue Muneo (1987: 283) refers to *all* the unattributed verses as anonymous, implying reservations regarding which are by Sōchō.

187. Kidō (1984: 342–43) argues that it was originally a longer sequence because the first verse sounds like a hokku and because of certain variations in verse order between manuscripts. The *GSRJ* ms. indicates there is a lacuna after the second verse, implying that the editor believed the work was originally a long sequence. Oda Takuji (1947: 79) concurs. Kidō further theorizes, however, that the long sequence was composed along the lines of a maekuzuke session, with various poets contributing tsukeku to each previous verse, the best of which was then selected.

188. Proponents of the maekuzuke alternative include Kaneko (1987: 365) and Harada (1979: 406).

189. Bakhtin 1984.

190. Suzuki Tōzō 1965: 54.

191. For a table of the shared verses, see Horton 1989: 627–29.

192. Harada 1979: 406.

193. The couplet appears in *Shinsen inu tsukubashū* (Tōkyō Daigaku Toshokan ms., Suzuki Tōzō 1965: 62) with the maeku given as *oitsukan / oitsukan to ya / omouran*.

194. The maeku appears only once in *The Journal of Sōchō*, but the possibility of different points of view in the two tsukeku necessitates a recasting of the verse in English.

195. Sōchō's tsukeku does not appear in *Shinsen inu tsukubashū*.

196. Tani 1952: 62.

197. Harada 1979: 357–58.

198. Kaneko 1987: 406.

199. This couplet appears in *Shinsen inu tsukubashū* (Tōkyō Daigaku Toshokan ms., Suzuki Tōzō 1965: 12), no. 4.

200. Suzuki Tōzō 1965: 12.

201. Harada 1979: 358.

202. Kimura and Iguchi 1988: 120–21.

203. Harada 1979: 358.

204. Tani 1952: 62.

205. Harada 1979: 358.

206. I am indebted to Kaneko Kinjirō for this interpretation, made in a personal communication.

207. Keene 1977: 277.

208. Kimura and Iguchi 1988: 294.

209. Kimura and Iguchi 1988: 196, 294.

210. Translation after Keene 1977: 276.

211. Shimazu 1969: 179–80.

212. Tani 1952: 66.

213. Harada 1979: 360–61.

214. *Yashima* 205.

215. One case in point is the tsukeku about the Kōya priest and the girl (*JS* no. 134), for which Sōchō explicitly took credit.

216. One modern compendium of haikai waka, *Kyōka taikan* (2: 27–29), includes forty-four verses from Sōchō's journal, with forty-one by Sōchō himself. But the total number may be closer to sixty.

217. Saigyō included in his *Kikigakishū* collection (nos. 165–77) a series of thirteen *tawabure uta* (playful poems); Reizei Tamemori may have been the composer of *Kyōka sake hyakushu*; and Nijō Yoshimoto is said to have composed *Mochi sake utaawase*, a short story that includes an entire kyōka poem competition. See also Fukuda 1972b and Kubota Shōichirō 1977.

218. *Kingon wakaawase* of 1493 and *Eishō gonen kyōkaawase* of 1508 are particularly well known.

219. Another important example is Dōkō (or Dōkyō), who included eleven haikaika among the approximately 350 verses in his travel diary, *Kaikoku zakki*, of 1486 (a volume once attributed to Sōgi). The kyōka in *Kaikoku zakki* are also found in *Kyōka taikan* (2: 14), and some of those in *Saishōsō* are found in *Kyōka taikan* as well (id. 2: 15–25). For more information on the unorthodox poetry in these two works, see Takahashi Yoshio 1984 and Takahashi Kiichi 1975.

220. Verses labeled haikai in the journal are the following: *JS* no. 16, *JS* no. 156, *JS* no. 169, *JS* no. 170, *JS* no. 194, *JS* no. 363, *JS* no. 430, *JS* no. 432, *JS* no. 442, *JS* no. 556, *JS* no. 566, and once to indicate the verse is *not* haikai, *JS* no. 484. For a preliminary study of these verses see Inazawa 1973.

221. Inoue 1971: 282.

222. Iguchi, in Kimura and Iguchi 1988: 249–50.

223. *Genji monogatari* 3: 149. Translation after Seidensticker 1976, 1: 298.

224. Shōtetsu, *Nagusamegusa* 584.

225. *Genji monogatari* 1: 106.

Epilogue

1. Arakida Morihira, *Nikonshū* 2: 175.

2. *Sanetakakōki* 1532:5:6 (8: 326).

3. Cf. JS no. 339.

4. *Tōgoku kikō* 827. Sōboku elegantly responds to Sōchō's poem by saying that Brushwood Cottage has indeed now become a thing of the past as Sōchō had foreseen, and he evokes the ephemerality of the bridge, and of the lives of Sōchō and himself, by re-

ferring to the floating bridge of dreams (*yume no ukihashi*), title of the last chapter of *Genji monogatari*. His phrase *mukashi nagara* evokes the Bridge of Nagara in Sōchō's verse, as well as *mukashinagara no yume* (dreams from the past).

5. *Jōha Fujimi michi no ki* 799.

6. *Jōha Fujimi michi no ki* 791. The translation is taken from Keene 1989: 248–49. Keene also translated a later section of the work (793) in which Jōha encounters an old friend of Sōchō: "I have an acquaintance who lives near the Seiken Temple, the lay priest Okitsu Bokuun. He related that long ago he was loved by Sōchō and said that he still carried with him the love letters he had received. His story made me feel as if the fragrance of the sleeves of his ink-dyed robes had penetrated me" (Keene 1989: 249). The identity of Bokuun is unclear, but Sōchō had several friends among the Okitsu family, and he mentions them a number of times in his journal, which gives support to the anecdote. The Saiokuji portrait of Sōchō that illustrates the translation of *The Journal of Sōchō* that accompanies this volume indeed shows him with light-green robes covered by a black cloak.

7. For a translation, see Appendix B.

8. Takeuchi Gengen'ichi, *Haika kijindan, Zoku haika kijindan* 21, 213.

9. Bakhtin 1981: 418.

10. See Bloom 1973.

11. Harada Yoshioki (1979: 399ff) has observed that the style of Sōchō's diaries in general is much closer than that of Sōgi's to the travel writing of Bashō. The relationship between between *The Journal of Sōchō* and early Edo travel literature invites further research.

12. The prescription is found in Hattori Dohō's record of Bashō's teachings, entitled *Sanzōshi* (Three Books, 1702) (546).

13. Harada 1979: 399.

14. Narugami Katsumi (1943: 211), for example, in his ground-breaking study of travel literature, writes the following about *The Journal of Sōchō*: "This is travel writing (*kikōbun*), but it cannot be called travel literature *kikō bungei*. It is a chronicle (*kiroku*), not a literary work. But it is a perfect source for investigating the nature of the diarist's journeys."

15. Tani Hiroshi (1952) whose opinions about Sōchō's haikai were quoted at length in Chapter Four, is one such example.

Appendix B

1. Yoshimoto is an error for Yoshitada.

2. Compare *Sōchō hyakuban rengaawase* (86), where Sanetaka equates Sōchō with the famous *Shinkokinshū* poet Jichin (Jien; see p. 231).

3. This is a standard metaphor for living a rustic life. A related phrase appears in Sōkyū, *Miyako no tsuto* (348).

4. *Hokkoku no michi no ki* is most likely another name for *The Journal of Sōchō*, taken from its first line.

5. This is an error for the fifth year of Kyōroku (1532). *Sōchō Kojiden*, Kurokawa Dōyū's kanbun account, likewise gives this incorrect date.

6. Current opinion holds that Sōchō did not study at Daigoji, but that his religious instructor in his early years did, a man Sōchō refers to as the Suruga Counselor (JS: 114).

7. Sōchō actually built his Brushwood Cottage in 1504 (the first year of Eishō) or 1506.

8. The poem is based on *Man'yōshū* 1: 19, which was read in Sōchō's day as follows:

somakata no	My love holds my eye
hayashihajime no	fast as a robe holds color
sanohagi no	made from bush clover
kinu ni tsukunasu	growing straight as timber
me ni tsuku waga se	and just beginning to flourish.

Sōchō also uses the poem as a honka for JS no. 200.

Bibliography

Abbreviations are listed on pp. xii–xiii. Unless otherwise indicated, all publishers are located in Tokyo. Multiple works by modern authors are listed chronologically, but multiple works by premodern authors appear alphabetically. *Renga* sequences are listed alphabetically, but chronologically within each era name. For the reader's convenience, alternate published manuscripts of select titles are provided in addition to the specific versions used in this text (the latter are in each case cited first). Rare, unprinted manuscripts are cited together with the published work that makes reference to them.

Abe Yoshio 阿部吉雄 et al., eds. 1976. *Rōshi, Sōshi* 老子・荘子 (C: *Laozi, Zhuangzi*). Vol. 7 of *Shinshaku kanbun taikei*.

Abutsu-ni 阿仏尼. *Izayoi nikki*. Ed. Fukuda Hideichi 福田秀一. In Fukuda et al. 1990: 179–209. See also *Izayoi nikki*, ed. Iwasa Miyoko 岩佐美代子, in Nagasaki et al. 1994: 265–304 and *Journal of the Sixteenth-Night Moon*, in McCullough 1990: 340–76.

Adachi Shūtarō 足立鍬太郎. 1931. *Imagawa Ujichika to Jukeini* 今川氏親と寿桂尼. Shizuoka: Yajimaya.

Akimoto Taiji 秋本太二. 1984. "Imagawa Ujichika no Tōtōmi keiryaku" 今川氏親の遠江軽略. In Arimitsu 1984: 113–35.

Alsop, Joseph. 1982. *Rare Art Traditions: The History of Art Collecting and Its Linked Phenomena*. New York: Harper and Row.

Amino Yoshihiko 網野善彦. 1977. "Chūsei ni okeru muen no igi" 中世における無縁の意義. *Chūsei bungaku* 22 (May): 11–21.

Anrakuan Sakuden 安楽庵策伝. 1986. *Seisuishō* 醒睡笑. Ed. Suzuki Tōzō 鈴木棠三. 2 vols. Iwanami Bunko.

Arai Eizō 新井英蔵. 1976. "Sakuramachi Jōkō chokufū Manjuinzō *Kokin denju* hitohako" 桜町上皇勅封曼殊院蔵古今伝授一箱. *Kokugo kokubun* 45.7 (July): 43 56.

Araki Yoshio 荒木良雄. 1941. *Sōgi* 宗祇. Sōgensha.

Bibliography

———. 1947. *Chūsei Nihon no shomin bungaku* 中世日本の庶民文学. Osaka: Shin Nihon Tosho.

Arakida Morihira 荒木田守平, comp. *Nikonshū* 二根集. Ed. Okuno Jun'ichi 奥野純一. Vols. 335 and 343 of *KB*.

Arakida Moritake 荒木田守武. *Gatten no ku* 合点の句. In Yamada 1951: 83–123.

———. *Moritake senku* 守武千句. See Iida 1977.

———. *Sōchō tsuizen senku* 宗長追善千句. In Yamada 1951: 55–82.

Arimitsu Yūgaku 有光有学, ed. 1984. *Imagawashi no kenkyū* 今川氏の研究. Vol. 11 of Nagahara 1983–85.

Arnesen, Peter Judd. 1979. *The Medieval Japanese Daimyo: The Ouchi Family's Rule of Suō and Nagato*. New Haven: Yale University Press.

Arntzen, Sonja, trans. 1986. *Ikkyū and the Crazy Cloud Anthology*. University of Tokyo Press.

Asukai Masayasu 飛鳥井雅康. *Fuji rekiranki* 富士歴覧記. In *GSRJ* 18: 621–26.

Auerbach, Erich. 1968. *Mimesis: The Representation of Reality in Western Literature*. Trans. Willard R. Trask. Princeton: Princeton University Press.

Bakhtin, Michael M. 1981. *The Dialogic Imagination: Four Essays by M. M. Bakhtin*. Trans. Caryl Emerson and Michael Holquist. Ed. Michael Holquist. Austin: University of Texas Press.

———. 1984. *Rabelais and His World*. Trans. Helene Iswolsky. Bloomington: Indiana University Press.

Barthes, Roland. 1977. "An Introduction to the Structural Analysis of Narrative." In *Image, Music, Text*, trans. Stephen Heath, pp. 79–124. New York: Hill and Wang.

Bashō 芭蕉. *Sanseizu no san* 三聖図讃. In Imoto, Hori, and Muramatsu 1972: 538–39.

Becker, Howard S. 1982. *Art Worlds*. Berkeley: University of California Press.

Berkowitz, Alan. 1989. "Patterns of Reclusion in Early and Early Medieval China: A Study of the Formulation of the Practice of Reclusion in China and its Portrayal." Diss. University of Washington.

Berry, Mary Elizabeth. 1982. *Hideyoshi*. Cambridge, Mass.: Harvard University Press.

———. 1994. *The Culture of Civil War in Kyoto*. Berkeley: University of California Press.

Birch, Cyril, ed. 1965. *Anthology of Chinese Literature from Early Times to the Fourteenth Century*. New York: Grove Press.

Biyanlu 碧岩録. See Cleary and Cleary 1992.

Bloom, Harold. 1973. *The Anxiety of Influence: A Theory of Poetry*. New York: Oxford University Press.

Blue Cliff Record, The. See Cleary and Cleary 1992.

Bokusai 墨斎 (Motsurin Jōtō 没倫紹等). *The Chronicle of Ikkyū*. In Sanford 1981: 69–117.

Bontō 梵灯. *Bontōanshu hentōsho* 梵灯庵主返答書. *ZGSRJ* 17b: 1041–55.

Botanka Shōhaku 牡丹花肖柏. See Shōhaku.

Bourdieu, Pierre. 1984. *Distinction: A Social Critique of the Judgement of Taste.* Trans. Richard Nice. Cambridge, Mass.: Harvard University Press.

Bowring, Richard, trans. 1982. *Murasaki Shikibu: Her Diary and Poetic Memoirs.* Princeton: Princeton University Press.

Brazell, Karen, trans. 1973. *The Confessions of Lady Nijō.* Stanford: Stanford University Press.

Brewster, Jennifer, trans. 1977. *The Emperor Horikawa Diary: Sanuki no Suke Nikki.* Honolulu: University of Hawaii Press.

Brower, Robert, trans. 1985. "Fujiwara Teika's *Maigetsushō.*" *Monumenta Nipponica* 40.4 (Winter): 399–425.

———, trans. 1987. "The Foremost Style of Poetic Composition: Fujiwara Tameie's *Eiga no ittei.*" *Monumenta Nipponica* 42.4 (Winter): 391–429.

———, trans. 1992. *Conversations with Shōtetsu.* With an Introduction and Notes by Steven D. Carter. Ann Arbor: Center for Japanese Studies, The University of Michigan.

Brower, Robert, and Earl Miner. 1961. *Japanese Court Poetry.* Stanford: Stanford University Press.

Bruss, Elizabeth W. 1976. *Autobiographical Acts: The Changing Situation of a Literary Genre.* Baltimore: The Johns Hopkins University Press.

Burke, Peter. 1978. *Popular Culture in Early Modern Europe.* New York: Harper and Row.

Carter, Steven D. 1981. "*Waka* in the Age of *Renga.*" *Monumenta Nipponica* 36.4 (Winter): 425–44.

———, trans. 1983. *Three Poets at Yuyama.* Japan Research Monograph 4. Berkeley: Institute of East Asian Studies / Center for Japanese Studies, University of California.

———. 1984. "A Lesson in Failure: Linked-Verse Contests in Medieval Japan." *Journal of the American Oriental Society* 104.4 (Oct.–Dec.): 727–37.

———. 1987a. *The Road to Komatsubara: A Classical Reading of the Renga Hyakuin.* Cambridge, Mass.: Council on East Asian Studies, Harvard University.

———, trans. 1987b. "Sōgi in the East Country: *Shirakawa kikō.*" *Monumenta Nipponica* 42.2 (Summer): 167–209.

———. 1988. "Mixing Memories: Linked Verse and the Fragmentation of the Court Heritage." *Harvard Journal of Asiatic Studies* 48.1 (June): 5–45.

———, trans. 1989. *Waiting for the Wind: Thirty-Six Poets of Japan's Late Medieval Age.* New York: Columbia University Press.

———, trans. 1991. *Traditional Japanese Poetry: An Anthology.* Stanford: Stanford University Press.

———, ed. 1993. *Literary Patronage in Late Medieval Japan.* Michigan Papers in Japanese Studies. Ann Arbor: Center for Japanese Studies, The University of Michigan.

Chaki meibutsushū 茶器名物集. See Yamanoue Sōji.

Chance, Linda H. 1990. "An Aesthetics of Formlessness: Kenkō's 'Tsurezuregusa' and the *Zuihitsu* Genre of Japanese Prose." Diss. University of California, Los Angeles.

Chapman, R. W., ed. 1952. *The Letters of Samuel Johnson*. 3 vols. Oxford: Clarendon Press.

Chikuba kyōginshū 竹馬狂吟集. In Kimura and Iguchi 1988: 9–115.

Chikurinshō. See Sōgi, *Chikurinshō*.

Childs, Margaret H. 1980. "Chigo monogatari: Love Stories or Buddhist Sermons?" *Monumenta Nipponica* 35.2 (Summer): 127–51.

———. 1985. "*Kyōgen-kigo*: Love Stories as Buddhist Sermons." *Japanese Journal of Religious Studies* 12.1 (Mar.): 91–104.

———, trans. 1991. *Rethinking Sorrow: Revelatory Tales of Medieval Japan*. Ann Arbor: Center for Japanese Studies, The University of Michigan.

Cleary, Thomas, and J. C. Cleary, trans. 1992. *The Blue Cliff Record*. Boston: Shambala Publications.

Cogan, Thomas J., trans. 1987. *The Tale of the Soga Brothers*. Tokyo: University of Tokyo Press. See also *Soga monogatari*.

Collcutt, Martin. 1981. *Five Mountains: The Rinzai Zen Monastic Institution in Medieval Japan*. Cambridge, Mass.: Council on East Asian Studies, Harvard University.

———. 1990. "Zen and the *Gozan*." In Yamamura 1990b: 583–652.

Covell, Jon Carter, in collaboration with Abbot Sobin Yamada. 1980. *Unraveling Zen's Red Thread: Ikkyū's Controversial Way*. Elizabeth, N.J. and Seoul: Hollym International.

Cranston, Edwin, trans. 1969. *The Izumi Shikibu Diary: A Romance of the Heian Court*. Cambridge, Mass.: Harvard University Press.

Davis, David L. 1974. "*Ikki* in Late Medieval Japan." In John W. Hall and Jeffrey Mass, eds., *Medieval Japan*, pp. 221–47. New Haven: Yale University Press.

Dobbins, James C. 1989. *Jōdo Shinshū: Shin Buddhism in Medieval Japan*. Bloomington: Indiana University Press.

Dōkō (or Dōkyō) 道興. *Kaikoku zakki* 廻国雑記. In *GSRJ* 18: 678–715.

Dokushi biyō 読史備要. 1978. Ed. Tōkyō Daigaku Shiryō Hensanjo. Kōdansha.

Drake, Christopher. 1992. "The Collision of Traditions in Saikaku's Haikai." *Harvard Journal of Asiatic Studies* 52.1 (June): 5–75.

Eakin, Paul John. 1985. *Fictions in Autobiography: Studies in the Art of Self-Invention*. Princeton: Princeton University Press.

Easthope, Anthony. 1991. *Literary into Cultural Studies*. London and New York: Routledge.

Eikyū hyakushu 永久百首. In *KT* 4: 248–63.

Eishō gonen kyōkaawase 永正五年狂歌合. In *Kyōka taikan* 1: 39–42.

Elbaz, Robert. 1983. *The Changing Nature of the Self: A Critical Study of the Autobiographical Discourse*. Iowa City, Iowa: University of Iowa Press.

Elison, George, and Bardwell L. Smith, eds. 1981. *Warlords, Artists, and Commoners: Japan in the Sixteenth Century*. Honolulu: University of Hawaii Press.

Endō Tetsuo 遠藤哲夫, and Ichikawa Yasushi 市川安司, eds. 1976. *Sōshi* 荘子 (C: *Zhuangzi*). Vol. 8 of *Shinshaku kanbun taikei*.

Etō Yasusada 江藤保定. 1952. "Sōgi no tabi." *Kokugo to kokubungaku* 338 (June): 39–49.

———. 1957. "Sōgi no haikai to shominsei" 宗祇の俳諧と庶民性. *Chūsei bungaku* 3: 6–9.

———. 1967. *Sōgi no kenkyū*. Kazama Shobō.

Fiévé, Nicolas. 1996. *L'architecture et la ville du Japon ancien*. Paris: Éditions Maisonneuve & Larose.

Fothergill, Robert A. 1974. *Private Chronicles: A Study of English Diaries*. London: Oxford University Press.

Fuboku wakashō 夫木和歌抄. Comp. Fujiwara Nagakiyo 藤原長清. In *KT* 2: 477–858.

Fūga wakashū 風雅和歌集. In *KT* 1: 554–99.

Fujii Manabu 藤井學. 1979. *Ikkyū Sōjun: hankotsu to fūkyō ni ikita zensō* 一休宗純―反骨と風狂に生きた禅僧. Heibonsha.

Fujioka Tadaharu 藤岡忠美, Nakano Kōichi 中野幸一, Inukai Kiyoshi 犬養廉, and Ishii Fumio 石井文夫, eds. 1971. *Izumi Shikibu nikki, Murasaki Shikibu nikki, Sarashina nikki, Sanukinosuke nikki* 和泉式部日記・紫式部日記・更級日記・讃岐典侍日記. Vol. 18 of *NKBZ*.

Fujiwara Akihira 藤原明衡. *Shinsarugakuki* 新猿楽記. Ed. Ōsone Shōsuke 大曽根章介. In Ōsone 1979: 133–52.

Fujiwara Kiyosuke 藤原清輔. 1976. *Fukurozōshi* 袋草紙. Eds. Ozawa Masao 小沢正夫 et al. 2 vols. Hanawa Shoten.

Fujiwara Masayoshi 藤原正義. 1983. "Sōgi no tabi." *Bungaku* 51.5 (May): 66–74.

———. 1984. *Sōgi josetsu* 宗祇序説. Kazama Shobō.

Fujiwara Norikane 藤原範兼. *Godaishū utamakura* 五代集歌枕. In *NKT bekkan* 1: 302–465.

Fujiwara Shunzei 藤原俊成. *Korai fūteishō* 古来風体抄. In Hisamatsu 1934: 7 158.

Fujiwara Tameaki 藤原為顕. *Chikuenshō* 竹園抄. In *NKT* 3: 410–28.

Fujiwara Tameie 藤原為家. *Eiga ittei* 詠歌一体. In Hisamatsu 1934: 196–216.

Fujiwara Teika 藤原定家. *Eiga taigai* 詠歌大概. In Hisamatsu 1934: 188–89. See also Sato and Watson 1981: 202–04 and Tsunoda, de Bary, and Keene 1958: 183–84.

———. *Maigetsushō* 毎月抄. In Hisamatsu 1934: 172–87. See also Brower 1985.

———. *Meigetsuki* 明月記. See Imagawa Fumio 1977–79.

Fujiwara Yoshitsune. See Gokyōgoku Yoshitsune.

Fukuda Hideichi 福田秀一. 1972a. *Chūsei waka shi no kenkyū*. Kadokawa Shoten.

———. 1972b. "Gyōgetsubō Tamemori to sono *Kyōka sake hyakushu*" 暁月房為守とその『狂歌酒百首』. In *Chūsei wakashi no kenkyū* 中世和歌史の研究, pp. 344–80. Kadokawa Shoten.

———. 1975. *Chūsei bungaku ronkō*. Meiji Shoin.

Fukuda Hideichi, and Herbert Plutschow. 1975. *Nihon kikō bungaku benran* 日本紀行文学便覧. Musashino Shoin.

Fukuda Hideichi et al., eds. 1990. *Chūsei nikki kikōshū* 中世日記紀行集. Vol. 51 of *SNKBT*.

Fukui Kyūzō 福井久蔵, ed. 1938. *Minase sangin hyōshaku* 水無瀬三吟評釈. Mizuho Shoin.

———. 1969. *Renga no shiteki kenkyū* 連歌の史的研究. Yūseidō.

Furokuki. See *Imagawaki*

Fusō shūyōshū 扶桑拾葉集. 1898. Ed. Tokugawa Mitsukuni 徳川光圀. 4 vols. Osaka: Shiyūkan.

Gans, Herbert J. 1974. *Popular Culture and High Culture*. New York: Basic Books.

Gatten, Aileen. 1977. "A Wisp of Smoke: Scent and Character in *The Tale of Genji*." *Monumenta Nipponica* 32.1 (Spring): 35–48.

Genji monogatari. 1964–75. Murasaki Shikibu. Ed. Tamagami Takuya 玉上琢彌. 10 vols. Kadokawa Shoten. See also Seidensticker 1976.

Genpei seisuiki 源平盛衰記. 1991. Eds. Ichiko Teiji et al. Miyai Shoten.

Gessonsai Sōseki 月村斎宗碩. See Sōseki.

Ginzburg, Carlo. 1992. *The Cheese and the Worms*. Trans. John and Anne Tedeschi. New York: Penguin Books.

Goffman, Erving. 1959. *The Presentation of Self in Everyday Life*. New York: Doubleday Anchor Books.

Gokashiwabara 後柏原. *Hakugyokushū* 柏玉集. In *ST* 6: 692–757.

Gokyōgoku Yoshitsune 後京極良経. *Akishino gesseishū* 秋篠月清集. In *KT* 3: 633–56.

Goodwin, Janet. 1994. *Alms and Vagabonds: Buddhist Temples and Popular Patronage in Medieval Japan*. Honolulu: University of Hawaii Press.

Gosen wakashū 後撰和歌集. In Kubota Jun and Kawamura 1986: 55–122.

Goshirakawa 後白河, comp. 1993. *Ryōjin hishō* 梁塵秘抄. Eds. Kobayashi Yoshinori 小林芳規 and Takeishi Akio 武石影夫. Vol. 56 of *SNKBT*. See also Kim 1994.

Goshūi wakashū 後拾遺和歌集. 1983. Ed. Fujimoto Kazue 藤本一恵. 4 vols. Kōdansha.

Greenblatt, Stephen. 1980. *Renaissance Self-Fashioning: From More to Shakespeare*. Chicago and London: The University of Chicago Press.

Grossberg, Kenneth A., and Kanamoto Nobuhisa, trans. 1981. *The Laws of the Muromachi Bakufu*. Sophia University Press.

Guhishō. 愚秘抄. In *NKT* 4: 291–312.

Gunsho ruijū 群書類従. 1959–60. Ed. Hanawa Hokiichi 塙保己一. 30 vols. Zoku Gunsho Ruijū Kanseikai.

Gusdorf, George. "Conditions and Limits of Autobiography." Trans. James Olney. In Olney 1980: 28–48.

Gyokuyō wakashū 玉葉和歌集. In *KT* 1: 421–81.

Haga Kōshirō 芳賀幸四郎. 1948. *Kinsei bunka no keisei to dentō*. Kawade Shobō.

———. 1960. *Sanjōnishi Sanetaka* 三条西実隆. Yoshikawa Kōbunkan.

Hall, John Whitney. 1981. "Japan's Sixteenth-Century Revolution." In Elison and Smith 1981: 7–21.

———, ed. 1991. *The Cambridge History of Japan, Volume 4: Early Modern Japan*. Cambridge: Cambridge University Press.

Hall, John Whitney, and Toyoda Takeshi, eds. 1977. *Japan in the Muromachi Age*. Berkeley: University of California Press.

Hamachiyo Kiyoshi 浜千代清. 1961. "*Arakidashū* ni tsuite." *Joshidai kokubun* 21 (May): 56-62.

Hara Katsurō 原勝郎. 1978. *Higashiyama jidai ni okeru ichishinshin no seikatsu* 東山時代に於ける一縉紳の生活. Kōdansha.

Harada Yoshioki 原田芳起. 1979. *Tankyū Nihon bungaku: chūko, chūsei hen* 探究日本文学一中古・中世編. Kazama Shobō.

Hare, Thomas Blenman. 1989. "Reading Kamo no Chōmei." *Harvard Journal of Asiatic Studies* 49.1 (June): 173-228.

Harries, Phillip. 1980. "Personal Poetry Collections: Their Origin and Development Through the Heian Period." *Monumenta Nipponica* 36.3 (Autumn): 299-317.

Hashimoto Fumio 橋本不美男, and Takizawa Sadao 滝沢貞夫, eds. 1977. *Horikawain ontoki hyakushu waka to sono kenkyū: kochū, sakuin hen* 堀河院御時百首和歌とその研究一古注, 索引編. Collated ed. (*kōhon* 校本). Kasama Shoin.

Hattori Dohō 服部土芳. *Sanzōshi* 三冊子. Ed. Kuriyama Riichi 栗山理一. In Ijichi, Omote, and Kuriyama 1973: 517-629.

Hayakawa Jinzō 早川甚三. 1943. *Kōdō* 香道. Yakumo Shorin.

Hayashiya Tatsusaburō 林屋辰三郎, ed. 1986. *Kodai chūsei geijutsuron* 古代中世芸術論. Vol. 23 of *Nihon shisō taikei*. Iwanami Shoten.

Heike monogatari. 1959-60. Eds. Takagi Ichinosuke 高木一之助 et al. Vols. 33-34 of *NKBT*. See also McCullough 1988.

Higuchi Hideo 樋口秀雄. 1954. "Jūyō bunkazai Botanka Shōhaku gazō to sono san" 重要文化財牡丹花肖柏画像とその讃. *Renga haikai kenkyū* 7-8 (June): 56-58.

Hirano Akio 平野明夫. 1987. "Taigen Sūfu Sessai no chii to kengen" 太源崇孚雪斎の地位と権限. In *SI* 10: 191-207.

Hisamatsu Sen'ichi 久松潜一. 1934. *Chūsei karonshū*. Iwanami Shoten.

———. 1948. "Ushin renga to waka no ushintei to no kankei" 有心連歌と和歌の有心躰との関係. *Nihon Gakushiin kiyō* 6.2-3 (Nov.): 147-55.

———. 1976. *Nihon bungaku hyōron shi: kodai, chūsei hen*. Vol. 1 of *Nihon bungaku hyōron shi*. Rev. ed. 5 vols. Shibundō.

Hoff, Frank, trans. 1982. *Like a Boat in a Storm: A Century of Song in Japan*. Hiroshima: Bunka Hyoron Publishing Company.

Hokekyō 法華経. 1976. Eds. Sakamoto Yukio 坂本幸雄 and Iwamoto Yutaka 岩本裕. 3 vols. Iwanami Shoten.

Holquist, Michael. 1990. *Dialogism: Bakhtin and his World*. London: Routledge.

Hori Akira 堀暁. 1982. "Imagawashi jūshin no kon'in kankei" 今川氏重臣の婚姻関係. In *SI* 6: 115-36.

Horton, H. Mack. 1989. "Poetry in Motion: The Linked-Verse Master Sōchō and His Journal, *Sōchō shuki*." Diss. University of California, Berkeley.

———. 1993a. "Japanese Spirit and Chinese Learning: Scribes and Storytellers in Premodern Japan." In Jonathan Boyarin, ed., *The Ethnography of Reading*, pp. 156–79. Berkeley: University of California Press.

———. 1993b. "Renga Unbound: Performative Aspects of Japanese Linked Verse." *Harvard Journal of Asiatic Studies* 53.2 (Dec.): 443–512.

———. 1993c. "Saiokuken Sōchō and Imagawa Daimyō Patronage." In Carter 1993: 105–61.

Hosoi Yasuko 細井泰子. 1959. "Botanka Shōhaku kenkyū" 牡丹花肖柏研究. *Tōkyō Joshi Daigaku Nihon bungaku kenkyūkai* 13 (Nov.): 34–52.

Hosokawa Yūsai 細川幽斎. *Jiteiki* (or *Niteiki*) 耳底記. Transcribed by Karasumaru Mitsuhiro 烏丸光広. In *NKT* 6: 142–208.

Hurvitz, Leon, trans. 1976. *Scripture of the Lotus Blossom of the Fine Dharma* (*The Lotus Sutra*). New York: Columbia University Press.

Hyakunin isshu. 百人一首. Comp. Fujiwara Teika. In *KT* 5: 933–34. See also "One Hundred Poems by One Hundred Poets," in Carter 1991: 203–38.

Ichijō Kaneyoshi (or Kanera) 一条兼良. *Renju gappekishū* 連珠合璧集. In Kidō 1972–, 1: 25–202. See also *Renju gappekishū*, in *ZGSRJ* 17b: 1134–204.

Ichikawa Hakugen 市川白弦. 1982. *Ikkyū: ransei ni ikita zensha* 一休—乱世に生きた禅者. Nihon Hōsō Shuppan Kyōkai.

Ichiko Teiji 市古貞次, et al. 1983–85. *Nihon koten bungaku daijiten*. 6 vols. Iwanami Shoten.

Ii Haruki 井伊春樹. 1980. *Genji monogatari chūshakushi no kenkyū* 源氏物語注釈史の研究. Ōfūsha.

Iida Shōichi 飯田正一, ed. 1977. *Moritake senkuchū* 守武千句注. Furukawa Shobō.

Iio (or Inō) Sōgi 飯尾宗祇. See Sōgi.

Ijichi Tetsuo 伊地知鉄男. 1936. "Sōchōden kōsetsu" 宗長伝考説. *Renga to haikai* 4 (Nov.): 14–25.

———. 1943. *Sōgi* 宗祇. Seigosha.

———. 1952. "Sōchō no kushū *Kabekusa* sono ta ni tsuite no oboegaki" 宗長の句集『壁草』その他についての覚書. *Kokubungaku kenkyū* 7 (Oct.): 70–83.

———. 1953. "Waka, renga, haikai." *Shoryōbu kiyō* 3 (March): 1–17. Reprinted in Ozaki Yūjirō, Shimazu, and Satake 1985: 277–94.

———. 1955. "Sōgi, Sōchō." In *Chūsei bungaku*, pp. 281–92. Vol. 3 of Origuchi Shinobu 折口信夫 et al., eds., *Nihon bungaku kōza*. Kawade Shobō.

———. 1968. *Rengashū*. Vol. 39 of *NKBT*.

———. 1973. "Sōchō no *Azumaji no tsuto* shohonkō" 宗長の『東路の津登』諸本考. In *Nagasawa Sensei koki kinen toshogaku ronshū* 長沢先生古希記念図書学論集, pp. 255–74. Sanseidō.

———, ed. 1975. *Renga hyakuinshū*. Facsimiles of sequences in *Renga shūsho* 連歌集書 (Seikadō Bunko 静嘉堂文庫). Kyūko Shoin.

———, ed. 1985. *Rengaronshū*. 2 vols. Iwanami Shoten.

Ijichi Tetsuo, Omote Akira 表章, and Kuriyama Riichi 栗山理一, eds. 1973. *Rengaronshū, nōgakuronshū, haironshū*. Vol. 51 of *NKBZ*.

Ijichi Tetsuo et al., eds. 1957. *Haikai daijiten*. Meiji Shoin.

Ikkyū shokoku monogatari 一休諸国物語. 1976. In Vol. 3 of Mutō Sadao 武藤禎夫 and Oka Masahiko 岡雅彦, eds., *Hanashibon taikei* 噺本体系, pp. 247-318. Tōkyōdō.

Ikkyū Sōjun 一休宗純. 1976. *Kyōunshū, Kyōunshū shishū, Jikaishū* 狂雲集・狂雲詩集・自戒集. Ed. Nakamoto Tamaki 中本環. Vol. 5 of *Shinsen Nihon koten bunko*. Gendai Shichōsha. See also Arntzen 1986.

Ikkyūbanashi 一休咄. Ibid., pp. 3-62. See also Oka 1995.

Imagawa Fumio 今川文雄. 1977-79. *Kundoku Meigetsuki* 訓読明月記. 6 vols. Kawade Shobō Shinsha.

Imagawa kafu 今川家譜. In *ZGSRJ* 21a: 141-60.

Imagawa Norimasa 今川範政, attrib. *Fuji goran nikki* 富士御覧日記. In Shirai 1976: 162-68.

Imagawa Ryōshun 今川了俊. *Imagawajō* 今川状. In Ozawa Tomio 1985: 238-42.

———. *Rakusho roken* 落書露顕. In *SKGSRJ* 13: 407-24.

Imagawaki 今川記. In *ZGSRJ* 21a: 216-51.

Imagawaki (Furokuki 富麓記). In *ZGSRJ* 21a: 161-215.

Imoto Nōichi 井本農一. 1974. *Sōgi: rōman to yūshū* 宗祇―浪漫と優愁. Vol. 5 of *Nihon no tabibito*. 15 vols. Tankōsha.

Imoto Nōichi, Hori Nobuo 堀信夫, and Muramatsu Tomotsugu 村松友次, eds. 1972. *Matsuo Bashōshū*. Vol. 41 of *NKBZ*.

Inazawa Yoshiaki 稲沢好章. 1973. "*Sōchō shuki* ni miru renga sakusha no haikai shikō ni tsuite"『宗長手記』にみる連歌作者の俳諧嗜好について. *Kokugo to kokubungaku* 50.12 (Dec.): 50-65.

Inō (or Iio) Sōgi 飯尾宗祇. See Sōgi.

Inoue Muneo 井上宗雄. 1969. "Nanbokuchō, Muromachi jidai no waka." In vol. 6 (*Chūseihen* 2) of Zenkoku Daigaku Kokugo Kokubun Gakkai, ed., *Kōza Nihon bungaku*, pp. 25-60. Sanseidō.

———. 1971. "Chūsei no kyōka" 中世の狂歌. *Rikkyō Jogakuin Tanki Daigaku kiyō* 3: 273-88.

———. 1987. *Chūsei kadanshi no kenkyū: Muromachi kōki* 中世歌壇史の研究―室町後期. Rev. ed. Meiji Shoin.

Inu tsukubashū 犬つくば集. See *Shinsen inu tsukubashū*.

Ise monogatari. 1984. Ed. Ishida Jōji 石田譲二. Kadokawa Shoten. See also McCullough 1968.

Ishida Yoshisada 石田吉貞. 1955. "Sōan bungakuron" 草庵文学論. *Kokubungaku kaishaku to kanshō* 234 (Nov.): 13-17.

———. 1958. "Chūsei no nikki, kikō bungaku." Vol. 4 of *Iwanami kōza Nihon bungaku shi*. Iwanami Shoten.

———, ed. 1960. *Shinkokin wakashū zenchūkai*. Yūseidō.

———. 1965. "Chūsei kikō bungaku no mondaiten" 中世紀行文学の問題点. *Bungaku gogaku* 37 (Fall): 16-22.

———. 1969. *Inja no bungaku* 隠者の文学. Hanawa Shobō.

———. 1970. *Chūsei sōan no bungaku* 中世草庵の文学. Rev. ed. (*kaitei* 改訂). Kitazawa Tosho Shuppan.

Issunbōshi 一寸法師. In Ōshima 1974: 394-402.

Itō Hiroyuki 伊藤博之 et al. 1976. *Chūsei no inja bungaku* 中世の隠者文学. Vol. 6 of *Shinpojiumu Nihon bungaku*. Gakuseisha.

Itō Kei 伊藤敬. 1969. "Muromachi kōki uta shoshi: Sanetaka, Mototsuna, Naritsugu, Muneaki, Sōgi, Dōken" 室町後期歌書誌―実隆・基綱・済継・統秋・宗祇・道堅. *Tomakomai Kōgyō Kōkō Senmon Gakkō kiyō* 4 (March): 116-34.

———. 1972. "Shinkei *Oi no kurigoto* shichū" 心敬『老のくりごと』私注. *Fuji Joshi Daigaku kokubungaku zasshi* 12 (Oct.): 72-97.

Iwashita Noriyuki 岩下紀之. 1976. "*Nachigomori* ni kansuru oboegaki" 『那智籠』に関する覚え書. *Renga haikai kenkyū* 51 (July): 1-8.

———. 1978. "*Sōchō shuki* no chosaku ito ni tsuite" 『宗長手記』の著作意図について. *Kokubungaku kenkyū* 65 (June): 13-23.

———. 1985. "*Oi no mimi* ni kansuru oboegaki" 『老耳』に関する覚え書. In Kaneko Kinjirō, ed., *Renga kenkyū no tenkai* 連歌研究の展開, pp. 303-28. Benseisha.

Iwashita Noriyuki, and Kishida Yoriko. 1978. "Honkoku Sōseki kaishō to Sōchō shōkushū shūsei" 翻刻宗碩回章と宗長小句集集成. In Ijichi Tetsuo, ed., *Chūsei bungaku: shiryō to ronkō* 中世文学―資料と論考, pp. 435-505. Kasama Shobō.

Izumi Shikibu nikki. Ed. Fujioka Tadaharu. In Fujioka, Nakano, Inukai, and Ishii 1971: 83-151. See also Cranston 1969.

Jōha 紹巴. *Jōha Amanohashidate kikō* 紹巴天橋立紀行. In Okuda Isao 奥田勲, "*Jōha Amanohashidate kikō* ni tsuite," *Kokubungakukō* 53 (May, 1970): 35-46.

———. *Jōha Fujimi michi no ki* 紹巴富士見道記. In *GSRJ* 18: 783-801.

———. *Renga kyōkun* 連歌教訓. In Ijichi 1985, 2: 261-85.

———. *Shihōshō* 至宝抄. In Ijichi 1985, 2: 231-59.

Johnson, David. 1985. "Communication, Class, and Consciousness in Late Imperial China." In David Johnson, Andrew J. Nathan, and Evelyn S. Rawsky, eds., *Popular Culture in Late Imperial China*, pp. 34-72. Berkeley: University of California Press.

Juntokuin 順徳院. *Yakumo mishō* 八雲御抄. In *NKT* 3: 9-91.

Kagerō nikki 蜻蛉日記. In Matsumura, Kimura, and Imuta 1973: 125-409. See also Seidensticker 1964.

Kai no kuni rekidaifu 甲斐国歴代譜. 1974. Vol. 2 of Kai Sōsho Kankōkai, ed., *Kai sōsho* 甲斐叢書, pp. 269-314. Daiichi Shobō.

Kaidōki 海道記. Ed. Tamai Kōsuke 玉井幸助. In Tamai and Ishida 1951: 59 139. See also *Kaidōki*, eds. Ōsone Shōsuke and Kubota Jun, in Fukuda et al., eds., 1990: 69-124 and *Kaidōki*, ed. Nagasaki Ken, in Nagasaki et al. 1994: 11-84.

Kamo no Chōmei 鴨長明. *Hōjōki* 方丈記. In Miki Sumito 三木紀人, ed., *Hōjōki, Hosshinshū*, pp. 13–39. Vol. 5 of *SNKS*. See also "An Account of My Hut," in McCullough 1990: 379–92.

———. *Hosshinshū*. Ibid., pp. 40–385. See also Ury 1972.

Kana mokuroku かな目録 (also known as *Imagawa kana mokuroku*). In *Imagawaki (Furokuki)*, pp. 204–13. See also Matsudaira Norimichi 1982 and Ozawa Seiichi 1977.

Kaneko Kinjirō 金子金治郎. 1965–72. "Kohaikai chūshaku" 古俳諧注釈. *Chūsei bungei* 32: 15–24; 33: 26–30; 34: 13–20; 37: 39–44; 41: 35–40; and 50: 1–28.

———. 1967. "Rengashi no raibaru ishiki" 連歌のライバル意識. *Kokubungaku kaishaku to kyōzai no kenkyū* 2.10 (Aug.): 88–92.

———. 1969. *Shinsen tsukubashū no kenkyū* 新撰筑波集の研究. Kazama Shobō.

———. 1971. "Renga sōshō no yukue" 連歌宗匠の行くえ. *Kokugakuin zasshi* 72.11 (Nov.): 104–16.

———. 1974. *Renga kochūshaku no kenkyū* 連歌古注釈の研究. Kadokawa Shoten.

———. 1976. *Sōgi tabi no ki shichū* 宗祇旅の記私注. Ōfūsha.

———. 1977a. "*Hokku kikigaki*" 発句聞書. In Kaneko 1977c: 10–46.

———. 1977b. *Rengashi Kensai den kō* 連歌師兼載伝考. Rev. ed. Ōfūsha.

———, ed. 1977c. *Renga to chūsei bungei*. Kadokawa Shoten.

———, ed. 1978–83. *Renga kichō bunken shūsei* 連歌貴重文献集成. 16 vols. Benseisha.

———, ed. 1979. *Renga kochūshakushū* 連歌古注釈集. Kadokawa Shoten.

———. 1982. *Shinkei no seikatsu to sakuhin* 心敬の生活と作品. Ōfūsha.

———. 1983. *Sōgi no seikatsu to sakuhin* 宗祇の生活と作品. Ōfūsha.

———. 1985a. "Sōgi no kichō" 宗祇の基調. *Chūsei bungaku* 30: 38–50.

———. 1985b. *Sōgi meisaku hyakuin chūshaku* 宗祇名作百韻注釈. Ōfūsha.

———. 1987. *Renga sōron* 連歌総論. Ōfūsha.

———. 1988. "Renga sakuhin no nintei" 連歌作品の認定. *Kokugo to Kokubungaku*, 65.12 (Dec.): 36–45.

———. 1990. *Rengashi to kikō* 連歌師と紀行. Ōfūsha.

———. 1993. "Sōgi and the Imperial House: One Model of Medieval Literary Patronage." Trans. H. Mack Horton. In Carter 1993: 63–93.

———. 1995. "Sōgi no chichi to haha to" 宗祇の父と母と. *Kokugo to kokubungaku* 72.7 (July): 30–46.

Kaneko Kinjirō, Nakamura Shunjō 中村俊定, and Teruoka Yasutaka 暉峻康隆, eds. 1974. *Renga haikaishū*. Vol. 32 of *NKBZ*.

Kaneko Kinjirō et al., eds. 1986. *Tōen Bunko mokuroku* 桃園文庫目録. Vol. 1. Tōkai Daigaku Fuzoku Toshokan.

Kanginshū 閑吟集. In Usuda and Shinma 1976: 353–472. See also *The Kanginshu*, in Hoff 1982: 29–131.

Kankyo no tomo 閑居の友. In *ZGSRJ* 32b: 483–524.

Bibliography

Karaki Junzō 唐木順蔵. 1982. "Sōchō oboegaki." Vol. 16 of *Karaki Junzō zenshū*, pp. 398-418. Chikuma Shobō.

Katagiri Yōichi 片桐洋一. 1969. *Ise monogatari no kenkyū*. Meiji Shoin.

———. 1983. *Utamakura utakotoba jiten* 歌枕歌ことば辞典. Kadokawa Shoten.

Katō, Eileen, trans. 1979. "Pilgrimage to Dazaifu: Sōgi's *Tsukushi no michi no ki*." *Monumenta Nipponica* 34.3 (Autumn): 333-67.

Katō Kiyomasa 加藤清正. *Katō Kiyomasa okitegaki* 加藤清正掟書. In Ozawa Tomio 1985: 338-40.

Katsuranomiyabon sōsho 桂宮本叢書. 1949-62. Eds. Shiba Katsumori 芝葛盛 and Yamagishi Tokuhei 山岸徳平. 21 vols. Yōtokusha.

Kawai Masaharu 河合正治. 1985. *Chūsei buke shakai no kenkyū* 中世武家社会の研究. Yoshikawa Kōbunkan.

Kawamura Teruo 川村晃生, Kashiwagi Yoshio 柏木由夫, and Kudō Shigenori 工藤重矩, eds. 1989. *Kin'yō wakashū, Shika wakashū* 金葉和歌集, 詞花和歌集. Vol. 9 of *SNKBT*.

Kawazoe Shōji 川添昭二. 1982. *Chūsei bungei no chihōshi* 中世文芸の地方史. Heibonsha.

Kazue Kyōichi 数江教一. 1985. *Wabi* わび. Hanawa Shobō.

Keene, Donald, comp. and ed. 1955. *Anthology of Japanese Literature: From the Earliest Era to the Mid-Nineteenth Century*. 2 vols. New York: Grove Press.

———, trans. 1967. *Essays in Idleness: The* Tsurezuregusa *of Kenkō*. New York: Columbia University Press.

———. 1977. "The Comic Tradition in Renga." In Hall and Toyoda 1977: 241-77.

———. 1978. *Some Japanese Portraits*. Kodansha.

———. 1981. "Jōha, A Sixteenth-Century Poet of Linked Verse." In Elison and Smith 1981: 113-31.

———. 1989. *Travelers of a Hundred Ages*. New York: Henry Holt and Company.

———. 1993. *Seeds in the Heart*. New York: Henry Holt and Co.

Kensai 兼載. *Baikunshō* 梅薫抄. In Ijichi Tetsuō, ed., *Rengaron shinshū*, pp. 188-216. Vol. 113 of *KB*.

———. *Kensai zōdan*. 兼載雑談. In *NKT* 5: 390-425.

Ki no Tsurayuki 紀貫之. *Tosa nikki* 土佐日記. In Matsumura, Kimura, and Imuta 1973: 27-68. See also McCullough 1990: 73-102.

Kidō Saizō 木藤才蔵. 1958. "Renga no keisei to tenkai" 連歌の形成と展開. Vol. 5 of *Iwanami kōza Nihon bungakushi*. Iwanami Shoten.

———. 1971. "Shōhaku denki shōkō" 肖柏伝記小考. *Kokugo to kokubungaku* 48.7 (July): 39-62.

———. 1971-73. *Rengashi ronkō* 連歌史論考. 2 vols. Meiji Shoin.

———. 1972-. *Rengaronshū*. 4 vols. to date. Vol. 1 co-edited with Shigematsu Hiromi. Miyai Shoten.

———. 1972. "Sengoku shoki ni okeru rengashi no seikatsu: Sōchō, Shōhaku, Sōseki no baai" 戦国初期における連歌師の生活—宗長・肖柏・宗碩の場合. *Bungaku* 40.10 (Oct.): 75–90.

———. 1984. *Chūsei bungaku shiron* 中世文学試論. Meiji Shoin.

Kidō Saizō, and Imoto Nōichi 井本農一. 1964. *Rengaronshū, haironshū*. Vol. 66 of *NKBT*.

Kidō Saizō, and Shigematsu Hiromi, eds. 1979. *Renga yoriaishū to kenkyū (ge)* 連歌寄合集と研究 (下). Vol. 2. Toyohashi: Mikan Kokubun Shiryō Kankōkai.

Kim, Yung-Hee. 1994. *Songs to Make the Dust Dance: The Ryōjin hishō of Twelfth-Century Japan*. Berkeley: University of California Press.

Kimura Miyogo 井村三四五, and Iguchi Hisashi 井口壽, eds. 1988. *Chikuba kyōginshū, Shinsen inu tsukubashū* 竹馬狂吟集・新撰犬筑波集. Vol. 77 of *SNKS*.

Kingon wakaawase 金言和歌合. 1983. In vol. 1 of *Kyōka taikan*, pp. 17–30.

Kinkō 禁好. In Kaneko 1978–83, 3: 189–334.

Kinoshita Motoichi 木下資一. 1985. "Tonsei" 遁世. *Kokubungaku kaishaku to kyōzai no kenkyū* 30.10 (Sept.): 94–95.

Kin'yō wakashū 金葉和歌集. In Kubota Jun and Kawamura 1986: 253–352.

Kirihioke 桐火桶. In *NKT* 4: 264–290.

Kishida Yoriko 岸田依子. 1980a. "Sōchō nikki no kōsei" 『宗長日記』の構成. *Waseda Daigaku Daigakuin Bungaku kenkyūka kiyō* 7: 59–67.

———. 1980b. "Sōchō hikashō shohonkō" 『宗長秘歌抄』諸本考. *Kokubungaku kenkyū* (Waseda University) 72 (Oct.): 56–71.

———. 1982. "Sōchō hikashō no chūshaku taido" 『宗長秘歌抄』の注釈態度. *Renga haikai kenkyū* 63 (July): 1–13.

Kishida Yoriko et al., eds. 1985. Vol. 6 of *Senku rengashū* 千句連歌集. Vol. 467 of *KB*.

Kitanosha ichimanku onhokku waki daisan shidai narabi ni jo 北野社一万句御発句第三次第并序. In *KNS* 18: 315–46.

Kodama Kōta 児玉幸多, Inoue Mitsusada 井上光貞, and Nagahara Keiji 永原慶二, eds. 1972–77. *Nihon no rekishi*. Shōgakukan.

Kojiki. Ed. Ogihara Asao 荻原浅男. In Ogihara and Kōnosu Hayao 鴻巣隼雄, eds., *Kojiki, jōdai kayō* 古事記・上代歌謡, pp. 1–367. Vol. 1 of *NKBZ*. See also Philippi 1969.

Kojima Yoshio 小島吉雄. 1936. "Rengashi to *Shinkokinshū*." *Kokugo kokubun* (March): 68–79.

Kokin waka rokujō 古今和歌六帖. In *KT* 2: 193–255.

Kokin wakashū 古今和歌集. In Kubota Jun and Kawamura 1986: 3–54. See also McCullough 1985.

Kokka taikan 国歌大観. 1983–92. Ed. Shinpen Kokka Taikan Henshū Iinkai. New ed. (*shinpen* 新編). 10 vols. Kadokawa Shoten.

Kokubungaku Kenkyū Shiryōkan, ed. 1985. *Renga shiryō no konpyūta shori no kenkyū* 連歌資料のコンピュータ処理の研究. Meiji Shoin.

Kokumin Tosho, ed. 1976. *Kokka taikei* 国歌大系. Collated and annotated (*kōchū* 校註). 28 vols. Rinsen Shoten.

Bibliography

Kokusho sōmokuroku 国書総目録. 1963–76. Eds. Ichiko Teiji et al. 9 vols. Iwanami Shoten.

Konishi Jin'ichi 小西甚一. 1951. *Tosa nikki hyōkai*. Yūseidō.

———. 1958. "Association and Progression: Principles of Integration in Anthologies and Sequences of Japanese Court Poetry, A.D. 900–1350." Trans. Robert H. Brower and Earl Miner. *Harvard Journal of Asiatic Studies* 21: 67–127.

———. 1975. "The Art of Renga." Trans. with an introduction by Karen Brazell and Lewis Cook. *Journal of Japanese Studies* 2.1 (Autumn): 29–61.

———. 1976. *Sōgi*. Vol. 16 of *Nihon shijinsen* 日本詩人選. Chikuma Shobō.

———. 1978. "The Genesis of the *Kokinshū* Style." Trans. Helen C. McCullough. *Harvard Journal of Asiatic Studies* 38.1: 61–170.

———. 1984. *A History of Japanese Literature, Volume One: The Archaic and Ancient Ages*. Trans. Aileen Gatten and Nicholas Teele. Ed. Earl Miner. Princeton: Princeton University Press.

———. 1991. *A History of Japanese Literature, Volume Three: The High Middle Ages*. Trans. Aileen Gatten and Mark Harbison. Ed. Earl Miner. Princeton: Princeton University Press.

Konjaku monogatarishū 今昔物語集. 1971–76. Eds. Mabuchi Kazuo 馬淵和夫, Kunisaki Fumimaro 国東文麿, and Konno Tōru 今野達. Vols. 21–24 of *NKBZ*.

Konoe Masaie 近衛家政. *Gohōkōinki* 後法興院記. Ed. Hiraizumi Kiyoshi 平泉澄. Vols. 5–8 of *Zoku shiryō taisei*.

Konparu Zenpō 金春禅鳳. 1986. *Zenpō zōdan* 禅鳳雑談. Ed. Kitagawa Tadahiko 北川忠彦. In Hayashiya Tatsusaburō, ed., *Kodai chūsei geijutsuron*, pp. 479–509. Vol. 23 of *Nihon shisō taikei*.

Koten bunko 古典文庫. 1946–. 517 vols. to date.

Kraft, Kenneth Lewis. 1992. *Eloquent Zen: Daitō and Early Japanese Zen*. Honolulu: University of Hawaii Press.

Kubo Tadao 久保忠夫. 1966. "*Muanki*" 夢庵記. In vol. 19 of Zoku Gunsho Ruijū Kanseikai, ed., *Gunsho kaidai*, pp. 98–99.

Kubo Tenzui 久保天髄, Shaku Seitan 釈清潭, and Iwatare Noriyoshi 岩垂憲徳, eds. 1978. *So Tōba zenshishū* 蘇東坡全詩集. 6 vols. Seishinsha.

Kubota Jun 久保田淳, ed. 1976–77. *Shinkokin wakashū zenhyōshaku*. Kōdansha.

———, ed. 1979. *Shinkokin wakashū*. Vols. 24 and 30 of *SNKS*.

Kubota Jun, and Kawamura Teruo 川村晃生, eds. 1986. *Gappon Hachidaishū* 合本八代集. Miyai Shoten.

Kubota Masaki 久保田昌希. 1977. "Imagawa Ujichika kōshitsu Jukeini hakkyū no monjo ni tsuite" 今川氏親後室寿桂尼発給の文書について. *Komazawa shigaku* 24: 135–48.

———. 1978. "Imagawa Ujiteru to sono monjo" 今川氏輝とその文書. *Komazawa Daigaku Daigakuin shigaku ronshū* 8: 37–46.

Kubota Shōichirō 窪田章一郎. 1977. "Saigyō no tawabureuta" 西行のたはぶれ歌. In vol. 5 of Waka Bungakukai, ed., *Waka bungaku no sekai*, pp. 95–111. Kasama Shoin.

Kubota Utsubo 久保田空穂, ed. 1964. *Kanpon Shinkokin wakashū hyōshaku* 3 vols. Tōkyōdō Shuppan.

Kubukihara Rei 久富木原令. 1985. "*Ushin, mushin*" 有心・無心. *Kokubungaku kaishaku to kyōzai no kenkyū* 30.10 (Sept.): 72–73.

Kumakura Isao. 1989. "Sen no Rikyū: Inquiries into His Life and Tea." Trans. Paul Varley. In Paul Varley and Kumakura Isao, eds., *Tea in Japan: Essays on the History of Chanoyu*, pp. 33–69. Honolulu: University of Hawaii Press.

Kurokawa Dōyū 黒川道祐. *Sōchō Kojiden* 宗長居士伝. In *ZZGSRJ* 3: 392–94.

Kurosawa Osamu 黒澤脩. 1975. "Imagawake shikken Sessai Chōrō to Jukeini" 今川家執権雪斎長老と寿桂尼. In *SI* 1: 73–85.

———. 1977. "Zōzenjidono Kyōzan Jōki Daizenjōmon Imagawa Ujichika nenpyō." 増善寺殿喬山紹僖大禅定門今川氏親年表. In *SI* 2: 159–79.

Kuwata Tadachika 桑田忠親. 1969. *Yamanoue no Sōjiki no kenkyū* 山上の宗二記の研究. Kawara Shoten.

———. ed. 1980. *Sengoku shi jiten* 戦国史事典. Akita Shoten.

Kyōka taikan 狂歌大観. 1983–85. Ed. Kyōka Taikan Kankōkai. 3 vols. Meiji Shoin.

LaFleur, William. 1983. *The Karma of Words*. Berkeley: University of California Press.

Legge, James, trans. 1871. *The She King*. London: Trubner and Co.

Lejeune, Philippe. 1989. *On Autobiography*. Trans. Katherine Leary. Ed. Paul John Eakin. Minneapolis: University of Minnesota Press.

Li Chi. 1962–63. "The Recluse in Chinese Literature." *Harvard Journal of Asiatic Studies* 24: 234–47.

Linjilu 臨済録. See Ruth Sasaki 1975.

Lotus Sutra. See Hurvitz 1976 and *Hokekyō*.

MacDonald, Dwight. 1957. "A Theory of Mass Culture." In Bernard Rosenberg and David M. White, eds., *Mass Culture: The Popular Arts in America*, pp. 59–73. Glencoe, Ill.: The Free Press.

Mandel, Barrett J. "Full of Life Now." In Olney 1980: 49–72.

Man'yōshū. Ed. Sakurai Mitsuru 桜井満. 3 vols. Ōbunsha, 1974–75.

Marra, Michele. 1993. *Representations of Power: The Literary Politics of Medieval Japan*. Honolulu: University of Hawaii Press.

Masukagami 増鏡. 1979. Ed. Inoue Muneo. 3 vols. Kodansha.

Matsudaira Norimichi 松平乗道. 1982. *Imagawa kana mokuroku* 今川仮名目録. In *SI* 1: 36–48.

Matsudaira Sadanobu 松平定信. 1973. *Shizuka naru amari* 閑なるあまり. In vol. 4 of Sekine Masanao 関根正直 et al., eds., *Nihon zuihitsu taisei*, pp. 331–38. 2nd. series. 24 vols. Yoshikawa Kōbunkan.

Matsue Shigeyori 松江重頼. 1988. *Kefukigusa* 毛吹草. Ed. Takenouchi Waka 竹内若. Iwanami Shoten.

Bibliography

Matsumoto Masako 松本真子. 1980. "Utsunoyamajō no Asahinashi ni tsuite" 宇津山城の朝比奈氏について. In *SI* 5: 103–33.

Matsumura Seiichi 松村誠一, Kimura Masanori 木村正中, and Imuta Tsunehisa 伊牟田経久, eds. 1973. *Tosa nikki, Kagerō nikki*. Vol. 9 of *NKBZ*.

Matsunaga Teitoku 松永貞徳. *Enokoshū* 犬子集. Eds. Morikawa Akira 森川昭 and Katō Sadahiko 加藤定彦. In Morikawa, Katō, and Inui Hiroyuki 乾裕幸, eds., *Shoki haikai-shū* 初期俳諧集, pp. 1–281. Vol. 69 of *SNKBT*.

Matsushita Shōkō 松下正広. See Shōkō.

McCullough, Helen C., trans. 1959. *The Taiheiki: A Chronicle of Medieval Japan*. New York: Columbia University Press.

———, trans. 1968. *Tales of Ise: Lyrical Episodes from Tenth-Century Japan*. Stanford: Stanford University Press.

———. 1985a. *Brocade by Night: "Kokin Wakashū" and the Court Style in Japanese Classical Poetry*. Stanford: Stanford University Press.

———, trans. 1985b. *Kokin Wakashū*. Stanford: Stanford University Press.

———, trans. 1988. *The Tale of the Heike*. Stanford: Stanford University Press.

———, trans. 1990. *Classical Japanese Prose: An Anthology*. Stanford: Stanford University Press.

McCullough, William H., and Helen Craig McCullough, trans. 1980. *A Tale of Flowering Fortunes*. 2 vols. Stanford: Stanford University Press.

McElrath, Miles Kenneth. 1971. "The *Seisuishō* of Anrakuan Sakuden: Humorous Anecdotes of the Sengoku and Early Modern Periods." Diss. University of Michigan.

Meikōawase 名香合. In *GSRJ* 19: 536–600.

Mezaki Tokue. 1985. "Aesthete-Recluses During the Transition from Ancient to Medieval Japan." Trans. Matthew Mizenko. In Earl Miner, ed., *Principles of Classical Japanese Literature*, pp. 151–80. Princeton: Princeton University Press.

Mikazuki 箕かづき. In Koyama Hiroshi 小山弘志, ed., *Kyōgenshū* 狂言集, pp. 32–36. Vol. 43 of *NKBT*.

Miki Sumito 三木紀人. 1983. "Inja" 隠者. In Ichiko et al. 1983–85, 1: 246–47.

Minamoto Sanetomo 源実朝. *Kinkaishū* 金槐集. Vol. 29 of *NKBT*.

Minamoto Toshiyori 源俊頼. *Toshiyori zuinō* 俊頼髄脳. In *NKT* 1: 118–221.

Minegishi Sumio 峰岸純夫, ed. 1977. *Chihō bunka no shintenkai* 地方文化の新展開. Vol. 5 of *Chihō bunka no Nihonshi*. Bun'ichi Sōgō Shuppan.

Minemura Fumito 峰村文人, ed. 1974. *Shinkokin wakashū*. Vol. 26 of *NKBZ*.

Miner, Earl. 1968. *An Introduction to Japanese Court Poetry*. Stanford: Stanford University Press.

———. 1969. *Japanese Poetic Diaries*. Berkeley: University of California Press.

———. 1979. *Japanese Linked Poetry*. Princeton: Princeton University Press.

———. 1990. "Waka: Features of its Constitution and Development." *Harvard Journal of Asiatic Studies* 50.2 (Dec.): 669–706.

Mitatsu 未達. 1915. *Sōgi shokoku monogatari* 宗祇諸国物語. In Sasa Masakazu 佐々政一 and Iwaya Sueo 巖谷季雄, eds., *Haijin itsuwa kikōshū* 俳人逸話紀行集, pp. 1–77. Vol. 6 of *Haikai sōsho* 俳諧叢書. Hakubunkan.

Mizaki Tokio 見崎関雄. 1983. "Imagawashi no Kai shinkō" 今川氏の甲斐侵攻. In *SI* 7: 121–35.

Mizukawa Yoshio 水川喜夫. 1985. *Asukai Masaari nikki zenshaku* 飛鳥井雅有日記全釈. Ed. Tanaka Norio 田中祝夫. Kazama Shobō.

Monokusa Tarō ものくさ太郎. In Ōshima 1974: 231–61.

Montrose, Louis. 1992. "New Historicisms." In Stephen Greenblatt and Giles Gunn, eds., *Redrawing the Boundaries: The Transformation of English and American Literary Studies*, pp. 392–418. New York: The Modern Language Association of America.

Moriya Takeshi 守屋毅. 1984. *Nihon chūsei e no shiza* 日本中世への視座. Nihon Hōsō Shuppankai.

Morozumi Sōichi 両角倉一. 1982. "Sōgi nenpukō" 宗祇年譜稿. *Yamanashi Kenritsu Joshi Tanki Daigaku kiyō* 15 (March): 41–72.

———. 1985. *Sōgi renga no kenkyū*. Benseisha.

Morris, Ivan, trans. 1967. *The Pillow Book of Sei Shōnagon*. 2 vols. London: Oxford University Press.

———, trans. 1971. *As I Crossed a Bridge of Dreams: Recollections of a Woman in Eleventh-Century Japan*. New York: The Dial Press.

Morris, V. Dixon. 1977. "Sakai: From Shōen to Port City." In Hall and Toyoda 1977: 145–58.

Morson, Gary Saul and Caryl Emerson. 1990. *Mikhail Bakhtin: Creation of a Prosaics*. Stanford: Stanford University Press.

Motsurin Jōtō. See Bokusai.

Murasaki Shikibu. *Genji monogatari*. See *Genji monogatari*.

———. *Murasaki Shikibu nikki*. Ed. Nakano Kōichi 中野幸一. In Fujioka, Nakano, Inukai, and Ishii 1971: 153–274. See also Bowring 1982.

Nagahara Keiji 永原慶二. 1975. *Sengoku no dōran* 戦国の動乱. Vol. 14 of Kodama, Inoue, and Nagahara 1972–77.

———, ed. 1983–85. *Sengoku daimyō ronshū*. 18 vols. Yoshikawa Kōbunkan.

———. 1990. "The Decline of the *Shōen* System." Trans. Michael P. Birt. In Yamamura 1990b: 260–300.

Nagai Yoshinori 永井義憲. 1960. "Jishū to bungaku geinō" 時衆と文学芸能. *Kokubungaku kaishaku to kanshō* 25.13 (Nov.): 61–69.

Nagakura Chieo 長倉智恵雄. 1978. "Imagawa Yoshitada Fujin Kitagawadono ni tsuite" 今川義忠夫人北川殿について. In *SI* 3: 59–93.

Nagasaki Ken 長崎健 et al., eds. 1994. *Chūsei nikki kikōshū* 中世日記紀行集. Vol. 48 of *Shinpen Nihon koten bungaku zenshū*. Shōgakukan.

Nagoya kassenki 名古屋合戦記. In *ZGSRJ* 21a: 104–07.

Bibliography

Nakagawa Yoshio 中川芳雄. 1981. "Rengashi Sōchō." In Owada et al. 1981: 1269-1370.

Nakamikado Nobutane 中御門宣胤. *Nobutanekyōki* 宣胤卿記. Vols. 44-45 of *Zōho shiryō taisei* and vol. 22 of *Zoku shiryō taisei*.

Nakamoto Tamaki 中本環. 1967. "Ikkyū Sōjun to Saiokuken Sōchō." In *Renga to sono shūhen: Kaneko Kinjirō Hakase kanreki kinen ronbunshū* 連歌とその周辺―金子金治郎博士還暦記念論文集, pp. 254-71. Hiroshima: Hiroshima Chūsei Bungei Kenkyūkai.

─── et al. 1976. "Chūsei shūkyō no kaitaiki ni tatsu Ikkyū" 中世宗教の解体期に立つ一休. Supplement (*Bessatsu*) to Ikkyū 1976.

Nakamura Yukihiko 中村幸彦. 1963. "Bunjin to sōshō" 文人と宗匠. *Bungaku* 31.5: 509-17.

Narugami Katsumi 鳴神克巳. 1943. *Nihon kikō bungeishi* 日本紀行文芸史. Tsukuda Shobō.

Nihon kagaku taikei 日本歌学大系. 1956-63; *Bekkan*, 1958-86. Ed. Sasaki Nobutsuna 佐々木信綱. 9 vols. Plus *Bekkan*. Ed. Kyūsojin Hitaku 久曽神昇 (vol. 1 co-edited with Higuchi Yoshimaro 樋口芳麻呂). 8 vols. Kazama Shobō.

Nihon koten bungaku taikei. 1957-68. 102 vols. Iwanami Shoten.

Nihon koten bungaku zenshū. 1971-76. 51 vols. Shōgakukan.

Nihon koten zensho. 1953-. Asahi Shinbunsha.

Nihon shisō taikei 日本思想体系. 1970-82. 67 vols. Iwanami Shoten.

Nijō Yoshimoto 二条良基. *Kinrai fūteishō* 近来風体抄. In Hisamatsu 1934: 262-81.

───, attrib. *Mochi sake utaawase* 餅酒歌合. In *Kyōka taikan* 1983-85, 2: 9-11.

───. *Tsukuba mondō* 筑波問答. In Kidō and Imoto 1964: 69-106.

Nijō Yoshimoto, Ichijō Kaneyoshi (or Kanera), and Shōhaku. *Renga shinshiki tsuika narabi ni shinshiki kon'an tō* 連歌新式追加並新式今案等. In *GSRJ* 17: 103-14. See also Carter 1987a.

Nijōgawara no rakusho 二条河原落書, in *Kenmu nenkanki* 建武年間記, in *SKGSRJ* 19: 753-54.

Nikonshū. Comp. Arakida Morihira 荒木田守平. Ed. Okuno Jun'ichi 奥野純一. 2 vols. Vols. 335 and 343 of *KB*.

Nishida Masayoshi 西田正好. 1977. *Ikkyū: fūkyō no seishin* 一休―風狂の精神. Kōdansha.

Nitta Shōjun 新田尚純. *Renga kaiseki shiki* 連歌会席式. In Tsurusaki 1980: 18-22. See also Horton 1993b: 506-12.

Nōin 能因. *Nōin utamakura* 能因歌枕. In *NKT* 1: 73-107.

Nussbaum, Felicity. 1989. *The Autobiographical Subject: Gender and Ideology in Eighteenth-Century England*. Baltimore: The Johns Hopkins University Press.

Oda Takuji 尾田卓次. 1947. *Renga bungeiron*. Kōtō Shoin.

Ōe Masafusa 大江匡房. 1978. *Gōdanshō* 江談抄. In *Kohonkei Gōdanshō chūkai* 古本系江談抄注解. Eds. Taguchi Kazuo 田口和夫 et al. Musashino Shoin.

───. *Kairaishiki* (also read *Kairaishi no ki* or *Kugutsuki*) 傀儡子記. 1979. Ed. Ōsone Shōsuke. In Ōsone et al. 1979: 157-59.

───. *Yūjoki* (or *Yūjo no ki*) 遊女記. Ibid., pp. 153-56.

Oka Masahiko 岡雅彦. 1995. *Ikkyūbanashi: tonchi kozō no raireki* 一休ばなし―とんち小僧の来歴. Heibonsha.

Okami Masao 岡見正雄. 1940. "Tonseisha: Jishū to rengashi" 遁世者―時衆と連歌師. *Kokubungaku ronkyū* 13 (Nov.): 10–28.

———. 1951. "Muromachigokoro" 室町ごころ. *Kokugo kokubun* (Nov.): 7–26.

———. 1955. "Mono: demono, monogi, hananomoto renga" もの―出物・物着・花の本連歌. *Kokugo kokubun* (Feb.): 31–36.

Okuda Isao 奥田勲. 1963. "Renga sakuhin nenpyōkō" 連歌作品年表稿. *Tōkyō Daigaku Kyōyō Gakubu jinbun kagaku kiyō* 32: 133–282.

———. 1966. "Renga sakuhin nenpyōkō hoi, sono ichi" 連歌作品年表稿補遺、その一. *Tōkyō Daigaku Kyōyō Gakubu jinbun kagaku kiyō* 39: 157–75.

———. 1976. *Rengashi: sono kōdō to bungaku* 連歌師―その行動と文学. Vol. 41 of *Nihonjin no kōdō to shisō* 日本人の行動と思想. Hyōronsha.

———. 1977. "Rengashi no tabi." In Minegishi 1977: 347–74.

———. 1995. "'Joryū' renga ryakunenpyō"「女流」連歌略年表. *Seishin Joshi Daigaku ronsō* 84 (Jan.): 101–32.

Ōkuma Yoshikuni 大熊喜邦. 1979. *Tōkaidō shukueki to sono honjin no kenkyū* 東海道宿駅とその本陣の研究. Nihon Shiryō Kankōkai.

Okumura Tsuneya 奥村恒哉. 1977. *Utamakura*. Heibonsha.

Okuno Jun'ichi 奥野純一. 1975. *Ise Jingūkan renga no kenkyū* 伊勢神宮官連歌の研究. Nihon Gakujutsu Shinkōkai.

Okuno Takahiro 奥野高広. 1952. "Sengoku jidai ni okeru kyūtei no koten kenkyū" 戦国時代に於ける宮廷の古典研究. In Kokugakuin Daigaku, ed., *Koten no shinkenkyū*, pp. 252–72. Kadokawa Shoten.

Olney, James, ed. 1980. *Autobiography: Essays Theoretical and Critical*. Princeton: Princeton University Press.

Origuchi Shinobu 折口信夫. 1966. "Nyōbō bungaku kara inja bungaku e" 女房文学から隠者文学へ. In vol. 1 of *Origuchi Shinobu zenshū*, pp. 273–320. Chūōkōronsha.

Ōshima Tatehiko 大島建彦, ed. 1974. *Otogizōshishū* 御伽草子集. Vol. 36 of *NKBZ*.

Ōshima Toshiko 大島俊子. 1962. "Sōchō nenpu" 宗長年譜. *Joshidai bungaku* 24 (Feb.): 38–54.

———. 1963–64. "Sōchō no shūhen" 宗長の周辺. *Joshidai bungaku* 28 (Feb., 1963): 28–40; 32 (Feb., 1964): 29–33; 33 (May, 1964): 20–28; and 35 (Oct., 1964): 76–85.

Ōsone Shōsuke 大曽根章介 et al., eds. 1979. *Kodai seiji shakai shisō*. Vol. 8 of *Nihon shisō taikei*. Iwanami Shoten.

Ōtsuka Isao 大塚勲. 1977. "Sengoku jidai Imagawashi jōsō kashin meibo" 戦国時代今川氏上層家臣名簿. In *SI* 2: 143–58.

———. 1987. "Rengashi Sōchō no wakaki koro" 連歌師宗長の若き頃. In *SI* 10: 168–90.

Owada Tetsuo 小和田哲男. 1981a. "Rugū suru kuge" 流寓する公家. In Owada et al. 1981: 1216–29.

———. 1981b. *Sengoku bushō* 戦国武将. Chūōkōronsha.

———. 1981c. "Shugo daimyō Imagawashi no hatten" 守護大名今川氏の発展. In Owada et al. 1981: 949–1057.

———. 1983. *Suruga Imagawa ichizoku* 駿河今川一族. Shin Jinbutsu Ōraisha.

———. 1984a. "Imagawa Ujichika to sono monjo" 今川氏親とその文書. In Arimitsu 1984: 94–112.

———. 1984b. *Sengoku kassen jiten* 戦国合戦事典. Sanseidō.

Owada Tetsuo et al. 1981. *Shizuokashi shi: genshi, kodai, chūsei* 静岡市史―原始・古代・中世. Shizuoka: Shizuoka Shiyakusho.

Ozaki Yūjirō 尾崎雄二郎, Shimazu Tadao, and Satake Akihiro 佐竹昭広. 1985. *Wago to kango no aida: Sōgi jōji hyakuin kaidoku* 和語と漢語のあいだ―宗祇畳字百韻会読. Chikuma Shobō.

Ozawa Seiichi 小沢誠一. 1977. "Imagawa kana mokuroku no kaidoku" 今川仮名目録の解読. In *SI* 1: 29–35.

Ozawa Tomio 小沢富夫, ed. 1985. *Kakun* 家訓. Kōdansha.

Oze Hoan 小瀬甫庵. *Taikōki* 太閤記. Ed. Yoshida Yutaka. 4 vols. Kyōikusha, 1979.

Parker, Joseph D. 1995. "The Hermit at Court: Recluses in Early Fifteenth-Century Japanese Zen Buddhism." *The Journal of Japanese Studies* 21.1 (Winter): 103–20.

Pascal, Roy. 1960. *Design and Truth in Autobiography*. Cambridge, Mass.: Harvard University Press.

Philippi, Donald L., trans. 1969. *Kojiki*. University of Tokyo Press.

Plutschow, Herbert, and Fukuda Hideichi, trans. 1981. *Four Japanese Travel Diaries of the Middle Ages*. Cornell University East Asia Papers 25. Ithaca, New York: China-Japan Program, Cornell University.

Powys, John Cowper. 1934. *Autobiography*. New York: Simon and Schuster.

Ramirez-Christensen, Esperanza. 1981. "The Essential Parameters of Linked Poetry." *Harvard Journal of Asiatic Studies* 41.2 (Dec.): 555–95.

———. 1983. "Shinkei: Poet-Priest of Medieval Japan." Diss. Harvard University.

———. 1994. *Heart's Flower: The Life and Poetry of Shinkei*. Stanford: Stanford University Press.

Redfield, Robert. 1956. *Peasant Society and Culture: An Anthropological Approach to Civilization*. Chicago: University of Chicago Press.

Reizei Masatame 冷泉政為. *Hekigyokushū* 碧玉集. In *ST* 6: 618–59.

Reizei Tamemori 冷泉為守, attrib. *Kyōka sake hyakushu* 狂歌酒百首. In *Kyōka taikan* 1976–85, 1: 13–16.

Renga gasshū 連歌合集. Kokkai Toshokan. A catalogue of this collection of *renga* manuscripts is found in Kokubungaku Kenkyū Shiryōkan 1985.

Renga shūsho 連歌集書. Seikadō Bunko 静嘉堂文庫. A limited number of *renga* sequences reproduced from this collection of manuscripts is found in Ijichi 1975.

Renga tsukeai no koto 連歌付合の事. In Kidō 1972-, 1: 203–20.

Renza, Louis. 1980. "The Veto of the Imagination: A Theory of Autobiography." In Olney 1980: 268–95.

Resshi 列子 (C: *Liezi*). 1976. Ed. Kobayashi Shinmei 小林信明. Vol. 22 of *Shinshaku kanbun taikei*.

Rongo 論語 (C: *Lunyu*). 1963. Ed. Kanya Osamu 金谷治. Iwanami Shoten.

Rosenfield, John M. 1977. "The Unity of the Three Creeds: A Theme in Japanese Ink Painting of the Fifteenth Century." In Hall and Toyoda 1977: 205–25.

Ruch, Barbara. 1977. "Medieval Jongleurs and the Making of a National Literature." In Hall and Toyoda 1977: 279–309.

———. 1990. "The Other Side of Culture in Medieval Japan." In Yamamura 1990b: 500–543.

Sadler, Arther L., trans. 1940. *The Ise Daijingū Sankei-ki or Diary of a Pilgrim to Ise*. Tōkyō: Meiji Japan Society.

Saigyō 西行. *Kikigakishū* 聞書集. In *KT* 3: 613–18.

———. *Mimosusogawa utaawase* 御裳濯河歌合. 1947. In Minegishi Yoshiaki 峯岸義秋, ed., *Utaawaseshū*, pp. 337–58. *NKZ*.

———. *Miyagawa utaawase* 宮河歌合. Ibid., pp. 359–80.

———. *Saigyō Shōninshū* 西行上人. 1983. In Kubota Jun 久保田淳, ed., *Saigyō zenshū*, pp. 353–421. Nihon Koten Bungakkai.

———. *Sankashū* 山家集. 1982. Ed. Gotō Shigeo 後藤重郎. Vol. 49 of *SNKS*.

Saiokuken Sōchō 柴屋軒宗長. See Sōchō.

Saitō Kiyoe 斎藤清衞. 1968. "Rengashi Sōchō nenpu tsuikō" 連歌師宗長年譜追考. In Hisamatsu Sen'ichi 久松潜一, ed., *Nihon bungei no sekai*, pp. 248–69. Ōfūsha.

Saitō Sakae 斎藤栄. 1985. "Sōchō." In *Henreki* 遍歴, pp. 201–45. Vol. 9 of *Rekishi no gunzō* 歴史の群像. Shūeisha.

Saitō Yoshimitsu 斎藤義光. 1979. "Renga ni arawareta haikaisei." In *Chūsei renga no kenkyū*, pp. 20–41. Yūseidō.

Saka Jūbutsu 坂十仏. *Ise Daijingū sankeiki* 伊勢大神宮参詣記. In *GSRJ* 27: 379–97. See also Sadler 1940.

Saku Misao 佐久節, ed. 1978. *Haku Rakuten zenshishū* 白楽天全詩集. 4 vols. Seishinsha.

Sakurai Yoshirō 桜井好郎. 1967. *Inja no fūbō* 隠者の風貌. Hanawa Shobō.

Sanetaka. See Sanjōnishi Sanetaka.

Sanford, James H. 1981. *Zen-Man Ikkyū*. Vol. 2 of *Studies in World Religions*. Chico, Calif.: Scholars Press.

Sangoki 三五記. In *NKT* 4: 313–61.

Sanjōnishi Sanetaka 三条西実隆. *Kōya sankei nikki* 高野参詣日記. In *GSRJ* 18: 716–23.

———. *Saishōsō* 再昌草. 1949–53. Vols. 11–13 of *KNS*.

———. *Sanetakakōki* 実隆公記. 1957–67. Eds. Shiba Katsumori 芝葛盛, Sanjōnishi Kin'masa 三条西公正, and Korezawa Kyōzō 是沢恭三 (vols. 1–6); Takahashi Ryūzō 高橋隆三 (vols. 7–13). 13 vols. Zoku Gunsho Ruijū Kanseikai.

Bibliography

———. *Setsugyokushū* 雪玉集. In *ST* 7: 194–424.

Sansom, George. 1984. *A History of Japan, 1334–1615*. Rutland, Vt., and Tokyo: Tuttle.

Santaishi 三体詩 (C: *Santishi*). Ed. Murakami Tetsumi 村上哲見. 4 vols. Asahi Shinbunsha, 1978.

Sanukinosuke nikki 讃岐典侍日記. Ed. Ishii Fumio 石井文夫. In Fujioka, Nakano, Inukai, and Ishii 1971: 369–456. See also Brewster 1977.

Sarashina nikki 更級日記. Ed. Inukai Kiyoshi 犬養廉. In Fujioka, Nakano, Inukai, and Ishii 1971: 281–362. See also Morris 1971.

Sasaki Harutsuna 佐々木治綱. 1955. "Sōan no bungaku." In *Chūsei no bungaku*, pp. 93–107. Vol. 3 of Origuchi Shinobu et al., eds., *Nihon bungaku kōza*. 8 vols. Kawade Shobō.

Sasaki Kōji 佐々木孝二. 1987. "Chūsei bungaku ni okeru ba no seishitsu" 中世文学における場の性質. *Nihon bungaku* 36.2: 40–49.

Sasaki, Ruth Fuller, trans. 1975. *The Recorded Sayings of Ch'an Master Lin-chi Hui-chao of Chen Prefecture, Compiled by His Humble Heir Hui-jan of San-sheng*. Kyōto: Institute of Zen Studies.

Sato, Hiroaki, and Burton Watson. 1981. *From the Country of Eight Islands: An Anthology of Japanese Poetry*. Introduction by Thomas Rimer. Garden City, N.Y.: Anchor Press/Doubleday.

Satomura Jōha 里村紹巴. See Jōha.

Sei Shōnagon. *Makura no sōshi*. Eds. Matsuo Satoshi 松尾聰 and Nagai Kazuko 永井和子. Vol. 11 of *NKBZ*. See also Morris 1967.

Seidensticker, Edward, trans. 1964. *The Gossamer Years*. Rutland Vt. and Tōkyō: Charles E. Tuttle Co.

———, trans. 1976. *The Tale of Genji*. 2 vols. Rutland, Vt. and Tōkyō: Charles E. Tuttle Co.

Seisuishō. See Anrakuan Sakuden.

Semoto Hisao 瀬本久雄. 1983. "Reizei Tamekazu to Imagawa Ujiteru, Yoshimoto" 冷泉為和と今川氏輝・義元. In *SI* 7: 137–67.

Sen no Sōtan 千宗旦. 1981. *Zencharoku* 禅茶録. In Saigusa Hiroto 三枝博音 and Shimizu Ikutarō 清水幾太郎, eds., vol. 16 of *Nihon tetsugaku shisō zensho*, pp. 239–55. Heibonsha.

Senda Ken 千田憲. 1964–69. "Sōchō, Sōseki ryōgin no *Daijingū hōraku onsenku ni tsuite*" 宗長・宗碩両吟の『大神宮法楽御千句』について. *Mizukaki* 62–84 (except numbers 68, 72, 79, and 81).

Senjūshō 撰集抄. In *ZGSRJ* 32b: 324–482.

Senzai wakashū 千載和歌集. 1986. Ed. Kubota Jun. Iwanami Shoten.

Shichijūichiban shokunin utaawase 七十一番職人歌合. 1993. Ed. Iwasaki Kae 岩崎佳枝. In Iwasaki et al., eds., *Shichijūichiban shokunin utaawase, Shinsen kyōkashū, Kokon ikyokushū* 七十一番職人歌合・新撰狂歌集・古近夷曲集, pp. 1–146. Vol. 61 of *SNKBT*.

Shigematsu Hiromi 重松裕巳. 1973. "*Sōchō renga jichū*: shohon oyobi seiritsu o chūshin ni" 『宗長連歌自注』―諸本および成立を中心に. *Kumamoto Joshi Daigaku kokubun kenkyū* 19: 27-43.

―――. 1978. "*Sōchō nikki* kōchū oboegaki" 『宗長日記』校注覚書. *Kumamoto Joshi Daigaku gakujutsu kiyō* 30 (March): 9-17.

―――. 1979. "Saiokuken ketsuan nenji shiron" 柴屋軒結庵年次試論. *Renga haikai kenkyū* 56 (Jan.): 9-19.

―――. 1981. "*Amayo no ki* shohonkō" 『雨夜記』諸本考. *Kumamoto Joshi Daigaku gakujutsu kiyō* 3 (March): 1-11.

―――. 1982. "Yūtokubon *Sōchō michi no ki* o megutte" 祐徳本『宗長道之記』をめぐって. In *Imai Gen'e Kyōju taikan kinen ronbunshū* 今井源衛教授退官記念論文集, pp. 117-39. Kyūshū Daigaku.

―――, ed. 1983. *Sōchō sakuhinshū: nikki, kikō* 宗長作品集―日記・紀行. Vol. 443 of *KB*.

―――, ed. 1990. *Sōchō sakuhinshū: renga gakusho hen* 宗長作品集―連歌学書編. Vol. 517 of *KB*.

Shika wakashū 詞花和歌集. 1988. Ed. Matsuno Yōichi 松野陽一. Izumi Shoin.

Shikashū taisei 私家集大成. 1973-76. Eds. Hashimoto Fumio 橋本不美男 et al. 7 vols. Meiji Shoin.

Shikyō 史経 (C: *Shijing*). Ed. Takada Shinji 高田真治. Vol. 2 of *Kanshi taikei* 漢詩大系. Shūeisha, 1964. See also Legge 1876.

Shimazu Tadao 島津忠夫. 1953. "Reizei kafū no yukue" 冷泉歌風のゆくえ. *Kokugo kokubun* 22.6 (June): 41-53.

―――. 1955. "Renga no hyōgen to waka no hyōgen" 連歌の表現と和歌の表現. *Gobun* 14 (March): 10-18.

―――. 1969. *Renga shi no kenkyū* 連歌史の研究. Kadokawa Shoten.

―――. 1970. *Ōsaka Tenmangū Bunko rengasho mokuroku* 大阪天満宮文庫連歌書目録. Osaka: Ōsaka Tenmangū Shamusho.

―――. 1972. Bannen no Shinkei (kaikō) 晩年の心敬 (改稿). *Setsurin* 21: 31-41.

―――. 1973. *Renga no kenkyū*. Kadokawa Shoten.

―――. 1975. *Sōchō nikki*. Iwanami Shoten.

―――. 1979. *Rengashū*. Vol. 33 of *SNKS*.

―――. 1987. *Chūsei bungaku shiron* 中世文学史論. Osaka: Izumi Shoin.

―――. 1991. *Rengashi Sōgi*. Iwanami Shoten.

Shimazu Tadao, and Fujita Hideo 藤田秀雄. 1963. "Matsudaira Bunkobon San'aiki" 松平文庫本三愛記. *Saga Daigaku bungakuronshū* 5 (Feb.): 34-54.

Shimazu Tadao, and Shigematsu Hiromi, eds. 1965. *Renga haikaishū*. Nishi Nihon Kokugo Kokubungakkai.

Shin Nihon koten bungaku taikei. 1989-. Iwanami Shoten.

Shinchō Nihon koten shūsei. 1976-89. 82 vols. Shinchōsha.

Shinchokusen wakashū 新勅撰和歌集. In *KT* 1: 259-88.

Shingyō Norikazu 新行紀一. 1977. "Mikawa bushi" 三河武士. In Minegishi 1977: 157-81.

Shinjō Tsunezō 新城常三. 1943. *Sengoku jidai no kōtsū* 戦国時代の交通. Unebi Shobō.

Shinkei 心敬. *Hitorigoto* ひとりごと (Kokkai Toshokan 国会図書館 ms.). In Kidō 1972-, 3: 291-310. See also *Hitorigoto* ひとりごと (Ōsaka Tenmangū 大阪天満宮 ms.), ed. Shimazu Tadao, in Hayashiya 1986: 465-78.

———. *Oi no kurigoto* 老のくりごと (Shoryōbu 書陵部 ms.). Kidō 1972-, 3: 367-85. See also *Oi no kurigoto*, in *GSRJ* 17: 68-75 and *Oi no kurigoto* (Jingū Bunko 神宮文庫 ms.), ed. Shimazu Tadao, in Hayashiya 1986: 409-22.

———. *Sasamegoto* ささめごと (Sonkeikaku Bunko 尊経閣文庫 ms.). In Kidō and Imoto 1964: 119-204. See also *Sasamegoto*, in *GSRJ* 17: 31-67; *Sasamegoto* (Shoryōbu ms.), ed. Ijichi Tetsuo, in Ijichi, Omote, and Kuriyama 1973: 63-160; and *Sasamegoto* (Shoryōbu ms.), in Kidō 1972-, 3: 177-257.

Shinkei et al. *Kawagoe senku* 河越千句. In *ZGSRJ* 17a: 432-58.

———. *Shinkei Sōzu hyaku ta* 心敬僧都百句他. Ms. in Fukui Bunko, Hiroshima Daigaku.

Shinkō gunsho ruijū 新校群書類従. 1928-38. Eds. Hanawa Hokiichi 塙保己一 et al. 24 vols. Naigai Shoseki.

Shinkokin wakashū 新古今和歌集. In Jun Kubota and Kawamura 1986: 440-529. See also Ishida Yoshisada 1960, Kubota Jun 1976-77, id. 1979, Kubota Utsubo 1964, Minemura 1974, and Tanaka and Akase 1992.

Shinsen inu tsukubashū 新撰犬筑波集 (also called *Inu tsukubashū*). Attributed to Yamazaki Sōkan 山崎宗鑑. See Kimura and Iguchi 1988: 117-227 and Suzuki Tōzō 1965.

Shinsen tsukubashū 新撰筑波集 (Meiō 明応 ms.). 1958. Eds. Yokoyama Shigeru 横山重 and Noguchi Eiichi 野口英一. Kazama Shobō.

Shinshaku kanbun taikei 新釈漢文大系. 1976-85. 96 vols. Meiji Shoin.

Shinshoku kokin wakashū 新続古今和歌集. In *KT* 1: 722-69.

Shirai Chūkō 白井忠功. 1976. *Chūsei no kikō bungaku*. Bunka Shobō Hakubunsha.

Shiryō sōran 史料総覧. 1936. Ed. Tōkyō Daigaku Shiryō Hensanjo Naikaku Insatsukyoku Chōyōkai.

Shively, Donald. 1991. "Popular Culture." In Hall 1991: 706-69.

Shōhaku 肖柏. *Muanki* 夢庵記. In *GSRJ* 17: 393. See also *Muanki*, in *SKGSRJ* 21: 187 (the *GSRJ* ms. collated with the *Fusō shūyōshū* 扶桑拾葉集 ms.) and *Muanki*, in *Fusō shūyōshū* 3: 88-89.

———. *San'aiki* 三愛記. In *GSRJ* 17: 394-95. See also *San'aiki*, in *SKGSRJ* 21: 188 (the *GSRJ* ms. collated with an unnamed ms.) and *San'aiki*, in *Fusō shūyōshū* 3: 89-90.

———. *Shunmusō* 春夢草. In *ZGSRJ* 17b: 846-944.

Shōkō 正広. *Shōkō nikki* 正広日記. In *GSRJ* 18: 643-47.

Shokusenzai wakashū 続千載和歌集. In *KT* 1: 481-525.

Shōtetsu 正徹. *Nagusamegusa* なぐさめ草. In *GSRJ* 18: 583-95. See also *Nagusamegusa* (Waseda Daigaku Toshokan ms.), ed. Inada Toshiyuki 稲田利徳, in Nagasaki et al. 1994: 427-53.

Shūi wakashū 拾遺和歌集. In Kubota Jun and Kawamura 1986: 123–84.

Shuten Dōji 酒呑童子. In Ōshima Tatehiko 1974: 444–74.

Smits, Ivo. 1995. *The Pursuit of Loneliness: Chinese and Japanese Nature Poetry in Medieval Japan, Ca. 1050-1150*. Stuttgart: Franz Steiner Verlag.

Sōboku 宗牧. *Shidō kuhon* 四道九品. In Kidō 1972-, 4: 365–83. See also Ijichi 1985, 2: 195–208.

———. *Tōfu renga hiji* 当風連歌秘事. Ed. Ijichi Tetsuo. In Ijichi, Omote, and Kuriyama 1973: 161–200. See also Ijichi 1985, 2: 209–29 and Kidō 1972-, 4: 385–411.

———. *Tōgoku kikō* 東国紀行. In *GSRJ* 18: 802–42.

Sōchō 宗長. *Amayo no ki* 雨夜の記. In *ZGSRJ* 17b: 1205–236. See also Kidō 1972-, 4: 221–305 and Shigematsu 1990: 99–231.

———. *Azumaji no tsuto* 東路の津登. In *GSRJ* 18: 770–82. See also *Azumaji no tsuto*, in *SKGSRJ* 15: 246–54 (the *GSRJ* ms. collated with the Fujino 藤野 ms.); *Azumaji no tsuto*, in Shigematsu 1983 (containing five manuscripts: Ōta Takeo 太田武男 ms. 25–40, Shōkōkan 彰考館 ms. 41–63, Ijichi Tetsuo ms. 65–87, Dazaifu Tenmangū 太宰府天満宮 ms. 89–113, and Yūtoku Inari Jinja 祐徳稲荷神社 ms. 115–48); and *Azumaji no tsuto* (Yūtoku Inari Jinja ms.), ed. Itō Kei, in Nagasaki et al. 1994: 483–512.

———. Bunmei 12 [1480]:8 *Nanimichi hyakuin*. In Etō 1967: 195–98.

———. *Chōka* 長歌 (Ōta Takeo 太田武男 ms.). Cited in Shigematsu 1982: 119.

———. *Ei gojisshu waka* 詠五十首和歌 (Tenri Toshokan ms.). Cited in *RSR* 2: 945.

———. *Genji monogatarishō* 源氏物語抄. See *Genjichū*.

———. *Genjichū* 源氏注. Tenri Toshokan ms. Cited in Ōshima Toshiko 1962: 51.

———. *Hosokawake senku* 細川家千句. Cited in *RSR* 2: 925.

———. *Hyakunin isshuchū* 百人一首注. Cited in Shigematsu 1982: 119.

———. *Ise monogatari Sōchō kikigaki*. In Katagiri 1969: 651–710.

———. *Kabekusa* 壁草. In *Kabekusachū* 壁草注 (Shoryōbu ms.). In Kaneko 1979: 371–512. See also *Kabekusa* (Mite Bunko 三手文庫 ms.), ed. Shigematsu Hiromi, vol. 424 of *KB*; *Kabekusa*, in *ZGSRJ* 17b: 945–1011; *Kabekusa* (Masamune Bunko 正宗文庫 ms.), in Okamoto Noriko 岡本史子, 1969, "Honkoku Masamune Bunkozō *Kabekusa*," *Nōtoru Damu Seishin Joshi Daigaku kokubungakka kiyō* 3: 91–135; and *Kabekusa* (Ōsaka Tenmangū ms.), ed. Shigematsu Hiromi, vol. 398 of *KB*.

———. *Kabekusachū* 壁草注 (Shoryōbu ms.). See *Kabekusa*.

———. *Mikawa kudari* 三河下り. See *Sōchō kawa*.

———. *Nachigomori* 那智籠 (Hiroshima Daigaku ms.). Ed. Shigematsu Hiromi. Vol. 379 of *KB*. See also *Nachigomori* (Kitano Tenmangū ms.), ed. Shigematsu Hiromi, vol. 376 of *KB*.

———. *Nagabumi* (or *Nagafumi*) 永文. In Ijichi 1985, 2: 188–93. See also Kidō 1972-, 4: 159–68.

———. *Oi no higagoto* 老のひがごと (Yūtoku Inari Jinja 祐徳稲荷神社 ms. of *Utsunoyama no ki*). In Shigematsu 1983: 149–74.

Bibliography

———. *Oi no mimi* 老耳. Ed. Shigematsu Hiromi. Vol. 362 of *KB*.

———. *Renga sakurei* 連歌作例 (two Kyōto Daigaku mss.). In Shigematsu 1989: 5-44, 45-98.

———. *Renga tsukeyō* 連歌付用. In Iwashita and Kishida, 1978: 464-79.

———. *Rengashū* 連歌集. In Iwashita and Kishida 1978: 480-87.

———. *Sengen senku* 浅間千句 (*Renga shūsho* ms.). Cited in *RSR* 2: 936.

———. *Shijin zanshō* 紫塵残抄 (Tōen Bunko 桃園文庫 ms.). Tōkai University. See Kaneko et al., eds. 1986: 145.

———. *Shutsujin senku* 出陣千句. In *ZGSRJ* 17a: 1359-67.

———, attrib. *Sōchō hikashō* 宗長秘歌抄 (Manjuin 曼殊院 and Kyōto Daigaku mss.). 1983. Ed. Imanishi Yūichirō 今西祐一郎. Vol. 412 of *Kyōto Daigaku kokugo kokubun shiryō sōsho*. Kyoto: Rinsen Shoten.

———. *Sōchō kawa* 宗長歌話. In Kidō and Shigematsu 1979: 7-48.

———. *Sōchō michi no ki* 宗長道之記 (an abridged version of *Sōchō shuki*, Yūtoku Inari Jinja ms.). Shigematsu 1983: 201-273.

———. *Sōchō nikki* (Shoryōbu 書陵部 ms.). In Shimazu 1975: 145-164. See also *Sōchō nikki*, in *ZGSRJ* 18b: 1252-266.

———. *Sōchō renga jichū* 宗長連歌自注. In *KNS* 18: 95-183.

———. *Sōchō rengashū*. In Iwashita and Kishida 1978: 446-50.

———. *Sōchō shuki* 宗長手記 (Shōkōkan 彰考館 ms.). In Shimazu 1975: 7-143. See also *Sōchō shuki*, in *GSRJ* 18: 256-327; *Sōchō shuki*, in *SKGSRJ* 14: 645-701 (the *GSRJ* ms. collated with a ms. in the Naikaku Bunko); *Sōchō michi no ki*; and *Sōchō Suruga nikki* and *Sōchō Suruga zoku nikki*.

———. *Sōchō Suruga nikki* 宗長駿河日記 and *Sōchō Suruga zoku nikki* 宗長駿河続日記 (Naikaku Bunko ms.). Ed. Uzawa Satoru 鵜沢覚. Vol. 344 of *KB*.

———. *Sōgi shūenki* 宗祇終焉記 (the *GSRJ* ms. collated with the Naikaku Bunko ms.). In Kaneko 1976: 101-25. See also *Sōgi shūenki*, in *GSRJ* 29: 442 48; *Sōgi shūenki* (the *GSRJ* ms. collated with the Naikaku Bunko ms.), in *SKGSRJ* 22: 673-77; *Sōgi shūenki* (Ōta Takeo 太田武男 ms.), in Shigematsu 1983: 7-23; and *Sōgi shūenki* (Naikaku Bunko ms.), eds. Tsurusaki Hiroo and Fukuda Hideichi, in Fukuda et al., eds., 1990: 449-61.

———. *Utsunoyama no ki* 宇津山記. In *GSRJ* 17: 395-405. See also *Utsunoyama no ki*, in *SKGSRJ* 21: 189-95 (the *GSRJ* ms. collated with the Naikaku Bunko ms.); *Utsunoyama no ki* (Matsudaira Bunko 松平文庫 ms.), in Shigematsu 1983: 174-200; and *Oi no higagoto*.

———. *Yamaga hyakuin* 山家百韻 (*Renga sōsho* ms.). Cited in *RSR* 2: 935. Ms. copy in the possession of Kaneko Kinjirō.

———. *Wakashū* (Kawagoe Shiritsu Toshokan ms.). Cited in Inoue Muneo 1987: 286.

Sōchō, Sanjōnishi Sanetaka, and Shōhaku. *Sōchō hyakuban rengaawase*. In *KNS* 18: 21-93.

Sōchō, Sanjōnishi Sanetaka, and Sōseki. *Gessonsai senku* 月村斎千句. See id., *Iba senku*.

———. *Iba senku* 伊庭千句. Ed. Tsurusaki Hiroo. In Tsurusaki et al., eds., vol. 7 of *Senku rengashū*, pp. 7–112. Vol. 471 of *KB*.

Sōchō, and Sōboku. Daiei 7 [1527]:1:18 *Yashima Shōrin'an naniki hyakuin* 矢嶋小林庵何木百韻. In *KNS* 18: 201–30.

Sōchō, and Sōgi. *Guku wakuraba* 愚句老葉. In Kaneko 1979: 7–153.

———. *Shitakusachū* 下草注. In Kaneko 1979: 215–43.

Sōchō, Sōgi, and Shōhaku. *Minase sangin* 水無瀬三吟 (*Renga shūsho* ms.). In Kaneko Kinjirō, ed., *Minase sangin hyakuin chūshaku*, in id. 1985b: 83–187. See also *Chōkyō ninen Minase sangin hyakuin* 長享二年水無瀬三吟百韻, in *ZGSRJ* 17a: 576–78; Fukui 1938: 11–68; *Three Poets at Minase*, in Keene 1955, 1: 314–21 (partial translation); Yasuda 1956; *Minase sangin hyakuinchū* (Konishi Jin'ichi ms.), in Ijichi 1968: 343–66; *Minase sangin* (Tsurumai Toshokan 鶴舞図書館 ms.), in Shimazu 1979: 211–46; *Three Poets at Minase*, in Miner 1979: 171–225; and *Three Poets at Minase*, in Carter 1991: 303–26.

———. *Yuyama sangin* 湯山三吟 (Tenmangū ms.). In Kaneko Kinjirō, *Yuyama sangin hyakuin chūshaku*, in id. 1985b: 189–288. See also *Yuyama sangin hyōshaku*, in Fukui 1938: 69–115; *Yuyama sangin* (Daitōkyū Kinen Bunko 大東急記念文庫 ms.), in Shimazu 1979: 247–79; *Three Poets at Yuyama*, in Sato and Watson 1981: 254–61; and Carter 1983.

Sōchō, and Sōseki. *Ise senku* 伊勢千句 (Naikaku Bunko ms.). In Kaneko 1974: 340–421. See also *Ise senku* (Jingū Bunko ms.), in Senda 1964–69.

Sōchō et al. Bunmei 12 [1480]:8 *Nanimichi hyakuin* (Ōsaka Tenmangū ms.). In Etō 1967: 195–8.

———. *Hamori senku* 葉守千句 (Kitano Tenmangū ms.). Ed. Hamachiyo Kiyoshi. In Kishida et al., eds., 1985: 9–116.

———. *Higashiyama senku* 東山千句 (Naikaku Bunko ms.). Ed. Kishida Yoriko. In Kishida et al., eds., 1985: 227–332.

———. *Hosokawake senku* 細川家千句. Cited in *RSR* 2: 925.

———. *Jikka senku* 十花千句 (Ōta Takeo 太田武男 ms.). In Kaneko 1974: 308–39.

———. *Renga hikyōshū* 連歌比況集. In Ijichi 1985, 2: 161–85. See also *Renga hikyōshū*, in Kidō 1972-, 4: 169–95; *Hikyōshū*, in Kaneko 1978–83, 9: 3–110; and *Hikyōshū*, in Shigematsu 1989: 233–76.

———. *Settsu senku* 摂津千句. The first three verses of each of the ten hundred-verse sequences are preserved in the Ōsaka Tenmangū ms., reproduced in Tsurusaki 1971b: 4–5.

———. *Shichinin tsukeku hanshi* 七人付句判詞. In Kidō 1972-, 2: 297–314.

Soga monogatari 曽我物語. Eds. Ichiko Teiji and Ōshima Tatehiko 大島建彦. Vol. 88 of *NKBT*. See also Cogan 1987.

Sōgi 宗祇. *Azuma mondō* 吾妻問答. In Kidō and Imoto 1964: 205–37. See also *Azuma mondō*, in *GSRJ* 17: 17–30.

———. *Bun'yōshū* 分葉集. In Kidō 1972-, 2: 207–224.

Bibliography

———. *Chikurinshō* 竹林抄. 1991. Ed. Shimazu Tadao et al. Vol. 49 of *SNKBT*. See also *Chikurinshō*, in *ZGSRJ* 17a: 270-354.

———. *Chōrokubumi* 長六文. In Kidō 1972-, 2: 109-30.

———. *Hyakunin isshushō* 百人一集抄. Kasama Shoin, 1969.

———. *Kokin wakashū ryōdo kikigaki* 古今和歌集両度聞書. See Sōgi and Tō no Tsuneyori, *Kokin wakashū kikigaki*.

———. *Mishima senku* 三島千句. In Etō 1967: 71-103.

———. *Oi no susami* 老のすさみ. In Kidō 1972-, 2: 139-86.

———. *Shirakawa kikō* 白河紀行. In Kaneko 1976: 7-26. See also *Shirakawa kikō*, in *ZGSRJ* 18b: 1276-282 and Carter 1987b.

———. *Shitakusa* 下草. In *ZGSRJ* 17b: 697-735. See also *Shitakusa*, ed. Morozumi Sōichi 両角倉一, vol. 387 of *KB*.

———. *Sōgi jōji hyakuin* 宗祇畳字百韻 (also titled *Haikai Sōgi dokugin hyakuin*). In Ozaki, Shimazu, and Satake 1985: 12-14.

———. *Sōgi hokkushū*. Ed. Hoshika Sōichi 星加宗一. Iwanami Shoten, 1985.

———. *Sōgi rengashū wakuraba* 宗祇連歌集老葉. Eds. Konishi Jin'ichi and Mizukami Kashizō 水上甲子三. Vol. 74 of *KB*. See also *Wakuraba*, in *ZGSRJ* 17b: 627-74.

———. *Sōgi rengashū wasuregusa* 宗祇連歌集萱草. Ed. Konishi Jin'ichi. Vol. 40 of *KB*. See also *Wasuregusa*, in *ZGSRJ* 17b: 675-96.

———. *Sōgi sodeshita* 宗祇袖下. In Kidō 1972-, 2: 225-79.

———. *Sōgishū*. In *ST* 6: 453-62.

———. *Tsukushi michi no ki* 筑紫道記. In Kaneko 1976: 27-100. See also *Tsukushi michi no ki*, in *GSRJ* 18: 651-69; *Tsukushi michi no ki*, in *SKGSRJ* 15: 167-77 (the *GSRJ* ms. collated with the *Zoku Fusō shūyōshū* and Ban Kōjun 伴光淳 mss.); *Tsukushi michi no ki* (*GSRJ* ms.), eds. Kawazoe Shōji and Fukuda Hideichi, in Fukuda et al., eds., 1990: 405-32; and Eileen Katō 1979.

———. *Wakuraba*. See *Sōgi rengashū wakuraba*.

———. *Wasuregusa*. See *Sōgi rengashū wasuregusa*.

———. *Yodo no watari* 淀渡. In Kidō 1972-, 2: 281-96.

Sōgi, and Tō no Tsuneyori 東常縁. 1981. *Kokin wakashū kikigaki*. In vol. 3b of Katagiri Yōichi, ed., *Chūsei Kokinshū chūshakusho kaidai* 中世古近集注釈書解題, 545-846. Kyoto: Akao Shōbundō.

Sōgi et al. *Kawagoe senku*. See Shinkei et al.

Sōgi shokoku monogatari 宗祇諸国物語. See Mitatsu.

Sōkyū 宗久. *Miyako no tsuto* 都のつと (Fusō shūyōshū ms.). Ed. Fukuda Hideichi. In Fukuda et al., eds., 1990: 345-61. See also *Miyako no tsuto*, in *GSRJ* 18: 529-40 and *Miyako no tsuto (Souvenir for the Capital)*, in Plutschow and Fukuda 1981: 61-75; 105-12.

Sone Yoshitada 曽禰好忠. *Yoshitadashū* (also called *Sotanshū* 曽丹集). Ed. Matsuda Takeo 松田武夫. In Hisamatsu Sen'ichi et al., eds., *Heian Kamakura shikashū*, pp. 41-130. Vol. 80 of *NKBT*.

Sōseki 宗碩. *Sano no watari* 佐乃々和太利. In *ZGSRJ* 524: 1282–87. See also *Sano no watari* 佐野のわたり (Bunsei shichinen 文政七年 ms.), eds. Tsurusaki Hiroo and Fukuda Hideichi, in Fukuda et al., eds., 1990: 463–72.

Spacks, Patricia Meyer. 1976. *Imagining a Self: Autobiography and Novel in Eighteenth-Century England*. Cambridge, Mass.: Harvard University Press.

Starobinski, Jean. 1980. "The Style of Autobiography." In Olney 1980: 73–83.

Stevens, John. 1986. "Brush Strokes of Enlightenment." *The Transactions of the Asiatic Society of Japan*. Fourth series, 1: 79–107.

———. 1993. *Three Zen Masters: Ikkyū, Hakuin, Ryōkan*. Kodansha International.

Strassberg, Richard E. 1994. *Inscribed Landscapes: Travel Writing from Imperial China*. Berkeley: University of California Press.

Sugiyama Hiroshi 杉山博. 1974. *Sengoku daimyō*. Vol. 11 of *Nihon no rekishi*. Chūōkōronsha.

Suruga no Imagawashi 駿河の今川氏. 1975–87. Ed. Imagawashi Kenkyūkai. 10 vols. Shizuoka: Yajimaya.

Suzuki Mitsuyasu 鈴木光保. 1973. "Mikawa ni okeru Sōchō oboegaki" 三河における宗長覚え書き. In *Matsumura Hiroshi Kyōju taikan kinen kokugo kokubungaku ronshū* 松村博司教授退官記念国語国文学論集, pp. 311–32. Nagoya: Nagoya Daigaku.

Suzuki Torao 鈴木虎雄, ed. 1978. *To Ho zenshishū* 杜甫全詩集. 4 vols. Seishinsha.

Suzuki Tōzō 鈴木棠三, ed. 1965. *Inu tsukubashū* 犬つくば集. Comp. Yamazaki Sōkan. Kadokawa Shoten.

Tahara, Mildred, trans. 1980. *Tales of Yamato: A Tenth-Century Poem-Tale*. Honolulu: University of Hawaii Press.

Taiheiki 太平記. 1960–62. Eds. Gotō Tanji 後藤丹治 and Kamada Kisaburō 釜田喜三郎. Vols. 34–36 of *NKBT*. See also McCullough 1959.

Takahashi Kiichi 高橋喜一. 1975. "*Saishōsō* no kyōka" 『再昌草』の狂歌. *Ashiya zemi* 2 (Nov.): 22–37.

Takahashi Yoshio 高橋良雄. 1984. "*Kaikoku zakki* no haikaika" 『廻国雑記』の俳諧歌. *Gakuen* 529 (Jan.): 83–95.

Takakura Toshiaki 高倉聡明. 1986. "Imagawashi to Shimada kaji" 今川氏と島田鍛冶. In *SI* 9: 99–1.

Takeuchi Gengen'ichi 竹内玄玄一. 1987. *Haika kijindan, Zoku haika kijindan* 俳家奇人談・続俳家奇人談. Ed. Kira Sueo 雲英末雄. Iwanami Bunko.

Tamai Kōsuke 玉井幸助, and Ishida Yoshisada, eds. 1951. *Kaidōki, Tōkan kikō, Izayoi nikki* 海道記・東関紀行・十六夜日記. *NKZ*.

Tanaka Takahiro 田中隆裕. 1993. "Sōchō no bannen no seikatsu to kufū" 宗長の晩年の生活と句風. *Renga haikai kenkyū* 84 (March): 1–10.

Tanaka Yutaka 田中裕. 1969. "Renga no haikai." In *Chūsei bungakuron kenkyū*, pp. 416–30. Hanawa Shoten.

Tanaka Yutaka, and Akase Shingo 赤瀬信吾, eds. 1992. *Shinkokin wakashū*. Vol. 11 of *SNKBT*.

Tani Hiroshi 谷宏. 1952. "Haikai no renga." *Bungaku* 20.11: 61–72.

Tani Sōboku 谷宗牧. See Sōboku.

Tatoezukushi たとへづくし. 1979. Ed. Shōyōken Tōsei 松葉軒東井. Dōbōsha.

Thornhill, Arthur H. III. 1993. *Six Circles, One Dewdrop: The Religio-Aesthetic World of Komparu Zenchiku*. Princeton: Princeton University Press.

Toda Katsuhisa 戸田勝久. 1969. *Takeno Jōō kenkyū* 武野紹鴎研究. Chūōkōronsha.

Tōkaidō gojūsan tsugi 東海道五十三次. Illustrated by Utagawa Sadahide 歌川貞秀. Collection of Tanaka Takahiro 田中隆裕.

Tōkan kikō. 東関紀行. In Tamai and Ishida, eds., 1951: 141–201. See also *Tōkan kikō*, eds. Ōsone Shōsuke and Kubota Jun, in Fukuda et al., eds., 1990: 125–53; *Tōkan kikō*, ed. Nagasaki Ken, in Nagasaki et al., eds., 1994: 105–41; and "An Account of a Journey to the East," in McCullough 1990: 421–46.

Tosa nikki. See Ki no Tsurayuki.

Towazugatari とはずがたり. By Nijō 二条. Ed. Fukuda Hideichi. Vol. 20 of *SNKS*. See also Brazell 1973.

Toyohara Muneaki 豊原統秋 (also read Toyohara Sumiaki). *Shōkashō* 松下抄. In *ST* 6: 660–91.

Tsuchihashi Yutaka 土橋寛 and Konishi Jin'ichi. 1957. *Kodai kayōshū* 古代歌謡集. Vol. 3 of *NKBT*.

Tsuda Sōkyū 津田宗及. *Sōkyū takaiki* 宗及他会記. In Toda 1969.

Tsuge Kiyoshi 柘植清 et al. 1931. *Shizuokashi shi* 静岡市史. 5 vols. Shizuoka: Shizuoka Shiyakusho.

Tsukubashū 筑波集. Comp. Nijō Yoshimoto. Ed. Fukui Kyūzō. 2 vols. *NKZ*.

Tsunoda, Ryusaku, William Theodore de Bary, and Donald Keene, eds. 1958. *Sources of the Japanese Tradition*. New York: Columbia University Press.

Tsurusaki, Hiroo 鶴崎裕雄. 1969a. "Sengoku bushi bungei no ichikōsatsu: *Sōchō shuki* o chūshin to shite" 戦国武士文芸の一考察―『宗長手記』を中心として. In *Senriyama bungaku ronshū* 2: 39–51.

——. 1969b. "Sōchō to Echizen Asakurashi: Sengoku bunka ni kansuru ichikōsatsu" 宗長と越前朝倉氏―戦国文化に関する一考察. *Tezukayama Gakuin Kōtōbu kenkyū ronshū teoria* 17 (Nov.): 1–18.

——. 1971a. "Chūseishi kenkyū ni okeru bunkazai hogo no mondai: rengashi Sōchō to Ise Sekishi no kōshō o chūshin to shite" 中世史研究における文化財保護の問題―連歌師宗長と伊勢関氏の交渉を中心として. *Tezukayama Gakuin Chūgakubu, Kōtōbu kenkyū ronshū teoria* 20 (July): 1–18.

——. 1971b. "Sengoku shoki no Settsu kokujinsō no dōkō: Akutagawajōshu Noseshi to sono bungei, toku ni renga o chūshin to shite" 戦国初期の摂津国人層の動向―芥川城主能勢氏とその文芸、特に連歌を中心として. *Shisen* 43 (Sept.): 1–36.

———. 1973a. "Owari Atsutagū ni okeru rengashi Sōchō" 尾張熱田宮における連歌師宗長. *Tezukayama Gakuin Tanki Daigaku kenkyū kiyō* 21: 13-34.

———. 1973b. "Rengashi no egokoro: renga to suiboku sansuiga, toku ni Shōshō hakkeizu ni tsuite" 連歌師の絵ごころ—連歌と水墨山水画, 特に瀟湘八景図について. *Geinōshi kenkyū* 43 (Oct.): 38-49.

———. 1976a. "Kokujin ryōshu to yoriai no bungei" 国人領主と寄合の文芸. In Ōsaka Rekishi Gakkai, ed., *Chūsei shakai no seiritsu to tenkai*, pp. 485-534. Yoshikawa Kōbunkan.

———. 1976b. "Ōmi kokujinshū no senku renga kōgyō" 近江国人衆の千句連歌興行. In *Nihon bunkashi ronsō*, pp. 586-99. Shibata Minoru Sensei Koki Kinenkai.

———. 1977. "Suruga ni okeru Saiokuken Sōchō" 駿河における柴屋軒宗長. *Nihon bungaku kenkyū* (March): 25-39.

———. 1978. "Araara muge no niwazuki sōrō kana: rengashi Sōchō no bannen" あらあら無下の庭数寄候哉—連歌師宗長の晩年. *Tezukayama Gakuin Tanki Daigaku kenkyū nenpō* 26: 1-22.

———. 1979. "Seki Kajisai to rengashi Sōchō" 関何似斎と連歌師宗長. "Shōhōjiato hakkutsu chōsa hōkoku, dainiji" 正法寺跡発掘調査報告第二次, pp. 8-16. Sekichō Kyōiku Iinkai.

———. 1980. "Kōzuke no kuni kokujin ryōshu Iwamatsu Shōjun no renga to sono shiryō" 上野国国人領主岩松尚純の連歌とその資料. *Tezukayama gakuin tanki daigaku kenkyū nenpō* 28: 1-36.

———. 1983. "Rengashi Sōchō to Ōmi Kokujinshū" 連歌師宗長と近江国人衆. In *Chūbu daimyō no kenkyū* 中部大名の研究. Ed. Katsumata Shizuo 勝俣鎮夫. Vol. 4 of Nagahara 1983-85: 265-91.

———. 1987a. "Rengashi Sōboku to sannin no Jishutachi" 連歌師宗牧と三人の時衆たち. In *Yokota Ken'ichi Sensei koki kinen bunkashi ronsō* 横田健一先生古希記念文化史論叢, pp. 396-415. Sōgensha.

———. 1987b. "Oi no kurigoto" *Kokubungaku kaishaku to kyōzai no kenkyū* 32.4 (March): 144-45.

———. 1988. "*Sōgi shūenki* ni kansuru ni, san no mondai" 『宗祇終焉記』に関する二, 三の問題. *Kokugo to kokubungaku* 65.5 (May): 45-57.

———. 1993a. "The Poet Shōkō and the Salons of Sakai." Trans. Steven D. Carter. In Carter 1993: 45-62.

———. 1993b. "*Sanetakakōki Saishōsō* ni miru rengashi Sōchō" 『実隆公記』『再昌草』に見る連歌師宗長. *Tezukayama Gakuin Tanki Daigaku kenkyū nenpō* 41: 36-57.

———. 1996. "Sōchō nenpu kō: tanjō yori Eishō jūyonen made" 宗長年譜稿—誕生より永正十四年まで. *Tezukayama Gakuin Tanki Daigaku kenkyū nenpō* 44: 52-76.

———. 1997. "Ise Yamada ni okeru rengashi Sōchō: hitotsu no chihō bunka shiron" 伊

勢山田における連歌師宗長――一つの地方文化史論. In *Nihon bungaku shiron: Shimazu Tadao Sensei koki kinen ronshū* 島津忠夫先生古希記念論集, pp. 214–29. Sekai Shisōsha.

Tsurusaki Hiroo et al., eds. 1985. Vol. 7 of *Senku rengashū* 千句連歌集. Vol. 471 of *KB*.

Ury, Marian, trans. 1972. "Recluses and Eccentric Monks: Tales from *Hosshinshū* by Kamo no Chōmei." *Monumenta Nipponica* 27.2 (Summer): 150–73.

———. 1993. "The Ōe Conversations." *Monumenta Nipponica* 48.3 (Autumn): 359–80.

Usuda Jingorō 臼田甚五郎, and Shinma Shin'ichi 新間進一, eds. 1976. *Kagurauta, Saibara, Ryōjin hishō, Kanginshū* 神楽歌・催馬楽・梁塵秘抄・閑吟集. Vol. 25 of *NKBZ*.

Uzawa Satoru 鵜沢覚. 1956. "Sōchō shuki oboegaki." *Chiba Daigaku Bunrigakubu kiyō (Bunka kagaku)* 2.1 (Feb.): 1–10.

———. 1961. "Sōchō renga no hōhō" 宗長連歌の方法. *Chiba Daigaku Bunrigakubu Bunka Kagaku kiyō* 3: 65–84.

Varley, H. Paul. 1967. *The Ōnin War: History of its Origins and Background with a Selective Translation of The Chronicle of Ōnin*. New York: Columbia University Press.

———. 1977. "Ashikaga Yoshimitsu and the World of Kitayama: Social Change and Shogunal Patronage in Early Muromachi Japan." In Hall and Toyoda 1977: 183–204.

———. 1990. "Cultural Life in Medieval Japan." In Yamamura 1990b: 447–99.

Wakan rōeishū 和漢朗詠集. 1985. Comp. Fujiwara Kintō 藤原公任. Ed. Kawaguchi Hisao 川口久雄. Kōdansha.

Watson, Burton, trans. 1994. *Four Huts: Asian Writings on the Simple Life*. Boston: Shambhala.

Weinstein, Stanley. 1973. "The Concept of Reformation in Japanese Buddhism." In vol. 2 of Saburo Ota, ed., *Studies in Japanese Culture*. P.E.N. Club.

Yakame Norikatsu 矢亀師勝. 1983. "Kyaku hokku, teishu waki" 客発句・亭主脇. *Kokubungaku kaishaku to kyōzai no kenkyū* 28.1 (Jan.): 58–62.

Yamada Yoshio 山田孝雄. 1932. *Renga oyobi rengashi* 連歌及び連歌史. Vol. 13 of *Iwanami kōza Nihon bungaku*. Iwanami Shoten.

———, ed. 1951. *Arakida Moritakeshū* 荒木田守武集. Mie Prefecture, Uji Yamada: Jingūjichō.

———. 1980. *Renga gaisetsu* 連歌概説. Iwanami Shoten.

Yamada Yoshio, and Hoshika Sōichi 星加宗一. 1985. *Renga hōshiki kōyō* 連歌法式綱要. Iwanami Shoten.

Yamaguchi Sodō 山口素堂. *Sōchō koji no ki* 宗長居士の記 (provisional title). Saiokuji 柴屋寺 ms.

Yamamoto Takeshi 山本大, and Owada Tetsuo. 1984. *Sengoku daimyō kashindan jiten: tōgoku hen* 戦国大名家臣団事典―東国編. Shin Jinbutsu Ōraisha.

Yamamura, Kozo. 1990a. "The Growth of Commerce in Medieval Japan." In Yamamura 1990b: 344–95.

———, ed. 1990b. *The Cambridge History of Japan, Volume 3: Medieval Japan*. Cambridge: Cambridge University Press.

Yamanoue Sōji 山上宗二. *Yamanoue no Sōjiki* 山上の宗二記. In Kuwata 1969: 241–92. See also *Chaki meibutsushū* 茶記名物集, in *ZGSRJ* 19b: 466–501.

Yamato monogatari 大和物語. Ed. Takahashi Shōji 高橋正治. In Takahashi et al., eds., *Taketori monogatari, Ise monogatari, Yamato monogatari, Heichū monogatari*, pp. 267–434. Vol. 8 of *NKBZ*. See also Tahara 1980.

Yamazaki Masakazu 山崎正和. 1984. *Muromachiki* 室町記. Asahi Shinbunsha.

Yamazaki Sōkan 山崎宗鑑, attrib. *Shinsen inu tsukubashū* (also known as *Inu tsukubashū*). See Kimura and Iguchi 1988 and Suzuki Tōzō 1965.

Yanase Kazuo 簗瀬一雄, ed. 1964. *Kamo no Chōmei zenshū* 鴨長明全集. Annotated and collated (*kōchū* 校注). Kazama Shobō.

———. 1980. *Hōjōki*. Kadokawa Shoten.

Yasuda, Kenneth, trans. 1956. *Minase sangin hyakuin: A Poem of One Hundred Links Composed by Three Poets at Minase*. The Tosho Insatsu Printing Company.

Yasuraoka Kōsaku 安良岡康作. 1982. "Tonseisha no bungei to sono tenkai" 遁世者の文芸とその展開. *Senshū kokubun* 31 (Sept.): 1–33.

Yokoi Kiyoshi 横井清. 1979. *Higashiyama bunka*. Kyōikusha.

Yokomichi Mario 横道萬里男, and Omote Akira 表章, eds. 1972. *Yōkyokushū* 謡曲集. Vols. 40–41 of *NKBT*.

Yokota Ken'ichi 横田健一. 1957. "Daitokuji Shinjuan to Asakurashi" 大徳寺真珠庵と朝倉氏. *Shiseki to bijutsu* 27.6 (July): 202–9.

Yokoyama Haruo 横山晴夫. 1978. "Chūbu no gun'yū" 中部の群雄. In vol. 3 of Kuwata Tadachika, ed., *Nihon no kassen*, pp. 323–94. Shin Jinbutsu Ōraisha.

Yonehara Masayoshi 米原正義. 1979. *Sengoku bushi to bungei no kenkyū* 戦国武士と文芸の研究. Ōfūsha.

Yoshida Kenkō 吉田兼好. 1971. *Tsurezuregusa* 徒然草. Ed. Yasuraoka Kōsaku. Ōbunsha. See also Keene 1967.

Yoshida Yukata 吉田豊 ed. 1983. *Buke no kakun* 武家の家訓. Tokkan Shoten.

Yoshikawa Ichirō 吉川一郎. 1955. *Yamazaki Sōkanden* 山崎宗鑑伝. Yōtokusha.

Yoshikawa Kōichirō 吉川幸一郎, ed. 1977–83. *To Ho shichū* 杜甫詩注. 5 vols. Chikuma Shobō.

Yoshishige Yasutane 慶慈保胤. 1968. *Chiteiki* 池亭記. In vol. 2 of Kakimura Shigematsu 柿村重松, ed., *Honchō monzui chūshaku* 本朝文粋注釈, pp. 693–708. 2 vols. Fūzanbō.

Yotsutsuji Yoshishige 四辻善成. *Genji monogatari chidorishō* 源氏物語千鳥抄. In *ZGSRJ* 18b: 842–900.

Yōyōki 養鷹記. In *GSRJ* 19: 483–85.

Yūki senjō monogatari 結城戦場物語. In *GSRJ* 20: 712–34.

Yunoue Sanae 湯之上早苗. 1972. "Sōgi kushū *Wasuregusa* zōbu no mondai" 宗祇句集『萱草』雑部の問題. *Kokubungaku kō* 60 (Dec.): 20–30.

Zenpo zōdan. See Konparu Zenpō.

Bibliography

Zōho shiryō taisei 増補資料大成. 1965–75. Ed. Zōho Shiryō Taisei Kankōkai. 48 vols. Rinsen Shoin.

Zōki 増基. *Ionushi* いほぬし. In *GSRJ* 18: 348–60.

Zoku gunsho ruijū 続群書類従. 1957–72. Eds. Hanawa Hokiichi et al. Rev. ed. (*teisei* 訂正). 37 vols., with three supplements (*hoi* 補遺). Zoku Gunsho Ruijū Kanseikai.

Zoku Gunsho Ruijū Kanseikai, ed. 1962–66. *Gunsho kaidai* 群書解題. 22 vols. Zoku Gunsho Ruiju Kanseikai.

Zoku shiryō taisei 続資料大成. 1967. Ed. Takeuchi Rizō 竹内理三. 22 vols. Kyoto: Rinsen Shoin.

Zoku zoku gunsho ruijū. 1978. Ed. Kokusho Kankōkai. 17 vols. (vol. 17 ed. Kosho Hozonkai 古書保存会). Zoku Gunsho Ruijū Kanseikai.

Index

Page numbers in boldface type indicate the most important reference.

Abeyama gold mines, 59, 99
Abutsu, 113, 219, 242, 321, 332
Ageku (final verse), 217
Agriculture, 15
Aiwa. See Tragic anecdotes
Allusive variation (*honkadori*), 228–29, 250, 287
Akahito. See Yamanobe Akahito
Amaterasu (Sun Goddess), 255
Amayo no ki (A Rainy Night Record), 203, 220, 225, 304, 353, 355
Anecdotes, 23
Anonotsu, 71, 128
Anrakuan Sakuden, 332, 360
Arakida Morihira, 69, 354, 365
Arakida Moritake, 17, 53, 254–57, 266, 293, 360, 363
Arakida Moritoki, 183
Arakidashū, 360
Arima, Mount, 228
Ariwara Motokata, 286
Ariwara Narihira, 128, 171, 201, 207
"Asahina Battle Chronicle," The, 64, 98–102, 332
Asahina house, 5, 14, 28, 60–61, **64–65**, 70, 76, 84, 127, 300
Asahina Tokishige, 15, 17, 19, 44, 63–65, 76, 103, 127, 150, 300
Asahina Yasuhiro, 64, 98, 300
Asahina Yasumochi, 63–65, 75–76, 98, 300, 337
Asahina Yasuyoshi, 60, 64, 98, 127, 300, 331–32

Asakura house, 5–6, 19, 28, 33, 35, 53, 56, 67, 69, 71, 319
Asakura Norikage, 5–6, 19, 69, 73
Asakura Takakage. See Asakura Toshikage
Asakura Toshikage (Takakage), 32, 56, 323
Ashikaga house, 12–13, 16, 27, 61, 320
Ashikaga Yoshiharu, 13, 74, 100, 320, 325
Ashikaga Yoshihisa, 320, 339
Ashikaga Yoshimasa, 13, 30, 32, 329
Ashikaga Yoshimitsu, 326, 329
Ashikaga Yoshinori, 98, 329
Ashikaga Yoshitaka. See Ashikaga Yoshizumi
Ashikaga Yoshitane, 319–20
Ashikaga Yoshizumi, 303, 320
Association (*yoriai*), 209, 214
Asukai Masaari, 321
Asukai Masayasu, 330
Asukai Masayo, 330
Atami, 77
Atsuta Shrine, 73, 139–41
Awaji, 101
Awa Province (now Tokushima Prefecture), 101
Azuchi Castle, 319
Azumaji no tsuto (Souvenir of the Eastland), 65, 71, 84, 104, 305, 330, 332, 336
Azuma kudari (Down to the Eastland), 113
Azuma michi no ki (Travels in the Eastland), by Saigyō, 124, 339
Azuma michi no ki, by Shōtetsu, 146, 339

Index

Azuma mondō (Eastland Questions and Answers), 200, 242, 267, 333, 352, 355, 359

Background. See *Ji*
Bakhtin, Mikhail x–xii, 22, 117–20, 126, 130–33, 139, 272, 296, 321, 337–38, 364, 366
Bakufu (or shogunate), 12–13, 15–16, 19, 31–32, 40, 42, 99, 100
Ballad drama. See *Kōwakamai*
Bashō, 232, 266, 295–97, 301, 363, 366
Basic essence (*hon'i*), 25, 199, 219
Beneath the blossoms linked verse (*hananomoto renga*), 198, 351
Ben no Naishi, 26, 322
Benzaiten, 18, 320
Bishamondō, 173
Bitchūnokami, 129
Biwa, 24
Biwa, Lake, 68, 74
Biyanlu (The Blue Cliff Record), 192
Black-Hair Mountain (Kurokamiyama), 108, 333
Blind performers, 279
Bo Juyi (Letian), 159, 162–63, 167, 171, 342, 345, 349, 360
Bokuō, 111, 335
Bokurin, 111, 335
Bokusai, 14, 326
Bokuun, 366
Bontō, 223, 333, 355
Bontōanshu hentōsho (Answers from the Master of Bontō Cottage), 223, 333, 355
Book of Songs, The (C: *Shijing*; J: *Shikyō*), 3, 58, 328
Bōshū, 91
Botanka Shōhaku. See *Shōhaku*
Brushwood Cottage (Saioku), 37, 65, 76–77, 148–49, 169, 172–75, 181, 191–92, 293–95, 301, 324, 340, 358
Buddhism, 6, 15, 17–19, 43, 47, 68, 79, 92, 104, 116, 138, 147–48, 151–53, 156–57, 164–67, 170–71, 175, 182–83, 192, 226, 230, 265, 269, 320, 341–42, 345–46, 350–51, 354, 362. See also Esoteric Buddhism; Ji sect; Pure Land sect; Shingon; Tendai; True Pure Land sect; Zen
Bunmei 12 [1480]:8 *Nanimichi hyakuin* (A Hundred-Verse Sequence Entitled "A Kind of Path"), 33, 303

Bunmei no naikō, 31
Bun'yōshū (Separating Leaves), 263
Cadastral surveys (*kenchi*), 58
Caotangji, 345
Chakaiki (tea diaries), 82
Chaki meibutsushū (Tea Utensils and Famous Pieces), 329
"Changhenge," 361
Chengdu, 166
Chikamasa. See *Ninakawa Chikamasa*
Chikuba kyōginshū (Hobbyhorse Collection of Mad Song), 254–55, 359–60
Chikurinshō (Bamboo Grove Collection), 32, 34, 151, 199, 352–53
Chikuzennokami, 139
Chikuzen Province (now part of Fukuoka prefecture), 142, 145
China, 17, 19, 22, 24, 29, 44, 58, 148, 159–60, 162–65, 167–68, 171, 185, 192, 225, 320, 326, 342–51, 353–54
Chinzō (portrait of a Zen master), 47
Chiun, 34, 207, 324
Chōka (long poem), 8, 95, 150, 175, 193, 290–91
Chōka, 359
Chōku. See *Kami no ku*
Chōrakuji, Abbot of, 241
Chōrokubumi (Letter to Nagao Magoroku), 122, 333, 337, 339
Chronicles, 28–29, 61, 98–100, 366
Chuang Tsu. See *Zhuangzi*
Clash (*uchikoshi*), 210–11, 263
Close link (*shinku*), 218, 355
Commissioner of Linked Verse at Kitano Shrine (Kitano Renga Kaisho Bugyō), 36, 38, 325
Conclusion (in a renga sequence, *kyū*), 213
Configuration (*sugata*), 200–201
Confucianism, 164–65, 167–68, 342–43, 351
Constable (military constable, *shugo*), 13–14, 58
Conviction. See *Ushin* verse
Corner Dwelling (Kadoya), 351
Cottage in a Mountain Village (Sanrian), 351
Cottage of Floral Delights (Rōkaken), 165
Currency, 15; Eirakusen, 264, *hiki*, 50, 63, 67, **327**, 328; *kan* or *kanmon*, 328; *mon*, 328
Cutting word (*kireji*), 203, 353

Dai. See Topic
Daigoji, 123, 322, 367
Daiō, 327
Daisan (the third verse in a linked-verse sequence), 204, **210–11**, 354
Daisen'in (in Daitokuji), 135
Daitō, 42, 45, 326–27
Daitokuji (see also Shinjuan, Plum Cottage), 5–7, 18, 34–35, 41–42, 46, 48, 51, **54–56**, 63, 68, 74–75, 87, 135, 149, 177–78, 192, 302, 324, 326–28
Daoism. *See* Taoism
Dazaifu, 142, 144, 338
Deep feeling. *See Ushin* verse
Den'a dokugin jōji hyakuin, 361
Desultory conversation (*zōdan*), 8, 103
Development (in a renga sequence, *ha*), 213, 262
Diary literature (*nikki bungaku*), 93; *kanbun nikki* (diary in Chinese), 8, 82, 93, 96, 138; *wabun nikki* (diary in Japanese), 8, 80–83, 93–94, 96; female diary, 93
Distant link (*soku*), 137, 218, 355
Dōbōshū (artistic companion), 61, 329
Dōjō (courtly) poets, 197
Dōken. *See* Iwayama Dōken
Dōkō (or Dōkyō), 365
Dokugin. See Solo sequence
Dōkyō. *See* Dōkō
Dōri. See Principle
Dōsha (wayfarer), 116
Dōshin (religious aspiration), 163
Dosō. *See* Pawnbroker
Dream Cottage (Muan), 148, 163–65, 168, 193, 346
Dreams, 79, 85–86, 91, 110, 112, 116, 126, 151, 159–61, 166, 168, 179, 189–90, 200, 261, 294, 344, 346–47, 366; the dream of a butterfly (*Zhuangzi*), 346–47
Du Fu, 168, 347–48
Du Xunhe, 344

Echigo Province (now part of Niigata Prefecture), 32, 36, 121
Echizen Province (now part of Fukui Prefecture), 5, 32, 56, 66, 96, 123
Edo, 23
Edo period, 53, 60, 71, 78, 96, 103, 254, 257–58, 266, 295–97, 322, 330, 348, 366

Eiga taigai (Essentials of Composing Waka), 49
Ei gojusshu waka (Fifty-Waka Compositions), 359
Eight Bridges, 126
Eight Peaks Pass, 72
Eiraku coins (*Eirakusen*). *See* Currency
Eishō gonen kyōkaawase (Kyōka Contest of the Fifth Year of Eishō), 365
Elegance (*yū*), 237
Epic, epical, x, 117–20, 122, 126, 128, 130–35, 139–41, 162, 167, 169, 185, 193, 218, 337, 350
Eremitic literature (or hermitage literature, *sōan bungaku*), x, 6, 9, 27, 48, 80, 82, 94, 96, 105, 146–93, 195, 235, 290–91, 340, 345, 349–50; and Shinkei, 158–63; and Shōhaku, 163–68; Sōchō's figuring of the poetic *sōan* orthodoxy, 151–57; the *sōan* in *The Journal of Sōchō*, 169–93; urban reclusion (*shichū no kakure*), 192, 350
Esoteric Buddhism (see also Shingon, Tendai), 17–18, 320, 341
Evangelists (*shōdōshi*), 18

Fei Zhangfang, 159, 162, 343
Festival of the Weaver Maid (Tanabata) 63, 150, 240, 274, 284–85
Fifth Ward, 273
First round (*ichijun*), 213, 217, 353, 357
Flower arranging, 24
Foundation poem (*honka*), 205, 210, 213, 219, 228–29, 356
Fudō, 271
Fūgashū (*Fūga wakashū*), 250, 358
Fuji, Mount, 159, 176, 226, 230–33, 251, 291, 323
Fuji goran nikki (Diary of Viewing Fuji), 98, 146, 305
Fuji rekiranki (An Account of Sightseeing at Fuji), 330
Fujiwara Akihira, 21
Fujiwara Ietaka, 112–13, 201, 216, 336
Fujiwara Kanesuke, 325
Fujiwara Kintō, 148
Fujiwara Kiyō, 284
Fujiwara Mototoshi, 223
Fujiwara Nagako, 141
Fujiwara Norikane, 336
Fujiwara Sanefusa, 341

Index

Fujiwara Shunzei, 130–31, 201, 222–23, 231, 250, 322, 340, 359
Fujiwara Tameie, 321
Fujiwara Teika, 199–201, 222, 231, 322, 328, 341, 352
Fujiwara Toshiyuki, 288
Fujiwara Yoshitsune, 201
Fukuda Hachirō, 91
Fūkyō (crazy, wild, free-spirited [or *kyōfū*]), 43, 45
Funi. See Nonduality
Fūryū. See Style
Furyū monji. See Nonverbalization
Fushimi, 72, 178
Fushimono (renga sequence title), 207

Ga (elegant, formal, precedented), 41, 44, 47, 79, 141, 198, 255–56, 264, 267–68, 283, 285, 287, 326, 351
Gardens, 115, 159, 162, 165, 167, 170, 173–75, 178, 184, 191–92, 215–16, 248, 258, 294, 302, 343, 351
Gatten no ku (Judged Verses), 360
Geiami, 329
Gekokujō (inferior overcoming superior), 11, 99, 319
Genjichū (Genji Commentary, *Genji monogatari-shō*), 39, 305, 325
Genji monogatari (The Tale of Genji), 24, 35, 39, 49, 55, 73, 228, 250, 262, 271, 273, 290–92, 304–5, 321, 325, 328, 335, 347, 362, 365–66
Gensei, 264
Gessonsai senku. See Iba senku
Gessonsai Sōseki. *See* Sōseki
Go, 278–79
Godaishū utamakura (*Utamakura* in the Collections of Five Eras), 336
Gōdanshō (The Ōe Conversations), 21, 320
Gojō Yoshisuke, 28, 301, 322
Gokashiwabara, Emperor (Crown Prince Katsuhito), 12, 49, 52, 238, 358
Gokokuji, 178, 245–46
Gonara, Emperor, 12
Gonsōjō Eien, 287
Gosenshū (*Gosen wakashū*), 197, 325, 335
Goshirakawa, Emperor, 21
Goshūishū (*Goshūi wakashū*), 114, 329
Gotsuchimikado, Emperor, 49, 324, 342, 361

Gozan (Five Mountains Zen), 17–18, 42, 54–55, 328
Grace (*uruwashiku*), 237
Guilds (*za*), 14
Guhishō (Ignorant Private Notes), 336, 352
Guku wakuraba (My Ignorant Blighted Verses), 304, 355
Gyokuyōshū (*Gyokuyō wakashū*), 250

Hachidaishū (the first eight imperial waka anthologies), 228
Haibun (haikai prose), 141, 296
Haikai (unorthodox or comic verse), x, 5, 8–9, 17–18, 22, 34, 41, 48, 56, 78, 87, 103–5, 122, 137–38, 139, 140–42, 163, 195, 198–99, 203, 226, 236–38, 240, 246, 253–92, 295–97, 328; haikai waka (haikaika or haikai uta), 105, 139, 253, 274, 277, 281, 283–90, 365; historical development of, 254–56; in *Shinsen inu tsukubashū*, 275–82; Sōchō's haikai renga, 267–92; Sōchō's haikai waka, 283–90; Sōchō's haikai chōka, 290–92; Sōgi's haikai, 257–67; Takigi haikai sequence, 203, 254, 268–82, 285–86
Haikaika. See Haikai
Haika kijindan (Anecdotes about Haikai Poets and Uncommon Characters), 295, 328, 366
Hakata, 142
Hakone Mountain, 301
Hakozaki, 142–43
Hakugyokushū (Collection of Oaken Jewels), 358
Hakusan Shrine, 226
Hall of No Renunciation (Fushain), 189–90
Hamamatsu, 129
Hamana, 87, 129
Hamori senku (*Shugyokuan senku*), 303
Hananomoto renga. See Beneath the blossoms linked verse
Hanashibon (collection of humorous poetry and prose), 103, 295, 332
Hannyaji Hill, 270
Hare no uta. See Public poetry
Hatted linked verse (*kasagi renga*), 198, 351
Hattori Dohō, 366
Hawking, 202
Heian period, 21, 26, 93, 114, 197, 345, 347
Heike house, 362

Heike monogatari (The Tale of the Heike), 20–21, 24
Hekigyokushū (Collection of Cyan Jewels), 358
Hiei, Mount, 17, 69, 226, 233
Hiesabi (cold and withered), 352
Higashiyama, 21
Higashiyama senku, 304
Hikima. *See* Hikuma
Hikuma, 60, 98, 100, 328
Hino, 123, 184
Hiraku (generic verses, numbers 4–99 in a hundred-verse sequence), 204, 212, 353
Hira Mountains, 180, 190, 249
Hirano, 109, 334
Hirao, 71
Hitomaro. *See* Kakinomoto Hitomaro
Hitorigoto (Talking to Myself), 34, 324, 333, 342
Hiwa. *See* Tragic anecdotes
Hōgaiken Dōken. *See* Iwayama Dōken
Hōjōki (An Account of My Hut), 157, 160, 184, 340–42
Hōjō Sōun, 30–31, 60, 77, 100, 300, 323
Hōjō Ujitsuna, 77
Hokekyō. *See* Lotus Sutra
Hokkoku no michi no ki (An Account of a Journey to the Northland), 301
Hokku (the first verse in a linked-verse sequence), 6, 8, 65, 67, 69, 80, 82–83, 96–97, 99, 105, 127, 130, 132, 150, 153, 160, 183, **202–4**, 205–7, 338–39, 353, 361
Homosexuality, 31, 46, 79, 134, 140, 277, 323. *See also* Young men
Hon'i. *See* Basic essence
Honka. *See* Foundation poem
Honkadori. *See* Allusive variation
Honnogahara, 129
Honsaka, 129
Hōraku verse. *See* Votive verse
Horikoshi Kubō, 337
Hoshizaki, 139
Hosokawa house, 33, 51
Hosokawa Katsumoto, 30
Hosokawake senku, 303, 320
Hosokawa Masamoto, 51, 303, 319
Hosokawa Takakuni, 5, 13, 51, 69, 74, 100–101, 181, 181, 304
Hosokawa Yūsai, 39, 325
Hosshinshū (A Collection of Religious Awakenings), 341

House laws (*kahō*), 58, 103
Humorous anecdotes, 102–3. *See also Hanashibon*
Hundred-verse sequences (*hyakuin*). *See* Linked verse
Hundred-*waka* sequences (*hyakushu*). *See Waka*
Hyakuin. *See* Hundred-verse sequences
Hyakunin isshu (A Hundred Poems by a Hundred Poets), 39
Hyakunin isshuchū (Commentary on *A Hundred Poems by a Hundred Poets*), 358
Hyakunin isshushō (Notes on *A Hundred Poems by a Hundred Poets*), 33
Hyakushu. *See* Hundred-*waka* sequences
Hyōbukyō, 130

Iba house, 321
Iba Sadakazu (Tanemura Nakatsukasanojō), 304, 357
Iba senku (*Gessonsai senku*), 53, 233, 304, 327, 357
Ibuki Mountains, 190, 249
Ichijōdani, 53
Ichijō Kaneyoshi, 32, 163, 209, 239, 345, 352
Ichijun. *See* First round
Ietaka. *See* Fujiwara Ietaka
Ihara Saikaku. *See* Saikaku
Iio Sōgi. *See* Sōgi
Iio Zenshirō Noritsura, 129
Iisute ("throw away") verses, 196
Ikeda, 163, 346
Iki no matsubara, 142
Ikki (leagues), 14, 16, 19
Ikkō ikki, 19
Ikkyū, 7, 17, **34–35,** 36, 38, 40, **41–48**, 54–56, 68, 74, 86–87, 92, 104, 141, 149, 168, 170, 177–78, 181, 183, 187, 189, 192, 249, 257–58, 272, 276, 295–96, 302, 323–24, 326–28, 350, 359; and sword, 43, 45, 47, 327
Ikkyūbanashi (Anecdotes about Ikkyū), 258, 324
Ikkyū Oshō nenpu (The Chronicle of Ikkyū), 326
Imagawa house, 5, 7, 12–14, 16, 28, **29–32**, 35–38, 40, 49–51, 54, **57–64**, 64–68, 74–76, 79, 84, 98–101, 127, 149, 187, 240, 302, 305, 323, 329, 331; and the linked-verse profession, 60–64. *See also* Jukei; Kitagawa, Lady; Imagawa Yoshitada; Imagawa Ujichika; Imagawa Ujiteru; *etc*.
Imagawajō (Imagawa Epistle), 58, 328

407

Index

Imagawa kafu (Lineage of the Imagawa House), 59, 63, 98, 305, 328–29, 332
Imagawa kana mokuroku. See *Kana mokuroku*
Imagawa keizu (Imagawa Lineage), 29
Imagawa Norikuni, 300
Imagawa Norimasa, 29, 59, 98, 146, 300, 305, 328
Imagawa Noritada, 300
Imagawa Noriuji, 300
Imagawake ryakki (Abbreviated Chronicle of the Imagawa House), 29
Imagawa Ryōshun, 29, 52, 58–59, 300, 327
Imagawa Ujichika (Honjosama, Ryūōmaro [Tatsuōmaro], Jōki, Kyōzan, Shōsaku, Shurinodaibu), 31, 36–37, 39, 49–51, 58–62, 64, 65, 74–77, 88, 91, 98–100, 241, 244, 300, 302–3, 323–24, 328–29, 331, 357
Imagawa Ujiteru (Gorō, Honjo, Ryūōmaro [Tatsuōmaro]), 31, 39, 60, 62–63, 75–76, 188, 230, 241, 300, 305, 330; coming of age, 63
Imagawa Ujitoyo, 60
Imagawa Ujizane, 60, 300
Imagawa Yasunori, 300
Imagawa Yoshimoto, 60, 300–301, 366
Imagawa Yoshitada (Chōhōjidono), 14, 28, **29–31**, 33, 57, 62, 74, 98, 300, 302, 322, 329, 366
Imahashi 70–71
Inano, 228, 346
Inasa Inlet, 129
Inawashiro Kensai. See *Kensai*
Incense, 23, 42, 91, 125, 165–66, 181, 231, 345, **347-48**; incense-matching competitions (*takimonoawase, meikōawase, kōawase*), 347; *jinkō* (aloe wood incense), 347; *kōdō* (the way of incense), 347; *nerikō* (blended incense), 347; six scents, 347
Ineffable beauty (*yūgen*), 20, 200, 204, 222, 237
Inohana, 70
Inō Sōgi. See *Sōgi*
Introduction (in a renga sequence, *jo*), 213
Inu tsukubashū. See *Shinsen inu tsukubashū*
Ionushi (Master of the Cottage), 95, 332
Ise, Lady, 136, 201
Ise Bay, 139
Ise Daijingū sankeiki (Diary of a Pilgrim to Ise), 333, 351
Ise haikai kikigakishū, 363

Ise house, 67, 300
Ise monogatari (Tales of Ise), 33, 39, 50, 95, 113, 126, 128, 146, 171, 226, 228, 246, 250, 329, 332, 362–63
Ise monogatari Sōchō kikigaki, 33, 304, 323
Ise Province (now part of Mie Prefecture), 64, 67, 159, 180, 285, 342
Ise Sadachika, 30
Ise senku, 51, 70, 203, 304, 327
Ise Shrine, 5–6, 17, 53, 69–70, 125, 135, 159, 181, 183, 186, 203, 207, 255, 304, 327, 330, 334–35, 351, 355; *Ise Daijingū sankeiki* (Diary of a Pilgrim to Ise), 333, 351
Ishikawa Shōrō, 338
Ishikura, 159
Issho fujū (not living in one place), 178
Issunbōshi (Little One-Inch), 320
Isuzu Mimosusogawa river, 125
Iwaki Minbunotaifu Yoshitaka, 191
Iwaki Province (now part of Miyagi and Fukushima Prefectures), 191
Iwayama Dōken (Hōgaiken), 69, 238, 358
Izanagi, 196
Izanami, 196
Izayoi nikki (Journal of the Sixteenth-Night Moon), 83, 95, 332
Izumi Province (now part of Osaka Prefecture), 135
Izumi Shikibu, 26
Izumi Shikibu nikki, 95
Izumigawa, 302
Izumigaya, 172
Izu Province (now part of Shizuoka Prefecture), 30, 66

Jakuren, 201
Ji (background), xi, 97, 214, 218, 355
Ji (Time) sect, 17–18, 69, 102, 135–36, 330
Jichin. See *Jien*
Jien (Jichin), 115, 152, 201, 231–32, 356
Jige (commoner) poets, 197
Jikka senku (A Thousand-Verse Sequence of Ten Blossoms), 53, 304
Ji-sho-i. See Season, place, and level
Jiteiki (or *Niteiki*, Deep in the Ear), 325
Jizamurai (small-scale samurai cultivators), 14
Jōan Ryūsū, 345–46, 349
Jōdo Shinshū. See True Pure Land sect
Jōdoshū. See Pure Land sect

Index

Jōfukuji, 135
Jōgyōji, 342
Jōha (Satomura), 26, 321, 325, 333, 353–54
Jōha (Sōchō's son, later Suian), 37, 66, 294, 325
Jōha Amanohashidate kikō (An Account of Jōha's Journey to Amanohashidate), 333
Jōha Fujimi michi no ki (An Account of Jōha's Journey to Fuji), 295, 333, 366
Jo-ha-kyū (introduction, development, conclusion), 213, 218
Jōji linked verse, 261–64, 266, 361; *Sōgi jōji hyakuin*, 261–64, 266, 269, 361
Jōsū, 135
Journal of Sōchō, The (*Sōchō shuki*; also *Hokkoku no michi no ki* [?], *Sōchō kikō, Sōchō kuku no ki, Sōchō michi no ki, Sōchō nikki, Sōchō Suruga nikki, Sōchō Suruga zoku nikki* [a sequel to the previous manuscript], *Sōchōki*), ix, xi, 5–9, 11, 15–16, 20, 23, 26–27, 29, 31, 35, 42, 48, 52–54, 57, 59–61, 63–67, 80, 84, 92, 93–98, 102–5, 107, 122–23, 129, 132–34, 137–38, 141–43, 146–47, 150, 168–69, 185, 187, 195, 204, 220–22, 230, 233, 237–40, 243, 247, 250, 253, 267, 280, 283, 293, 295–96, 305, 320, 322–24, 327, 330, 332, 337, 359, 364, 366–67; the journal in overview, 93–95; genres in, 8, 95–105; as travel literature, 107, **122–46**, 332, 337; travel and repose in, 148–51, 154, 169; as eremitic literature, 147–93, 340, 349; poetry in, 195–292, 359, 364
Jūjūshin'in, 158
Jūjūshin'in Shinkei kikō. See *Oi no kurigoto*
Jukei, 59–60, 76, 300, 328, 330
Jukkai. See Lament

Kabekusa (Wall Grass), 57, 105, 305, 327, 329
Kabekusachū (Wall Grass Commentary), 305
Kachiyama, 129
Kadoya. See Corner Dwelling
Kaeruyama. See Mountain of Returning
Kaga Province (now part of Ishikawa Prefecture), 19
Kagerō nikki (The Gossamer Years), 94
Kahō. See House laws
Kaidōki (Sea Road Account), 184
Kaikoku zakki (A Miscellaneous Record of Provincial Travels), 365
Kai no kuni rekidaifu (History of the Lords of Kai Province), 329

Kai Province (now Yamanashi Prefecture), 61–62, 99, 101
Kairaishiki (Of Puppeteers), 21
Kaisho (meeting place), 24
Kajisai. See Seki Kajisai
Kakegawa Castle, 64, 127, 129
Kakekotoba (pivot word), 136, 227–28, 230, 264
Kakinomoto Hitomaro, 200, 272, 301, 352, 360
Kakinomotoshū, 360
Kamakura, 23, 27, 159, 208
Kamakura period, 26, 197, 208, 240, 340
Kameyama Castle, 67, 69–71
Kamiji, Mount, 335
Kami no ku (or *chōku*, the 17-syllable verses in a *renga* sequence), 212
Kamo no Chōmei, 113, 151, 157, 160–61, 184, 341
Kana mokuroku (*Kana Code, Imagawa kana mokuroku*), 58, 328
Kanbun 8, 63, 98, 104, 135, 345, 349; *kanbun chokuyakutai*, 93; *kanbun kundoku*, 127
Kanginshū (Songs Sung in Tranquillity), 20
Kankyo no tomo (A Friend in Tranquil Solitude), 340
Kanō School, 19
Kanrei (shogunal deputy), 13
Kan Sanbon. See Sugawara Fumitoki
Karasumaru Mitsuhiro, 325
Kasagi renga. See Hatted linked verse
Kashii Shrine, 142
Kasō, 48
Kasuga, Mount, 237
Katada, 179
Katauta (an archaic poem type of 5-7-7 syllables), 196
Katsuyama Castle, 99
Kawagoe senku, 158, 323
Kawarabayashi Masayori, 101
Keeper of the Fires, 196
Kefukigusa (Splitting Hairs), 348
Kenchi. See Cadastral surveys
Kenkokuji, 125
Kenmu nenkanki, 354
Kenmu Restoration (*Kenmu no chūkō*), 13, 208
Kenninji, 166
Ken'ō, 42
Ke no uta. See Private poetry

409

Index

Kensai, 49, 256, 327, 360
Kensai zōdan, 103
Kenzan, 327
Kigin. *See* Kitamura Kigin
Kigo. *See* Seasonal word
Kii Province (now part of Wakayama and Mie Prefectures), 158, 335
Kikigakishū, 365
Kikō bungaku. *See* Travel literature
Kingon wakaawase (Waka Contest of Golden Words), 365
Kinkaishū, 334
Ki no Tadana (Seimei), 344
Ki no Toshisada, 284
Ki no Tsurayuki, 95, 127, 141, 201, 362
Kin'yōshū (*Kin'yō wakashū*), 287
Kireji. *See* Cutting word
Kirihioke (Paulownia Brazier), 352, 363
Kiryoka (travel waka), 112
Kitagawa, Lady, 30–31, 37, 62, 76, 300, 329, 337
Kitamuki, 30, 59, 300
Kitamura Kigin, 265, 360
Kitano Renga Kaisho Bugyō. *See* Commissioner of Linked Verse at Kitano Shrine
Kitanosha ichimanku onhokku waki daisan shidai narabi ni jo, 354–55
Kitano Shrine, 36, 160, 198, 355
Kiyohara Motosuke, 334
Kiyomi Gate, Strand, 29–30, 131, 146, 244–47. *See also* Seikenji
Koga Kubō, 337
Kojiki (Record of Ancient Matters), 196, 351
Kojōruri (puppet plays predating Chikamatsu's of the late seventeenth century), 20
Kokinshū (*Kokin wakashū*), 7, 21–22, 32, 38–39, 45, 49, 52, 63, 79, 88, 116, 120, 136, 140–42, 195, 152, 197–98, 206–7, 209–10, 211, 217, 225–26, 228, 236, 239, 250, 267, 283–88, 333–35, 353–54; *Kokinshū* preface, 116, 136, 356, 358–59; Secret Traditions of *Kokinshū* (*Kokin denju*), 7, 21–22, 32, 38–40, 45, 49, 52, 63, 79, 120, 142, 163, 239, 325, 348
Kokin wakashū ryōdo kikigaki, 323
Kokoro (sense, content, feeling, spirit), 201, 232, 252, 279–80
Kokorozuke. *See* Linking by meaning
Kokujin (men of the provinces), 14, 16, 19, 64–68, 330
Komachi. *See* Ono no Komachi

Konjaku monogatarishū (Tales of Times Now Past), 338
Konoe Hisamichi, 22
Konoe house, 294, 305
Konoe Masaie, 238
Konohama, 130, 249, 268
Konparu Zenchiku, 34, 324
Korai fūteishō (Notes on Poetic Style Through the Ages), 359
Kōsai, 322
Kotoba (rhetoric, diction, language), 201, 232, 252
Kotobazuke. *See* Linking by words
Kotsugawa, 72
Kouta (a type of popular song), 20
Kōwakamai (ballad drama), 20, 362
Kōya, Mount, 32, 269
Kōya monks, 269, 273, 276–77, 365
Kōya sankei nikki (Diary of a Pilgrimage to Kōya), 327
Koyorogi Strand, 288
Kubota, 71
Kumagai Echigonokami, 129
Kumano nuns (Kumano bikuni), 18
Kumozugawa, 71
Kuonji, 329
Kurinomotoshū, 360
Kurokamiyama. *See* Black-Hair Mountain
Kurokawa Dōyū, 29, 295, 331, 367
Kurokawa river, 109
Kyōgen (humorous play presented after a *nō* drama or as an entr'acte), 7, 20, 256, 322
Kyōgen kigo. *See* Wild words and fancy phrases
Kyōgoku house, 224
Kyōka (comic *waka*), 139, 283, 293, 365
Kyōka sake hyakushu, 365
Kyōku (comic linked verse), 264, 267
Kyoto (or capital, Upper Capital, Lower Capital), 5–6, 11–14, 16, 19–21, 23, 27, 29–34, 36, 38, 41–42, 49, 51–62, 66–69, 73–74, 87, 96, 100, 104, 108–13, 116, 120–21, 126–28, 130, 135, 140–41, 143–44, 147, 152, 156–58, 168–69, 171, 173, 175, 177–78, 180, 186–88, 192–93, 208, 226, 233–34, 243, 245, 247, 259, 262, 270, 289, 301–2, 319–20, 322, 324–25, 330, 334–35, 340, 342, 350–51, 353, 357, 358, 362
Kyōunshū (Crazy Cloud Collection), 324, 326–27

Index

Kyūsei, 22, 198–99, 209, 239, 338, 344, 351–52
Kyushu, 23, 33, 142, 159

Lament (*jukkai*), 148, 162
Lao Tsu. *See* Laozi
Laozi, 350
Latter Hundred-Waka Sequence at the Palace of the Retired Emperor Horikawa (*Horikawain godo hyakushu, Eikyū hyakushu*), 73, 139
Laureate (*Sōshō*), 36, 38, 45, 325
Lectures, 18, 23–24, 33, 35, 39, 47, 49, 63, 304–5, 325, 348
Letian. *See* Bo Juyi
Letters, 24, 103, 150
Lexical category, 208, 210, 213–14, 218, 263, 280, 354, 362
Linji (J: Rinzai), 42–43, 326
Linjilu (Linji Record), 326
Linked verse (*renga*), ix, 5–9, 11, 15, 18–19, 21, 23–24, **25-27**, 28–30, 32–41, 47–54, 57, 59–70, 73–74, 76–84, 88, 96–98, 100, 103, 105, 107–8, 113, 115, 117, 121–22, 129–31, 133–34, 136–40, 142–43, 147–48, 150–51, 153, 158, 161–63, 168, 170, 175, 183, 195–238, 239–40, 242–43, 247, 250, 252–57, 260–64, 266–69, 273, 277, 279–83, 285–88, 292, 295–96, 301–5, 321–23, 325, 327, 330, 333, 336, 338–40, 334, 344–63; history of, 196–201; contests (*rengaawase*), 51, 231, 327, 356, 366; hundred-verse sequences (*hyakuin*), 7, 25, 33, 35, 51, 53, 73, 78, 105, 108, 122, 148, 153, 156, 161, 164, 166–67, 169, 173, 184–85, 187, 197, 201–2, 204–5, 208, 215, 218, 261–62, 266, 282, 294, 303–4, 321, 331, 333, 336, 353, 355, 360–61, 371; in Japanese and Chinese (*wakan renku*), 8, 88, 196, 242, 294, 361; operation of a session, 25–27, 202–3; the profession of, 60–64; Sōchō's haikai renga (see *Haikai*); Sōchō's style of, 219–38; Sōgi's ushin, 199–201; *Yashima Shōrin'an naniki hyakuin*, 204–17
Linked-verse master (*renga* master, *rengashi, sōshō*), 5–7, 21, 23–27, 29, 36, 47, 49–50, 52, 57, 61, 63, 67, 69–70, 98, 108, 115, 121–22, 129, 133–34, 143, 147, 166, 168, 187, 189, 193, 199, 202, 205, 213–14, 239, 256–57, 282, 285, 302, 332, 351, 360
Linking by fragrance (*nioizuke*), 232
Linking by meaning (*kokorozuke*), 218, 280
Linking by words (*kotobazuke*), 218, 264, 281

Loftiness (*taketakaku*), 200–201, 203, 222, 224
Long poem. *See Chōka*
Lotus sect, 62, 183
Lotus Sutra (*Hokekyō*), 74, 170, 183, 226, 228, 336
Lower Capital. *See* Kyoto
Lower Capital Tea Coterie, 192
Lu, Mount (Lushan), 342, 345, 349
Lunyu (J: *Rongo*, The Confucian *Analects*), 342

Machishū (townsmen), 21
Maeku (previous link), 96, 205, 218, 258, 269, 274–75, 278–79
Maekuzuke (linking to a preexisting maeku), 269, 364
Maiden-Calling Slope (Tego no yobisaka), 171
Maigetsushō (Monthly Notes), 352
Makino Denzō, 70–71
Makino house, 129
Makino Kohaku Shigetoki, 71
Makino Shirōzaemonnojō, 129
Makurakotoba (lit., "pillow word," fixed epithet), 227
Makura no sōshi (The Pillow Book), 260, 360
Mansai Jugō, 322
Man'yōshū, 39, 109, 197, 228–29, 237, 250, 328, 333–35, 338, 351–52, 356, 367
Mariko, 31, 37, 65, 76–77, 128, 147–49, 169–70, 172, 177, 191, 293–94, 302, 324, 340, 358
Mariko Castle, 65
Masahisakyōki (The Diary of Lord Masahisa), 326
Matsudaira house, 71
Matsudaira Kiyoyasu, 71, 330
Matsudaira Nobutada, 330
Matsudaira Sadanobu, 329
Matsue Shigeyori, 348
Matsunaga Teitoku, 279, 325
Matsura, 144
Matsushita Shōkō. *See* Shōkō
Meikōawase, 347
Meitoku Discord, 100
Mengzong, 359
Mibuate. *See Sōchō renga jichū*
Mibu no Tadamine, 201, 354
Michiyuki (poetic travel sequence), 117
Miidera, 68
Mikawa kudari. *See Sōchō kawa*

Index

Mikawa Province (now part of Aichi Prefecture), 58, 70–71, 330
Mikazuki (The Winnow Hat), 322
Mimosusogawa river, 335
Mimosogawa utaawase, 231, 335
Minakuchi, 16
Minamoto house, 362
Minamoto Ienaga, 113
Minamoto Sanetomo, 334
Minamoto Shigeyuki, 338
Minamoto Tōfuru, 334
Minamoto Toshiyori, 336
Minamoto Tsunenobu, 112
Minase sangin (Three Poets at Minase), 7, 35, 51, 233, 303, 324, 345
Mishima senku, 266, 363
Mitsumono (lit., "three things," the first three verses in a *renga* sequence), 212
Mitsunaka, 362
Mitsuneshū, 197, 351
Miyagawa utaawase, 231
Miyagino, 115
Miyahara Moritaka, 70–71
Miyai Nyūdō Shinkan, 243
Miyako no tsuto (Souvenir for the Capital), 116, 336, 367
Miyako Yoshika (To), 343
Miwa, Mount, 272
Mizu no mimaki, 72
Mochi sake utaawase, 365
Momoyama period, 53
Mon (pattern), ix, 97, 214, 218, 355
Money. See Currency
Mongrel Tsukubashū. See *Shinsen inu tsukubashū*
Monjuin, 270
Monokusa Tarō (*Monogusa Tarō*, Lazy Tarō), 320
Mori (or Shin, Ikkyu's mistress), 38
Moritake. See Arakida Moritake
Moritake senku (or *Haikai no renga dokugin senku, Tobiume senku*), 254–55, 360, 363
Moruyama, 291
Mototsu Yamatonokami, 130
Mountain of Meeting (Gate at the) (Ōsaka [no seki]), 112, 188, 258, 259
Mountain of Returning (Kaeruyama), 123
Mountain Princess (Yamahime), 109, 335
Muanki (Dream Cottage), 148, 163–64, 167–68, 345; translation of, 164–65
Muko Crossing, 109

Muko River (Mukogawa), 334
Mumonkan (C: *Wumenguan*, The Gateless Gate), 324
Murasaki Shikibu, 39
Murasaki Shikibu nikki, 95, 332
Murasakino (site of Daitokuji in Kyoto), 55
Murata Jukō, 33, 192, 328, 350
Murata Sōju, 56, 192, 350
Muromachi Palace, 342
Muromachi period, xi, 15, 20, 26, 38, 278
Muromachi Street, 30
Musashino, 333
Musashi Plain, 109, 115, 118
Musashi Province (now Tokyo Metropolitan Prefecture, Saitama Prefecture, and part of Kanagawa Prefecture), 60, 158–59
Mushin verse (lit., "without heart"; humorous, "unorthodox" poetry), 197, 199, 255, 267, 360
Music, 19, 23–24, 130–31, 135–36, 213, 227
Musō renga (verse vouchsafed in a dream), 79, 330
Musō Sōseki, 329
Myōshōan, 149, 179, 190
Myōshōji, 327

Nachigomori (Beneath Nachi Falls), 73, 105, 305, 330, 332
Nagabumi (Long Letter; also *Nagafumi*), 35, 69, 203, 219–20, 232–33, 304, 353, 355, 357
Nagao house, 337
Nagao Magoroku, 333
Nagao Magoshirō, 333
Nagato Province (now part of Yamaguchi Prefecture), 142, 145, 359
Nagoya Castle, 60, 329
Nagoya kassenki (Nagoya Battle Chronicle), 329
Nagusamegusa (Consolations), 83–84, 146, 291, 365
Nakae Tosanokami, 137, 246
Nakagawa river, 109
Nakamikado house, 59–60
Nakamikado Nobuhide, 59, 190, 242, 300
Nakamikado Nobutane, 7, 59–60, 76, 90, 186–87, 240, 243, 300, 319, 328
Nakamikado Nobutsuna, 60, 300
Nakoso Gate, 188, 259
Nanku (puzzle verse), 234, 269
Nanquan, 346

Index

Nara (or Southern Capital), 32, 136, 192
Narihira. *See* Ariwara Narihira
Narumi, 139
Nasu Plain, 108, 115, 118, 125, 334
Nenchū gyōji (annual rites and ceremonies), 150
Nichiren (Lotus) sect, 329
Nihachi meidai wakashū (Selections from the Sixteen Collections), 59
Niibari, 196
Nijō, Lady, 26
Nijōgawara no rakusho, 354
Nijō house, 223
Nijōnoin Sanuki, 344
Nijō Princess, 363
Nijō Yoshimoto, 21–22, 26, 198–99, 209, 213, 223, 239, 283, 322, 344–45, 352, 355, 361, 365
Nikki bungaku. *See* Diary literature
Nikkō, 108, 333
Nikonshū, 69, 207, 236, 330, 354, 365
Ninakawa Chikamasa, 201
Nine-Fold Enclosure, 165, 346
Nioizuke. *See* Linking by fragrance
Nisho ga Myōjin, 335
Nisuiki, 350
Niteiki. See *Jiteiki*
Nitta Shōjun, 26
Nō (*sarugaku*), 19–22, 34, 103, 117, 140, 256, 327
Nōami, 329
Nobutanekyōki (The Diary of Lord Nobutane), 319
Nōin, 110, 114, 118, 329, 335–36
Nonduality (*funi*), 43, 46–47, 79, 86, 92, 104, 167–68, 180, 189, 191, 273, 296, 343, 346–47
Nonverbalization (*furyū monji*), 41, 47, 86
Northern and Southern Courts, Period of (Nanbokuchō), 21
Nose Yorinori, 51, 303
Noto Province (now part of Ishikawa Prefecture), 69
Novel, novelistic, x, 117, 126, 130–33, 141, 144, 146, 169, 185, 321, 337, 350
Nuns, 18–19
Nyoian (in Daitokuji), 42, 45

Ōan shinshiki (New Rules of the Ōan Era), 209, 342
Oda Nobunaga, 60, 319
Odawara, 77
Ōe Chisato, 211

Ōe Masafusa, 21
Oga Norimitsu, 31
Ōgimachisanjō Kin'e, 59, 88, 300, 328
Ōgimachisanjō Sanemochi, 30, 50, 59, 76, 88, 103, 240, 245, 300
Ohara Chikataka, 88, 240
Ōigawa river, 109, 128
Oi no higagoto. See *Utsunoyama no ki*
Oi no kurigoto (An Old Man's Prattle; also *Kokemushiro* [Bed of Moss] or *Jūjūshin'in Shinkei kikō* [The Travel Account of Jūjūshin'in Shinkei]), 148, 158, 160–64, 166–67, 173, 185, 193, 333, 342, 344; partial translation of, 158–60
Oi no mimi (Aged Ears) 73, 96–97, 105, 230, 305, 330, 332, 337, 355–57
Ōkawa river, 109
Okazaki Castle, 330
Okinoi Miyakoshima, 140
Okitsu, 149, 189–90
Okitsuate. See *Sōchō renga jichū*
Okitsu Hikokurō, 244, 246
Okitsu house, 366
Ōkōchi house, 98–99
Ōmi, Vice-Governor of, 284
Ōmi house, 99
Ōmi Province (now Shiga Prefecture), 15, 69, 130, 284–85, 320–21, 357, 363
Omote hachiku (eight verses, the first side of the first page), 321
Ōninki, 30
Ōnin War, 12, 30, 33, 51, 54–55, 98, 100, 108, 144, 158, 160, 319, 352
Ono no Komachi, 140, 201
Orality, 7, 22–25, 63, 196, 203, 205, 353
Osada Chikashige, 66
Ōsaka. *See* Mountain of Meeting
Osaka Castle, 319
Ōsaka Gate. *See* Mountain of Meeting
Ōshikōchi Mitsune, 197, 226
Ōta house, 342
Ōtawara (Ōdawara), 109, 334
Otogizōshi ("companion story," Muromachi short fiction), 20
Ōtōkan Zen, 327
Ōtomo Yakamochi, 351
Otowa Mountain, 188
Ōtsu, 130, 158, 178
Ōtsuki Masahisa, 326

413

Index

Ōuchi house, 33, 142–43, 329
Ōuchi Masahiro, 33, 68, 84, 143–45, 339
Overtones (*yojō, yosei*), 200, 237
Owari Province (now part of Aichi Prefecture), 71
Owa Sōrin, 327
Ōyama, Mount, 158–62, 342
Oze Hoan, 348

Painting, 19–20, 34, 64, 329, 366; paintings of trades and occupations (*shokunin zukushie*), 20; scenes in and around the capital (*rakuchū rakugaizu*), 20
Parting poem (*ribetsuka*), 113
Pattern. See *Mon*
Pawnbroker (*dosō*), 15, 18
Personal poetry collection (*jisen kashū, jisen kushū*), 7–8, 96
Personal waka anthology (*shikashū*), 253
Pivot word. See *Kakekotoba*
Plain verse (*uchihirame* verse), 355
Plum Cottage (in Shinjuan, Daitokuji), 55, 178
Poem-diary (*utanikki*), 253
Poem-tale (*utamonogatari*), 95
Poetic exchange (*zōtōka*), 104
Poetry contest. See Linked verse; *Waka*
Principle (*dōri*), 41
Private poetry (*ke no uta*), 359
Public poetry (*hare no uta*), 240, 359
Pure Land sect (*Jōdoshū*), 17, 45

Rakuchū rakugaizu. See Painting
Rakusho roken (Scribblings Made Public), 327
Random essay (*zuihitsu*), 103, 138
Reality Mountain. See Utsunoyama mountain
Recasting (*torinashi*), 218
Reizei house, 224, 331
Reizei Masatame, 358
Reizei Tamekazu, 330
Reizei Tamemori, 283, 365
Reizei Tamesuke, 351
Religious discipline (*shugyō*), 116
Renga. See Linked verse
Rengaawase (linked-verse contest). See Linked verse
Renga hikyōshū (Linked Verse Through Comparisons), 202, 239, 304, 353, 359
Renga jūmuyaku (Ten Vexations of Linked Verse), 351

Renga kaiseki shiki (Rules for Renga Sessions), 26, 322
Renga kyōkun (Instruction on Linked Verse), 353
Renga master. See Linked-verse master
Renga sakurei (Linked-Verse Composition Exemplified), 220, 304, 355
Rengashi. See linked-verse master
Renga shinshiki tsuika narabi ni shinshiki kon'an tō (New Rules of Linked Verse with Additions, Plus Current Ideas on the New Rules, etc.), 209, 345
Renga tsukeai no koto (Linking in Renga), 214, 354
Renga tsukeyō (Techniques for Linking Verses), 57, 96, 305
Renju gappekishū (Collection of Linked Pearls and Joined Jewels), 209–11, 214–16, 263, 354–55, 361–62
Repetition (*rinne*, lit., "rebirth"), 209
Re-renunciation (*saishukke*), 134, 186
Residence by the river, 37, 149, 324
Ribetsuka. See Parting poem
Rikijū, 102
Rinne. See Repetition
Rinsen'an, 149, 324
Rinzai. See Linji
Rokkaku house, 320
Rokkaku Sadayori, 357
Ruanjie, 342
Rules (*shikimoku*), 25, 202, 208–19, 354. See also Renga shinshiki tsuika narabi ni shinshiki kon'an tō
Ryōjin hishō (Songs to Make the Dust Dance), 21, 320
Ryōjusen (Eagle Peak), 226

Sabi, 20, 157
Saburōgorō, 102
Sadatoki, Prince, 284
Sagami Province (now part of Kanagawa Prefecture), 22, 30, 158–59, 162, 301
Saga no kayoi (Saga Visits), 321
Saigō house, 129
Saigyō, 27, 80, 114–16, 124–25, 129, 146, 151, 153, 165–67, 181–83, 184–86, 222–23, 231, 283, 335, 337, 339, 341, 349–50, 355, 365
Saigyō Shōninshū, 355
Saigyō Valley, 125–26, 181, 183
Saihen. See Second round

Saikaku, 320
Saioku. *See* Brushwood Cottage
Saiokuji, 301–2
Saiokuken Sōchō. *See* Sōchō
Saishōsō (Grasses of Recrudescence), 283, 327, 358, 365
Saishukke. *See* Re-renunciation
Saitō Yasumoto, 37, 65, 302
Sakai, 14, 21, 47, 55, 135, 167
Sakai denju, 45, 327
Saka Jūbutsu, 333, 351
Sakamoto, 130, 179
Sakanoshita, 70
Sake (sake brewers, wine), 10, 15–16, 20, 22, 50, 62, 67, 70–72, 79, 88, 130, 134, 165–67, 176–77, 203, 246, 264, 288, 291, 345, 348–49, 365; *dakurō, doburoku*, 348; *nerinuki, nerizake*, 348; *usuzake*, 348
Sakurai Motosuke, 327
San'aiki (Three Loves), 148, 163–64, 166–67, 185, 345–49; translation of, 165–66
San'ami (Three Ami), 329
Sanetaka. *See* Sanjōnishi Sanetaka
Sanetakakōki (The Diary of Lord Sanetaka), 50, 327, 329, 351, 362, 365
Sangoki (Three Fives Record), 352
Sangyokushū. *See* Three Jewelled Collections
Sanjōnishi Sanetaka, 12, 22, 26, 32, 39, 47, **49–50**, 51, 53, 60–61, 68, 74, 89–90, 101, 104, 180, 186, 193, 205–7, 209, 231–33, 238–39, 264–65, 283, 293, 304, 327, 329, 340, 347–48, 351, 353, 356–58, 366
Sankashū (Mountain Cottage Collection), 115, 182, 336
Sanmon gate (of Daitokuji), 54
Sano no watari (Sano Crossing), 327, 332
Sanrian. *See* Cottage in a Mountain Village
Sanseizu no san (Colophon for a Painting of Three Sages), 363
Santaishi. *See* Santishi
Santishi (J: *Santaishi*, Poems in Three Styles), 348
Sanukinosuke nikki (The Sanukinosuke Diary), 141, 338
Saohime, 281
Sao Mountain, 109, 334
Sarugaku. *See Nō*
Sasamegoto (Murmured Conversations), 158, 223, 344, 355
Sashiide Strand, 101

Satomura Jōha. *See* Jōha
Sayo no nakayama mountain (Sayo no nagayama, Nagayama, Sayonoyama, Saya no nakayama, Sayo Long Mountain), 123–24, 126, 182
Scenes in and around the capital (*rakuchū rakugaizu*). *See* Painting
Scribe (*shuhitsu*), 25–26, 202, 217
Season, place, and level (*ji-sho-i*), 203–4
Seasonal word (*kigo*), 203
Second round (*saihen*), 213
Second verse. *See Waki*
Secret Traditions of *Kokinshū* (*Kokin denju*). *See Kokinshū*
Seidō (orthodox way), 41
Seikenji, 132, 246–47, 366
Seimei. *See* Ki no Tadana
Sei Shōnagon, 260
Seisuishō (Laughs to Banish Sleep), 257, 266, 295, 332, 360
Seitaka, 271
Sekiguchi Ujikane, 88
Seki Kajisai, 6, **67–68**, 69–71, 73, 84, 149, 180, 285, 330
Sengen senku (A Thousand-Verse Sequence for Sengen Shrine), 60
Sengohyakuban utaawase (Waka Contest of One Thousand Five Hundred Rounds), 344
Sengoku daimyō, 13, 16
Senjun, 108, 201, 206
Senjūshō (Select Collection), 340
Senku. *See* Thousand-verse sequence
Sen no Rikyū, 192
Sen no Sōtan, 192, 350
Senzaishū (*Senzai wakashū*), 116, 131
Sesshū, 19, 145
Setsugyokushū (Collection of Snowy Jewels), 358
Setsuwa, 8
Settsu Province (now part of Osaka and Hyōgo Prefectures), 163, 165, 335
Settsu senku, 303
Seven Gentlemen of Linked Verse (Renga Shichishi), 49
Seven Sages of Linked Verse (Renga Shichiken), 34, 47, 206, 239, 352
Seven Sages of the Bamboo Grove, 167
Shakkyō (Buddhist) poetry, 148
Shakuhachi (also *hitoyogiri*), 19, 34, 73, 130–31, 135–36, 227, 302,

415

Index

Shiba house, 30–31
Shichinin tsukeku hanshi (Critique of Seven Poets' Links), 304
Shidō kuhon (Four Ways and Nine Stages), 336
Shigaraki, 137
Shihōshō (Ultimate Treasure Notes), 353–54
Shijing. See *The Book of Songs*
Shijin zanshō (Remaining Notes on Purple Dust), 35, 39, 73, 304
Shikimoku. See Rules
Shikyō. See *The Book of Songs*
Shimada, 27–28, 295, 301–2
Shimo no ku (or *tanku*, the 14-syllable verses in a renga sequence), 212
Shimotsuke Province (now Tochigi Prefecture), 108
Shina, 249
Shinagawa, 159, 342
Shinano Province (now Nagano Prefecture), 160
Shinchokusenshū (*Shinchokusen wakashū*), 228
Shin'eki, 140
Shingon, 17
Shinjuan (in Daitokuji), 34, 55–56, 88, 178, 192, 245
Shinkei, x, 29, 34, 47, 108, 148, 157, **158**, 160–63, 167–69, 173, 178, 184–85, 187, 193, 199, 201, 207, 222–23, 235, 239, 323–24, 327, 333, 342–45, 349, 352, 355, 358
Shinkokinshū (*Shinkokin wakashū*), 112–13, 124–25, 132, 152–53, 175, 195, 197, 199, 216, 227–28, 250, 252, 335, 338–41, 344, 349, 352, 356–57, 362, 366
Shinku. See Close link
Shinkyū kyōka haikai kikigaki (Notes on Old and New *Kyōka* and *Haikai*), 363
Shinsarugakuki (New Sarugaku Account), 21
Shinsen inu tsukubashū (Newly Selected *Mongrel Tsukubashū*; also *Inu tsukubashū, Haikai renga, Haikai rengashō*), 18, 34, 140, 266, 268, 272, 275–76, 280–82, 336, 359–60, 363–64
Shinsen tsukubashū (Newly Selected *Tsukubashū*), 35–36, 68, 122, 160, 199, 229, 254, 257, 301, 324, 327, 342, 345, 353, 359
Shintō, 17, 68, 254, 354
Shinzoku inu tsukubashū (New Sequel to Mongrel *Tsukubashū*), 265–66, 360, 362
Shio, Mount, 101

Shioya, 108
Shirakawa (in Uji), 267
Shirakawa Castle, 121
Shirakawa Gate (Shirakawa no seki), 23, 65, 71, 108–12, 114–22, 144, 162, 305, 335–37
Shirakawa kikō (An Account of a Journey to Shirakawa), **107–22**, 126–28, 131, 133–35, 139, 141–46, 158, 160, 162–63, 181, 199, 201, 327, 332–33, 337, 340; partial translation of, 108–11
Shirutani, 16
Shitakusa (Undergrowth), 336, 354–55
Shitakusachū, 304, 355
Shizuka naru amari (Too Quiet), 329
Shōgakuin, 89
Shogun, 18. See also Ashikaga house; Bakufu
Shōhaku (Muan, Botanka, Rōka Rōjin), x, 7, 35, 45, 49, **51–52**, 53, 148, 157, 163–64, 166–68, 169, 171, 178, 184–85, 187, 189, 191, 193, 209, 231–33, 235, 239, 261, 301, 303–4, 324, 327, 345–46, 348–49, 354, 356, 358
Shoin-style architecture, 19
Shōjū Ryūtō, 163, 166, 345, 348–49
Shōkashō (Beneath the Pines), 351, 358
Shōkō, 29, 146, 323
Shōkokuji, 47, 145
Shōkō nikki, 146
Shokugo meidai wakashū (Selections from the Five Later Collections), 59, 328
Shokunin zukushie. See Painting
Shokushi, Princess, 252
Shōmyōji, 192
Shōren'in, 325
Shōrin'an, 46, 53, 56, 69, 74, 78, 100, 149, 178–79, 190, 204, 282–83, 292, 304, 331–32
Shōshō no Naishi, 26, 322
Shōtetsu, 83, 146, 239, 291, 339, 344, 365
Shōzōbō, 130
Shrines of the Two Deities (Nisho ga Myōjin), 110, 118, 335
Shūa, 338
Shueki, 88
Shugo. See Constable
Shugyō (ascetic discipline), 27
Shuhitsu. See Scribe
Shūishū (*Shūi wakashū*), 329, 334–35, 361
Shunmusō (Grasses of Spring Dreams), 163–64, 345
Shunzei. See Fujiwara Shunzei

Shūon'an, 34–35, 41, 51, 54, 56, 69, 72, 74–75, 149, 178, 182, 186, 268, 275, 283, 286, 288, 324, 327

Shusse monogatari (tales of making one's fortune), 320

Shuten dōji (The Wine-Drinking Demon), 22

Shutsujin senku (A Thousand-Verse Sequence for the Campaign; also *Shin Mishima senku* or *Saiokuken senku*), 60, 69, 234, 303, 357

Sōami, 329

Sōan bungaku. See Eremitic literature

Sōboku, 49, **53–54**, 68, 78, 80, 204–19, 232, 235, 282, 293–94, 304, 325, 331, 333, 336, 353, 355, 357, 365

Sōchō (Chōa, Chōtō, Kōsai [?], Kuan or Kyūan, Saioku Rōjin, Sōkan); biographies of, 29, 301–2, 324, 335, 366–67; and Buddhist monks, 68–69; and daughter, 79; and father (Gojō Yoshisuke), 28, 301, 322; and Ikkyū, 7, 17, 34–35, 38–48, 54–56; and the Imagawa, 5–6, 28–32, 36–38, 58–64, 74–77; and the Ise poetic circle, 69, 330; major works by, 303–5; and mother, 301; and mother of his children, 37; and Sōgi, x, 7, 32–36, 38–41, 47–48, 57; and son (Jōha, later Suian), 37, 79, 294; in old age, 42, 51, 55, 62, 70, 72, 74–77, 81, 83–94, 105, 123–24, 127, 135, 147, 151–53, 169, 172, 174–77, 180–83, 185, 187, 190–93, 195, 218, 235–36, 243, 245, 247–48, 252, 284, 290, 293, 348; poetic development, 232–38; self-portrait in *The Journal of Sōchō*, 78–93; youth, 27–29

Sōchō hikashō (Private Notes on Waka, by Sōchō), 304, 330, 338, 358

Sōchō hyakuban rengaawase (Linked-Verse Contest in One Hundred Rounds, by Sōchō), 51, 231, 327, 356, 366

Sōchōji, 324

Sōchō kawa (Sōchō's Talks on Waka; also *Mikawa kudari* [Down to Mikawa]), 35, 69, 112, 151–52, 156–57, 184, 228, 239, 304, 330, 336, 340

Sōchō Kojiden (Biography of the Lay Priest Sōchō), 29, 323, 331, 367

Sōchō nikki (The Diary of Sōchō), 57, 76, 105, 253, 305, 326, 333, 337, 350, 359

Sōchō renga jichū (Personal Commentary on Sōchō's Linked Verse, first half subtitled *Okitsuate* [To Okitsu], second half subtitled *Mibuate* [To Mibu]), 57, 69, 96, 105, 218, 228, 237, 304, 355–56, 358, 363

Sōchō shuki. See *The Journal of Sōchō*

Soga Jasoku, 34

Soga school, 34

Sōgi (Jinensai, Shugyokuan), x, 7, 22–23, 29–31, **32–34**, 35–39, **40–41**, 44, 47–52, 54, 57, 63, 68, 74, 83–84, 104, 107–8, 110–13, 115–22, 124–29, 131–35, 137, 139–45, 145, 147, 149, 151, 158, 161–63, 181, 195, 199–201, 204, 206–7, 213, 218–20, 222–24, 228, 230–31, 233, 235–39, 242, 247, 253–54, 256–59, 261–67, 269, 273, 282, 293–97, 301–5, 321, 323–27, 331–40, 343–45, 348, 352–55, 358–63, 365–66; and *Shirakawa kikō*, 108–22, 126, 128, 131–36, 141–42

Sōgi hokkushū, 354

Sōgi jōji hyakuin, 261–64, 266, 269, 361

Sōgi shokoku monogatari (Tales of Sōgi's Travels Through the Provinces), 257

Sōgi shūenki (The Death of Sōgi), 36, 57, 104, 121, 305, 332, 337

Sōgi sodeshita (Sōgi's Notes Carried in the Sleeve), 362

Sōho, 165, 346

Sōi, 34

Sōkan, x, 34, 56, 80, 140, 254, 257, 266, 268, 273, 275–82, 297, 328, 359–60

Sōkei, 130

Soku. See Distant link

Sōkyū, 116, 336, 367

Solo sequence (*dokugin*), 51, 150, 153, 243, 303, 321, 340, 353, 357, 360. See also *Yamaga hyakuin*

Sōrōbun (epistolary style), 93, 104

Sōseki, 36, 38, 49, 51, **52–53**, 69–70, 130, 203, 233, 235, 289, 304, 325, 327, 332, 357, 360

Soshin Jōetsu, 56

Sōshitsu, 164–65, 345–46

Sōshō. See Linked-verse master

Sotanshū. See *Yoshitadashū*

Soto no Shirakawa, 70

Sōun. See Hōjō Sōun

Southern Barbarians, 166

Southern Capital. See Nara

Sōyo, 53

Sōyō yori kikigaki, 355

Sōzei, 199–200, 209, 327, 333, 352, 360

Style (*fūryū*), 256

417

Index

Su Dongpo, 346
Sugata. See Configuration
Sugawara Fumitoki (Kan Sanbon), 344
Sugawara Michizane (Tenjin), 18, 142, 144, 320, 346
Sugihara Iganokami, 126
Suian. *See* Jōha
Suki (taste), 157, 163, 192
Sumeru, Mount (Suminoyama), 230
Sumiyoshi Shrine, 142, 144, 335, 359
Sumō, 325
Sun Goddess. *See* Amaterasu
Sunpu (Suruga Capital), 6, 13, 29–31, 36, 59–60, 62–64, 66, 71, 100, 149, 169, 172–73, 175–77, 188, 233, 240, 291, 331, 340
Suō Province (now part of Yamaguchi Prefecture), 33, 142
Suruga Counselor (Suruga no Saishō), 322, 367
Suruga Province (now part of Shizuoka Prefecture), 5–6, 13, 23, 27–29, 31–32, 35–38, 41–42, 52, 57, 59–60, 64–67, 69, 74–77, 79–80, 82, 88, 96, 98, 100–102, 107, 123, 128, 130, 133, 139, 147, 150, 173, 176–77, 181, 188–90, 230, 233, 243, 251, 290, 302, 305, 322–25, 328, 331–32, 358
Suzhou, 343
Suzuka Mountains, 67, 70, 72, 124 25, 185–86
Suzuki Nagatoshi, 158, 342

Tadamine. *See* Mibu no Tadamine
Tada Mountain, 265
Tada no Mitsunaka, 362
Tago Bay, 243
Taiheiki (The Great Peace), 24, 117
Taijin, 39, 325
Taikōki (Chronicles of the Regent), 348
Taira Kanemori, 110, 118, 335
Taira Shinzaemonnojō, 354
Taira Tadamori, 110, 335
Takahashi house, 99
Take, 71
Takeda Nobutora, 61
Takeda Shingen, 332
Taketakaku. See Loftiness
Takeuchi Gengen'ichi, 325, 328, 366
Takigi, 34–35, 42, 54, 56, 66, 69, 72, 74–76, 87, 135, 149, 169–70, 177–78, 181–83, 186–88, 203, 254, 268–70, 275–76, 280, 282–83, 285–86, 340; Takigi *haikai* sequence, 203, 254, 268–82, 283, 285–86
Takinobō, 139
Takyōji, 322
Tale of Genji, The. See Genji monogatari
Tale of Heike, The. See Heike monogatari
Tamamatsu, god of, 335
Tanabata. *See* Festival of the Weaver Maid
Tanba Province (now part of Kyoto and Hyōgo Prefectures), 101
Tanemura Nakatsukasanojō. *See* Iba Sadakazu
Tani Sōboku. *See* Sōboku
Tanku. See Shimo no ku
Tanrenga ("short linked verse," one 17-syllable verse linked to one 14-syllable verse), 197, 361
Taoism, 164–65, 167–68, 342, 346–47, 349–50
Taste. *See Suki*
Tatoezukushi (A List of Exempla), 276
Taxation, 15–16, 56
Tawabure uta (playful poems), 365
Tea, 15, 19–21, 23–24, 34, 56, 82, 91, 176, 192, 272, 291, 302, 328, 350
Teika. *See* Fujiwara Teika
Teitoku. *See* Matsunaga Teitoku
Tenchūzan mountain, 301
Tendai, 17–18, 68, 158
Tenjin. *See* Sugawara Michizane
Tenkurō, 363
Tenmangū shrine, 338
Tenmyō, 92
Tenryūgawa river, 98
Third verse. See *Daisan*
Thousand-verse sequence (*senku*), 5, 7, 49, 51, 53, 60, 68–70, 99, 158, 203, 233–34, 254–55, 266, 303–4, 320–21, 323, 327, 357, 360
Three Crossings, 71
Three Jewelled Collections (*Sangyokushū*), 358
Three Laughers of Tiger Valley, 168, 343
Tiger Ravine (Huxi), 160, 162, 343
Time sect. *See* Ji sect
To. *See* Miyako Yoshika
Tōenbō, 130
Tōfū renga hiji (Private Matters Concerning Modern Linked Verse), 53, 355, 357
Tōgoku kikō (Journey to the Eastern Provinces), 54, 68, 294, 325, 330, 333, 365
Tōkaidō gojūsan tsugi (The Fifty-Three Stations of the Tōkaidō), 301, 322

Tōkaidō road, 27, 66, 71, 330
Tōkan kikō (An Account of a Journey to the East), 184
Tokugawa Ieyasu, 319, 330, 332
Tolls, 16
Tomorrow River (Asukagawa), 136, 177
Tō no Chūjō, 273
Tō no Sōjun, 32, 76, 328
Tō no Tsuneyori, 22, 32–33, 39, 47, 239, 348–49
Topic (*dai*), 240, 242, 248
Topical category, 148, 208, 212–15, 217, 234, 354–55
Toribeyama, 260
Torinashi. See Recasting
Tosa nikki (A Tosa Diary), 83, 95, 113, 141
Toshiyori zuinō (Toshiyori Medulla), 336
Tōtōmi Province (now part of Shizuoka Prefecture), 28, 30–31, 58, 60, 64, 98, 323, 332
Tōunken, 178
Toyohara Muneaki (or Sumiaki), **50**, 90, 104, 193, 238, 327, 351, 358
Towazugatari (Confessions of Lady Nijō), 7
Tragic anecdotes (*aiwa, hiwa*), 101
Travel, 6, 16–19, 23, 25–28, 33, 49, 61, 66–74, 77, 107–46, 154–55, 184–85, 301; mechanics of travel, 69–73
Travel literature (*kikō bungaku*), x, 6, 27, 82–85, 96, 107–46, 147–51, 158–59, 161, 166, 171, 173, 181, 184, 199, 201, 250–53, 256, 267, 291, 294–95, 301, 305, 325, 327, 332–33, 337, 366; and Saigyō, 124–25; Sōchō's figuring of the poetic travel orthodoxy, 112–13; and Sōgi, 107–22; travel works by linked-verse poets, 332–33
True Pure Land sect (Jōdo Shinshū), 19, 325
Tsuchiyama, 70
Tsugiuta. See *Waka* sequence
Tsujinobō, 267
Tsukeai (linking to a previous verse) 9, 207–18, 232, 234, 242, 250
Tsukeku (the link to a previous verse), 96, 105, 229, 231, 233, 235, 258, 272–73, 275, 278–80
Tsukuba, Mount, 108, 143, 196, 333
Tsukuba mondō (Questions and Answers about the Way of Tsukuba), 26, 198, 213, 322, 355
Tsukubashū, 151, 198–99, 255, 336, 352, 360
Tsukushi, 116
Tsukushi michi no ki (An Account of a Kyushu Journey), 33, 84, 142–46, 256, 297, 332, 338–39
Tsurayuki. See Ki no Tsurayuki
Tsurezuregusa (Essays in Idleness), 103, 138, 222

Uchihirame verse. See Plain verse
Uchikoshi. See Clash
Uchi no Shirakawa, 70
Uesugi Fusasada, 32–33, 323
Uesugi Fusayoshi, 323
Uesugi house, 33, 36, 52, 121, 337
Uji, 178, 183
Uji Bridge, 72
Ujigawa, 72–73
Umedo, 72
Upper Capital. See Kyoto
Urbanization, 15
Uruwashiku. See Grace
Ushin verse (lit., "with heart"; poetry with deep feeling or conviction; "orthodox" poetry), 117, 138, 197–202, 206, 219, 236–38, 245, 247, 253, 255, 257–62, 266–69, 271, 277, 279–80, 282, 287, 292, 295–96, 352, 359–60
Uta. See *Waka*
Utaawase (*waka* contest). See *Waka*
Utagawa Sadahide, 301
Utamakura (poetic places), 114–15, 118, 121, 124, 126, 129–31, 133, 139, 143–44, 150, 158, 203, 227, 243, 259, 272, 336–37, 339
Utamonogatari. See Poem-tale
Utanikki. See Poem-diary
Utsunoyama mountain (Reality Mountain), 123, 128, 169–70, 172, 174–75, 294
Utsunoyama no ki (Utsunoyama Chronicle; also Oi no higagoto [An Old Man's Delusions]), 28, 32, 34, 36–37, 62, 65–66, 104, 128, 236, 301, 305, 322, 329, 332, 357
Utsuyama Castle, 83

Vimalakirti, 350–51
votive (*hōraku*) verse, 5–6, 60–61, 145

Wabi (see also tea), 19–20, 157, 192, 350
Wabun (writing in pure Japanese), 82, 93, 117, 135–36
Waka (Japanese 31-syllable poems; also *uta*), 7–9, 16, 23–25, 29, 35, 48–50, 59, 69, 77–79, 81–82, 90, 95–96, 105, 112, 121–22, 136, 139, 143, 150–52, 162, 164, 170, 189, 195–201,

Index

209, 220, 223, 228–29, 231–32, 237, 238–53, 255–56, 260, 304, 323, 328, 330, 332, 337, 339–40, 342, 351–52, 354, 356, 358–60, 362; contests (*utaawase*), 197, 231, 238, 256, 335, 344, 365; *haikai waka* (see *haikai*); hundred-*waka* sequences (*hyakushu*), 73, 130, 139, 252, 340, 358–59, 365; public *waka*, 240–42; private *waka*, 242–49; waka in *The Journal of Sōchō*, 238–53

Wakamatsu Pond, 16

Wakankonkōbun (Japanese written with a mix of phonetic syllables [*kana*] and Sino-Japanese characters [*kanji*]), 8, 93, 117, 127, 136, 305, 345

Wakan kyōku (Mad Verses in Japanese and Chinese), 361

Wakan renku. *See* Linked verse

Wakan rōeishū (Japanese and Chinese Poems to Sing), 148, 162, 343–46

Waka sequence (*tsugiuta*), 240

Wakashū, 359

Wakashu. *See* Young men

Wakatsuki Jirō (Kunisada), 101

Wakatsuki Wakasanokami (Nagazumi), 101

Waki (or *wakiku*, the second verse in a linked-verse sequence), 203–4, 207–8, **210–11**, 234, 242, 250, 302, 354

Wakuraba (Blighted Leaves), 220–22, 236, 355

Wang Huizi. *See* Ziyou

Wang Xizhi, 343

Wangyin Bridge, 343

Wang Zhi, 159, 162, 343

Washinosuyama (Eagle Nest Mountain), 123, 226

Washio Takayasu, 50, 350

Wasuregusa (Grass of Forgetfulness), 30, 32, 120, 258, 260–61, 360–61

Way of Tsukuba, xi, 197, 333

Wenxuan Selections of Refined Literature), 344

White Mountain (Shirayama), 226

Wild words and fancy phrases (*kyōgen kigo*), 157, 163, 342

Wine. *See* Sake

Writerly text, 353

Wumen Huikai, 324

Yahagigawa river, 126

Yakumo mishō (Imperial Notes on Eight-Fold Clouds), 353

Yamabe Akahito, 200

Yamada, 71, 125, 135, 183, 249, 285, 330

Yamaga hyakuin (One Hundred Verses on a Mountain Hut), 148, 153–56, 161, 164, 166–67, 169, 173, 184–85, 187, 340

Yamaguchi, 142, 339

Yamaguchi Sodō, 295, 301

Yamana Sōzen, 30, 33

Yamanobe Akahito, 200, 301, 352

Yamanoue Sōji, 329

Yamashiro Province (now part of Kyoto Prefecture), 135, 169, 178

Yamato Takeru no Mikoto, 196

Yamazaki, 129

Yamazaki Sōkan. *See* Sōkan

Yanagimoto Kataharu, 74, 100

Yariku (a link designed to move the sequence in a new direction), 263

Yashima, 46, 53, 56, 67, 69, 100, 129, 133, 149, 169, 175, 178–81, 188–90, 206, 249, 283, 340, 353

Yashima Shōrin'an naniki hyakuin (A Hundred-Verse Sequence entitled 'A Kind of Tree,' Composed at Shōrin'an in Yashima), 53, 78, **204–17**, 304, 353, 365

Yawata (in Ise Province), 71

Yawata (in Mikawa Province), 129

Yawata Mountain, 7

Yodo no watari (Yodo Crossing), 218

Yojō. *See* Overtones

Yokooka, 109, 111–12, 120, 335

Yoriai. *See* Association

Yosei. *See* Overtones

Yoshida Kenkō, 103, 222

Yoshikawa Yorishige, 101

Yoshikawa Tōgorō, 101

Yoshimoto. *See* Nijō Yoshimot; Imagawa Yoshimoto

Yoshino mountains, 151, 166

Yoshitadashū (Sotanshū), 352

Yoshitsune. *See* Fujiwara Yoshitsune

Yōsō Sōi, 54

Young men (*wakashu*), 46, 79, 134, 140, 271

Yū. *See* Elegance

Yuan Jie, 349

Yuanwu Keqin, 192

Yūgao (Lady of the Evening Faces), 273

Yūgen. *See* Ineffable beauty

Yui Hōgo (Mimasakanokami), 88, 25

Yu Jian, 329
Yūjōki (Of Prostitutes), 21
Yūki house, 337
Yūki Nyūdō Dōchō (Naotomo), 337
Yukiyō (development in a linked-verse sequence), 9, 209, 218, 339. See also *Yashima Shōren'in Naniki hyakuin*
Yuyama sangin (Three Poets at Yuyama), 7, 35, 51, 233, 235, 260, 265, 303, 324, 345, 357

Za. See Guilds
Zaigo Chūjō no nikki (Diary of Middle Captain Ariwara of the Fifth Rank), 95
Zareuta (comic *waka*), 140
Zeami, 22
Zekkai Chūshin, 329
Zen, 5, 7, 17–18, 28, 34, 36, 38, 40–45, 47–48, 78–79, 86, 92, 103, 138, 163, 168, 187–88, 192, 217–18, 252, 293, 296, 302, 326–27, 350
Zencharoku (Record of Zen and Tea), 192, 350
Zenchiku. *See* Konparu Zenchiku
Zenna, 351
Zenpō zōdan, 103
Zhang Xiaobiao, 343
Zhaozhou, 324
Zhonghe, 164, 345
Zhuangzi, 168, 346–47, 350
Ziyou (Wang Huizi), 159, 162, 343
Zōdan. See Desultory conversation
Zōki, 332
Zoku (everyday, informal, unprecedented), 41, 44, 47, 79, 141, 198, 255–56, 258, 262, 264–65, 267, 269, 282–83, 285, 287, 326
Zoku haika kijindan (Anecdotes about Haikai Poets and Uncommon Characters, Continued), 325, 328, 366
Zōtōka. See Poetic exchange
Zuihitsu. See Random essay
Zushū, 91